End

Dr. Watson has undertaken a project that would make most men tremble: he has studied and explained some of the most daunting passages of Scripture, and then has demonstrated the courage to publish his explanations for all of the theologians of Christendom to evaluate and contest! He has done so with remarkable care and thoroughness, and you will profit by reading the outcomes and learning from his methods.

—Dr. James Maxwell
President, Faith Baptist College and Seminary
Ankeny, Iowa

I had the privilege of teaching with Dr. Watson in Haiti in 2011 and providentially was able to read several issues of TOTT. These articles not only gave me an appreciation for his scholarship but an understanding and gratitude for a resource that is desperately needed by the serious student of the Word of God. The perspicuity of the Bible has been challenged throughout Church History, but *Truth on Tough Texts: Expositions of Challenging Scripture Passages* brings clarity to difficult texts using a sound biblical hermeneutic.

—Dr. Allen Monroe
Equipping Leaders International
Former Professor, Cedarville University

Challenging. Insightful. Biblical. Three words that accurately describe Doc Watson's writing in his new book, *Truth on Tough Texts: Expositions of Challenging Scripture Passages*. In this compilation of excellent articles, the author does something that is rare these days: he lets the Bible speak for itself. By applying a sound biblical hermeneutic and taking the Bible seriously, truth clearly emerges from the tough texts of Scripture. Pastors and laymen alike will benefit from the hours of study and careful scholarship that went into these pages.

—Dr. James Bearss
President, On Target Ministry
Teaching Faithful Men through International Education

If you have not been blessed to sit under the teaching ministry of Dr. Watson, in one of the most beautiful venues in God's creation, then do the next best thing and read his books. TOTT is a much needed antidote for a culture that overwhelming calls itself Christian but cannot enumerate its most basic and important truths. I heartily recommend you wrestle through the tough texts of Scripture with Doc's enlightened coaching.

—JD Wetterling
Author of *No one . . .* and
No Time to Waste

The vast majority of Scripture is clear and understandable to even the simplest of readers, but there are those "hard sayings," those confusing sections, those tough texts that take extra care and study to discern. Dr. Watson examines many of these "tough texts" through the lens of Scripture, making every effort to determine their true meaning and eliminate the layers of inadequate teaching that has covered many of them over the ages. I recommend this book to the serious student of the Word of God.

—Dr. Gary E. Gilley
Pastor, Southern View Chapel; Springfield, Illinois
Author, *This Little Church* series

Doc Watson's TOTT has served me and our church family with his willingness to tackle not only tough *texts* but also tough *topics*. I often post his recent article on my office bulletin board. As a pastor, I am all about helpful resources for myself and others, and that's what this publication offers. Where the commentaries give a brief statement, Doc gives you a concise and thorough explanation. Keep this book within reach on your shelf because you will use this as a reference source when discussions lead to a question about a biblical text or topic.

—Kevin Kottke, MDiv
Pastor, Plainfield Bible Church
Plainfield, Indiana

Dr. Watson has taken from his extensive experience those biblical texts and issues that are most difficult and tackled them head-on. These are texts most commentaries skirt over or shy away from. Doc's manner is thorough and in-depth, using sound hermeneutic principles of exegesis. The results are profound studies and answers on important subjects. These rich studies have been very beneficial to me personally, and I recommend them to anyone who loves the truth of God's Word.

—Jim Bryant, MBS
Pastor, Grace Bible Chapel; San Antonio, Texas

Truth
on Tough Texts

Expositions of Challenging Scripture Passages

Brother Darstek,
Thanks so much for the
support. God bless you!

Dr. J. D. Watson

Dr. J. D. Watson
Eph. 1:6

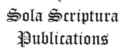

Sola Scriptura
Publications

Truth on Tough Texts: Expositions of Challenging Scripture Passages

Published by Sola Scriptura Publications
P. O. Box 235
Meeker, CO 81641

www.TheScriptureAlone.com

Cover Photograph: Barry Bishop/National Geographic stock

Unless otherwise noted, all Scripture quotations and word references are from *The Authorized King James Version.*

Copyrighted translations either quoted or referenced: **NKJV** (New King James Version. Copyright © 1982 by Thomas Nelson, Inc.); **NIV** (New International Version®. Copyright © 1973, 1978, 1984 Biblica); **NASB** (New American Standard Bible®. Copyright ©1995 by The Lockman Foundation); **ESV** (English Standard Version® Copyright ©2001 by Crossway Bibles, a publishing ministry of Good News Publishers, and the National Council of Churches); **NRSV** (New Revised Standard Version. Copyright ©1989 by the National Council of Churches); **NLT**(New Living Translation Copyright ©1996. Tyndale House Publishers); **CEV** (Contemprary English Version. Copyright ©1995. Amercian Bible Society); **GWT** (God's Word Translation. Copyright ©1995. World Publishing); **NCV** (New Century Version. Copyright ©1991. Word Bible); **MSG** (The Message: The Bible in Contemporary Language. Copyright ©2005. NavPress).

Library of Congress Cataloging-in-Publication Data

ISBN–13: 978-0615623054 (Sola Scriptura Publications)
ISBN–10: 0615623050

Dedication

This work is dedicated first to my dear Savior and
Lord, Jesus Christ,
and also to

Mark Phillippo, Jr.

whose love for Scripture
and commitment to godly living have
been a blessing to my heart for many years.

Acknowledgements

I want to thank each reader of the monthly articles that have appeared in *Truth On Tough Texts* since its premiere in August 2005. The response has been more encouraging than you can know.

Special thanks go out to my wife, Debbie, for her reading, editing, and critiquing of the monthly offerings. Special thanks also to Mark Phillippo, Jr. for his copy editing of the final book manuscript.

A particularly heart-felt thanks goes to Joe Bruce, who I have the joy of pastoring at Grace Bible Church, and who was of tremendous help in bringing this project to fruition. Warm thanks to several others who also greatly aided this endeavor: Rico Patterson, Russ Spees, Jim Spees, and Dr. James Bearss.

Soli Deo Gloria

Contents

Let this be a firm principle: No other word is to be held as the Word of God, and given place as such in the church, than what is contained first in the Law and Prophets, then in the writings of the Apostles; and the only authorized way of teaching in the church is by the prescription and standard of the Word.

John Calvin, *Institutes*, IV.9.8

Introduction

W as Matthias God's choice to replace Judas (Acts 1:15–26)? What is the identity of those "sons of God" referred to in Genesis 6? Are the "angels" of the seven churches real angels or pastors (Rev. 1:20)? Is there a so-called *call* to ministry (Eph. 4:11; 1 Tim. 3:1)? Is "deaconess" a valid church office (1 Tim. 3:11)? What is the "sealing" of the Holy Spirit (Eph. 1:13–14)? Is "regeneration" absent from the Old Testament, being a New Testament doctrine only (Isa. 57:15; Eph. 2:1)? What do other terms that appear in Scripture mean, such as: "fall away" (Heb. 6:4–6), "old man" (Rom. 6:6), and "new creature" (2 Cor. 5:17)?

Those are just a few of the "tough texts" we find in Scripture. While Scripture is infallible, never contradicting itself, and while it is literal and straightforward, not mysterious and ambiguous, there are some texts that raise questions and have therefore prompted varied "interpretations" throughout Church History. Again, such texts are certainly not "less inspired" than the rest of Scripture, rather simply more intricate and complex and thereby demand especially diligent investigation.

This book, therefore, addresses many texts of Scripture that have historically been debated, are particularly difficult to understand, or have generated questions among believers. The chapters that follow originally appeared in the monthly publication, *Truth on Tough Texts*, which was launched by the author in August 2005. They reappear here so that they might reach a wider audience, as well as provide a quick reference for longtime readers of the monthly offerings.

Why study such "tough texts"? There are several reasons. One is that we need to know *all* Scripture, not just the "easy parts." Another is that such study is an exercise in diligence, which hones the mind and stirs the heart. Correct biblical interpretation is a difficult and demanding discipline. This is one reason we have included the Appendix, "Principles of Biblical Interpretation," which was itself originally a two-part article in the monthly publication.

Perhaps the most important reason to study such "tough texts," however, comes from the words of our Lord, "Search the scriptures; for in them ye think ye have eternal life: and they are they which testify of me" (Jn. 5:39). In a day when the Bible is made to say literally anything people want it to say and is anything but the final and sufficient authority, correct interpretation has never been more crucial. As our chapter 6 ("Where Has Our Discernment Gone?") challenges, true discernment has all but vanished from the Church today. The studies in this book, then, are meant to encourage us to interpret and apply Scripture carefully and correctly.

It should be noted that while the positions presented on each subject are based on years of careful study and biblical principles of interpretation, we recognize that other respected men of God disagree. The godly men who so graciously endorsed this book, for example, would not agree with every "jot and tittle" that I have scribbled here. Further, you the reader might not always agree. That, however, is not the point. The point again is the encouragement to search the Scriptures, to be diligent in our study so we can "rightly divide it," that is, "cut it straight" (2 Tim. 2:15), and to discern truth from error (Eph. 4:14).

Certain conventions have been used in this book to aid in reading. *First*, each biblical text is noted at the beginning of the chapter and appears in **bold**. This is also true in the exposition itself. *Second*, each chapter title is footnoted to indicate its original place in the history of the monthly publication and any other pertinent information. *Third*, all other notes appear at the end of each chapter. *Fourth*, Greek, Hebrew, and Latin words appear in a different font (e.g., *charis*, "grace") to contrast them from normal text. *Fifth*, sprinkled throughout the book are short, powerful quotations from great men of the faith, most of which also appeared in the monthly issues.

Finally, while a popular notion among today's "church gurus" is that "you cannot start with a text," we are convinced that that is precisely where we must *always* begin. As we hope our exhaustive Scripture Index also demonstrates, Scripture is everything, and whatever the issue or subject, it's always about the text. We pray, therefore, that these studies of "tough texts" will deepen your love for God's Word and drive you to "cut it straight" and apply it thoroughly.

The Author
April 2012

Truth seldom goes without a scratched face.

Puritan John Trapp
A Puritan Golden Treasury, p. 300

1

The Sufficiency of Scripture*

Romans 4:3; Galatians 4:30

For what saith the scripture? Abraham believed God, and it was counted unto him for righteousness.

Nevertheless what saith the scripture? Cast out the bondwoman and her son: for the son of the bondwoman shall not be heir with the son of the freewoman.

Of all the issues that surround and inundate the church today—the redefining of the Gospel, the "seeker-sensitive" movement, the entertainment-orientation of ministry, the abandonment of preaching, the relativism and pragmatism that rule every aspect of Church life, etc.—I am absolutely convinced that it is *the doctrine of the sufficiency of Scripture* that is the key issue, that *every* issue and question, without exception, comes back to our attitude toward and approach to Scripture. *The bottom line is that what Scripture alone says is always the issue.* In contrast, when Scripture *alone* is not our *sole* authority, anything is possible.

If we may interject here, even more alarming, as documented by several recent polls, is the fact that "a major reason many people are leaving the church is because they no longer believe the Bible to be the absolute Word of God."[1] Is there any doubt of the Church's weakness?

When one, therefore, sits down and *objectively* (repeat, *objectively*) compares modern Christianity with Scripture, it does not take him long to see the places of departure. He quickly sees that men have removed many of the necessities, such as the primary one of strong expository preaching, and then added several tons of baggage. How many doctrinal statements, church constitutions, and denominational creeds *say*, "We believe the Holy Scriptures, the sixty-six books of the Old and New Testaments, to be the only verbally inspired, inerrant, infallible Word of God, the final authority for faith and life" (or words to that effect), but how many truly *practice* it? How many pastors are standing in pulpits and boldly and unapologetically preaching "all the counsel of God" (Acts 20:27) and following it *alone* as

---

* This chapter was originally issue 17 of *Truth on Tough Texts* (hereafter abbreviated TOTT), December 2006. Because of its critical importance to our theme, however, we have chosen to place it first in this collection.

their authority for every aspect of ministry? How many Christians live a life that follows *solely* the principles, precepts, and precedents of the Word of God? How many have a true *biblical worldview* (see chapter 49)?

In both our texts, we see Paul concerned with one thing only, namely, **what saith the scripture?**—that is, *what does Scripture say on a particular subject?* In the first instance (Rom. 4:3), he speaks of justification by faith and cites Abraham as the prime example. To emphasize his point, he quotes from Genesis 15:6. In the second instance (Gal. 4:30), he speaks again of justification by faith. Illustrating the principle that we are no longer under law but under grace (vv. 21–31), he again quotes from Genesis (21:10, 12).

Over and over again, we see Paul going to the Scripture as his *sole* authority. He uses the phrase "it is written," for example, thirty times (e.g. Rom. 1:17; 3:10; 9:13; 1 Cor. 1:19, 31; Gal. 3:10; etc.). Further, including all New Testament writers, we find that phrase a total of sixty-three times (KJV; 60 in the NASB; 62 in the NIV; 64 in the ESV; etc.). Similarly, we find the words "Scripture saith" six times (Jn. 19:37; Rom. 9:17; 10:11; 11:2; 1 Tim. 5:18; Jas. 4:5). All this demonstrates the *singular importance* of the declarations of Scripture.

We read something very different, however, in our day. One noted evangelical author and pastor, for example, writes the following in one of his many books (so not to offend, I give the source only in an endnote):

> There are four rather common misconceptions about spirituality and maturity that simply don't hold water. . . . Flaw 2: All the problems you will ever have are addressed in the Bible. They're not.[2]

To be fair, we'll give the author the benefit of the doubt by saying that perhaps he means that not every difficulty we will ever face is mentioned *by name*. For example, nowhere do we read, "Thou shalt not use tobacco products," but the principle of not doing anything that damages the temple of the Holy Spirit (1 Cor. 6:18–20) plainly teaches against this practice.

So we must object to the author's wording, for it immediately, whether intended or not, casts a doubt on the Scripture. This wording could easily cause someone to say, "Oh, since the Bible doesn't saying anything about this practice, then it must be okay," or, "Since I can't find the answer in the Bible, I must look elsewhere." We submit, however, *every single problem or question we might have is answered by either word or principle in Scripture*. The Word of God is sufficient! If the above author agrees with that truth, and we hope he does, why didn't he word it this way: "All the problems you will ever have are addressed either in Word or principle in the Bible?"

In contrast to today's attitude, oh, how different was that of many in bygone days! In the words of Puritan Thomas Gouge, for example:

There is not a condition into which a child of God can fall but there is a direction and rule in the Word in measure suitable thereunto.[3]

While the Puritan's were certainly not perfect, their devotion to the authority and application of the Word of God puts us to shame. It was from them that we received the *Westminster Confession of Faith* (1646), in which we read these statements (which also appear virtually verbatim in *The London Baptist Confession of 1689*):

. . . all the books of the Old and New Testament . . . are given by inspiration of God to be the rule of faith and life . . . (Chapter I, section II)

The authority of the holy Scripture, for which it ought to be believed, and obeyed, dependeth not upon the testimony of any man, or church; but wholly upon God (who is truth itself) the author thereof: and therefore it is to be received, because it is the word of God . . . (I.IV)

The whole counsel of God concerning all things necessary for his own glory, man's salvation, faith and life, is either expressly set down in scripture, or by good and necessary consequence may be deduced from scripture: unto which nothing at any time is to be added, whether by new revelations of the Spirit, or traditions of men . . . (I.VI)

The supreme judge by which all controversies of religion are to be determined, and all decrees of councils, opinions of ancient writers, doctrines of men, and private spirits, are to be examined, and in whose sentence, we are to rest, can be no other but the Holy Spirit speaking in the Scripture. (I.X)

The Puritans believed the Bible to be the *only* model for life and cited Scripture for *every area* of living: worship, family, government, economics, sex, church, education, and all others. Do we *really* believe Thomas Vincent's (1634–1678) answer to the question, "Why are the Scriptures called the rule to direct us how we may glorify and enjoy God?"

Because all *doctrines* which we are bound to believe must be measured or judged of; all *duties* which we are bound to practice as means in order to the attainment of this chief end of man, must be squared or conformed unto this rule.[4]

Among my favorites of the Puritans was Thomas Watson (no relation that I know of), who wrote:

> The Word is a rule of faith, a canon to direct our lives. The Word is the judge of controversies, the rock of infallibility. That only is to be received for truth which agrees with Scripture. . . . All maxims in divinity are to be brought to the touchstone of Scripture, as all measures are brought to the standard.[5]

Further, the Puritans mercilessly scorned (and rightly so) the traditions of Catholicism (in contrast to today's open tolerance of its heinous blasphemies and pagan practices). To them the Scriptures *alone* were to govern the Church. Watson continues:

> The Papists, therefore, make themselves guilty, who eke out Scripture with their traditions, which they consider equal to it. The Council of Trent says, that the traditions of the church of Rome are to be received . . . with the same devotion that Scripture is to be received; so bringing themselves under the curse. Rev xxii:18. "If any man shall add unto these things, God shall add unto him the plagues that are written in this book."[6]

We simply cannot avoid equating that with what we see today, even in Evangelicalism. Countless things have been and continue to be added to the Church and its ministry, and traditions often supersede the clear revelations of Scripture.

We should approach every question of life by turning to Scripture *alone*. If the Bible is absolutely authoritative, this therefore means that it is authoritative in *every* area. If, on the other hand, it is not authoritative in every area, then it's not authoritative at all. There can be no middle ground here, no "gray area." Therefore, when a question arises, we should turn to the Word of God *alone* for the answer.

Again, however, the grievous trend in the Church today is the idea that, "The Bible does not address every issue of life." To mention a single example, one of the most common things used to supplement Scripture today is psychology. I have heard many advocates say, "Psychology by itself is not enough and the Bible by itself is not enough; we need both for effective counseling." Such teaching is appalling and is no less than heresy; it flies in the face of Scripture by blatantly denying its sufficiency, that something else is needed to answer people's problems. If we may submit, whatever did poor ole Paul, or the Lord Jesus Himself for that matter, do without modern psychological techniques? How could they possibly have been effective without adequate training in psychology? (See chapter 47 for more on this issue.) We must face the question: *Is Scripture solely sufficient, or is it not?* Our answer to that question reveals our true attitude toward Scripture.

In an article titled, "The Finality and Sufficiency of Scripture," theologian John Murray wrote:

> Here, I believe, we have too often made the mistake of not taking seriously the doctrine we profess. If Scripture is the inscripturated revelation of the gospel and of God's mind and will, if it is the only revelation of this character that we possess, then it is this revelation in all its fullness, richness, wisdom, and power that must be applied to man in whatever religious, moral, mental situation he is to be found. It is because we have not esteemed and prized the perfection of Scripture and its finality, that we have resorted to other techniques, expedients, and methods of dealing with the dilemma that confronts us all if we are alive to the needs of this hour. . .

> . . . it is not the tradition of the past, not a precious heritage, and not the labours of the fathers, that are to serve this generation and this hour, but the Word of the living and abiding God deposited for us in Holy Scripture, and this Word ministered by the church. And we must bring forth from its inexhaustible treasures, in exposition, proclamation, and application—application to every sphere of life—what is the wisdom and power of God for man in this age in all the particularity of his need, as for man in every age. There will then be commanding relevance, for it will be the message from God in the unction and power of the Spirit, not derived *from* the modern mentality, but declared *to* the modern mentality in all the desperateness of its anxiety and misery.[7]

I am compelled here to cite another example of today's trend. My desire is not to be divisive or unkind, but to "[speak] the truth in love" (Eph. 4:15). The same writer mentioned earlier first makes this well-sounding and typical evangelical statement (source again in endnote):

> If I could have only one wish for God's people, it would be that all of us would return to the Word of God, that we would realize once and for all that His book has the answers. The Bible IS the authority, the final resting place of our cares, our worries, our sorrows, and our surprises. It is the final answer to our questions, our search.[8]

We whole-heartedly agree so far, but then in another book, he writes:

> Clearly my position is on the side of openness, allowing room for the untried, the unpredictable, the unexpected, all the while holding fast to the truth.

[My wife] and I are neither brilliant nor worldly wise, but we do learn fast and we stay flexible, always open to innovative ideas. . . . If a fresh idea, never tried before, makes sense, we'll give it a whirl! If it fails, we learned. If it works, we get all the more excited![9]

Again, our desire is unity, but if I may be lovingly blunt, that stetement is appalling. First, God doesn't ask us to be *brilliant*, and He certainly doesn't ask us to be *worldly wise*; He asks us to be *obedient*. Second, we must ask "makes sense" to whom, man or God? Third, "give it a whirl?" What verse of Scripture tells us to give things "a whirl"? On the other hand, how many verses outline what we are to do and how many more tell us to obey? Fourth, Christian ministry simply is *not a matter of trial and error*. We must disagree with the writer's statement, "If it fails, we learn," for he obviously *didn't* learn that when we do *what* God says and do it the *way* He says, we won't fail. Fifth, why can't the writer "get all the more excited" by just doing things God's way? Sixth, in light of the second paragraph, it's difficult to know what the writer means when he says "holding fast to the truth" in the first paragraph.

My Dear Christian Friend, God doesn't want simply our physical *activity*, nor does He need our mental *productivity*, rather He demands our total *reliability*. He wants to use us, but He wants to do it *His* way, and His way is outlined in His Word *alone*. We have flooded His church with man-made programs, gimmicks, humanistic psychology, worldly marketing, and a plethora of other "helps" just to get results, but what kind of results are they? They are not lasting results, for just as man's ideas come and go, so will the followers of such ideas. Only when we follow the Word *alone* will we have lasting, permanent results: "I [Paul] have planted, Apollos watered; but God gave the increase. So then neither is he that planteth any thing, neither he that watereth; but God that giveth the increase" (1 Cor. 3:6–7; cf. 2:1–5).

Of many Scriptural examples we could cite of those who just did things God's way and obeyed His Word without addition or subtraction, Noah is among my favorites. Here was a man who appeared to everyone outside his family to be either an eccentric at best or "a nut" at worst. Though totally land-locked, he built a huge boat, all the while proclaiming it was going to rain, even though it had never rained before. Why would anyone do such a thing? Did God give Noah any signs that it was going to rain—how about just a couple of cloudy days? Did He give Noah any evidence that what He said about the coming judgment was true—maybe just a lightening bolt or two? No. So why did Noah do it? *Simply and solely because God said to do it*. That was enough for Noah; his response to what God said was: "Thus did Noah; according to all that God commanded him, so did he" (Gen. 6:22).

How many of us today fear what people will think if we simply obey what God says? We fear that we will appear old-fashioned, behind the times, out of touch, naïve, simplistic, non-intellectual, or just plain silly if we quote and practice the Bible. Not Noah.

Noah teaches us another lesson. Notice that he did not build the ark because he saw "a need" for it—there wasn't one. There were no large bodies of water nearby, and Noah certainly didn't live in a port city, so there was absolutely no need for a big boat. In contrast, many today want to go out and "do something" just because they perceive a need. So using human reasoning they think up something to "meet the need." This is not what Noah did. *He did what God told him to do, no more and no less.* He didn't form a committee, he didn't found an organization, he didn't think up a method for ministry; he simply obeyed God by building the ark and preaching the Word. Likewise, if we would just do what God says to do, the way He says to do it, no more and no less, we will see God's blessings like never before.

Without doubt, most of Christianity today is totally pragmatic in its approach to ministry. To many, if not most, Christian ministers, "the end justifies the means." They, like Charles Finney, D. L. Moody, and others, will "do anything to get a man to God" (Moody's words). But is that what we see in God's Word? Is that what we learn from Noah? No. We see a man doing what God told him to do.

Consider what Noah would do today if he followed modern trends. To be successful, he would build several boats (or just one even bigger one) and then do anything to get people on one of them. He would run an attendance contest, give away balloons with dinosaur pictures on them, put on a stage play to dramatize the coming flood, make people feel comfortable by appealing to their "felt-needs," sing praise choruses for an hour, have a celebrity give his testimony, and then deliver a ten-minute talk on self-esteem and that "God has a wonderful plan for your life, so you really need to get on the boat." But Noah's ministry was not a *pragmatic* one; it was a *biblical* one. He did things God's way.

I'm also constantly reminded of another example, namely, the book of Nehemiah, where we read:

> And all the people gathered themselves together as one man into the street that was before the water gate; and they spake unto Ezra the scribe to bring the book of the law of Moses, which the LORD had commanded to Israel. (8:1)

The pivotal words here are "bring the book," the background of which we find in Deuteronomy 31:9–13, where Moses delivers a law stating that,

> At the end of every seven years, in the solemnity of the year of release, in the feast of tabernacles, When all Israel is come to appear before the LORD thy God in the place which he shall choose, thou shalt read this law before all Israel in their hearing. Gather the people together, men, and women, and children, and thy stranger that is within thy gates, that they may hear, and that they may learn, and fear the LORD your God, and observe to do all the words of this law: And that their children, which have not known any thing, may hear, and learn to fear the LORD your God, as long as ye live in the land whither ye go over Jordan to possess it. (vv. 10–13)

Note carefully that *all* the people—men, women, and children—were to listen to the Law of God. The accepted practice today, of course, is that we need "graded curriculum" and different classes and programs for each age group, an approach that is, according to historical fact, a by-product of evolutionary thought propagated by John Dewy and others. Here, however, all the people listened to the reading of God's Law. In fact, what we find in Scripture is that children of every age were *always*, without a single exception, with their parents when God's people met for worship; in other words, *families always worshipped together.*[10]

And what was (and is) the purpose? "That they may learn, and fear the LORD your God, and observe to do all the words of this law." While people were instructed every Sabbath and daily in their homes, this public reading served as a collective reminder to obey God's Law.

So the people's request to "bring the book" is extremely significant. During the seventy years of captivity in Babylon, the practice of publicly reading the Scriptures had been neglected, but was now reinstated. I am always struck by those words. The people did not say, "Ezra, bring entertainment," "Bring a celebrity," "Bring your opinion," "Bring psychology," "Bring a new method," or "Bring your experience"; rather they said, "Bring *the Book*!" Oh, how much we need the Book today! We bring everything under the sun into our assemblies except the one (and *only*) thing we should bring, the Word of God.

We also read that the people "gathered themselves together as one man." We hear much today about "unity," but it is the Word of God *alone* that provides the ground for true unity. If there is no unity around the Word of God, then there's no unity.

Also notice that the people were attentive to the Word (v. 3), and that they "stood up" when it was opened (v. 5). What reverence and awe they had for God's Word, in stark contrast to today's often nonchalant, flippant, and lip-serving attitude.

Further, the people listened from "the morning until midday." The Hebrew for "morning" (*owr*) means "light, light of day, daybreak, or dawn." So God's people stood and listened to the Word read, exposited, and applied for several hours. What an indictment on us today who barely have time to give God an hour on Sunday morning, or who don't want the sermon to go "too long" so as not to interfere with our plans for the afternoon, or who think nothing of attending a Christian concert or having an hour long song service but only a ten-minute "sermon" (or none at all).

What was the result of all this in Nehemiah's day? Did the Word of God make a difference in the lives of God's people?

> Now in the twenty and fourth day of this month the children of Israel were assembled with fasting, and with sackclothes, and earth upon them. And the seed of Israel separated themselves from all strangers, and stood and confessed their sins, and the iniquities of their fathers. And they stood up in their place, and read in the book of the law of the LORD their God one fourth part of the day; and another fourth part they confessed, and worshipped the LORD their God. (9:1–3)

Again the people gathered to read God's Law, this time for a fourth part of the day, that is, for three hours. They then spent another three hours in confession of sin and worship of God. What a contrast to our habit today! As Matthew Henry puts it, "They stayed together six hours . . . without saying, *Behold what a weariness it is!*"

Further, we often hear such clichés as, "Oh, we need revival," "We need renewal," "We need reformation," and so on. We then use every human idea we can think of to produce the desired effect. Charles Finney wrote in his autobiography, "A revival is not a miracle, nor dependent on a miracle in any sense. It is a purely philosophical result of the right use of the constituted means, as much so as any other effect produced by the application of means."[11] Likewise, today's basic philosophy of ministry is, "If it works, do it." But that is not what we see in Nehemiah. It was *only* when Ezra opened the Book, read it, and expounded it that true revival broke out. It was *only then* that the people of God repented and turned back to Him. Likewise, new life will come to the Church only when we "bring the Book" *alone*.

In his typical straightforward style, A. W. Tozer brings the issue down to this pointed and practical application:

> What Christian when faced with a moral problem goes straight to the Sermon on the Mount or other New Testament Scripture for the authoritative answer? Who lets the words of Christ be final on giving, birth control, the bringing up of a family, personal habits, tithing, entertainment, buying, selling, and other such important matters?[12]

What is the final conclusion of believing in Biblical authority and sufficiency? We *say* we believe it, but do we *really*?

> *The final conclusion of believing in biblical authority and sufficiency is that we do that which it says, refrain from doing what it forbids, and add nothing to it or subtract nothing from it in both doctrine and practice.*

It's one thing to say those words, but it's quite another, indeed, to live them.

NOTES

[1] From a poll taken by Answers in Genesis, as a follow-up to a 2002 Barna poll and a Southern Baptist poll of around the same time. Cited in "Answers Update", Volume 13, Issue 11 (Hebron, KY: Answers In Genesis, 2006), p. 2.

[2] Charles Swindoll, *Three Steps Forward, Two Steps Back* (1980). He adds (chap. 1), "The Bible simply does not offer a specific answer to every problem in life."

[3] Cited in Leland Ryken, *Worldly Saints: The Puritans As They Really Were* (Zondervan, 1986), p. 137.

[4] Thomas Vincent, *The Shorter Catechism Explained from Scripture* (Banner of Truth Trust, 1980), p. 22 (emphasis added).

[5] Thomas Watson, *A Body of Divinity* (Banner of Truth Trust, 1992 reprint), p. 30.

[6] Ibid.

[7] John Murray, *Collected Writings of John Murray* (Banner of Truth Trust, 1976), Vol. 1, pp. 21-22 (emphasis in the original).

[8] Charles R. Swindoll, *Growing Deep in the Christian Life* (Multnomah Press, 1986), 56.

[9] Charles R. Swindoll, *Living Above the Level of Mediocrity* (Word Publishing, 1989), pp. 162–165.

[10] See Josh. 8:35; 2 Chron. 20:13; Neh. 12:43; Joel 2:15–16; Matt. 18:1–5; Mk. 10:13–14; Lk. 2:41–42; Acts 2:46; 20:20.

[11] *Charles G. Finney: An Autobiography* (Revell, n.d.), p. 5.

[12] A. W. Tozer, "The Waning Authority of Christ in the Churches" in *God Tells the Man Who Cares* (Christian Publications).

The Holy Ghost rides in the chariot of Scripture, and not in the wagon of modern thought.

Charles Spurgeon, "The Sword of the Spirit"
The Metropolitan Tabernacle Pulpit

2

Was Matthias God's Choice?[*]

Acts 1:15–26

While I am more than aware that the majority of commentators are satisfied that Matthias was God's choice to replace Judas in Acts 1:15–26, I must go with the minority who have problems with this idea. I would offer, therefore, seven points that the choice of Matthias was premature and *not* God's choice.

First, and foremost, the Lord Jesus told His disciples to *wait*, nothing else, until the coming of the Holy Spirit. This point is totally ignored by most commentators but seems to me to be the key point of the whole issue. In Luke 24:49, our Lord commands, "And, behold, I send the promise of my Father upon you: but tarry ye in the city of Jerusalem, until ye be endued with power from on high." The Greek for "tarry" is *kathizō*. In Classical Greek, as one Greek authority writes, "Sitting was often a mark of honor or authority: a king sat to receive his subjects, a court to give judgment, and a teacher to teach. The general practice at meals in the Graeco-Roman world was not to sit on chairs but to recline on couches placed round three sides of the table."[1] All these meanings are also found in both the Septuagint and the New Testament. In light of how the disciples sat, that is, *reclined*, with Jesus at the last supper (Jn. 13:23, 25; 21:20), it seems clear that what Jesus is saying is, "I want you to sit like you normally would at supper and wait. I don't want you to preach or anything else. I just want you to sit down, pray together, and wait for Me to send the Holy Spirit as I've promised." This leads to a second point.

Second, our Lord did not tell His disciples to replace Judas. This, too, seems to be ignored by the majority. As one such commentator writes, "As the Holy Ghost, on the day of Pentecost, was to descend upon them and endue them with power from on high, it was necessary that the number twelve should be filled up previously, that the newly elected person might also be made partaker of the heavenly gift." But we are forced to ask, *Why?* If the twelfth Apostle was so necessary at that time, would not the Lord Himself appointed him or specifically instructed the others to do so? The fact is that our Lord already had the twelfth Apostle in mind.

Third, the disciples never chose other disciples before this, so why would they do so now? One writer simply shrugs this off by writing, "In the

[*] This was the main article in the premiere issue of TOTT in August 2005.

[NT] the Apostles were originally chosen by Christ (Lk. 6:13; Acts 1:2), but then after Christ's ascension, the church needed to fill the place of Judas." How can we accept such an offhanded comment? While verses 16 and 20 speak of David's prophecies that there would be a betrayer and the necessity that he be replaced (Pss. 69:25; 109:8), that doesn't mean the task fell to the disciples. The Lord Jesus, and He alone, chose His disciples (and then trained them we might add). One writer makes this point strongly:

> Some have supposed that the role of apostle in the early church can be parallel by an appeal to Jewish procedures. But it seems more likely that the special importance of the apostolic office was derived from the fact that Jesus himself appointed the twelve. It is curious in view of this that the replacement of Judas, selected by means of casting lots (Acts 1:26), was ranked on the same level as those personally appointed by Jesus.[2]

Some respond by arguing, "Since they prayed and asked the Lord to choose the right one, then Christ was there in essence." But that was never the precedent. Christ always chose His disciples in person. This is further confirmed when He called Saul, whom He chose in person, thereby following the pattern He'd laid down. In his commentary on the Greek text of Ephesians, John Eadie is at least doubtful: "Matthias was appointed [Judas'] successor and substitute (if a human appointment, and one prior to Pentecost, be valid)."[3]

Fourth, the Holy Spirit had not yet come upon them, so Spirit control is not indicated. One commentator writes, "Peter acted by inspiration," but we must ask, *where does the text say that*? This was still technically Old Testament times, and the usual indication of the Holy Spirit's work in the Old Testament were the words "the spirit came upon" (1 Chron. 12:18; cf. Jud. 3:10; 6:34; 13:25; 2 Sam. 23:2). Still many insist that "Matthias was the Holy Spirit's choice," but again, the text doesn't say that. Yes, it says he "was numbered with the eleven apostles," but any more than that is only an assumption. The beloved J. Vernon McGee writes:

> I can't see that this was the leading of the Holy Spirit, nor that it was God's leading in the casting of lots. Is Matthias actually the one who took the place of Judas? I don't think so . . . I think the Holy Spirit ignored Matthias.

We also agree with Martyn Lloyd-Jones who comments, "The *apostles* decided that *they* must appoint a successor," but it was Paul who was the Lord's choice.[4] How many wrong actions have been taken, how many unbiblical ministries have been founded, simply because men did things their way instead of allowing God to work His way?

Fifth, casting lots was of the Law and an immature practice in view of the coming Holy Spirit. Yes, this practice was accepted in the Old Testament for discovering God's will (Lev. 16:8–10; Prov. 16:33). Either different colored stones or stones with the candidates name on them were placed in an urn and shook. The first stone that fell was God's choice.

But it's truly puzzling why commentators go out of their way to defend this Old Testament practice even though it's used right on the threshold of a new era. In response, G. Campbell Morgan writes that here is "a revelation of their inefficiency for organization." Indeed, they had not yet comprehended what God was about to do and the way He would then work, namely, not by *lots* but by the *Spirit*. Again, this is why our Lord told them to *wait*. Morgan continues:

> These men were perfectly sincere, proceeding on the lines of revealed truth, but they were ignorant of God's next method; unable to bear their witness; unable to organize themselves for the doing of the work; and consequently needing the coming of the Paraclete.[5]

Likewise, that great theologian Charles Hodge adds:

> It is very doubtful whether this appointment of Matthias had any validity. What is here recorded (Acts 1:15–26), took place before the Apostles had been endued with power from on high (Acts 1:8), and, therefore, before they had any authority to act in the premises.[6]

Sixth, we never again read of Matthias in the Scripture record. Most interpreters are quick to say here, "But many of the other disciples never appear again either." While that is certainty true, one would think that an Apostle chosen under such extraordinary circumstances would figure prominently in the coming events in Acts. But such is not the case. There are even conflicting reports of what became of Matthias. One tradition says that he was stoned to death by the Jews in Judea for preaching the gospel, while others say he was martyred by crucifixion in Ethiopia or Cappadocia.[7] This seems odd for one chosen to be an Apostle under such extraordinary circumstance.

Seventh, clearly, Paul was the twelfth Apostle. Why fill up what the Lord Himself left vacant? He would fill the vacancy in His own time with His own choice, the Apostle Paul. As Hodge writes, "Christ in his own time and way completed the number of his witnesses by calling Paul to be an Apostle."[8] J. Vernon McGee concurs: "I believe that in His own time, the Lord Jesus Himself appointed one to take the place of Judas Iscariot. We don't hear another word about Matthias—nothing is recorded of his ministry . . . It is my conviction that the man the Lord chose was Paul."[9]

Many commentators insist that Paul always excludes himself from the original twelve. They argue, "In 1 Corinthians 12:5 and 8 Paul refers to the twelve and *then* to himself showing a separation of him from them" ("he was seen of Cephas, then of the twelve . . . And last of all he was seen of me also, as of one born out of due time").

But the term "the twelve" is used as a "collective term;" that is, whether there were twelve or not, the disciples as a group were called "the twelve." John 20:24, for example, declares that after the resurrection, "Thomas, one of the twelve, called Didymus, was not with them when Jesus came." Even though there was actually only ten disciples at that time—since Thomas was not with them and Judas was dead—they were still "the twelve." Further, 1 Corinthians 12:5 and 8 are clearly sequential; they simply deal with time and the sequence of events. He appeared *first* to the twelve (again, actually only eleven at that time), and *then* to Paul. This in no way implies that Paul was not Judas' replacement.

It is further argued that Paul's apostleship was different, that is, the other Apostles were for the Jews and Paul was for the Gentiles. While we agree that Paul was the Apostle to the Gentiles, we should be careful about pushing this too far. After all, those so-called "Jewish Apostles" entered the Church Age the next day, and Paul also preached to Jews. There is simply no justification whatsoever to say that Paul was so unique that he is to be considered separate from the other Apostles.

One other question remains: Why did the Holy Spirit allow this situation to be recorded? For the same reason any other wrongdoing is recorded—*for us to learn*. It teaches us to wait on the Lord's time and not take matters into our own hands. There are many today who say such things as, "I believe the Holy Spirit is leading me to do this thing," but what we must look to is what God's Word says (and what it doesn't say), for it is there that we find the will of God.

NOTES

[1] Colin Brown, (General Editor). *The New International Dictionary of New Testament Theology*, 3 Vol. (Grand Rapids: Zondervan, 1975), Vol. 3, p. 588.

[2] Donald Guthrie, *New Testament Theology* (Downers Grove: Inter-Varsity Press, 1981), p. 739.

[3] John Eadie, *Commentary on the Epistle to the Ephesians*. Grand Rapids: Zondervan, reprinted from Eadie's 1883 edition, p. 298.

[4] D. Martyn Lloyd-Jones, *Christian Unity: An Exposition of Ephesians4:1-16*. Grand Rapids: Baker, 1982, p. 186 (emphasis added).

[5] G. Campbell Morgan, *The Acts of the Apostles*, p. 21.

[6] Charles Hodge, *Systematic Theology* (Eerdmans Publishing, Reprinted 1989), Vol. 1, p. 140-141.

[7] *Unger's Bible Dictionary* and *Smith's Bible Dictionary*.

---

[8] Hodge, Vol. 1, p. 141.

[9] J. Vernon McGee, *Through the Bible*, Acts.

First, my friends, stand over this volume, and admire its authority. This is no common book. It is not the sayings of the sages of Greece; here are not the utterances of past ages. If these words were written by man, we might reject them; but O let me think the solemn thought, that this book is God's handwriting, that these words are God's! Let me look at its date; it is dated from the hills of heaven. Let me read the chapters; they flash glory on my eye. Let me read the chapters; they are big with meaning and mysteries unknown. Let me turn over the prophecies; they are pregnant with unthought of wonders. Oh, book of books! And wast thou written by God? Then will I bow before thee. Thou book of vast authority! Thou art a proclamation from the Emperor of Heaven; far be it from me to exercise my reason in contradicting thee. Reason, thy place is to stand and find what this volume means, not to tell what this book ought to say. Come thou, my reason, my intellect, sit thou down and listen, for these words are the words of God. I do not know how to enlarge on this thought. Oh! if you could ever remember that this Bible was actually and really written by God. Oh! if ye had been let into the secret chambers of heaven, if ye had beheld God grasping His pen and writing down these letters, then surely ye would respect them; but they are just as much God's handwriting as if you had seen God write them. This Bible is a book of authority; it is an authorized book, for God has written it. Oh tremble, tremble, lest any of you despise it; mark its authority, for it is the Word of God."

Charles Spurgeon
The New Park Street Pulpit, Vol. 1, page 111

3

How Often Should the Lord's Supper Be Observed?*

1 Corinthians 11:26

For as often as ye eat this bread, and drink this cup, ye do shew the Lord's death till he come.

It has amazed me for decades how this verse is dismissed with a shrug, as if it has absolutely no bearing at all on how **often** we should observe the Lord's Supper. It is argued, "The verse doesn't say *how* **often**, just *as* **often**." It is, therefore, very common in evangelical and fundamental churches to observe it only once a month, every two months, or even once a quarter. Let us, therefore, first honestly follow the New Testament progression, and then second prayerfully submit a conclusion.

The New Testament Progression

First, originally, in Acts 2 the Lord's Supper was observed daily. This doesn't necessarily mean in every house gathering, rather somewhere in the city every day. As Theologian Augustus Strong writes, "The Lord's Supper is to be repeated often,"[1] and this was certainly the case in Acts. But again, *how* often should it be observed?

Second, in Acts 20:7 we read, "And upon the first day of the week, when the disciples came together to break bread, Paul preached unto them, ready to depart on the morrow; and continued his speech until midnight." According to verse 6, Paul stayed in Troas seven days. Verse 7 is then the clearest verse about Sunday worship, and the Lord's Supper was observed on Sunday evening. This is shown by the fact that Luke's method of noting time here is not Jewish (sundown to sundown) but is Roman (midnight to midnight). Not only does Luke use the word "midnight" in verse 7, but "break of day" in verse 11. He undoubtedly did this in the spirit of when Christ instituted the Lord's Supper. As Matthew 26:26–30 indicates, it was in the evening of the night of His betrayal.

---

* This chapter was originally TOTT issue #2, September 2005. See chapter 48 for another discussion of the Lord's Supper.

So, the Lord's Supper was here observed on Sunday evening before the preaching. No longer were there daily meetings, but here is a clear reference to Sunday worship and observance of the Lord's Supper then. May we submit, then, *what better time could there be to remember our Lord's ordeal than on Sunday evening?*

Acts 2:42 further substantiates this: "And they continued stedfastly in the apostles' doctrine and fellowship, and in breaking of bread, and in prayers." The Greek construction shows that "breaking of bread" and "prayers" are what actually constitute fellowship. But the main point here is that consistency dictates we observe *all* of them on the Lord's Day, not just two out of three. Acts 2:42, therefore, gives the *principle* (or *precedent*), while 20:7 gives the *practice*.

Of course, it is argued that "breaking of bread" can refer simply to eating a regular meal, but that simply cannot be true here. As solid commentator William MacDonald rightly observes (and virtually every evangelical commentator agrees):

> This expression is used in the NT to refer both to the Lord's Supper and to eating a common meal. The meaning in any particular case must be determined by the sense of the passage. Here it obviously refers to the Lord's Supper, since it would be quite unnecessary to say that they continued stedfastly eating their meals. From Acts 20:7 we learn that the practice of the early Christians was to break bread on the first day of the week. During the early days of the church, a love feast was held in connection with the Lord's Supper as an expression of the love of the saints for one another. However, abuses crept in, and the "agape" or love feast was discontinued.[2]

So we ask again, why should we observe only two out of the three fundamental activities of the Church on the Lord's Day? As one commentator insists, "There is no command anywhere in the Bible that specifies how often the Supper should be observed." But may we ask, why does there need to be? Is not a biblical *precedent* just as binding as a biblical *command*? When there is a clear precedent, why would we need anything else? And if I may interject, how many so-called "ministries" and "methods" do we practice today that don't even *have* a precedent, much less a command, but we do them anyway? What is patently ignored today concerning the doctrine of Biblical Authority is that it includes *precedents*, not just commands.

Third, note specifically what our text *says* (and the text is always the issue): "For *as often* as ye eat this bread, and drink this cup, *ye do show the Lord's death till he come* (emphasis added). How often do we meet to celebrate the Lord's death and resurrection? *Every Lord's Day*, and the

Lord's Supper is here included. Many take **as often** to be infrequent, but the text implies the exact opposite.

Fourth, notice also that each time we observe the Lord's Supper, it *shows* **the Lord's death till he come**. The word **shows** is the Greek *kataggellō*, to announce publicly, proclaim. This word is a derivative of *kerux* and *kerussō*, which spoke of the imperial herald announcing the wishes of the King, as when Paul told Timothy to "preach the Word" in 2 Timothy 4:2. So, each time we observe the Lord's Supper, we are proclaiming the Gospel. Should this not, then, be practiced each Lord's Day?

Harry Ironside wonderfully illustrates this in a personal incident. A Japanese man who was attending some of Ironside's meetings in Sacramento was troubled about his soul, but it seemed impossible to bring him to Christ because of his love for money. A year later, Ironside was again in Sacramento for meetings and there was the man again. Ironside asked him if he'd received Christ yet, to which he answered no. He then asked an odd question, "Do you have a meeting on Sunday where you eat the bread and drink the wine showing how Jesus died?" Ironside answered yes, to which the man replied, "I come." At the meeting, the man sat close to the front, and Ironside prayed that God would speak to his heart. After the people had partaken of the elements and the elements were returned to the table, the man stood up and said, "I like to pray." Ironside winced, regretting that he didn't tell the man they he wouldn't be expected to take part in the meeting. But the man prayed like this: "Oh, God, I all broke up. For one year I fight You. I fight you hard. Your Spirit break me all to pieces. O God, today I see Your people eating the bread, drinking the wine, telling how Jesus died for sinners like me. O God, You love me so. You give Your Son to die for me. I cannot fight you anymore. I give up. I take Him as my Savior." As Ironside then writes,

> It did not spoil our meeting at all to have him take part with such a prayer. We realized that this simple ordinance had preached to him . . . The Lord's Supper, if given the place our Lord intended it to have, will constantly preach to the world, and will say more than any words of ours can say: "As often as ye eat this bread, and drink this cup, ye do *preach* the Lord's death till he come."[3]

Fifth, it's also noteworthy that this passage is the lengthiest discussion of the Lord's Supper in Scripture and was given to a church that had perverted virtually all church activity. It seems apparent, then, that the Lord's Supper, as Harry Ironside put it, "was intended to occupy a very large place in the minds of Christians in this dispensation."[4] It seems clear, then, that something that occupies such a large place should occur each Lord's Day.

Sixth, and finally, a principle that is overlooked on this issue is that any other frequency is totally subjective. We are left with no absolute but allowed to decide for ourselves how often we will remember the Lord's death and resurrection. Indeed, the common practice of our day on every issue is "to make it up as we go along."

Conclusion

I simply see no other conclusion than the observance of the Lord's Supper each Lord's Day as part of our worship and fellowship. Others of this "old school" agree. That was, for example, the view of Reformer John Calvin, who wrote in his *Institutes*:

> [The Lord's Supper] was not instituted to be received once a year and that perfunctorily (as is now commonly the custom); but that all Christians might have it in frequent use, and frequently call to mind the sufferings of Christ, thereby sustaining and confirming their faith . . . That such was the practice of the Apostolic Church, we are informed by Luke in the Acts . . . (Acts 2:42). Thus we ought always to provide that no meeting of the Church is held without the word, prayer, the dispensation of the Supper, and alms.[5]

This was also the view of the famous English non-conformist preacher Thomas Goodwin (1600–80),[6] as well as theological giant Francis Turretin (1623–87), who wrote:

> Christians are said to have come together upon the first day of the week to break bread (Acts 20:27), i.e., to celebrate the holy supper, which was customarily done on the Lord's Day when they assembled to hear preaching and to perform the other public exercises of piety.[7]

Likewise, this was the view of the Puritans, such as Matthew Henry (1662–1714):

> Our bodily meals return often; we cannot maintain life and health without this. And it is fit that this spiritual diet should be taken often too. The ancient churches celebrated this ordinance every Lord's Day, if not every day when they assembled for worship.[8]

It was also Charles Spurgeon's conviction that the Lord's Supper was to be observed every Lord's Day, as brought out in the Preface to his book, *Till He Come: Communion Meditations and Addresses*. He believed strongly that this was the "apostolic precedent; and it was his oft-repeated testimony that the more frequently he obeyed his Lord's command, 'This do in remembrance of Me,' the more precious did his Savior become to him."

Likewise, in his commentary on Acts, A. C. Gaebelein wrote:

> The Lord's Day and the Lord's Supper belong together, and there can be no doubt that the early church celebrated that feast of love each Lord's Day . . . Is it too much to carry out His loving request every Lord's Day, the day on which He left the grave?[9]

Theologian Louis Sperry Chafer concurs: "As the resurrection is celebrated by fitting observance of the Lord's Day each week, so it seems probable that it is well to celebrate Christ's death just as often."[10] John Murray also agrees when he writes, "The Lord's Day is ever recurrent and the Lord's supper should be frequently administered. . . . Acts 2:42 implies that the supper was an integral part of the worship of the early church."[11]

I we may also add, as theologian Wayne Grudem rightly points out, "It has been the practice of most of the Church throughout its history to celebrate the Lord's Supper every week when believers gather."[12] The change, for some odd reason, seems to have occurred after the Reformation, although as mentioned a moment ago, some retained it.

One more important question arises: is there a danger of this becoming ritual and mindless activity? *Certainly, but that would be our fault and to our shame.* This is an act of worship and remembrance that is observed by God's unified people. A wonderful aid that I have found to contribute to the worship atmosphere is to read an entry from the book, *The Valley of Vision: A Collection of Puritan Prayers & Devotions* (Banner of Truth Trust). One can find other good resources, of course. I've used, for example, the "Table Addresses" of John Murray in Volume 3 of *The Collected Writings of John Murray* (Banner of Truth Trust).[13]

Finally, the Lord's Supper is more than a remembrance for our *own* sakes; it is also a proclamation for the *world's* sake. It is a testimony to the world that we are not ashamed of our Lord or of His blood, that we belong to Him and are obedient to Him.

NOTES

[1] Augustus Strong, *Systematic Theology* (Valley Forge: Judson Press, 1907), p. 964.

[2] William MacDonald, *Believer's Bible Commentary* (Nashville: Thomas Nelson Publishers, 1995), p. 1588.

[3] H. A. Ironside, *1 Corinthians* (New York: Loizeaux Brothers, 1938), pp. 350-3 (emphasis in the original).

[4] Ironside, p. 342.

[5] *Institutes*, Book IV, Ch. 14, Section 44 (Beveridge translation).

[6] Thomas Goodwin, *Government of Churches*, b. 7, ch. 5, p. 328. Cited in John Gill, *A Body of Doctrinal and Practical Divinity* (Paris Arkansas: The Baptist Standard Bearer, 1995 Reprint of the 1839 Edition), p. 923.

[7] Francis Turretin, *Institutes of Elenctic Theology*. Three Volumes. (Phillipsburg, NJ: Presbyterian and Reformed Publishing, 1997), Vol. 3, p. 445..

[8] Matthew Henry, *Matthew Henry's Commentary on the Whole Bible*.

[9] A. C. Gaebelein, *Acts* (New York: Loizeaux Brothers), pp. 344, 67.

[10] Louis Sperry Chafer, *Systematic Theology*, (Dallas: Dallas Seminary Press, 1947-1948), Vol. VII, p. 229.

[11] *Collected Writings of John Murray* (Carlisle: Banner of Truth Trust, 1977), Vol. 2, pp. 376, 380.

[12] Wayne Grudem, *Systematic Theology* (Grand Rapids: Zondervan, 1994), p 999.

[13] We have posted these on our website (www.TheScriptureAlone.com) at the following link: www.TheScriptureAlone.com/murray_ls.htm.

Scripture has its authority from God, not from the church . . . But a most pernicious error widely prevails that Scripture has only so much weight as is conceded to it by the consent of the church. As if the eternal and inviolable truth of God depended upon the decision of men! . . . Thus these sacrilegious men, wishing to impose an unbridled tyranny under the cover of the church, do not care with what absurdities they ensnare themselves and others, provided they can force this one idea upon the simple-minded: that the church has authority in all things.

But such wranglers are neatly refuted by just one word of the apostle. He testifies that the church is "built upon the foundation of the prophets and apostles" (Eph. 2:20). If the teaching of the prophets and apostles is the foundation, this must have had authority before the church began to exist.

John Calvin
Institutes of the Christian Religion (I.VII.1, 2)

4

Temporary Spiritual Gifts[*]

1 Cor. 12:8–11; 13:8–13

For to one is given by the Spirit the word of wisdom; to another the word of knowledge by the same Spirit; To another faith by the same Spirit; to another the gifts of healing by the same Spirit; To another the working of miracles; to another prophecy; to another discerning of spirits; to another divers kinds of tongues; to another the interpretation of tongues: But all these worketh that one and the selfsame Spirit, dividing to every man severally as he will.

When we study spiritual gifts thoroughly, we see that they fulfill two major purposes.

First, *permanent gifts* edify the church. Paul lists these in his letter to the Romans (12:6–8): prophecy, ministry (serving), teaching, exhortation, ruling, and mercy. God will continue to give these gifts to believers for the duration of the church age, and these are to be ministered by His people at all times in the life of the church.

Second, the *temporary gifts* were signs to authenticate the apostolic message as being the very Word of God until the time when the Scriptures, His written Word, were completed and became self-authenticating.

After years of studying the Scriptures and the issue of spiritual gifts, I am convinced that the present passage is one of the most misunderstood in all the Bible. Most commentators insist that all the gifts spoken of here are still with us today.[1] If this is true, however, we are not only left with some inconsistencies in the list, but more seriously a very real weakening of the Word of God Itself.

To study this fine point of doctrine adequately, we'll also need to examine another passage in 1 Corinthians (13:9–13). Let's look at five principles, the first one of which is overlooked by many teachers on the issue of temporary spiritual gifts.

---

[*] This chapter was originally TOTT issues #3 and 4, October and November 2005.

The Finality of Inspiration

As 2 Timothy 3:16 declares, "All Scripture is given by inspiration of God." The Greek word for "inspiration" (*theopneustos*) is derived from two Greek words: *theos*, "God," and *pnein*, "to breath out, or to blow." The best way to understand these Greek words is to contrast them with two other words. One is *psuchin*, "to breath gently." In contrast, *pnein* speaks of a forceful expiration of air. Another word is the Hebrew *ah-ayrh*, "to breath unconsciously," but to contrast again, *pnein* speaks of a conscious breathing. All this provides a clear definition of Inspiration: *Inspiration is the forceful and conscious exhaling of God into the Scripture writers*. That definition reflects what is meant when we say the Scriptures are "God-breathed."

We also read in 2 Peter 1:20–21, "No prophecy of the scripture is of any private interpretation. For the prophecy came not in old time by the will of man: but holy men of God spake as they were moved by the Holy Ghost." Scripture didn't come by anyone's experience. It didn't come from anyone's private interpretation. It didn't even come from the men who wrote it. From whence did it come? *Holy men of God were moved by the Holy Spirit of God.*

"Moved" translates *pheromenoi*, which means to be "carried along." Luke used this word to describe how a ship is carried along by the wind (Acts 27:15, 17). It's also interesting to note that Peter evidently loved this word, for he uses it six times in his two Epistles. Being an outdoorsman, he wanted to paint us a picture, and what a picture it is! Men today are moved, motivated, and mastered by many things, but the men God used were driven by only one thing, the Holy Spirit.

So, the biblical view of inspiration is stated theologically as "Verbal, Plenary Inspiration." The term "verbal" means that the Holy Spirit guided the choice of the words. "Plenary" simply means full or complete and, therefore, describes the Bible as being the full, complete revelation of God. All this gives us a complete and conclusive definition of inspiration:

> Inspiration is the activity of God by which He superintended the reception and the communication of His message, even in the specific words used, while still allowing for the style and personality of each writer, with the results being the Word of God.

Now, the point of all this is to ask a question. Is inspiration still going on today *in any way, shape, or form*? Is man getting any "flashes of insight," any wisdom, any knowledge, or any discernment whatsoever from *any other source* except the Scriptures? If we say "yes" at any point, then we have just violated the doctrine of Verbal Plenary Inspiration.

With the words "but holy men of God spake as they were moved by the Holy Ghost," our text declares that the Scriptures, as they stand today, are the complete record. No new revelation is being given, no matter who claims otherwise. There is no other wisdom, no other tool for discernment, no other spiritual knowledge, no "flashes of insight," or anything else. This is proven by the tense of the verb translated "spake." The Greek verb (*elalesan*) is in the aorist tense, indicating punctiliar past action that occurred *then* not *now*.

This leads us to a second principle.

The Reason Some Spiritual Gifts Were Temporary

While we will deal with the passage again, it is essential that we here mention 1 Corinthians 13:8–13:

> Charity never faileth: but whether there be prophecies, they shall fail; whether there be tongues, they shall cease; whether there be knowledge, it shall vanish away. For we know in part, and we prophesy in part. But when that which is perfect is come, then that which is in part shall be done away. When I was a child, I spake as a child, I understood as a child, I thought as a child: but when I became a man, I put away childish things. For now we see through a glass, darkly; but then face to face: now I know in part; but then shall I know even as also I am known. And now abideth faith, hope, charity, these three; but the greatest of these is charity.

Verses 8 and 9 reveal that what has come before this passage, that is, the things of chapter 12, are partial knowledge, only temporary. Verse 10 says that there is something coming that is "perfect," that is, mature or complete. But the question is, "What exactly is coming?" No matter what the objections may be, this can refer to one thing only. The Greek for "perfect" is *teleio*, which literally means "perfect, full grown, complete." It is also important to see that the word appears in the *neuter* gender. Therefore, this is referring to a "thing" not a person. Because of that fact, "perfect" cannot refer to Christ as some have suggested. Faced with this textual fact, others have said that it refers to Christ's *Second Coming* (a thing). But that doesn't fit the context, nor is it spoken of elsewhere. It is poor exegesis to insist that Paul here throws a weak and uncertain reference to the Second Coming into a discussion of something entirely different. Violating the context is one of the chief reasons for error. One other view says that "perfect" refers to *eternity*, that is, the eternal state, but this falls for the same reason as the Second Coming View—it just doesn't fit. Paul is talking about that which is needed on earth, not what will be in heaven. Ultimately, this view, as all the others, weakens the absolute and sole authority and sufficiency of Scripture.

There is only one view that fits the context. The "mature, full-grown, complete thing" can refer only to *the completed New Testament Scriptures*. Throughout his letter Paul has been emphasizing preaching, teaching, and knowledge. Right here in verses 11 and 12 he speaks of immature and incomplete knowledge. But when the New Testament Scriptures were completed, there was then mature, full-grown, complete knowledge. Instead of being children, they would then be adults. Greek born scholar Spiros Zodhiatus makes this comment:

> The phrase "when that which is perfect is come" refers to the written revelation of Scripture. When this revelation was completed, there was no need for the temporary gifts (e.g., tongues, prophecies, and knowledge) which were given in order to substantiate the message that the apostles were preaching.[2]

Henry Morris agrees:

> Since the previous verse refers to the incompleteness of the divine revelation at that time, "that which is perfect [complete]" almost certainly refers to the completion of biblical revelation, as finally announced by John, the last of the apostles (Revelation 22:18,19). In the Scriptures, we now have all the prophetic truth needed for the guidance of the church until Christ comes again. With few, if any, exceptions, we also have all the attestation we need to its veracity and power, so there is little need any more for miraculous signs, even though many still desire them.[3]

In his book, *Decisions, Decisions*, Dave Swavely also concurs:

> Some commentators have suggested that "perfect" or "complete" is the eternal state, but it seems more likely that it is a reference to the completed canon of Scripture. Paul knew that when the Bible was completed, there would be no more need for any further revelation, and therefore no need for revelatory gifts.[4]

Consider also New Testament scholar Merrill Unger:

> But when that which is perfect is come [Greek, *to teleion*, the completed and final thing, which means "the New Testament Scripture;" the neuter in the Greek denotes neither Christ nor His second advent, both of which thoughts are foreign to the context], then that which is in part [partial or piecemeal revelation through the gift of directly inspired prophecy and knowedge before the New Testament was given] shall be done away with [*katargēthēstai*, shall be superseded, rendered uncecessary, and meaningless, because no longed needed and so shall be cancelled and done away with].[5]

This view has been criticized because some say it teaches that we have "all knowledge," but this view says no such thing. The Word of God nowhere says It contains all knowledge. There are many things about God's nature and workings that we know nothing about, things that are not revealed in His Word. Rather, the Word of God contains all the knowledge God wants us to have, all the knowledge we need to live correctly for Him. Indeed, the knowledge that existed before the completion of the Scriptures was incomplete, but with the Scriptures came a complete knowledge, complete in the sense that it is now adequate for all earthly purposes and absolutely authoritative.

We should also interject here that a cross reference to verse 11 is Ephesians 4:14 (a text we will examine in chapter 6), where we are told to "be no more children, tossed to and fro, and carried about with every wind of doctrine." In both of these texts and contexts Paul is speaking of maturity in the *present*, and the only thing that will bring that about is the Word of God.

Finally, the "eternity view" says that the "Word of God view" has a problem explaining the words "face to face" and that these words are best explained as the believer being with God in the eternal state. That is a nice thought, and we all look forward to that reality, but again, it does not fit the context. Why does Paul throw in something about eternity when the entire context speaks of something that is needed *now*? "Face to face" simply refers to the comparison that Paul makes between the Word of God and a "glass" (mirror). Mirrors of that day were often made of bronze, and because of the worldwide renown of Corinthian bronze, the analogy undoubtedly struck the Corinthians profoundly. Even the best mirrors, however, reflected images imperfectly, but the Scriptures would remove all obscurity and distortion. In other words, Paul is simply telling his readers that when they look at themselves and truth *now*, they see things unclearly, but when they look at them *then*, when they have the completed Word, the answers will be clear. No longer will they need the temporary things, for they will have the *exact* words that God wants them to have for life on earth.

The List Of Temporary Gifts

So, 13:9–13 sheds a tremendous amount of light on 12:8–10. As we saw in 13:9, Paul was referring to things before the completion of the New Testament Scriptures, even mentioning one of the gifts by name, **knowledge**. Therefore, we must conclude, beyond any question, that *all the gifts spoken of here were only necessary and were only in force before the completion of the New Testament Scriptures*. Let us look at each listed gift and demonstrate that this *must* be true.

Wisdom was the supernatural insight into and the understanding of spiritual truth. We have all heard someone say, "Oh, that person is so wise; he just has the gift of wisdom." But that is incorrect. A supernatural imparting of wisdom is no longer needed because wisdom is now found in the Word of God alone. We often think that just because someone is older in years or is knowledgeable in the affairs of the world he is therefore "wise." Not so! No one is wise if his words do not come from the Word of God.

"But James says," it is argued, "that 'If any of you lack wisdom, let him ask of God, that giveth to all men liberally, and upbraideth not; and it shall be given him.' (Jas. 1:5)." Yes, God *will* give us wisdom if we ask for it, and the way He will do so is by illuminating His Word to us.

May we also add that if wisdom is still a spiritual gift, it is the only one we are told to ask for, which flatly contradicts the fact that we are never instructed to ask for *any* spiritual gift.

Knowledge was the supernatural ability to communicate practical truth from doctrine. Such supernatural knowledge is no longer needed because the completed Scriptures alone contain all the knowledge we need to live.

This gift is perhaps the best example of why this list is temporary. Highly respected expositor John MacArthur, for example, writes of this gift being active today: "The gift of knowledge is the capability of grasping the meaning of God's revelation, which is mystery to the natural mind." But let us point out that such a gift is totally unnecessary because of the biblical doctrine of the Illumination of the Holy Spirit. Our brother goes on to write:

> The human writers of Scripture had the gift of knowledge in a unique way. God gave them truths directly, which they recorded as part of His written Word. Since the closing of the canon of Scripture, however, that gift has not involved the receiving of new truth but only understanding of truth previously revealed.[6]

Again, we respect this brother highly, but we lovingly submit that this is conjecture. Nowhere does the Bible say, either here or anywhere else, that there are two types of this knowledge, one for the writers and another for us today. The bottom line is that with the completed Scriptures, we need no other knowledge and no other understanding than the illumination of the Spirit. As Unger submits again: "The completed revelation of Scripture in the canonical books of the New Testament would eventually make prophecy, knowledge, and tongues unnecessary and useless."[7]

Faith was the supernatural ability for unusual reliance upon God. This, too, is misapplied today. Often we hear someone say, "Oh, that person has such great faith; he has the gift of faith." Those who teach that this is a gift for today cite great men such as Hudson Taylor and George Mueller as those who had an unusual reliance upon God.

Once again, that is not so. Men such as Taylor and Mueller were simply trusting in the promises of God in His Word. In fact, no Christian should have either more or less faith than another Christian. Why? Because our faith is based only upon what the Word of God says. Absolutely nothing else is needed. We need only believe what God says!

Healing was the supernatural ability to heal sickness *and* restore life. There are many today who claim to have this gift, but there are at least three features of the miraculous healing of Jesus and the Apostles that disprove those claims. *First*, they healed with a word or touch, without prayer, and sometimes without even being near the person. *Second*, they healed any affliction, even congenital disease, no matter how severe or long-standing. *Third*, they restored life to the dead. This gift was one of the "sign gifts" that was needed to confirm certain things to the Jews in the early days of the Church (more about this later). These "sign gifts" were replaced by the permanence of the Scriptures; once it was completed, it was the only confirmation anyone needed (more about this also in a moment).

Miracles was the supernatural ability to perform supernatural acts. This, too, was a temporary "sign gift." John tells us, for example, that Jesus' turning the water into wine at the wedding feast was the beginning of the "signs Jesus did in Cana of Galilee, and manifested His glory, and His disciples believed in Him" (John 2:11). That was the purpose. The miracle was not to improve the party or to show off great power to the curious. Even with Jesus, the working of miracles, just as the work of healing, was confirmation of His coming as Messiah, the carrier of God's power and message. This was also true of the Apostles. Paul later wrote the Corinthians, "The signs of a true apostle were performed among you with all perseverance, by signs and wonders and miracles" (2 Cor. 12:12). Miraculous signs were a mark of apostleship, authenticating the apostles' message and work as being of the Lord. We'll also return to this later.

Prophecy, in this context, was the supernatural ability to proclaim new revelation from God. The Greek behind **prophecy**" (*propheteia*) has the literal meaning of speaking forth with no specific reference to prediction or other supernatural significance. Some believe (as I once did) that this was only revelatory and was possessed only by the apostles. But while it did have revelatory aspects during Old Testament and apostolic times, it was not limited to those. It simply refers to the divine enablement to speak divine truth, whether *new* truth or previously revealed truth. We find both of these in Scripture, in fact. Silas, for example, was called a prophet but gave no prediction or new revelation, rather he "encouraged and strengthened the brethren with a lengthy message" (Acts 15:32).

The key, then, is the context. In the list of spiritual gifts in Romans 12:6–8, prophecy appears in reference to *speaking and serving* gifts. In contrast, in 1 Corinthians 12, it appears in the list of *sign* gifts, which are no longer needed. This distinction is extremely important. Without it, we are left with those who say, "God spoke to me in a dream," or "God revealed this new truth to me." This is simply unbiblical, not to mention outright dangerous. There are no new revelations. The Word of God is God's final authority. We'll return to this emphasis in our discussion of tongues below.

Discerning of spirits is one of the most important evidences of the temporary nature of these gifts. It was the supernatural ability to distinguish true revelation from God from that which comes from a satanic deceiver. The basic meaning of "discerning" has to do with separating out for examination and judging in order to determine what is genuine and what is error. Here is another common misnomer: "Oh, that person has the gift of discernment; he can see right through false doctrine." *No, the only reason anyone can see through false doctrine or discern any error is because he knows what Scripture says!* Hebrews 4:12 declares that the Word of God is "the Discerner of the thoughts and intents of the heart." With His Word, God has given us all the tools we need to discern the true from the false. The only way to discern truth from error is knowledge of the Word of God. Yes, before that was complete, a special gift was needed to expose error, but the Word of God does that now.

Tongues were the supernatural ability to speak a human language without previous knowledge of it. This gift also has direct bearing on our study, so we should address it here.

First, consider *exactly* what tongues were. Definitions are always essential when dealing with any issue. The Greek for "tongues" is *glossa*, which has three meanings: (1) the physical organ; (2) figurative for speech and language; (3) an obscure expression that needs explanation. Which one of those, then, is meant in a discussion of the spiritual gift of tongues? The physical organ is obviously not what is referred to since Paul points out that there are "different *kinds* of tongues" (1 Cor. 12:10). Neither can this refer to an "obscure expression" or an "unintelligible sound" because Paul clearly and sharply criticizes the Corinthians for using "unknown languages," that is, ecstatic utterances, because no one could understand them (14:2, 9, 11, 26). All gifts are for edification, so how can anyone be edified if they can't understand what is being said?

Therefore, there can be no valid argument against "tongues" being known, earthly languages. This is made quite plain in Acts 2:6 and 8:

> . . .the multitude came together, and were bewildered, because they were each one hearing them speak in his own language. And how is it that we each hear them in our own language to which we were born?

Verses 9–11 go on to list many of the regions from which these languages came. The dear, sincere Christians today who claim tongues to be "an ecstatic heavenly language" are simply wrong. *This is absolutely impossible by the words used in Scripture.* As we said, this was exactly the practice Paul condemned in the church at Corinth, and we'll see this in greater depth in a moment. Clearly, tongues were earthly languages that people, by supernatural means, were able to speak without having any previous knowledge of them.

Second, what was the purpose of tongues? If we may we say clearly and with no mistake: *the purpose of the "sign gifts" was always and only a sign to Jews.* Throughout their history the Jews have required "signs," outward proofs of what God was doing. That was the *only* purpose of the "sign gifts." This fact is proven beyond argument by the three occurrences of tongues in Acts.

The first occurrence of tongues was, of course, in Acts 2. This sign was to validate to the Jews who were present the partial fulfillment of Joel's prophecy of the coming Holy Spirit. Luke even quotes Joel's prophecy in verses 16–21 (we'll come back to Joel's prophecy later). The second occurrence is in Acts 10:44–47. At his conversion to Christ, Cornelius (a Gentile) spoke in tongues. This was not for his benefit but was for the benefit of the Jews who were present (v. 45). This sign was for the purpose of validating to the Jews God's acceptance of Gentiles. The third occurrence is in Acts 19:1–7. In Ephesus there were some disciples of John the Baptist who had not yet received the New Testament message of Christ. We are told that they believed, were baptized by Christian baptism (*baptizō*, which always means immersion), and spoke in tongues. The tongues were a sign to the Jews who were present that Paul's message was authoritative. So, we can conclude, *these three occurrences of tongues are the only valid occurrences on record.*

But the question arises, "What about the occurrence of tongues in 1 Corinthians?" Many base today's "tongues movement" on the situation in Corinth. But let us please remember that the Christians in Corinth were not doing *anything* right. I once heard a charismatic preacher on the radio who in his excitement blurted out: "Oh, I wish all our churches were just like the one at Corinth!" Indeed, many churches are striving for this, but what a grave error. There is nothing in that church after which we should pattern churches today. The believers there had perverted everything they touched.

To answer our question about how we should view the occurrence of tongues in Corinth, let us *carefully* trace the biblical history. The last occurrence of tongues (Acts 19) was at the beginning of Paul's three year ministry in Ephesus, and it was actually during that time period that Paul wrote his letter to the church at Corinth. So, since tongues had occurred in

Ephesus, and since Paul mentioned them in his letter to the Corinthians (far down on the list, we might add), tongues were not yet past at that time. But, as we have pointed out already, *Paul condemned the Corinthian practice.* The "tongues" in Corinth were clearly self-produced "ecstatic speech" only, not valid occurrences of the supernatural gift. First Corinthians 14:6–15 makes this clear. The tongues in Corinth were totally useless because no one could understand them. This is, in point of fact, exactly what we see in today's modern "tongues movement." The occurrences today do not even remotely resemble the biblical occurrences of tongues in the book of Acts.

There are at least two other reasons why the occurrence of tongues in Corinth was not valid. *First,* we repeat, tongues (and all "sign gifts") were for Jews and Jews only. There is no indication that there were Jews present in that church, nor is it even realistic to think that there *might* have been. How silly it is to see Gentiles today doing something that existed centuries ago only for the benefit of Jews. *Second,* in every valid occurrence of tongues, there was an Apostle present to authenticate and validate the occurrence. In fact, the occurrence of *any* "sign gift" was either *done* by or, at the very least, *confirmed* by an Apostle. There were no Apostles in Corinth at this time. If there had been, they certainly would not have allowed the terrible things that were going on there to continue. So, to conclude, tongues *could* have been valid in Corinth under the right circumstances, but under the circumstances that existed, they were far from it.

Finally, a point that is usually totally overlooked on this issue is that if tongues are so vital, so mandatory for spirituality, why are they not taught in *at least the majority* of the New Testament Epistles if not *all* of them? Why do we see them only in a single letter written to a totally messed up church? An important principle of biblical interpretation is *analogia scriptuea* (the analogy of Scripture, comparing Scripture with Scripture), but here we see an isolated practice in a twisted church that is used to build the foundation for an entire theology—Charismatic Theology.

Interpretation was the supernatural ability to translate a human language without previous knowledge of it. Our discussion of tongues, also applies here.

The Importance of this Position

Why is the position we have offered here so important? Why is this such an important issue? There are at least four reasons for taking the position that all the gifts listed in 1 Corinthians 12:8–11 were temporary.

First, and most important, this position emphasizes the *absolute* authority, completeness, and sufficiency of Scripture (a doctrine that is being attacked in every way possible in our day). Without this position, we can quite literally do anything we want with the "sign gifts." Why? Because most of the proponents of these gifts today say they are receiving new revelation. But if we accept the Word of God as authoritative and complete, then we immediately rule out any such "new revelation." Are we saying that God no longer heals, for example? Of course not. God still heals and does other supernatural things that confound the mind of man. What we are saying is that God no longer gives such power to men because the Word of God replaced any such need for outward signs.

Second, this position is the only one that fits the context of 1 Corinthians 12–14. This we have already emphasized.

Third, this position is the only one that is consistent. Here is an important point. Some evangelicals go down through the list of gifts in 1 Corinthians 12:8–10 and literally "pick and choose" which gifts are valid for today and which ones are not. Many will go through the list and say, "The gifts of wisdom, knowledge, faith, and discernment are for today, but the gifts of healing, miracles, prophecy (foretelling the future), tongues, and interpretation are not." Those in the Charismatic Movement are quite justified in their criticism of this practice. This kind of biblical interpretation is sad indeed. The position we have presented here, however, is consistent; it proves grammatically, contextually, and historically that *all* these gifts are past and no longer needed because we now have the completed Word of God, God's final revelation to man.

Fourth, this position destroys the false teachings about the "sign gifts" that are prevalent today. There are many today, both charismatic and non-charismatic, who are guilty of what we might call "Corinthianism," that is, the over-emphasis and/or the incorrect emphasis on spiritual gifts. Many evangelicals, for example, speak of "how to find your spiritual gift" and then list principles of how to ascertain the gifts in yourself and others. But the Word of God contains no such listing of principles, nor does it ever say to "seek your gift." True, it says we should *desire* spiritual gifts (1 Cor. 14:1), but it never says that we should in our own effort go out and *find* our gift. We don't need to find it because it was never lost. What the Scripture *does* say is that the Holy Spirit bestows gifts as He wills (1 Cor. 12:11). Therefore, as we yield to the Spirit and desire to serve the Lord, He will give us and make us aware of the gift(s) that will best glorify Him and edify the Church (1 Cor. 12:7; 14:12).

Further, let us for a moment examine the "sign gifts" in *historical perspective*. In 1 Corinthians 13:8 we read that certain gifts "shall cease." As examples, in fact, Paul even lists three such gifts: prophecy, tongues, and knowledge. The Greek construction indicates that these would literally "cease of themselves," that is, just fade away. The Greek also indicates that these would not return. As one studies Church History he finds that that is exactly what happened—the temporary gifts faded away, never to return. We offer the following historical facts.

One will find not even a hint in the writings of the Post Apostolic Fathers that tongues were valid after the 1st-century. Some of the great theologians of the ancient Church (Clement of Rome, Augustine, and others) considered tongues to be a practice of the early Church only. In the early centuries of the Church only followers of Montanus (who, along with his disciple Tertullian, was branded a heretic) spoke in "tongues." In the 17th-century a group called the Cevenol priests were also branded heretics when their "prophecies" went unfulfilled. One of the most shocking facts is that of the group called the Shakers. The founder, Mother Ann Lee (1736–1784), regarded herself as the female equivalent of Christ and established the Shaker community in Troy, New York. She claimed that God revealed to her that sexual intercourse, even within marriage, was wicked. So, to "mortify the flesh" and give victory over temptation, she had her followers, men and women alike, dance together in the nude while they spoke in "tongues." There was another group, the Irvingites (founded by Edward Irving in 1830), that declared prophecies (which went unfulfilled), claimed healings (which were followed by death), and practiced "tongues." I hope the reader notices that a supposed "new revelation" was claimed in most of these instances. That is one reason we strongly emphasize the passing away of such things when the Scriptures were completed.

But the focal point occurred in 1901 at the Bethel Bible College in Topeka, Kansas. A woman named Agnes Ozman claimed that she received the "baptism of the Holy Spirit" and proceeded to speak in "tongues." The practice quickly became part of the Holiness Movement and gave birth to the mainline Pentecostal denominations. The modern Charismatic Movement was born in an Episcopal church in Van Nuys, California in 1960.

One of the most disturbing and dangerous things about the Charismatic Movement is how "tongues" can be added to one's theology without affecting anything else. This practice has spread to many denominations such as Roman Catholic, Lutheran, Presbyterian, and even Baptist. It has become a common and dangerous ground for "fellowship."

At this point a question arises, "If tongues did cease back in the 1st-century, why are they so prevalent today?" Some Pentecostals and Charismatics view Montanus and Mother Ann Lee as their forerunners, but this puts them in an obviously heretical position. Realizing this fact, the majority of Charismatics say that tongues *did* cease but have returned as God pours out His Spirit once more upon the earth. Their strongest "proof" of this is Joel 2:28 and Peter's reference to that prophecy in his sermon on the Day of Pentecost (Acts 2:16–21). Joel prophesied that there would be a great outpouring of the Spirit in the last days. But as one reads those verses, he quickly finds that Joel's prophecy was *not* fulfilled on the Day of Pentecost. Furthermore, his prophecy has not been fulfilled since Pentecost nor can it be fulfilled in the Church Age. Why? Because that prophecy can only be fulfilled at the end of the Jewish age, which itself cannot come as long as the Church is on the earth. So, this prophecy will be fulfilled in connection with Christ's return to the earth for the Millennium.

Why, then, did Peter even refer to this prophecy? Peter was saying that what the people were witnessing on the Day of Pentecost was *similar* to what Joel prophesied. The coming of the Holy Spirit at Pentecost was only an "earnest," a first installment, of what was to come. Paul used this very word in Ephesians 1:14 to show that the Holy Spirit is the "earnest" (first installment) of our inheritance in Christ. The Holy Spirit was sent to "bind the contract." Additionally, Peter was saying to those people who thought the Spirit-filled believers were drunk that they *should* have recognized what they were seeing as the work of the Holy Spirit, not drunkenness.

May we lovingly say, the practice of speaking in tongues, as well as the other sign gifts, is clearly not valid today. Those who hold to these do so from incorrect exegesis and historical ignorance. We should not try to use that which God says is past. These gifts are from an immature age and are retained today only by immature Christians.

God's Sovereign Control of Spiritual Gifts (12:11)

But all these worketh that one and the selfsame Spirit, dividing to every man severally as he will.

What then of the gifts that remain? Let us close with three brief considerations.

First, the gifts in Romans 12:6–8 and two of the office gifts in Ephesians 4:11 still remain. If I might interject at this point, two gifts spoken of in 1 Corinthians 12:28, even though in the same context with the gifts that are past, are still valid today because they are mentioned elsewhere in Scripture (namely, in the Romans list).

Second, God wants us to manifest those gifts. Some might think, in light of our study, that there really aren't very many gifts left. But these gifts are more than enough to edify the body of Christ.

Third, let us beware of today's unbalanced emphasis on the spiritual gifts. May we please remember: as we are yielded to the Holy Spirit, He will empower us and impart to us the spiritual gifts that will glorify God and edify the Church. The Holy Spirit is the one **dividing to every man severally as he will**. It's not our place to seek the gifts, but to be yielded and wait for Him to give them.

Postscript

Since the first appeared in 2005 of the original articles on which this chapter is based, there has been an increasing number of evangelicals who have adopted a non-cessationist position on the sign gifts. Such a course is, indeed, a steep slippery slope, for it compromises biblical and historical precedent and ultimately biblical sufficiency itself. "God could still use these gifts," it is insisted. That, however, is not the issue. Of course, He *could*, but He *doesn't* because they have passed away. Yes, we have heard many "stories" of their supposed occurance, but anecdotes are not Truth.

NOTES

[1] Among those who do not (and with whom I agree) are S. Lewis Johnson in *Wycliff Bible Commentary*, and John Walvoord in Lewis Sperry Chafer, *Systematic Theology*, Vol. VI, 220.

[2] Spiros Zodhiates, *Hebrew-Greek Key Study Bible* (Chattanooga: AMG Publishers, 1984, 1991), 1436.

[3] Henry Morris, *The Defender's Study Bible* (Grand Rapids: World Publishing, Inc., 1995).

[4] Dave Swavely, *Decisions, Decisions* (P & R Publishing; 2003), 23.

[5] Merrill F. Unger, New Testament Teaching on Tongues (Grand Rapids: Kregel Publications, 1971), 95–96 (brackets are Unger's).

[6] *The MacArthur New Testament Commentary: 1 Corinthians* (electronic edition, WordSearch), comment on 12:8.

[7] Unger, 96.

In these days, when so many make their boast of "advanced thought," it may sound singular to speak of sticking to God's testimonies . . . Perseverance in the truth when it is unfashionable is the test of a real believer . . . Others may gad abroad after the novelties of human opinion; but the true-born child of God glories in saying to his heavenly Father, "I have stuck unto Thy testimonies."

Charles Spurgeon on Psalm 119:31
The Golden Alphabet: A Devotional Commentary on Psalm 119

5

Who In the World Were Those "Sons of God"?

and

Does Jude Quote from Pseudepigraphal Literature?[*]

Genesis 6:4; 1 Peter 3:18–20; 2 Peter 2:4; Jude 6

There were giants in the earth in those days; and also after that, when the sons of God came in unto the daughters of men, and they bare children to them, the same became mighty men which were of old, men of renown.

For Christ also hath once suffered for sins, the just for the unjust, that he might bring us to God, being put to death in the flesh, but quickened by the Spirit: By which also he went and preached unto the spirits in prison; Which sometime were disobedient, when once the longsuffering of God waited in the days of Noah, while the ark was a preparing, wherein few, that is, eight souls were saved by water.

For if God spared not the angels that sinned, but cast them down to hell, and delivered them into chains of darkness, to be reserved unto judgment.

And the angels who kept not their first estate, but left their own habitation, he hath reserved in everlasting chains under darkness unto the judgement of the great day.

Perhaps at the top of the list of debated texts is Genesis 6:4, which refers to the "sons of God" and "daughters of men." Along with it, however, are three related texts. Tragically, the debate over these verses has gone on for centuries. I say "tragically" because one view is based exclusively on

---

[*] This chapter was originally TOTT issues 5, 6, and 7, December 2005 and January and February 2006.

pagan myths instead of the sole authority of Scripture. Sadly, and shockingly, the most common view is that there was an invasion of the earth by fallen angels (the "sons of God," Gen. 6:4) who cohabited with earthly women (the "daughters of men") and produced a race of giants. It is absolutely incredulous to me that a large portion of Evangelical Christianity today holds this view when the fact of the matter is, as we will demonstrate, it is totally pagan in origin.

To explore this great debate, let's first consider why the "sons of God" were not fallen angels, second their true identity, and third the identity of the angels in Jude 6.

Why the "Sons of God" Were Not Fallen Angels

Let us examine three reasons why the "sons of God" in Genesis 6 cannot possibly refer to fallen angels.

This View Is Untenable

By *untenable* we, of course, mean that the view is difficult to maintain and is even indefensible. To put it simply, this theory is just plain fanciful. Respected pastor and author Warren Wiersbe puts it this way: "The whole explanation, though held by teachers I respect, to me seems a bit fantastic."[1] And that is putting it mildly. Joseph Exell (1849–1909), a British clergyman who compiled the monumental, multi-volume work, *The Biblical Illustrator*, rightly brings out the fact that Jewish rabbis tended toward views that were fantastic. He writes, "Hence Apocryphal Jewish literature assumes this [theory] constantly . . . which, nevertheless, seems fanciful and ungrounded."[2]

Actually, the Jewish Scriptures themselves assume this. The Tanakh Translation of Genesis 6:4, for example, reads: "It was then, and later too, that the Nephilim appeared on earth—when the divine beings cohabited with the daughters of men, who bore them offspring. They were the heroes of old, the men of renown." But "translating" the Hebrew *ben elohim* as "divine beings" is total conjecture and is not really translating at all, rather it is interpretation. *Ben* clearly means "son" and *elohim*, while it sometimes refers to any god, usually refers to the supreme "God." There is absolutely no linguistic support for "divine beings," and such translation is indefensible.

We'll come back to this later, but we need to point out here that this view has its roots in Old Testament pseudepigraphal books. These are books that have been proven over and over again to be unreliable, extremely fanciful, mythological, mystical, and pagan. So, as we'll see, this theory, in the final analysis, is of pagan origin and has no Scriptural support whatsoever.

This View Is Unthinkable

I submit this point out of real burden. For not only is this theory *unthinkable*, it is also quite *objectionable*. The Word of God makes it very clear that angels are "sexless," that is, incapable of physical relations. Matthew 22:30 plainly declares that angels "neither marry nor are they given in marriage." Of course, the proponents of this theory immediately say, "Angels took human form." That is certainly true; angels have, more than once, appeared in human form. These appearances are called "theophanies," physical presentations of Deity. But may we submit that *appearance* is one thing while *incarnation* is quite another. Angels that *appeared* human did not necessarily *become* human.

This is further demonstrated by the fact that Jesus was the only *incarnate* manifestation of God. No angel was ever an incarnation. They were not *human*; they were *spirit*. In his book, *Studies in Problem Texts*, J. Sidlow Baxter includes a lengthy chapter on the identity of the "sons of God," which is the best study I have read on the subject. In it he writes:

> As for the suggestion that these evil angels somehow took human bodies to themselves and thus became capable of sex functions, it is sheer absurdity, as anyone can see. Both on psychological and physiological grounds it is unthinkable.[3]

"Fallen Angel Theory" proponents try to answer this problem by saying that Matthew 22:30 only says that angels "do *not* marry," but that it doesn't say they *could* not or *did* not. Others insist that the verse only says that angels *in heaven* don't marry, so perhaps they can *on earth*. But is this not just playing word games? Is not the implication clear that angels are sexless? Why in the world would angels be capable of sex anyway? The whole subject is utter nonsense. And if we may add, no other Scripture states that angels married humans. As any first year seminary student knows, to base a teaching on a single Scripture reference (Gen. 6) is bad hermeneutics.

Additionally, this theory is extremely *objectionable*. Think of it! Our dear Savior was an incarnation. Are we to believe that these wicked angels were like Him? In the final analysis this theory brings our Savior down to the level of these fallen angels. In fact, the incarnation of God is no longer something unique. Put bluntly, it makes His incarnation "old news" because it had been done before. No, a thousand times no! We must not allow our Savior to be thus defamed.

This View Is Unscriptural

Again, the "Fallen Angel Theory" maintains that the "sons of God" in Genesis 6 refer to fallen angels who assumed human bodies, cohabited with human women, and produced a race of giants on the earth. It also maintains, however, that *this sin was the main reason for the flood*, and that Jude 6 (along with 1Pet. 3:18–20 and 2 Pet. 2:4) also refers to this. Let us deal with a few of what the proponents of this theory call "proofs" and compare them with Scripture.

First, it maintains that the term "sons of God" (Gen. 6:2) is a title used for angels. Again, this is absolutely true; we find this title used for angels in Job 1:6, 2:1, and 38:7. But the fact that many ignore is that all three of these refer to *unfallen* angels, not *fallen* angels. Is it not unthinkable that God would ever refer to Satan as "a son of God?" He is, indeed, "the son of perdition," but he would never be a Son of God. Why then would a Scripture writer refer to any other fallen angel as a "son of God?"

We can also point out that Moses mentions angels some fifteen times in the Pentateuch, but not once does he refer to them as "sons of God." The "Fallen Angel Theory" proponent, however, leads us to believe that just this once Moses is referring to "fallen angels." But why? Are we to conclude that Moses was inconsistent or that he had a lapse in thinking?

Second, it maintains that these angels cohabited with human women and produced a race of giants. But this is a violation of Genesis 6:4, which is simply misread by the angel theorist:

> There were giants in the earth IN THOSE DAYS; and also AFTER THAT, when the sons of God came in unto the daughters of men, and they bare children to them, the same became mighty men which were of old, men of renown (emphasis added).

This clearly shows that the "giants" were already on the earth when these events were taking place. *They were not the offspring of this cohabitation.*

It is also important to understand the word "giant," which has been greatly misunderstood and abused. It simply does not *necessarily* mean "giant" as we think of the word. One reliable Hebrew source makes this clear:

> Actually, the translation "giants" is supported mainly by the LXX [the Septuagint, the Greek Old Testament] and may be quite misleading. The word may be of unknown origin and mean "heroes" or "warriors," etc. The . . . transliteration "Nephilim" is safer and may be correct in referring the noun to a race or nation.[4]

So, these were not necessarily "giants," rather they were "warriors," "men of violence." This is further substantiated, in fact, by the context—"the earth was filled with violence" (6:11). Why? Because the earth was filled with these "men of violence." Right in line with this is our next point.

Third, the "Fallen Angel Theory" maintains that these "giants" were the main reason God destroyed the earth through the flood. But if we may submit: *that is simply not what the Scripture text says*. Genesis 6:3 and 5 clearly declare:

> And the LORD said, My spirit shall not always strive with MAN, for that HE also is flesh: yet HIS days shall be an hundred and twenty years . . . And God saw that the wickedness of MAN was great in the earth, and that every imagination of the thoughts of HIS heart was only evil continually (emphasis added).

God's judgment was poured out on *man*, not angels. While this theory says the "giants" were destroyed in the flood, if this were true, why do we see "giants" in Numbers 13:33? The twelve spies saw "giants" (*Nephilim*, "men of violence") in the land of Canaan. But how could this be true if these "giants" were killed in the flood some 800 years earlier? Charles Ryrie well summarizes our thoughts thus far:

> *Nephilim*. From a root meaning "to fall;" i.e., to fall upon others because these individuals were men of strength (only other use of this Hebrew word is in Num. 13:33). Evidently they were in the earth before the marriages of Gen. 6:2 and were not the offspring of those marriages from which came the mighty men (military men) and men of renown (of wealth or power).[5]

Fourth, the "Fallen Angel Theory" maintains that the clauses "even as" and "in like manner" in Jude 6 show that Sodom and Gomorrah sinned in like manner as the "angels" in Genesis 6. But this not only violates the *grammar* but also the *context*. Verses 5–7 contain *three separate historical examples that serve as warnings*. They do not overlap, neither is one like the other; they are completely separate. The angel theorist, however, insists that "even as" and "in like manner" indicate that Sodom and Gomorrah sinned in the same way as the fallen angels of Genesis 6. But, again, both clauses are used simply to emphasize the phrase "are set forth for an example." We'll see later who those angels were who "kept not their first estate," but for now just consider these two verses this way:

> The angels who kept not their first estate are set forth as an example, even as and in like manner as Sodom and Gommorah and the cities about them are set forth as examples.

In the same vein, the fallen angel theory also has a very serious problem with the specific sins present in each of these instances. To put it simply, even *if* Jude were saying that these fallen angels sinned in exactly the same way as the Sodomites did, then the angels in Jude *cannot possibly* be the same ones as in Genesis 6. Why? Because the Sodomites were guilty of homosexuality, while the so-called "fallen angels" of Genesis 6 are not guilty of homosexual acts, rather relations with earthly women.

Fifth, the "Fallen Angel Theory" maintains that 1 Peter 3:18–20 shows that the fall of the angels took place "in the days of Noah." E. W. Bullinger, who was notorious for his fanciful views in several areas, even maintained that Christ, in His resurrection body, went and preached to these fallen angels! How absurd! If the above passage isn't enough, farther along in the context we read: "For this cause was the gospel preached also to them that are dead" (4:6). All this clearly shows that *men* were being preached to, not angels. This passage is simply saying that the Spirit of the preincarnate Christ was preaching *through* Noah. But because these men rejected God's message, they are in prison (*hades*) awaiting final judgment. This view is, in fact, the position of many reliable writers. Older scholarship includes, among others, the rock-solid Puritan commentator Matthew Henry. Twentieth century scholarship includes the beloved Harry Ironside, Charles Ryrie, Roger Raymer in Dallas Seminary's *The Bible Knowledge Commentary*, and others.

Sixth, the "Fallen Angel Theory" maintains that 2 Peter 2:4 also shows that the angels fell "in the days of Noah." Of course, the reason these proponents want to show that the angels fell in Noah's day is because they think this gives credence to the angel's "invasion" of the earth and their cohabitation with human women. But all this is wasted effort. Note the verse again along with its context (vv. 5–6):

> For if God spared not the angels that sinned, but cast them down to hell, and delivered them into chains of darkness, to be reserved unto judgment; And spared not the old world, but saved Noah the eighth person, a preacher of righteousness, bringing in the flood upon the world of the ungodly; And turning the cities of Sodom and Gomorrah into ashes condemned them with an overthrow, making them an ensample unto those that after should live ungodly;

It is so obvious that these verses are presenting three separate historical incidents that it's ridiculous to argue otherwise. In fact, here is one of the several similarities between Jude and 2 Peter 2. The passage in 2 Peter 2 is not teaching that the angels fell in the days of Noah because the incidents are presented as being separate and independent from one other.

Much confusion is eliminated when this principle is observed here *and* in Jude 6.

Theologian Louis Berkoff also points out that the "Fallen Angel Theory" actually teaches "a double fall" of the angels: Satan fell through pride, but the other angels fell because of "their lusting after the daughters of men." He goes on to say, however, that this teaching was "gradually discarded . . . during the Middle Ages" and then adds, "in view of this it is rather surprising to find that several modern commentators are reiterating the idea in their interpretation."[6] Indeed, how tragic that many today are still holding to a once discarded view.

The Identity of the "Sons of God"

Before dealing with the identity of these "sons of God," a brief word is in order concerning one other alternate view of their identity, a view that is gaining popularity. Recent archeological discovery supposedly suggests that the "sons of God" were sometimes used to describe kings. But the main problem with that view is that the Scripture nowhere else describes human rulers using this term, so why would it be so here?

Who then were the "sons of God" and "Daughters of Men" in Genesis 6? The simple, natural, and Scriptural answer is: "the sons of God" represent the godly line of Seth, and "the Daughters of Men" represent the ungodly line of Cain. *The strongest proof of this is the context*, that is, chapters 2–7. More problems of biblical interpretation arise from taking Scripture out of context than from any other reason. All one has to do is look at the surrounding context in Genesis and the meaning becomes obvious:

- ❏ Chapter 2 details the creation of man;
- ❏ Chapter 3 records the fall of man;
- ❏ Chapter 4 presents the line of Cain (a man);
- ❏ Chapter 5 presents the line of Abel (a man);
- ❏ Chapter 6 records the time when the two lines crossed, represented by the terms "sons of God" and "daughters of men."
- ❏ Chapter 7 shows the judgment of man through the flood showing that the whole world was corrupted by the mixture of the godly with the ungodly.

The most amazing thing about the "Fallen Angel Theory" is that it seems to cast aside the context as though it were irrelevant. *But without exception, the surrounding context speaks of MAN.* Then, all of a sudden, according to the angel theory, like magic, angels appear to corrupt man. *But man did not need fallen angels to corrupt him.* He was already corrupt to the core, with "every imagination of the thoughts of his heart [being] only evil continually" (Gen. 6:5). This view is held by that great British scholar and commentator, W. H. Griffith Thomas:

> It is . . . in every way better and truer to the context to explain the passage of the two lines of Seth and Cain, and as giving the explanation of the judgment and the flood.[7]

Neither was there a question in the mind and heart of Puritan Matthew Henry:

> The posterity of Seth did not keep by themselves, as they ought to have done, both for the preservation of their own purity, and in detestation of the apostasy; they intermingled themselves with the . . . race of Cain.

Warren Wiersbe also writes:

> When the Sethites compromised by mingling with the Cainites, they fell from God's blessing. God was grieved that they married godless Cainites, choosing wives as they pleased without considering God's will (Gen. 6:2). In doing this, they endangered the fulfillment of the 3:15 promise; for how could God bring a Redeemer into the world through an unholy people? The people of that day "married and were given in marriage" (Matt. 24:37–39) and thought nothing of the warning that Enoch and Noah gave about the coming judgment. Human history was now at the place where only Noah and his family—eight people—believed God and obeyed His Word. God's spirit was striving with lost people, but they resisted the call of God; and God was grieved at what man was doing.[8]

This is likewise the view of theologians Augustus Strong,[9] Millard Erickson,[10] and the great 17th-century Francis Turretin, who first writes that the angel theory is "false and immodest," which underscores this theory's objectionable character, as we noted earlier. Turretin goes on to write:

> the "sons of God" referred to are no other than the posterity of Seth, who on account of still retaining the purer worship of God, are distinguished from the profane posterity of Cain or "the sons of men."[11]

Finally, contemporary theologian Wayne Grudem makes this comment on the context:

> In fact, there is an emphasis on sonship as including likeness to one's father in Genesis 5:4. Moreover, the text traces the descendents from God through Adam and Seth to many "sons" in all

of chapter 5. The larger purpose of the narrative seems to be to trace the parallel development of the godly (ultimately messianic) line of Seth and the ungodly descendants of the rest of mankind. Therefore, the "sons of God" in Gen. 6:2 are men who are righteous in their imitation of the character of their heavenly father, and the "daughters" of men are the ungodly wives whom they knew.[12]

If we may ask, then, *could the context be clearer?*

One objection to this view is why is the term "sons of God" not used with this meaning in any other place? J. Sidlow Baxter brilliantly answers:

> But we may even turn this objection back upon the objectors, for in the New Testament the title "sons of God" (in the exact Greek equivalent of the Hebrew) is used again and again of *men*, that is, of the regenerate in Christ. [Angel theorists] "explain" this as being because all who are the direct creation of God are called His "sons," and the new nature which is in us as regenerate believers is a direct creation of God. So the regenerate are "sons of God." Look back, then, over the Seth line. Were not the worshipping Seth and Enos and the sanctified Enoch and the "just" and "perfect" (upright) Noah who "walked with God"—were not *these* men regenerate? Who will dare say "No?" And were they not, then, truly "sons of God?"[13]

Another objection is how can these men be considered holy when the Bible says that only Noah was holy (Gen. 6:8, 9)? But as mentioned earlier, the Sethites were clearly the *godly* line but "intermingled themselves with the . . . race of Cain" (Matthew Henry).

Others ask why is it that only "sons" and not "daughters" are associated with the line of Seth? This demonstrates an ignorance of the patriarchal system in Scripture, which views the male as the family representative. Just as Paul included women when he wrote, "For as many as are led by the Spirit of God, they are the sons of God" (Rom. 8:14; cf. Phil. 2:15; 1 Jn. 3:1–2), the "sons of God" in Genesis would also include women.

The Identity of the Angels in Jude 6

In the final analysis, it is actually Jude 6 that forms the foundation of the entire "Fallen Angel Theory." As one authority puts it, "This ancient viewpoint hinges in part on the assumption that Jude 6 and 7 refer to these angels."[14]

The extremely important point here is, as stated earlier, the "Fallen Angel Theory" is based upon *the mythology of the Pseudepigrapha.* The Pseudepigraphal books were those books rejected by virtually everyone as being part of the canon of Scripture. These books claim biblical authors, but are full of religious fancy and magic from 200 B.C. to A.D. 100. Now, it is an incontrovertible fact that this theory first appeared in the Pseudepigraphal book, *The Book of Enoch*, a spurious book that is full of far-fetched stories. The author without doubt got his ideas from pagan myths, which are full of stories about "the gods" cohabiting with human women. In fact, the story in *The Book of Enoch* goes so far to say that the number of angels in Genesis 6 was 200. Why don't the proponents of the "Fallen Angel Theory" believe and teach this? One writer recounts the story thusly:

> Two hundred angels in heaven, under the leadership of Semayaz, noticed that the humans had unusually beautiful daughters. These they desired for themselves, so they took a mutual oath to go down to earth together, and each took a wife. They taught these wives magical medicine, incantations, the cutting of roots and the care of plants. When the women became pregnant, they gave birth to giants that reached three hundred cubits. The giants in turn consumed all the food, thereby arousing the deep hatred of the earthlings. The giants turned to devouring the people along with the birds, wild beasts, reptiles and fish. Then it was that the earth, having had enough of these huge bullies, brought an accusation against them.[15]

Now may we ask, are we to believe that Jude is following such pagan myth? Are we to believe that a man writing under the inspiration of the Holy Spirit would be so tainted by such superstition? Why would anyone want to hold to something so ridiculous? Why not just believe the plain language and context of Scripture and hold only to that? It is because of these very questions that the next section will answer the question: "Does Jude Quote from Pseudepigraphal Literature in Jude 6, 9, and 14?"

Finally, to what then does Jude 6 refer? The answer is simple: The angels in Jude 6 can refer only to *the angels who followed Lucifer at his fall*. Satan's fall is described in Isaiah 14:12 and Ezekiel 28:12–19. His sin was, of course, pride and arrogance. He was going to exalt his throne above God's Throne. We then read in Revelation 12:4 that one-third of the angels followed Lucifer and were cast out of heaven.

Jude 6 bears this out. Note the words "kept not their first estate." "Estate" is the Greek, *archē*, which carries the basic meaning "beginning." But it also refers to "the beginning or first place of power." Hence, it gives the ideas of sovereignty, dominion, and elevated position. Jude is saying, then, that these angels had an elevated position, a place of dominion, and a certain degree of sovereign power. This same word is translated "principalities" in Ephesians 6:12.

The word "habitation" is *oiketerion*, which means "dwelling place," that is, heaven. These angels left heaven behind and left the position and dominion they once had.

We should make note of the judgment of these fallen angels. Some of these angels are right now confined in "darkness," which is the Greek *zophos*, "Used of the darkness of the nether world."[16] Peter calls this place "Tartarus" (2 Pet. 2:4). These angels are awaiting "the judgment of the great day," that is, the final judgment at the Great White Throne (Rev. 20:11–15.).

The question now arises, why are these angels reserved in judgment? As we've seen, some speculate and then insist that it is because these angels cohabited with human women. But, of course, the main problem with this is *the Word of God doesn't say that.* So, what *is* the reason? We are not told the reason! God, for some reason unknown to us, has not chosen to tell us the specifics. Consider 2 Peter 2:4 once again: "God spared not the angels that sinned." These angels did *something*, we know not what, for which God severely punished them. Warren Wiersbe wisely comments on this verse:

> It is not necessary to debate the hidden mysteries of this verse in order to get the main message: God judges rebellion and will not spare those who reject His will.[17]

Let us not concoct a story based on pagan mythology just so we can explain a verse of Scripture. Rather, let us look to the main message of the verse. One thing is clear: the doom of all the fallen angels is sealed. *That is really all we need to know.* Whether some of them are chained in darkness now awaiting judgment, or whether some are loose and doing Satan's bidding while they, too, await judgment, their doom is clear. Let us not violate God's Word by adding something that isn't there.

In the same vein, however, we also see that *the doom of all men who reject God is already sealed.* Note very carefully John 3:18: "He that believeth on Him is not condemned, but he that believeth not is condemned ALREADY, because he hath not believed in the name of the only begotten Son of God" (emphasis added). Those who reject Christ don't have to wait for judgment—it is already marked out. What still awaits is the actual *punishment*, but the *judgment* is already sealed.

Note also John 16:8–11:

> And when he is come, he will reprove the world of sin, and of righteousness, and of judgment: Of sin, because they believe not on me; Of righteousness, because I go to my Father, and ye see me no more; Of judgment, because the prince of this world is [HAS BEEN] JUDGED (literal translation and emphasis added).

Verses 11 does not read, "The ruler of this world is *going to be* judged." No, he has *already been judged*. He is guilty and now only awaits sentencing. What then of apostasy? At first glance we might think, "Well, God is going to condemn them for their perversion of His truth." On the contrary, God has *already* condemned the apostate. We can stand before an apostate today and say, "You may blaspheme God, but you are already condemned because Jude 6 says that you are just like the fallen angels, already condemned."

So, with this historic incident, Jude warns us about apostasy. To reject the Word of God results in condemnation both now and forever. Let us, therefore, truly hate paganism and traditionalism! We find that Christianity today, in many ways, is *bathed in* and sometimes even *based on* both of those. Let us not be guilty of thus tainting the Word of God.

*   *   *

Does Jude Quote from Pseudepigraphal Literature?

With the above in mind, as scholars have studied the Epistle of Jude, the question has often been raised whether Jude is actually referencing such literature in verses 6, 9, 14, and 15. Incredulously, the tendency has actually been to lean in the direction of the affirmative—that Jude, indeed, relies heavily on this literature.

In this final section, therefore, I wish to submit that Jude does *not* quote, refer to, or otherwise rely on Pseudepigraphal literature. In a very real sense, this issue lies at the very core of the whole debate about the identity of the "sons of God." Are we to think that an inspired writer actually relied on pagan literature? Is that what Bible believing Christians should defend? For those readers who still lean toward the "Fallen Angel Theory," or who are still undecided on the whole issue, I pray that what follows will demonstrate the serious consequences of viewing Jude as in any way relying on pagan literature.

Jude 6

And the angels which kept not their first estate, but left their own habitation, he hath reserved in everlasting chains under darkness unto the judgment of the great day.

Since we dealt at length earlier with the question of what angels are being referred to here, we will not repeat that material. What we are concerned with here is that some believe that Jude is, as one commentator puts it, "making use of the APOCRYPHAL *Book of Enoch*" (emphasis added).

The first thing we must note about the above statement is the use of the word "apocryphal." The *Book of Enoch*, as well as the *Assumption of Moses* (which we will encounter later) are *not apocryphal* books. They are *pseudipgraphal books*. There is, in fact, a *vast* difference between the two. Rene Pache provides a good summary of the Apocrypha:

> The word Apocrypha is the name given to the Jewish religious books of obscure origin (*apocrypha*, meaning "secret, hidden"); these were late books (between the second century B.C. and the first, or even the second century after Christ), which were never included in the Hebrew canon. They had no place in the Masoretic text and were not interpreted by any Targum [Aramaic paraphrases of the Old Testament]. According to the general opinion of the Jews, the prophetic voice died with Malachi. After that, which they called "the seal of the prophets," they estimated that no other inspired writings appeared. Josephus declared this expressly (*Against Apion* I. 8); and even the book of 1 Maccabees stresses it (9:27; 14:41).[18]

While the Apocrypha is considered to have some historical value (especially 1 Maccabees), as a whole it is not reliable enough to be considered authentic Scripture. Even in light of the evidence, the Roman Catholic Church canonized the Apocrypha at the Council of Trent (1546) "in an obvious polemic action against Protestantism."[19]

This brings us to the Pseudepigrapha (literally, "false writings"). Here is an excellent summary by one scholar of biblical introduction:

> The Pseudepigrapha books are those books which are distinctly spurious and unauthentic in their overall content: While they claim to have been written by Biblical authors, they actually express religious fancy and magic from the period between 200 B.C. and A.D. 200. In Roman Catholic circles these books are known as the Apocrypha, a term not to be confused with an entirely different set of books known in Protestant circles by the same name . . . ; although at times Protestants have referred to these same books as the "wider Apocrypha," or "Apocalyptic Literature." Most of these books are comprised of dreams, visions, and revelations in the apocalyptic style of Ezekiel, Daniel, and Zechariah.[20]

The same scholar adds that these books are those that were "rejected by all"; that is, no one would seriously contend for their authority.[21]

So, there is a great difference between the Apocrypha and the Pseudepigrapha. The former has *some* value while the latter has *none*. It is, therefore, erroneous to say Jude is "making use of the apocryphal *Book of Enoch*," when, in fact, the book in question is *pseudepigraphal*, not apocryphal.

Why then would Jude base his writing on such mystical and obviously pagan, worthless literature? As pointed out earlier, the "Fallen Angel Theory" of Genesis 6 was first recorded in the *Book of Enoch* and some believe that Jude is referring to that book. As we observed, the Greek *archē* is used for "estate" and means "sovereignty, dominion, or elevated position." One Greek scholar says, "*Archē* is used in the *Book of Enoch* (12:4) of the watchers (Angels) who have *abandoned the high heaven and the holy eternal place* and defiled themselves with women," which is supposed to lead us to believe that one Greek word that happens to be used in both places "proves" that Jude is quoting the *Book of Enoch* (a book which has been proven to be full of magic, mysticism, and pagan beliefs). Wow! That is quite a leap, indeed!

Some teachers argue at this point that there is no difference between saying that Jude refers to the Pseudepigrapha and Paul quoting some heathen poets. Now, Paul did indeed do that; he quoted Aratus (Acts 17:28), Menander (1 Cor. 15:33), and Epimenides (Titus 1:12). Basically, this would be like a preacher today saying that a statement by Shakespeare illustrates a biblical principle. That would be a valid illustration. But we would submit: it is far different to say that Shakespeare *illustrates* a biblical principle than to say we shall base our *interpretation*, or even our *writing*, of Scripture on what Shakespeare said. When Paul quotes a Greek poet, he does not base truth upon what the poet said; rather he merely illustrates God's Truth. But to say that Jude quotes a pseudepigraphal book, and to say he bases what he writes on that information, is to say that Jude *bases* Truth on what some pagan wrote.

We would also submit, it does no good at this point to say, "Well, God just controlled how much material Jude quoted." As we'll see later, *the damage to inspiration has already been done*.

Jude 9

Yet Michael the archangel, when contending with the devil he disputed about the body of Moses, durst not bring against him a railing accusation, but said, The Lord rebuke thee.

It has been conjectured that the story of Michael contending with the Devil is taken from the pseudepigraphal book *Assumption of Mosis* (i.e., *Moses*). Origen (c. 185–c. 254) has been credited with being the first one to offer this view. He maintained that a book was in existence in his time called *The Assumption of Moses*, but commentator Albert Barnes brings out a devastating observation:

> There can be no reasonable doubt that such a book as Origen refers to, under the title of *The Assumption of Moses*, was extant [in

existence] in *his* time, but that does not prove by any means that it was extant in the time of Jude, or that he quoted it. There is, indeed, no positive proof that it was *not* extant in the time of Jude, but there is none that it was; and all the facts in the case will be met by the supposition that it was written afterwards, and that the tradition on the subject here referred to by Jude was incorporated into it.[22]

In other words, there is no way of knowing exactly when this pseudepigraphal book was penned. Some insist that Jude quoted from this book, *but who is to say that this unknown author didn't quote from Jude?* Moreover, as Barnes points out, there is more reason to believe the latter than there is the former.

Jude 14–15

And Enoch also, the seventh from Adam, prophesied of these, saying, Behold, the Lord cometh with ten thousands of his saints, To execute judgment upon all, and to convince all that are ungodly among them of all their ungodly deeds which they have ungodly committed, and of all their hard speeches which ungodly sinners have spoken against him.

Once again, some maintain that Jude here quotes from the *Book of Enoch*. But let us compare the above quotation (KJV) with that of the *Book of Enoch*:

> Behold he comes with ten thousands of his saints, to execute judgement upon them, and destroy the wicked, and reprove all the carnal, for everything which the sinful and ungodly have done and committed against him.(1:9).[23]

While one writer makes the ridiculous statement, "Jude quotes almost verbatim" from the *Book of Enoch*, who can honestly say that those two are the same? Commentator Maxwell Coder points out a serious difference:

> It is interesting to note that the unknown writer of the [pseudepigraphal] *Book of Enoch* revealed his ignorance of the truth by making Enoch say: "[He comes with ten thousands of his saints] to execute judgment on them . . ." Jude knew better than this. His epistle does not contain the error that the Lord will come to visit judgment on His people.[24]

We should also add that, like verse 9, there is no proof that this spurious book even existed in Jude's day. In fact, as William MacDonald submits in his excellent *Believer's Bible Commentary* (quoting William Kelly):

> [The *Book of Enoch*] has every mark of having been written subsequent to the destruction of Jerusalem [and therefore after Jude's Epistle was written], by a Jew who still buoyed himself up with the hope that God would stand by the Jews.[25]

As with verse 9 there is far more reason to think that the *Book of Enoch* was copied from Jude than vice versa.

"How, then, would Jude have learned of this ancient prophecy?" one might ask. *By verbal inspiration!* And to even *ask* such a question demonstrates one's doubt of that very doctrine and his reliance upon human reason.

It should be crystal clear, therefore, that saying Jude quoted from the *Book of Enoch* is not only an "unwarranted assumption,"[26] but that it's also a statement that leaves one in a completely indefensible position. The facts simply do not warrant such a view.

Correlation

Finally, perhaps one might wonder, "Why take the time and space to argue pseudepigraphal origins in Jude's writing? Why is this a big deal?"

The reason is this: *To allow the view that Jude quoted from the Pseudepigrapha does damage to the doctrine of the inspiration of Scripture.* We are not saying that those who hold the pseudepigraphal view are deliberately trying to undermine inspiration. On the contrary, this view is held by some solid evangelical teachers. But we must maintain that this view "waters down" or, at the very least, detracts from supernatural, verbal inspiration. Proponents of this view at times seem to try and "harmonize" these false books with inspiration by offering a caution such as this:

> It should be noted that Jude's use of this quotation from the Book of Enoch [referring to Jude 14–15] does not vouch for the reliability of the entire *Book of Enoch*. The same is true of . . . *The Assumption of Moses* from which Jude may have taken the information about Michael contending with Satan. This specific information is accurate, but Jude's use of it does not guarantee the reliability of the rest of the book.

The first problem with such a statement is that the information given in these pseudepigraphal books is *not* accurate. Second, even if the information were accurate, who would (or could) trust these books anyway, especially an inspired writer? (Ponder also, the Lord Jesus refused to allow demons to vindicate his ministry [Mk. 3:12].)

At any rate, the statement above, and others like it, is a compromise for the sake of "being scholarly." At first appearance the "pseudepigraphal view" *seems* scholarly; it appeals to the logical mind. But on close examination, this view is *not* scholarly, rather a compromise of Scripture.

Furthermore, we submit that the aforementioned quote presents an *inconsistency in inspiration.* If God has given all other Scripture by revealing to the writer what He wanted written, then why did God allow the writer to quote from books that are mystical and clearly pagan in origin? These books contradict and violate Scripture at every turn. Why would God want to allow His Perfect Word to be based on such literature? We ask again, is this really what we want to defend?

We offer this analogy: a particular statement from the *Book of Mormon* might be true, but an evangelical writer would hardly quote from it. Why? Because of association! We would in no way want to associate ourselves with apostasy. Likewise, we cannot fathom God associating Himself with these mystical, apostate writings. We'll end with these words from Maxwell Coder:

> Those who love the Word of God and trust it implicitly need not fear that any attack upon Jude will succeed in showing that he took any part of his epistle from such a volume.[27]

From whence, then, did Jude get his information? FROM GOD!

NOTES

[1] Warren Wiersbe, *Be Alert* (Wheaton: Victor Books), 1984, p. 140.

[2] Joseph Excell, *The Biblical Illustrator, Genesis* (Grand Rapids: Baker Book House, 1956), p. 401.

[3] J. Sidlow Baxter, *Studies in Problem Texts* (Grand Rapids: Zondervan Publishing House, 1974), p. 152.

[4] Laird R. Harris, et. al. (Editors), *Theological Wordbook Of The Old Testament* (Chicago: Moody Press, 1980), Vol. 2, p. 587.

[5] *Ryrie Study Bible* (NASB edition).

[6] Louis Berkhof, *Systematic Theology* (Grand Rapids: Eerdmans Publishing Company, 1993 reprint), pp. 141, 148.

[7] W. H. Griffith Thomas, *Genesis: A Devotional Commentary* (Grand Rapids: Eerdman's Publishing Co., 1971), p. 66.

[8] Warren Wiersbe, *Be Basic* (Wheaton: Victor Books), 1998, p. 89-90.

[9] Augustus Strong, *Systematic Theology* (Valley Forge: Judson Press, 1907), p. 445.

[10] Millard J. Erickson, *Christian Theology* (Grand Rapids: Baker Book House, 1998), p. 467.

[11] Francis Turretin, *Institutes of Elenctic Theology*, three Volumes, (Phillipsburg,

NJ: Presbyterian and Reformed Publishing, 1997), Vol 1, p. 548.

[12] Wayne Grudem, *Systematic Theology* (Grand Rapids: Zondervan, 1994), p. 414.

[13] J. Sidlow Baxter, *Studies in Problem Texts* (Grand Rapids: Zondervan Publishing House, 1974), p. 177 (emphasis in the original).

[14] Spiros Zodhiates and Warren Baker (General Editors), The Complete Word Study Old Testament (Iowa Falls, IA: World Publishing, 1994), p. 17 (footnote).

[15] Walter C. Kaiser, et. al., *Hard Sayings of the Bible*, (Downer's Grove, IL: InterVarsity Press) 1997.

[16] Joseph Thayer, *Thayer's Greek–English Lexicon of the New Testament*, (Grand Rapids: Associated Publishers and Authors, Inc.).

[17] Warren Wiersbe, *Be Alert* (Wheaton: Victor Books), 1984, p. 42.

[18] Rene Pache, *The Inspiration And Authorty Of Scripture* (Chicago: Moody Press, 1971), p. 171-2.

[19] Norman L. Geisler and William E. Nix, *A General Introduction To The Bible, Revised and Expanded* (Chicago: Moody Press, 1971), p. 269.

[20] Ibid, p. 262-3.

[21] Ibid, p. 262.

[22] Albert Barnes, *Barnes Notes On The New Testament*, One Volume Edition (Grand Rapids: Kregal Publications, 1974), p. 1516..

[23] Ibid, p. 1519, quoting Chapter 2 of *Biblical Repository*, Vol. 15, p. 86.

[24] Maxwell S. Coder, *Jude: The Acts Of The Apostates. Everyman's Bible Commentary* (Chicago: Moody Press, 1958), p. 91.

[25] William Kelly, "Lectures on the Epistle of Jude," *The Serious Christian*, Vol. I (Charlotte, NC: Books for Christians, 1970), as cited in William MacDonald, *Believer's Bible Commentary* (Nashville: Thomas Nelson Publishers, 1995), p. 2343.

[26] Coder, p. 85.

[27] Ibid.

Compare Scripture with Scripture. False doctrines, like false witnesses, agree not among themselves.

Puritan William Gurnall
A Puritan Golden Treasury, p.36

6

Where Has Our Discernment Gone?[*]

Ephesians 4:14

That we henceforth be no more children, tossed to and fro, and carried about with every wind of doctrine, by the sleight of men, and cunning craftiness, whereby they lie in wait to deceive.

The great conqueror Napoleon often told the tale of when he was visiting a certain province and came upon an old soldier with one severed arm. On his uniform he displayed the coveted Legion of Honor. "Where did you lose your arm?" Napoleon asked. "At Austerlitz, Sire," came the soldier's brisk reply. "And for that you received the Legion of Honor?" "Yes, Sire. It is but a small token to pay for the decoration." Then the emperor said, "You must be the kind of man who regrets he did not lose both arms for his country." "What then would have been my reward?" asked the one-armed man. "Then," Napoleon replied, "I would have awarded you a double Legion of Honor." With that the proud, old fighter drew his sword and immediately cut off his other arm. The story was circulated for years, until one day someone asked, "How?"[1]

Ponder further, sometimes we accept sayings simply because they are pithy, such as the Earl of Kent's remark in Shakespeare's *King Lear*, "The stars above us govern our conditions."[2] This is just one of many references to that day's common belief in Astrology. Other times we accept a proverb because it matches our own philosophy, such as the famous declaration often attributed to Greenbay Packer coach Vince Lombardi but actually said by another football coach, Red Sanders, in 1953, "Winning isn't everything; it's the only thing."[3]

People accept such ideas and uncounted more simply because they lack *discernment*, form the Latin *discernere*, comprised of *dis*, "apart," and *cernere*, "to sift." As we'll see in detail, the Bible constantly, over and over again, emphasizes this principle, to separate and distinguish between in order to see and understand the difference. But far worse is how the lack of discernment has marched into the church like a plague of Driver Ants consuming everything in its path. Lost in the Church today is the ability to

---

[*] This chapter was originally TOTT issues 8, 9, and 10, March–May 2006.

discern, to see the difference between truth and error. And the few who do dare discern are labeled "unloving," "divisive," and "intolerant."

So what does Scripture say about discernment? I would humbly submit my burdened evaluation.

Characteristics of Spiritual Children

Our text declares: **That we henceforth be no more children, tossed to and fro, and carried about with every wind of doctrine, by the sleight of men, and cunning craftiness, whereby they lie in wait to deceive**. While this verse is not a "Tough Text" because of a grammar problem, historical uncertainty, controversial issue, or other such matter, it's tough for another reason. This is a "Tough Text" because it's a verse that is hard to face, a verse that *demands* that we "grow up" and make narrow judgments about doctrine and practice.

Ephesians 4:14 is probably the most graphic description in Scripture of the immature, unguided, undiscerning Christian. As the words **henceforth be no more** indicate, the Ephesian believers obviously had previously been **children**, so the first thing Paul says is that this must cease. There are several characteristics of children that apply to the spiritually immature Christian.

First, children are *ignorant*. The Greek for **children** is *nēpios*, which is a combination of *nē* ("not") and *epos* ("word"), so the literal idea is "one who cannot speak, that is, an infant." Metaphorically, it pictures one who is "unlearned, unenlightened, simple, innocent,"[4] and even "foolish"; when the ancient Greek philosophers wished to dismiss someone who was foolish in his views, they would use *nēpios* with biting sarcasm.[5] Writing to Christians in Greek society, Paul challenged the Corinthians, "When I was a child, I spake as a child, I understood as a child, I thought as a child: but when I became a man, I put away childish things" (1 Cor. 13:11).

This point is, indeed, profound. After becoming a father, I often found myself thinking, "This child ought to know *something*, but he doesn't; we've got to teach him *everything*." And children will believe anything. They'll *believe* there is a Santa Clause because we tell them there is (which really doesn't say much for us, does it?). They'll also *try* anything. They'll try to see what small objects will fit into an electrical outlet, they'll run into the street, they'll eat the family dog's food, and other things we wouldn't believe unless we saw them. *And that is precisely Paul's point.* The immature Christian knows either nothing at all or so little that he constantly gets himself into trouble.

Second, children are *impulsive*; they are **tossed to and fro**. This phrase is a single word in the Greek, *kludōnizomai*, an old nautical term "meaning to be tossed by the waves."[6] Children have a short attention span. They bounce from one thing to another. Babies will be drawn to a moving object one minute and a shiny one the next. Toddlers will play with a toy one minute and the box it came in the next. Immature Christians are the same, bouncing from one opinion to another, one teaching to another, with no discernment of which is better or even right. They'll just grab onto anything and run with it. This leads to another characteristic.

Third, children are *impressionable*; they are **carried about with every wind of doctrine**. **Carried about** is *periphero*, which pictures being carried around in circles, that is, being directionless, just driven here and there with no guidance. As Greek expositor John Eadie puts it, "The billow does not swell and fall on the same spot, but it is carried about by the wind, driven hither and thither before it—the sport of the tempest."[7] It's also significant that the definite article ("the") appears before **doctrine** in the Greek (*tēs didaskalias*)—"every wind of *the* doctrine"—showing that false teachers are very deliberate; they don't have a general doctrine, rather a definite, calculated, and well formulated doctrine to teach. Most cults illustrate this vividly; as wrong as the doctrine is, it is nonetheless systemized, organized, and well devised. As a result, whatever the false teacher's **doctrine** is, the immature, undiscerning Christian is just carried along by it until the next teaching blows in and carries him somewhere else. One pastor boldly asserts the habits of the spiritually immature Christian when he writes:

> There is a flightiness and instability to their lives . . . They dash in a dither toward every new religious fad, they seem more excited about the latest religious book than about the one Great Book, they rush from seminar to conference, hanging on to the words of the latest Christian guru, they change their spiritual and doctrinal mindset as often as they change their socks. With them, prophecy becomes a hobby, and spirituality becomes the latest craze.[8]

How true! From the days of Bill Gothard's "Institute in Basic Youth Conflicts" decades ago, to Bill McCartney's "Promise Keepers" more recently, to Rick Warren's "Purpose Driven Life" today, it's been this fad, that book, and this other movement, one after the other, year after year. The picture painted by **wind** is also graphic. Just as the **wind** surrounds us when it blows, so all kinds of teaching surround us. This demands, therefore, that we discern its direction—we must examine where it *comes from*, what it *carries*, and where it's *headed*.

Another pastor, theologian, and professor tells of being at a denominational meeting one day when a pastor rose and shared his heart about the evil results of para-ecclesiastical movements. As is frequently true, parishioners, who often know little of God's truth, go to some large popular meeting, learn something new and exciting, and return to their church and boldly announce that the pastor is not doing things right. After all, the popular speaker has a huge following, and the pastor only a little one. As this writer rightly observes, "These popular movements violate every principle of church organization."[9] Far worse, however, these tear down the Local Church and undermine the leadership of such faithful shepherds.

Fourth and finally, children are *indulgent*. If there is one thing that characterizes a child more than anything else, it's that he wants to play, he wants to be entertained, he wants to have fun, he's self-absorbed. And that's not only true of the immature Christian today but most of the Church as a whole. The seeker-sensitive movement has inevitably led to entertainment as the driving force of Church "ministry." This started decades ago with just children and youth ministries that kept the kids entertained, but now *it defines the whole Church*. There is literally every form of entertainment in the Church today that is found in the world: all genres of music concerts, dramas, movies, standup comedy, dances, sports, and even—I'm not making this up—gambling and strippers.

To raise money, one church in Surrey, England sponsored "Rodent Roulette," in which they put a mouse in a box that has several holes in the sides of it, put a cup over the mouse, spin the box around a few times, take bets on which hole the mouse will use to exit the box, and then release it.

Christianity Today once reported of an incident that took place in Richardson, Texas. On one Sunday, Pastor William Nichols of the First Unitarian Church invited Diana King, a Unitarian from Fort Worth, to take part in the service. She did, and when she was through, all that she was wearing was a G-string. The congregation of 200 adults and children watched in fascinated silence as Miss King—an exotic dancer at a Dallas nightspot—shed her clothes in time with recorded music. The pastor said that the dance fit "very well into our service" and nobody complained. He also said he didn't think anyone was aroused, "but I don't consider the erotic aspect of the dance wrong. After all, that's the way we were conceived." Miss King said it was something she wanted to do for a long time, and she would like to conduct classes for women church members. She commented, "I would like to do a sermon using the exotic dance, and members of the congregation could join me if they liked."

At this point, many would say, "Oh, those are just isolated incidents in liberal churches." Really? Consider Glide Memorial Methodist Church in San Francisco, a church that once preached the Gospel and was soundly evangelistic. Today it has this "Call to Worship" in its printed bulletin on Sunday and recited by the leader: "We are all of us Christians—Jews, liberals, Bolsheviks, anarchists, socialists, Communists, Keynesians, Democrats, Civil Righters, Beatniks, ministers, moderate Republicans, pacifists, teach-inners, doctors, scientists, professors, Latin Americans, New Africans, Common Marketers, even Mao Tse-Tung. Doubtless. From Lyndon Johnson to Mao Tse-Tung, we are all Christians." Its services are performed in the mode of the modern dance. Participants gyrate suggestively, and the church has become a haven for dope addicts, homosexuals, and sexpots.

Or how about one great New York City church that was originally built in honor of the great missionary to Burma, Adoniram Judson? Apostasy has closed in on that church, and from what goes on there it has no right to be called a church. They put on a show one Flag Day, a show supposedly "dedicated to the stars and stripes." There were depraved and obscene exhibits defiling the flag, and according to Max Geldman in the conservative political publication *National Review*, there were exhibits that were "simply unquotable." The show was so offensive that the police closed it. On another occasion, the pews were removed to make room for dancing and the people sat in circles of folding chairs. The pulpit had been removed for a presentation of "Winnie the Pooh" and had not been replaced. The place where the choir used to be is vacant. On one Sunday a nude couple danced there during the service.[10]

Yes, I freely admit that those are extreme examples, *but I also submit that* **philosophically** *they are no different than any church today that resorts to entertainment in any form.* So-called "ministry" today is built on "giving people what they want," "appealing to felt-needs," and "user-friendliness." It is specifically geared to the flesh and thrives in an atmosphere of spiritual immaturity.

But Paul is not done yet!

The Sources of False Doctrine

Paul adds that such false doctrine comes in three ways.

First, **by the sleight of men.** Here is a fascinating term. The word **sleight** is by far the best translation of the Greek *kubeia*, from *kubos* (English "cube") and appears only here in the New Testament. The Greek literally means "playing dice" and the translation **sleight** graphically pictures the implication of the gambling, trickery, and fraud that is involved. We can picture this easily by thinking of how many people throw away billions of dollars on gambling. In 1946 the gangster Ben "Bugsy" Siegel opened the Flamingo Hotel in Las Vegas, which was at first a disaster—nobody came to a hotel/casino in the middle of nowhere. The price tag that began at two million dollars swelled to six, for which Siegel was eventually murdered by his associates because they figured he was skimming money. The casino turned around, however, and made four million dollars in its first year, which grew to tens of *billions* to the present day, and all of it by *kubos*. The house edge in Roulette, for example, is 2.7% for single zero and 5.26% for double zero. The edge is even worse for other games: 4.5% for Sportsbook Betting, 3.9% to 15.2% for various slot machines, and an unbelievable 25% for Keno.

I was also reminded of the old scam, Three-Card Monte, in which the expert scam artist lays three cards on the table, one of which is a queen, shuffles them back and forth, and then asks you to "find the lady." You'll win at first, but when the bet increases, you'll lose because of a sleight of hand trick. The dealer picks up two cards with his right hand, the upper card between his thumb and his forefinger and the lower card between his thumb and his middle finger, with a small gap between both cards. According to common sense, and is, in fact, what he did before, the dealer should drop the lower card first, but this time his forefinger smoothly and slyly ejects the upper card first, which causes you to lose track of the queen. This is especially difficult to see if the dealer's hand makes a sweeping move from his left side toward his right side while he drops the cards. The moral of the story is: *you are going to lose.*

That is the false teacher. By "sleight of mouth" he tricks the unwary without their even knowing it because they are gullible and over-confident in their knowledge. Pride gets the Three Card Monte victim every time; he's confident he can follow the Queen, but he can't because of the **sleight** of hand—the hand *is* quicker than the eye. Likewise, immature Christians are over-confident in their supposed knowledge and are easy prey for false teachers. That is precisely why Paul warned the Ephesian elders in Miletus that "grievous wolves [will] enter in among you, not sparing the flock. Also of your own selves shall men arise, speaking perverse things, to draw away disciples after them" (Acts 20:29–30).

Second, false doctrine comes by **cunning craftiness**, which is one word in the Greek, *panourgia*, a compound word from two roots, *pan* ("all") and *erg* ("work"), yielding the meaning "capable of all work," or as Aristotle viewed it, "an unprincipled [capability] to do anything."[11] *That* is the false teacher. He will do anything, stoop to any level needed to manipulate error, to make something look like truth and thereby lead others away from truth. Paul also uses this word in 2 Corinthians 2:2, where believers should "[renounce] the hidden things of dishonesty, not walking in craftiness, nor handling the word of God deceitfully; but by manifestation of the truth commending ourselves to every man's conscience in the sight of God."

The Jehovah's Witness, for example, deceitfully alters the Greek text of John 1:1 to read, "In [the] beginning the Word was, and the Word was with God, and the Word was a god." Where does *The New World Translation* get this rendering? Supposedly, it is based on the "oldest manuscripts," which can be easily shown to be patently false. Also, it was translated thusly from the German by Johannes Greber in 1937, a former Catholic priest turned spiritist who claimed the translation came from God's spirits. Indeed, men will do anything to make their teaching look like truth when it is the very opposite.

Third, false doctrine comes by delusion and deception (**they lie in wait to deceive**). The Greek behind **lie in wait** (*methododeia*, English "method") does not appear in Greek literature prior to the New Testament,[12] where it means "to investigate by settled plan" or "a deliberate planning or system." [13] There is, therefore, a settled plan, an elaborate system, a deliberate scheme behind those who teach false doctrine. Their desire to is to **deceive**, Paul says, which translates *planē*, "a wandering out of the right way" and, therefore, figuratively delusion and error. First Thessalonians 2:10–11 speak of the lost multitude that will believe the Antichrist, and for that very reason God will "send them strong delusion, that they should believe a lie." While that day is not yet here, delusion, error, and seduction are everywhere.

What is even more tragic is how many true believers there are who are gullible and will believe virtually anything and follow almost anybody. Even with our unequaled education, freedom, sophistication, access to God's Word, Christian books, and a multitude of Bible translations (which I am convinced is actually part of the problem), it seems that *anybody, no matter what he teaches*, can get a following and even financial support from not only individual Christians, but entire Local Churches and even whole denominations, associations, and fellowships. Like little children, they are captivated by something new: a new interpretation, a new idea, a new catchy phrase or term, a new method of "ministry," and countless other things.

What, then, is the key to discernment? There is only a single principle: *What does the Word of God say?* It doesn't matter if some new idea or teaching "sounds good," but whether or not it's right according to Scripture. At the very heart of the Reformation was *Sola Scriptura* ("Scripture Alone") that dictates all we believe and practice, not Church Tradition, human opinion, or anything else. For centuries Roman Catholicism has been adding its traditions to Scripture, and even incorporating pagan practices (and even gods) into its system, but Evangelicalism is not much better as it also adds men's teachings, methods, and ministries to Scripture. How we need a new Reformation today!

Tests of Discernment

Let's practice our discernment skills for a few moments. One popular speaker, for example, gives this description of one whose "felt need" should be addressed:

> You have a guy sitting in church and he's figuring out, "Okay, how am I going to make payroll? How am I going to finance my lifestyle? I've got these two kids that are rebellious; they're caught up in this lack of authority thing. My emotional connection with my wife is really running dry. I'm sitting with three strangers next to me listening to this sermon. I need some help for my life right now." I believe that's the way Jesus taught. I mean Jesus started at the point of the real and felt need that a person would have.

That certainly sounds good, noble, and caring, but is it *right* according to Scripture? No, it is *not*. The Lord Jesus simply did *not* start with a person's "felt need," which has become a term on which many churches are built today. In His dealing with the woman at the well (Jn. 4:1–26), he very specifically confronted her with her sin and then even taught her some doctrine on worship. He most certainly did not start with a "felt need," rather *real sin*.

Another popular voice boldly says this:

> People are always telling me that we should go back to the New Testament church where they were pure. Are you crazy? Where they loved each other. You're out of your mind. Where they joined hands and walked off into the sunset together. That's not the way it was. You haven't taken the time to read the Bible. They were as bad as we are, and sometimes they were worse. And I get along better with people at the seminary than Paul got along with Barnabas.

That sounds authoritative coming from the mouth of a well-know Bible teacher, but is it *right*? No, it is *not*. In fact, it borderlines on blasphemy. It is that man who has "not read the Bible," for Luke records that the early church

> *continued stedfastly* in the apostles' doctrine and fellowship, and in breaking of bread, and in prayers. And fear came upon *every* soul: and many wonders and signs were done by the apostles. And *all that believed* were together, and had *all things* common; And sold their possessions and goods, and parted them to all men, as every man had need. And they, *continuing daily* with one accord in the temple, and breaking bread from house to house, did eat their meat with gladness and singleness of heart, Praising God, and having favour with all the

people. And the Lord added to the church daily such as should be saved" (Acts 2:42–47, emphasis added).

Were there controversies and problems as the Church continued? Of course, there were, as in Acts 6 and 15, as well as other mentions of doctrinal and practical issues, such as as in most of 1 Corinthians. But those were exceptions to the general rule. This man's comment clearly implies that he knows a better way, that we can actually improve on the biblical record, *and that is heresy.*

Here is another quote, which is, in fact, one of the most common teachings of our day:

> The unity of the faith is more important than doctrinal opinion.

Again, that sounds loving, but is it *right*? No, it is *not*. As Paul told Titus, a pastor of a local church, the pastor has been entrusted with God's word and is, therefore, *required* to, "[Hold] fast the faithful word as he hath been *taught*, that he may be able *by sound doctrine* both to *exhort* and to *convince* the gainsayers [i.e., refute those who oppose that doctrine]" (Titus 1:7a, 9; emphasis added). Unity is most certainly not more important than correct doctrine, no matter who says anything to the contrary.

Another speaker, who was shouting in a hateful tone, said this:

> I *refuse* to argue any longer with any of you out there! Don't even call me if you want to argue doctrine, if you want to straighten somebody out . . . Get out of my life! I don't want to even talk to you or even hear you! I don't want to see your ugly face! I say get out of God's way, quit blocking God's bridges. Or God's going to shoot you if I don't. Let Him sort out all this doctrinal doodoo. I don't care about it!

Even if we ignore the ranting and raving, is such teaching about doctrine *right*? No, it is *not*. 1 Timothy 4:16 could not be clearer: "Take heed unto thyself, and unto the doctrine; continue in them: for in doing this thou shalt both save thyself, and them that hear thee." Neither could Proverbs 30:5–6, "Every word of God is pure: he is a shield unto them that put their trust in him. Add thou not unto his words, lest he reprove thee, and thou be found a liar."

Still another speaker explained "doctrine" this way:

> I want you to know the word doctrine. Circle it. It happens to be the matter of, if you're taking notes, the how you do the what you do. That's what it means—doctrine, the way you do the what you do. Yea, there's a certain way I get dressed, there's a certain way you get dressed. Men, you put your socks on first and then your pants or you put your pants on first and then your socks. So, let me tell you

something, depending upon how you dress, that happens to be your doctrine. The way you brush your teeth—do you squeeze the tube from the bottom, from the top, do you roll it? That would happen to be a matter of doctrine. You see, doctrine is just a word that describes your daily routine.

We shouldn't even have to ask if such a notion is biblical because it is so foolish, so childish, so contrary to even the simplest dictionary definition of "doctrine" that it's unbelievable that anyone would listen to a man like that.

Another well-known speaker counsels Christians with these sage words:

> If you're sure that you're right, for God's sake don't correct those who are wrong. If you're sure that you're pure, for God's sake don't correct those who aren't. If you're sure that you've got it together, for God's sake don't try to fix somebody who isn't. From your position of righteousness and purity and balance, you'll kill the church.

Yes, this sounds loving and unifying, but is it *true* biblically? No, it is *not*. As Paul declared to the Corinthians: "Do not ye judge them that are within [the church]? But them that are without God judgeth. Therefore put away from among yourselves [i.e., the church] that wicked person" (1 Cor. 5:12–13). And as he likewise commanded Pastor Timothy, "As I besought thee to abide still at Ephesus, when I went into Macedonia, that thou mightest charge some that they teach no other doctrine" (1 Tim. 1:3). He goes on to state in verse 5 that the goal of such action is true, biblical love.

To illustrate, if I knew that a flashflood had washed out a bridge, would it be loving and compassionate for me to stand by the railroad tracks smiling and waving at the passengers on an Amtrak train as it hurtled toward the chasm? Of course not! True love desires to warn people of coming doom.

Paul even goes so far to mention *by name* those who were teaching false doctrine in verses 18–20 ("Hymenaeus and Alexander"). Today such an act is considered unloving and divisive, even if what they are teaching is hurting people and destroying biblical Truth. Commenting on Paul's challenge to Timothy to "preach the Word" and "reprove, rebuke, exhort with all longsuffering and doctrine" (2 Tim. 4:2), theologian Gordon Clark writes:

> Paul denounced heretics publicly by name. It is not enough to give diplomatic, spineless, uninformative warnings against unidentified errors. They must be clearly explained and clearly refuted. Some in the congregation may think refutation is useless and

tedious. But Paul commands the preachers to persevere in their instruction with all patience.[14]

In spite of that absolutely crystal clear Truth, the Senior Pastor of a mega-church in California writes:

> How tragic it is when we become more concerned with being "right" than being "loving." I would rather have the wrong facts and a right attitude, than right facts and a wrong attitude.

That is not only childishly foolish, but it blatantly contradicts Ephesians 4:15, where Paul says we do *both*: we *speak the truth* and we do so *in love*. One without the other will always bring heresy.

Still another teacher authoritatively declares:

> [One] big lie is that God only wants three things from us; he wants "the three G's:" He wants groveling, groaning, and He wants grieving; He wants us to cry and grieve over our sin. What a big lie!

While that might certainly liberate us in our way of living our lives, is it biblically *true*? No, it is *not*. As God declares in James 4:9–10, "Be afflicted, and mourn, and weep: let your laughter be turned to mourning, and your joy to heaviness. Humble yourselves in the sight of the Lord, and he shall lift you up," and in Isaiah 66:2, "To this man will I look, even to him that is poor and of a contrite spirit, and trembleth at my word."

Another teacher characterizes God this way:

> God is a God of grace. You can curse Him and disobey Him and spit in His face and reject Him, and you can do it over and over and over again, and He keeps coming back for more.[15]

Is such a characterization of God *biblical*? No, it is *not*. It flies in the face of the Truth that "the LORD said, My spirit shall not always strive with man" (Gen. 3:6) and that "the wrath of God is revealed from heaven against all ungodliness and unrighteousness of men, who hold the truth in unrighteousness" (Rom. 1:18). But even more profound are God's words in Hebrews 10:26–31:

> For if we sin wilfully after that we have received the knowledge of the truth, there remaineth no more sacrifice for sins, But a certain fearful looking for of judgment and fiery indignation, which shall devour the adversaries. He that despised Moses' law died without mercy under two or three witnesses: Of how much sorer punishment, suppose ye, shall he be thought worthy, who hath trodden under foot the Son of God, and hath counted the blood of the covenant, wherewith he was sanctified, an unholy thing, and hath done despite unto the Spirit of grace? For we know him that hath said, Vengeance

belongeth unto me, I will recompense, saith the Lord. And again, The Lord shall judge his people. It is a fearful thing to fall into the hands of the living God.

Another vivid example of the gullibility and undiscerning nature of Christianity today is the virtual cult that has arisen around the hugely popular book *The Prayer of Jabez*. One author's indictment is right on the mark, calling this book "the most mesmerizing deception to be launched on American Christianity in the modern era."[16] Why? Because, as another author puts it, the basic, underlying error of the book is "that the repetition of a prayer, any prayer, even a biblical prayer, unlocks the power of God in our lives."[17] The whole thrust of the book is that by repeating this obscure Old Testament prayer (a clear violation of the prohibition of "vain repetition" in Matt. 6:8), the Christian can unlock blessing and miracles. All it boils down to be is old prosperity teaching in a new wrapper, and to be blunt once more, it's heresy plain and simple. Over and over again (*ad infinitum, ad nauseam*) the author promises prosperity and miracles with such statements as the following:

- ❏ "God wants [us] to be 'selfish' in [our] prayers. To ask for more—and more again—from our Lord . . . [and is] exactly the kind of request our Father longs to hear" (*although Scripture nowhere says any of that*).

- ❏ "A guaranteed by-product" of saying the Jabez prayer will be that "your life will become marked by miracles" (*but again, that's not promised either in the so-called "Jabez Prayer" or anywhere else in Scripture*).

- ❏ "Seeking God's blessing is our ultimate act of worship" (*but not one verse of Scripture says that; it is totally the author's conjecture*).[18]

And on we could go. While this book is filled with warm anecdotes, personal experience, and boundless conjecture, totally absent are solid theology and hermeneutics, Scripture exposition, and Divine Truth. When I first read this book, my immediate reaction was, "Where has our discernment gone?" Hence the title of this chapter.

I also never cease to be amazed at how something novel, clever, pithy, and even shocking is received with glorious excitement by the Church today. An example of this is found in another popular book, *Desiring God*, written by John Piper. While he does say some very good things, his entire premise is based on an absolutely ridiculous term, "Christian Hedonism." What he means by this term is a call to abandon the short-term, low-yield pleasures of the world for the magnificent joys of knowing God in whom is fullness of joy, but to use the term "hedonism" is utterly ludicrous.

In Classical Greek, the term *hēdonē* (from which hedonism is derived) ultimately came to refer "to the pleasure of the senses, of sex, and then the unrestricted passions." This meaning is clearly carried over into the New Testament, where the term appears only five times, all in "later books," and *always* with "a bad connotation."[19]

The point here is why *invent* a term that you then have to spend several pages (or even a whole book) defending and explaining? Why not write a book on a *biblical* term, such as the word *joy* (Greek *chara*)? Piper could have written his entire book based on that *biblical* word and done it much more easily. Why not do so? Why manufacture a provocative and contradictory term that has nothing whatsoever to do with real joy? Is the reason simply cleverness and marketability or is it a misunderstanding of language? In either case, it misses the Truth.

It is because of such shallowness and faddishness in the Church today that I read far more of the older, tried and tested expositors than I do contemporary writers, though there are, of course, some good authors today. In the present case, for example, the reader would be much better off reading 17th-century Puritan Stephen Charnock's classic, *The Existence and Attributes of God*, which provides a lifetime of meditation.

Let me share one more discernment test. A well-known husband and wife team, whose desire is to reach millions for Christ, claim that an angel appeared to the woman and told her how to get instant decisions for Christ. For example, if you are talking to a waitress, you should ask her, "Do you know that there are two kinds of beautiful waitresses?" "Really?" she would probably respond. "Yes, those who are saved and those who are about to be. Which one are you?" If she says anything except, "I am saved," then say, "Repeat this after me, 'Father forgive me of my sins. Jesus come into my heart. Make me the kind of person You want me to be. Thank You for saving me'" Now ask the waitress, "Where is Jesus right now?" If she answers, "In my heart," say, "Congratulations on being a child of God!" If her answer is anything else, have her repeat the prayer after you again. This couple also insists, "When you talk to someone, use the same words the angel said. It works! If you change the words, it does not work."[20]

That approach and ones similar to it are commonplace. While some teachers would never say that an angel revealed their new method to them, they might as well because they think they can improve on God's method of confronting the sinner with his sin, showing him God's demand for repentance or eternity in Hell, and then sharing with him God's gracious provision in Christ.

The Challenge to Discernment

All the examples we offered earlier, and a myriad of others, demonstrate how completely undiscerning the Church has become. Now we could understand this if the Bible only mentioned discernment once or twice, but the fact is that *the discerning of Truth from error is a recurring theme throughout Scripture.*

When God asked Solomon what he wanted most, Solomon answered, "Give therefore thy servant an understanding heart to judge thy people, that I may discern between good and bad: for who is able to judge this thy so great a people?" (1 Kings 3:9). We, too, have access to such discernment. As we'll come back to in a moment, Hebrews 4:12 declares that God's Word is the "discerner of the thoughts and intents of the heart." As is the pastor's responsibility today, one of the chief duties of the priests was to "teach [God's] people the difference between the holy and profane, and cause them to discern between the unclean and the clean" (Ezek. 44:23).

Most people are aware of the old adage, "Red sky in morning, sailors take warning; red sky at night, sailor's delight," which is based upon Matthew 16:2–3. The occasion was when the Pharisees tempted Jesus to perform a sign from heaven. But He turned it around on them and said, "O ye hypocrites, ye can discern the face of the sky; but can ye not discern the signs of the times?" In other words, they could discern a simple natural phenomenon, but they had no spiritual discernment of who Jesus really was. The Greek for "discern" is *diakrinō*, one of several similar words that speak of judgment and discernment. It literally means "to make a distinction," something the Pharisees *could not* do and something many Christians today *will not* do.

A graphic picture of discernment appears in Acts 17:11. After leaving Thessalonica because of much bitter treatment from Jews there, Paul and Silas headed for Berea, about forty-five miles away. Upon entering the synagogue, they found a group of new believers who "were more noble than those in Thessalonica, in that they received the word with all readiness of mind, and searched the scriptures daily, whether those things were so." While many in Thessalonica had "received the word of God which [they] heard" (1 Thes. 2:13), the Bereans were totally dedicated to the study of Scripture to see if what Paul said was true. *That* is discernment.

Paul also declared to the Corinthians, who were anything but mature, discerning, or spiritual, "He that is spiritual judgeth all things" (1 Cor. 2:15). "Spiritual" is *pneumatikos*, which means "non-carnal"[21] or "dominated by the Spirit, in contrast to [the] natural."[22] To really be spiritual, then, means that we are characterized not by our natural instincts or opinions but by the Holy Spirit.

That is why Paul further says that the spiritual person "judgeth all things." Here is a crucial principle. "Judgeth" is the same word translated "discerned" in the previous verse: "But the natural man receiveth not the things of the Spirit of God: for they are foolishness unto him: neither can he know them, because they are spiritually discerned." The Greek for "discerned" here is *anakrinō*. From about 400 BC onwards, it expressed "the questioning process which leads to a judgement: to examine, cross-examine, interrogate, enquire, and investigate." Other concepts in the word are "scrutinize" and "sift."[23] To discern something means that we don't say, "Well, as long as that Bible teacher talks about God or Jesus, then he's okay." True spirituality and maturity means that we examine *everything*, that we investigate, question, scrutinize, and sift through every aspect of what is being taught and practiced, not from the perspective of the flesh, natural inclination, or personal opinion, but by the domination of the Holy Spirit and God's Word. Most people are, just like the Corinthians, anything but *spiritual*; they are, in fact, the very opposite, looking at everything from their perspective not God's. The truly spiritual person does not accept everything that comes along; rather he or she first examines it biblically to see if it's right or wrong.

Paul likewise wrote the Thessalonians, "Prove all things; hold fast that which is good. Abstain from all appearance of evil" (1 Thes. 5:21–22). "Prove" is *dokimazō*, which means "test, pronounce good, establish by trial." A related word, *dokimos*, was originally used as a technical term for coins that were genuine.[24] So Paul is saying, "Examine everything, put everything to the test, verify each item to see if it is genuine or if it's a fake." If it's good, seize it and hold on to it. If not, however, we are to withdraw from it. As the master expositor John Gill wrote 100 years before Spurgeon in London:

> Abstain from all appearance of evil, of doctrinal evil. Not only open error and heresy are to be avoided, but what has any show of it, or looks like it, or carries in it a suspicion of it, or may be an occasion thereof, or lead unto it; wherefore all new words and phrases of this kind should be shunned, and the form of sound words held fast.

The Apostle John echoes Paul's mandate to discernment by also using *dokimazō*: "Beloved, believe not every spirit, but *try* the spirits whether they are of God: because many false prophets are gone out into the world" (1 Jn. 4:1, emphasis added). How much clearer could Scripture be? *Don't believe every spirit*. There are several teachers today we could list who can say anything and people will believe it. They are never questioned, never doubted. Likewise, there are countless claims to spiritual authority today, innumerable assertions that "this is what the Bible says," but every single one of these is to be examined, tested, and verified.

As I shared this with the sheep under my care, I told them that their pastor must also be tested and verified. That is why all pastors should stick with the Scripture alone, expositing only that. We should not want anything new or novel, no new terms or new philosophies. We should want only what *the text says*. If we stick with Scripture alone, that leaves little room for error.

Finally, Hebrews 4:12 is among the strongest New Testament statements about discernment: "For the word of God is quick, and powerful, and sharper than any two-edged sword, piercing even to the dividing asunder of soul and spirit, and of the joints and marrow, and is a discerner of the thoughts and intents of the heart." The Greek for "discerner" is *kritikos*, which appears only here in the New Testament and which from Plato's day onward referred to "a competent, experienced judge."[25] What a perfect description of the Word of God!—The Discerner, The Judge of men's thoughts and even their "intents" (Greek, *ennoia*), that is, intentions, ideas, notions, and purposes.

Before we go on, we should also address one other verse that always arises with this issue, Matthew 7:1: "Judge not, that ye be not judged." This is used by most people to say, "See there, Jesus says we are not supposed to be critical of anyone; we should not criticize what they believe or say." That is always the cry of tolerance: "Just leave me alone; don't judge what I say; don't ask any questions; just let things be."

But is that what the verse says? Of course not. If it did, Paul contradicted the Lord Jesus many times. What such people fail to do is *read the context* (vv. 2–5):

> For with what judgment ye judge, ye shall be judged: and with what measure ye mete, it shall be measured to you again. And why beholdest thou the mote that is in thy brother's eye, but considerest not the beam that is in thine own eye? Or how wilt thou say to thy brother, Let me pull out the mote out of thine eye; and, behold, a beam is in thine own eye? Thou hypocrite, first cast out the beam out of thine own eye; and then shalt thou see clearly to cast out the mote out of thy brother's eye.

What Jesus is very clearly saying is that we are not to judge and discern *hypocritically* or judge someone's *motives and attitudes*, which have nothing to do with what someone *teaches*. They might have the purest motive and sweetest attitude, but that is not the issue; *the issue is what they teach*. Each of us is tempted to hold others to a higher standard than we hold ourselves, which is hypocrisy, so we must first make sure of our own life, make sure our standard is consistent, and *then* discern actions. In fact, that is exactly what Jesus says: "First, get the *log* out of your own eye and *then* you can remove the *splinter* that's in your brother's eye." Our Lord did not say, "Leave the splinter where it is." He said, "Deal with the error in your life first and then address the error in your brother."

Paul's command to Timothy to "preach the Word" in 2 Timothy 4:2–4 also includes the result of *not* doing so. When people *willingly* "turn away their ears from the truth," they *un*willingly are "turned unto fables." Most significant is that while "shall turn away" is in the Active Voice (subject doing the action), that is, they willfully choose to do this, the words "shall be turned unto fables" is in the Passive Voice (subject being acted upon), which means that they don't choose this result; they are being acted upon and have no choice. Because they willfully turned away, they now will unwillingly be deceived by "fables." This is a staggering truth! The Greek is *muthos*, where we get the English words "myth" and "mythology" and is always used in the New Testament to denote a cunning fable full of falsehoods and pretenses for the purpose of deceiving others.[26]

That is why we have mentioned so many errors in this chapter. Because so many people have *willingly* turned away from the Truth, they have in turn *un*willingly been deceived into countless false teachings, and there's virtually no discernment left in the Church. Besides what we've already listed, doctrinal error is everywhere: God's sovereignty has been redefined in the "Open Theism" movement, Christians seek extra-biblical revelation through mysticism and so-called prophecies, hell is denied as a reality, the roles of men and women are blurred or destroyed altogether, homosexuality, fornication, abortion, and other immorality is condoned and even defended, and on it goes.

I doubt that anyone in our day has said it better than has John MacArthur: "A half truth presented as if it were a whole truth is an untruth." To apply that, think of a courtroom setting. A witness swears to "tell the truth, the whole truth, and nothing but the truth." If that witness does not tell the whole Truth, if he leaves something out, or if he omits something to try to hide what really happened, he is, therefore, lying. To withhold the Truth is a lie. Likewise, if men today are not preaching all of God's Truth, that is, "all the counsel of God," they are committing a sin of omission and, therefore, are in the final analysis preaching a lie.

Paul warned of the subtle danger of satanic lies, describing their sources as

> false apostles, deceitful workers, transforming themselves into the apostles of Christ. And no marvel; for Satan himself is transformed into an angel of light. Therefore it is no great thing if his

ministers also be transformed as the ministers of righteousness; whose end shall be according to their works (2 Cor. 11:13–15).

The word "transforming" is an interesting one. Please follow this carefully. The Greek is *metaschematizō*, to change the outward form or appearance of something. It's actually best understood by contrasting it with *metamorphoō* (English "metamorphosis"), which we find in Romans 12:2 ("transformed by the renewing of our minds"). One Greek scholar puts it this way:

> If one were to change a Japanese garden into an Italian one, this would be *metaschematizō*. But if someone were to transform a garden into something wholly different, as a baseball field, it is *metamorphoō*. It is possible for Satan to *metaschematizō*, transform himself into an angel of light . . . that is, change his whole outward [appearance]. But it would be impossible to apply *metamorphoō* to any such change, for this would imply an internal change, which lies beyond his power.[27]

In other words, while Satan can't change his *nature*, he can change his *appearance*. He appears as something different than he really is.

I was immediately reminded here of how the word "virtual" is used in computer technology, such as "Virtual Reality," which is technology that enables us to be "near reality." We can totally design a house, for example, with so much detail and realism that we can "walk around inside it" and take a "virtual tour." That is exactly what Satan does—he creates *virtual light*. It's so near the real light that the majority of people think it's real. *It therefore takes careful discernment by Christians to see that virtual light is really darkness.* The prophet Isaiah's first test of any teacher was, "To the law and to the testimony: if they speak not according to this word, it is because there is no light in them" (Isa. 8:20). If men do not preach the Scripture alone, there is no light in them, and *we should not even listen to them.*

Besides all those, Scripture over, and over, and over again emphasizes discernment and the dangers of false doctrine. Let us quote just a few:

> Beware of false prophets, which come to you in sheep's clothing, but inwardly they are ravening wolves. Ye shall know them by their fruits . . . (Matt. 7:15–16).

> Then if any man shall say unto you, Lo, here is Christ, or there; believe it not. For there shall arise false Christs, and false prophets, and shall show great signs and wonders; insomuch that, if it were possible, they shall deceive the very elect. Behold, I have told you before. Wherefore if they shall say unto you, Behold, he is in the

desert; go not forth: behold, he is in the secret chambers; believe it not (Matt. 24:23–26)

Take heed therefore unto yourselves, and to all the flock, over the which the Holy Ghost hath made you overseers, to feed the church of God, which he hath purchased with his own blood. For I know this, that after my departing shall grievous wolves enter in among you, not sparing the flock. Also of your own selves shall men arise, speaking perverse things, to draw away disciples after them. Therefore watch, and remember, that by the space of three years I ceased not to warn every one night and day with tears. (Acts 20:28–31).

But I fear, lest by any means, as the serpent beguiled Eve through his subtlety, so your minds should be corrupted from the simplicity that is in Christ . . . For such are false apostles, deceitful workers, transforming themselves into the apostles of Christ. And no marvel; for Satan himself is transformed into an angel of light (2 Cor. 11:3, 13–14).

O Timothy, keep that which is committed to thy trust, avoiding profane and vain babblings, and oppositions of science falsely so called: Which some professing have erred concerning the faith (1 Tim. 6:20–21).

Beware of dogs, beware of evil workers, beware of the concision [*katatomē*, a mutilation, a butchering] (Phil. 3:2).

Beware lest any man spoil you through philosophy and vain deceit, after the tradition of men, after the rudiments of the world, and not after Christ (Col. 2:8).

But there were false prophets also among the people, even as there shall be false teachers among you, who privily shall bring in damnable heresies, even denying the Lord that bought them, and bring upon themselves swift destruction. And many shall follow their pernicious ways; by reason of whom the way of truth shall be evil spoken of (2 Pet. 2:1–2).

Conclusion

Never before has the Church been in such need of discernment and pure **doctrine** as it is today. One of the best statements on the place of doctrine in the Church was written back in 1983 by pastor and theologian Gordon Clark. Commenting on 1 Timothy 6:1—"Let as many servants as are under the yoke count their own masters worthy of all honour, that the name of God and his doctrine be not blasphemed"—he writes:

> What the speed-reader is apt to miss in this verse is the repetition of the importance of doctrine. Doctrine and the name of God, that is, God Himself and His truth, must not be blasphemed. Today liberals, humanists, behaviorists, and the neo-orthodox attack doctrine; but what is worse, those who think of themselves as devout evangelicals strongly insisting on the inerrancy of Scripture, ignore doctrine. They favor pastoral counseling, they prate about four spiritual laws, sing Gospel dance tunes, testify to their happiness, even read some of the Bible, but they read it without trying to understand it. Nor is the major blame to be put on the congregation; most of whom know no Greek; the major blame lies on ministers who know no Greek and not much theology. They do not speak evil of God's work: they simply do not speak. A friend of mine, who did his best to preach the whole counsel of God, had a conversation with a very popular preacher and author. Said the popular idol to my friend, "I believe the same doctrines you do." Said my friend, "I am delighted, I wouldn't have known it, if you hadn't told me."[28]

Indeed, in many circles today, doctrine is avoided at all costs. *What folly!* Doctrine is the foundation on which we stand, and we must discern it carefully. If we fail in this, we "reap the whirlwind" (Hosea 8:7).

NOTES

[1] Cited in Paul Lee Tan, *Encyclopedia of 7,700 Illustrations*, (Garland, Texas: Bible Communications, Inc., 1996).

[2] IV.iii.32–33.

[3] The actual saying by Vince Lambardi in a 1962 interview was, "Winning isn't everything, but wanting to win is." Both cited in *Bartlett's Familiar Quoations*, 16th Edition, p. 783.

[4] Zodhiates, *The Complete Word Study Dictionary, NT*, p. 1009-10.

[5] Colin Brown, *The New International Dictionary of New Testament Theology*, Vol. 1, p. 281.

[6] Kenneth Wuest's *Word Studies*. (John Eadie, *A Commentary on the Greek of Text of Ephesians*: "tossed about as a surge," p. 315).

[7] Eadie, p. 315.

[8] Ray Stedman, *Our Riches in Christ: Ephesians*, p. 229.

[9] Gordon Clark, *Ephesians*, p. 141.

[10] Four preceding illustrations from Paul Lee Tan, *Encyclopedia of 7,700 Illustrations*.

[11] Brown, Vol. 1, p. 412.

[12] Brown, Vol. 3, p. 943.

[13] Joseph Thayer's *Greek/English Lexicon* and Wuest respectively.

[14] Gordon Clark, *The Pastoral Epistles* (Jefferson, MD: The Trinity Foundation, 1983), p. 188.

[15] The seven preceding examples taken from actual radio and TV broadcasts of either interviews, sermons, or other public presentations by nationally known Bible teachers and authors.

[16] Steve Hopkins, *The Cult of Jabez* (Bethal Press, 2002).

[17] Gary E. Gilley, *"I Just Wanted More Land" —Jabez* (Xulon Press, 2001).

[18] Bruce Wilkinson, *The Prayer of Jabez* (Sisters, OR: Multnomah Publishers, 2000), pp. 19, 24-25, 49.

[19] Colin Brown, *The New International Dictionary of New Testament Theology*, Vol. 1, pp. 458-9.

[20] Cited in Kirk Cameron and Ron Comfort, *The Way of the Master* (Wheaton, IL: Tyndale House Publishers, 2002) p. 87.

[21] *Strong's Concordance.*

[22] Spiros Zodhiates, *The Complete Word Study Dictionary, NT*, p. 1185.

[23] Colin Brown, *The New International Dictionary of New Testament Theology*, Vol. 1, Vol. 2, p. 362.

[24] Brown, Vol. 3, p. 808.

[25] Brown, Vol. 2, p. 362.

[26] Zodhiates, p. 999.

[27] Zodhiates, p. 973.

[28] Gordon Clark, *The Pastoral Epistles* (Jefferson, MD: The Trinity Foundation, 1983), pp. 106-107.

[Truth] is the great treasure, which God delivers to His saints, with a strict and solemn charge to keep against all that undermine or oppose it. Some things we trust God with, some things God trusts us with. . . . That which God trusts us chiefly with is His Truth.

Puritan William Gurnall
The Christian in Complete Armour, Vol. I, p. 306

7

Does the Authorship of Hebrews Matter?*

2 Peter 3:15–16

And account that the longsuffering of our Lord is salvation; even as our beloved brother Paul also according to the wisdom given unto him hath written unto you; As also in all his epistles, speaking in them of these things; in which are some things hard to be understood, which they that are unlearned and unstable wrest, as they do also the other scriptures, unto their own destruction.

Concerning the authorship of Hebrews, commentators often write such things as, "This great epistle is anonymous . . . This, however, does not affect the genuineness of the epistle."[1] Another writes, "Today [Pauline authorship] is consider very unlikely."[2] Still another says, "Current scholarship admits the puzzle still has no solution."[3]

Such statements, as well as the overall nonchalant attitude toward this issue, have puzzled (and troubled) me for several years. As the beloved Harry Ironside writes:

> May we be certain as to its human authorship, or is it merely a matter of intellectual speculation at best? I believe God has given us definite information on this point.[4]

I wholeheartedly agree. It's absolutely unthinkable that God would "hide" the authorship of such a critical book of His Word.

But does this really matter? What difference does it make who wrote Hebrews? It's still in the Bible, right? I am convinced that it matters a great deal and that there is a point here that is not often addressed. Few seem to realize that without knowledge of the author, *we have a New Testament letter with no apostolic authority and which therefore simply cannot be Scripture.* Among other writers, commentator E. Schuyler English, in his excellent "Introduction" to Hebrews, makes this very point:

> If Paul is not the author, but Apollos, or Clement, or another, then we have in the New Testament an inspired writing that does not have apostolic authority.[5]

---

* This chapter was originally TOTT issues 11 and 12, June and July 2006.

Is such a strong statement justified? I believe it is when we consider the requirements for a book of the Bible to be considered a part of the "Canon" of Scripture. "Canon" (from the Greek *kanōn* and the Hebrew *keneh*) literally means "cane" or "rod of measurement," since such was used in ancient times for measuring purposes, much like we still do today. The term came to be used for testing writings to determine whether or not they "measured up" to the standards required to be considered the Word of God.

Briefly, there were four major tests for the canonicity of a New Testament book.[6] One test was whether the book agreed with the books already in the canon. There certainly was no question here concerning Hebrews "in view of its agreement with all of the Scriptures and its revelation of Christ's Deity, His grace, His sacrificial death, His present mediatorial work, and His coming again."[7] At first, however, Hebrews *was* questioned because chapter 6 seemed "out of sorts with apostolic teaching," but this was actually resolved "when the early church concluded that Hebrews was written by Paul."[8]

A second test that goes along with that one is inspiration. Does the book give clear, unmistakable evidence of being "God-breathed" (2 Tim. 3:16)? In light of the above subjects, the answer was yes to Hebrews.

A third test was that a book had to be gladly received by the Early Church, which Hebrews was. By the time of Clement of Alexandria (c. 150–215) and Origen (c. 185–253), the Eastern Church accepted the Epistle (as well as attributed it to Paul), while the Western Church came along a little later. We will come back to this point in more detail.

A final test of canonicity was apostolic origin, that is, a book either had to be written *by* or attested *to* by an apostle. The two examples here, of course, are Mark and Luke, neither of whom were apostles, but were *sanctioned* by an apostle, Peter in Mark's case and Paul in Luke's case.

It is that last test, in my view, that is really at the heart of this issue. Without knowing who the author of Hebrews is, how can anyone attest to him? How can someone sanction an unknown writer? This is the equivalent of me writing a letter to recommend a man for a job without knowing who the man is. The whole idea is just plain silly. Further, who is doing the attesting anyway?

Again, it is often said that, "Hebrews is anonymous," but we agree with J. Sidlow Baxter who adds "it is only superficially so."[9] I, for example, could write a letter and not sign it, but still be recognized as the author by people who know me or know my writing habits. Likewise, I, with others, see no doubt whatsoever that the Apostle Paul was the author of the Book of Hebrews. I would offer the following evidences, after which we will come back to our main question: "Does it really matter?"

The Testimony of Peter

This point and the next are on almost equal ground, but this one must be first because it deals with Scripture itself. One of the most underrated indications of Pauline authorship (which is virtually ignored by some and even missed by others) is our text, 2 Peter 3:15–16. The brilliant Puritan John Owen, who exhaustively defends Pauline authorship in his monumental and mammoth exposition of Hebrews, writes of this verse:

> Amongst the arguments usually insisted on to prove this Epistle to have been written by St Paul, the testimony given unto it by St Peter deserves consideration in the first place, and is indeed of itself sufficient to determine the inquiry about it.[10]

In other words, *this verse alone is enough to settle the whole matter.*

Peter is here writing, of course, to Jews of the dispersion (that is, Jews scattered in lands outside Israel). In his clear reference to Paul, he not only accepts Paul's letters as "Scripture," but also refers to the fact that Paul has already written to these very same Jews. Therefore, if Paul did not write Hebrews, where is the letter that he wrote to the dispersed Jews? Arthur W. Pink concurs:

> That this Epistle *was* written by Paul is clear from 2 Peter 3:15. Peter was writing to saved Jews as the opening verses of his first Epistle intimates; 2 Peter 3:1 informs us that this letter was addressed to the same people as his former one had been. Then . . . he declares that his beloved brother Paul "also according to the wisdom given unto him hath written *unto you.*" If the Epistle to the Hebrews be not *that* writing, where is it?[11]

The great 18th-century expositor John Gill likewise agrees:

> Above all, the testimony of the Apostle Peter is greatly in favour of [Hebrews] being [Paul's], (2 Peter 3:15,16) from whence it clearly appears, that the Apostle Paul did write an epistle to the Hebrews; for to them Peter wrote; (see 1 Peter 1:1; 2 Peter 3:1) and what epistle could it be but this?[12]

We could add to these quotations others from commentators such as: Jamison, Fausset, and Brown; Matthew Poole; B. W. Johnson; and E. Schuyler English. The point, however, is clear: if Hebrews isn't the letter that Paul wrote to the same Jews of the dispersion that Peter wrote to, where is the other letter? Are we to believe he wrote another such letter that didn't make it into the Canon? John Owen answers that question by offering a scenario that would be just as ridiculous:

> [If] we give place to such rash and presumptuous conjectures, we shall quickly have nothing left entire or stable; for why may not another as well say, "It is true Moses wrote five books; but they are lost, and those that we have under his name were written by another?"

One other point can be made here, namely, Peter specifically says that Paul wrote a letter that contained "some things hard to be understood," which immediately, of course, brings to mind such passages as Hebrews 6 and 10. It's significant, then, that Paul also makes mention of this point in Hebrews 5:11: "Of whom we have many things to say, and hard to be uttered." And in point of fact, Peter and Paul speak of some of the same things. Compare, for example, 6:2 with 1 Peter 3:20–21, and especially 10:26–27 with 2 Peter 2:20–22.

The Testimony of the Early Church

Another underrated indication of Pauline authorship is the testimony of the Early Church. As Baxter puts it, "We believe that the Pauline *tradition* is much weightier than is generally allowed."[13] In other words, it seems irrelevant to many that the Early Church, especially the Eastern branch, unhesitatingly recognized Paul as the author. By A.D. 150, in fact, only 70 years after Paul's death, Panteanus (the head of the celebrated Christian school at Alexandria) referred to it as a generally accepted Epistle of Paul. Of Panteanus, trusted commentator Albert Barnes writes that he

> lived near Palestine. He must have been acquainted with the prevailing opinions on the subject, and his testimony must be regarded as proof that the epistle was regarded as Paul's by the churches in that region.[14]

While virtually every doubter falls back on the overused statement by the famous 3rd-century Origen ("As to who wrote the Epistle, the truth God knows"), few even acknowledge, much less quote, the *context* of that remark, which actually argues *for* Paul's authorship:

> I, to declare my own opinion, should say that the thoughts are the apostle's, but the diction and composition that of some one who recorded from memory the apostle's teaching, and, as it were, interpreted [or "wrote a commentary on"] what had been spoken by his master. If, then, any Church receives this Epistle as Paul's, let it be well esteemed, even also on this account [i.e., let it not for this

reason lose any recognition as a witness to the truth]; for not without good reason have the men of old handed it down as Paul's. But as to who wrote the Epistle, the truth God knows. The account that has reached us is, on the part of some, that Clement, who became Bishop of the Romans, wrote the Epistle; on the part of others, that Luke, who wrote the Gospel and the Acts, did so.[15]

Turning again to John Owen, the great Puritan tallies the rest of this external evidence for Pauline authorship. In the *Alexandrian* church, besides Pantaenus and Origen, there was "Dionysius, Theognostus, Peter, Alexander, Hierax, Athanasius, Theophilus, Serapion, Didymus, and Cyril of Alexandria." In the *Western* church, "from the fourth century, this view was held by Hilary, Ambrose, Jerome, Augustine, Rufinus, Chromatius, Innocent of Rome, Paulinus, Cassian, Prosper, Eucherius, Salvian, and Gelasius." In the *Greek* church, "the synod at Antioch A.D. 264, Gregory Thaumaturgus, the council of Nice A.D. 315, Gregory of Nazianzum, Basil the Great, the council of Laodicea A.D. 360, Gregory of Nyssa, Titus of Bostra, Epiphanius, Chrysostom, and Theodore of Mopsuestia, assign it to the same author." In the *Syrian* church, "the same opinion generally prevailed, as appears from Justin Martyr, Eusebius of Caesarea, Cyril of Jerusalem, Jacob of Nisibis, Ephraim Syrus." Finally, in the *African* church, "the council of Hippo A.D. 393, the third council of Carthage A.D. 397, and the sixth council of Carthage A.D. 419, decide in favor of the same view."

Special note should be made of Eusebius, that well-known bishop of Caesarea and historian in Palestine (4th-century). As Barnes points out, his testimony is extremely significant:

> He took pains, from all quarters, to collect testimony in regard to the Books of Scripture. He says, "There are fourteen epistles of Paul, manifest and well known: but yet there are some who reject that to the Hebrews, alleging, in behalf of their opinion, that it was not received by the church of Rome as a writing of Paul." The testimony of Eusebius is particularly important. He had heard all the objection to its canonical authority. He had weighed that objection. Yet, in view of the testimony in the case, he regarded it as the undoubted production of Paul. As such it was received in the churches in the East.

So, are we to shrug our shoulders at all that and say, "I guess we'll just never know?" Is it not obvious that the knowledge of Paul's authorship was known and then handed down by "the men of old?" On this point, Baxter writes, "Decades *before* Panteanus those who immediately followed the apostles regarded it as truly Paul's."[16]

Still there are those who insist, "But Paul nowhere identifies himself as the author, so we can't be sure." Really? Can we be sure that he wrote Ephesians? "Of course," we answer, "he says so in the first verse." Ah, yes, but "modern scholarship" tells us that he didn't! Contemporary commentator Andrew L. Lincoln writes, "The more I have worked on the text as a whole, the more persuaded I have become that seeing the letter as the work of a later follower of Paul makes better sense of its contents." He then even adds, "This is now the consensus view in New Testament scholarship, though a sizable minority [?] continues to uphold Pauline authorship."[17] Based on five ridiculous reasons that he goes on to detail, this man *denies what the text clearly says*,[18] despite the fact that, similar to Hebrews, Eusebius recognized that the entire Orthodox Church considered Ephesians as belonging to Paul. (See chapter 11, "Who Were the Recipients of the Epistle to the Ephesians?") So, if we "can't be sure" when Paul says he *is* the author, should we be unsure when he *doesn't* say he is?

The Testimony of Paul

It is consistently argued that Paul was the Apostle to the *Gentiles*, not to the Jews, so he would have had no reason to write this Epistle. While it's true that Paul was the Apostle to the Gentiles, he also clearly considered himself "an Hebrew of Hebrews" (Phil.3:5). As he also makes plain in his Epistle to the Romans (9:3; 10:1), he had a great burden for his fellow Jews. He consistently taught that the Gospel should go "to the Jew first" (Rom. 1:16). In fact, he always went to the synagogue first when he arrived in a new city (Acts 17:1–2). It certainly stands to reason that Paul would write a detailed exposition of the doctrine of Christ for the benefit of his fellow Christian Jews. God revealed the depths of the doctrine of the New Covenant to Paul, so it seems obvious that he would be the one to pass it on to both Jew and Gentile. Arthur W. Pink comments on this point:

> Though he was distinctively and essentially the "apostle of the Gentiles" (Romans 11:13), yet his ministry was by no means confined to them, as the book of Acts clearly shows. At the time of his apprehension the Lord said, "He is a chosen vessel unto Me, to bear My Name before the Gentiles, and kings, and the children of Israel" (Acts 9:15).[19]

E. Schuyler English (a Dispensationalist) is even more convincing:

> Was the commission that the Lord Jesus Christ left for His apostles, to go to the Gentiles *only*, or to Israel *only*? No, it was to all nations. It had no bound but was wholly catholic [that is, universal or general]. Peter was "the apostle of the Circumcision" (cf. Gal. 2:7);

yet it was he, first of all, who proclaimed the Gospel of Christ to the Gentiles, in the house of Cornelius (Acts 10). God, who is not respecter of persons, is not limited in the employment of His messengers. He gave Paul the apostolic, prophetic, and evangelistic gifts. He also gave him the teaching gift. Could He not, then, have used him in this capacity to the Hebrews, rather than in that of prophet or apostle announcing the future of some new revelation?[20]

The Testimony of Internal Evidence

Added to the foregoing, there are several internal pointers to Paul's authorship in the Epistle itself.

First, style differences are not as insurmountable as some critics would have us believe. A common objection to Pauline authorship is that the style of this letter is supposedly far different than Paul's. Ignored, however, are the similarities. Consider, for example, several parallels with other Pauline Epistles, such as 5:13 ("For every one that useth milk is unskilful in the word of righteousness: for he is a babe") with 1 Corinthians 3:2 ("I have fed you with milk, and not with meat: for hitherto ye were not able to bear it, neither yet now are ye able"). Consider also 10:1 ("For the law having a shadow of good things to come, and not the very image of the things, can never with those sacrifices which they offered year by year continually make the comers thereunto perfect") with Colossians 2.17 ("Which are a shadow of things to come; but the body is of Christ")? We could also note: 8:6, 9 with Galatians 3:19–20; 13:10 with 1 Corinthians 9:13 and 2 Corinthians 10:18; and others.

There is also the interesting similarity between Romans, Galatians, and Hebrews, all of which quote Habakkuk 2:4: "the just shall live by his faith" (Rom. 1:17; Gal. 3:11; Heb. 10:38). Does this have no significance?

Should we also ignore 13:25 ("Grace be with you all"), a statement that is so typical of Paul that it appears multiple times, in various forms, in every one of his Epistles? Is not this as good as a signature? Compare it with the closing of Paul's other 13 letters: Romans 16:24; 1 Corinthians 16:23–24; 2 Corinthians 13:14; Galatians 6:18: Ephesians 6:24; Philippians 4:23; Colossians 4:18; 1 Thessalonians 5:28; 2 Thessalonians 3:18; 1 Timothy 6:21; 2 Timothy 4:22; Titus 3:15; Philemon 25. We ask again: *Is not this as good as a signature?*

Ironically, the so-called "stylistic differences" argument is voiced by the liberal commentator mentioned earlier who denies Pauline authorship of Ephesians. But just as his ridiculous, Bible-dishonoring attacks are easily answered by the fact that different letters call for different emphases, words, and even style, so it is with Hebrews.

Now we readily admit that there are some style differences. A notable one is that Hebrews is an extremely polished letter, much more so than Paul's other letters. This is easily answered, however, by two points. First, most of Paul's other letters were written earlier, during a busy life filled with traveling, conflict, struggle, and danger. In contrast, Hebrews was a later letter, one which Paul could have taken much more time to compose.

One other comment on the style question is in order, of which a friend of mine reminded me.[21] Higher critics have been challenging Scripture for many years. One of the ways they do so is by rejecting the traditional view that Isaiah wrote the book that bears his name and instead insist on a dual- (or even tri-) authorship. And what is one of their major arguments? *Style!* The point to be made is that while conservative scholars won't allow Isaiah to be ripped apart (or while we're at it, the Pentateuch by the long ago refuted "Documentary Hypothesis" of four authors), then why do they entertain any doubt about Hebrews for supposed style differences?

Second, as J. Sidlow Baxter offers,[22] we could even concede, without doing any damage to Paul's authorship, that Luke aided Paul in polishing the letter, just putting some finishing touches on it. Alternately, we could concede, as noted scholar R. Laird Harris writes, this is "a genuine Epistle of Paul with Barnabas as his secretary."[23]

Further, Paul was writing to different people and with a different purpose, which would in-turn demand different language. Another example of different language, in fact, is 1 Corinthians, which contains expressions that do not occur in any other of the Apostle's letters. This was part of Paul's genius. Baxter offers another illustration using the Apostle John:

> What a difference between the Greek of the Gospel according to John and the Apocalypse!—yet on weighty evidence, both external and internal, John is accepted by first rank scholars as the author or both.[24]

Let us also note again the closing of the letter. Who can deny that this is Paul?

> And I beseech you, brethren, suffer the word of exhortation: for I have written a letter unto you in few words. Know ye that our brother Timothy is set at liberty; with whom, if he come shortly, I will see you. Salute all them that have the rule over you, and all the saints. They of Italy salute you. Grace be with you all. Amen. (13:22–25)

This leads us right to a second internal evidence.

Second, as noted in 13:23 above, the writer refers to "our brother Timothy," which is typical of Paul since Timothy was his convert, disciple, and co-worker. As Owen, Gill, and Barnes all point out, in light of the fact that Timothy was with Paul in Rome during the latter's imprisonment (Phil. 1:1, 13–14; 2:19–24), who but Paul would not only mention Timothy, who was unknown to the letter's recipients, but also make special note of him being released from prison? This is, in fact, as the old expression goes, "a dead giveaway" of the author's identity.

Third, as Baxter observes, there is the striking use of the pronoun "we" in addressing his readers, "as though he speaks representatively of a group (5:11; 6:9, 11; 13:18, 23)." This is characteristic of Paul alone, as it "is never found in John, Peter, James, [or] Jude." Baxter explains:

> It often occurs, of course, in verses where the writer includes himself with his readers in some large class, as for instance in 1 John 1:7, "If *we* walk in the light," where the writer includes himself with *all* Christian believers; but not once is it used by the writer as associating others cooperatively with himself. Yet it is found everywhere in *Paul's* epistles, and again in Hebrews.[25]

Fourth, the writer speaks of himself in 2:3 as one who had not witnessed Jesus earthly ministry. While this verse is used by critics to "prove" that Paul *wasn't* the author, it actually indicates he *was*! It is argued that the verse implies that Paul never *heard* the Lord, which, of course, he did on the road to Damascus. But the verse goes deeper than just a single incident: "How shall we escape, if we neglect so great salvation; which at the first began to be spoken by the Lord, and was *confirmed unto us by them that heard him*" (emphasis added). The picture here is obviously what people heard and saw over a period of time, that is, during Jesus' earthly ministry, nothing of which, to our knowledge, did Paul ever witness. Paul didn't witness Jesus' miracles or teaching, but others did and subsequently "confirmed" it to Paul and his readers.

Fifth and finally, we might also add here that the date of writing (62–65) fits Pauline authorship. Since there is no mention of the Roman destruction of Jerusalem in 70 A.D., the letter had to be written before that. This coincides with Paul's writings. His last letter (2 Tim.), for example, was written in about 68 A. D.

The Testimony for Alternative Authors

If Paul didn't write Hebrews, who did? Many alternatives have been offered through the centuries, but no more than four are worth mention: Luke, Barnabas, Clement of Rome, and Apollos.

Luke is, if not impossible, highly improbable since he was a Gentile and would, therefore, not have been qualified to write such a letter, much less been be accepted by Jewish readers.

Barnabas, on the other, was a Jew, a Levite, in fact, but the only ancient writer to even suggest him was Tertullian (160–230) and he had no proof.

How about Clement of Rome, who we know wrote an excellent letter to the Corinthians? For one thing, there are absolutely no similarities between his letter to the Corinthians and the Epistle of Hebrews, and for another, there is no ancient support for his authorship.

Finally, Apollos has been suggested. The first one to suggest him was actually Martin Luther, but again with no ancient support. Frankly, Apollos is almost as ridiculous a suggestion as Priscilla, who also has been offered because of "'certain dainty feminine touches,' which a lady expositor thinks she has seen in it"![26]

The truth of the matter in all these and all others is that there is not one shred of evidence that any of them penned this Epistle. Men's conjectures have served only to muddy the water.

Conclusion

To conclude, I would offer three points:

First, one question that still remains is, "Why didn't Paul just *say* he was the author of the Epistle and clear up any confusion?" For one thing, *there* wasn't *any confusion in that day*. As we've demonstrated, Paul's authorship becomes clear to the discerning reader, and Paul's readers were discerning. For another, however, it is quite reasonable that Paul didn't mention his name "up front" because it would have immediately put off certain Jews who were prejudiced against him and viewed him as having become an enemy of the Mosaic Law. Both Matthew Poole[27] and Harry Ironside make this point, but Ironside makes it much better:

> Paul is here writing to his own brethren after the flesh. They were greatly prejudiced against him and his ministry, though he yearned after them with all the fervor as a devoted brotherly love. Yet many of them repudiated his apostleship and feared his attitude toward their ancient ritual. He had tried to overcome this opposition. Upon the occasion of his last visit to Jerusalem [Acts 21:18–40], he went so far, in accordance with the suggestion of James, as to pay for the sacrificial offering of certain brethren about to be released from Nazarite vows. But God would not permit this, for it would have been a virtual denial of the sufficiency of the one offering of the Lord Jesus Christ upon the cross, and so the divinely permitted insurrection against Paul saved him from this apparent inconsistency. Probably during the time of his release, after his first imprisonment and before his second arrest (cf. Heb. 13:23), he was chosen of God

to write this letter calling upon believers in the Lord Jesus to separate completely from Judaism, as the entire system was about to be definitely rejected with the destruction of the Jewish temple so soon to take place. Paul therefore acts in accordance with the principle laid down elsewhere, "Unto the Jews I became a Jew that I might gain the Jews" (1 Cor. 9:20). And so he hides his identity for the time being and does not insist upon his own apostolic authority, but rather makes his appeal to the Old Testament Scriptures, in the light, of course, of the new revelation.[28]

Second, I think E. Schuyler English best summarizes our discussion:

> We recapitulate: (1) Peter, writing to the Hebrews, declares that Paul wrote to them also, a communication that teaches the same truths and has some things hard to be understood; (2) the Epistle to the Hebrews is a letter that teaches the same truth and contains in it some things hard to be understood. In other words, (a) Paul *wrote* to the Hebrews; (b) we *have* a letter to the Hebrews; and (c) there is *no other* letter to the Hebrews extant. Therefore this must be Paul's letter. If not, where is it?[29]

Third, and finally, we come full circle back to our original question: "Does all this really matter? Why is the authorship of Hebrews important?" As stated when we began, without knowledge of the author, *we have a New Testament letter with no apostolic authority and which therefore simply cannot be Scripture.*

In his book, *Inspiration and Canonicity of the Bible*, scholar R. Laird Harris makes a vital point concerning how the Early Church recognized Scripture:

> Our conclusion is that the Early Church was not misled when it used the principle that that is inspired which is apostolic. They clearly included in their concept that which was prepared under direction of the apostles.[30]

We must conclude, then, if that which is inspired is apostolic, it must also be true that that which is not apostolic is not inspired. I submit, therefore, that for the Epistle of Hebrews to be inspired we *must* know the Apostolic authority behind it, and that authority can be no one else but the Apostle Paul.

One Final Consideration

In his classic *Halley's Bible Handbook*, Henry Halley makes a very significant statement:

> In the King James Version [Hebrews] is called, in the title, the Epistle of Paul. In the American Revised Version [ASV of 1901] it is anonymous, because in the older manuscripts, found since the King James Translation was made, the Author is not named.

While some readers would conclude that Halley says that in order to *deny* Pauline authorship and attack the KJV, that is not the case, for he goes on to add:

> On the whole, the traditional view, held through the centuries, and still widely held, is that Paul was the Author.[31]

Why is that significant? We submit that it is so because Halley rightly states *the traditional view*, the view that is quite frankly obvious and has been recognized through the ages. *It was not until the rise of rationalistic textual criticism that this view was seriously challenged.* It was, in fact, not until the rise of so-called "older and more reliable manuscripts," which omit the traditional view of Pauline authorship, that this view was categorically denied. Does no one see a problem here?

That question serves to prepare us for the question in our next chapter.

NOTES

[1] Merrill F. Unger, *Unger's Bible Handbook* (Chicago: Moody Press, 1967), p. 748.

[2] *Eerdman's Concise Bible Handbook* (Minneapolis, MN: Worldwide, 1973), p. 365.

[3] John MacArthur, *MacArthur's Quick Reference Guide to the Bible* (Nashville: W Publishing Group, 2001), p. 291.

[4] H. A. Ironside, *Studies in the Epistle to the Hebrews and the Epistle to Titus* (Neptune, NJ: Loizeaux Brothers, 1932, 1958), p. 9.

[5] E. Schuyler English, *Studies in the Epistle to the Hebrews* (Findlay, OH: Dunham Publishing Company, 1955), p. 17.

[6] See, for example, such discussions in Merrill Unger, *Unger's Bible Handbook* (Chicago: Moody Press, 1966), p. 885, and Henry Thiessen, *Introduction to the New Testament* (Grand Rapids: Eerdmans, 1943, 1989), p. 10.

[7] English, p. 14.

[8] R. C. Sproul, *Foundations: An Overview of Systematic Theology* (Orlando, FL: Ligonier Ministries, 1999), p. 23.

[9] J. Sidlow Baxter, *Explore the Book* (Grand Rapids: Zondervan Publishing House, 1960), p. 277.

[10] John Owen, "The Works of John Owen," Vol. 17: *Concerning the Epistle to the Hebrews* (Rio, WI: Ages Software CD-ROM, 2000). Other quotations are from this work.

[11] Arthur W. Pink, "The Arthur W. Pink Collection," *An Exposition of Hebrews*

(Rio, WI: Ages Software CD-ROM, 2000) (emphasis in the original). Other quotations are from this work.

[12] John Gill, "The Collected Writings of John Gill," *Exposition of the Old and New Testaments* (Rio, WI: Ages Software CD-ROM, 2000). Other quotations are from this work.

[13] Baxter, p. 275 (emphasis in the original).

[14] Albert Barnes, *Barnes Notes on the New Testament* (electronic edition in *The Online Bible*). Other quotations are from this work.

[15] Eusebius, *Ecclesiastical History*, 6.25.

[16] Baxter, p. 276 (emphasis in the original).

[17] Andrew T. Lincoln, *Word Biblical Commentary: Ephesians* (Dallas: Word Publishing, 1990), p. lx, lxii.

[18] See my "Introduction and Overview of Ephesians" on our web site for this detailed discussion.

[19] Arthur W. Pink, *An Exposition of Hebrews*.

[20] E. Schuyler English, *Studies in the Epistle to the Hebrews* (Findlay, OH: Dunham Publishing Company, 1955), p. 23 (emphasis in the original).

[21] Thanks to my friend and colleague Dr. James Bearss, former pastor and now director of On Target Ministry, an international education ministry founded in 2006 (www.OnTargetMinistry.org).

[22] J. Sidlow Baxter, *Explore the Book* (Grand Rapids: Zondervan Publishing House, 1960),, p. 279

[23] R. Laird Harris, *Inspiration and Canonicity of the Bible* (Grand Rapids: Zondervan, 1957), p. 269.

[24] Ibid, p. 279.

[25] Baxter, p. 277 (emphasis in the original).

[26] Cited in H. A. Ironside, *Studies in the Epistle to the Hebrews and the Epistle to Titus* (Neptune, NJ: Loizeaux Brothers, 1932, 1958), p. 8.

[27] Matthew Poole, *Matthew Poole's Commentary of the Bible* (electronic edition in *The Online Bible*).

[28] Ironside, pp. 13-14.

[29] English, p. 26 (emphasis added).

[30] Harris, p. 270.

[31] Henry H. Halley, *Halley's Bible Handbook*, New Revised Edition (Grand Rapids: Zondervan, 1965), p. 646.

8

What's *Really* At Stake in the Textual Issue?*

This chapter is a little different than usual. While we won't be examining a particular text, we will be looking rather at "the text," that is, the Scripture itself. My reason for this will, I hope, become clear as we continue. Before we can ever trust any "text" of Scripture, we must be clear on "*the* text" of Scripture, because *the TEXT is always the issue.*

There has been for many years a great deal of controversy, not to mention heated argument, concerning the "textual issue," that is, modern translations of the Bible and the Greek text on which they are based.

The point of this article, however, is to explore what is *really* at stake here. While, "text types," "older versus newer manuscripts," "translation approach," and other matters are most certainly important, there is another matter that is, I am absolutely convinced, the *real* issue and far outweighs all the others *combined.* It is this issue, in fact—an issue I've been studying for almost 20 years—that really drives both sides of the controversy, even though many people involved in the fray are not even aware of it. While the issue is admittedly a complex one, my goal here is to put it the matter as simply as possible.

Foundational Terms

Before getting to that real issue, we must understand two basic foundation stones and put them as simply as possible.

First, we must define the term *textual criticism.* An easy definition appears in Henry Halley's classic *Bible Handbook*: "This is the comparison of various manuscripts to ascertain the exact original text from which they are copied."[1] Another scholar goes into more detail by writing that this is an "[attempt] to restore the readings of the original text, the autographs." It attempts to "[recover] the original text" since "there are no known extant [i.e., still existing] autographs of the New Testament." This is done by "the study of numerous manuscripts" and the formulating of "principles of textual criticism that are applied to many different sorts of literary works."[2] So, in short, the point of *textual criticism* is to study the various

---

* This chapter was originally a two-part article (issues 13 and 14) that began the second year of TOTT, August and September 2006.

manuscripts that *do* exist of a literary work (the Bible in this case) and recreate as close as possible the original text that does *not* exist.

It is actually those "principles of textual criticism that are applied to many different sorts of literary works" that are the point of this article. In other words, what are those principles, or as we'll see, the *underlying principle*, the underlying *approach*, of modern textual criticism? But we must look at a second foundational term first.

Second, there are two basic schools of thought concerning textual criticism, that is, *how to go about* "reconstructing the original text."

(1) The first camp is what is called the Traditional, Ecclesiastical, or Majority Text theory. This approach follows the vast majority of manuscripts to support its Greek text of the New Testament. While the manuscripts themselves do not date before the 5th-century, this majority comprises 80–95% of the over 5,000 extant (still existing) manuscripts, and essentially agree among each other. It is this manuscript tradition that forms the basis of the Authorized King James Version. This approach, as we'll see, does not actually *reconstruct* the text, rather it *recognizes* that the authoritative text *already* exists and that we have it in our hands *now* and have *always* had it.

(2) In dramatic contrast, the other camp (the Critical Text camp) follows a very small number of *early* manuscripts that date from the 3rd- to the 5th-century. The logic used in this theory is that because the manuscripts in this group are older than those in the majority, they must be closer to the originals even though they are *much* fewer in number. The oddity in those manuscripts, however, is that not only do they not agree with the ones in the majority, but in literally thousands of instances they don't even agree with each other. Nonetheless, this theory maintains that "older is better" (although any first year student of logic would recognize such a false premise). It is this second camp, however, that has dominated the scholarly world for over a century, and it is this camp that has produced almost all the modern translations.

NOTE: Before I go any further, I want to make something as clear as I possibly can. I received an email from one visitor to our web site that said, "How sad, you're just another King James Only website." I cannot express how distressed that made me because it could not be further from the truth. The typical "KJV only" advocate is an embarrassment as he "foams at the mouth" and casts aspersion upon anyone who does not agree with him. *That is not my platform and is not what I'm presenting in this article.*

The Underlying Approach of Modern Textual Criticism

Again, what's *really* at stake in this controversy transcends "text types" and all the other technical matters. *The real issue is the underlying approach that modern textual criticism takes to reconstructing the original text and its underlying attitude toward the Bible itself.*

Now, lest I be accused of misrepresentation, I will be quoting textual critics verbatim as we progress. I'm not reading anything into their statements, rather quoting their own clearly stated attitude toward Scripture and its reconstruction.

To state the matter simply and succinctly: *the basic underlying approach to Scripture held by modern textual criticism is that the method of restoring the original text of Scripture is no different than for any other literature.* That was stated plainly in our earlier quotation concerning "principles of textual criticism that are applied to *many different sorts of literary works.*"

It is that very fact that many, if not most, people either do not *realize* or simply do not *recognize*. But it is that issue that is really at the core of this controversy.

Among the first "textual critics," for example was Johann A. Bengel (1687–1752). While an orthodox German Lutheran in other areas of doctrine, when it came to New Testament textual criticism, he took a totally rationalistic approach. Read carefully what he wrote:

> Concerning the care of the early Church for the purity of the manuscripts and concerning the fruits of this care, whatever is clearly taught must be eagerly and piously maintained. But it is certainly difficult to explain through what churches and ages this care extended, and whatever it was it did not keep from coming into existence those variant readings which circulate today and which are more easily removed when their origin is known.[3]

That statement makes clear the core belief of modern, rationalistic textual criticism, which is: instead of there being a text that has been recognized down through the ages as the preserved text of God's Word, what must be done is to compare various classes of manuscripts with each other, along with their "variant readings," to reconstruct the original text, whatever that might be. We repeat: *that is and always has been the very root and foundation of textual criticism.*

This is nowhere better illustrated than in one of the chief tenets of that approach, which not only Bengel advocated but every critic since supports. Second only to the first tenet that "the older reading is to be preferred," another chief rule is that "the more difficult reading is to be preferred."[4] In other words, as Bengel decided, and as every critic since argues, when there is a choice between a reading that is hard to understand and a reading that is easy to understand, the hard reading must be the genuine one because orthodox scribes always changed the hard readings to make them easy. While that should sound absurd to the ear of any Christian, it is, in fact, the second rule of textual criticism. Is it spiritual or based on God's sovereignty? Hardly! It is entirely humanistic, as it is based on *total conjecture* that has no authority whatsoever. It is the creation of human reason, and nothing more.

"But what is really the harm in that?" we might ask. Simply the inescapable conclusion that orthodox Christians deliberately corrupted their own New Testament text by making readings easier. In other words, let's call it what is—*They lied!* As scholar Edward Hills (who we shall examine later) points out, there was even in Bengel's own day an outcry by conservative Christians because his view was a blatant "denial of the doctrine that God by His special providence had preserved the true text down through the ages in the usage of believers."[5] *Where is the outcry today?* Bengel's attitude was not that *GOD preserved* the true text but that *WE must discover* the true text. And that attitude continued.

Johann J. Griesbach (1745–1812) took up the baton from Bengel (as well as J. S. Semler [1725–91], who was known as the "Father of German Rationalism").[6] Griesbach was, by his own admission, a skeptic of the New Testament text, that is, the Received (or Traditional) Text. Of that text he wrote, "The New Testament abounds in more glosses, additions, and interpolations purposely introduced than any other book."[7] He agreed with Bengel that early Christians corrupted the Scriptures. He also stated that when a variation appeared, the Traditional reading was to be immediately rejected. But may we humbly ask, "On whose authority, sir?"

Critics who followed, such as Johann L. Hug (1765–1846), Martin L. Scholtz (1794–1852), Karl Lachmann (1793–1851), Lobegott F. C. von Tischendorf (1815–1874), and others agreed on the essential point early made by Bengel.

Of special note is Samuel P. Tregelles (1813–1875) "who was chiefly instrumental in leading England away from the *Textus Receptus* ['Received,' or Traditional, Text], during the mid 19th-century."[8] Additionally, Henry Alford (1810–1871) is well known for his work to bring about "the demolition of the unworthy and pedantic reverence for the received text, which stood in the way of all chance of discovering the genuine word of God."[9]

The pattern here can be seen by even a blind man—*it is clear that early in the modern era any thought of an already existing, divinely preserved, definitive text of the New Testament has never existed and, as we'll see, still does not exist today.* In this view, it is left totally up to man to "[discover] the genuine Word of God."

The baton then passed to two Cambridge scholars, Brooke F. Westcott (1825–1901) and Fenton J. A. Hort (1828–1892), and Christianity has never been the same. While "their views were not original but were based on the work of Lachmann, Tregellas, Griesbach, Tischendorf, and others,"[10] they made clearer than anyone else their approach to "rediscovering the original text." Not only did they believe that orthodox scribes altered the text, but Hort added:

> The principles of criticism . . . hold good for all ancient texts preserved in a plurality of documents. In dealing with the text of the New Testament no new principle whatever is needed or legitimate...
>
> For ourselves we dare not introduce considerations which could not reasonably be applied to other ancient texts, supposing them to have documentary attestation of equal amount, variety, and antiquity.[11]

I strongly encourage you to read that again. It could not be clearer that Westcott and Hort believed that the Bible could, and actually *should*, be approached like any other literature for the purpose of reconstructing the text. This fact, of course, is not at all surprising since both men rejected biblical infallibility, as stated unambiguously in their biographies. Hort was the most outspoken, scoffing at that doctrine and saying that anyone who believed it was perverted.[12] While both men professed faith in the Deity of Christ, His saving death, and His resurrection, their low view of Scripture simply cannot be ignored (*or tolerated*). To trust their attitude toward and treatment of Scripture is absolute folly!

Another example, believe it or not, was B. B. Warfield (1851–1921). While one of the Church's greatest defenders of the faith, he actually helped forever change the doctrine of Verbal Inspiration. After returning from Germany, where he studied textual criticism under German rationalists, he virtually turned his back on Verbal Inspiration. His view changed to that of Westcott and Hort, that when reconstructing any text, the method is the same, "Whether the writing before us be a letter from a friend, or an inscription from Carchemish, or a copy of a morning newspaper, or Shakespeare, or Homer, or the Bible."[13]

An almost unconscionable move by Warfield was his reinterpreting a statement in the *Westminster Confession of Faith* (1646) to actually "prove" the validity of textual criticism. The *Confession* reads:

> The Old Testament in Hebrew . . . and the New Testament in Greek . . . being immediately inspired by God, and, by His singular care and providence, kept pure in all ages, are therefore authentical .

. . so as, in all controversies of religion, the Church is finally to
appeal unto them. (Ch. I, Sec. 8)

Here, then, is what Warfield wrote in 1891 about that statement:

> The Confession (sect. 8) asserts that final appeal in all
> controversies is to be made to the original Hebrew and Greek
> Scriptures, which are alone safeguarded in their accuracy by Divine
> inspiration, and it asserts that these originals have been, "by His
> singular care and providence, kept pure in all ages."[14]

"What's wrong with that?" you might ask. Only that the Confession had
never been interpreted that way in its 245 year history.

Dr. Theodore P. Letis, a contemporary textual scholar with a Ph.D. in
Ecclesiastical History from the University of Edinburgh, has done extensive
research on Warfield. He writes of Warfield's "ingenious new
interpretation" of the Confession," that "which had once taught the
providential *preservation* of the extant [presently existing] Church texts,
was now used to affirm the providential *restoration* of an inerrant original
text, by means of modern text criticism."[15] In other words, before
Warfield's reinterpretation, the Confession had *always* referred to already
existing Greek texts as being inspired, *not just the originals*. Warfield's
reinterpretation of the Confession, in fact, is now mimicked by virtually
every evangelical today. *And it's wrong!*

It's equally unmistakable that, like their predecessors, Westcott and
Hort's descendents today hold a demonstrably rationalistic view of
Scripture. One noted contemporary scholar, for example, writes:

> . . . in general the most difficult reading (that is, more difficult
> to the scribe) is to be preferred, since a scribe is more likely to
> emend a difficult reading than an easy one.[16]

Another contemporary writer reaches into thin air and invents the term
"expansion of piety" to refer to the *third* artificial rule of the critics, that
"the shorter reading is to be preferred." He writes, "Additions have been
made to the text that flow from the desire to protect and reverence divine
truths." He goes on to call this a "logical explanation" for longer readings,
such as: "Jesus" in the *Textus Receptus* versus "He" in the Critical Text
(Matt. 4:18; 12:25; Mk. 2:15; 10:52), "Jesus Christ" in the *Textus Receptus*
versus just "Jesus" in the Critical Text (Acts 19:4; 1 Jn. 1:7; Rev. 1:9;
12:17), and so forth.[17]

The same writer (whose book is a totally one-sided presentation of the
whole subject) elsewhere makes it glaringly apparent that he does not hold
to true Providential Preservation. He does so by first lumping *all* defenders
of the Received Text, even the embarrassing "foam-at-the-mouth" type,

into one group (an unfair tactic he uses many times throughout his book, as do many writers on this issue). He writes:

> Almost all KJV Only books will contain a section on how God has promised to preserve His words, and they will, of course, assume that these "words" are found in the KJV. At this point they believe themselves to be holding the "high ground" in the debate . . .

It's wholly incomprehensible to me that someone who believes in Providential Preservation is actually *"guilty"* of something, namely, taking the "high ground." Yes, the writer veils his sarcasm with the widely-held accusation that all defenders of the *Textus Receptus* believe that "the KJV were the words of Paul" (which is most certainly *not* true of all defenders), but his general attitude to true Providential Preservation comes through loud and clear—*he doesn't believe in it.*

What he says next, however, is the real key: "What if God preserved His Word in a much less flashy way?" The "flashy way" he refers to, of course, is the *Textus Receptus.* His alternative, therefore, is this:

> Instead, God worked with His people over time, leading them to recognize what He had already done through the act of inspiration. It took time, and some might wish for a more "spectacular" method, but God did it in His way, in His time.[18]

There are three things wrong with that statement. First, it's as guilty of conjecture as the writer accuses the *Textus Receptus* advocate of doing. It states authoritatively that God did it "over time," *but that is the writer's opinion.* Second, are we to actually believe that God preserved the true text in such a way that it can be discovered only by the efforts of rationalism "over time"? Third, it ignores the plain fact, as we've outlined, that from Bengel to Westcott and Hort, such critics have rejected *the whole idea* of Providential Preservation. By offering his own theory of "preservation" (however erroneous), he betrays his own confederates and is more in the Textus Receptus camp than in the Critical Text camp (a thought that would appall him). His argument is absurd and self-refuting.

The underlying approach of modern textual criticism that we've shown has resulted in the inevitable conclusion: *if man is responsible to discover the true text, he will NEVER reach that goal.*

Is such a radical statement true, or is it just more rambling of the "KJV Only Cult," an accusation unfairly leveled by some?

Well, consider the following and judge for yourself. In 1963 Robert M. Grant, a well-known Bible scholar, wrote:

> The primary goal of New Testament textual study remains the recovery of what the New Testament writers wrote. We have already

suggested that to achieve this goal is well-nigh impossible. Therefore we must be content with what [many scholars call] an "impossible possibility."[19]

If the double-talk ("impossible possibility") were not bad enough, *here is a statement that destroys any possibility of an authoritative Bible.* Even before that, Grant wrote in 1947, "It is generally recognized that the original text of the Bible cannot be recovered."[20] Likewise, scholar Gunther Zuntz remarked in 1953, "The optimism of the early editors has given way to that skepticism which inclines towards regarding the original text as an unattainable mirage."[21]

Again, in their rationalistic pride, men are merely grasping smoke to think that they will discover the "original text." *That ship sailed when they rejected Providential Preservation*, and the honest critic admits it.

If the above quotations don't get our attention, how about one by James Moffatt, who has been lauded by many for his contribution to Christianity? He was one of the first to offer a modern translation, but consider what he wrote in the Preface to that work in 1913:

> Once the translation of the New Testament is freed from the influence of the theory of verbal inspiration . . . difficulties cease to be formidable.

That is the issue, my Dear Reader. Once we get rid of Verbal Inspiration, we can do anything with the Bible and its text that we want, *and that is precisely what we're doing*. It continues to baffle me how any evangelical can *tolerate*, much less *advocate*, such an attitude toward Scripture, but the majority does just that.

This leads us to one more consideration, which is, in fact, the very heart of the whole issue.

The Contribution of Edward F. Hills

Edward Freer Hills (1912–81) was without question a scholar of the highest caliber. Not only graduating from Yale and Westminster Seminary, Hills also earned a Ph.D. in textual criticism from Harvard Divinity School. In spite of those impeccable, world-class credentials, however, Hills is laughed at, or just simply ignored, if I may be so blunt, by arrogant modern textual critics. That kind of dishonesty is unconscionable.

I would go so far as to say that any person who thinks he "knows all about the textual issue" (a statement I've heard many times), but who has not read (and answered) Hills, needs to think again because, he does not know the complete story. In his two books (*Believing Bible Study* and *The*

King James Version Defended), Hills confronts and exposes modern textual criticism to be what it really is—*veiled unbelief.*

Edward F. Hills was, in fact, the first "textual critic" to approach the text from a *Godly* perspective instead of a *rational* one, from a presupposition of *belief* instead of *skepticism.* It's for that reason that I don't even like to call Hills a "textual critic" because of what the term automatically implies. I prefer the term "textual scholar" because of what he believed about the sacred text and how he approached its preservation. As scholar Dr. Theodore Letis comments in the Preface to Hill's book:

> While Hills was the only recognized, published New Testament text critic to advocate the primacy of the Byzantine text either in his day or in the present, no one since has been more innovative than he was in attempting to integrate his confessional, theological perspective with the discipline of New Testament text criticism.[22]

In other words, Hills looked at this issue *theologically* instead of *rationally.* What a concept! Here is where Hills began:

> In science, in philosophy, in New Testament textual criticism, and in every other field of intellectual endeavor, our thinking must differ from the thinking of unbelievers. *We must begin with God.*[23]

While Hills is called naïve and antiquated in this thinking, he uncompromisingly and unconditionally recognized God's sovereign providence over *everything.* Correct me if I'm wrong, but isn't that what evangelicals are supposed to believe?

Hills goes on to call this reliance on God's sovereignty concerning the Traditional Text "the logic of faith." He asks, "How do we take our stand upon divine revelation?" and then answers that question with profound clarity:

> Only in one way, namely through the logic of faith. *For God so loved the world, that He gave His only begotten Son, that whosoever believeth in Him should not perish, but have everlasting life* (John 3:16). Since this Gospel is true, these conclusions logically follow: *First*, the Bible is God's infallibly inspired Word. This must be so, because if our salvation depends on our believing in Christ, then surely God must have left us an infallible record telling us who Jesus Christ is and how we may believe in Him truly and savingly. *Second*, the Bible has been preserved down through the ages by God's special providence. This also must be so, because if God has inspired the holy Scriptures infallibly, then surely He has not left their survival to chance but has preserved them providentially down through the centuries. *Third*, the text found in the majority of the

biblical manuscripts is the providentially preserved text. This too must be true, because if God has preserved the Scriptures down through the ages for the salvation of men and the edification and comfort of His Church, then He must have preserved them not secretly in holes and caves but in a public way in the usage of His Church. Hence the text found in the majority of the biblical manuscripts is the true, providentially preserved text. *Fourth*, the providential preservation of the Scriptures did not cease with the invention of printing. For why would God's special, providential care be operative at one time and not at another time, before the invention of printing but not after it? Hence the first printed texts of the Old and New Testament Scriptures were published under the guidance of God's special providence.

Thus when we believe in Christ, the logic of our faith leads us to the true text of holy Scripture, namely, the Masoretic Hebrew text, the Textus Receptus, and the King James Version *and other faithful translations* [Ed: emphasis added; note that Hills was not "KJV Only"]. It is on this text, therefore, that we take our stand and endeavor to build a consistently Christian apologetic system.[24]

In comparing his approach to that of Modernism, Hills later writes:

In New Testament textual criticism, therefore, we must start at the highest point. We must begin with God, the supreme and eternal Truth, and then descend to the lower, temporal facts which He has established by His works of creation and providence. We must take all our principles from the Bible itself and borrow none from the textual criticism of other ancient books. It is only by following this rule that we will be able to distinguish facts from the fictions of unbelievers.[25]

Finally, Hills submits that this approach will provide something that the modernistic approach can *never* provide—namely, *certainty*.

If we believe in the special providential preservation of the Scriptures and make this the leading principle of our biblical textual criticism, we obtain *maximum certainty*, all the certainty that any mere man can obtain, all the certainty that we need. For we are led by the logic of faith to the Masoretic Hebrew text, to the New Testament Textus Receptus, and to the King James Version. But what if we ignore the providential preservation of the Scriptures and deal with the text of the Holy Bible in the same way in which we deal with the texts of other ancient books? If we do this, we are following the logic of unbelief, which leads to *maximum uncertainty*

. . . In short, unless we follow the logic of faith, we can be certain of nothing concerning the Bible and its text.[26]

Dear Reader, if we do not trust in the sovereignty of God to preserve the true text, on what else can we rely? As we've seen, the foundation of modern textual criticism, from Bengel to the present, is that the Bible is treated like any other historical document, from a purely rationalistic and naturalistic approach. Should Christians embrace that? Should we defend such humanistic philosophy? If we do, we are wallowing with unbelievers in the mire of uncertainty and unbelief.

Conclusion

During the writing of this article, I came across J.I. Packer's book *God Has Spoken* (1979) in which I read something rather amazing, yet typical of our day. In a section titled "The Infection of Uncertainty" he makes this truly excellent point:

> At no time, perhaps, since the Reformation have Protestant Christians as a body been so unsure, tentative and confused as to what they should believe and do. Certainty about the great issues of Christian faith and conduct is lacking all along the line. The outside observer sees us as staggering on from gimmick to gimmick and stunt to stunt like so many drunks in a fog, not knowing at all where we are or which way we should be going. Preaching is hazy; heads are muddled; hearts fret; doubts drain our strength; uncertainty paralyses action.[27]

While we certainly say a hearty "Amen" to that, five pages before Packer sabotages his own statement by praising the existence and use of the plethora of Bible translations, giving *equal admiration* for word-for-word, dynamic equivalence, and everything in between. He even manages to throw in the unwarranted attack that those who "feel swamped" by all the variety and "are resolved to trust none of them, but stick to the King James Version" are "irrational."

What Packer either fails to recognize or refuses to acknowledge, however, is that *the textual issue is part of the very uncertainty he talks about.* There is, in fact, as we've seen, absolutely no certainty whatsoever about the text in modern criticism, *and there NEVER will be.* If you think I'm wrong, just keep watching the contemporary scene. The text is *always* in flux, updated periodically with a "new edition" of the Greek text, not to mention the latest "translation *du jour.*" A contemporary of B. B. Warfield (who we examined earlier), Professor N. M. Wheeler of Lawrence University, well sums up the scene both historically and today. He said that

Warfield's view (and today's) implies that "we must ask the critics every morning what is the latest conclusion in order to know what is that Scripture inspired of God."[28] *Oh, where are the Wheelers today?*

Packer also goes into some detail about how "Higher Criticism" has caused the uncertainty he outlines. "Higher Criticism," of course, questions the historical accuracy of the Bible and has been practiced by inarguably unsaved critics, while "Lower Criticism" is another term for Textual Criticism.

But again, what is totally ignored, and even scoffed at, is the incontrovertible fact that *both* Higher Criticism *and* Lower Criticism were *the spawn of unbelief.* Both approach the Bible like any other piece of literature and "evaluate" it according to rationalistic principles. I repeat—*that is a fact!*

While we will not deal with it here, it can be historically demonstrated, if truth be told, as does Dr. Theodore Letis, that Higher Criticism was actually introduced in England "as a direct development of the *lower criticism.*"[29] Many people think that Higher Criticism came first, but that simply is not so. It was the seemingly "harmless" and even "helpful" Textual Criticism that came first, and it paved the way for the full-blown Higher Criticism that rejected the very veracity of the Bible.

So, what's *really* at stake in the textual issue?

Answer*: the very underpinnings of Scripture.* What grieves me to the core of my soul is that what I have shared in this article categorically refuses to be acknowledged by the majority of evangelicals today. What is so appalling is that these evangelicals willfully align themselves with men and a philosophy that undermines the very Scripture they profess in their "Statements of Faith" to love and defend.

It continues to amaze my mind and burden my spirit that while some Christian leaders are quite rightly sounding a warning about "seeker-sensitive" Christianity, the diluted Gospel, and other key issues, some of the very same leaders refuse to recognize that *the REAL core of these problems is men's attitude toward the Bible.* If we have a low view of Scripture, which modern criticism most certainly does, it is actually this that produces other problems. What is needed today more than anything else is *a high view of Scripture,* but that will *never* be found in modern textual criticism.

Where do you stand, my Dear Christian Friend? Are you following the rationalists who handle Scripture the same way they handle any other literature and reconstruct it according to their own rules? If you are a pastor, it is my burden to *implore* you that if you adhere to modern textual criticism and embrace the text and translations it produces, then you are, my Dear Brother, defending a philosophy that is rooted in unbelief. I *beg* you to look honestly at what is really going on concerning the text of Scripture.

Or do you already recognize how vital it is that we trust a text that has been providentially and miraculously preserved by God through the ages? It is time we all make that choice, and I pray that it's this one.

One final question, I think, will put the matter succinctly: Do you believe that the Bible *IS divinely preserved* or do you believe that it *MUST BE humanly reconstructed*?

May God richly bless you, and I pray that I'll hear from you on this pivotal issue (see "Contact" at www.TheScriptureAlone.com).

NOTES

[1] Henry Halley, *Halley's Bible Handbook* (Grand Rapids: Zondervan Publishing House, 1927, 1965), p. 747.

[2] Norman Geisler and William Nix, *A General Introduction to the Bible*, Revised and Expanded (Chicago: Moody Press, 1968, 1986), pp. 433, 435, 465.

[3] J. A. Bengel, *Novum Testamentum, Graecum* (Tubingae: George Cotta), p. 420. Cited in Edward F. Hills, *The King James Version Defended* (Des Moines, IA: Christian Research Press, 1956, 1984), p. 64.

[4] Geisler and Nix (p. 478) listing the seven principles, according to priority, offered by Gleason Archer, *A Survey or Old Testament Introduction*, Revised Edition (Chicago: Moody Press, 1974), pp. 57-60.

[5] Hills, p. 64.

[6] Geisler and Nix, p. 454.

[7] J. J. Griesbach, *Opuscula Academica*, Jena, 1824, vol. 1, p. 317. Cited in Hills, p. 65.

[8] Geisler and Nix, p. 455.

[9] Henry Alford, "Prolegomena," *The Greek Testament*, 1:76. Cited in Geisler and Nix, p. 455.

[10] Geisler and Nix, p. 455.

[11] *Introduction, The New Testament in the Original Greek* (London: Macmillan, 1881), pp. 73, 277.

[12] Arthur Westcott, *The Life and Letters of Brook Foss Westcott*, Vol. 1, (London: Macmillan, 1903), p. 207 and Hort's own *The Life and Letters of Fenton John Anthony Hort*, Vol. 1 (London: Macmillan), p. 400.

[13] B.B. Warfield, *An Introduction to Textual Criticism*, 1886, p. 10.

[14] B. B. Warfield, "Westminster Doctrine of Holy Scripture" in *Selected Shorter Writings of B. B. Warfield*, edited by John Meeter (Phillipsburg: P & R Publishing, 1970, 1973), Vol. II, p. 569.

[15] Theodore P. Letis, *The Ecclesiastical Text: Text Criticism. Biblical Authority, and the Popular Mind* (Philadelphia, Edinburgh: The Institute for Renaissance and Reformation Biblical Studies, 1997), p. 22 (emphasis in the original). We highly recommend this book. (My thanks to Dr. Letis for originally reviewing

this article for historical and technical accuracy before publication. He went into eternal glory in 2005, and this chapter is dedicated to his memory.)

[16] D.A. Carson, *The King James Version Debate: A Plea for Realism* (Grand Rapids: Baker Book House, 1979), p. 30.

[17] James White, *The King James Only Controversy* (Minneapolis: Bethany House Publishers, 1995), pp. 43, 46

[18] White, pp. 47.

[19] Robert M. Grant, *A Historical Introduction to the New Testament* (New York: Harper and Row, 1963), p. 51. Also cited in Wilbur Pickering, *The Identity of the New Testament Text*, Revised Edition (Nashville: Thomas Nelson, 1977, 1980), pp. 18-19.

[20] Robert M. Grant, "The Bible of Theophilus of Antioch," *Journal of Biblical Literature* (LXVI, 1947), p. 173. Also cited in Pickering, p. 19.

[21] G. Zuntz, *The Text of the Epistles* (London: Oxford University Press, 1953), p. 9. Also cited in Hills, p. 67.

[22] Preface in Edward F. Hills, *The King James Version Defended* (Des Moines, IA: Christian Research Press, 1956, 1984), p. vi.

[23] Hills, p. 61 (emphasis added).

[24] Hills, p. 86 (emphasis in the original except for editor's note).

[25] Hills, p. 115.

[26] Hills, pp. 224-225 (emphasis in the original).

[27] J.I. Packer, *God Has Spoken* (Downers Frove, IL: Intervarsity Press, 1979), p.20.

[28] N. M. Wheeler, "Uncanonical Inspiration," *Sunday School Times* 25 (Jan. 6, 1883), p. 4. Cited in Theodore P. Letis, *The Ecclesiastical Text*, p. 16.

[29] Theodore P. Letis, *From Lower Criticism To Higher Criticism*, an essay based on a lecture delivered at the Annual Meeting of the Society of Biblical Literature before the History of Exegesis Section, San Francisco, California, 22 November 1992. Essay published in *Journal of Higher Criticism*, 9/1 (Spring 2002), pp. 31-48. Read it at www.depts.drew.edu/jhc/LetisPriestly.pdf.

It was said by some of old, that the "Scripture hath fords where a lamb may wade, and depths where an elephant may swim."

John Owen
Works, Vol. 20, Ch. 3, Heb. 3:15

9

What Does "It" and "That" Refer to in Ephesians 2:8?[*]

For by grace are ye saved through faith; and that not of yourselves: it is the gift of God:

Paul not only says that salvation is by grace, but adds the phrase, **that not of yourselves**. Theologian John Murray states the case very well when he comments on this verse:

> When [Paul] says "and that not of yourselves," he is reminding us of the true nature of grace, that its whole urge and explanation reside in God. It may be easy to give formal assent to this text. Every evangelical Christian will do so. But how ready we are to shy away from its implications! In reality we deny the truth here asserted when we introduce at any point in the whole span and process of salvation a decisive autonomy on the part of man. If salvation at any point is contingent upon some contribution which man himself makes, then at that point it is *of ourselves*, and to that extent it is not of grace. Paul's definition "and that not of yourselves" is thereby effaced and the true nature of grace is denied.[1]

Indeed, Murray cuts to the heart of the matter. *Grace that is not ALL grace is NO grace.* Grace means that God has done everything; if He does not do everything, then it is not grace.

There is a common teaching today that says, "Christ's crucifixion is a proof of our worth." In other words, God could see worth in us so He bought us. But as verses 1–3 make clear in their description of man's deparavity, such teaching is patently false and a heretical distortion of grace. The cross is not proof of *our worth* but *God's grace*. We were undeserving and even dead. Where is the worth in a corpse?

One key, if not *the* key to this passage, lies in the debate over the words **that not of yourselves: it is the gift of God**. The debate is: to what exactly does **it** and **that** refer? Do they refer to grace, faith, or just the whole concept of salvation in general? Perhaps Charles Hodge puts the answer best:

---

[*] This chapter was originally TOTT issue #15, October 2006.

What is said to be the gift of God? Is it [the whole concept of] salvation, or faith? To say that faith is the gift of God best suits the purpose of the passage. The object of the Apostle is to show the unmerited nature of salvation. This is most efficiently done by saying, "Ye are not only saved by faith in opposition to works, but your very faith is not of yourselves, it is the gift of God." The other interpretation makes the passage repetitive. To say, "Ye are saved by faith; not of yourselves; your salvation is the gift of God; it is not of works," is saying the same thing over and over again without any progress.[2]

Holding this view, a more contemporary expositor is equally sound here:

Some have objected to this interpretation, saying that "faith" (*pistis*) is feminine, while "that" (*touto*) is neuter. That poses no problem, however, as long as it is understood that "that" does not refer precisely to the noun "faith" but to the act of believing. Further, this interpretation makes the best sense of the text, since if "that" refers to "by grace you have been saved through faith" (that is, to the whole statement), the adding of "that not of yourselves, it is the gift of God" would be redundant, because grace is defined as an unearned act of God. If salvation is of grace, it has to be an undeserved gift of God.[3]

We should also note that "faith" being feminine is actually irrelevant, simply because both "grace" and "salvation" are also feminine. The Greek alone, therefore, does not prove the issue.[4]

At any rate, the main thrust of both the above quotations is that to say that **it** and **that** refer to grace or the whole concept of salvation results in the verses being redundant. Paul's central concept is that we have been saved by grace, which he states plainly in the first clause. Is he then going to just repeat the same thing by saying "grace is a gift of God," or "salvation is a gift of God?" No, he has already said that. What is Paul trying to get across here? He's emphasizing that even "faith" is a gift of God.

Ponder it this way a moment. How can two unsaved people sit under the same salvation message, hear the preacher pour out his heart, listen to the Gospel message of sin, wrath, and salvation, and then one person believe and the other not? The answer is simple when we realize that left to themselves neither person would believe, but one does because God gives him the faith to do so. Because they are both dead, neither can respond until God gives them the power.

Further, faith *must* be of God, for if we say that faith is of ourselves, then faith becomes a human work, as much a human work as partaking of a sacrament or just "being a good person." *Faith* does not determine salvation; *grace* determines salvation. God has done it all. As John MacArthur rightly puts it: "When we accept the finished work of Christ on our behalf, we act by the faith supplied by God's grace." From where does our faith come? It comes from grace.

Several other Scriptures strongly substantiate this principle:

> And he said, Therefore said I unto you, that no man can come unto me, *except it were given unto him of my Father.* (Jn. 6:65, emphasis added)

> For unto you it is *given* [granted] in the behalf of Christ, not only to *believe* on him, but also to suffer for his sake. (Phil. 1:29, emphasis added)

> And when [Apollos] was disposed to pass into Achaia, the brethren wrote, exhorting the disciples to receive him: who, when he was come, helped them much which had *believed through grace.* (Acts 18:27, emphasis added)

Something else that many do not consider is that if *our* faith is the basis of salvation, what if we one day choose not to believe anymore? Taken to its logical conclusion, this view results in a lack of assurance and security, which may we interject, is exactly what many Christians lack. But if *God* has done it all, if God gives us faith, there is total security.

Another often quoted verse is John 1:12: "But as many as received him, to them gave he power [i.e., right] to become the sons of God, even to them that believe on his name." Many Gospel preachers quote this verse, but they stop without quoting the very next one: "Which were born, not of blood, nor of the will of the flesh, *nor of the will of man,* but of God." Where did we get the will to believe? In ourselves? No, because we were dead. Rather it was God's grace that gave us the will to believe. Man's will has nothing to do with salvation, not even with believing. It is all of God. Were we born again *because* of our will? No, thank God, we were born again *in spite* of our will.

That beloved Puritan commentator Matthew Henry (1662–1714), who could read the Bible when he was only three years old, and of whose commentary Spurgeon said, "Every minister ought to read it entirely and carefully through once at least," said it well when he wrote:

> We do not become the children of God as we become the children of our natural parents. Grace does not run in the blood, as corruption does. It is not *produced* by the natural power of our own will. As it is not of *blood*, nor of *the will of the flesh*, so neither is it

of the *will of man*. It is the grace of God that makes us willing to be His.[5]

Before going on, we can answer this controversy about faith even more simply: when we read, "By grace are ye saved," is this not enough to show that *everything* is from God? If *everything* is not from God, then why do we need grace at all? If I can do *something*, why does God have to do *anything*? In the final analysis, then, it really doesn't matter how you read the verse grammatically. Theologically, salvation, from beginning to end and everything in between, is of God. As one theologian writes:

> Does [*that*] refer to salvation? Or does [*that*] refer to faith. Is Paul saying that salvation is a gift of God? Or is he saying that faith is a gift of God. Although Greek scholars argue about which of these is the preferred rendition of the Greek text, theologically it really doesn't matter. In both ways of reading that sentence, we have to come to the conclusion that faith is a gift of God. It is not an expression of human achievement, or of human effort, or of human ability. This is why every believer should be praising God daily for the fact that he has received as a gift not only the salvation that comes through faith, but the gift of faith itself.[6]

To that we must say, "Amen." A common notion on the relationship of grace and faith is that, "Grace is God's part and faith is man's part," but such a notion is shallow sentimentality and theological foolishness. Yes, man believes, but even his faith must originate in God's power, not his own. Salvation is not partly God and partly you; it is all of God.

NOTES

[1] John Murray, *Collected Writings of John Murray: Volume 1, The Claims of Truth* (Carlisle, PA: The Banner of Truth Trust, 1976), p. 120 (emphasis in the original).

[2] Hodge, p. 63.

[3] MacArthur, *Ephesians*, p. 61. Gordon Clark adds, "Grammatically, neuter demonstrative pronouns, even in the more precise classical Greek, often refer to feminize nouns, especially to abstract feminine nouns. Hence it is false to say that *touto* [that] cannot mean faith" (*Ephesians*, p. 73).

Also J. N. Darby: "I am quite aware of what critics have to say here as to gender; but it is equally true as to grace, and to say, 'by grace... and that not of yourselves,' is simply nonsense; but by faith might be supposed to be of ourselves, though grace cannot. Therefore the Spirit of God adds, 'and that [not it] not of yourselves: it is the gift of God.' That is, the believing is God's gift, not of ourselves. And this is confirmed by what follows, 'not of works.' But the object of the apostle is to shew that the whole thing was of grace and of God-God's workmanship-a new creation. So far, grace and faith and all go together."

4 In spite of that fact, however, Adam Clark, Wesley, and other Arminians strenuously held onto this argument simply because to admit anything else would destroy their system.

5 Emphasis in the original. Calvin also: "Ought we not then to be silent about free-will, and good intentions, and fancied preparations, and merits, and satisfactions? There is none of these which does not claim a share of praise in the salvation of men; so that the praise of grace would not, as Paul shews, remain undiminished." (*Commentaries*)

6 R. C. Sproul (*Ephesians*, p. 55). Martyn Lloyd-Jones agrees: "It is not a question of grammar, it is not a question of language . . . And there is a sense in which it really does not matter at all, because it comes down to much the same thing in the end. In other words, what is important is that we should avoid turning faith into 'works'" (*God's Way of Reconciliation*, p. 135).

As rivers, the nearer they come to the ocean whither they tend, the more they increase their waters, and speed their streams; so will grace flow more fully and freely in its near approaches to the ocean of glory.

Puritan John Owen
A Puritan Golden Treasury, p. 102

10

Is the Bible Unclear on the Deity of Christ?[*]

Ephesians 4:5; John 1:1

One Lord, one faith, one baptism,

In the beginning was the Word, and the Word was with God, and the Word was God.

A pastor once said to me, "It's too bad the Bible doesn't just say, 'Jesus was God' and therefore clear up all the confusion." I can't express how that grieved me because it was based upon ignorance not only of what the term **one lord** (Eph. 4:5) means but also of several other statements in Scripture. I would interject that it's also sad because it implies an insufficiency in Scripture, that Scripture is ambiguous and therefore weak. Such an implication, even if unintended, is serious error.

So is the Bible unclear about the Deity of Christ? Is this idea just something men have read into the Bible? Did the disciples mishear what Jesus claimed and falsely conclude that he was claiming Deity? After all, several cults and religions teach against it, so is it something that is so unclear that the issue can "go either way"?

A pivotal term concerning this doctrinal reality is the term **one lord** in Ephesians 4:5. The Greek behind lord is *kurios*. In early Classical Greek, while the word was applied to the gods, there was no general belief of a creator God. The word, therefore, was used in a broad way of someone who had power or authority. It was different in Eastern thought, however. To the Oriental mind, the gods were "the lords of reality." By Jesus' day, Eastern kings, such as Herod the Great (c. 73–74 BC), Agrippa I (10 BC.–44 AD, and Agrippa II (27 AD–c. 100) came to be called lord. Most Roman emperors resisted such temptation, but others, such as Caligula (37–41 AD) and Nero (54–48) found it appealing. It was this very attitude of implied divinity that caused both Jews and Christians to refuse to use the term lord of the emperor.

Turning to the Septuagint (the Greek translation of the Old Testament), *kurios* appears over 9,000 times, some 6,156 of which translate the Hebrew YHWH (Yahweh, Jehovah), thus reemphasizing the meaning of divinity.

---

[*] This chapter was originally TOTT issue 16, November 2006.

In the New Testament, then, *kurios* appears 717 times, the majority of which occur in Luke's Gospel and Acts (210) and Paul's Epistles (275). The reason for this, of course, was that they both wrote for readers who were dominated by Greek culture and language and who, therefore, understood the deep significance of this word in implying deity.

Finally, while **lord** is sometimes used as simply a title of honor, such as Rabbi, Teacher, Master (Matt. 10:24; cf. Lk. 16:3), or even a husband (1 Peter 3:6), *when used of Jesus in a confessional way, it without question refers to His divinity.* The confession *Kurios Iesous* (Lord Jesus) is rooted in the pre-Pauline Greek Christian community and is probably the oldest of all Christian creeds.

Early Christians unarguably recognized Jesus as God, as Paul wrote to the Philippians: "And that every tongue should confess that Jesus Christ is *Lord*, to the glory of God the Father" (2:11, emphasis added). Even more significantly, when Thomas saw the risen Jesus, he called Him, "My *Lord* and my God" (Jn. 20:28, emphasis added). As we'll see in a moment, even salvation is based on a confession of Jesus as **Lord**, as Divine (Rom. 10:9–10).[1]

The Deity of Christ is an absolutely cardinal doctrine of Christianity; without it, Christianity collapses of its own weight. But it's also a doctrine that is clearly taught in Scripture without any ambiguity. For example, at the very foundation of this doctrine is the birth of Jesus. Matthew 1:23, a quotation of Isaiah 7:14, declares: "Behold, a virgin shall be with child, and shall bring forth a son, and they shall call his name Emmanuel, which being interpreted is, God with us." As C. I. Scofield rightly observes:

> Why was Jesus not actually called "Immanuel"? According to Hebrew usage the name does not represent a title but a characterization, as in Isa. 1:26 and 9:6. The name "Immanuel" shows that He really was "God with us." Thus the Deity of Christ is stressed at the very beginning of Matthew.[2]

We are then immediately drawn to John 1:1: **In the beginning was the Word, and the Word was with God, and the Word was God.** Charles Ryrie well sums up the deep significance of this verse:

> Before time began, Christ was already in existence with God. That is what is meant by the term "the pre-existent Christ." See Gen. 1:1 and 1 John 1:1. *Logos* [Word] means "word, thought, concept, and the expressions thereof." In the OT the concept conveyed activity and revelation, and the word or wisdom of God is often personified (Ps. 33:6; Prov. 8). In the Targums (Aramaic paraphrases of the OT) it was a designation of God. To the Greek mind it expressed the ideas of reason and creative control. Revelation is the

keynote idea in the *logos* concept. Here it is applied to Jesus, who is all that God is and the expression of Him (1:1, 14). In this verse the Word (Christ) is said to be *with God* (i.e., in communion with and yet distinct from God) and to be God (i.e., identical in essence with God).[3]

John 1:14 goes on to declare, "The Word was made flesh, and dwelt among us, (and we beheld his glory, the glory as of the only begotten of the Father,) full of grace and truth." Only the most dishonest or foolish "interpreter" would deny what these verses unmistakably declare concerning Jesus Christ.

Besides the many confessions of Jesus as God by his followers—Peter (Matt.16:16–17), Martha (Jn. 11:27), Nathaniel (1:49), Stephen (Acts 7:59), and Paul (Acts 20:28; Heb. 1:8)—more importantly Jesus *Himself* claimed He was God. This silences those who argue, "Well, Jesus' followers were deluded; they thought He was God, but He didn't really claim deity." One key passage is John 5:16–18, where Jesus had just healed a lame man on the Sabbath:

> And therefore did the Jews persecute Jesus, and sought to slay him, because he had done these things on the sabbath day. But Jesus answered them, My Father worketh hitherto, and I work. Therefore the Jews sought the more to kill him, because he not only had broken the sabbath, but said also that God was his Father, making himself equal with God.

While our culture might understand these words to mean, "Big deal. My father is working and I'm working. So what?" the Jews heard something far different. Based on their culture and traditions, what those religious leaders heard was this: "By using the term *my* Father instead of *our* Father, this man is claiming *equality* with God. This man is, in fact, claiming to *be* God." And that is what enraged them.

The same thing happened on another occasion:

> I and my Father are one. Then the Jews took up stones again to stone him. Jesus answered them, Many good works have I showed you from my Father; for which of those works do ye stone me? The Jews answered him, saying, For a good work we stone thee not; but for blasphemy; and because that thou, being a man, makest thyself God (John 10:30–33; cf. 17:11; 17:21–23).

The Jews knew *exactly* what Jesus was claiming to be. His statement, in fact, becomes all the more offensive to the Jewish ear because the Greek for "one" is neuter not masculine, which therefore means not one in *person* but one in *essence or nature*. Jesus was clearly saying that He was the same as God, and the Jews went berserk.

Perhaps the most unmistakable claim of all that Jesus made to deity appears in John 8:58: "Verily, verily, I say unto you, Before Abraham was, I am." To use the term "I am" denotes not just existence before Abraham, but rather a claim to be Yahweh of the Old Testament, as God revealed Himself to Moses in Exodus 3:14. And once again, the Jews understood immediately what Jesus claimed and "took they up stones to cast at him" Jn. 8:59).

Still another statement from our Lord's own mouth appears in John 14:10: "Have I been so long time with you, and yet hast thou not known me, Philip? he that hath seen me hath seen the Father." Jesus claimed that He was so like the Father that to see Him was to see the Father. There is, in fact, even a mild note of rebuke in our Lord's words, namely, to fail to recognize that Jesus is God is to fail to know Jesus at all.

One author tells of a businessman who scrutinized the Bible to verify whether or not Jesus actually claimed to be God and said, "For anyone to read the New Testament and not conclude that Jesus claimed to be God, he would have to be as blind as a man standing outdoors on a clear day and saying he can't see the sun."[4]

That is why we can only come to one of three conclusions about Jesus. He was either a *liar*, the biggest fraud who ever lived, or He was a *lunatic* because He ultimately died for His false claim, or He was exactly what He said He was—*Lord*. He *repeatedly* spoke of His equality with the Father:

All men should honour the Son, even as they honour the Father. · He that honoureth not the Son honoureth not the Father which hath sent him (Jn. 5:23).

Ye neither know me, nor my Father: if ye had known me, ye should have known my Father also (8:19).

And he that seeth me seeth him that sent me (12:45).

He that hateth me hateth my Father also (15:23).

To this we should also add that according to Jewish law, only God could forgive sins, but this is precisely what Jesus did in Mark 2:5: "When Jesus saw their faith, he said unto the sick of the palsy, Son, thy sins be forgiven thee." Once again the religious leaders were horrified and asked, "Doth this man thus speak blasphemies? who can forgive sins but God only?" (v. 7), to which the Lord Jesus asked, "Whether is it easier to say to the sick of the palsy, Thy sins be forgiven thee; or to say, Arise, and take up thy bed, and walk?" (v. 9).

So to answer that pastor's statement, "It's too bad the Bible just doesn't say, 'Jesus was God,'" that's precisely what it *does* say. To the Jews' ears, Jesus' statements were just as clear as the words "Jesus was God" are to our ears. They knew exactly what He was claiming, and they went berserk; likewise many are still doing so today because they refuse to admit Jesus was (and is) God.

Turning to the New Testament Epistles, Paul wrote to the Philippians: "[Christ], being in the form of God, thought it not robbery to be equal with God" (2:6). That clearly states that Jesus was God before His incarnation. Charles Ryrie offers this paraphrase, "Who, though of the same nature as God, did not think this something to be exploited to His own advantage." Another writer adds that the words "thought it not robbery to be equal with God" is "an expression which means 'did not think it necessary to grasp at deity.' No ambition to become God could plague Christ since He was in fact God!"[5] Further, while He took on human form—the words "form of a servant" in verse 7 are the Greek *morphen doulou*, "the nature or essence of a slave"—and while He set aside His divine glory for a time, His divine nature was in no way less than it had ever been. "The incarnation was not a subtraction of deity, but an addition of humanity."[6]

Paul likewise wrote to the Colossians, "[Christ] is before all things, and by him all things consist" (1:17), thereby asserting both His preexistence and position as Creator. He again writes, "For in [Christ] dwelleth all the fulness of the Godhead bodily" (2:9). That is another important verse. The Greek behind "fullness" is *plērōma*, which refers to "that which is filled" and was used of a ship being filled with sailors, rowers, soldiers, and even cargo. Paul is, therefore, saying that Christ is filled with everything that God is, His very nature and character.

While we could examine much more, Paul well summed it up in his letter to Titus: "Looking for that blessed hope, and the glorious appearing of the great God and our Saviour Jesus Christ" (2:13). Could Scripture be any plainer as to Jesus being God in the flesh? Those who reject that are apostate indeed.

NOTES

[1] The preceding portion of our study adapted from the author's book, *A Word for the Day: Key Words from the New Testament* (AMG Publishers, 2006), April 8 devotional.

[2] *Scofield Reference Bible*; note on Matt. 1:23.

[3] *Ryrie Study Bible* (NASB; Moody Press; emphasis in the original).

[4] *Cited in Josh McDowell, More Than a Carpenter*, p. 14.

[5] W. A. Criswell, *The Believer's Study Bible* (Criswell Center for Biblical Studies,

1991), comment on Philippians 2:6.

[6] Ibid.

So, following the saintly fathers, we all with one voice teach the confession of one and the same Son, our Lord Jesus Christ: the same perfect in divinity and perfect in humanity, the same truly God and truly man, of a rational soul and a body; consubstantial with the Father as regards his divinity, and the same consubstantial with us as regards his humanity; like us in all respects except for sin; begotten before the ages from the Father as regards his divinity, and in the last days the same for us and for our salvation from Mary, the virgin God-bearer as regards his humanity; one and the same Christ, Son, Lord, only-begotten, acknowledged in two natures which undergo no confusion, no change, no division, no separation; at no point was the difference between the natures taken away through the union, but rather the property of both natures is preserved and comes together into a single person and a single subsistent being; he is not parted or di-vided into two persons, but is one and the same only-begotten Son, God, Word, Lord Je-sus Christ, just as the prophets taught from the beginning about him, and as the Lord Je-sus Christ himself instructed us, and as the creed of the fathers handed it down to us.

Council of Chalcedon (451 AD)

11

Who Were the Recipients of the Epistle to the Ephesians?*

Ephesians 1:1

Paul, an apostle of Jesus Christ by the will of God, to the saints which are at Ephesus, and to the faithful in Christ Jesus:

How could this verse possibly be a tough text? Well, believe it not, there is a major controversy concerning the Epistle to the Ephesians that has arisen in recent years. While some do not consider this very important or crucial, I am convinced that it is a significant issue. The issue is this: exactly *to whom* was Ephesians written?[1] "But doesn't this verse clearly tell us?" you ask. Ah, but that is precisely the problem. The key words **at Ephesus** are the words under dispute!

From a personal perspective, I am greatly troubled by this issue. In my early study and exposition of Ephesians back in the late 1980s, I was sucked into and accepted the view I am about to refute. In my second study and exposition during 2003–06, I spent weeks studying this issue and am convinced of its importance. Like Pauline authorship (which is denied by liberal scholarship), in spite of the fact that the entire Early Church regarded this as a letter that had been sent to the *Ephesians* by *Paul*, this has been challenged in recent years. It is believed by many that it was not, in fact, addressed to the Ephesians but was rather a circular letter.

The first extremely significant fact about this is that the first man to question the recipients of the letter was the 2nd-century Gnostic heretic Marcion. Reading Paul's request in Colossians 4:16 that the Colossians and Laodiceans should exchange letters, he concluded that "the letter to Laodicea" mentioned there actually refers to this letter to the Ephesians. Based on that single opinion, he actually altered the copy of the Greek text he had from "at Ephesus" to "at Laodicea." But this was conclusively proven to be an absurd conclusion. Except for his altered copy, not one single manuscript contains the heading, "to the saints that are at Laodicea."[2] It has been further shown that Marcion, as one writer puts it, "cut and

---

* This chapter was originally TOTT issue 25, August 2007. It was taken from the author's three-and-one-half year exposition of Ephesians, which Sola Scriptura Publications plans to publish in the future.

slashed texts to suit his purposes in an astounding manner."[3] Tertullian, a contemporary of Marcion, wrote: "Instead of a stylus, Marcion employed a knife." He went on to say that Marcion even changed the title of the letter.[4]

I mention this not only because of its historical importance, but also to say that modern thought is really not much different. The whole question of the destination of this letter actually revolves around a textual issue. The real issue is this: because the words "at Ephesus" do not appear in the oldest Greek manuscripts, then some other destination is implied. But when we *objectively* and *honestly* analyze the textual evidence, we must conclude otherwise. The simple fact of the matter is that only six manuscripts omit the words "at Ephesus" while all others, thousands in fact, contain them. Among these six are the revered, but arguably corrupt, 4th-century codices Sinaiticus and Vaticanus. It is argued that since they are the oldest, they are the best, which is the foundation of the modern Textual Criticism and modern translations. But this argument has been shown by several conservative scholars to be illogical. How can it possibly be rational to accept a handful of manuscripts—which are in fact suspicious to begin with and actually contradict each other some 3,000 times—over thousands of other copies that say something different and agree among themselves? The fact is, to say that older is always better is absurd, and any first semester student of logic would recognize it.[5]

We might also add, it has also been shown by two scholars that it's very possible that the reason these wrongly revered 4th-century manuscripts omit the words "at Ephesus" might well be the result of Marcion's tampering with the text 200 years earlier.[6]

It's also conveniently ignored that while Sinaiticus and Vaticanus omit the words "at Ephesus" in the text, they still retain the title of the letter, *"The Epistle of Paul to the Ephesians."*[7] The same is true of the Chester Beatty papyrus manuscript (P46) dated A.D. 200, which is the earliest extant manuscript of Paul's epistles. It, too, has *Pros Ephesious* ("to Ephesians") at the top of the first page (see the picture of that first page in the back of this book). Why the contradiction? Why is it retained in the title but not in the text? We also should note that Vaticanus includes the words "in Ephesus" in the margin.

Another manuscript that is cited as not containing the words "in Ephesus" is the 12th-century Codex 67. But the truth here is that originally it actually *did* contain the words but some later "correctionist" deleted them apparently to make it conform to Vaticanus![8] Doesn't this bother anyone?

It is further argued that since Paul sends no greetings to the people in a church he labored in for three years, this implies that Ephesians was actually a circular letter, that is, not one sent to the single church but a general one sent to many churches. "Surely he knew everybody," it is argued, "so why wouldn't he send greetings?" As mentioned earlier, this is not proof because other epistles lack such greetings. But one scholar adds another perceptive point:

> [This] argument is two-edged, for Paul's long years of labour at Ephesus must have made him acquainted with so many Christian people there, that their very number may have prevented him from sending any salutation. A roll far longer than the epistle itself might have been filled, and yet the list would have been by no means exhausted. Omissions might have given offence . . .[9]

Still another commentator makes this observation:

> The better he knows the parties addressed, and the more general and solemn the subject, the less he seems to give of these individual notices.[10]

In other words, personal greetings are far from being the most important issue, rather the lofty truths that the epistle presents. This reminds me of the "user friendly" churches in our day, which are more concerned about being "touchy-feely" than they are about Truth. In this Epistle, Paul presents some of the grandest truths he ever penned, so it is easy to assume that presenting these far exceeded any need for personal greetings.

Henry Alford, 19th-century biblical scholar, adds another objection to the circular theory. He writes that it is "[improbable] that the apostle, who in two of his Epistles (Second Corinthians and Galatians) has so plainly specified their encyclical character, should have here omitted such specification."[11] Indeed, Galatians 1:2 makes it clear that Paul is writing to "the churches of Galatia," and 2 Corinthians 1:1 declares that that letter was meant not only for "the church of God which is at Corinth" but also "with all the saints which are in all Achaia." In both cases Paul makes it clear that the letter is meant to be circular, so if Ephesians was purposely designed to be such a letter, why does he not make that equally clear?

One verse that is cited as "proof" that Paul didn't write this letter directly to the Ephesians is 1:15, "Wherefore I also, after I heard of your faith in the Lord Jesus, and love unto all the saints." Albert Barnes sums up the argument and then answers it this way:

> The argument is, that he writes to them as if they were strangers to him, and that it is not language such as would be used in addressing a people among whom he had spent three years . . . But this inference is not conclusive. Paul had been some years absent from Ephesus when this epistle was written. In the difficult communication in those times between distant places, it is not to be

supposed that he would hear often from them. Perhaps he had heard nothing after the time when he bade farewell to the elders of Ephesus at Miletus (Acts 20), until the time here referred to. It would be, therefore, a matter of great interest with him to hear from them; and when, in some way, intelligence was brought to him at Rome of a very gratifying character about their growth in piety, he says that his anxiety was relieved, and that he did not cease to give thanks for what he had heard, and to commend them to God in prayer.

Likewise, Charles Hodge writes:

> As Paul was the founder of the church in Ephesus and had labored long in that city, it has always caused people to wonder that he should speak of having heard of their faith, as though he had no personal acquaintance with them. This expression is one of the reasons why many people think, as mentioned in the Introduction, that this letter was addressed not to the Ephesians alone or principally, but to all the churches in the western part of Asia Minor. It is, however, not unnatural that the apostle should speak in this way about so large and constantly changing a congregation after being absent from them for a time. Besides, the expression need mean nothing more than that he continued to hear about their general welfare.

John Eadie agrees and boldly states:

> It is wrong to argue from this expression, with Olshausen and De Wette, that the apostle had no personal knowledge of the persons whom he addressed. This was an early surmise, for it is referred to by Theodoret. Some, says he, have supposed that the apostle wrote to the Ephesians, *os medepo theasamenos autous*, (as having never seen them.) But some years had elapsed since the apostle had visited Ephesus, and seen the Ephesian Church; and might he not refer to reports of their Christian steadfastness which had reached him? Nay, his use of the word may signify that such intelligence had been repeatedly brought to him.

Jamieson, Fausset, and Brown make still another point:

> "Ever since I have heard." Not implying that he had only heard of their conversion: an erroneous argument used by some against the address of this Epistle to the Ephesians; but referring to the report he had heard since he was with them, as to their Christian graces. So in the case of Philemon, his "beloved fellow laborer" (Phm 1:1), he uses the same words (Phm 1:4,5).

We could also cite R. C. H. Lenski, who makes the same point, as well as Eadie's. Finally, Matthew Poole puts the matter very simply with this comment:

> He was an eyewitness of their first believing, but here he speaks of their increase and constancy in the faith since, of which he had heard by others.

All these comments should demonstrate just how ridiculous this whole theory is.

Another important point here is that omitting "at Ephesus" makes the verse grammatically incorrect and even unintelligible. The verse therefore says, "to the saints which are," a statement that makes no sense and one which we find hard to accept that Paul would write. Paul always includes the destination of his letters, so why not here?

To answer this, the critic argues—and this is perhaps the most absurd theory of all—that the two clauses "to the saints that are . . . and to the faithful" imply a blank space; perhaps multiple copies were made and the name of each church was inserted in the copy sent to it. But this just begs the question and assumes that these few manuscripts are correct in omitting "at Ephesus." If we may add, in fact, such a fill-in-the blank document was, as one writer puts it, "without parallel in the annuals of the primitive Church. It is, as far as I am aware, essentially a modern notion."[12] In other words, to prop up their position, somebody just made up the idea of a blank space in the manuscript, despite the fact that such a practice was unknown in that day.

That writer was 19th-century textual scholar Dean John W. Burgon, a contemporary of Westcott and Hort. Burgon thoroughly dismantled their Critical Theory of textual criticism but is ignored today by liberal critics and even by the majority of Evangelicals who have bought into the liberal theories.

I must say again, this issue greatly troubles me. It does so because it is important in view of biblical authority. *This theory challenges the clear text of Scripture that is supported by the majority of the Greek manuscripts.* As we'll mention later, the majority of modern commentators and expositors spew out this unfounded theory. In essence, they say, "Well, since those six manuscripts don't have 'at Ephesus,' then this was probably just a circular letter in which they perhaps just wrote in the name of the church before they sent the copy." Every time I read such a statement, written by a godly and intelligent man, it simply amazes me at how undiscerning we have become. Why do we want to hold on to some ridiculous theory that has not one shred of support?

As I pondered this, I thought of an analogy. The same evangelicals who most certainly reject evolution because it is a God-rejecting and totally improvable theory, then turn right around and accept a ridiculous and pointless theory such as this. After careful examination of this theory, I am totally appalled at its widespread acceptance and the cavalier attitude with which it is treated.

May we also point out, not only do the majority of Greek manuscripts include "at Ephesus," but so do all the ancient versions (translations) of Ephesians *without exception*, as do the all the ancient commentaries on Ephesians.

Another 19ᵗʰ-century scholar, John Eadie, who wrote one of the most authoritative commentaries on Ephesians, *A Commentary on the Greek Text of the Epistle of Paul to the Ephesians*, is very difficult to argue with when he sums up this matter:

> We are therefore brought to the conclusion that the Epistle was really meant for and originally entituled [sic] to the church at Ephesus. The strong external evidence is not weakened by internal proof or statement; the seal and the inscription are not contradicted by the contents. Such was the opinion of the ancient church as a body, as seen in its [manuscripts], quotations, commentaries, and all its versions; of the mediaeval church; and in more modern times of the commentators Calvin and [many others].[13]

It could not be clearer, therefore, that the Church has, through the ages, universally accepted the fact that this Epistle was written *by* Paul and addressed *to* the Church at Ephesus.

Why make such an issue of this? I do so because only in recent years have both of these been challenged, and challenged even by Evangelicals. I for one refuse to be sucked into anything that in any way weakens, waters down, compromises, or casts doubt upon Scripture. *And that is exactly what this theory does.* Evangelicals and Fundamentalists today have been sold a bill of goods by so-called "scholars" who in reality merely undermine the Word of God with their speculations.

The fact is that for people today to argue against the authenticity of the words "at Ephesus" is total folly. We say again, the real issue here is textual. This whole thing would not even arise were it not for modern Textual Criticism that ignores (and even scoffs at) the Traditional (Majority) Text theory, which holds that the true text of Scripture has been providentially preserved in the majority of Greek manuscripts. Burgon again writes:

> In the face of this overwhelming mass of unfaltering evidence to insist that [Sinaiticus and Vaticanus] must yet be accounted right, and all the rest of Antiquity wrong, is simply irrational. To uphold the authority, in respect of this nonsensical reading, of *two*

[manuscripts] confessedly untrustworthy in countless other places,—against *all* the [manuscripts]—*all* the versions,—is nothing else but an act of vulgar prejudice . . .

> It is absolutely unreasonable for men to go out of their way to invent a theory wanting every element of probability in order to account for the omission of the words [in Ephesus] . . .[14]

What a significance statement! *They have truly gone "out of their way" to explain a problem where no problem exists.* Against simple and overwhelming evidence, they have created a ridiculous theory—and please get this—*a theory that has no positive end and no good purpose.* As I researched, pondered, and wrote about this hour after hour, I finally asked, "What possible good can come out of denying the words 'at Ephesus' and coming up with some preposterous theory to explain the absence?" I could find only one answer—*none.* It accomplished nothing good. *All it ultimately accomplishes is to cast one more doubt on the veracity and trustworthiness of our present translations.* This, Dear Reader, upsets me, and it ought to upset every Christian who loves God's Word. We should all be sick and tired of the constant subtle challenges to the veracity of Scripture today made by not only liberals but even Evangelicals and Fundamentalists. Instead of accepting the simple facts before them, they create theories that ultimately dishonor God's Word.

As mentioned already, it is most interesting and instructive that most modern commentators and expositors have swallowed this view of Ephesians against the ancient evidence. It's tragic just how gullible and undiscerning we have become. One refreshing exception, however, is the commentary on Ephesians contained in *The Bible Knowledge Commentary*, written by the faculty of Dallas Seminary. Harold W. Hoehner writes:

> It seems better to accept "in Ephesus" as genuine because of the wide geographical distribution of the Greek manuscripts that do include those words. Also no manuscripts of this epistle mention any other city, and none have only the word "in" followed by a space to insert a city's name. The prescript or title "To the Ephesians" appears in all manuscripts of this epistle. Furthermore, all the letters Paul wrote to churches mention their destinations.

Another comment in the *Wycliffe Bible Commentary* is also worth mentioning:

> Some believe that this epistle may have been a circular letter addressed to a number of different churches. It seems more likely, however, that a particular congregation was in view, and there is no strong reason for rejecting the traditional destination—Ephesus.[15]

Still another respected commentator, Jamieson, Fausset, and Brown, who actually leans on the Critical Text, accepts "in Ephesus" as genuine.

May I share one other quotation. Writing in 1891, *after* the discovery of Vaticanus and Sinaiticus, B. W. Johnson writes in his work *The People's New Testament with Explanatory Notes*:

> The absence of at Ephesus in a few manuscripts of the fourth century, and in the Vatican, as well as all other difficulties, can be explained without the necessity of denying that the Epistle was addressed to the Ephesians. Hence the great majority of critics have agreed in following the authority of existing manuscripts and of the ancient church in the statement that the Epistle was addressed to the great congregation founded by its writer in the capital of proconsular Asia, which had enjoyed his apostolic labors for a longer period than any other of which a record has come down to us.

Two things struck me as I read that. First, any difficulties that arise can be explained without denying that the letter was addressed to the Ephesians. We have, in fact, dealt with these difficulties. The second thing that struck me, however, is even more profound, namely, "the great majority of critics have agreed in following the authority of existing manuscripts and of the ancient church in the statement that the Epistle was addressed to [the Ephesians]." In other words in *his* day, 1891, just like throughout Church history, the majority of the church accepted this letter as being addressed to the Ephesians. In other words, in *his* day there was no problem. In *our* day, however, there *is* a problem, namely, we have rejected time-honored Truth and have been sold a lie by liberal criticism.

As I continued pondering all this, I asked myself, why don't more of us see this development? Why aren't more of us bothered by it? Why aren't more of the intelligent, educated, and godly men of today concerned about all this? Why can't we get it through our heads that the Bible is under attack from every direction? Some might ask, "So what? What's the big deal that the words 'at Ephesus' aren't there? What difference does it make?" The difference is that it is just one more subtle attack on the veracity of the Word of God. Instead of looking at Scripture rationally, may we just look at the text—*the issue is always the text*. Those who reject these well-attested words are, whether they recognize it or not, undermining the text. They say they believe in the authority of Scripture, but then tolerate and even embrace something manufactured by the liberal critic.

Another reason we make an issue of all this is because as one embarks on the study of this wondrous epistle, like any other study, what is the first prerequisite? It is this: before we can study it, we must first believe that it is God's Word. And if we swallow some liberal criticism, we might as well stop now because other doubts will arise. There are, in fact, other challenges to the text of Ephesians by the critic,[16] so we better decide "up front" whether we will stand or compromise.

Before going on, I would submit one more thought. This seemingly insignificant attack has accomplished something else, namely, that the Critical Text, and therefore the modern translations based on it (such as the NIV),[17] have been so elevated that most people today simply ignore the facts of something basic to New Testament history, namely, the recipients of the Epistle that Paul obviously wrote to the Ephesians. How tragic it is! What is the matter with us that we ignore such a danger?

In summary, there is absolutely no valid reason whatsoever to doubt that the Epistle to the Ephesians was written by the Apostle Paul to the Church at Ephesus. It is, in fact, foolish, irrational, and destructive to do otherwise. Might it still have been circulated among other churches? That is certainly possible,[18] but that in no way detracts from the fact that it was addressed *by* Paul *to* the Ephesians.

NOTES

[1] The defense that follows of Ephesians being the destination of the letter is based on: John Eadie (*A Commentary on the Greek Text of the Epistle of Paul to the Ephesians* [Wipf and Stock Publishers, 1998; reprint of 2nd Edition, 1861] xx-xxxiii); R. C. H. Lenski (*Commentrary on the New Testament: Galatians, Ephesians, Philippians* [Hendrickson Publishers, 1937, 2001], 331–342); and John Burgon (*The Last Twelve Verses of Mark* [James Parker and CO, 1871, Reprinted by The Dean Burgon Society], 91–113); but many other points are made by this writer. William Hendrickson (*New Testament Commentary: Exposition of Ephesians* [Baker Book House], 56–61) is also helpful but indecisive.

[2] Jamieson, Fausset, and Brown, *A Commentary, Critical, Experimental, and Practical*, three volumes (Eerdmans Publishing, 1993 Reprint).

[3] Lenski, p. 337.

[4] Cited in Burgon, p. 106.

[5] Theologian and philosopher Gordon Clark, who taught logic for 50 years, provides an excellent example (*Ephesians* [Trinity Foundation, 1986], p. 3): "It is not true that the oldest manuscripts are always the best. If the original X were copied in A.D. 110, and this copy was copied in A.D. 120, and so on to A.D. 200, there would be ten generations between the original and the final copy. Each step would incorporate an error or two. But suppose another copy was made directly from X in A.D. 210. This manuscript would be *later* than A.D. 200, but it would be only *one* step away from the original, not ten steps; and would therefore be better than the more ancient copy. This would be true even if all errors were accidental. But now suppose that *two* copies of the original were made: one contains a few accidental mistakes, but the other was written by a man who wanted to change the message and who therefore deliberately altered the

text. In this case, and this case did in fact occur, the earlier manuscript would be *worse* than the majority of very late copies with their purely accidental mistakes. Manuscripts [Sinaiticus and Vaticanus] are *supposed* to be two copies of the same earlier manuscript. They attest the same readings. But can it be shown that this earlier, now non-existent manuscript was a good copy? Might it not be the one Marcion mutilated?" (emphasis added).

[6] Lenski (338) and Clark (3).

[7] Noted in *Wycliffe Bible Commentary*.

[8] Lenski (337) and Eadie (xxii).

[9] Eadie, p. xxx.

[10] Jamieson, Fausset, and Brown.

[11] Cited in Jamieson, Fausset, and Brown.

[12] Burgon, p. 104.

[13] Eadie, p. xxxiii.

[14] Burgon, pp. 99 and 108 (emphasis in original).

[15] Charles Pfeiffer and Everett Harrison (Editors), *The Wycliffe Bible Commentary* (Chicago: Moody Press, 1975).

[16] For example, some doubt and challenge "through Jesus Christ" in 3:9 and "with his flesh and blood" in 5:30, both of which are addressed in the complete exposition of Ephesians.

[17] The NIV, for example, and others, casts doubt on the text with this note: "Some early manuscripts do not have *in Ephesus*."

[18] Charles Hodge writes: "The assumption that this letter was designed specially for any one church but intended equally for all the churches in that part of Asia Minor has met with more favor. This view, first suggested by Archbishop Ussher, has been adopted, and variously modified, by many others. The great objection to it is the overwhelming authority in favor of the reading "in Ephesus" in the greeting and the unanimous testimony of the early church. Perhaps the most probable solution of the problem is that the letter was written to the Ephesians and addressed to them, but being intended specially for the Gentile Christians as a class, rather than for the Ephesians as a church, it was designedly thrown into such a form as to suit it to all such Christians in the neighboring churches, to whom no doubt the apostle wished it to be communicated. This would account for the absence of any reference to the peculiar circumstances of the saints in Ephesus" (*Commentary on the Epistle to the Ephesians*).

D. Edmond Hiebert also writes: "The Epistle was written to the Ephesians and addressed to them, but . . . the Apostle intentionally cast it into a form which would make it suitable to the Christians in the neighboring churches and intended that it should be communicated to them." (*An Introduction to the Pauline Epistles*, p. 266).

Harold Hoehner concurs: "Even so, the epistle may still be considered a circular letter, with Ephesus being the primary church addressed since Paul had stayed there so long and since it was the capital city of the province of Asia. This helps explain the absence of personal names of Ephesian believers. If this epistle were routed to other churches after the Ephesians read it, it may have gone to

Laodicea and Colosse, for Paul in writing Colossians urged the believers there to "read the letter from Laodicea" (Col. 4:16), possibly a reference to the Ephesian epistle."

The scripture is the library of the Holy Ghost [Spirit]; it is a pandect of divine knowledge, an exact model and platform of religion [true religion, i.e., biblical Christianity]. The Scripture contains in it the credenda, *"the things which we are to believe," and the* agenda, *"the things which we are to practice."*

Thomas Watson
How We May Read the Scriptures with Most Spiritual Profit,
Direction 11

12

Who are the "Angels" of the Seven Churches?*

Revelation 1:20

The mystery of the seven stars which thou sawest in my right hand, and the seven golden candlesticks. The seven stars are the angels of the seven churches: and the seven candlesticks which thou sawest are the seven churches.

In light of a literal approach to the book of Revelation, God *strongly* emphasizes the messages to the seven churches of chapters 2 and 3. So important are these messages, in fact, that they comprise a little over twelve-and-one-half percent (or about one eighth) of the content of the book. Moreover, there is a lot of "Church Truth" in these messages that matches the Church Truth contained in other New Testament Epistles. Let us not neglect these two chapters in favor of the more "spectacular" parts of Revelation. These two chapters will honestly be of far more help to local churches and individual believers than will the remainder of the book.

In this chapter and the next, we will examine the four-fold application of these letters, the first of which provides us with our first "tough text."

The Contemporary Application

By this is meant that Christ was concerned with the state of each of these physical, 1st-century local churches. As one commentator observes, "The order of scriptural presentation was geographic. A messenger would naturally travel the route from the seaport Ephesus, 35 miles north to another seaport, Smyrna, proceed still farther north and to the east to Pergamos, and then would swing further to the east and south to visit the other four cities (1:11)."[1] These cities, of course, were located in the Roman province of Asia Minor (modern Turkey) and were undoubtedly selected because they were the key cities of the seven postal districts of that region. They were the cities one would choose if he wanted to spread information.

---

* This chapter was originally TOTT issue 22, May 2007.

The Lord Jesus makes observations and counsels each one of them. Revelation 1:20 makes this clear: **The mystery of the seven stars which thou sawest in my right hand, and the seven golden candlesticks. The seven stars are the angels of the seven churches: and the seven candlesticks which thou sawest are the seven churches.**

As this verse declares, each church was viewed as a lampstand. The Greek here for "lampstand" is *luxnos,* which refers to the hand-lamp that was fed by oil. As we know, "oil" is used in Scripture as a symbol of the Holy Spirit, so the thought here is that the churches themselves do not create light; rather, each church bears the light of Christ through the power of the Holy Spirit.

We now notice the word "angels." The Greek here is *angeloi,* meaning "messengers." The identity of these "angels" has been a matter of much discussion through the years. A clue to this identity lies in the fact that Jesus holds them **in His right hand.** As the **right hand** is used in Scripture as a symbol of honor and authority (Eph. 1:20; Heb. 8:1; 12:2; 1 Pet. 3:22; etc.), the idea here is that Jesus is controlling His church through the authority of these "messengers." While **angels** is the common translation of *angeloi,* and while there are some valid arguments that these are literal **angels,** we are compelled to disagree for several reasons.

First, literal angels are never spoken of in Scripture as being the "authorities" in churches. In other words, they are never involved in church leadership; God does not rule churches through **angels.** Nowhere is this indicated in the Epistles. Angels don't lead churches; God's *men* lead churches and are responsible for how they lead.

Second, all but two of these churches, and obviously their leadership, have been disobedient to God's Word and are commanded to repent of their sin (□2:4–5□, □14□, □20□; □3:1–3□, □15□, □17□, □19□). Angels, however, do not sin and, therefore, have no need to repent.

Third, and perhaps most significantly, saying that these are literal **angels** actually means that God is sending messages to **angels** *through* John, but such an idea has no precedent in Scripture. Not once do we read that God spoke to angels through men.

Fourth, while it is argued that *angelloi* always means **angels,** that simply is not so; there are several instances in Scripture where *angelloi* clearly speaks of "messengers," that is, *human* messengers. Luke 7:24, for example, declares, "And when the messengers [*angelloi*] of John were departed, [Jesus] began to speak unto the people concerning John." A few verses before, in fact, we read that these same messengers were John's disciples, that is, men (v. 19). Then in verse 27, our Lord Himself uses *angellos* to refer to John as His "messenger." Likewise, James 2:25 recounts, "Was not Rahab the harlot justified by works, when she had received the messengers [*angelloi*], and had sent them out another way?" The spies sent in to reconnoiter the Promised Land were men, not angels. As one Greek authority points out, an argument could be made that even Hebrews 13:2—"Be not forgetful to entertain strangers: for thereby some have entertained angels unawares"—might be referring to hospitality "to itinerate preachers rather than angels."[2]

Further, we see the same idea in the Old Testament, both in the Hebrew and the Greek (Septuagint), which provides a clear precedent for the New Testament use. While most references in the Old Testament are to literal angels, several are not. Commentator William Newell well points out some of those. While Genesis 32:1, for example, says that Jacob encountered literal **angels**, verse 3 says he sent his own "messengers" to Edom. In both verses, the Hebrew word is the same, *malāk*, which in-turn is translated as the Greek *angelloi*. Likewise, in Numbers 20:14, Moses sent his own "messengers from Kadesh unto the king of Edom," while God sent an "angel" to Moses. The Hebrew is again *malāk* in both verses and is translated as the Greek *angelloi* (and *angellos*). Again, in Judges 6:10–23, the literal "Angel of the Lord" is referred to seven times by the Hebrew *malāk* (vv. 11, 12, 20, 21 [twice], 22 [twice]), while the messengers Gideon sent are also called *malāk* (v. 35); in all cases the Greek is again *angellos*. And still again, Sennacherib's representative are called "messangers" in Isaiah 37:9 and 14, while in verse 36 the Angel of the Lord is in view, and the same Hebrew and Greek words are used.[3]

Most significant in all those examples is the fact that the Hebrew and Greek words refer to *both* angels and men *in the same context*. Some argue, "Since the word 'angel' occurs 67 other times in Revelation, and since every one of those refers to heavenly angels, then it must also be true here in 1:20." But that obviously is not so.

Fifth, the context clearly seems to argue against literal **angels**. Christ is speaking about *earthly* matters to an *earthly* messenger, who will in-turn pass on those matters to other *earthly* messengers. Why would He bring heavenly beings into a discussion of earthly issues? Further, the *responsible parties* in these letters are earthly beings, not heavenly beings.

Sixth, one final problem with the literal angel idea is that there is no way to explain how the angels then conveyed Christ's message to the churches. It seems more than obvious that men would carry these messages to the churches.

We must conclude, therefore, that the messengers of Revelation 2—3 were, indeed, the pastors of the seven churches. These men were those who were responsible for the leadership of those churches and those to whom the challenges and encouragements of the letters were given. It is through such men that the Lord (who holds these **in His right hand**) leads and rules His Church.

If we may submit, therefore, this is precisely why the qualifications and requirements for leadership in the Church are *extremely* high, according to 1 Timothy 3:1–7 and Titus 1:6–8 (see chapter 14 and 15). God could not be clearer on this issue of qualified leadership. In spite of that, however, we increasingly see people today leading who, frankly, should not be doing so. The common attitude is that anyone can lead, but this is worse than dangerous. In fact, the precedent in Scripture for training to be a leader seems to be three years. The disciples spent three years with the Lord, Paul spent three years in training before being sent out to preach and plant churches (Gal. 1:11–18), and Timothy was with Paul three years during the second missionary journey (Acts 15:36—18:22). We would also add, as Paul wrote to Timothy—"And the things that thou hast heard of me among many witnesses, the same commit thou to faithful men, who shall be able to teach others also" (2 Tim. 2:2)—can there be any doubt that he was saying, "As I trained you for leadership, you train others for leadership?" (see chapters 33 and 34 for a deeper look at this verse).

NOTES

[1] *The Bible Knowledge Commentary.*

[2] Spiros Zodhiates, *Word Study Dictionary: New Testament,* p. 68.

[3] William Newell, *The Book of Revelation* (Chicago: Moody Press, 1935), pp. 33-34.

I sometimes think if I were in heaven I should almost wish to visit my work at the Tabernacle, to see whether it will abide the test of time and prosper when I am gone. Will you keep in the truth? Will you hold to the grand old doctrines of the Gospel? Or will this church, like so many others, go astray from the simplicity of its faith, and set up gaudy services and false doctrines? Methinks I should turn over in my grave if such a thing could be. God forbid it!

Charles Spurgeon
Metropolitan Tabernacle Pulpit, Vol. 23, p. 514

13

Do the Seven Churches Have a Historical Application?*

Revelation 2 and 3

In our last chapter, we began what must be a *very* brief look at the seven churches of Revelation 2 and 3. (We hope to publish a complete exposition of these chapters in a future book, *The Seven Churches of the 21st Century*.) Last time we examined the first of four applications that these churches provide, the first of which, the *contemporary* application, includes a "tough text," namely who are the "angels" of these churches. In this conclusion, we will mention the other three applications, the last of which, the *chronological*, is our second "tough text."

The Collective Application

By this we mean that these letters are an admonition to all churches of all time. In other words, by extension, not only did they apply to the seven specific churches in Asia Minor, they apply to all churches everywhere both then and in the future. These messages provide us with the seven possible appearances of any church. Every individual local church throughout this age fits into one of seven types.

It is interesting to observe that except for Smyrna and Philadelphia, our Lord rebuked all the churches for some sin that existed within them. How many churches is that true of today? Further, the specific evils in those five churches varied in seriousness from a lack of love at Ephesus that progressively grew in severity until it reached the total apostasy at Laodicea. Further still, and even worse, a church can be plagued by more that just one of these problems. Let us briefly overview the seven possible types of local church.

First, there was Ephesus, which had no love for the Lord (2:1–7). They hadn't "*lost*" their first love," as some incorrectly quote verse 4, rather they had "*left*" their love for the Lord behind. While they were busy and free of heresy, it was all mechanical and lacked a genuine love for the Lord.

---

* This chapter was originally TOTT issue 23, June 2007.

Second, there was Smyrna, which was willing to suffer tremendous persecution for the Lord (2:8–11). No sin is mentioned for this church, which shows us that suffering for Christ keeps us pure, faithful, and humble and makes us gloriously triumphant.

Third, there was Pergamum, a church that was tolerant of the world (2:12–17), tolerant of false teaching and had compromised key principles of God's Truth.

Fourth, Thyatira was clinging to paganism (2:18–29). While Pergamum was *entangled with* the world, Thyatira was *absorbed into* the world. Pagan teachings had actually been embraced.

Fifth, there was Sardis, the church that was dead and buried (3:1–6). The inevitable result of Pergamum and Thyatira was dead orthodoxy, a church where there was *liturgy* but no *life*.

Sixth, the church at Philadelphia is a breath of fresh air in the progression, for here we see a church that is faithful in all things (3:7–13). Here is a church with great works, a consistent witness, and a guarding of God's Truth.

Seventh, after a moment of respite in Philadelphia, the church at Laodicea was overtaken by apostasy (3:14–22). Here the church was people-centered and had become the authority in place of God's Word.

The Characteristic Application

Each of these messages also carries with it a personal application to every individual believer. After all, a church is comprised of people who will make that body what it is. As each of these churches, therefore, applies collectively to other churches, the lessons of each likewise apply to every individual Christian. Note Revelation 2:7, for example: "He that hath an ear let him hear what the Spirit saith unto the churches." This admonition is used, in fact, at the close of each letter showing that every Christian is responsible for the message he has heard. Each letter, then, is a challenge to believers to ascertain what "characteristics" are true in their lives.

The Chronological Application

Here is truly one of the most fascinating things in all the Word of God. These seven churches also present the entire history of the Church (Christ's body) from its beginning in the 1st-century right to the time of Christ's return for His Church at the Rapture. I spent countless hours studying Church History in light of these seven letters and saw this fact unfold before me. The Church has gone through seven distinct periods in her long history. The number "7" is "the number of perfection" in Scripture, and

Revelation 2 and 3 are, indeed, the "perfect historical record" of Christ's Church.

It should be said at this point that there are, of course, Bible teachers who do not agree that the seven churches picture Church History. There are various reasons for this skepticism, but one of the main ones is that some feel the parallels are not close enough to prove this idea. I think, however, that as our study unfolds the reader will see that just the opposite is true.

Others do not agree with this historical presentation because they are not ready to face the conclusion that we find in the letter to the church at Laodicea. Many simply do not want to face the sad condition of the Church today. While many people in Christianity today think the Church has never been in better shape, the very opposite is true. The Church as a whole has never been further away from *the absolutes of Scripture* since before the Reformation.

While it has been observed that only Dispensationalists hold this view, that seems quite irrelevant in the final analysis. From Pentecost until now, Church History is Church History. The more one studies these letters and Church History, in fact, the more glaringly obvious it becomes that these letters anticipate that history. I for one simply do not understand how someone can miss this application or why they would want to argue against it. Having said that, however, some interpreters, such as Postmillennialists and others, miss this simply because they do not take a literal view of the Book of Revelation. And, in point of fact, if we reject the literalness of Revelation, as well as *all* Bible prophecy, the Bible becomes virtually incomprehensible. In such a case, we cannot know what is literal, allegorical, mystical, real, false, or much of anything else.

So, as one commentator writes:

> Obviously these churches were specially selected and providentially arranged to provide characteristic situations which the church has faced throughout its history. . . . There are some remarkable similarities in comparing these letters to the seven churches to the movement of church history since the beginning of the apostolic church.[1]

Another writes: "It can be no mere coincidence that these Epistles do set out the salient characteristics of the Church through the centuries, and no one can deny that they are presented in historic sequence."[2] Commentator William MacDonald also observes the obvious: "The letters give a *consecutive preview* of the history of Christendom, each church representing a distinct period. The general trend of conditions is downward."[3] And even a cursory viewing of Church History proves that statement to be absolutely correct.

First, the church at Ephesus pictures the history of the Church from Pentecost to A.D. 100, a time of great growth, great labor, and purity of doctrine, but also a time when it all eventually became mechanical.

Second, the church at Smyrna pictures the Church from A.D. 100 to 313. The "Ephesian Period" was characterized by a waning love for the Lord, so God allowed great persecution to come on the Church to bring it back to Him. It was during this time that the Church experienced its greatest suffering—Satan tried to destroy Christianity from *without* using a series of ten periods of persecution under ten Roman emperors—but we also see some of the greatest growth the Church has ever known.

Third, the church at Pergamum is vivid indeed, as it pictures the period of Church History when the Church and the state were united under the Roman emperor Constantine and his successors (313–590). While Satan tried to destroy the Church from without in the "Smyrnan Period," here he tried to do it from *within*. A. C. Gaebelein puts it well: "When the devil found that the 'blood of the martyrs is the seed of the church' he stopped his work as the roaring lion and took on the form of an angel of light."[4]

One of Satan's great attempts came in 313 when the Roman emperor Constantine succeeded Diocletian (the worst of the Roman persecutors). Constantine supposedly had a vision of a fiery cross in the sky and a voice saying, "In this sign conquer." He wondered what this meant and was told that this was the sign of the Christian religion. He took this to mean that God was calling him to be the champion of this religion, and that if he obeyed, he would become emperor of the world. Though we cannot view Constantine as being a true believer, since he was never weaned from the cult of Apollo and at times consulted the pagan sooth-sayers (fortune tellers), he did, in fact, become emperor of the "world" (i.e. the known world of his day). He liberated all Christians and stopped all persecution, although Christianity merely became one more of the many religions of the empire.

As time went on, however, Constantine discovered that Christians were more trustworthy than his pagan subjects and were not causing him constant problems as were the pagans. In 324 he ordered Christianity to be the one and only religion of the empire. He threw all the pagans out of the government, and filled every post with a Christian. Our first reaction to that might be, "Oh, how wonderful!" But in reality, this was the worst event to occur in Church History, for in this way the Church was "married" to the world; it was here that the Church stopped looking for the Second Coming of Christ; it said, "Constantine's empire must be Christ's kingdom." Moreover, Christians had to tolerate many pagan superstitions and customs to get along with priests who had become "Christian," literally, at the point of the sword. The effects of that unholy alliance continued right up to the Reformation and, may we point out, still continue today in many respects.

Fourth, the church at Thyatira is extremely significant in viewing Church History, for it pictures "The Middle Ages" (590–1517), the latter of which was "The Dark Ages." The church at Thyatira is, without any shadow of a doubt, a picture of the rise of "Romanism," Papal Rome (Roman Catholicism). Catholics quite boldly say: "The first and *only* church was the Roman Catholic Church." All the different branches of the Protestant Church, they argue, have simply broken away from Rome, the true Church. It is insisted that there was no Protestant Church until Martin Luther. That is a lie that is easily proven to be a lie! Historically, there was no Roman Church (or Papacy) until the 7th-century. For six centuries before that the one true Church, the body of Christ, was continually growing more corrupt as it drifted away from the Word of God. Between 313 and 590, the bishop at Rome was considered "first among equals," but in 590 the Roman bishop was given supremacy over all other bishops. In the strict sense of the word, this bishop (who in 590 was Gregory I) became the first "Pope." The Papacy then had to go back through history and arbitrarily choose certain men through whom they could trace "apostolic succession" back to Peter.

One of the greatest tragedies of our day—and I can't emphasize this strongly enough—is the continued tolerance of Catholicism by evangelicals. When one honestly and biblically analyzes Catholicism, he finds that virtually every doctrine, holy day, rite, dogma, ceremony, vestment, and title in the Roman Church has its roots in ancient pagan religion; it is the ultimate perversion of "Christianity," the "continual sacrifice" of the "mass" being perhaps the greatest of all. During *every* mass Christ is again offered up in sacrifice for the sins of the living and the dead. The priest supposedly calls Christ down from Heaven and sacrifices Him again, a "power," that is supposedly bestowed up the priest at his ordination. This parallels the pagans as they made "continual sacrifice" to their gods. Such teaching is unimaginable, and it is equally appalling that any true Christian today can tolerate such teaching and even encourage "unity" of any kind with Romanism. The Word of God clearly declares that Christ's sacrifice was *once-for-all* (Heb. 9:28; 10:10–14), never to be repeated. To do so is to "crucify to themselves the Son of God afresh, and put him to an open shame" (6:6). Think of it! Tens of millions of times our Lord has been blasphemed by the Roman mass.

Fifth, the church at Sardis clearly pictures the period of Church History called "dead Protestantism," the time of the great state churches of the Reformation (1517–1790). *The importance of the Reformation should never be discounted or understated.* While men in *southern* Europe wallowed in the Humanism of the Renaissance, another movement was arising in the *north*. The men there struggled with the same questions of morals and life, but they came to a *conclusion*, and therefore *results*, that were the polar opposite of Renaissance man. The reformers recognized the biblical teaching of man's totally fallen and perverse nature, that his entire being—intellect, emotions, and will—is hopelessly depraved. The reformers also considered the Bible as the Word of God and the only authority over men's lives. By removing Humanism from their thought, the reformers rediscovered the Truth of the Gospel.

As one writer words it, however, "The Reformation was not a golden age. It was far from perfect."[5] That is an understatement. While the Reformers tried hard to make Scripture their only standard, there were inconsistencies that seriously marred the movement. Space does not permit the many details, but the bottom line is that *the Reformers came out, but they didn't come out far enough*. Gaebelein says it well:

> The reformation itself was of God and the great men of God who were used were the most mighty instruments of the Holy Spirit. It was the greatest work, up to that time, since the days of the apostles. But out of it came the human systems which go by the name Protestantism. The reformation began well, but soon developed in the different Protestant systems into a dead, lifeless thing.[6]

Indeed, the Reformation *was* of God and had a glorious beginning, but its leaders fell short by failing to return to the principles of Church government and ministry that were evident in the 1st-century and which are recorded in the Word of God. The majority of what we see in much of Christianity today was originally founded, not upon biblical authority, but upon human reasoning and human ideas. We still suffer today because of the Reformers not coming out far enough.

Sixth, the church at Philadelphia pictures the time of great revival and great preaching that took place in the eighteenth, nineteenth, and may we add, the *very* early 20th-century. Think of some of the great preachers and theologians of those days: Charles Haddon Spurgeon, Robert Murray McCheyne, Matthew Henry, Andrew Bonar, Thomas Chalmers, Charles Hodge, Robert Haldane, Richard Fuller, John Henry Jowett, Andrew Murray, C. H. Mackintosh, Alexander Maclaren, and others. Though there were still a few problems that remained from Reformation thought, men like this nonetheless stood on the Word of God more firmly than anyone had in some 1800 years of Church History. Some folks would ask here, "But isn't this true today?" To that we must answer, *absolutely not*! Sad to say, the Word of God and the strong preaching of doctrine and practice are not the emphasis today. How churches today need the depth of the Word and strong doctrinal preaching!

Seventh, the church at Laodicea, the "lukewarm," apostate church, pictures the period of Church History in which we are right now. This period began in the early 20th-century and will continue until Jesus comes. As John R. W. Stott wrote in 1980:

> Perhaps none of the seven letters is more appropriate to the twentieth-century church than this. It describes vividly the respectable, sentimental, nominal, skin-deep religiosity which is so widespread among us today. Our Christianity is flabby and anaemic. We appear to have taken a lukewarm bath of religion.[7]

Even the word *Laodicea* demonstrates the lukewarmness of this church and our own age. The Greek *Laodikeus* is comprised of two words: *laos*, meaning "people," and *dikē*, meaning (depending upon the context) "law, right, custom, and even prescribed punishment." The idea in this word, then, is "the law of the people" or "the people ruling." The society of that day (and today) was *people centered*. People had become the authority instead of the Word of God being the authority. The modern term for this is "Humanism," which says, "Man is the center of all things." More up-to-date terms include "seeker sensitive" and "user-friendly."

Dear Christian, is there any doubt that we are right now living in the "Laodicean Age" of Church History? We are living in the age of Humanism, in which man has set himself up as the final authority on every subject and every question. This is the age of "people ruling." Sadly, this is true even in the Church. Never before in Church History has the Church been as "people centered" as today. We build entire churches and ministries based upon what people want, not upon the sole authority and sufficiency of Scripture. We are more concerned about "felt needs" and appealing to the "unchurched" than with proclaiming Truth.

Finally, we must accept these churches as a picture of Church History because of Christ's words to John, "Write the things which are in this age." These words indicate that our Lord is speaking of the *entire age*, not just a limited geographical area. We submit that our Savior was being much more farsighted than to be looking only at Asia Minor. Are we to think that while the great prophets of the Old Testament looked centuries into the future, our Lord was looking only at the contemporary scene or at only the 1st-century, as some argue? Surely not! He was concerned about His Church, His Body, throughout the centuries to come. As commentator A. C. Gaebelein observes, while there were hundreds of churches in existence at that time, only seven letters were sent. Our Lord

> knew the entire history of the Church from the beginning. . . . He saw in seven of them conditions which were in embryo, the condition through which the whole church on earth would pass, so

that we have in these seven messages, which uncover the state of the different churches, the spiritual and religious history of Christendom.[8]

Why would anyone want to ignore the obvious? Why would we wish to close our eyes to the deep significance of this "Prophetic History?" *We do so, in fact, at our peril.* As the notable quote goes, "Those who cannot remember the past are condemned to repeat it."[9] We have had to be brief, but even our brief look at this "Prophetic History" explains much of the error that has existed in the Church through the centuries and explains where the Church is today and why it is there.

NOTES

[1] *The Bible Knowledge Commentary* (Wheaton, IL: Victor Books, 1984).

[2] R. H. Clayton. Cited in Lehman Strauss, *The Book of Revelation* (Neptune,NJ: Loizeaux Brothers, Inc., 1964), p. 33.

[3] *Believer's Bible Commentary* (Nashville: Thomas Nelson Publishers, 1995), p. 2355.

[4] A. C. Gaebelein., *The Revelation* (New York: Loizeaux Brothers, Inc., 1961),

[5] Francis Scheaffer, *How Should We Then Live* (Old Tappen: NJ: Fleming H. Revell Company, 1976), p. 84.

[6] Gaebelein, p. 40.

[7] John R. W. Stott, *What Christ Thinks of the Church* (Grand Rapids: Eerdmans, 1980), p. 116.

[8] Gaebelein, p. 33-34.

[9] George Santayana, *Life of Reason*, Ch. 12, "Reason in Common Sense" (Scribner's, 1905), p. 284.

I will give you this as a most solemn observation, that there never was anything of false doctrine brought into the church, or anything of false worship imposed upon the church, but either it was by neglecting the Scripture, or by introducing something above the Scripture.

Puritan John Collins
A Puritan Golden Treasury, p. 33

14

Is There a So-called "Call" to Ministry?*

Ephesians 4:11; 1 Timothy 3:1

And he gave some, apostles; and some, prophets; and some, evangelists; and some, pastors and teachers;

This is a true saying, If a man desire the office of a bishop, he desireth a good work.

Between 1982 and 1986, my wife and I were in a traveling ministry of music and preaching. It was during that time that I occasionally heard the statement, "There's no such thing as God's 'inward call' to the ministry; that whole concept is nothing more than a person's subjective feeling." Once in a while someone would even add, "Anyone can be in the ministry simply if they choose to be."

Some twenty years later, however, that once infrequent statement has now been transformed into a full-blown teaching that is being propagated by many evangelical leaders. A growing number insist that "the call" is only outward. As one writer puts it:

> This call may be the call of the congregation to the pastorate, or the call of the representative Church to the mission field or to professorships in a theological seminary, or executive offices in the Church, or to any other work in which the Church may be engaged, or which it may find it necessary to perform. . . .[1]

We'll come back to that statement and quote another by the same teacher a little later, but the result of such a view, as I hope to show, is not only a departure from clear biblical teaching and historical precedent but is also a serious weakening of the Church by putting people in leadership who do not belong there.

The Biblical Teaching

Does the Bible teach an inward call to ministry? *First*, there is a sense in which *all* believers are called "to *ministry*." The word "call" is *kaleō* or

---

* This chapter was originally TOTT issue 18, January 2007.

kaleomai. Basically, these speak of an "invitation," but more specifically "a summons." A call, therefore, is not just a *request*; it is a *demand.* Of course, all the elect are called (summoned) to salvation (Rom. 8:30; 1 Pet. 2:9; etc.). Further, however, *all* believers are called to ministry (service). For example, 1 Peter 1:15 and 2 Peter 1:3 say we are called (summoned) to virtue and holy living. Likewise, 1 Peter 3:9, says we are called (summoned) to be a blessing to others, which is another way of saying we are to minister to (serve) others.

Second, however, it is essential to recognize that there is what is called "the call to *the ministry*," that is, God's call to what has been termed "full-time ministry," that is, as one's vocation. Is this "subjective," as goes the accusation? Of course it is because it is what God is doing in a man's heart and mind to compel him to the ministry, but that doesn't prove that it doesn't exist. As we'll see, this is the precedent we see throughout Scripture.

It is also insisted that any kind of ministry is simply one's personal choice, but we humbly and categorically disagree because that simply is not the biblical precedent. Nowhere in Scripture is this a man's choice; it is always God's choice alone. Yes, a local church is to *train* and *ordain* men to the ministry and thereby show that it *recognizes their call and qualifications*. But the actual call is God's and He works it out between Himself and His servants. Let's consider two points.

First, we see this *doctrinally* in Ephesians 4:11: **And he [Christ] gave some, apostles; and some, prophets; and some, evangelists; and some, pastors and teachers**. That verse, of course, lists four "office gifts" that have been given to the Church (the first two, which have passed away, and the two that replaced them). The words **He gave** are pivotal. The Greek here includes an "intensive pronoun" (*autos edōken*) that yields the literal idea "**He** Himself **gave**," that is, *He and no one else.* In other words, these offices are given by God alone, not by the Church, not by a school, not even by the person who wants to fill an office. Again, the common attitude today is that anyone can say, "I want to teach," and is thereby qualified to teach. While such willingness is commendable, it does *not* qualify. As none of the Apostles appointed themselves but were chosen by Christ, neither does any man appoint himself to any of these offices. As commentator aptly John Eadie puts it, "The Jesus who ascended—this, and none other, is the sovereign donor. The provider and bestower are one in the same."[2] *It is Christ alone Who calls to ministry.*

This principle is even more graphic in 1 Timothy 3:1–7 and Titus 1:6–8, where there are twenty-four qualifications a man must meet to hold the office of Pastor (Bishop and Elder). The key to understanding 1 Timothy 3:1–7 is that the qualifications Paul lists are set against the backdrop of the unqualified leaders in Ephesus. Some interpreters view these qualifications as "the ideal"; that is, no one can measure up to all of them so we must simply find as many as possible in each person. Such a view is obviously erroneous because the text neither *says* nor even *implies* such an idea. What Paul does here is place God's standards against what the Ephesians had allowed the leadership to degenerate into in the approximately six years since he had written the Ephesian letter to them. As expostitor John MacArthur summarizes, "Some of the leaders were teaching false doctrine (1 Tim. 1:3; 4:1–3, 7; 6:3–5), turning aside to 'fruitless discussion' (1:6), they misused the law, and misunderstood the gospel (1:7–11). Some were women (2:12), though that was forbidden by God's Word [which Paul notes also in verse 11]. Others were guilty of sin, and needed public rebuke (5:20)."[3]

Paul, therefore, says, "Here is what you must look for. If a man does not have these qualities, he is not qualified to lead"—period. These are not "the ideal"—they are the *standard*.

The problems we see in Christianity today—the redefining of the Gospel, the "seeker-sensitive" movement, the entertainment-orientation of ministry, the Relativism and Pragmatism that rule all aspects of Church life, and so on—all come, in part, from the breakdown of leadership, which in-turn comes from *putting people in leadership who biblically should not be there*. As Martyn Lloyd-Jones put it, "It is largely because the true conception of the work of a minister has become so debased that the ministry has lost its authority and counts so little at the present time."[4]

To illustrate, it is noteworthy that when one goes back in Church History, he finds that pastors were great theologians, and when they spoke people listened. Was that because of *their* authority? No, it was because *Scripture alone* was their authority, and they were there because they were called, qualified, trained, and ordained to be there. In stark contrast, today we find very few theologians in the pulpit, and anyone who wants to be "in the ministry" is permitted to be. We have hundreds of voices saying thousands of things, we have mega-churches doing whatever they want, we have celebrities with their own television shows, and we have every "church program" under the sun. As a result, the ministry means virtually nothing anymore. One voice is just as good as another because the Word of God is simply not the final authority for all we believe, think, say, and do.

So again, Paul, therefore, gives Timothy (and Titus) specific requirements for leadership. Out of a total of twenty-four, there are 14 *character* requirements, four *social and family* requirements, five *spiritual* requirements, and one *vocational* requirement for those who are to fill the office of Pastor (also Bishop and Elder—we'll examine these three terms in the next chapter). It is that *vocational* requirement that is at the root of

Church leadership. We use the word "vocational" here in a stronger sense than it is often used today. Webster tells us that this is "an impulse to enter a certain career." So, the word means more than most people think. In truth, as Webster indicates, a *vocation* is that to which one is totally dedicated, that for which he has a passion, that which he does because he cannot even imagine doing anything else.

While the list of qualifications in 1 Timothy 3:1–7 does not *grammatically* begin until the word "then" in verse 2, *contextually* speaking verse 1 also speaks of a qualification: **This is a true saying, If a man desire the office of a bishop, he desireth a good work.** Oh, how this verse has been abused! The word **desire** has been twisted to mean that anyone can preach or teach as a "side-line" just because he "wants to." The Greek words behind **desire** and **desireth**, however, say something quite different. **Desire** is *oregō*, which means "to stretch." One Greek authority tells us: "to stretch one's self out in order to grasp something; to reach after or desire something."[5] Another adds that metaphorically the idea is to "long after, try to gain, be ambitious (in a benign manner)."[6] So this means far more than what we usually mean by **desire**. It speaks of a deep longing, a complete disregard for all else. This is exactly what the call to the ministry is: *a desire to preach that disregards all else one could do.* There is in this a sense of constraint; one can do nothing else. How well Charles Spurgeon said it in one of his lectures to pastoral students:

> In order to [be] a true call to the ministry there must be an irresistible, overwhelming craving and raging thirst for telling to others what God has done to our own souls . . . "Do not enter the ministry *if you can help it*," was the deeply sage advice of a divine to one who sought his judgment. If any student in this room could be content to be a newspaper editor, or lawyer, or a grocer, or a farmer, or a doctor, or a senator, or a king, in the name of heaven and earth let him go his way; he is not the man in whom dwells the Spirit of God in its fulness, for a man so filled with God would utterly weary of any pursuit but that for which his inmost soul pants.[7]

In other words, if a man can do anything else and be satisfied with it, and have peace in it, then he is not called to preach. Spurgeon goes on to describe the full extent of such a desire:

> This desire should be one which *continues with us*, a passion which bears the test of trial, a longing from which it is quite impossible for us to escape, though we may have tried to do so; a desire, in fact, which grows more intense by the lapse of years, until it becomes a yearning, a pining, a famishing to proclaim the Word.[8]

Anecdotes do not constitute Truth, but if I may interject a personal example, I did not start out to be a preacher—no way. I was headed for another vocation entirely, a surgeon. The ministry was not my plan, but it was God's. He called me to the ministry and put within me that compulsion. We find the same story of men throughout Scripture (e.g., Jeremiah; 20:9) and throughout Church History.

Now notice the word **desireth**, which translates *epithumeō*, "to long after, to have a passionate compulsion." This word often speaks of something bad and lustful, but the word "good" and the surrounding context make it clear that this is for good rather than for evil. In contrast to *oregō*, (which doesn't imply inner motive only outward pursuit) this verb refers to the inward feeling of desire. Taken together, then, *the two terms describe the man who pursues the ministry outwardly because of a driving compulsion inwardly.*

That, Dear Reader, is the call to ministry.

Second, we see all this proven *practically* everywhere we look. It was true of the Apostle Paul, for example. Second Corinthians 5 is about the compulsion of the ministry. In verse 14 he declares: "The love of Christ constraineth us." Even more pointed is 1 Corinthians 9:16, where Paul writes, "Necessity is laid upon me; yea, woe is unto me, if I preach not the gospel!" *This kind of desire transcends mere human desire; it is placed by God; it is given according to His grace.* This is not any man's idea, not something that he desires before the call, not something he chooses to do because it is as good as anything else. Rather, it is something God does in a man's life, and that man can do nothing else. If a man does what Scripture demands of him, a mere human desire will fade, just as we see increasingly today.

We see this principle throughout Scripture for men God called to preach. Not only does it describe God's calling of several prophets (e.g., Jer. 1:1–10; Ezek. 2:1–3; Jonah 1:1–3), it also records the calling of Jesus' disciples by the Lord Jesus Himself (e.g., Matt. 4:18–22; cf. Mk. 1:16–20; Lk. 5:1–11; Jn. 1:35–42). While the specific call of each one is not recorded, Matthew 10:5 specifies that "these twelve Jesus sent forth," emphasizing Jesus' sole power to call and commission. Luke 9:1–2 goes further to say, "Then he called his twelve disciples together, and gave them power and authority over all devils, and to cure diseases. And *he sent them* to preach the kingdom of God" (emphasis added).

At this point, some insist that such examples were only for that time when God called directly and not for today. But such a position is not only inconsistent, it is also dangerous because it clearly implies that biblical precedent (on any issue) is meaningless.

Another key verse is Hebrew 5:4: "And no man taketh this honour unto himself, but he that is called of God, as was Aaron." This verse, of course, speaks of God's calling of the Old Testament priest, but the picture is no less graphic—God calls His servants.

A very unpopular application arises at this point, namely, that God's calling immediately and fundamentally implies that not just anyone can preach, which is the exact opposite of modern opinion. Why? Because not just anyone can disregard all else to *fill* that office and then *fulfill* its responsibilities. A preacher is called of God to preach and *does nothing else.* Many, if not most, people today believe in "lay-preachers," "lay-pastors," and "lay-elders." But these simply do not match the Scripture, no matter how one tries to justify them. Preaching and teaching the Scripture takes the majority of a man's time to prepare for; it is not something that can be done as a "sideline."

Many disagree with that, but please think of it this way: would any of us want a surgeon to operate on us simply because he had read a couple books on how to perform surgery (perhaps one titled, *General Surgery for Dummies*)? Anyone, in fact, could ask the same question of their vocation, such as this: "Could just anyone walk into my office and say, 'Well, I read a couple of books on your job, so I think I can do it as well as you?'" How ridiculous, and if we may be frank, how arrogant! But this is precisely what many do with teaching the Bible. They think that just a little time in the Word, such as reading their Sunday School lesson or reading a couple of commentaries, qualifies them to preach and teach. How tragically wrong (not to mention dangerous) that is! Yes, a pastor has many duties, but the majority of his time must be invested in the study of the Word and prayer so he can adequately prepare to feed God's people. We submit, if this isn't a man's attitude, he does not belong in a pulpit. Martyn Lloyd-Jones comments on "lay-preaching" in his classic book, *Preaching and Preachers*:

> What is the ultimate criticism of what is called 'lay-preaching?' The answer comes to this, that it seems to miss completely the whole notion of a 'call.' There are also other reasons. . . . My main argument is that the picture I have given of the preacher, and what he is doing, insists not only that this is something to which a man is called, but also something that should occupy the whole of his time apart from exceptional circumstances. It is not something which can be done as an aside, as it were; that is a wrong approach and a wrong attitude to it.[9]

The teacher I quoted at the beginning of this article adds this statement, which demonstrates a serious error: "The so-called inner call is due to Calvinistic or Reformed influence." Shouldn't such a statement greatly trouble us? Does it not clearly attack the basic underlying doctrine of the sovereignty of God? Are we to think that a sovereign God leaves the whole matter up to men to decide who will preach? Is this the only area in which God is not sovereign?

The same teacher again objects to the "inward call" based upon the idea that it "[divides] the Church into two classes, the clergy and the laity." Now I must choose my next words very carefully, for I do not want to be misunderstood. Yes, Roman Catholicism (and even Protestantism) have created an artificial and destructive hierarchy of "clergy and laity," but we should also recognize that there *is* a difference between a *shepherd* and a *sheep*—shepherds are to lead and sheep are to follow, and God does call certain men to be shepherds. Some folks really bristle at the word "layman," but that word is neither an insult nor a term that implies inferiority. How many of us, for example, have heard a doctor first describe a medical condition with half a dozen ten-syllable words and then say, "Now to the layman, here's the problem"? Webster, in fact, defines *layman* as "a person who does not belong to a particular profession or who is not expert in some field." *That* is all the word means in this context. As I would be a layman when it comes to the vocations of the men in my church, so is each one of them a layman when it comes to my vocation.

Many people today still react to this by saying, "You just think you are part of an elite group. Or maybe it is just that you're proud and don't want to share the glory with anyone else." On the contrary, one of the main reasons we make this so clear is *for their own protection*. As James declares, "My brethren, be not many masters [i.e., *didaskalos*, teachers], knowing that we shall receive the greater condemnation" (Jas. 3:1). Here is a serious warning that seems to be overlooked by many today. Such would-be teachers, whether a Sunday School teacher, lay-preacher, or other teaching position, have no idea what responsibility they take on when they presume to teach the Scripture. Every person who takes on that task will give an account of it and will be strictly judged for it. James is telling us, in effect, "Be warned! Don't take this on unless God has called you and you have been properly trained for it."

As a pastor, this principle hits me every time I sit down to study in preparation for preaching and teaching. I will answer for what I teach, and it is for that reason that I spend so many hours in study. There are times when I will spend hours, or even days, on one verse, or even a single word, because I want to get it right.

The above attitude of the ministry being a "glorious profession" also shows a total misunderstanding of the ministry. If a man preaches the pure, unaltered Truth, especially in our modern pragmatic, relativistic society, *the last thing he will receive is glory*; rather he will experience resistance, rebellion, and even rage from many, if not most, hearers.

So once again, we are brought back to a distinct call of God, which takes place between Him and His servants. We see once more that this was true of Paul, as Luke records in Acts 13:2: "As they ministered to the Lord, and fasted, the Holy Ghost said, Separate me Barnabas and Saul for the work whereunto *I have called them*" (emphasis added).

Calling is not the end, only the beginning of a long journey. A man must secondly be tested according to the qualifications for leadership (1 Tim. 3:1–7; Titus 1:6–8), thirdly be trained in doctrine and practice (1 Tim. 3:6; 2 Tim. 2:2), fourthly be ordained by other leaders (Acts 14:21–25; 1 Tim. 4:14; 5:22; Titus 1:5;) and then finally be sent forth by the Church (Acts 13:2–3). In other words, *his call must be confirmed by others and then nurtured into use*. But at the very foundation is the irresistible call of God in his life.

The Historical Testimony

As I scoured my library on this issue, a very interesting (and troubling) pattern emerged. While older theologians and commentators consistently recognize the biblical principle of the inward call, most contemporary writers either deny the inward call outright or, more often, simply don't mention the issue at all, as if it is not important enough to deal with. John Calvin, for example, wrote in the 16th-century of "that secret call of which every minister is conscious before God."[10] A century later, the great theologian Francis Turretin wrote:

> The [internal call] is that by which the heart itself is excited by God to consecrate itself to the work of the ministry (of which Paul speaks in 1 Tim. 3:1). . . . By it, a man is conscious before God that he is impelled to undertake this office not by ambition or avarice or any other carnal affection, but from a sincere love of God and a desire to build up the church.[11]

About another century later the great expositor and theologian John Gill wrote:

> There must be a call to the ministry of the Word, both inward and outward, previous to this office; *no man*, under the law, took to himself the honour of the priest's office, but he that was called of God, as was Aaron, Heb. 5:4, 5. Nor ought any man to take upon him the office of a prophet, or minister of the word, without a call; there were some in the times of Jeremiah, complained of by the

Lord, who were not sent nor spoken to by him; and yet prophesied, Jer. 23:21.[12]

Space does not permit us to cite others here,[13] but thankfully, there are also some contemporary Christian leaders who agree. One asks, "How important is the assurance of a special call?"

> The work of the ministry is too demanding and difficult for a man to enter it without a sense of divine calling. Men enter and then leave the ministry usually because they lack a sense of divine urgency. Nothing less than a definite call from God could ever give a man success in the ministry.[14]

Indeed, what man who has been in the ministry for twenty years cannot remember times when he would have quit if it had not been for the fact that *God called him to the ministry no matter what*? Another writes:

> A man who is called to the ministry has an internal desire so strong that it motivates him toward external pursuit of that goal. His desire to minister is so strong that he doesn't have any other option. Ministry is his consuming passion, and he pursues preparation and qualification for that task.[15]

Still another writes this excellent summary:

> The call of God to vocational ministry is different from God's call to salvation and His call to service issued to all Christians. It is a call to selected men to serve as leaders in the church. To serve in such leadership capacities, recipients of this call must have assurance that God has so selected them. A realization of this assurance rests on four criteria, the first of which is a confirmation of the call by others and by God through the circumstances of providing a place of ministry. The second criteria is the possession of abilities necessary to serve in leadership capacities. The third consists of a deep longing to serve in the ministry. The final qualification is a lifestyle characterized by moral integrity. A man who fulfills these four qualifications can rest in the assurance that God has called him to vocational service.[16]

While we rejoice in those statements, and some others we could cite, for the most part the Church is drifting away from this biblical and historical position, and she is reaping the tragic consequences. I would submit, therefore, that Christian leaders who reject the principle of God's sovereign, inward calling of men to His service are (whether knowingly or unknowingly) aligning themselves with *a distinctly modern trend*, a trend that is eroding biblical leadership.

NOTES

[1] C. H. Little, D.D., S.T.D, *Disputed Doctrines: A Study in Biblical and Dogmatic Theology* (The Lutheran Literary Board, 1933).

[2] John Eadie, *A Commentary on the Greek Text of the Epistle of Paul to the Ephesians* (Wipf and Stock Publishers, 1998; reprint of 2nd Edition, 1861), p. 297.

[3] John MacArthur, *New Testament Commentary: 1 Timothy* (Moody, 1995).

[4] D. Martyn Lloyd-Jones, *The Unsearchable Riches of Christ* (Baker), p. 53.

[5] J oseph Thayer, *Thayer's Greek-English Lexicon* (Hendrickson), p. 452.

[6] Spiros Zodhiates, *The Complete Word Study Dictionary: New Testament* (AMG Publishers), p. 1056.

[7] C. H. Spurgeon, *Lectures To My Students* (Zondervan, 1974), pp. 26-27 (emphasis in the original).

[8] Ibid, p. 28 (emphasis in the original).

[9] D. Martyn Lloyd-Jones, *Preaching and Preachers* (Zondervan, 1972), p. 103. This work is highly recommended. It quickly and cuttingly goes to the heart and speaks of what the ministry is and how it's been perverted in recent history.

[10] *Institutes* (Beveridge translation), IV, iii, 11

[11] Francis Turretin, *Institutes of Elenctic Theology* (Presbyterian and Reformed Publishing, 1997), Vol. 3, p. 215.

[12] John Gill, *A Complete Body of Doctrinal and Practical Divinity* (The Baptist Standard Bearer, 1995 reprint of the 1839 edition), p. 866.

[13] E.g., William Ames, William Perkins, Robert L. Dabney, Louis Berkof, and others.

[14] Howard F. Sugden and Warren W. Wiersbe, *When Pastors Wonder How* (Moody, 1973), p. 9.

[15] John MacArthur, *New Testament Commentary: 1 Timothy* (3:1).

[16] James M. George, chapter 6, "The Call to the Ministry," in John MacArthur, Richard Mayhue, and Robert Thomas (editors), *Rediscovering Pastoral Ministry* (W Publishing Group, 1995), p. 102.

Not to desire [Truth] is to despise it.

William Gurnall, *The Christian in Complete Armour*, Vol. I, p. 294

15

Pastor, Bishop, and Elder*

Ephesians 4:11; 1 Timothy 3:1–2; 5:17

And he gave some, apostles; and some, prophets; and some, evangelists; and some, pastors and teachers;

This is a true saying, If a man desire the office of a bishop, he desireth a good work. A bishop then must be blameless, the husband of one wife, vigilant, sober, of good behaviour, given to hospitality, apt to teach;

Let the elders that rule well be counted worthy of double honour, especially they who labour in the word and doctrine.

There is no doubt that one of the most misunderstood, misinterpreted, and misapplied areas of Scripture is that of Church leadership. This is nowhere more vivid than in the identity of three terms: **pastor**, **bishop**, and **elder**. In this chapter, we will briefly examine the meaning of these terms, identify to whom they refer, and note the chief responsibility of the position involved.

The Meaning of These Terms

In our first text we note the word **pastors** (Latin *pāstor*, shepherd), which translates the Greek *poimēn*, which means "shepherd." In Classical Greek, it referred to the herdsman who tended and cared for the sheep. It was also used metaphorically to refer to a leader, a ruler, or a commander. Plato, for example, compared "the rulers of the city-state to shepherds who care for their flock."[1] That meaning was carried over into the New Testament. A pastor is a man who cares for and feeds God's flock.

Teachers, then, is *didaskalos*, which from Homer (8th–7th-century B.C.) onwards was used in the sense of a teacher or tutor. The term covered "all those regularly engaged in the systematic imparting of knowledge or technical skills: the elementary teacher, the tutor, the philosopher, also the

---

* This chapter was originally TOTT issues 19 and 20, February and March 2007.

chorus-master who has to conduct rehearsals of poetry for public performance." This is the sense in which it is used in the New Testament: "Men holding this office had the task of explaining the Christian faith to others and of providing a Christian exposition of the Old Testament."[2] So the Christian teacher is one who systematically imparts Divine Truth and practical knowledge based on the Word of God.

The key to understanding both these terms, however, is that *they refer to the same office; they are not to be separated.* A misunderstanding of this principle leads to a great deal of error. One Greek authority makes this abundantly clear by explaining what is called the "Granville Sharp's Rule":

> . . . when there are two nouns in the same case connected by *kai* (and), the first noun having the article [the], the second noun not having the article, the second noun refers to the same thing the first noun does and is a further description of it.[3]

The same Greek scholar repeats this rule elsewhere and then adds:

> This construction requires us to understand that the words "pastor's and teachers" refer to the same individual, and that the word "teacher" is a further description of the individual called a "pastor." The expression, therefore, refers to pastors who are also teachers, "teaching pastors."[4]

It's interesting that more liberal interpreters either downplay this fact or deny it altogether.[5] This is no doubt due, at least in part, to the fact of little teaching and weak leadership in such groups. To deny this fact of the language, however, is blatant folly. The evidence is overwhelming, and this position is held by the majority of commentators.[6] Martyn Lloyd-Jones excellently summarizes this office:

> Were there two separate offices we would expect to read, "He gave some, apostles; some, prophets; some, evangelists; some pastors; some teachers;" but the apostle writes, "some, pastors and teachers," linking the two together; and generally speaking, these two offices are found in the same man. They apply to a more settled state of the Church, and have persisted throughout the centuries. The office of a pastor is generally concerned about government and instruction and rule and direction. It is borrowed, of course, from the picture of a shepherd. The shepherd shepherds his flock, keeps the sheep in order, directs them where to go and where to feed, brings them against enemies liable to attack them. It is a great office, but unfortunately it is a term which has become debased. A pastor is a man who has been given charge of souls. He is not merely a nice, pleasant man who visits people and has an afternoon cup of tea with

them, or passes the time of day with them. He is the guardian, the custodian, the protector, the organizer, the director, the ruler of the flock. The teacher gives instruction in doctrine, in truth. The Apostle [Paul] proceeds to elaborate this [in verses 12–15], showing that we need to build up, and that we must not remain "babes." We must be protected against "every wind of doctrine," and the way to do so is to give instruction and teaching.[7]

The great 19th-century theologian and commentator Charles Hodge concurs, citing one historical example of those who deviated from the biblical precedent:

> According to one interpretation we have here two distinct offices: that of pastor and that of teacher, but there is no evidence from Scripture that there was a set of men authorized to teach but not authorized to exhort. The thing is almost impossible. The one function includes the other. The man who teaches duty and the basis of it, at the same time admonishes and exhorts. It was, however, on the ground of this unnatural interpretation that the Westminster Directory made *teachers* a distinct class of officers in the Church. The Puritans in New England endeavored to put the theory into practice, and appointed *doctors* [or "lecturers"] as distinct from preachers. But the attempt proved to be a failure. The two functions could not be kept separate. The whole theory rested on a false interpretation of Scripture. *Pastors and teachers*, therefore as most modern commentators agree, must be taken as a twofold description of the same officers, who were simultaneously the guides and instructors of the people. [See note for a further technical discussion.][8]

As much as I love the Puritans, I am compelled to agree with Hodge in pointing out their error in this area.

May we also add that the whole point of the "shepherd" imagery (*poimēn*) is that he meets *all* the needs of the sheep: care, feeding, protecting, exhorting, etc. To divide pastors and teachers into two offices destroys the entire picture. This would have been crystal clear to readers in Paul's day. The idea of one shepherd who fed the sheep and another who tended to their needs would have been totally foreign to them because a shepherd does both. May we further add that 1 Timothy 5:17 clearly puts the two functions together: "Let the elders that rule well be counted worthy of double honour, especially they who labour in the word and doctrine." "Labour" is *kopiaō*, so the idea is literally "to labor to the point of exhaustion in word and teaching." These two functions define the teaching shepherd.

To understand the term *pastor* fully, it is essential that we also understand two other terms, how all three of these relate to each other, and how they came to be used throughout Church History. Few terms are more misunderstood today than these.

First, is the term **elder**, which has Jewish origins. The usual Hebrew word is *zaqen*, which was used to refer to the leaders of Israel, such as the seventy tribal leaders who assisted Moses (Num. 11:16; Deut. 27:1) and through whom Moses communicated with the people (Ex. 19:7; Deut. 31:9). The elders of Israel were mature men. They were heads of families (Ex. 12:21); God-fearing men of truth and integrity (Ex. 18:20–21); full of the Holy Spirit (Num. 11:16–17); and were impartial and courageous men who could be counted on to intercede, teach, and judge righteously and fairly (Deut. 1:13–17).

The New Testament uses the Greek *presbuteros* (English "presbyterian"), which basically means "one who is advanced in years or of mature age." How old exactly we do not know, but the main emphasis in Israel and the early Church was *maturity*. This word was the only commonly used Jewish term that was free from any connotation of either the monarchy or the priesthood. So since the early church was Jewish, it was only natural for this concept to be adopted.

Second, is the term **bishop**, a term that in our day has been encumbered with a lot of ecclesiastical trappings. As we'll see in our next section, however, in the New Testament the term **bishop** (which we find, for example, in that list of leadership qualifications in 1 Timothy 3:1–7) refers to the same person as **pastor** and **elder**. The Greek is *episkopas* (English "Episcopal"), which means "overseer, guardian." Its basic roots are in Greek culture. Emperors appointed bishops to oversee captured or newly-formed cities. I also read that it's possible that it had roots in the Essene Jews of the Qumran community. The Essenes preached, taught, presided, exercised care and authority, and enforced discipline. In either case, the idea is basically the same. The biblical usage is that **elder** refers to the man's person, that is, his *character*, while **bishop** refers to his *position*, that is, a ruler and guardian.

The Identity of These Terms

A major issue in Church History and today is in the division over whether **elder** and **bishop** refer to the same person or different people. *But there is absolutely no doubt whatsoever that biblically they refer to the same person.* While that sounds like a very narrow and dogmatic statement, it is merely historical fact that cannot be disproved. Ninetieth century Church historian Philip Schaff, for example, writes:

The terms elder and bishop denote in the New Testament one and the same office, with this difference only, that [elder] is borrowed from the Synagogue, [bishop] from the Greek communities; and that [elder] signifies the dignity, [and bishop signifies] the duty.[9]

Another 19th-century historian, E. De Pressense, provides further light:

This identity of the office of bishop with that of elder is so very apparent in the New Testament that it was admitted by the whole ancient church, even at the time of the rise of the episcopate . . .[10]

The "episcopate" refers to the practice of a bishop ruling over many churches and their pastors or priests. In other words, even when this practice arose, men knew full well that it was not taught in the New Testament. In short, the rise of the episcopate occurred in deliberate departure from the Scriptural precedent. Still another 19th-century writer, J. M. Hoppin, adds:

. . . [these terms] stand for essentially the same office, and are employed as convertible terms. . . . Neither can it be proved . . . from the New Testament that a higher official standing was assigned to one than to another . . . so that we conclude that these titles all denote the ordinary office of the ministry, as different phases of one office, viewing it from different historical points of view.[11]

Going back further, one of the greatest theologians who ever lived was the 17th-century Francis Turretin, a direct descendent of the 16th-century Reformers. His mammoth three-volume *Institutes of Elenctic Theology* (which I have the blessing to own) were the fruit of some 30 years of teaching at the Academy of Geneva. He dedicates several pages to this important issue. Here are a few highlights:

Bishop and presbyter [elder] are everywhere in Scripture taken for one and the same (so that the difference is only in the name, not in the thing—bishop, with regard to his office and function; presbyter, with regard to his age and dignity), the same characters and the same functions are ascribed to both. . . . We read in Scripture of no ordination of a bishop apart from that of a presbyter . . . *the ancients [Church Fathers] do not attribute this distinction to divine right, but to human custom.*[12]

Turretin then goes on to detail the witness of the Church Fathers, some of whom I'm going to mention in a moment.

Going back even further, John Calvin (writing of course in the 16th-century) maintained that Scripture uses "bishops," "presbyters," and "pastors," interchangeably, and then details some of the particulars of the issue.[13]

The reason we make so much of this is because very early in Church History men deliberately departed from this unmistakably clear biblical truth. As Turretin put it earlier, this distinction did not come from "divine right," but from "human custom." In other words, this did not come by *Divine revelation* but by *human reason*. Men took it upon themselves, by human reason alone, to create a distinction where God never made one and to alter the very foundations of Church order. Men decided that a bishop was to be superior to a priest, elder, or pastor. In fact, this was no doubt the first serious departure from the Word of God after the apostolic days. J. M. Hoppin again tells us:

> . . . the system [of one bishop over] a plurality of churches or of a district . . . began to appear as early as the second century and was fully established in Cyprian's time [i.e., the beginning of the third century].

Is it, therefore, any wonder why we have today every conceivable ministry, program, church office, and method that men can think of? Why? Is it by "divine right?" No. It's because once men began changing what God designed, they continued doing so until what we have today does not even resemble the biblical model.

If that evidence is not enough, the most devastating witness to this change was the 4th-century Roman scholar Jerome, who was unarguably one of the greatest students of the biblical languages in the early centuries of the Church. He states quite boldly and against all the traditions of his day that bishops and elders were originally the same. He wrote:

> A presbyter [elder] and a bishop are the same . . . the churches were governed by a joint council of the [elders]. . . . If it be supposed that this is merely our opinion and without scriptural support that bishop and [elder] are one . . . examine again the words the apostle addressed to the Philippians [1:1, where Paul addresses his letter to bishops and deacons]. Now Philippi is but one city in Macedonia, and certainly in one city there could not have been numerous bishops. It is simply that at that time the same persons were called either bishops or [elders].[14]

But Jerome was not alone. Even before him, the Church Father Hilary stated the same truth. Contemporary theologians of Jerome (such as Chrysostom), as well as his successors (such as Pelagius, Theodore of Mopsuestia, and Theodoret) all acknowledged this fact of Scripture.

So what happened? Again, Jerome gives us the answer. Commenting on the Epistle to Titus, he writes:

> A bishop is the same as a presbyter [elder]. And before dissensions were introduced into religion by the instigation of the devil, and it was said among the people, I am of Paul, and I of Cephas, churches were governed by a common council of presbyters. Afterwards, that the seeds of dissension might be plucked up, all oversight was committed to one person. Therefore, as [elders] know that by the custom of the Church they are subject to him who presides, so let bishops know that they are greater than [elders] *more by custom than in consequence of our Lord's appointment*, and ought to rule the Church for the common good (emphasis added).

While the motive was pure, the action was still wrong. Let us ask a simple question: *does it make sense to combat error by using another error?* It's preposterous! The way to deal with error is to use the Truth.

So again, we see here a deliberate, calculated departure from the authority of the Word of God, a departure that formed the beginning of a clerical hierarchy that continues to this day even in many Protestant and some Evangelical denominations. In his book, *Biblical Eldership*, Alexander Strauch, provides a concise historical summary:

> At the start of the 2nd Century, the overseer (bishop) presides over one local church, not a group of churches. Thus he is called the monarchial bishop. Through the centuries, inordinate authority became concentrated in the bishop. *Unchecked by the New Testament Scriptures*, his role continued to expand. The bishop became a ruler over a group of churches. Some bishops emerged as supreme over other bishops. Eventually they formed councils of bishops. Finally, in the West, one bishop emerged as head over every Christian and every church. But in the churches of the New Testament period, there was no clearly defined, three office system. Instead, there were only two offices as found in Philippians 1:1 . . . elders and deacons.[15]

If I may make an application here, the more I study and observe the Church, both in history and the present, the more I am convinced that most of the problems in Christianity *were* and *are* rooted in this early departure from New Testament Truth. This one change altered the entire course of Church History. When men departed from biblical authority concerning church order, other problems were inevitable, inescapable, and incalculable. That one change *set the precedent* that it was no longer Scripture alone that matters, rather man's opinion about what "fits our needs," or what "will work best in our situation." Instead of God's Word alone being absolute and sufficient, it is considered relative and inadequate.

Putting all three terms together, then, **elder** refers to the man's *character*, **bishop** refers to his *position*, and **pastor** (and "pastor-teacher") refers to his *duty*.

If we now reference other Scripture, there is again no question that all these refer to the same office and person. Acts 20:28 declares:

> Take heed therefore unto yourselves, and to all the flock, over the which the Holy Ghost hath made you overseers, to feed the church of God, which he hath purchased with his own blood.

This is part of Paul's farewell to the Ephesian elders, so he addresses them by this title. He tells them that they are "overseers" (bishops) and that they are to "feed" (*poimēn*, shepherd) the Church of God.

Likewise, Titus 1:5 speaks of appointing elders, verse 7 calls the same men bishops, and verse 9 speaks of the duty of this man, namely, teaching. Peter does the same thing. In 1 Peter 2:25 he views Jesus as Shepherd (feeder) and Overseer (ruler), while in 5:1–4 he uses the words "shepherd the flock," "elder," and "overseers."

The Chief Responsibility of This Office

Our primary "tough text" here is 1 Timothy 3:2, where Paul states that one of the *qualifications* (not just *duties*) of the pastor is that he is **apt to teach**. We submit that it *is* a tough text because its real meaning and significance are often missed or simply ignored.

Those three words are actually only one word in the Greek, *didaktikos*, which appears in the New Testament only here and in 2 Timothy 2:24, where we find the same phrase. Many look at this as superficially as they do the word "desire" in verse 1 and think that anyone can do this just because he wants to (see chapter 14 for a study of this verse and the call to ministry). But this word specifically means "*skilled* in teaching." As one expositor puts it:

> Not merely *given to* teaching, but able and skilled in it. All *might teach* to whom the Spirit imparted the gift: but *skill* in teaching was the especial office of the minister on whom would fall the ordinary duty of instruction of believers and refutation of gainsayers.[16]

The meaning is clear. The point is *not* that "it is a nice quality if a pastor is a good teacher" or that "being a good teacher is certainly a plus," rather *being a good teacher is an absolute requirement to hold that office at all*. If that quality does not exist, a man is not qualified to be a pastor, regardless of how gifted he might be in other areas. In light of our study of the "call" to the ministry, the ability to teach well is an evidence of whether or not a man is truly called. He must be a highly skilled teacher, who works hard in his studies and proclamation. Later in this letter (5:17) Paul writes:

Let the elders that rule well be counted worthy of double honour, *especially* **they who labour in the word and doctrine** (emphasis added).

That is the one qualification that sets him apart from the "deacon" (see our next chapter). Since the primary duty of the overseer is to preach and teach the Word of God, being gifted for that is essential.

Further, it's crucial to note that *this qualification is the only one in the list that relates specifically to a candidate's giftedness and function.* The implication is clear: while this leader has several duties, the primary one, and the one he *must* be specifically gifted for, is teaching.

I have heard certain preachers say, "I'm not really much of a teacher, but I sure love my flock," and have heard certain sheep say, "Well, he's not a good teacher, but he does have a pastor's heart." If I might lovingly submit, while loving God's people is most certainly commendable, if a man is not a skilled teacher, he simply is not qualified for that ministry, for he can't do *the number one thing* his job requires. This is equivalent to a surgeon who does not know how to make an incision or a carpenter who can't use a tape measure.

It's interesting, in fact, that in that entire list of qualifications, "love" is not even mentioned, while being a skillful teacher is high on the list. Now, of course, the pastor loves the sheep, which is understood in the shepherd/sheep analogy and is certainly implied in the word "patient" (v. 3), but Paul specifically says that the candidate *must* be a good teacher. *That is his function!* Men who are not doing that today betray the office and bring shame to Christ.

Unlike today, when many pastors do everything under the sun *except* teach, Paul *repeatedly* emphasized the mandate of teaching in the Pastoral Epistles:

> *1 Timothy 4:6:* If thou put the brethren in remembrance of these things, thou shalt be a good minister of Jesus Christ, nourished up in the words of faith and of good doctrine, whereunto thou hast attained.

> *11–13:* These things command and teach. Let no man despise thy youth; but be thou an example of the believers, in word, in conversation, in charity, in spirit, in faith, in purity. Till I come, give attendance to reading, to exhortation, to doctrine.

v.16: Take heed unto thyself, and unto the doctrine; continue in them: for in doing this thou shalt both save thyself, and them that hear thee.

5:17: Let the elders that rule well be counted worthy of double honour, especially they who labour in the word and doctrine.

2 Timothy 2:24: And the servant of the Lord must . . . be apt [skilled] to teach.

4:1–2: I charge thee therefore before God, and the Lord Jesus Christ, who shall judge the quick and the dead at his appearing and his kingdom; Preach the word; be instant in season, out of season; reprove, rebuke, exhort with all longsuffering and doctrine.

Titus 2:1: But speak thou the things which become sound doctrine.

Even a quick look at the statistics of the Pastoral Epistles, in fact, reveals how central this is. In searching for various related terms, we find the following in the Authorized Version: "teach" (9 times); "teaching" (twice); "preach" (once); "preaching" (twice); "speak" (3 times); "exhort" (8 times); "doctrine" (16 times); "rebuke" (5 times); "reprove" (once).[17] That is a total of at least 47 references to the teaching and preaching ministry of the pastor-teacher, bishop, and elder. Is there any doubt? Should there be any question today?

Still there are those nowadays who think other things are more important. The "minister," or whatever you prefer to call him, is viewed as part administrator, part manager, part philanthropist, and even part entertainer. He is expected to be, and even aspires to be, "well-rounded," that is, someone who can wear many hats, including: businessman, media figure, psychologist, and philosopher. As one commentator astutely observes:

> . . . many of today's ministers spend a great deal of time pastoring and shepherding in the restricted form of pastoral counseling; and few spend much time teaching. The old Scottish ministers used to go from home to home catechizing. They then had an educated congregation.[18]

Oh, how well that would go over in most churches today! Indeed, how few Christians today really know God's Truth. While there is not one single word of Scripture that even implies any of those other so-called "qualities" for a pastor, it makes it clear what he *must* be, from beginning to end—a *teacher.* If he has no teaching ability, if he cannot clearly convey God's truth, he does not belong in the ministry. He, in fact, is not *called* to the ministry at all, for God would not call someone who is not qualified and can be proven to be qualified by other observers.

Showing his continuing concern, the above commentator goes on to write about this qualification:

> [The elder] must be "didactic." The usual translation is "apt to teach." Many elders today, as everyone knows, are not apt to teach . . . the deliberate attack on New Testament regulations shows that some denominations are apostate. They no longer are Christian churches.

Those are certainly strong words for our day, but they are true. If a church does not have preaching and teaching as the core of its ministry, and if it does not have qualified people carrying on that ministry, it is a perversion of the New Testament standard.

A direct corollary to this mandate of the pastor's primary responsibility to teach is stated in Acts 20:32: "And now, brethren, I commend you to God, and to the word of his grace." The context of this verse (vv. 28–35), of course, is that Paul, in a hurry to get to Jerusalem for Pentecost, sends for the elders (pastors) of the church at Ephesus. In one of the most touching scenes in Scripture, we read the counsel and parting challenges Paul gives these dear men of God. Of the six basic responsibilities of the pastor-teacher,[19] the one in verse 32 involves the pastor's responsibility to *study*. "Commend" (*paratithēmi*) speaks of "a deposit, a trust." Preachers have been entrusted with the Word of God, put in charge of its use. What a responsibility this is and one we had better not take lightly!

Again we emphasize 1 Timothy 5:17: **Let the elders that rule well be counted worthy of double honour, especially they who labour in the word and doctrine. Labor** is *kopiaō*, "labor to the point of exhaustion." This must be our approach to the study of God's Word. Most preaching today shows the shallow study of the preacher (if he studies at all). This is so important that Paul said again in his second letter to Timothy (2:15): "Study [Old English, 'be in a state of absorbed contemplation'] to show thyself approved unto God, a workman that needeth not to be ashamed, rightly dividing the word of truth."

So while the number one *responsibility* of the pastor is to feed the sheep, his number one *priority* must be his study time. A preacher who does not spend the majority of his "ministry time" in study and prayer will simply not be able to adequately feed his people. It is as simple as that. Today's "seeker-sensitive," movement where "preaching" is not preaching at all, rather "motivational speaking," accomplishes absolutely nothing spiritual. What God demands from pastors is hours of studying Truth and then feeding it to His sheep. Harry Ironside relates an incident that perfectly illustrates the trend of our day, even though it occurred around 1935:

> I listened to a widely advertised man the other day who was said to be one of the outstanding religious leaders of our day, and for nearly an hour he was telling ministers how to preach. I listened carefully, but I did not hear him quote one verse of Scripture. He quoted from Shakespeare, from George Bernard Shaw, and a number of trashy novels, and he drew his illustrations from ancient and modern literature. Yet he was supposed to be a teacher of preachers. If preachers have to listen to that kind of a teacher it is no wonder they deliver sermons that never could convert one poor sinner.[20]

And look where we are today! It gets harder every day to find men who are truly preaching the Word of God instead of philosophy, politics, pop-psychology, and "warm-fuzzies." Families who have had to leave our church because of the demand of job relocation have shared with me the terrible frustration they've suffered in trying to find a church where the Bible is preached. I once heard pastor and author Dr. Steve Lawson say at a Bible conference that there are some families in his church (Christ Fellowship Baptist Church; Mobile, Alabama) that drive over an hour every Sunday, and even through two other towns, just to hear the Word of God expounded.

Worse is the fact that men are actually being trained to disregard preaching and teaching. Many Bible colleges, seminaries, and pastor's conferences revolve around the latest marketing tools instead of the revealed Truth of God.

Ironside goes on to relate another trend of his day that again parallels ours. He recalls how several years earlier a very well known American pulpit orator stated that "expository preaching is the poorest type of preaching in the world because it leaves so little scope for the imagination." While Ironside doesn't give the name, I strongly suspect he was referring to Henry Ward Beecher (1813–1887), whose philosophy of preaching changed the pulpit forever. Beecher was an orator, showman, and ad-libbed most of what he preached. He prepared his Sunday morning sermon an hour before the service and his evening sermon in the afternoon. His message was dominated by love and the universal fatherhood of God and brotherhood of man, and his delivery was nothing but drama and entertainment. Oh yes, he was enormously popular, as many are today, but he said little that was biblical. Not surprisingly, his theology got progressively more liberal until ultimately he accepted evolution and higher criticism and even rejected eternal punishment and verbal inspiration. And that is exactly what we are seeing today, a steady drift away from Scripture. Ironside is correct when he writes:

Thank God for any kind of preaching that leaves little scope for man's imagination, for the Word of God says, "And God saw that the wickedness of man was great in the earth, and that every imagination of the thoughts of his heart was only evil continually."

Indeed, thank God for any kind of preaching that leaves man out of it. And, oh, would that pastors today recognize the mandate that God has given them!

NOTES

[1] Colin Brown (General Editor), *The New International Dictionary of New Testament Theology* (Zondervan, 1975), Vol. 3, p. 564.

[2] Brown, Vol. 3, p. 766, 768.

[3] Cited by Kenneth Wuest, *The Pastoral Epistles In The Greek New Testament* (Eerdmans, 1952), p. 195.

[4] Kenneth Wuest, Chapter IV, "Greek Grammar and the Deity of Christ," *Treasures from the Greek New Testament* (Eerdmans, 1945).

[5] E.g., Andrew Lincoln, *Word Biblical Commentary: Ephesians* (Word Publishing, 1990), p. 250.

[6] This position held by the majority of theologians and Ephesians commentators: e.g., Augustine, Barclay, Blaikie, Chrysostom, Boice, Gordon Clark, Hendrickson, Hodge, Eadie, Earle, Grant, Grudem, Hoehner, Hughes, Chafer, Lloyd-Jones, MacArthur, Robertson, Roustio, Sproul, Stedman, Vaughn, Vincent, Wiersbe, Wood ("*often* coordinated in the same person"), and Wuest.

[7] Martyn Lloyd-Jones *Christian Unity* (Baker), p. 193.

[8] Hodge, *Ephesians*, pp. 120-1. He continues: "It is true the article is at times omitted between two substantives referring to different classes, where the two constitute one order—as in Mark 15:1 (KJV); the elders and scribes formed one body. But in such a list as that contained in this verse, the rules of the language require "of the teachers" if the apostle had intended to distinguish the teachers from the pastors. Pastors and teachers, therefore, must be taken as a twofold name for the same officers, who were both the guides and instructors of the people."

We should also mention John Eadie's excellent discussion (*Ephesians*, pp. 303-4). As he points out, "those who make a distinction" between the two "vary greatly in their definitions." After outlining several, he concludes that "none of these distinctions can be scripturally and historically sustained."

[9] Philip Schaff, *History of the Christian Church*, Vol. 1, p.491-2.

[10] E. De Pressense, *Early Years of Christianity* (1890).

[11] J. M. Hoppin, *Pastoral Theology* (1884).

[12] Francis Turretin, *Institutes of Elenctic Theology* (Presbyterian and Reformed Publishing, 1997), Vol 3, pp. 200-3 (emphasis added).

[13] *Institutes*, IV.3.8.

[14] *Faith of the Early Fathers*, Vol. 2, p.194

[15] Alexander Strauch, *Biblical Eldership* (Littleton, CO: Lewis and Roth Publishers, 1995), p. 310, Note 26 (emphasis added).

[16] Henry Alford, *Alford's Greek Testament* (emphasis in the original).

[17] "Teach" (1 Tim. 1:3; 2:12; 3:2; 4:11; 6:2, 3; 2 Tim. 2:2, 24; Titus 2:4); "Teaching" (Titus 1:11; 2:12); "preach" (1 Tim. 4:2); "preaching" (2 Tim. 4:7; Titus 1:3; "speak" (1 Tim. 2:7; Titus 2:1; 2:15 2 Tim. 5:14 and Titus 3:2 not appropriate]); "exhort" (1 Tim. 2:1; 6:2; 2 Tim. 4:2; Titus 1:9; 2:6, 9, 15; "Doctrine" (1 Tim 1:3, 10; 4:6, 13, 16; 5:17; 6:1, 3; 2 Tim. 3:10, 16; 4:2, 3; Titus 1:9; 2:1, 7, 10); "rebuke" (1 Tim. 4:1; 5:20; 2 Tim. 4:2; Titus 1:13; 2:15) "reprove" (2 Tim. 4:2).

[18] Gordon Clark, *Ephesians* (Trinity Foundation), p. 138.

[19] 1. Guard his own life and ministry (v. 28); 2. "Feed the church of God" (v. 28); 3. "Oversee," that is, lead the sheep (v. 28); 4. Protect the sheep (vv. 29-31); 5. Study and pray (v. 32); 6. Be free of self-interest (vv. 33-35).

[20] Harry Ironside, *1 Corinthians* (New York: Loizeaux, 1938), pp. 407-8.

Pin not your faith upon men's opinion; the Bible is the touchstone.

The Works of John Owen, Vol. 13, pp. 40–41

16

What About the Deacon and Deaconess?[*]

Acts 6:1–6 and 1 Timothy 3:11

And in those days, when the number of the disciples was multiplied, there arose a murmuring of the Grecians against the Hebrews, because their widows were neglected in the daily ministration. Then the twelve called the multitude of the disciples unto them, and said, It is not reason that we should leave the word of God, and serve tables. Wherefore, brethren, look ye out among you seven men of honest report, full of the Holy Ghost and wisdom, whom we may appoint over this business. But we will give ourselves continually to prayer, and to the ministry of the word. And the saying pleased the whole multitude: and they chose Stephen, a man full of faith and of the Holy Ghost, and Philip, and Prochorus, and Nicanor, and Timon, and Parmenas, and Nicolas a proselyte of Antioch: Whom they set before the apostles: and when they had prayed, they laid their hands on them.

Even so must their wives be grave, not slanderers, sober, faithful in all things.

If there is one area in which the church has clearly departed from biblical authority and sufficiency, it is in the area of church government. Today we have created an entire hierarchy of church government. We seem to think that we must organize and structure everything we do so that nothing gets left out.

As pure as that motive is, however, Scripture is not ambiguous here. In very clear words it declares that there are only *two* recognized offices that cover everything. This is nowhere more clearly stated than in Philippians 1:1: "Paul and Timotheus, the servants of Jesus Christ, to all the saints in Christ Jesus which are at Philippi, with the bishops and deacons." As the trusted commentator Albert Barnes writes on this verse:

> The apostle here mentions but two orders of ministers in the church at Philippi; and this account is of great importance in its

---

bearing on the question about the way in which Christian churches were at first organized, and about the officers which existed in them.[1]

Having briefly examined the "pastor," along with the related terms "bishop" and "elder," we turn to the office of **deacon** (and another supposed one called "deaconess").

The Office of Deacon

During the writing of the original article on which this chapter is based, I had the joy of teaching a deacon training course in our church, which outlined the *reality, requirements, responsibilities,* and *rewards* of the office of deacon. To summarize, as I shared with our men, this office is absolutely crucial to the church. So important is it that the standards for it are no less than those for the elder (pastor and bishop). The only difference between the two is *function*, the latter being required to be a good teacher.

Diakonos (**deacon**) and the related terms *diakoneō* ("to serve"), and *diakonia* ("service") appear approximately 100 times in the New Testament. Only in 1 Timothy 3:11 and Philippians 1:1 are they transliterated "deacon" or "deacons." The rest of the time they are translated by various English words. In other words, only in those two passages is the deacon elevated to official status. The rest of the time the terms are used in a general, nonspecific sense.

So how did the translators know to transliterate the word as the name of an office? The context makes this clear. *First*, Paul has already dealt with the known office of bishop (elder, pastor) and then another is mentioned immediately after that. *Second*, a list of qualifications follows the first office, and then another list appears after that. The list must be referring an office.

Diakonos itself is found twenty-nine times in the New Testament. Let us note three things about this term.

First, its primary meaning was "one who serves at table," but probably included other menial tasks. That definition gradually broadened until it came to include any kind of service in the church. The word group's versatility can be seen in its divergent usage in the New Testament. *Diakonos, diakoneō*, and *diakonia* are variously translated "administration," "cared for," "minister," "servant," "serve," "service," "preparations," "relief," "support," and "deacon," among others. The root idea of serving food comes across in John 2:5, where *diakonos* is used of the waiters at a wedding. *Diakoneō* is used in the same sense in Luke 4:39, where Peter's mother-in-law served a meal. Luke 10:40, 17:8, and John 12:2 also use this word group to refer to serving food.

Diakonos is used to refer to soldiers and policemen who enforce justice

(Rom. 13:4). In John 12:26, Jesus equated *following* Him with *serving* Him; anything done in obedience to Him is spiritual service. In the general sense of the term, all Christians are deacons, for all are to be actively serving Christ and His church. That is Paul's point in 1 Corinthians 12:5, where he writes that "there are varieties of ministries" (*diakoniōn*). Every Christian is to be involved in some form of spiritual service. Leaders, through both teaching and practice, are to equip believers to perform that service (Eph. 4:12).

Second, however, *diakonos, diakoneō,* and *diakonia* □□ are also used in a more specific sense. The list of spiritual gifts in Romans 12:6–8 includes a gift for service. Those with that gift are specially equipped for service, though they may not hold the office of deacon. Stephanas and his family were so gifted. Paul wrote of them, "they have addicted [devoted] themselves to the ministry (*diakonia*) of the saints" (1 Cor. 16:15). These are people that God has especially gifted and seem to just materialize from nowhere when a need for service arises.

Third, this word group refers to the officially recognized responsibility of the office of **deacon.** Yes, first everyone is a deacon in the general sense, and second the Holy Spirit specially gifts for service, but there are still others who are appointed to the office of deacon. They are the models of spiritual service for everyone else to follow. What is their function? *They work alongside the elders, implementing their preaching, teaching, and oversight in the practical life of the church.*

This brings us to a key text, Acts 6:1–6. In spite of what seems to be an obvious reference to deacons here, there are some who, for some inexplicable reason, make it an issue and argue against it. In fact, the basic meaning of "serving tables" is right in the passage, which sets the perfect precedent of what the deacon does—he takes care of temporal matters. Going against older expositors (such as Calvin and many others), however, one contemporary expositor, who I do respect and admire, writes:

> Many hold that the seven men chosen to oversee the distribution of food in Acts 6 were the first official deacons. The text, however, nowhere calls them deacons.[2]

But I must respectfully disagree. While the English *noun* "deacon" is not used for the seven men appointed to serve, the Greek *verb diakoneō* is used twice in verse 1 and the infinitive *diakonia* is used once in verse 2, which as we've seen come from the same root. So why doesn't Luke use the noun here? Undoubtedly because the church is still in its infancy and the office has not yet been defined. The same expositor takes his argument farther and comments:

The book of Acts nowhere uses the term *diakonos* (**deacon**), which seems strange if an order of deacons was initiated in Acts 6. Elders are mentioned several times in Acts (cf. 11:30; 14:23; 15:2, 4, 6, 22–23; 16:4; 20:17), making the omission of any reference to deacons even more significant.

But what is bothersome here is that this is an argument from silence, which is always weak and often even dangerous. Just because the office is not *named* doesn't mean that it didn't *exist*. The Epistles build on the Book of Acts, and the office of deacon that is *named* in the Epistles seems clearly *rooted* in that early situation of Acts 6. This is the consistent position of almost all commentators and expositors and is simply the natural conclusion. We'll come back to this in a moment.

First, let us understand the historical situation. By this time, the Church had already filled Jerusalem and was on the threshold of world evangelism, as stated in 1:8: "But ye shall receive power, after that the Holy Ghost is come upon you: and ye shall be witnesses unto me both in Jerusalem, and in all Judaea, and in Samaria, and unto the uttermost part of the earth." There was now simply too much for the Apostles to handle alone.

Specifically, there were two kinds of Jews in the early Church: Native-born Palestinian (Hebrews) and Grecian-born (Hellenistic). There was, therefore, a natural strain between them. Not only were their languages different, but also the Hebrews looked down on the Hellenists because they assumed the Hellenists had been polluted by heathen culture. Culturally, however, it was actually the Hellenists who were more concerned about widows. They said (and rightly so), "It's wrong to neglect widows." Since the Apostles did not deny this observation, it was obviously a legitimate problem that needed to be addressed.

Verse 2, however, tells us that the Apostles could not take care of this work. In essence, they were saying: "We certainly recognize the problem, but we can't handle it. It's too big and would demand too much of our time. If we spend all our time on temporal matters, we will have to neglect the ministry of the Word of God and prayer, and that we simply cannot do for any reason."

Therefore, seven men were appointed to do this work. But who appointed them? This passage has been used, among other things, to "prove" congregational government—people voting on issues and officers. But the language doesn't support that idea. While it's true that they "set before the apostles" these seven men, it was the *Apostles* who appointed them. In other words, if these men had not been qualified, they would not have been appointed. Congregational rule often elects people who are not qualified and is also quite often not much more than a popularity contest.

Second, we would, therefore, submit four indications that this *is* the first instance of deacons.

1. As noted earlier, the Greek term is present—once in verse 1—"Widows were neglected in the daily ministration [verb *diakoneō*]"—and once in verse 2— "Not reason that we should leave the word of God, and serve [infinitive *diakonia*] tables." Again, some insist, "This is not referring to an *office* because the words are verbs." No, but it is referring to the *function* of the office, which is most certainly named in the Epistles.

2. Early Church History confirms this. We find that the Early Church assigned not only the distribution of food to deacons, but also many other administrative affairs. In fact, the Church at Rome for many years limited the number to seven.

3. Strict qualifications are given even here in Acts 6, not just 1 Timothy 3 and there are obvious similarities. While the office is in its primitive state, strict requirements were still laid down. The tie between the men here and those referred to in 1 Timothy seems so obvious that, frankly, I find arguments against it not only pointless, but just downright silly.

4. Viewing this as the beginning of deacons *sets a precedent* for both the *existence* and *duties* of this office. As to their existence, while the office of pastor (bishop and elder) has a clear precedent in Acts, without Acts 6, we have the office of deacon mentioned in the Epistles but have no precedent in Acts. As to their duties, the expositor I mentioned earlier makes this statement about deacons in 1 Timothy 3 that appears to us to be contradictory:

> No specifics are given in Scripture as to the duties of deacons. They were to carry out whatever tasks were assigned to them by the elders or needed by the congregation.

But a question comes to mind: "If there aren't any specifics as to their duties, then how do we know that they were to carry out whatever tasks that the elders assigned them or that were needed by the congregation?" Acts 6, however, clearly speaks of their duties involving temporal matters. Without Acts 6, therefore, there is no precedent for either the *duties* of the deacon or even the *existence* of deacons. Acts 6 is needed to show both.

What About the Deaconess?

Before leaving this subject, it is essential that we deal with the issue of what is commonly called in our day "the deaconess." The basic reason for the controversy is that the word **wives** (1 Tim. 3:11) is the Greek *gunaikas* (plural of *gunē*), which can also be translated "women." There are some, therefore, who believe that the reference to these women in verse 11 supports the idea of "the female deacon," that is, a specific office called "deaconess."

Frankly, I was shocked to read this view even by one very respected contemporary expositor. By doing so, however, he takes the same position as every liberal does. I believe this to be an important issue, so I want to take a few moments to share ten reasons why I can't even imagine that this refers to an office. The first four reasons directly answer the major arguments that are offered for this being another distinct group.

First, it is argued, the use of **likewise** argues strongly for a third and distinct group here in addition to elders and deacons. But frankly this argument is just plain ridiculous. **Likewise** does not necessarily do any such thing. Paul could have phrased this, "Deacons must have the following qualifications, and their wives likewise." Besides, if these women are deaconesses, why do they need additional qualifications? Paul has already given the qualifications for being a deacon. Should not every person in an office have the same qualifications? As Gordon Clark illustrates, "One does not state the qualifications of a US Senator and then add something additional for red-haired senators, western senators, or women senators."[3]

Second, it is argued, there is no possessive pronoun or definite article connecting these women with deacons. In other words, if Paul were talking about wives, he would have said "their wives." But it's really not unusual for the Greek to omit an article or a demonstrative pronoun. There is, in fact, a possible reason that Paul omitted the pronoun "their." Had Paul inserted "their," a reader would have immediately assumed that he was referring only to the deacon's wives. But instead, before going on with other qualifications for deacons in verse 12 (qualifications that women cannot meet, I might add), he inserts a note regarding the wives of *both* bishops and deacons. As noted earlier, Calvin and many others maintain that this as the natural meaning.

Third, it is further argued, Paul used the word "women" because there was no Greek word for "deaconess," and therefore the word "women" was the only way to differentiate the male office from the female office. But that statement is more accurately only *half* true. While it is true that there is no word for deaconess in the *New Testament*, there is a word in extrabiblical Greek—*diokonissa*—although, to be honest, it is uncertain as to whether this word existed during New Testament times or after. If it did, Paul would surely have used it if he meant "deaconess."

Fourth, one other argument is that Phebe in Romans 16:1–2 is an example of a deaconess:

> I commend unto you Phebe our sister, which is a servant of the church which is at Cenchrea: That ye receive her in the Lord, as

becometh saints, and that ye assist her in whatsoever business she hath need of you: for she hath been a succourer of many, and of myself also.

The word servant is *diakonos*, and some view this as an instance of a deaconess. But this is weak to say the least. The context speaks of service in general and there is no implication whatsoever that this is an office. Phebe was a wealthy and generous woman who simply ministered to the needs around her. And, oh, how we need to understand that this is what service is all about! People today make such an issue of organizing this ministry and that outreach, when that isn't the New Testament standard. As we each see needs, we do what we can to meet them. It is as simple as that.

In addition to answering those four arguments, I would further submit six other points.

Fifth, if this is supposed to be an office, why is it never mentioned again? Why is it not *clearly* defined instead of ambiguously referred to in this one single verse? If it's so important, why not make it unquestionably clear?

Sixth, if deaconess is supposed to be a separate office, why didn't Paul finish listing the qualifications for deacon and then go to deaconess? Why does he deal with deacons in verses 10 and 12 but insert a new office, which he doesn't name, in verse 11? This would be confusing to readers, and some today seem to want to be confused.

Seventh, in the final analysis, why is the office of deaconess even necessary? Any temporal or physical needs are to be met by the deacons. Their wives, as God designed it in the Garden of Eden, are their helpmeets and will aid them as needed. When we keep in mind this original design, this is the most natural and biblical way to view this passage. As John Gill wrote some 200 years ago:

> Some instead of "wives" read "women", and understand them of deaconesses, such as were in the primitive churches; whose business it was to visit the poor and sick sisters of the church, and take care of things belonging to them; but it is better to interpret the words of the wives of the deacons, who must be as their husbands.

Eighth, Scripture does not allow women in place of leadership or authority. The whole concept of deaconess in our day, for the most part, is a way of putting women in such places.

I know this is a very unpopular position in our day of Egalitarianism, but Scripture is clear. Now I want to weigh my next words carefully so as not to be misunderstood—and I certainly do not want to offend—but try as I might, I do not understand how a principle that is so clear, so unambiguous, so beyond any doubt, can be so ignored. Paul could not have been clearer when he wrote these three separate clauses to Timothy: "But I suffer not a woman to teach, nor to usurp authority over the man, but to be in silence" (1 Tim. 2:2). In the meeting and ministry of the Church, a woman is *neither* to teach *nor* have a position of leadership. Men are to lead, and women are to follow. In short, women are to be *learners*, not *leaders*.[4] While many in the Church today don't like this teaching, *that is what the text says*. Even Acts 6:1–6 clearly indicates that only men filled the office of deacon. Despite these facts of the text, however, fewer principles are violated more today than this one. While it is argued that women can lead and teach *women* in public meetings, *not one Bible text says that*. Such interpreters are clearly reading their own views into the text.

Does all this mean that women are inferior to men? NO, NO, a thousand times *NO*. God simply commands this as being in line with His design for the weaker vessel. The issue is not *superiority*, rather *authority*, which in turn results in *responsibility* and *accountability*. That is why God said through James, "Be not many [teachers], knowing that we shall receive the greater condemnation" (Jas. 3:1). Countless Christians today, both men and women, have no idea how foolish they are being to take on the responsibility of teaching, which they are not *called to*, *qualified for*, or *trained in*. It is a sad commentary on the Church that a principle so crystal clear, an issue so beyond doubt that it can still be totally ignored or readjusted for the express purpose of conforming to modern thought.

We would humbly submit, therefore, that to read "deaconess" into 1 Timothy 3:11, which appears in the context of exclusively *male* leadership of the Church, is to pry open the context with a crowbar and hammer the idea into place.

Ninth, I just cannot get past the simplicity of a deacon having to be the "husband of one wife," but a deaconess doesn't have to be the "wife of one husband." If deaconess is an office, then Paul first says that the office of deacon demands that the officer is devoted to his wife, but then says that that there can be female deacons. Huh? It simply does not make sense.

Tenth, and finally, as theologian Charles Ryrie points out:

> No deaconesses are mentioned in any literature until the third-century writing called the *Didascalia*. Here deaconesses appear as a well-recognized and established order of helpers who were either to be virgins or once-married widows."[5]

That statement truly sheds a lot of light. The 3rd-century *Didascalia* ("Teaching of the Apostles") was a revision of the 2nd-century writings called the *Didache* ("Teaching of the Twelve Apostles"). These had much biblical Truth in them dealing with morals, ethics, church practice, and the hope of Jesus' return, but they were not Scripture and added things that were not in Scripture. This clearly demonstrates, therefore, that at the very least, unbiblical *qualifications* were added to a so-called office of deaconess—"virgins or once-married widows" are not listed by Paul but added by men. Is it not very possible, therefore, that even the *office* had been created by men? Indeed, the absence of the office in literature until the 3rd-century *Didascalia* strongly implies that it was a totally man-made position.

I would like to close on a positive note. Whichever position we take on the "tough texts" of this study, what is important is our service to God. No matter who we are, we are to serve and glorify God according to His prescribed methods.

Soli deo gloria (to God alone be the glory).

NOTES

[1] *Barnes Notes on the New Testament.*

[2] John MacArthur, *The MacArthur New Testament Commentary: 1 Timothy* (electronic edition), comment on 1 Timothy 3:8–13.

[3] Gordon Clark, *The Pastoral Epistles* (Trinity Foundation), p. 61.

[4] See chapter 27, "What Does Scripture Say About Women Teachers?" for a deeper study of these issues.

[5] Charles Ryrie, *Basic Theology* (Victor Books, 1986), pp. 419-421.

For God, requiring the first born for His offering and the first-fruits for His service, requireth the first labours of His servants.

Puritan Henry Smith
The Sermons of Mr. Henry Smith, Vol. II, p. 74.

17

What Does the Phrase "Led Captivity Captive" Mean?*

Ephesians 4:8–10

Wherefore he saith, When he ascended up on high, he led captivity captive, and gave gifts unto men. (Now that he ascended, what is it but that he also descended first into the lower parts of the earth? He that descended is the same also that ascended up far above all heavens, that he might fill all things.)

At first glance these verses seem to be an interruption of thought. One would think that after writing the thoughts of verse 7, Paul would just go right to the gifts in verse 11, but he does not do that. Why? Because he thought it necessary to carefully emphasize exactly who bestows these gifts—the Lord Jesus Christ Himself.

This point is crucial. *All spiritual gifts, and especially the leadership gifts in this context, are based upon what God is doing.* Paul emphasizes here how vital leadership is and that it is God alone who is appointing and gifting these leaders, not men who just decide to appoint themselves, not just people in the church who decide that they would like to teach a little bit. The point is, are you gifted to do this, are you called of God and qualified for such leadership? *That* is the question, and it is the question that few today are willing to ask. Men such as Charles Spurgeon in his classic book *Lectures to My Students*, Martyn Lloyd-Jones in his equally enduring *Preaching and Preachers*, and others in the past were aware of this foundation to ministry, but today it is all but lost. (See chapter 14, "Is There a So-Called "Call" to Ministry?")

So it is for that reason that Paul writes what he does in verses 8–10. As the words **Wherefore he saith** indicate, verse 8 is actually a "semi-quotation" of Psalm 68:18 ("Thou hast ascended on high, thou hast led captivity captive: thou hast received gifts for men; yea, for the rebellious also, that the LORD God might dwell among them"). The scene here is that of a victory hymn celebrating God's conquest of the Jebusites and His ascent (represented by the Ark of the Covenant) up Mount Zion (2 Sam. 6—7; 1 Chron. 13). At that time of conquest, soldiers who had been

---

* This chapter was originally TOTT issue 24, July 2007.

captured by the enemy became "re-captured captives," and the spoils of war became the property of the conqueror to give as he wished.

There is obviously a slight discrepancy between Psalm 68:18 and our text. The Psalm reads "*received* gifts *for* men," but Paul writes "*gave* gifts *unto* men." The liberal critic immediately sees a contradiction here, which he thinks argues against the inspiration and infallibility of Scripture. But there is no problem because our Lord did *both*: He received *and* gave. On the one hand, the Son received them from the Father, and on the other, the Son gave them to the Church. As a victorious king would first receive the spoils of war and then distribute them to those who aided in the conquest, so the King of Kings received of His Father and distributed to His Church.[1]

So Paul's words picture the risen, triumphant Savior going into heaven after His battle on earth. With Him He takes certain captives and then gives **gifts** to those who remain on earth. What a thrilling picture!

This does, however, bring up a question: What is the meaning of that odd phrase, **He led captivity captive**? There has been some debate on this phrase. A common teaching views "captivity" as referring to Old Testament saints who though saved were held in some sort of captivity. It is further taught that the Lord Jesus went into Hades (Hell), retrieved them from their captivity, and took them to Heaven.

Such a teaching, however, is rooted in Roman Catholic tradition, *not* Scripture *as it claims.* The Latin term is *limbus patrum*, that is, "limbo of fathers." The literal idea of *limbus* is "fringe or border," and the basic idea in the word "limbo" is "a state or place of confinement." So the teaching in the term *limbus patrum*, which was chosen in the Middle Ages, refers to a place on the border of Hell that, as the *Catholic Encyclopedia* puts it, was the place where "the just who had lived under the Old Dispensation, and who, either at death or after a course of purgatorial discipline, had attained the perfect holiness required for entrance into glory, were obliged to await the coming of the Incarnate Son of God and the full accomplishment of His visible earthly mission. Meanwhile they were 'in prison'" . . . awaiting "the higher bliss to which they looked forward."[2]

We might also interject that a similar teaching is called *limbus infantium* ("children's limbo"), which is the place where unbaptized infants go, according to Catholicism; since they weren't baptized, they can't go to heaven, but because they have done no wickedness, they go a place of happiness and no "positive pain." This is why infant baptism is so strongly emphasized to parents, so that they will be able to see their children again in Heaven.

Further, such teaching does not come even remotely close to the imagery of the phrase. The Greek (*ēchmalōteusen aichmalōsian*) more literally says, "he led captive captivity." *Ēchmalōteusen* is the aorist indicative active of *aichmalōteuō*, to capture, and *aichmalōsian*, the state of being captive, is a noun from *aichmalōtos*, a captive. The picture is rooted in the public triumphs of conquerors, especially as celebrated by the Romans. The language clearly describes the conqueror who took captives, led them away in chains, and then made them part of his triumphal procession.

We find the same expression elsewhere in the Old Testament. In Judges 5:12, for example, Deborah praises the Lord for giving victory over Canaan: "Awake, awake, Deborah: awake, awake, utter a song: arise, Barak, and lead thy captivity captive." The idea is clear, that you will now lead captive him who held you captive. Also in Amos 1:3–6 we read God's pronouncement of judgment on the nations around Israel because they had "carried away captive the whole captivity, to deliver them up to Edom," that is, the Philistines had handed over a large number of Israelites to the cruel Edomites.

So what is Paul saying? As Martyn Lloyd-Jones puts it,

> It is a picture of the Lord Jesus Christ leading in His triumphal train the devil and hell and sin and death—the great enemies that were against man and which had held mankind in captivity for so long a time. The princes which had controlled that captivity are now being led captive themselves.[3]

What a picture! Our Lord is, indeed, the Conqueror of Conquerors, the King of Kings, the Lord of Lords. Those who once held us in bondage are now captives to the Great Conqueror and march in chains before Him.

Paul continues the thought in verses 9–10: **(Now that he ascended, what is it but that he also descended first into the lower parts of the earth? He that descended is the same also that ascended up far above all heavens, that he might fill all things.)** Some interpret this to mean that Christ **descended** into Hell (Latin, *descensus ad inferos*) to accomplish certain things, such as preaching to Old Testament saints or even preaching to lost people, such as those before Noah, to give them a "second chance," or perhaps to proclaim His victory to Satan. But, as John Gill puts it, such ideas are "fictitious and fabulous." They are, of course, usually propped up with 1 Peter 3:19, "By which also he went and preached unto the spirits in prison." But when viewed in its context, the verse obviously does not say anything of the sort, nor does any other Scripture. The verse is best understood as referring to our preincarnate Lord "preaching through Noah to those who, because they rejected that message, are now spirits in prison."[4]

So, then, to where is Paul saying our Lord **descended**? The answer obviously is the earth itself. After all, can one "*ascend*" who did not first "*descend*?" This principle is expressed, in fact, in other Scriptures. Our

Lord Himself declared, "And no man hath ascended up to heaven, but he that came down from heaven, even the Son of man which is in heaven" (Jn 3:13), and then again, "For the bread of God is he which cometh down from heaven, and giveth life unto the world" (6:33), and still again in 6:38, 41, 42, 50, 51, and 58.

With that in mind, however, does **descended** perhaps mean something even deeper? After all, if all Paul wanted to say was that Christ came to the Earth, he could have said it in much simpler terms than referring to **the lower parts of the earth**. We submit, therefore, that it is not just Christ coming to Earth, but *His coming to Earth in the deepest, most profound humiliation possible*. As Philippians 2:7–8 declares:

> But made himself of no reputation, and took upon him the form of a servant, and was made in the likeness of men: And being found in fashion as a man, he humbled himself, and became obedient unto death, even the death of the cross.

This is further substantiated by the Greek for **descended** (*katabainō*), which in its literal meaning simply means "to go down," as when Jesus came down from the mountain after His Sermon on the Mount (Matt. 8:1) or when the angel of the Lord told Philip to go down from Jerusalem to Gaza (Acts 8:26). But as Greek authority Joseph Thayer writes, there is a figurative meaning of this word, "to be cast down to the lowest state of wretchedness and shame."[5] This meaning is found in Matthew 11:23, where our Lord said of Capernaum that though it had been "exalted unto heaven," since He had chosen it as His headquarters, it would "be brought down to hell: for if the mighty works, which have been done in thee, had been done in Sodom, it would have remained until this day." It's interesting that there is no record that the inhabitants persecuted Him or even mocked Him, but simply because of their indifference, their sin was more wretched than even Sodom's.

Think, then, of the humiliation of our Lord. He set aside His heavenly glory and was born a man, was born of peasant stock in stable, was born in the less than significant Nazareth (Jn. 1:46), experienced all the weaknesses and temptations of humanity, was mocked by the masses, scorned by His own family, rejected by His own nation, nailed to a Roman cross as the worst of criminals, buried in a borrowed tomb, and then forgotten by everyone except only a few loyal followers.

That is the view of several expositors,[6] and I am convinced that it is correct because only against that backdrop could we then see the true glory of His ascension, for He **ascended up far above all heavens**. As Calvin put it, "If ever there was a time when, after appearing to lay aside the brightness of his power, God ascended gloriously, it was when Christ was raised from our lowest condition on earth, and received into heavenly glory." In other words, if there is anything that illustrates the lowest ascending to the highest, it is our Lord. Paul here adds to the ascension story told by Luke (Lk. 24:50–52; Acts 1:9–11) by telling us more specifically where our Lord went. While John 3:13 (and the other texts mentioned earlier) declare that He "ascended *up* to heaven" and "came *down* from heaven," Paul specifies that He went **far above all heavens**, that is, above the atmosphere, above the stars, beyond the universe, into the third heaven and to the very Throne of God, where He now sits at the Father's right hand (Heb. 8:1; 10:12; 12:2). As commentator John Eadie aptly phrases it, "As His humiliation was so low, His exaltation is proportionately high."[7] As noted earlier, Philippians 2:7–8 speaks of His humiliation, but verses 9–11 immediately go on to declare:

> Wherefore God also hath highly exalted him, and given him a name which is above every name: That at the name of Jesus every knee should bow, of things in heaven, and things in earth, and things under the earth; And that every tongue should confess that Jesus Christ is Lord, to the glory of God the Father.

And what was the purpose of this? Paul tells us that Christ did it to **fill all things**. Fill is *plēroō*, "to render full, to complete." He did it all to complete God's plan of salvation and to fulfill God's plan for the Church. And what a completion it is! Our Lord **descended** to the lowliest state and suffered the lowliest death, but then He rose again, led our enemies into captivity, **ascended** gloriously into Heaven, and left behind great **gifts** that His redeemed people can use to carry on ministry.

We emphasize this in dramatic contrast to today's distorted emphasis on spiritual gifts. There are many today who teach that every believer must "seek their spiritual gift." We hear such things as, "Here are four principles on how to find your spiritual gift," or, "You have got to find your gift before you can ever serve God." But we would humbly submit that this emphasis is incorrect. Nowhere in Scripture are we instructed to "seek our gift." Spiritual gifts are not to be *sought*; they are to be *received*. Receiving a spiritual gift is like receiving any other gift; we do not solicit it or expect it, rather we receive it when the giver decides to give it. The single key to understanding this is found in the word *yieldedness*. We are to be totally yielded to Christ. When we are yielded, God will then give the gift or gifts (in the amounts He wills) that will glorify Him and edify the Church the most.

NOTES

[1] This seems further indicated by the reading of the ancient Syriac Peshitta (a 2nd Century Bible version), which translates the Hebrew word as "gave." As John R. W. Stott writes, "Evidently this was already a traditional interpretation" (*God's New Society* [Downers Grove: IL: Intervarsity Press, 1979), p. 157).

F.F. Bruce is even more significant: "An early targumic rendering [Targums are oral paraphrases of the OT committed to writing in 2nd and 3rd Century A.D.] is found in the Peshitta:

'Thou hast ascended on high;
thou hast led captivity captive;
thou hast given gifts to men.'

"A later amplification appears in the traditional Targum on the Psalter, which provides the text with a life-setting far removed from Jerusalem under the monarchy:

'Thou hast ascended to the firmament, prophet Moses;
thou hast led captivity captive;
thou hast taught the words of the law;
thou hast given gifts to men.'

"Paul and other NT writers occasionally give evidence of using targumic renderings (or renderings known to us nowadays only from the Targums), especially where such renderings are better suited to the argument to which they are applied than the Hebrew or Septuagint wording would be. Even when a written Targum is quite late, the renderings it presents often had a long oral prehistory. However far 'thou hast given gifts to men' deviates from 'thou hast received gifts among (from) men,' it circulated as an acceptable interpretation in the first century A.D." (F. F. Bruce, *The Epistles to the Colossians, to Philemon, and to the Ephesians* (Grand Rapids, MI: Eerdmans, 1984).pp. 342-3).

In the typical liberal fashion of modern textual critics, Andrew Lincoln prefers to call the Peshitta reading a possible "corruption, which makes its value as evidence precarious" (*Word Biblical Commentary: Ephesians* [Dallas: Word Publishing, 1990], p. 242).

[2] "Limbo" in *Catholic Encyclopedia*, Classic 1914 Edition (http://www.newadvent.org/cathen).

[3] Martyn Lloyd-Jones, *Christian Unity: An Exposition of Ephesians 4:1-16* (Grand Rapids: Baker, 1982), p. 153.

[4] *Ryrie Study Bible* (NASB). John Gill expands, "The plain and easy sense of the words is, that Christ, by his Spirit, by which he was quickened, went in the ministry of Noah, the preacher of righteousness, and preached both by words and deeds, by the personal ministry of Noah, and by the building of the ark, to that generation who was then in being; and who being disobedient, and continuing so, a flood was brought upon them which destroyed them all; and whose spirits, or separate souls, were then in the prison of hell, so the Syriac version renders it . . . in hell . . . so that Christ neither went into this prison, nor preached in it, nor to

spirits that were then in it when he preached, but to persons alive in the days of Noah, and who being disobedient, when they died, their separate souls were put into prison, and there they were when the apostle wrote: from whence we learn, that Christ was, that he existed in his divine nature before he was incarnate, he was before Abraham, he was in the days of Noah; and that Christ also, under the Old Testament, acted the part of a Mediator, in his divine nature, and by his Spirit discharged that branch of it, his prophetic office, before he appeared in human nature; and that the Gospel was preached in those early times, as unto Abraham, so before him" (*John Gill's Exposition*).

[5] *Thayer's Greek – English Lexicon of the New Testament*, p. 329

[6] E.g., Albert Barnes, John Calvin, John Gill, William Hendrickson, William Kelly, Martyn Lloyd-Jones.

[7] John Eadie, *A Commentary on the Greek Text of the Epistle of Paul to the Ephesians* (Eugene, OR: Wipf and Stock Publishers, 1998; reprint of 2nd Edition, 1861), p. 296.

The Papists, therefore, make themselves guilty, who eke out Scripture with their traditions, which they consider equal to it. The Council of Trent says, that the traditions of the church of Rome are to be received pari pietatis affectu, with the same devotion that Scripture is to be received; so bringing themselves under the curse. Rev xxii:18. "If any man shall add unto these things, God shall add unto him the plagues that are written in this book."

Puritan Thomas Watson
A Body of Divinity, 1992 reprint, p. 30

18

What About the Head Covering?*

1 Corinthians 11:2–16

As noted in the Appendix—the reader might want to read it first before continuing here—there are no less than twelve priciples for interpreting literature, including biblical literature. Using those principles, this chapter develops the biblical teaching on a specific subject. While we could choose from many subjects, one that caught my interest during the original writing of these studies on interpretation was that of head coverings on women. What does Scripture really say about this? Should women today wear a head covering? Let us apply these principles (except the Paradox Principle, as it does not apply) to find out.

The Reverence, Diligence, and Illumination Principles

These three principles must always be the foundation of any study we do. We must not approach the Word of God flippantly or nonchalantly. Neither should we approach it with any preconceived ideas. Further, we must not approach it without a dependence upon the Holy Spirit's teaching. So, as we approach our main text, 1 Corinthians 11:2–16, let us do so with reverence, diligence, and dependence.

The Plain Principle

Applying this principle immediately reveals one important truth: *this passage does not command women to wear a covering*. There are those who use this text to teach that a woman must wear a hat, a scarf, or other article to cover the head, but the text clearly does not say that. In other words, this passage does not *mandate* a head covering.

It's also significant that the covering Paul speaks of is simply a metaphor, or illustration, of submission. Unlike the allegorical approach to interpretation, which *reads* allegory *into* the text, Paul clear *states* that the covering *is* symbolic. When he says **the head of the woman is the man**, it's obvious that a man is not the literal head of a woman, rather he is the authority over her, as Christ is the authority over him.

---

* This chapter was originally TOTT issue 28, November 2007.

Applying the Plain Principle here also destroys today's common teaching that women can preach, teach, and lead in church meetings (see chapter 27). The teaching comes from the words **every woman that prayeth or prophesieth with her head uncovered dishonoureth her head** (v. 5). But if we take the Scripture plainly, this verse says nothing about church worship. We must not read anything into the text that is not there. As we'll point out later, Paul refers here to a woman praying or **prophesying** (that is, proclaiming the Truth) in public places, not in congregational meetings.

The Grammatical Principle

The Greek word translated **uncovered** in verse 5 is the Greek *akataka-luptos*. The root *katakaluptos* means "to cover with a veil." This veil was not just a hat or other such article that covered the top of the head, rather it was the common eastern veil that covered the entire face except for the eyes. This word appears in the Septuagint (the Greek translation of the Old Testament) in Exodus 26:34, where Moses hides the ark behind a curtain, and in Isaiah 6:2, where the seraphim cover their faces before the glory of God. So, the language clearly demonstrates that the **covering** was actually a veil. Those who teach that the covering is for today are clearly not doing what the language teaches. Why do they not teach that the woman should be veiled? Because, as we'll see in a moment, Paul was dealing here with a local custom. How many Christian ladies today would be willing to go out of their houses with their faces totally veiled?

The word **covering** in verse 15 is a different Greek word, *peribolaion*, which refers to a cloak, wrap, cape, outer garment, or a mantle. It seems that Paul uses it here to reemphasize a covering for the head. In this case, as we'll see later, it is actually the woman's hair that can be her **covering**. The Greek behind **for** (*anti*) in verse 15 substantiates this fact, as it carries the normal meaning of "in place of" or "instead of." In Luke 11:11, for example, where Jesus asks, "If a son shall ask bread of any of you that is a father, will he give him a stone? or if he ask a fish, will he *for* [instead of] a fish give him a serpent?" James also uses this word. He points out that some people say, "To day or to morrow we will go into such a city, and continue there a year, and buy and sell, and get gain." He then adds, "*For* [instead] that ye ought to say, If the Lord will, we shall live, and do this, or that" (Jas. 4:13, 15). So, Paul is saying that a woman's hair can be worn as a symbol of submission *instead* of a literal veil. (We will see another grammatical point in the next principle.)

The Historical Principle

This principle strongly substantiates the Grammatical Principle, for again, the so-called **covering** was actually a veil. As the classic work *Manners and Customs of Bible Lands* points out:

> The veil was the distinctive female wearing apparel. All females, with the exception of maidservants and women in a low condition of life, wore a veil. They would usually never lay it aside, except when they were in the presence of servants, or on rare occasions. This custom has prevailed among the Eastern women down to the modern era. When traveling, women may throw the veil over the back part of their head, but if they see a man approaching, they place it back in its original position. Thus Rebekah, when she saw Isaac approaching her camel caravan, covered her face with her veil (Gen. 24:64, 65). When women are at home they do not speak to a guest without being veiled and in the presence of maids. They do not enter the guest's chamber, but rather, standing at the door, they make it known to the servant what is wanted (See 2 Kings 4:12, 13). It is well to remember that prostitutes went unveiled. Today, as in olden times, virgins and married women may be seen wearing veils in Bible lands. The old customs are not being observed strictly by some Moslem Women, for they are now going unveiled.[1]

Furthermore, the weight of historical evidence indicates that the wearing of a veil was a universal custom in the 1st-century in both Jewish[2] and Greco-Roman[3] culture. This historical fact has been understood for centuries. Puritan Matthew Henry (1662–1714), for example, taught, "To understand this, it must be observed that it was a signification either of shame or subjection for persons to be veiled, or covered, in the eastern countries, contrary to the custom of ours, where the being bare-headed betokens subjection, and being covered superiority and dominion."

Even the briefest historical look at the city of Corinth reveals what the situation was. Corinth was an extremely pagan and immoral city. Women of loose morals, especially the prostitute priestesses in the Temple of Aphrodite, didn't wear veils and kept their hair short to differentiate them from other women. There was also a strong spirit of feminism (women's liberation). Women didn't want children because it ruined their bodies and restricted their freedom, they demanded the same jobs as men, they dressed and acted like men, and they cast off all signs of femininity. History records, for example, that women of that time did such masculine things as wrestling, sword throwing, and running bare–breasted while hunting wild boars. One of the first symbols of this liberation was that they took off their veils. So, the feminists took off their veils as a protest and the prostitutes took them off to advertise.

Apparently, Christian women were lured into this practice, as they have been in our day in different expressions. It's quite possible that the principle of Christian liberty ("all things are lawful") had been turned into license. As a result, the women threw off their veils and their place of submission. Again, just like today. Paul, therefore, reminds them that the veil was a symbol of their submission to their husbands.

Another extremely important historical and grammatical point in the passage is the Greek word behind **such** (*toioutos*) in verse 16, which means "such as this, of this kind, or sort." What is particularly interesting is that most of the popular English translations wrongly translate the word as "other" (NIV, NASB, NLT, NCV, RSV), despite the clear fact that it means **such**, *never* "other." The implication then is, "There is no need to argue with anyone on these issues because we have no *other* custom." But that is an *interpretation*, not a translation and is not what Paul is saying. To illustrate, as does commentator Gordon Clark, "If someone asks me, does your family always eat turkey on Thanksgiving?—and I answer, we have no *other* custom, it means that we eat turkey. However, if I reply, "We have no *such* custom, it means that we do not eat turkey."[4] So, if we follow the modern translations, Paul is saying that we do, indeed, follow the customs mentioned earlier, *but that is the exact opposite of what he is saying.* He is saying, in fact, we have **no *such* custom** (as the KJV, NKJV, Young's Literal, ASV, and ESV rightly say), which underscores again that such practices are cultural. In other words, there is no reason to be **contentious** because the covering issue is a cultural one.

This leads us right to the Contextual Principle.

The Contextual Principle

The point of this entire passage is *submission*, not the wearing of clothing. Just as there was nothing right or wrong in the eating or not eating of meat that had been sacrificed to idols, which Paul just dealt with in 10:23–33 (see also Rom. 14:1—15:6), there was nothing intrinsically right or wrong in wearing or not wearing a veil. As long as clothing is modest, it meets the Scriptural demand (1 Tim 2:9).

The purpose of the veil, then, was to be a public testimony of a woman's submission to her husband. The word **head** is the key here. A man is responsible directly to Christ as his head and doesn't wear a veil because he is the image of God as a ruler. A woman, however, is directly responsible to her husband as her head. This is dramatically illustrated in verse 7. Here we see that the man is *both* **the image and glory of God**, while the woman is only the **image of God**, but the **glory of man**. While the *man* was made to demonstrate *God's* authority, will, and glory, the *woman* was made to demonstrate the *man's* authority, will, and glory. Further, the man illustrates the magnificent creature God created from Himself, while the woman illustrates the magnificent creature God made from a man. Many people today don't like this principle, and neither did most Corinthians like it, but it's still true.

In light of the throwing off of this principle in Corinth, it was absolutely necessary for Paul to restate it, just as God stated it when Adam sinned. Genesis 3:16 plainly declares, "Unto the woman he said, I will greatly multiply thy sorrow and thy conception; in sorrow thou shalt bring forth children; and thy desire shall be to thy husband, and he shall rule over thee." The Hebrew for "rule" (*masal*) means "to install in an office, to elevate to official position." Man and woman were once "co-rulers," as the word "them" in Genesis 1:27–28 clearly demonstrates, but the husband was now installed as the ruler.

Even more dramatic, however, is the phrase "your desire shall be for your husband." This phrase does not mean what we might first think; it doesn't mean "a desire to please." In fact, it means quite the opposite! "Desire" comes from an Arabic word which means "to compel, to urge, or to seek control." It appears in only one other place, where we find it in the same construction as here. In Genesis 4:7 we read of Cain's anger and God's encouragement that he could still bring the correct offering. The latter part of the verse reads, "If thou doest not well, sin lieth at the door. And unto thee shall be his desire, and thou shalt rule over him." The same meaning is here in 3:16. Literally, it says, "Your desire will be to control your husband, but he will rule over you." We therefore see that *this is the curse*! It is from here that the "battle of the sexes" came. "Women's Liberation" is nothing but women trying to rule, and "Male Chauvinism" is nothing but men trying to squelch the rebellion.

If I may interject, the home life of many Christians today is in shambles because the wife "rules the roost." Neither does this mean that the husband should act like Napoleon. It means that he is to lead his home in accordance with God's Word. And may we add, every man will stand before God and give an account for how he led his family.

So again, the veil was a symbol of a wife's submission to her husband. It was a public testimony of a wife's recognition of her husband as being her head, a testimony that was in direct contrast to the spirit of rebellion that prevailed in Corinth.

Perhaps the pivotal verses concerning this issue are verses 14–15, **Doth not even nature itself teach you, that, if a man have long hair, it is a shame unto him? But if a woman have long hair, it is a glory to her: for her hair is given her for a covering**. These verses should clear up any question about the veil being a mandate for today. As mentioned earlier, the word **for** is the Greek *anti*, which carries the normal meaning of "in place of" or "instead of." Why is long hair a shame for man? Because it's a covering, and a man is not to be covered (v. 7). How ridiculous a man would look in a veil! But a woman has long hair simply because she needs "a veil." Her hair is a glory to her as she is a glory to her husband, and it serves as a veil, a symbol of her submission. When you compare the first part of the passage with the last part, it becomes clear that regarding the head covering Paul first talks about *custom* but then talks about *nature*, that is, what God designed. If custom does not require a veil to symbolize submission, as it did because of the situation in Corinth, then a woman's hair is enough to symbolize that submission.

The Comparison Principle

As we saw in the Plain Principle, this passage does not mandate or command the wearing of a veil. When we now apply the Comparison Principle, we discover that no such command appears anywhere in Scripture. We must not mandate that which God does not mandate, for when we do, we degenerate into legalism.

As also pointed out in the Plain Principle, some teachers use this passage to teach that women can preach, teach, and lead in church meetings, but plainly the text does not say that. Other Scriptures clearly forbid women from teaching in church meetings (1 Cor. 14:34) or usurping authority over a man (1 Tim. 2:12). This praying and **prophesying** (that is, proclaiming the Truth) must refer to a women's public witnessing. This, too, coincides with other Scripture. A woman can teach children and other women (Titus 2:3–4), and nowhere does the Scripture prohibit a woman from witnessing even to a man, but she is never permitted a leadership role over men.

The Outline Principle

As one reads this passage, Paul's progression of thought emerges. As we've seen, the point of this passage is submission, not the wearing of clothing. With that in mind, then, we see at least three points. First, we see The Statement of the Principle (v. 3), which is that of headship. Second, we see The Development of the Principle (vv. 4–12), which is that a man does not veil himself because he is the image of God as a ruler, but a woman is to veil herself because she is to demonstrate the man's authority, will, and glory. Third, we see The Application of the Principle (vv. 13–16), which is that to demonstrate her submission, the woman is to be veiled. The method of the veiling might demand a literal veil, as was the case in Corinth, or her veil can be her hair if no other symbol is needed.

The Progressive Principle

This passage provides us with another example of the Progressive Principle, that God reveals His Truth in steps. As mentioned earlier, the custom of wearing a veil goes back millennia, but Paul now reveals the next step in the progression. He emphasizes that it is not the *symbol* of submission that is the most important, rather the *reality* of submission that's crucial. If custom permits, a woman's hair can just as effectively demonstrate her submission to her husband as can a literal veil. Why? Because submission is a matter of attitude. After all, is it possible for a woman who wears a covering to still be unsubmissive? Of course. So, as always, Paul takes us past forms and symbols to emphasize reality and truth.

The Practical Principle

As always, we do not apply this principle until last. Oh, how much damage is done by quick application! We must first see what God says by painstaking study before we can apply it. And again, the interpretation process uncovers the application. We don't have to *look* for the application, for it becomes self-evident. At least three applications flow from the study of this issue. First, every man should be reminded of his submission to God. Second, every woman should be reminded of her submission to her husband. Third, every Christian should be reminded not to add artificial symbols to Christian living.

As we close this issue, let us notice that we did not come to our position quickly. Indeed, we have taken several pages to examine this subject. This should again emphasize that biblical interpretation demands diligence. This should encourage us to practice such diligence always in our study of the Word of God.

NOTES

[1] Fred Wight, *Manners and Customs of Bible Lands*, CD-ROM computer version; electronic text (c) 1995 Epiphany Software.

[2] As in the apocryphal book 3 Maccabees 4:6; the Mishna, *Ketuboth* 7.6; and the Babylonian Talmud, *Ketuboth* 72a-b. Cited by David K. Lowery in *The Bible Knowledge Commentary* (Wheaton: Victor, 1983), p. 529.

[3] As in Plutarch, *Moralia* 3.232c; 4.267b; and Apuleius, *The Golden Ass* 11.10.

Cited by David K. Lowery in *The Bible Knowledge Commentary*, p. 529.

[4] Gordon H. Clark, *1 Corinthians* (Jefferson, Maryland: The Trinity Foundation, 1975), p. 177.

"And the Philistines were afraid, for they said, God is come into the camp. And they said, Woe unto us! for there hath not been such a thing heretofore." The Israelites probably made the same mistake, fixing their hope on this new method of fighting the Philistines, which they hoped would bring them victory. We are all so apt to think that the new plan of going to work will be much more effective than those that have become familiar; but it is not so. It is generally a mistake to exchange old lamps for new. "There hath not been such a thing heretofore." There is a glamour about the novelty which misleads us, and we are liable to think the newer is the truer. If there has not been such a thing heretofore, some people will take to it for that very ready. "Oh," says the man who is given to change, "that is the thing for me!" But it is probably not the thing for a true-hearted and intelligent Christian, for if "there hath not been such a thing heretofore," it is difficult to explain, if the thing be a good one, why the Holy Ghost, who has been with the people of God since Pentecost, and who came to lead us into all truth, had not led the Church of God to this before. If your new discovery is the mind of God, where has Holy Scripture been all these centuries? Believing in the infallible Word and the abiding Spirit, I rather suspect your novelty; at least, I cannot say that I endorse it until I have tested it by the Word of God.

Charles Spurgeon
Metropolitan Tabernacle Pulpit, Vol. 38, pp. 25-36

19

What Does "Fall Away" Mean?[*]

Hebrews 6:4–6

For it is impossible for those who were once enlightened, and have tasted of the heavenly gift, and were made partakers of the Holy Ghost, And have tasted the good word of God, and the powers of the world to come, If they shall fall away, to renew them again unto repentance; seeing they crucify to themselves the Son of God afresh, and put him to an open shame.

Right up there with the identity of the "Sons of God" in Genesis 6 (see chapter 5 for a study of this), the meaning of "fallen away" in Hebrews 6:4–6 is among the major "tough texts" of Scripture. This is, indeed, a puzzling passage.

Before we begin our study, I want to mention again the TOTT mission statement that we print in every issue. We recognize that godly and scholarly men differ with the views we share here, and we respect each one. We reemphasize this here because this text is particularly controversial.

That said, it is insisted by some Bible teachers that this passage means that a Christian can lose his salvation, whether through apostasy, willfully turning one's back on Jesus Christ and returning to the old life, or some other sin. That idea must be rejected immediately, however, because the only teaching that is more heretical than the idea of losing salvation is one that teaches that salvation comes either wholly or partly by works. The evidences for the security of the believer are numerous and unmistakable (e.g., Jn. 10:27–29, Rom. 8:15–17; 35–39; Heb. 10:10, 12, 14; 1 Peter 1:3–5; etc.). To deny the security of the believer is not only to deny grace but even question the very character of God.

We should also point out that those today who teach that it is possible to *lose* one's salvation also teach that one can *get it back*. This passage, however, says that it is impossible for those who have fallen away to be [renewed] again unto repentance. The view that this passage teaches the loss of salvation is, therefore, self-refuting.

Another interpretation is that this refers only to a purely hypothetical situation, that is, *if* a Christian *could* lose his salvation, there remains no

---

[*] This chapter was originally TOTT issue 29, December 2007.

provision for repentance because Christ died only once, which is therefore another proof for the security of the believer.

Again, while we respect those who differ with the view we will defend in just a moment, we humbly submit that it is puzzling that any interpreter would read salvation into this passage, for it clearly is not here. No one is spoken of as exercising saving faith, being justified, redeemed, saved, born again, sanctified, or any other term normally used in Scripture to indicate true salvation. The reverse is also true, namely, that no term that is used here is ever used elsewhere to refer to salvation.

Still another view is that this refers not to *salvation* but to *Christian service*; that is, it is a warning of the danger of a Christian moving from a position of true faith and life to the extent of becoming disqualified for further service. This, however, as we will see, does not fit the context. Let us, therefore, examine this controversial passage by first examining the text and then considering an implication that some teachers do not wish to face.

The Text

What is this passage all about? In light of our recent study of biblical interpretation, it is the principle of *context* that is the foundation for understanding this passage. The word **For** immediately points back to what has already been stated. While we will go deeper in a moment, Harry Ironside writes this summary:

> There were many Hebrews who in the beginning professed to acknowledge the Messiahship of Jesus and were eye-witnesses of the marvelous things that took place at Pentecost and afterwards. But as the Lord did not return and the promised Kingdom was not immediately established, it was easy to understand how many of these, if lacking personal faith in Christ as Saviour, would eventually give up the Messianic confession and go back to Judaism which they knew to be a divinely revealed religion. This was a very serious thing, and yet it was something to which all these Hebrews would be exposed if they did not make a clean break with Judaism and go on to the perfection of Christianity. As to those who had already apostatized, it was too late to help them. They had made their choice and acted accordingly; and having experienced so much that was new and wonderful and then turned away from it all, they would be the hardest people on earth to change again. It is impossible, we are told, to renew again to repentance those once enlightened.[1]

Another expositor, E. Schuyler English, likewise emphasizes the word **For** as taking "us back to what has been discussed." He goes on to explain exactly what that was:

> ... there were some who ... while professing to be Christians, were still clinging to the ordinances and typology of the old economy, still relying upon the Old Testament sacrifices and Mosaic institutions, and still looking at Christ in His life rather than in His death and resurrection; and it is a warning lest some of the readers of the epistle might be in such a classification.[2]

This "explanation," as another commentator puts it, "seems most consistent with the context and with the rest of the New Testament."[3]

Let us now turn to the five specific privileges these people enjoyed, *while still not exercising saving faith.*

First, they **were once enlightened**. The Greek verb here is *phōtizō* (English "photo"), which means "to give light, to shine" and does not imply salvation, that is, what someone *does* with the light. Just as one might close their eyes in a lighted room, for example, and choose not to use the light, a person can choose to ignore the spiritual light that God has given.

John 1:9–10, for example, declares that "the true Light, which lighteth every man that cometh into the world. He was in the world, and the world was made by him, and the world knew him not." While Christ's coming **enlightened** the whole world, not every person believes. Just two verses before, we read that John the Baptist "came for a witness, to bear witness of the Light, that all men through him might believe," but again, while the Light came, not all believe it. As commentator E. Schuyler English points out, in fact, "whenever a man or woman hears the gospel of salvation in Christ, he is enlightened . . . but many, loving darkness rather than light, flee from its radiance."[4] Another example appears in Matthew 4:16, where Jesus declares that He had come to fulfill the prophecy of Isaiah 6:2, which declares, "The people that walked in darkness have seen a great light." Just because the people *saw* the Light does not mean that they *believed* the Light.

"Enlightenment," therefore, simply refers to intellectual awareness of something and does not imply either accepting it as true or, much less, receiving it as life changing. The people pictured in our text saw the light, were mentally aware of it, and perhaps even mentally assented to it, but they most certainly did not receive the light in the fullest sense; saving faith is nowhere to be found here. So strong was their mental state, in fact, that they were **once** (that is, "once for all," aorist tense) **enlightened**; that is, as Greek authority Kenneth Wuest points out, they

> understood these issues perfectly. . . . They were enlightened as every sinner is enlightened who comes under the hearing of God's Word. But as the unsaved in an evangelistic meeting today clearly understand the message of salvation but sometimes refuse the light

and turn back into the darkness of sin and continued unbelief, so these Hebrews were in danger of doing a like thing.[5]

Just hearing is not enough. Intellectual understanding is not enough. Only faith is enough, and these hearers had not truly believed anything they saw.

Second, these people had **tasted of the heavenly gift**. What is **the heavenly gift**? Without doubt, it is salvation in Christ. It is, indeed, "the gift of God" (Eph. 2:8), God's truly "unspeakable gift" (2 Cor. 9:15). But to *taste* something is far different than actually eating or drinking it, that is, fully *receiving* it. Some teachers object to this observation by pointing out that the Greek behind **tasted** (*geuomai*) is also used in Hebrews 2:9, where God permitted Jesus to "taste death for every man." Surely then, it is argued, Jesus did not simply *sample* death on the cross. No, indeed, He did not just *taste* it; He went on to *drink all of it*. To force the word here, however, to mean the same is not warranted. Just as the spies who went into Canaan saw its incredible fruit, and perhaps tasted it (I would have), and yet did not believe they could ever possess it, how many people have done the same with Christ? How many have been deeply stirred by a Gospel message, sampled the blessings it has to offer, but then say, "No thank you?" Jesus, who is the Living Bread, must be *eaten*, not just *tasted* (John 6:51).

Third, and most controversial of all, these people were **made partakers of the Holy Ghost**. Some insist that this clearly implies that these people were believers. We submit, however, that this simply does not mean the same thing as being "born of the Spirit" (Jn. 3:5–6, 8), "sealed with the Spirit" (Eph. 1:13), indwelt by the Spirit (Rom. 8:9), baptized by the Spirit into the body of Christ (1 Cor. 12:12–13), or the believer being the "temple of the Holy Spirit" (1 Cor. 6:19). And again, nowhere in the New Testament is this term used to indicate salvation. In short, "'partakers' does not mean 'possessors.'"[6] The Greek *metochos* has to do with sharing, association, or participation, but *not* possession. Commentator William MacDonald puts the matter very well:

> Before we jump to the conclusion that this necessarily implies conversion, we should remember that the Holy Spirit carries on a preconversion ministry in men's lives. He sanctifies unbelievers (1Cor. 7:14), putting them in a position of external privilege. He convicts unbelievers of sin, of righteousness, and of judgment (John 16:8). He leads men to repentance and points them to Christ as their only hope. Men may thus partake of the Holy Spirit's benefits without being indwelt by Him.[7]

Fourth, these people had also **tasted the good word of God**. The word *geuomai* (**tasted**) is used again, this time to show that these people had sampled God's Word. I have met many a lost person who loves to debate Scripture, is intrigued by its subject matter, who enjoys a lively discussion about its ethics and morality, and even admits its fascinating historical content. But alas, all this is merely *tasting*, not *receiving*. As commentator John MacArthur illustrates:

> Herod was like this. In spite of the prophet's hard message, including accusations directly against the king, Herod enjoyed listening to John the Baptist preach (Mark 6:20). He was perplexed but fascinated by this dynamic preacher. He liked to sample the message of God. But when pressed into decision, he forsook God's man and God's message. He reluctantly, but willingly, agreed to have John beheaded. His taste of God's Word only brought on him greater guilt.[8]

Others taste it with even more sincerity. They listen to it carefully, are moved by it, are enthusiastic about it, and even appear to receive it. But in the end, they are merely the "stony ground hearer," who endures for a while but falls away when persecution comes (Matt. 13:20–21).

Fifth and finally, these people had also **tasted . . . the powers of the world to come**. The word **world** translates the Greek *aiōn*, which literally means "age," that is, a period of time or even a dispensation. **Powers** is *dunamis*, which speaks of inherent or raw power, the ability to do wonders. **The [age] to come**, then, is the future Millennial Kingdom, when great wonders and miracles will be commonplace. These people, therefore, had actually **tasted** of such a time, as Jesus did miracles here on earth. In spite of that savory taste, however, they would not fully eat and receive the One who performed such wonders. These wonders, in fact, proved that Jesus was who He said He was. By their rejection, they reaffirmed their guilt and sealed their fate.

In spite of those five great privileges, the writer goes on to say that such people had **fall way**, and here is the key to the issue. The Greek *parapiptō*, which appears only here in the New Testament, is a compound comprised of the root *piptō*, "to fall," and *para*, "near or beside." The full idea in the word, then, is "to fall beside a person or thing, to slip aside, hence, to deviate from the right path, to turn aside, to wander."[9] One Greek authority makes the important point that this word does not "indicate errors of weakness, faults or accidents," but rather "in every case [signifes] deliberate acts of sin."[10] What is, therefore, in view here is a deliberate departure from the privileges that are listed. It is a calculated decision to reject what is known, and such a decision, as we have shown, simply cannot come from a regenerated person.

The writer[11] then writes of the horrendous consequence of such a decision—**it is impossible . . . to renew them again unto repentance.** Some have tried to soften the word **impossible** to "difficult" or "hard," but the Greek *adunatos* is unmistakable. The root *dunatos* means possible, able, or powerful, so the alpha negative (*a-*) makes it the polar opposite: impossible, unable, powerless. The same word, in fact, appears elsewhere in Hebrews. In 6:18, for example, it is "impossible for God to lie," in 10:4, it is "not possible that the blood of bulls and of goats should take away sins," and in 10:6, "without faith it is impossible to please [God]." So by making this decision, these Hebrews "would render their hearts so hard that they would be impervious to the ministry of the Holy Spirit. They would be irrevocably lost. There would be no more hope for them."[12] **Repentance** would, indeed, be **impossible**.

Finally, the writer adds why these Hebrews cannot be brought back: by rejecting these grand privileges, choosing rather to return to the old sacrificial system, **they crucify to themselves the Son of God afresh, and put him to an open shame.** Of all the horrific aspects of Roman Catholicism, for example, surely the worst of all is "the Mass," which crucifies our Savior over and over again, and has done so incalculable millions of times through the centuries. Spitting in the face of the Savior, mocking His finished work, such people have stripped Him naked again, lifted Him up before the mocking crowd, and **put him to an open shame**. This phrase is one word in the Greek (*paradeigmatizō*) that means "to make a public example of or expose to public humiliation." Joseph, for example, chose to divorce Mary privately so as not "to make her a public example" (Matt. 1:19), that is, so as not to shame and humiliate her.

This passage is, indeed, a horrifying scene. E. Schuyler English concludes his exposition of it by writing:

> They have been convinced of their sin and their need. They have had opportunity to become recipients of God's loving provision in Christ. They have, by their profession, acknowledged the truth as truth. Then deliberately and willfully, they turn back, turn away from the Lord of glory. Like their fathers, they crucify the Son of God; afresh He is nailed to the cross in rejection and put to an open shame, and there is no hope for them. They were never Christians. They were those who had ample opportunity to become children of God in Christ through faith, who have professed to be converted, but they have turned away to their condemnation.[13]

The Implication

Once again, while we respect those who teach other views of this passage, we cannot help but wonder if at least part of the reason for other views in the minds of *some* interpreters (not all but *some*) is that they do not like the implications of the view we have submitted here. We live in a day of unprecedented tolerance and perhaps the broadest definition of salvation that has ever existed in Church History. A passage like this one, therefore, is not well accepted. Many today find the view we have offered as narrow and "judgmental."

We would submit, however, that other passages underscore the narrow road of true salvation. One passage, in fact, uses those very words:

> Enter ye in at the strait gate: for wide is the gate, and broad is the way, that leadeth to destruction, and many there be which go in thereat: Because strait is the gate, and narrow is the way, which leadeth unto life, and few there be that find it. (Matt. 7:13–14).

A few verses later, we then read some of the most sobering and terrifying words in all of Scripture:

> Not every one that saith unto me, Lord, Lord, shall enter into the kingdom of heaven; but he that doeth the will of my Father which is in heaven. Many will say to me in that day, Lord, Lord, have we not prophesied in thy name? and in thy name have cast out devils? and in thy name done many wonderful works? And then will I profess unto them, I never knew you: depart from me, ye that work iniquity. (vv. 21–23)

Just *saying* one is a Christian does not make it so (see chapter 48). That is why Paul writes elsewhere that we must "examine [ourselves], whether [we] be in the faith; prove [our] own selves" (2 Cor. 13:5), and why Peter wrote that we should "give diligence to make [our] calling and election sure" (2 Pet. 1:10). It is not enough to *call* yourself a Christian or even *say* Jesus is Lord. What *proves* you are a Christian? *Doing "the will of My Father in heaven."* As the old expression goes, "Words are cheap," and they seem to get cheaper every day as the Gospel is redefined in increasingly broader terms. But our Lord is in no way ambiguous: the two greatest evidences of true conversion are obedience to God's Word (Jn. 14:15, 23; 1 Jn. 2:1–5) and holiness of life (Eph. 4:24; 1 Thes. 4:17; etc.).

The Hebrews addressed in this "tough text" were in danger of becoming what others had already become, namely, "beyond salvage." We need the same warning today, regardless of how painful the implication.

NOTES

[1] Harry Ironside, *Hebrews and Titus* (Loizeaux Brothers, Inc., 1932), pp. 77-78.

[2] E. Schuyler English, *Studies in the Epistle to the Hebrews* (Dunham Publishing Company, 1955), p. 162.

[3] William MacDonald, *Believer's Bible Commentary* (Thomas Nelson Publishers, 1995), p. 2172.

[4] English, p. 163.

[5] Kenneth Wuest, *Hebrews in the Greek New Testament* (Eerdmans, 1947), p. 114.

[6] Ibid.

[7] MacDonald, p. 2174.

[8] John MacArthur, *The MacArthur New Testament Commentary, Hebrews.*

[9] Wuest, p. 117.

[10] Spiros Zodhiates, *The Complete Word Study Dictionary: New Testament* (AMG Publishers, 1992), entry #3895.

[11] We believe the writer of Hebrews was, indeed, the Apostle Paul. See our chapter 7, "Does the Authorship of Hebrews Matter?"

[12] Wuest, p. 118.

[13] English, p. 167.

As to their question, How can we be assured that this has sprung from God unless we have recourse to the decrees of the church?, it is as if someone asked: Whence will we learn to distinguish light from darkness, white from black, sweet from bitter? Indeed, Scripture exhibits fully as clear evidence of its own truth as white and black things do of their color, or sweet and bitter things do of their taste.

John Calvin
Institutes, I.7.4

20

What is the "Old Man"?*

Romans 6:6

Knowing this, that our old man is crucified with him, that the body of sin might be destroyed, that henceforth we should not serve sin.

In this chapter we turn to a "tough text" that is without question one of the most important verses in Scripture concerning sanctification and Christian living. Sadly, however, this verse is also among the most misunderstood and most often misinterpreted verses of Scripture.

Understanding the Issue

Again, this verse (and it's context, of course) is the very foundation for living a holy life. Why? Because it serves to remind us every day that we are no longer this **old man**, that he is gone. It reveals that the **old man** *was* crucified (past tense in the Greek) and has been destroyed. But what exactly *is* the **old man**? *That* is the issue. And until that is understood, the doctrine of sanctification itself cannot be understood.

This verse has been a battleground for centuries. The question has been not whether we become holy in Christ—all agree there—rather *how* this holiness is brought about.

One theory of sanctification has been dubbed the *Eradication Theory*. Ever since the esteemed John Wesley formulated it, this doctrine has been widely believed and taught. The teaching is that "entire sanctification," that is, sinlessness, the complete purging of "inbred sin," "the old nature," "the flesh," comes through a "second blessing." Through a process of continually purging sin and the **old man**, the Christian, *by his efforts*, finally reaches the goal of sinlessness. This teaching is based, oddly enough, on Romans 6:6, that having yielded everything to Christ, we by faith identify ourselves with Him in His death and believe that our "old nature" is "crucified with Him" and therefore "destroyed." Since we "reckon" ourselves "dead indeed unto sin" (v. 11), we will actually experience the eradication of sin. But as we'll see, this teaching is inarguably based upon a basic misreading of the text.

---

* This chapter was originally TOTT issue 37, August 2008, and began our fourth year in this ministry.

A second view of sanctification is the *Counteraction Theory*. Simply stated, this teaches that sanctification comes not by *eradicating* our inherited sin-bias, but by *counteracting* it, working against it, suppressing it; by our daily efforts of "dying to self" and "crucifying the old man," we suppress the "old nature." This comes, it is taught, by an inward "joint crucifixion with Christ" that counteracts the "old nature," "renders it inoperative," for the time being, but which can be reactivated at any moment. We must then crucify ourselves again to render the "old nature inoperative" again. Like the Eradication Theory, however, this too is based on a fundamental misreading of Romans 6:6 and its context.

What is so strange about both these views is that they are based on the idea that Romans 6:6 refers to something in the present, something that happens in our own experience; in other words, it is something that we do in our efforts, something that comes as result of our own struggling against sin. *But that is the exact opposite of what the text SAYS.* This leads us to consider first what the old man is *not*, and then what it *is*.

What the "Old Man" is *Not*

Now, I want to say the following as clearly and as singularly biblically as I possibly can. My reason for that little introductory statement is because the term **old man** has been sorely misunderstood, so much so, in fact, that it is often called by another completely different name that is not once used in Scripture.

Terminology is essential on any issue. Some teachers, however, seem to disagree with that truth when it comes to this issue and just dismiss it by saying, "Well, we are just arguing semantics. Why make a big deal of terms?" We submit, however, that words matter very much when Truth is at stake. One of the passions of my life and ministry is that *words matter*; they make a difference in doctrine. How many false doctrines, and even entire cults, have been created because of the lack of precision?

One such term that has been around for many years in the teaching concerning sanctification and holiness is the term "old nature," as in the expression, "The Christian has two natures, the *old* nature and the *new* nature." But that is an extremely unfortunate statement. To make matters worse, there are some organizations that make this a matter of fellowship, inexplicably insisting that anyone who denies the "two natures" is virtually anathema.

That attitude has greatly puzzled me for several years, because the clear fact of the matter is that to be accurate in our terminology—and if words matter we must be accurate—we must recognize that *Scripture simply does not SAY we have two NATURES*. The common teaching is that we have two *natures* that are warring against one another. But we repeat, and are compelled to insist, that *Scripture does not say that*. Yes, we most certainly do have a war going on (Rom. 7), and we will examine that later, but *to be precise*, the Bible does not say that this war is between two *natures*.

In fact, Scripture doesn't even use the word "nature" either in our text or in another important text on this issue: "That ye put off concerning the former conversation the **old man**, which is corrupt according to the deceitful lusts" (Eph. 4:22). In both cases, we find the Greek *palaios* (**old**), which means "old in the sense of worn out, decrepit, useless," and then *anthropos*, which means **man**, not a mere "part" of a man, such as a "nature" or "self," but the whole man, every aspect of him.

There is absolutely no argument to be made, therefore, that **old man** refers to anything except something old in the person that is now gone, not a supposed "nature" that cannot be controlled. This, then, leads us to consider what the **old man** really is.

What the "Old Man" *Is*

Let us examine four major points on Romans 6:6.

First, Romans 6 is located in what can be called the "judicial section" of the Epistle, not the "experiential." In other words, just as Ephesians, for example, is divided into *doctrine* (1–3) and *practice* (4–6) Romans has a similar structure. While chapters 1–8 are *judicial* (i.e., *doctrinal*), as they show how God saves the sinner, and chapters 9–11 are unique to Romans as they are *national*, explaining how the Gospel relates to Israel, chapters 12–16 are *experiential* (practical), as they demonstrate how the Gospel bears on our practical conduct. *Romans 6, therefore, deals with what GOD alone has accomplished JUDICIALLY, not what WE do EXPERIENTIALLY.*

Second, and this is the key to the whole issue, *all the verb tenses in Romans 6 are past tenses*, either the aorist or the perfect. In other words, every verb tense that refers to our identification with Christ in His death refers to that identification being *completed in the past*. Romans 6:6, therefore, does not say that our "old man *is being* crucified" or that our "old nature *must be* crucified," rather it says that our "old man *was* crucified" way back when Christ died and that it was *completed* then and there. It does *not* say (as some teachers insist) that we must each morning get up and "crucify ourselves again to sin." Rather it inarguably says that by *God's judicial act*, not by our experiential effort, the **old man** was **crucified** and therefore **destroyed**.

Third, this brings us to the precise meaning of the term **old man**. If this doesn't mean "old nature" or "inbred sin" that we must either eradicate or suppress—and it does *not* mean either one of those—what does it mean? The **old man** can refer to one thing and one thing only: *all that we were in Adam*, that is, all the guilt, penalty, power, and dominion of sin that was in Adam.

Now, we immediately want to ask, "But I *do* still sin—why?" We'll deal with that in a moment. The point that *must* be understood first is that *sin is not the rule of life like it was before*. We are not dominated by sin as we once were. The **old man**, the person we were before salvation is gone because of what Christ accomplished on Calvary. We are not sinless, but we are *no longer dominated and controlled by sin*. While sin used to rule, it is now Christ who rules.

To make this practical, how often have we all used the excuse, "Well, I just can't help it; I'm a Christian, but because of my old nature, I just can't help but sin?" Such an attitude is defeatist and actually justifies our sin. The fact is, as we'll see, we most certainly can "help it" because we are no longer dominated by sin. Sin is no longer the *rule*, it is the *exception*.

Paul then continues, **that the body of sin might be destroyed**. **Destroyed** is *katargeō*, "to render inactive, put out of use, cancel, bring to nothing, do away with."[1] Because it is in a past tense, like all the verbs in the passage, it declares that **the body of sin** (a synonym for **old man**) has been nullified, put out of use, done away with completely in the past. It was through the cross that God put the **old man** out of action. That **body of sin** no longer hangs on us as like an anchor to sink us into the ocean of sin; God has removed it and freed us from sin's dominion.

As J. Sidlow Baxter masterfully summarizes, here is the *positional* meaning of Romans 6:6 according to the language of the text:

- ❑ OUR OLD MAN—all that we were in position and relation to Adam, with all our culpability and condemnation.

- ❑ WAS CRUCIFIED WITH HIM—was judged and executed in the once-for-all death of Christ.

- ❑ THAT THE BODY OF SIN—the whole Adam humanity as guilty before God.

- ❑ MIGHT BE DESTROYED—completely done away in the judicial reckoning of God.

- ❑ THAT WE SHOULD NO LONGER BE IN BONDAGE TO SIN—that is, no longer in *legal* bondage through *judicial* guilt.[2]

With that *positional* truth firmly established, how does this work in *practice*? That leads us to our final point.

Fourth, we now consider the role of what is called "the flesh." This answers the question, "If I was crucified with Christ in the past, and the **old**

man is dead, and **the body of sin** has been put out of action, why do I still sin?" Paul knew this question would arise, so right after he writes Romans 6, he writes Romans 7, where he laments over "the flesh." Even though the **old man** is gone, even though sin doesn't rule and dominate, "the flesh" remains.

Some insist here, "It's the same thing to say 'the flesh' and 'the old nature." But to that we ask in response, how can these be the same when they are different words? We must be precise. We still sin not because of the "old nature"—*a term that immediately implies something inbred that we can't control*—but because the new spiritual man is still in the physical body and must still contend with the infirmities of "the flesh."

The Greek for "flesh" is *sarx*, which occurs 96 times in Paul's Epistles (including five in Hebrews). It refers to the physical body 37 times (e.g, Rom. 2:28), to humanity or that which is human 25 times (e.g., 3:20), and to *inherent evil in the human nature* 27 times (e.g., 7:5). Romans 7:5, in fact, clearly defines this third use of "flesh": "For when we were [Greek imperfect tense, "were and continue to be"] in the flesh, the motions of sins, which were by the law, did work in our members to bring forth fruit unto death." "Motions" is an Old English term for "impulses," which is the idea in the Greek *pathēma*, from *pathos* (English, "pathology"), "which describes the emotions of the soul, i.e., human feelings, and impulses which a man does not produce within himself but finds already present, and by which he can be carried away." In Classical Greek, "it acquired a predominately negative meaning, that of passion."[3] We can, indeed, be carried away by our passions. In short, *"the flesh" is the animal and selfish inclinations, the self-centered perversity and propensity inherent and co-existing in our humanity.*

How often do we think that Satan is our greatest enemy? While in the spiritual realm, he is certainly the ultimate foe, our greatest enemy in our personal experience is ourselves, our flesh. As Martin Luther wrote, "I dread my own heart more than the pope and all his cardinals, for within me is the greater pope, even self."

So, it's not that we have "two natures" or "two minds." We are not spiritual schizophrenics. We are not beings with a split personality or bipolar disorder, where one nature or personality is trying to suppress the other. Rather we have two "states of mind," the *spirit* and the *flesh*. We are now "partakers of the *divine* nature, having escaped the corruption that is in the world through lust" (2 Pet. 1:4; emphasis added). The divine nature is present because the Holy Spirit regenerated our dead spirit, now making it alive and empowering it by His continuous indwelling. But at the same time, while our "spirit indeed is willing . . . the flesh is weak" (Matt. 26:41). This explains why the words "pride," "proud," and "self" are *never* used in a positive way in Scripture. Pride is of the flesh, and it is the flesh, our passions, our impulses, that are our problem.

Recognizing this distinction enables us to understand the truth of the text by expanding the translation of Romans 7:15–25. Meditate on the willingness of the *spirit* (the divine nature) but the weakness of the *flesh*:

> For that which I [*the flesh*] do, I [*the spirit*] allow not: for what I [*the spirit*] would, that [I] [*the flesh*] [do] not; but what I [*the spirit*] hate, that do I [*the flesh*].

> If then I [*the flesh*] do that which I [*the spirit*] would not, I [*the spirit*] consent unto the law that it is good.

> Now then it is no more I [*the one undivided personality*] that do it, but sin that dwelleth in me [the one me, not "us"]. For I [*the spirit*] know that in me (that is, in my flesh,) [*the flesh*] dwelleth no good thing: for to will is present with me [*the spirit*]; but how to perform that which is good I [*the spirit*] find not. . . .

> For I [*the spirit*] delight in the law of God after the inward man [*the spirit*]: But I [*the spirit*] see another law in my members, warring against the law of my mind [*the spirit*], and bringing me [the one me, not "us"] into captivity to the law of sin which is in my [*not "our"*] members. O wretched man that I [*the flesh*] am! who shall deliver me [*the total me*] from the body of this death? I thank God through Jesus Christ our Lord. So then with the mind I myself [*the total me*] serve the law of God; but with the flesh the law of sin.[4]

So within the one "total me" there is *the spirit* and *the flesh*. The question that now arises is, "How does *the spirit* rule? How do we deal with those passions and impulses that remain? How do we deal with this flesh?" Indeed, if Paul had stopped with Romans 7, we would have cause for deep depression. But Paul did not stop there. He goes on in Romans 8 to reveal the wondrous truth that the indwelling Holy Spirit provides the victory over the flesh. *In fact, "the flesh" is never mentioned in chapter 8 without the Holy Spirit also being mentioned* (vv. 1, 3–4, 5, 8–9, 12–13).

We have, therefore, been freed from sin in two ways: freed from the **old man** *positionally* by the past action of Christ (Rom. 6) and then *practically* (experientially) from "the flesh" by the indwelling Holy Spirit (Rom. 7–8). Ponder this:

> *We do not have the inability to sin, but we do have the ability not to sin.*

Did you get it? Have we reached sinless perfection? Have we reached the point where we no longer sin? Certainly not. But we still have the ability not to sin; we can still claim the victory over sin by the power of the Holy Spirit. No longer can we say, "I just couldn't help it. It's just part of my nature. It's just who I am." Yes, we *can* "help it" because of the Holy Spirit. Even though our passions and impulses are strong, we can claim the victory, something that is impossible to claim when we insist that sin is still part of our *nature*. We are now "partakers of the divine nature, having escaped the corruption that is in the world through lust" (2 Pet. 1:4).

As 1 Corinthians 10:13 then declares: "There hath no temptation taken you but such as is common to man: but God is faithful, who will not suffer you to be tempted above that ye are able; but will with the temptation also make a way to escape, that ye may be able to bear it." God promises that temptation to sin will never overwhelm us, that even our passions and impulses do not control us.

How often do we try to run and hide from the sins that defeat us, or worse, try to excuse them? Each one is the wrong approach. We can and must face our passions and impulses. In the power of the Holy Spirit, we can say, "I'm not afraid of you. I'm not going to run away from you. I claim God's power in my life to deliver me from myself. I'm *not* the **old man**, so I'm not going to *act* like the **old man**. I am 'the new man, which after God is created in righteousness and true holiness' (Eph. 4:24)"

NOTES

[1] Colin Brown, *The New International Dictionary of New Testament Theology* (Zondervan, 1975), Vol. 1, p. 73.

[2] In my humble opinion, Baxter's trilogy on the Christian doctrine of sanctification is unequalled: *A New Call To Holiness*, *His Deeper Work In Us*, and *Our High Calling* (Zondervan).

[3] Brown, Vol. 3, p. 719.

[4] Adapted from Baxter, *His Deeper Work in Us* (p. 136).

The devil can cite Scripture for his purpose.

William Shakespeare
The Merchant of Venice, Act I, Sc. 3

21

Apologetics and the Gospel[*]

1 Peter 3:15

But sanctify the Lord God in your hearts: and be ready always to give an answer to every man that asketh you a reason of the hope that is in you with meekness and fear:

B ack in my first year of theology in 1972, my professor required a 3,000 word research paper on any subject that had been covered during that year. (Actually, I think my passion for writing was ignited partially by that event.) The topic I chose was one that had been bothering me ever since we had dealt with it in class, namely, the logical proofs for the existence of God. Those classic arguments were originally designed to prove God's existence rationally.

But even as a naïve, know-nothing neophyte, this idea bothered me. "Is this the way we should approach God?" I asked in my paper. "Is this how we should 'argue' to a lost world?" It is now, three-and-a-half decades later, that I am still troubled by this in a very popular form of evangelism called *apologetics*.

What Is Apologetics?

When we do something that offends or hurts someone, we "apologize" or "make an apology," which is an admission of error. The source of those English words, however, has a very different meaning.

Here we turn to our text. The word **answer** translates the Greek *apologia*, which is comprised of *apo*, "from," and *logos*, "speech." In Classical Greek, it was used as a legal term referring to an attorney presenting a defense for his client.

That idea is carried over into the New Testament. Paul, for example, made a "defense" before the people of Jerusalem for his speaking against the Law in Acts 22:1. He also "answered" Festus in defense of his faith (25:8; cf. v. 15), as well as Agrippa (26:1).

The question that arises, however, is what does such a "defense" or "answer" mean? Does it mean that in order to be an effective witness for Christ we each must memorize reams of facts about creation science so we

---

* This chapter was originally TOTT issue 38, September 2008.

can shoot down every argument the evolutionist raises? Does it mean that we can't possibly be effective in evangelism if we can't prove the accuracy of the Bible to the atheist by reciting all the archeological evidences for the existence of ancient cities mentioned in the Bible?

A few months ago, I heard a noted speaker say, "There is no [Church office] of Apologist," but he went on to insist nonetheless that this kind of "elder" is crucial for the church today. His ministry consists, then, of debates and open forums with every ilk of unbeliever, outspoken (even violent) enemy of Christianity, and the most vile and immoral people of society. What is this if it is not "[casting] . . . pearls before swine," thereby not only *allowing* but even further *empowering* such people to "trample [God's truth] under their feet" (Matt. 7:6)?

The Major Approaches to Apologetics

Apologetics is defined, as one noted author writes, as "the reasoned defense of the Christian religion. Christianity is a faith, to be sure; but there are reasons for this faith. Faith is not be confused with reason; but neither is it to be separated from it."[1] There are three major approaches to apologetics that have been advocated through the years.

Classical Apologetics

This approach defends the faith through rational arguments for the existence of God, using evidence to substantiate biblical claims and miracles. Early classical apologists include Augustine, Anselm, and Thomas Aquinas (which actually should bother us because they all, especially Aquinas, tried to blend Scripture with pagan Greek philosophy). Such an apologetic might go something like this:

Steve: Can you give me any logical evidence that God exists?

Jim: Well, I can sure try. After all, the universe exists, and it's not very rational to think it made itself.

Steve: Well, maybe. Do you have any other argument?

Jim: Well, to take that a little farther, there is the Cosmological Argument. Everything has a cause, so if you continue to trace back through each cause, you must get to the First Cause, and it is there you find God.

Steve: Is that all you have?

Jim: Oh, no. There's also the Teleological Argument, which says everything must have a designer, such as a watch, for example. Who then designed the complexity of the universe? We must conclude God.

And so the arguments continue but without proving anything, quite frankly. Such arguments no more prove God exists than does the evolutionist's assertion that there was a big bang prove that it happened.

What many advocates of this approach either fail to recognize, or refuse to admit, is that this is actually the foundation of *Deism*, which every true evangelical, of course, rejects as apostasy. Deists maintain that reason is the essential element in all knowledge and flatly reject both organized and revealed religion. And what is the foundation of their belief? *The logical proofs for God's existence.* The practical outworking of Deism is that while God created the world, He does not intervene or take an active part in it. We must ask, therefore, is this really the approach we should advocate?

Evidential Apologetics

Similar to the classical approach, this one defends the faith through the evidence of the miracles of the Bible, especially the evidences for Christ's resurrection, as well as fulfilled prophecies and scientific evidence for creation. Such an apologetic session might go like this:

Steve: Can you give me any logical evidence that God exists?

Jim: Absolutely. The miracles of the Bible demonstrate it clearly.

Steve: But all that is just a bunch of stories.

Jim: Oh, but the Bible accurately records various cities, customs, and other things that have been verified by outside sources. Besides, such things were recorded by eyewitness.

Steve: Maybe, but such stories, even by eyewitness, could be mistaken, exaggerated, or plagiarized.

Jim: That's not likely. With thousands of Greek manuscripts that essentially say the same thing, that's pretty good evidence that the accounts are reliable.

Steve: Well, I've still got a problem with miracles. That's just not rational thinking.

Jim: But what do you do with all those witnesses?

And again it goes on. It could now go into the historical evidences of Jesus resurrection, creation, and so forth, but nothing is necessarily *proven* in the strict sense of the word because nothing can be *demonstrated*.

Presuppositional Apologetics

This approach abandons the rational method of the preceding approaches. It seeks to prove nothing because nothing can be proven. Why? *Because of a person's presuppositions.* Fallen man is unable to *see* truth much less *believe* it. His sinful mind doesn't even think straight. Unless a person starts with God, he cannot know Truth. Oh, yes, he can certainly know that the universe exists, that gravity will kill him if he jumps off a tall building, and so forth, but his presuppositions force him to deny that God made any of it. Proverbs 1:7 seems to clearly indicate just such a reality: "The fear of the LORD is the beginning of knowledge: but fools despise wisdom and instruction." Such a conversation with an unbeliever might go like this:

Steve: Can you give me any logical evidence that God exists?

Jim: Actually, no, I can't.

Steve: Why not? How do you expect me to believe anything you say?

Jim: I can't prove anything to you because of your presuppositions.

Steve: What do you mean by that?

Jim: I mean that what you already assume to be true forbids you to look without bias at any evidence I might give you that God exists.

Steve: That's because there *is* no evidence God exists.

Jim: See what I mean? Your mind is already made up and refuses to allow any alternative.

Steve: No, that's not true. I'll believe enough evidence.

Jim: I don't mean to be confrontational, but no you wouldn't. If I told you that 1,000 witnesses saw Jesus rise from the dead, you might say (just as many skeptics have in the past) that it was just mass hysteria. If I said that hundreds of Old Testament prophecies have been fulfilled, you could say (again like many critics have) that they were forged, post-dated, or whatever. Even if I had a videotape, you'd say it was just special effects. Your presuppositions simply will not allow you to believe.

Steve: Sure I can if you give me enough evidences.

Jim: And how many would that take? No, regardless of how much I offer, you will still say no because your presuppositions absolutely demand it.

Steve: Well, then how can I believe?

That last question is really the heart of the whole issue. How *do* we get someone to believe? This leads us to our main point.

The Application

So how *do* we get someone one to believe? The answer is: *we don't.* Does it not seem quite odd that we think that our well reasoned arguments, however compelling or convincing they might be, can actually persuade someone to believe apart from the power of God? And if it is the power of God that saves, why do we need compelling arguments in the first place? Or is it that we need both?

Please consider this: Our Lord did literally thousands of miracles. Now *there* was positive, irrefutable, convincing proof, right? But did that compel anyone to believe? No. In fact, despite all those miracles, when the Lord Jesus began to preach about righteousness and salvation, and then even had the "audacity" to say that He *alone* is the "bread of life" (Jn. 6:22–71), many left Him (v. 66), just as most people today are offended by the preaching of a narrow Gospel (Matt. 7:13–14; Jn. 14:6; Acts 4:1–12). Our Lord went on to make it clear that it is the Holy Spirit who gives life (v. 63) and "that no man can come unto me, except it were given unto him of my Father" (v. 65). He went on to add another very unpopular notion nowadays: "No man can come to me, except the Father which hath sent me draw him" (v. 44), indicating that God alone is at work in salvation.

No, it is not arguments that win anybody to Christ, rather it is "the Gospel of Christ" *itself* (the Gospel *in and of itself* without anything added) that is "the power of God unto salvation to every one that believeth; to the Jew first, and also to the Greek" (Rom. 1:16). Paul, in fact, prefaced that statement with the assertion that he wasn't ashamed of that Gospel, rather he preached *that alone* as God's power to save.

I fear that just the opposite is true today, that many *are* ashamed of preaching the Gospel alone. I fear that they think that doing so is to be simplistic, naïve, unscholarly, and not socially relevant or intellectually challenging. I also fear that we have become so Arminian, so man-centered in our theology, that we no longer believe that it is God *alone* who performs the *entire* work of salvation.

Paul went on in 1 Corinthians 1 to deal with this exact situation. Yes, preaching the Gospel alone will be *very* offensive to Jews and foolishness to Gentiles (v. 23). What about knowledge, argument, and thought provoking debate? Paul says that "[God] will destroy the wisdom of the wise." What, then, is the power to save? "The preaching of the cross is to them that perish foolishness; but unto us which are saved it is the power of God" (v. 18).

Commentator Gordon Clark tells the story of a University of Pennsylvania history professor who read Jonathan Edward's great sermon, "Sinners in the Hands of an Angry God" to his students. His motive was to reveal how harsh and morose the Puritans were, but the result was that one student was converted.[2] *That* is the power of Gospel preaching!

As if that were not enough, Paul goes on in 2:1–5 to make the matter even less ambiguous by using his own ministry as an illustration. Now let us not forget that Paul was extremely educated. He was familiar with Greek culture and philosophy. In 1 Corinthians 15:33, for example, he quotes a proverb that first appeared in a play by the Greek poet Menander (ca. 342–291 BC). He also quotes the semi-mythical 6th-century BC Cretan philosopher-poet and reputed prophet Epimenides in Titus 1:12.

In spite of such education, not to mention an obviously brilliant mind that could have debated the Greek orators in Corinth right out of the forum if he had chosen that methodology, Paul wrote:

> I, brethren, when I came to you, came not with excellency of speech or of wisdom, declaring unto you the testimony of God. For I determined not to know any thing among you, save Jesus Christ, and him crucified. And I was with you in weakness, and in fear, and in much trembling. And my speech and my preaching was not with enticing words of man's wisdom, but in demonstration of the Spirit and of power: That your faith should not stand in the wisdom of men, but in the power of God.

What could possibly be clearer than that? The key word is "enticing," which translates the Greek adjective *peithos*, which in-turn comes from the verb *peithō*, "to persuade, prevail upon, win over, or bring about a change of mind by the influence of reason or moral considerations" (e.g., Matt. 27:20).[3] He didn't philosophize or debate in the Greek forum. He didn't give any logical proofs for God's existence. He didn't even try to prove Jesus' deity or resurrection. *He just preached the Gospel.* Why? Because saving "faith" is "the power of God," as well as even "the gift of God" (Eph. 2:8; see chapter 9).

At this point, some teachers immediately bring up Acts 19:8, where Paul "went into the synagogue, and spake boldly for the space of three months, disputing and persuading the things concerning the kingdom of God." They insist that since "persuading" is also *peithō*, then this proves that Paul was doing "apologetics." We submit, however, that if that is true, we have a serious contradiction, for what Paul did there in the lecture hall at Ephesus was the very thing he said he refused to do in Corinth. Please read it again. What he was doing in Ephesus was debating with the Jews concerning the *kingdom*, a focal point for the Jews, *not* the existence of God or other such apologetic subject. This verse simply does not justify modern apologetics.

I was blessed in the depths of my soul by these simple words from the beloved J. Vernon McGee:

> There are many people today who try to prove that the Bible is the Word of God. There are also those who try to prove that the Bible is not God's Word. My ministry at the beginning was an apologetic ministry. I tried to prove that the Bible was the Word of God. I learned, however, that I do not need to prove it; I am to give it out, and the Spirit of God takes care of that. I have already come to the definite, dogmatic conclusion that the Bible is indeed the Word of God. I don't *think* it is—I *know* it is. And I know what it can do for you today. Therefore it does not need my weak support. The Bible will take care of itself.[4]

It would appear that Charles Spurgeon agreed. When asked one day how he would defend the Bible, he replied, "Defend the Bible? I would just as soon defend a lion. Just turn the Bible loose. It will defend itself."

We come full circle back to our main text. What does Peter mean when he says **be ready always to give an answer to every man**? John Gill well explains:

> Now, a "reason" of this is to be given; not that they are to account for the Gospel, upon the foot of carnal reason; for that is not of men, nor according to the carnal reason of men; nor is it to be thought that every Christian should be capable of defending the Gospel, either in whole, or in part, by arguments and reasons, in a disputatious way, or to give a reason and argument for every particular truth; but that he should be *well acquainted with the ground and foundation of the Christian religion*; at least, with the first principles of *the oracles of God*, and be *conversant with the Scriptures*, and be able to point out that in them, which is the reason of his holding this and the other truth, though he is not able to give a gainsayer satisfaction, or to stop his mouth: and this is to be done with meekness and fear; with meekness, before men; in an humble modest way; not with an haughty air, and in a morose and surly manner, which serves only to irritate and provoke.[5]

In other words, we don't use *reason*; we use *revelation*. We don't *debate* the issues in arrogance; we *deliver* the truth in humility. One of the tendencies in modern apologetics is to think our arguments are actually helpful, or to word it even more spiritually, "God uses our arguments." *But where does Scripture say that?* Further, it is extremely easy for us to become puffed up in our knowledge and think that we are responsible for "winning someone to Christ."

We should also address another use of *apologia*: "I am set for the defence of the gospel" (Phil. 1:17). What does this mean? Does it imply the modern idea? Hardly. Lehman Strauss well puts it:

> I have heard it said that the gospel needs no defense. No doubt there is some truth in that statement, but certainly there needs to be a defense against the misrepresentations of the gospel. . . . The full truth should be preached with singleness and purity of purpose.[6]

Paul was not talking about argumentation and proof-preaching, rather defending the preaching of the true Gospel. What we should be doing today is defending the true Gospel in light of how it is being diluted and perverted by so many teachers. Those are the people who are doing the greatest damage, not the foolish evolutionist and atheist. If I may be so blunt, it is the Joel Osteens, Robert Schulers, and Rob Bells that are destroying the Gospel message.

I am convinced, in fact, that at least part of this issue has to do with our no longer knowing what the Gospel is and exactly what it is we are to be proclaiming. The Gospel is not about proving God's existence or demonstrating evolution to be ridiculous (not to mention "meeting people's felt needs"). Scripture doesn't try to do any of that. Genesis 1:1 states that God created the universe and makes no attempt to prove either that fact or even God's existence. The only verses that can possibly be defined as "apologetic" (in the modern sense of the word) are ones such as, "The heavens declare the glory of God; and the firmament showeth his handiwork" (Ps. 19:1), and, "For the invisible things of him from the creation of the world are clearly seen, being understood by the things that are made, even his eternal power and Godhead; so that they are without excuse" (Rom. 1:20). That is "proof enough." Anyone, therefore, who rejects that glaringly obvious truth, who defiantly rejects the God of the universe, is a helpless, hopeless, and hapless *fool* (Ps. 14:1).

So strong is the word "fool" in that verse, in fact, that it is the third level of fool in the Hebrew.[7] The first (*'ewîl*) is the person who is thick-brained, likes to argue, and despises instruction (Prov. 1:7; 12:15; 20:3). The second (*kesîl*) is the dull, obstinate fellow who even if you put truth right in front of his eyes, he will not see it (17:24). But here the fool is *nābāl*, which adds to the others the idea of "an arrogant bore," a totally insensitive, immoral, and ungracious person. He speaks well of nothing

(Prov. 17:7), is a disgrace to all that is good (Ps. 74:22), and his mind is closed. Again, even though all creation loudly proclaims not only God's *existence*, but also His eternal, sovereign *power* and even *Godhead*, that is, His glorious character and attributes (Rom. 1:20), this depraved, obstinate wretch shakes his fist and says, "There is no God." Such people willfully refuse (because of their presuppositions) "to retain God in their knowledge" (1:28). Should we actually give such people an open forum for their blasphemy? They already own our school campuses and monopolize the news media. Why empower them further?

What, then, are we to do? *We are to proclaim the Gospel.* We are to *tell* the lost that they *are* lost, that they have sinned against a holy God, and are destined for an eternity in hell. We are to tell them that Jesus Christ alone is "the way, the truth, and the life" and that "no man cometh unto the Father, but by [Him]" (Jn. 14:6), for "neither is there salvation in any other: for there is none other name under heaven given among men, whereby we must be saved" (Acts 4:12). We must boldly proclaim that only in Him is there "forgiveness of sins" (Col. 1:14).

Now, should we know the arguments of the unbeliever? Should we know how they will attack? Should we equip our church people and our children for the dangers that exist? Of course! Any military man knows the importance of knowing his enemy. But our answer must always be, "Thus saith the Lord," not, "So says science."

Are apologetics worthless and a waste of time, effort, and brain storage? Absolutely not! They are a wonderful blessing to the Christian heart. I am fascinated, for example, by fulfilled Bible prophecy. My favorite example is how it has proven the accuracy of the prophecy against the city of Tyre (Ezek. 26) and how Alexander's conquest fulfilled it to the letter. Archaeology is also a great blessing; the existence of many biblical cities has been proven by the archeologist's spade, such as, Ur of the Chaldees and the cliff city of Petra. Further, as a backyard astronomer, every deep space object I observe gives me joy in how it "[declares] the glory of God" (Ps. 19:1).

But none of that saves anyone. The only hope man has is regeneration. He will know nothing apart from God. It is our responsibility, therefore, as God's Word declares, to "plant" the seed and "water" the seed, but it is the Sovereign God who will "[give] the increase." We are nothing; He is everything (1 Cor. 3: 6–7).

One writer, who oddly enough is an evidentialist, puts it well: "Some people say the best offense is a good defense, but I say unto you that the best defense is a good offense. . . . The best defense of Christianity is a clear, simple presentation of the claims of Christ and who He is in the power of the Holy Spirit."[8] Let's leave it there.

NOTES

[1] R. C. Sproul, John Gerstner, Arthur Lindsley, *Classic Apologetics* (Zondervan, 1984), p. 13.

[2] Gordon Clark, *Philippians* (The Trinity Foundation, 1996), p. 29.

[3] *Vine's Expository Dictionary of Old and New Testament Words.*

[4] *Thru the Bible* (electronic edition), comment on Neh. 3:26 (emphasis in the original).

[5] *John Gill's Exposition of the Entire Bible* (emphasis added).

[6] Lehman Strauss, *Devotional Studies in Philippians* (Loizeaux Brothers, 1959), p. 72.

[7] For a deeper study of these three words, see the author's *A Hebrew Word for the Day* (AMG Publishers, 2010), 86–87.

[8] Josh McDowell, *The New Evidence That Demands a Verdict* (Thomas Nelson, 1999), p. xxxi.

Why are the Scriptures called the rule to direct us how we may glorify and enjoy God? Because all doctrines *which we are bound to believe must be measured or judged of; all* duties *which we are bound to practice as means in order to the attainment of this chief end of man, must be squared or conformed unto this rule.*

Puritan Thomas Vincent
The Shorter Catechism Explained from Scripture, p. 22.

22

The Sealing of the Holy Spirit[*]

Ephesians 1:13–14

In whom ye also trusted, after that ye heard the word of truth, the gospel of your salvation: in whom also after that ye believed, ye were sealed with that holy Spirit of promise, Which is the earnest of our inheritance until the redemption of the purchased possession, unto the praise of his glory.

To understand the subject of this study, it is essential to note first the basic organization of the surrounding context. These two verses usher us into the third "stanza" of Paul's "Song of Praise" (vv. 3–14, which is actually one long and amazing sentence in the Greek). While verses 4–6 focus on the *Father* and speak of *past* ELECTION, and verses 7–12 focus on the *Son* and speak of *present* REDEMPTION, verses 13–14 focus on God the *Holy Spirit* and speak of *future* INHERITANCE. In that passage, we see the whole picture: salvation was *planned* by the Father, *provided* by the Son, and *powered* by the Holy Spirit.

Before continuing, we should make one general observation about this "stanza": *this stanza on the Holy Spirit is the shortest of the three*. Is there a reason for this? We are inclined to think there is. We should make it clear that the reason is not because the Holy Spirit is less *important*, but rather He has less *emphasis*. We point this out because the Word of God clearly declares that the Holy Spirit came to glorify Christ (Jn. 16:13–14), not be elevated above Him. Many today want to glorify the Spirit to such an extent that Christ (His person and work) is obscured. Many elevate the spiritual gifts and other "manifestations of the Spirit" so high that they become the test of spirituality. That type of thinking, therefore, makes the Holy Spirit the ultimate reality instead of the objective Truth of Christ being the ultimate reality. This is serious error, however. Any time a teaching elevates the Holy Spirit over Christ, there is a serious problem with its foundational Theology.

Even here in Ephesians 1 we see the Holy Spirit's subservient position. As Christ is the emphasis of verses 8–12, so He is here. If I may I

---

[*] This chapter was originally TOTT issues 39 and 40, October and November 2008.

say again, *we are in no way belittling the Holy Spirit*. On the contrary, we are showing exactly why the Spirit came; we are presenting the purpose for which He was sent.

This is further underscored by the fact that verse 13 contains a reference *first* to the **word of truth** (that is, Christ) and *then* to the **Holy Spirit**. Expositor Ray Stedman says it well:

> Some groups and individuals emphasize the Spirit and ignore the Word. They say, "We don't need the Word. All we need is the Spirit within. All we need is to trust our feelings—the indwelling Spirit will lead us." This is almost invariably a prescription for error and heresy as people drift away from the revealed truth of the Bible and into all sorts of confused, mystical, cultic views and practices, all in the guise of "following the spirit within."[1]

That is an excellent statement. There are countless Christians running around today saying, "Well, I am lead by the Spirit to do this thing," but we can without hesitation respond, "Wait just a minute. It doesn't matter what you *think* the Spirit is telling you to do; what matters is what Christ says in His Word." The issue is *always* the Word of God. The Holy Spirit is here to illumine us to the Truth of God's Word, never to give new Truth or lead us to do anything that contradicts God's Word. Truth is found only in the Word of God, not science, philosophy, religion, or anything else.

We should also recognize, however, the opposite danger—that is, the **word** without the **spirit**. The **word** is foundational and must be our guide, but we can become so mechanical that our vitality dies and we just wallow in empty orthodoxy. This is simply duty without love, agreement without fellowship, and depth without warmth. To put it succinctly: The **spirit** without the **word** is *heresy*, but the **word** without the **spirit** is *sterility*.

With those introductory thoughts in mind, we can now study the riches that we do, indeed, have in the **Holy Spirit**. Again, these riches are *centered* in Christ but *provided* through the Spirit.

The key to understanding our riches from the Spirit is to understand the doctrine of the "sealing" of the Holy Spirit.

It is truly sad (and somewhat inexplicable) that most theology books deal only briefly with the doctrine of *sealing*, and some actually do not mention it at all. Even in Louis Sperry Chafer's mammoth eight-volume *Systematic Theology*, there is only a scant 2-1/2 pages of coverage (III, pp. 338–39 and VI, pp. 136–37). This is true also of Charles Ryrie's *Basic Theology*. Even the old standbys, Augustus Strong's and Charles Hodge's *Systematic Theology*, mention it not at all. Neither do several modern works, such as *Foundations of the Christian Faith* (James Mongomery Boice), *Christian Theology* (Millard Erickson), and Wayne Grudem's *Systematic Theology* (only quotes Eph. 1:13 in the NIV). Disappointing also is even Francis Turretin's massive and usually thorough three-volume *Institutes of Elenctic Theology* (17th-century), which contains less than a page on the subject.

Neither is there much preaching on this extremely important and crucial doctrine. This surely is one of the reasons for much of the misunderstanding and false teaching on this subject and the subject of the Holy Spirit in general. How tragic it is that so many Christians do not understand the sealing of the Holy Spirit!

The reason I find this so tragic is that this doctrine is actually a key doctrine in understanding the Holy Spirit. Further, it is a key doctrine in understanding salvation. As we'll see in this study, the sealing of the Holy Spirit at our conversion is one of the most (if not *the* most) comforting and irrefutable doctrines in Scripture when it comes to our security in Christ. *No other doctrine makes the believer's security so vivid and undeniable.*

Let us, therefore, take the time to study the sealing of the Holy Spirit by looking at two divisions: the *reality* of sealing (v. 13) and the *result* of sealing (v. 14).

The Reality of Sealing (v. 13)

We need to study several things, so we will break our study down into four basic thoughts.

The Meaning Of Sealing

Besides our text here in Ephesians 1, there are two other references to the sealing of the Spirit in the New Testament:

> Now he which stablisheth us with you in Christ, and hath anointed us, is God; Who hath also sealed us, and given the earnest of the Spirit in our hearts. (2 Cor. 1:21–22).

> And grieve not the Holy Spirit of God, by whom ye are sealed unto the day of redemption (Eph. 4:30).

While most theologians and expositors get it right when they do mention it, there are others who muddy the water so badly that the concept of sealing is totally misunderstood. This is puzzling because the concept of sealing is actually quite ancient and *very* simple. In fact, this concept can be traced back centuries before Christ. Herodotus, the first of the great Greek historians (5th and 6th centuries BC), wrote in his book, *History*, that ancient man possessed not only his staff but his seal.

The Greek for **sealed** is the verb *sphragizō*, which means "to set a seal" or "to "mark with a seal." This comes from the noun *sphragis*, which refers to a signet ring that possessed a distinctive mark. There are many illustrations of a seal, both from ancient and modern times. We can see many of these by showing the four pictures sealing gives.

First, sealing pictures *Acquisition*. By this we mean that sealing pictures a finished transaction. First and foremost, sealing paints a legal picture; it shows the completion of a *legal transaction*. The Ephesian believers understood this since Ephesus was a seaport and supported a large lumber trade. We should interject that this was also true in Corinth, which explains why Paul mentioned sealing to the Corinthians as well as the Ephesians. A raft of logs would be brought from the Black Sea and notice sent to the various lumber firms that the raft had arrived. A lumber merchant would come, purchase his timber, and than stamp it with his seal. Usually he would leave his purchase in the harbor, sometimes for several weeks, and would send a trustworthy agent later to identify the master's seal and take away the purchased property.

This is actually true in more modern times. Harry Ironside recounts an incident in his own experience here in America around 1930:

> I was standing on a high bridge at St. Cloud Minn., watching a lumber jam, and as I saw the men working I said to my friend, "Do all these logs belong to one firm?" "Oh, no," he said; "there are representatives from many different firms working here in the Minnesota woods." "Well," I asked, "how on earth can they distinguish between the logs?" He showed me from the bridge how they were marked, so that when they reached their destination down the river, the various firms would be able to select their own logs.[2]

Another modern illustration of a seal, is a "notary public." A notary signs and seals a document, thereby finishing the transaction and sealing the agreement.

The spiritual parallel is that we have been "bought with a price" (1 Cor. 6:19–20), and we have been redeemed by Christ (Eph. 1:7). The indwelling Holy Spirit is now proof of that finished transaction. Again, as Ironside put it, "Though you and I are still tossing about on the waters of this poor scene we have been sealed by the Holy Spirit of promise." This leads us right to another picture.

Second, sealing pictures *Absolute Ownership*. The ancients would put their seal on animals and even slaves to prove ownership. In fact, the branding of animals is thought to have been practiced as early as 2,000 BC. Of course, branding cattle and horses is still done today. A brand is registered with the particular state in which the owner lives and that brand shows legal ownership. The same is true today of a patent or a copyright. In many books today, for example, one will find (along with the copyright symbol, date, and copyright holder) the words, "All rights reserved." This means only the copyright holder and the publisher are entitled to the benefits of the sale of the book.

This carries over into the spiritual parallel. The indwelling Holy Spirit shows that we belong to Christ. "All rights are reserved" to Him; only He is entitled to the benefits of ownership. As 2 Timothy 2:19 declares, "The foundation of God standeth sure, having this seal, The Lord knoweth them that are His." We do not belong to ourselves. Man today wants to "pull his own strings," "be his own boss," and "do his own thing." But the believer belongs to the Lord, for He purchased us with His own blood.

Third, sealing pictures *Authenticity*. A seal attests to the authenticity of a signature; likewise, a signature proves the genuineness of a letter.

Graphology, the scientific study of handwriting, is a fascinating subject. While some argue about whether handwriting reveals personality traits, "forensic graphology," the technical study of handwriting, is considered to be reliable. It is often used, in fact, in judicial proceedings to determine the authenticity of a signature or document. Though someone might be able to copy your signature accurately, it's highly improbable that they can copy the lines exactly or press on the paper with the same amount of pressure as you do.

The spiritual parallel is obvious. The indwelling Holy Spirit proves that the believer is genuine. Think of it! The Spirit's presence within us is "God's signature." There are arguments today about such things as "Lordship Salvation," what a Christian can and can't do, legalism verses antinomianism, grace and law, but doesn't this truth about sealing make it all obvious? The Holy Spirit within us is God's signature. With God's signature upon us, our lives will be different. It, indeed, declares that we are "new creatures" and that old things have passed away" and "all things have become new" (2 Cor. 5:17). Romans 8:9 is so very clear: "Now if any man have not the Spirit of Christ, he is none of His." The words "Spirit of Christ" refer without question to the Holy Spirit Whom Christ sent (Jn. 14:26; 15:26; 16:7). This is the **Holy Spirit of promise** spoken of in our text. If the Spirit is not present, if God has not "signed the document," that person does not belong to God. How many professing Christians today are merely a "close copy" instead of the "genuine article?" If they are genuine, people will be able to see the seal, God's signature. They will be able to see the "fruit of the Spirit" (Gal. 5:22–23).

Fourth, sealing pictures *Assurance*. By "assurance" we mean that sealing pictures absolute security. Matthew 27:62–66 tells us of the Roman seal that was placed on Jesus' tomb. No one in that day would have dared to break that seal as that would have resulted in certain death, specifically, being crucified upside down, a hideous death where the internal organs would end up in the victim's throat. So, that seal protected the contents; it made the contents secure by order of Rome. The same was true of the seals of King Darius and his nobles that they put on the stone placed over the entrance to the lion's den into which they threw Daniel (Dan. 6:17).

Today there is what is called a "registered letter." The addressee and the sender of the letter are recorded in a book. On the back of the letter is what is called a "return receipt" which is removed, signed by the addressee, and returned to the sender. The letter is also hand delivered and signed for by the addressee. All this protects and secures the contents of the letter.

The spiritual application is clear: *we are sealed eternally in Christ by the Holy Spirit's sealing.* One of the most important aspects of sealing is this one concerning assurance. All three New Testament references to sealing are aorist tense, a once-for-all past action. As Ephesians 4:30 indicates, we are "sealed [once for all] unto the day of redemption." We shall examine this in more depth when we get to the "Result of Sealing."

We should point out, however, that sealing is not the "baptism" of the Holy Spirit. These two are similar but also quite distinct. The word "baptism" is from the Greek *baptizō*, which literally means "immerse; place into." Originally the word was used of dying a garment, that is, placing a garment *into* the dye. This is why immersion is obviously and unarguably the only biblical method of baptism. To argue for sprinkling or pouring is simply foolish and pointless. No one dyes a garment by sprinkling or pouring the dye onto it.

The Baptism of the Holy Spirit, therefore, does two things. First, it places us into Christ. At one time we were in Adam, but now we are in Christ (see Col. 2:12 and Rom. 6:3–4). Second, it places us into the Body of Christ, the Church. First Corinthians 12:13 is clear: "For by one Spirit were we all baptized [placed into] one Body [the Body of Christ]." The word "baptized" is in the aorist tense showing that this is a once-for-all act which has been accomplished by God. Also, right here in Ephesians speaks of the fact that there is "one Spirit" and "one baptism" (4:4–5). The context of that passage shows this to be Spirit baptism (see chapter 31). The Scriptures are clear; all believers have been baptized by the Spirit. There is not one single exhortation or command in Scripture to "seek the baptism" as some teach today. Why? Because it is aorist tense. God alone accomplished this work in the past. Paul is here writing to the Corinthians, whom he calls carnal, fleshly infants, but still assures them that they, even in their immaturity, have been baptized, place into, the Body of Christ.

Putting all this together, we observe:

❑ *Baptism* of the Spirit places us into Christ and into His Body;

❑ *Sealing* of the Spirit shows God's ownership of us.

While similar, they are still distinct. And, as we will see later, both of these occur at the moment of salvation.

A wonderful example of this picture of assurance appears in Esther 8:8–12. While Haman had already been hanged for his evil plot against Mordecai, Queen Esther was still distressed. Because of Haman's treachery, he had persuaded King Ahasuerus to decree that anyone in his kingdom was allowed to attack and destroy the Jews. The key here is since *even the King himself could not reverse a decree that he had marked with his seal,* he had to issue and seal *another decree* that declared that the Jews could arm and defend themselves from attackers. This vividly pictures that a sealed decree was authoritative, binding, and *irreversible.* That is the picture in our sealing. God will not break His own decree that He sealed with His Spirit.

Before God called him to preach, pastor and author John Phillips was in the business world and worked for a large multinational British bank. Recalling those days, he writes:

> . . . when contracting parties entered into a legal agreement, the documents were "signed, sealed, and delivered." On numerous occasions the bank manager called for the sealing wax. Both contracting parties would sign the documents and the bank manager would sign as a witness. Then he would affix the heated sealing wax to the documents. After being signed and sealed, the documents were "delivered" to the contracting parties. The agreement, ratified by the seal, was then in force and was binding on all parties . . .
>
> In my banking days, the manager would usually deliver the original contract to a bank officer who would place it in the vault for safekeeping. Everything that could be done was done to ensure that the contract was preserved and its terms were put into effect. We can rest assured that God has taken every precaution against His promise ever being broken. As far as we are concerned, God has sealed us with that Holy Spirit of promise. Our salvation is as certain as God's character and throne can make it.[3]

How wonderful that last statement is—"Our salvation is as certain as God's character and throne can make it." Mark it down: *To say that we can lose our salvation is an attack on the very character of God.* It is saying that God isn't powerful enough to save us *and* keep us. It is saying that even with God's signature upon us, we are not guaranteed. We will return to this theme as we continue.

The Method of Sealing

By this we mean who exactly is the one who seals us. All three of the passages we have mentioned make it clear that sealing is accomplished entirely by God. Just like the Baptism of the Spirit, we are never exhorted to be sealed. Sealing is the work of God from start to finish.

It is also important to note that the verse reads "*with* **the Holy Spirit**, not "*by* the Holy Spirit." This indicates that the Holy Spirit is the *seal* not the *sealer*. It is God the Father who does the sealing. He is the "Lumber Merchant," while the Holy Spirit is the "Merchant's signet." Second Corinthians 1:21–22 bears this out:

> Now he which stablisheth us with you in Christ, and hath anointed us, is God; Who hath also sealed us, and given the earnest [guarantee] of the Spirit in our hearts.

We also should note that the definite article ("the") appears before **promise**, so the idea is that we **were sealed with that holy Spirit of [the] promise**. This, of course, refers to the Lord Jesus' promise to send His Spirit (Jn. 14:16; Jn. 16:7–14; Acts 1:4, 8). So **the Holy Spirit** was *sent*; He was sent to do certain tasks that would glorify Christ. One of those tasks was to be God's Seal upon the purchased possession.

To illustrate, I recall the days when my father-in-law owned and operated a little country store where he would buy food items in bulk and package them for resale. One item he carried was cheese, in various varieties, which he would buy in large blocks and then cut to a customer's wishes. To preserve some blocks for aging purposes (and, oh, how good is a 12-year-old, extra-sharp cheddar!) he would seal a block in wax. So in that case the *substance* of the seal was wax, and it was my father-in-law who did the actual *act* of sealing. Likewise, God the Father has done the sealing with (or, by means of) the Spirit.

Another modern illustration is when you go down to the store and buy a large item, such as an appliance, you receive a piece of paper called a "Guarantee." This is the manufacture's promise of quality. Infinitely deeper, the Holy Spirit is God's guarantee of quality. And we can also be thankful that God's guarantee is not just 90 days parts and labor, but is forever.

To summarize: First, the Father is the *Sealer*; second, the Holy Spirit is the *Seal*; third, Christ is the *Strength* of the seal (as He is the One who sent the Spirit and the One whose work made the Spirit's indwelling possible); fourth, the believer is the *Sealed*.

The Measure of Sealing

The main point we need to make here is that the sealing of the Holy Spirit is *universal among believers*. Some claim that they have had "an experience" that confirmed their sealing and that sealing is not necessarily true of every Christian. But there are three very plain proofs that *all* believers are sealed.

First, 2 Corinthians 1:21–22 declares that even the Corinthians were sealed. The Corinthians were not as carnal when Paul wrote his second letter as they were when he wrote his first, but they were still a carnal lot indeed. Paul, however, makes no exception; even in their carnality, the Corinthians were sealed. The same thing is true of the "baptism of the Spirit;" the Corinthians were not exempt from this either, as we noted earlier.

How we need to grasp the truth that the acts of sealing and baptism are the work of God! It is tragic, indeed, that Christians today live in a constant need of an "experience." Our salvation is not based on how we feel or what we have experienced, rather on what God has done. It is based upon the finished work of the Lord Jesus Christ on Calvary, and the assurance of that is based upon the indwelling, sealing power of the Holy Spirit.

Second, there is no Scripture exhortation to be sealed. This is a strong indication that sealing is universal. If sealing were not universal, then surely God would command us to seek it. There is no believer who knows how to go about "getting sealed" simply because there is no instruction on how to do it. *Sealing has nothing to do with experience*; it is a work that God accomplishes. In contrast, we *are* commanded to be "filled" (controlled) by the Holy Spirit (Eph. 5:18), as this is a repeated experience. But we are never told to be either sealed or baptized.

Third, Ephesians 4:30 exhorts us not to grieve the Holy Spirit by whom we are sealed. It is obvious here that Paul's attitude is that he assumes all believers are sealed. Remember, Paul is writing to all believers, so he says here to all those sealed believers that they should not grieve (sadden) the Holy Spirit. If only "spiritual people" were sealed, Paul's exhortation would make no sense. He would then be saying "do not grieve the Holy Spirit" to people who were already grieving the Holy Spirit.

We say again, *all* believers are sealed. Right in line with this is our fourth principle.

The Moment of Sealing

It is essential to recognize that *sealing occurs at the moment of salvation*. Again, there are those who maintain that sealing occurs sometime after salvation. This view, in fact, is quite troubling. The great expositor Martyn Lloyd-Jones is one of my personal heroes. His book on preaching (*Preaching and Preachers*) is unmatched on that subject and is greatly needed in our day. In my humble opinion, however, his otherwise stellar teaching was marred by his weakness on the doctrine of the Holy Spirit. With the deepest respect, I must say that his muddled (sometimes almost mystical) views on sealing, indwelling, infilling, and baptism (*God's Ultimate Purpose*, pp. 243–311 and other works) opened the door wide for errant charismatic teaching. It's undoubtedly significant that soon after his departure from Westminster Chapel in London, that church went the way of the charismatic Vineyard Movement.

Mystical ideas about sealing violate the simple purpose of this act, which is to be a guarantee. The Holy Spirit is the guarantee that we are genuine. Further, there are no New Testament examples of a person being sealed at some time subsequent to salvation. There are no instances of people being *filled*, but not sealed. While Lloyd-Jones, for example, discusses several Scriptures as "proof" (pp. 250–254), *not one of them mentions sealing by name*. It's amazing and tragic that one so solid in his overall theology was so confused about the work of the Holy Spirit. For example, the statement, "I am suggesting therefore that the 'baptism of the Spirit' is the same as the 'sealing with the Spirit'" (p. 264), reveals some very serious misunderstanding.

The main cause of this misunderstanding is the failure to examine the Greek text (again, something that Lloyd-Jones usually did not fail to do). The construction of the verb **believed** is the aorist participle in the Greek.[4] This actually shows *cause* more than it does *time*. In other words, believing is what *caused* the sealing. Therefore, both happened at the same time. The literal translation of this is, "in whom also having believed, ye were sealed."

This is not an isolated case of this Greek construction. Another example appears in Acts 1:8: "Ye shall receive power, after the Holy Spirit is come upon you." Again, "is come" is the aorist participle showing cause; that is, receiving power is caused by the indwelling Holy Spirit. Literally the verse reads, "Ye shall receive power, the Holy Spirit coming upon you."

We must also add, not only does sealing occur at the moment of salvation, it also happens once-for-all and forever. For example, a letter is designed to be sealed only once. Likewise, down through the centuries a seal of any kind was designed to be used only once. This has always been the value of a seal and is the case with God's seal; it has been given once-for-all. As mentioned earlier, all three references to sealing in the New Testament are aorist tense (punctiliar action in the past). But, in addition, Ephesians 4:30 says we are sealed (once-for-all) "unto the day of redemption." This refers to our final redemption, which is yet future. What redemption is this? Romans 8:23 tells us: "We ourselves groan within ourselves, waiting for the adoption, that is, the redemption of our body." Back in verse 5 we learn that we are "predestined" to final adoption, which is yet future. Now we see that redemption not only involves the present (in that Christ's blood was the purchase price for our redemption), but that redemption also involves our going to be with the Lord in glory.

The Results of Sealing (v. 14)

How marvelous verse 14 is! We've seen that sealing pictures acquisition, absolute ownership, and authenticity. But the most significant picture of sealing is *assurance* (security). If I may, I say again that I have found no other principle more assuring to salvation than this doctrine. Verse 14 teaches two results of sealing, both of which having to do with security.

Sealing Secures *Our Inheritance*

One of the saddest realities in Christianity today is the fact that many deny the biblical doctrine of the security of the believer. This doctrine has been called "that damnable doctrine that gives people license to sin." It is argued, "If you are eternally secure, you can go out and live any way you want to and just ask God to forgive you." But this doctrine says no such thing, for anyone who has that idea of salvation cannot possibly be a Christian. Salvation involves a new person, a new creature in Christ (2 Cor. 5:17; see chapter 23). We no longer live the way we once did.

But this verse tells us exactly where our security lies—*in the Holy Spirit*. We might be forced to agree with those who deny security if it were not for the Holy Spirit. But our text tells us that He is the **earnest** of our inheritance. That wonderful word **earnest** is *arrabōn*, a word that came into the Greek from Phoenician traders and means "first installment, down payment, deposit."

It's interesting to note that this was more than just a mere "pledge," as it is translated in the Roman Catholic Douay-Rheims translation and the Revised Standard Version. That mistranslation was the result of the inaccurate and often corrupt Latin Vulgate's use of the word *pignus* (pledge),[5] which is not the equivalent of the Greek *arrabōn*. This earnest is not just a *pledge* or *promise*; it's actually a *portion* of the inheritance, the first installment. As one commentator puts it, "The earnest, in short, is the inheritance in miniature."[6]

So it was that this term was used in secular Greek as a legal term in business and trade; it was with this advance payment that a contract became lawfully valid and binding. In fact, we have this term "earnest money" even today. The same Greek word is used in modern Greek for an engagement ring; it is more than just a promise to marry; it is the first installment of the coming marriage.

Now let us couple this thought with a deeper look at the word **inheritance**. This is the same basic word as back in verse 11—"In [Christ] also we have obtained an inheritance." The literal sense of the Greek *klēros* is "a lot" (as in "casting lots"). The word then came to mean "a share," "a plot of land," and finally "an inheritance." What then is our inheritance?—*the salvation described in verses 3–14*. Most of us have viewed our future inheritance as pots of gold sitting in various places throughout our heavenly mansion, but that is because our minds have been polluted by the world's ideas of wealth. Our true inheritance is the salvation Paul has been describing, and *the Holy Spirit is the guarantee of that salvation*. Just as "earnest money" is binding and not returnable, the Holy Spirit is not withdrawn from the believer; He is God's deposit, God's *first installment* of eternal salvation.

There has been much confusion and question about the sealing of the Holy Spirit in past years, but we must honestly ask, "Why?" How could anything be clearer? We first see all we have in Christ in verses 3–14, and then we see that the Holy Spirit is the promise, the guarantee, and the first installment of that salvation. What more could Paul have said to make it plainer? Those who reject the security of the believer must either ignore or willingly reject the plain analogy that Paul offers here. If someone can see that God has given us the first installment of our inheritance, that He has given us the down payment of glory, that He has given us the deposit of what is to come, but still think that we can lose all that, they are to be pitied indeed.

We, of course, are the purchased possession (v. 7), and our final redemption is yet future (Rom. 8:23). Therefore, we are absolutely secure in the knowledge of our future home in heaven. We not only have eternal salvation in the here and now, but this salvation is also going to usher us right into the redemption of the body, the final redemption of the purchased possession.

Dear Christian, can we ever lose our salvation? Absolutely not! Why? Because we have been sealed with "God's earnest money"—His indwelling Holy Spirit. Does that thought cause us to clap our hands in glee that we can now live any way we want? On the contrary, it ignites a humble submission and holiness of life.

Sealing Secures *God's Possession*

Not only is *our inheritance* in view in verse 14, but so is *God's possession*. Paul declares, **until the redemption of the purchased possession**. The word **possession** translates the Greek *peripoiēsis*, which speaks of gaining possession of property for one's self. To review one of our earlier illustrations, when the lumber merchant went to Ephesus, he purchased his timber and placed his seal upon it so that it would come directly to him and no one else. Likewise, we are God's purchased possession and His Seal (the Holy Spirit) secures that purchase and brings it directly to Him.

Finally, Paul closes by reminding us once again of God's ultimate purpose. While the spiritual riches God has given us are awesome, indeed, and while it is all guaranteed by God's down payment in the person of the Holy Spirit, that is not the primary purpose. Why is God bringing us to Himself? The answer is: it is all **unto the praise of his glory**. There is that marvelous phrase once again; this is the third and the most glorious usage in this passage; it culminates the entire passage. As Isaiah declared: "My people, my chosen. This people have I formed for myself; they shall show forth my praise" (Isa. 43:20–21). Yes, that speaks specifically of Israel, but God also "did visit the Gentiles, to take out of them a people for his name" (Acts 15:14), and so we too are His elect, His chosen, and we shall "show forth His praise."

We are reminded here of God's ultimate purpose as outlined in Ephesians 1—*to restore the unity between God and man so that man can glorify Him.* God did not save us primarily for our benefit, but rather saved us so we could praise Him. Let us never forget that truth!

Oh, is it not wonderful to know we are sealed? Man's seals can be broken. I used to hear my father say, "Locks only keep the honest people out." How true, for if someone wants into a place bad enough he will get in. But God's Seal will not and cannot be broken.

NOTES

[1] Ray Stedman, *Our Riches in Christ* (Discovery House Publishers, 1998), p. 50.

[2] Harry Ironside, *In The Heavenlies: Practical Expository Addresses on the Epistle to the Ephesians* (Loizeaux Brothers, 1977), p. 79.

[3] John Phillips, *Exploring Ephesians* (Loizeaux Brothers, 1993), electronic edition, comment on 1:13b.

[4] For a detailed explanation, see A. T. Roberson, *A Grammar of the Greek New Testament in the Light of Historical Research* (Nashville: Broadman Press, 1934), pp. 520-525. We would briefly mention the Greek case "locative of sphere." Basically, "locative" (Latin *locus*) speaks of "local" or "location." The "locative of sphere" then indicates the sphere, realm, or location in which something or some one exists. So, the words "in Whom . . . ye believed" show the location of belief.

[5] John Eadie, *A Commentary on the Greek Text of the Epistle of Paul to the Ephesians* (Wipf and Stock Publishers, 1998; reprint of 2nd Edition, 1861), p. 67.

[6] Eadie, p. 68.

The television performer watches his ratings, the politician his votes, the public speaker his applause, but the prophet who speaks for God is not governed by such response. He delivers his message though it may fall on deaf ears and gain him only scorn and maybe a prison cell. Amos did not rate with the bigwigs of Bethel, nor did John the Baptist win applause in the courts of Herod. The forerunner had crowds but he stepped aside and left the center of the stage to One greater than himself. We live in a day when men will not endure sound doctrine but look instead for pleasant ticklers of itching ears. Is there not somewhere a coming prophet who will forget comfort and security and status and retirement benefits for the loneliness of a Jeremiah, the perils of a Savonarola, the conflicts of a Luther, to speak for God in these last days? [William] Barclay says that the settled ministry has always resented wandering prophets who disturb their congregations. So the wilderness voice is not welcome either at home or abroad. But his reward is in the approval of God and the verdict of history.

Vance Havner
Pepper and Salt, pp. 104–105

23

"New Creature" and the Lordship Debate[*]

2 Corinthians 5:17

Therefore if any man be in Christ, he is a new creature: old things are passed away; behold, all things are become new.

This "tough text" is difficult only because of those who miss its critical application. The pivotal nature of this verse simply cannot be overstated. What does it mean to be a Christian? It means to be a **new creature**. The word **new** is the Greek *kainos*. While another word for **new** (*neos*) refers to something new in *time*, something that recently has come into existence, *kainos* refers to something new in *quality*, as it would be distinguished from something that is old and worn out, something that has never existed before.

Creature, then, is *ktisis*. In Classical Greek it meant the act of creation, the created thing, or the result of the act. It (and the verb *ktizō*) was often used in the Septuagint (Greek translation of the Old Testament) to translate the Hebrew *bara* "to create from nothing."

So what does it mean to be a **new creature**? It means that the Christian is not new in the sense of *time* (*neos*)—as in the date he received Christ as Savior—rather new in *quality* (*kainos*), a creature that has never existed before, a creature with a new character. When Christ comes into a life, *that life changes*. God's Word everywhere declares, in fact, that a change is automatic when someone truly believes.

The issue of "Lordship Salvation" (an unfortunate term that has been used to criticize some teachers who are desperately fighting against today's continued diluting of the gospel) has been a subject of much debate. If I may interject, I find it to be one of the most distressing debates I've witnessed in my 35 years of ministry. It is a sad state of affairs when many today actually teach that there is a difference between "accepting Jesus" as *Savior* and then at some later date making Him *Lord*, when there is absolutely no such dichotomy or distinction in Scripture. While their motive is inarguably pure—namely, they wish to avoid any appearance of salvation by works—their conclusion is tragically faulty.

---

[*] This chapter was originally TOTT issue 41, December 2008. See chapter 48 for another study on this topic.

Taken to its logical conclusion, in fact, such a teaching—which is actually an American invention and not a historical position of the church—results in a new form of Universalism, which teaches that ultimately everyone will be saved. The teaching is that all one must do is "believe in Jesus" (whatever that means) to be saved. No repentance is necessary, no change of life is expected, and no responsibility is demanded. What is this if not a form of Universalism? How many people do you know whom you could in some way persuade to say, "Oh, yes, I believe in Jesus." That's easy. Why? Because He was a historical figure, just as real and easy to believe in as Abraham Lincoln. He lived, He taught, and He had a "religion." You might even get a Buddhist to say, "Sure, I believe in Jesus," and it's certainly easy to get a Roman Catholic or a Mormon to say it. But does that mean they are truly saved? Further, one could even believe in Jesus' teachings and accept His resurrection as authentic, but does that mean he or she is a true Believer?

After all, we should also add, "the devils also believe, and tremble" (Jas. 2:19). They believe in the facts concerning Christ, and that is exactly what many today view salvation to be. How many people are relying on some vague "profession," "commitment," or some prayer they recited in Bible School when they were seven years old?

Our text, therefore, cuts to the very heart of this issue. All so-called "Lordship Salvation" means is that *true salvation results in an automatic change in the person who believes.* Is it not silly to talk about a "conversion" that doesn't change anything? The word "convert" is from the Latin *convertere,* "to turn around, transform." True salvation is, indeed, a conversion. This verse (and its context) says the believer (obviously from the moment of salvation on) *is* a new creature, not *will* be a new creature.

The story is told of a missionary who asked a Chinese merchant, "Have you ever heard the Gospel?" The merchant replied, "No, but I have seen it. I know a man who was a terror in this region. He was as fierce as an animal. He was an opium addict. But when he accepted the Jesus religion, he changed completely. Now his wickedness is gone. He is quiet and gentle."[1] Countless illustrations like that one demonstrate the automatic change that comes in the true believer.

It is the height of contradiction to say that a person can believe in Jesus as Savior but reject Him as Lord simply because *a change of life automatically results in a change of lordship.* Before salvation, *we* were lord, but after salvation, *Christ* is Lord, not because we *make* Him Lord by some subsequent "decision," but because He *is* Lord. That is what the Scripture says. If there hasn't been a change of lordship, there has been no change at all.

One of the most vivid examples of this principle appears in Acts 19:8–10, where we read that Paul encountered many "hardened" (*sklērunō*, to make hard or stiff) hearts while preaching the Gospel in the synagogue for three months. But there were also those in Ephesus who believed. As verses 18–20 recount, the Gospel turned Ephesus on its ear; it changed that society. Those who were involved in occult practices burned their books on spells, sorcery, and other such things. Their life change was dramatically demonstrated by the value of those books. Five thousand pieces of silver today would be worth hundreds of thousands of dollars. (We're reminded here of how even some Christians today ignorantly dabble in such things as horoscopes and Ouija boards, things that ought to be burned.)

Verses 23–29 go on to say that believers no longer invested money in pagan practices or paraphernalia, which was a devastating blow to local commerce. Silversmiths were being driven out of business because people no longer bought silver shrines of Diana, which were household idols. Paul's statement that these were "no gods" at all and the stir churned up by the silversmiths combined to trigger a riot. So serious was the situation that there was the danger of Diana worship being destroyed altogether.

That is what the Gospel does. It changes lives. If one chooses to call this "Lordship Salvation," so be it, but the fact is: true *conversion* means real *change*. Christianity is not a creed, code, or a system of ethics. Christianity is a *life*, a new reality that comes when we trust Christ as Savior *and* Lord.

Another point that many overlook is that justification and sanctification are inseparably linked together, for they occur at the same time. We are not justified at conversion and then sanctified at a later date by some other "decision" or "experience." While sanctification is in a sense *progressive* as we grow in grace and knowledge of Christ (2 Pet. 3:18), it is first and foremost *positional*. When we come to Christ and are, therefore, justified in Him, we are at the same moment made holy, "set apart," as we receive the righteousness of Christ (Rom 3:22; 4:11; 5:18; 2 Cor. 5:21). There is then an outworking of this holiness in everyday living: "But now being made free from sin, and become servants to God, ye have your fruit unto holiness, and the end everlasting life" (Rom. 6:22). After all, what does it mean to "be saved"? It means being saved *from* sin and *unto* holiness.

So, contrary to the "easy believism" that is prevalent today, there is no such thing as being *justified* without being *sanctified*. There is no such thing as spiritual *life* without spiritual *living*. Some immediately object by saying, "But you are adding to the Gospel; all one must do is believe." On the contrary, we are not *adding* to the Gospel, that *is* the Gospel. Yes, all one must do is "believe," but such *belief always results in obedience* (Rom.

1:5; 16:26; 1 Pet. 1:2). Faith and obedience are, in fact, so inseparable that we often find them used synonymously. Hebrews 5:9, for example, declares: "And being made perfect, he became the author of eternal salvation unto all them that obey him" (cf. 11:8). What's more, as we will detail later, the Greek behind "faith," contrary to modern teaching, clearly and irrefutably implies obedience. Good works never *save* (Eph. 2:8–9; Titus 3:5), but good works are always a *result*, an *evidence* of salvation (Eph. 2:10; Jas. 2:14–26).

It is, therefore, totally incongruous to say that we can believe in Christ but have absolutely no intention of following Him, obeying Him, or surrendering to Him. Certainly there is growth and an ever deeper understanding of what discipleship is, but to say that we can believe in Christ without becoming disciples is not only illogical, it borders on the heretical. While there are some disciples of Christ who are not true believers (Matt. 7:21–23 [see our chapter 48]; 8:21–22; Jn. 6:66), there is no true believer who is not a disciple, a follower, an imitator, an obedient servant of Jesus Christ. An acid-test of true salvation is a desire to obey Christ. If that desire is not present, something is seriously wrong.

Still there are those who want to divorce Christ's Saviorhood from His Lordship, but the Apostles certainly didn't do so. Paul echoes our Lord's words when he writes of salvation in Romans 10:9–11:

> That if thou shalt confess with thy mouth the Lord Jesus, and shalt believe in thine heart that God hath raised him from the dead, thou shalt be saved. For with the heart man believeth unto righteousness; and with the mouth confession is made unto salvation. For the scripture saith, Whosoever believeth on him shall not be ashamed.

Verse 9 clearly emphasizes that salvation involves two actions: confessing (*homologeō*, "declare the same thing") Jesus as Lord, and believing in the resurrection of Christ. But is this principle unique to the New Testament? No. It is rooted in Old Testament thought. To emphasize Lordship even more, Paul adds in verse 13, "For whoever calls on the name of the LORD shall be saved," which is actually a quotation of Joel 2:32. In the Old Testament, the phrase "call upon the name of the Lord" was specially identified with worship of the true God. It spoke of worship, adoration and praise and drew attention to God's holiness, power, and majesty.

Please read and consider how it is also used in the following verses: Psalm 79:5–6; 105:1; 116:4–5. Those verses emphasize that calling on the name of the Lord is to recognize who God is and to submit to His power, authority, and holiness. To say, as many do today, "Just call on Jesus to be saved," betrays an ignorance of what that phrase truly means. It means to call on Him as *God*, as *Sovereign*, and as *Lord*.

Still there are those who insist, "All you have to do is believe in Jesus," but this again shows a total ignorance of the meaning of the words they're using. I have read several Bible teachers who say such things as, "Faith does not mean obey," or "Obedience has no part in believing something." This, however, is patently false and demonstrates the increasing lack of study of the original languages by Bible teachers today. It is no wonder that there is so much false teaching on so many issues.

"Believe" and "faith" translate the Greek verb *pisteuō*. Its basic meaning is "to have faith in, trust; particularly, to be firmly persuaded as to something."[2] But as one Greek authority points out, *pisteuō* also implicitly and indisputably carries the idea "to obey":

> The fact that "to obey," as in the OT, is particularly emphasized in Heb. 11. Here the *pisteuein* [faith] of OT characters has in some instances the more or less explicit sense of obedience. . . . Paul in particular stresses the element of obedience in faith. For him *pistis* [faith] is indeed *hupakon* [obey] as comparison of Rom. 1:5, 8; 1 Thes. 1:8 with Rom. 15:18; 16:19, or 2 Cor. 10:5 with 10:15 shows. Faith is for Paul to *hupakouein tō euangeilō* [literally, "obedient to the good news"], Rom. 10:16. To refuse to believe is not to obey the righteousness which the Gospel offers by faith, Rom. 10:3. . . . He coins the combination *hupakon pisteuō* [literally, "obedience of faith"], Rom. 1:5.[3]

It is, therefore, an incontrovertible fact that the word "believe" immediately and fundamentally demands lordship, because it has the underlying foundation of obedience, commitment, and submission.

It should be clear from such language that *this issue should not be an issue at all*. It is truly puzzling (and distressing) why some evangelicals argue otherwise. It should deeply grieve us all, for it most certainly grieves our Lord. It is ludicrous, if not even blasphemous to the very character of Christ, to teach a distinction between His Saviorhood and His Lordship. To "believe" fundamentally demands Lordship because it includes the desire to submit and obey.

We can put this in the form of an axiom: *when someone believes something, regardless of what it is, that belief somehow changes them and results in some action or behavior that is characteristic of the belief.* In other words, true belief results in actions that reflect that belief.

How can one read Hebrews 11 and miss this truth? Every one of those characters had "faith," but that faith *always*, without exception, resulted in an outward action. Noah did not say, "Well, if God said it's going to rain, then I believe it's going to rain, but that doesn't really affect me or demand anything from me." No, Noah built an ark as a result of believing what God said (v. 7). Was Noah and his family saved because he built a boat? Absolutely not, because God could have destroyed the boat like everything else. Noah was saved because He believed what God said, and that belief resulted in obedience. Works do not *save* us, but when we believe our works *prove* it. That is what the book of James is all about: faith without the evidence of works is a dead faith.

Columbus, for example, believed the earth was round and that he could sail to the New World, so he acted upon it and left Spain. To make it even more practical, all of us believe in gravity, and we act upon it by not jumping off tall buildings. We can put the matter another way: *truly believing something, being fully persuaded of it, and trusting in it automatically demands behavior that conforms to the belief.* To deny this, if I may be brutally frank, is just plain foolishness.

Applying this to salvation, to "believe in Jesus" means three things. *First*, it means to believe in who He *is*, that He is God incarnate, Savior, and Sovereign Lord. *Second*, it means to believe in what He *did*, that He died for your sins and rose again from the grave. *Third*, it means to believe in what He *says*, that is, to trust Him and His Word implicitly and desire to obey Him in all respects. To obey Him means we acknowledge His lordship and submit to His authority.

Before going on, let me make something clear. Lordship teachers are *not* saying "belief plus works equals salvation," as some other teachers blatantly accuse us of saying. We are *not* saying that to be saved you must not only believe but also obey. Such an idea is unscriptural because it says that salvation is not all of grace. This was, in fact, the issue in Galatia, as the Judaizers were teaching that not only did one have to believe to be saved but also had to obey the Law.

Rather, what the Lordship view is saying is that believing *results* in obedience and an intention to obey. If you are truly born again, if you truly believe, then there will be evidence of this in your life. Obedience does not *cause* your salvation, rather it *proves* your salvation.

How clear the Apostle John was when he wrote:

> And hereby we do know that we know him, if we keep his commandments. (1 Jn. 2:3).

> And he that keepeth his commandments dwelleth in him, and he in him. And hereby we know that he abideth in us, by the Spirit which he hath given us. (1 Jn. 3:24)

There is one sure way to know if someone is a true believer, a true disciple of Jesus Christ: whether or not he (or she) obeys the Word of God.

There are countless people walking around today who claim to be "Christian," but they no more obey the Word of God than a thief obeys laws about burglary. Certainly, there are many who don't know the Word of God (often because preachers aren't telling them), but the numbers are increasing of those who, when they hear the Word, do not obey. Such willful and continuous disobedience, a lack of any intention or desire to obey God's Word, indicates a lost condition.

Turning to our Lord Himself, He constantly emphasized that before someone believes, they must "count the cost" and then follow Him *unconditionally* (Lk. 14:26–33; see also Matt. 7, in which the whole context is a progression concerning salvation; also 10:34–39; Lk. 6:46–49; etc.). People are being told today to, "Just believe in Jesus," but Jesus said, in effect, "Stop and count the cost before you believe; following Me will cost you something."

Our Lord also made it clear that just saying you are a Christian doesn't make it so. In Matthew 7:21–23 He makes this sobering and frightening statement (see chapter 48 for an exposition of this passage):

> Not every one that saith unto me, Lord, Lord, shall enter into the kingdom of heaven; *but he that doeth the will of my Father which is in heaven.* Many will say to me in that day, Lord, Lord, have we not prophesied in thy name? and in thy name have cast out devils? and in thy name done many wonderful works? And then will I profess unto them, I never knew you: depart from me, ye that work iniquity.

What a terrifying passage! This is why Paul writes elsewhere that we need to "examine [ourselves], whether [we] be in the faith; prove [our] own selves" (2 Cor. 13:5), and why Peter wrote that we should "give diligence to make [our] calling and election sure" (2 Pet. 1:10) and lists the evidences of that in the context (vv. 5–9). It's not enough to *call* yourself a Christian or even *say* Jesus is Lord. What *proves* you are a Christian? *Doing "the will of My Father in heaven."* As the old expression goes, "Words are cheap," and they seem to get cheaper every day as the Gospel is redefined in increasingly broad terms. But our Lord is in no way ambiguous—*the proof of salvation is obedience.*

Earlier in Matthew (7:14) our Lord says that few go through the narrow gate that leads to life. He also adds that there are many wolves that *look* like sheep (v. 15) but are not, and that we can identify them by their fruits (vv. 16–20).

Indeed, the two greatest evidences of true conversion are obedience to God's Word (Jn. 14:15, 23; 1 Jn. 2:1–5; 3:21–24) and holiness of life (Eph. 4:24; 1 Thes. 4:3–4, 7; etc.). Those who do neither one are simply not true believers. If one chooses to call this "Lordship Salvation," so be it, but the fact remains.

Martyn Lloyd-Jones well says:

> We must emphasize that you cannot separate the Lord and Jesus. The person is one and indivisible. He is always the Lord. There is no such thing as "coming to Jesus." In one sense, a man cannot even come to Christ. He can only come to the Lord Jesus. . . . A man cannot accept Him as Saviour only, and then perhaps later decide to accept Him as Lord, for He is always the Lord. . . . We do not "come to Jesus," and we do not believe in Jesus: we come to the Lord Jesus, we believe in Him as He is.[4]

The New Testament nowhere separates Jesus as *Savior* from Jesus as *Lord*. He is either both, or He is neither. We say again in closing, the so-called "Lordship Salvation" controversy shouldn't even be a controversy. The true believer knows Christ not only as Savior but also as Lord. The true Christian is a **new creature**.

NOTES

[1] Cited in Roy L. Laurin, *Life Matures! Devotional Exposition of the Book of First Corinthians* (Stationers Corporation, 1941), p. 93.

[2] Spiros Zodhiates *The Complete Word Study Dictionary: New Testament* (AMG Publishers, 1992), p. 1160.

[3] Gerhard Kittle (Editor). *Theological Dictionary of the New Testament* (Eerdmans, 1964; reprinted 2006), Vol. VI, p. 205.

[4] *God's Ultimate Purpose: An Exposition of Ephesians 1* (Baker Book House, 1983), p. 321.

The faith will totter if the authority of the Holy Scripture loses its hold on men. We must surrender ourselves to the authority of Holy Scripture, for it can neither mislead nor be misled.

Augustine of Hippo
The Westminister Collection of Christian Quotations, p.19

24

The Sabbath or Sunday?[*]

Exodus 20:8–11

Remember the sabbath day, to keep it holy. Six days shalt thou labour, and do all thy work: But the seventh day is the sabbath of the LORD thy God: in it thou shalt not do any work, thou, nor thy son, nor thy daughter, thy manservant, nor thy maidservant, nor thy cattle, nor thy stranger that is within thy gates: For in six days the LORD made heaven and earth, the sea, and all that in them is, and rested the seventh day: wherefore the LORD blessed the sabbath day, and hallowed it.

What was instituted as the Sabbath in the Mosaic Law continues to be a misunderstood concept in our day. Some sincere, well-meaning Christians, in fact, insist on worshipping on the Sabbath (Saturday) instead of the Lord's Day (Sunday). To address this issue, let us examine four emphases.

The Old Testament Sabbath

The root of the Hebrew *shabbāt* (**Sabbath**) is the verb *shābat*, which means to cease or rest. It first occurs in Genesis 2:2, where God "rested on the seventh day from all his work which he had made." That, of course, set the precedent that God desires His people to cease work (implying rest), but how they do so is not the same in all ages.

Based on *shābat* in Genesis, therefore, some teachers conclude that the Sabbath *day* (*shabbāt*) is perpetual and the same in every age, but Scripture simply does not say that. Yes, while *shābat* occurs in Genesis in reference to *God*, *shabbāt* occurs not a single time in Genesis to indicate a prescribed Sabbath day for *man*. There is, in fact, neither a *command* nor even an *implication* that man was required to observe (or ever did observe) the Sabbath day until the Mosaic Law was given after Israel came out of Egypt (Ex. 16:23–29; **20:8–11**). Not one of the patriarchs of Genesis, for example, is said to have observed the Sabbath.

---

[*] This chapter was originally TOTT issue 42, January 2009.

Job is another crucial example. Several factors date the events of Job as occurring sometime after Babel but before, or perhaps contemporaneously, with Abraham. In other words, Job lived before the Mosaic Law was given. It is, therefore, significant, as theologian Louis Sperry Chafer puts it, that while "Job discloses the religious life and experiences of the patriarchs, and though their various responsibilities to God are therein discussed, there is never a reference to a Sabbath-day obligation."[1] In dramatic contrast, it is distinctly stated that the Sabbath was given to *racial* Israel through Moses (Ex. 16:29; **20:8–10**; Neh. 9:13–14; Ezek. 20:11–13). The remainder of the OT is permeated with references to the **Sabbath**, the word appearing some seventy-seven times (all the other books of the Pentateuch, 2 Kings, 1 and 2 Chron., Neh., Ps., Isa., Jer., Ezek, and Amos). So complete was such cessation from any labor to be (Ex. 20:10), for example, that the people couldn't gather sticks for a fire (Num. 15:32–36) or even light a fire in their homes (Ex. 35:3).

The Place of the Mosaic Law

When the above point arises, another immediately follows, namely, the place of the OT Law, which also is greatly misunderstood today. Some teachers (as did the Judaizers of old: Acts 15:5; Gal. 2:11–13; 3:1, 3; 5:1) insist that Christians must keep the Mosaic Law. It is *essential* to a proper understanding of Scripture, however, to recognize that the recipients of the law were those whom God "brought . . . out of the land of Egypt" (Ex. 20:2), that is, Israel *alone*. It was *never* meant for the Church or Gentiles in general. It was a covenant made *with* Moses *for* racial Israel.

The purpose of the Law was basically four-fold and is summarized in Galatians 3:19–25. *First*, it was to make sin known (v. 19, "added because of transgression"), "for by the law is the knowledge of sin" (Rom. 3:20). *Second*, it demonstrates that "all [men are] under sin" (v. 22; cf. Rom. 3:23) and sin's horribleness (Rom. 7:7–13). *Third*, it actually imprisons men and inhibits sin: "Before faith came, we were kept under the law, shut up unto the faith which should afterwards be revealed" (v. 23; cf. 1 Tim. 1:9). "Kept" is *phroureō*, which means to keep inward under lock and key. The law was a jailer who held in custody those who were subjected to sin, and who kept them that way until Christ came to free them.

Fourth, and most significantly, because God is holy (1 Pet. 1:16), the law was a schoolmaster that pointed men to Christ and His righteousness (vv. 24–25). The end of the Law came when Christ was crucified. One of the most basic principles of understanding the Bible is that the Mosaic Law ended in Christ. If that is not recognized, the result will be enormous confusion and serious error. Paul, therefore, makes the matter absolutely clear with the word "schoolmaster." The Greek is *paidagogos,* which was a person (usually a slave) who was assigned as a tutor and guardian for young boys. By its very definition, it was both a *temporary* and *lowly* position. When the son came of age into full sonship at about eighteen, the schoolmaster's responsibilities ended. Paul's imagery, then, is unmistakable. The Mosaic Law was a temporary schoolmaster that was designed to lead Israel to maturity, that is, *Christ.* Once Christ arrived, He became the controlling force in the believer's life.

The Mosaic Law, therefore, including the **Sabbath,** was *never* intended to be the rule in the Christian's life. The Christian is under a "new law." One school of Bible teaching is fond of saying, "We are no longer under law but under grace," which while true when we are speaking of the Mosaic system, is not true if we conclude that there is *no law at all.* In other words, just as grace existed in the Old Testament, law still exists today, but just as grace was manifested differently under the Old Covenant, law is manifested differently in the New Covenant.

So basic is the truth that the Mosaic Law is passed that our Lord Himself declared, "Think not that I am come to destroy the law, or the prophets: I am not come to destroy, but to fulfil" (Matt. 5:17). "Fulfil" is *plēroō,* a verb that speaks of filling a container to capacity and means to influence fully, control, or satisfy. The entire Mosaic Law pointed to Christ, so when He came, He "filled it up," He satisfied it, so it passed away.

Even more significant, our Lord later even summarized the *entire* law (all 613 commands of it!) into two: love God and your neighbor, on which "hang *all* the law and the prophets" (Matt. 22:36–40; emphasis added). What is the key word here? What law is now in force that replaces and supercedes the old? *The law of love.* As Paul wrote, "He that loveth another hath fulfilled the law. . . . Love worketh no ill to his neighbour: therefore love is the fulfilling of the law" (Rom. 13:8, 10).

Oh, how far superior this law is to the old! Jesus declared, "except your righteousness shall exceed the righteousness of the scribes and Pharisees, ye shall in no case enter into the kingdom of heaven" (Matt. 5:20), and then went on to illustrate how superior. While the old law said not to murder, the new says not to have rash anger (vv. 21–26; cf. Ex. 20:13). While the old said not to commit adultery, the new says to not even look with lust (vv. 27–28; cf. Ex. 20:14). While the old said not to swear falsely, the new says, "Swear not at all," that is, carelessly or profanely (vv. 33–34; cf. Lev. 19:12). While the old said "an eye for an eye," the new says "turn the other cheek" (vv. 38–39; cf. Ex. 21:24). Let us glorify our Lord by keeping *His* law, not the one He fulfilled.

For a little more study, what did Paul tell the Galatians about how the law is fulfilled (Gal. 5:14)? What does he call that law, in fact (6:2)?

New Testament Rest

Coming back to the **Sabbath**, if we may we reemphasize, the Mosaic Law, including the **Sabbath**, was given to *racial* Israel (Ex. 20:2). *None* of the Mosaic system was meant for the church or Gentiles in general. This includes the **Sabbath**, which was not commanded until the Mosaic system, and is never repeated in the NT, as are the other nine commandments that are written on men's hearts (Rom. 2:15).[2]

So what about the NT? While it is quite true that there are sixty occurrences of the word **Sabbath** in the New Testament (*sabbaton*), all but one are in the Gospels and Acts, where it is simply used as historical reference (e.g., as in "such-and-such a thing happening on the Sabbath"). The *only* occurrence in the Epistles is Colossians 2:16: "Let no man therefore judge you in meat, or in drink, or in respect of an holyday, or of the new moon, or of the Sabbath days." It is beyond any doubt whatsoever that the Sabbath is not in force in the NT.

That being said, however, since God's resting in Genesis established the precedent that He wanted His people to enjoy rest, is the Lord's Day the Christian "day of rest" in this age, or as some word it, "the Christian Sabbath"? No, as Hebrews 4:1–11 wonderfully demonstrates. There we read of the perfect rest provided by the finished work of Christ. "The rest under Christ," Chafer writes, "is not for one day in the week, nor is it that Sabbath rest which was due after a six-day strain. . . . It is rather the abiding rest of faith in Another. . . . It is rather the rest of Christ's imparted, resurrection life, and that life is ceaselessly active."[3]

Thanks be to God that because of grace through Christ, no longer do we need a prescribed *day* of rest because our Lord fulfilled the Mosaic System, including the **Sabbath**. Whenever we need rest, therefore, we take it. We live not by *legalism* but by *liberty* (Gal. 2:4; 5:1, 13).

Again for further study, read Hebrews 7:18–19, 22 and 8:6–13, noting how the writer declares that the Mosaic Law (the old covenant) had passed its usefulness because of its own weakness and that "a better testament" of "Jesus" (the New Covenant) replaced the Mosaic System.

The Centrality of the Lord's Day

This brings us to a final emphasis, that of the place of the Lord's Day (Sunday). While not "the day of rest," the first day of the week, the day of our Lord's resurrection, became the day for public worship of the church. While some teachers adamantly argue, this is the clear precedent (Jn. 20:19; Acts 20:7; 1 Cor. 16:2; Rev. 1:10).

While modern "Sabbath keepers" insist that Sunday did not become the day of worship until Constantine in the 4th-century, that is historically false. Writing in the middle of the second century, apologist Justin Martyr described a typical worship service of his day:

> And on the day called Sunday, all who live in cities or in the country gather together to one place, and the memoirs of the apostles or the writings of the prophets are read, as long as time permits; then, when the reader has ceased, the president verbally instructs, and exhorts to the imitation of these good things. Then we all rise together and pray, and, as we before said, when our prayer is ended, bread and wine and water are brought, and the president in like manner offers prayers and thanksgivings, according to his ability, and the people assent, saying Amen.[4]

We should also interject here that while lost in most churches today, Martyr demonstrates that preaching was central to the Early Church (note the primacy of "doctrine" in Acts 2:42) and its immediate descendents. Mark it down—unlike today's seeker-sensitive, entertainment driven, music saturated church growth philosophy, the reading and exposition of the Word of God was the absolute center of the worship service.

If Justin Martyr is not enough, the even earlier writings of Barnabas and Ignatius prove Sunday worship beyond the slightest doubt. *The Epistle of Barnabas* 15:8–9 (100 AD) states:

> Finally, [the Lord] says to them: "I cannot bear your new moons and Sabbaths" [Isa. 1:13]. . . . This is why we spend the eighth day in celebration, the day on which Jesus both rose from the dead and, after appearing again, ascended into heaven.[5]

Further, *The Letters of Ignatius: To Magnesians* 8:1–9:1 (AD 107) declares:

> Do not be deceived by strange doctrines or antiquated myths, since they are worthless. For if we continue to live in accordance with Judaism, we admit that we have not received grace. . . . If, then, those who had lived in antiquated practices came to newness of hope, no longer keeping the Sabbath but living in accordance to the Lord's Day, on which our life also arose through him and his death.[6]

Following is one of the most devastating statements I have ever read on this issue. It comes from the late David Baron (1857–1926), who at one time was one of the most eminent and learned Jewish converts to the Christian faith and who founded, along with C.A. Schönberger, the *Hebrew Christian Testimony to Israel* missionary organization in London:

> How can a Hebrew Christian be shown that he must not keep the Seventh-day Sabbath seeing it is written: "Wherefore the children of

Israel shall keep the sabbath, to observe the sabbath throughout their generations, for a perpetual covenant" (Ex. 31:16)?

There is no necessity to "show" or teach the Jewish believers that they "must" not "keep the Sabbath." . . . When more fully instructed, and as he grows in grace and in the knowledge of Christ, he will be brought to see for himself that the Jewish Sabbath has not significance in this dispensation and in relation to those whose calling is a heavenly one, and whose destinies are bound up not with time but with eternity. . . .

The Sabbath is thus essentially connected with the old marred creation, with the imperfect Mosaic dispensation, and with the typical redemption from Egypt. But Christians are children of the new creation, and are in the dispensation not of Law but of the Spirit. "With Christ's resurrection," says one writer, "the Seventh-day Sabbath expired, transmitting its sanctity and its privileges . . . to the first day of the week."[7]

Again, that is from a saved Jew. If a *Jewish* believer can so easily recognize that "the old marred" system is past, why can't *Gentile* believers see it and stop their insistence on the Sabbath?

The simple fact is that the first day of the week is so obvious in the NT, so clearly the precedent set for *all* believers, both Jew and Gentile, and then so unmistakably observed by the church from the resurrection, through the Church Fathers, and to the present, that to argue against it is the height of folly and an insult to our Lord.

Finally, to further support the straw man of "Sabbath keeping," some teachers are so desperate that they even challenge the fact that Jesus rose on the first day of the week. There are two incontrovertible passages, however, that state this without doubt.

First, Mark 16:9: "Now when Jesus was risen early the first day of the week, he appeared first to Mary Magdalene, out of whom he had cast seven devils." While this is clear, rationalistic textual criticism challenges this passage (vv. 9–20), saying that it's not in the so-called "best manuscripts." (Some "Sabbath-keepers," in fact, rely on such criticism to get around this verse.) Sadly, this is only one of many passages that have been damaged because of such criticism. I have been studying and writing on the textual criticism issue for some twenty years, so I could go into some detail, but I will just submit here the very brief facts concerning this passage.

1) The vast majority of Greek manuscripts (about 1800) include this passage. 2) It appears in many ancient versions of the Bible (e.g., the 2nd-century Peshitta Syriac). 3) *Nineteen* of the early Church Fathers (100–500) supported it; Justin Martyr (151), for example, quotes verse 20 in his first

Apology, proving that this passage was familiar to believers within 50 years of the last of the evangelists. 4) All the approximately 2,000 surviving Lectionaries (portions of the Greek NT that were read in the churches on special days) include it. 5) It has stood through the centuries as being unquestionably genuine only until modern textual criticism.

This verse, then, is clear, authentic evidence of Jesus' resurrection on the first day of the week. To reject it is pure folly. *But*, if people insist on rejecting it, we can still turn to another irrefutable proof.

Second, please turn to Luke 24 (for the sake of space, we will not quote the entire passage). What is essential to note here is that *all the events from verses 1–21 occurred on the same day*. Verse 1 sets the stage:

> *Now upon the first day of the week*, very early in the morning, they came unto the sepulchre, bringing the spices which they had prepared, and certain others with them. (Emphasis added here and in the following verses.)

While *this* verse does not actually *state* that Jesus rose on the first day of the week, when we read on, we discover that the other events that happened *on that same day* make the issue inarguably clear. Please read verses 2–6 and then note verse 7:

> The Son of man must be delivered into the hands of sinful men, and be crucified, and *the third day* rise again.

This obviously establishes that Jesus would rise on the third day, which no one questions. When we continue reading, however, *we find out what day that was*. Read verses 8–12 and then note verse 13, where the scene in this drama changes to when Jesus appears to two men who are on their way to Emmaus on this same day:

> And, behold, two of them went *that same day* to a village called Emmaus, which was from Jerusalem about threescore furlongs [about 7-1/2 miles].

Again, on the *same day* that the women went to the tomb, Jesus appeared to these men. So what day is this? The *first day*, our "Sunday." Finally, read verses 14–20, and then note the clincher, verse 21:

> But we trusted that it had been he which should have redeemed Israel: and beside all this, *to day is the third day* since these things were done.

Let us put it all together: Since verse 1 says the ladies went to the tomb on the *first* day of the week, since verse 7 says He would rise on the *third* day, since verse 13 says this is the *same* day, and since verse 21 says this *is* the third day, what day is this?—*the first day of the week.* It is just that simple.

Oh, that we would rejoice in the true rest we have in Christ and revere each Lord's Day as we worship together (cf. Heb. 10:25).

NOTES

[1] Louis Sperry Chafer, *Systematic Theology* (Dallas Seminary Press, 1947–1948), Vol. IV, p. 254.

[2] The Moral Law was written in the hearts of men everywhere (Rom. 2:15), demonstrating that men know in their heart (i.e., by their conscience) not to lie, steal, murder, and violate the other moral commands. Such moral law is found in legal codes of nations throughout history prior to the Mosaic Law. These moral laws (except for keeping the Sabbath) are also found restated several times in the NT: having no other gods (Ex. 20:3; Deut. 5:7; Acts 5:29); making no idols or images" (Ex. 20:4–6; Deut. 5:8–10; Acts 17:29–31; 1 Cor. 8:4–6; 10:14; Col. 3:5; I Jn. 5:21); not profaning God's name (Ex. 20:7; Deut. 5:11; Jas. 5:12); honoring one's father and mother (Ex. 20:12; Deut. 5:16; Eph. 6:1–3; Col. 3:20); not murdering (Ex. 20:13; Deut. 5:17; Rom. 13:9–10; Jas. 2:11); not committing adultery (Ex. 20:14; Deut. 5:19; Rom. 13:9–10; 1 Cor. 6:9; Heb. 13:4; Jas. 2:11); not stealing (Ex. 20:15; Deut. 5:19; Rom. 13:9–10; Eph. 4:28); not lying (Ex. 20:16; Deut. 5:20; Eph. 4:25,31; Col. 3:9; Tit. 3:2); not coveting (Ex. 20:17; Deut. 5:21; Rom. 7:7; 13:9; Eph. 5:3–5; Heb. 13:5 Jas. 4:1–3).

[3] Chafer, Vol. IV, p. 110.

[4] *The Ante-Nicene Fathers*, Vol. 1; Ages Digital Library, "The First Apology Of Justin," Chapter 67.

[5] J. B. Lightfoot and J. R. Harmer (translators), *The Apostolic Fathers*, Second Edition (Baker Books, 1989], p. 183.

[6] *Ibid*, p. 95.

[7] From *The Witness* (Scotland). Cited in William C. Irving, *Heresies Exposed*, Third Edition (Loizeaux Brothers, 1921), p. 167.

25

Was There Regeneration in the Old Testament?*

Isaiah 57:15; Ephesians 2:1

For thus saith the high and lofty One that inhabiteth eternity, whose name is Holy; I dwell in the high and holy place, with him also that is of a contrite and humble spirit, to revive the spirit of the humble, and to revive the heart of the contrite ones.

And you hath he quickened, who were dead in trespasses and sins;

As theologian Millard Erickson puts the matter, "Regeneration is a particularly problematic issue with regard to Old Testament believers."[1] Some teachers insist that because regeneration is an act of the Holy Spirit, and because the Holy Spirit would not be given until Pentecost, it therefore follows that regeneration was not at work in the Old Testament.

One problem with that view, it seems to me, is that it assumes that *regeneration* is inseparably linked with *indwelling*. In other words, it assumes that the only way the Holy Spirit can regenerate is if He also indwells (Jn. 14:16–20; Rom. 8:9, 11, 23; 1 Cor. 6:19; 1 Jn. 4:13).

But this also assumes that the Holy Spirit never indwelt Old Testament believers, but in some cases it appears He did. David cried, "Take not thy holy spirit from me" (Ps. 51:11), indicating the Holy Spirit's presence in him. "The Spirit of the LORD departed from Saul" (1 Sam. 16:14), indicating that the Holy Spirit had to be there before He could depart. While some teachers argue here that the Holy Spirit didn't actually dwell within, rather exerted an external influence, that doesn't seem to agree with the language.

So, while the Holy Spirit never leaves the New Testament believer—He abides with us *forever* (Jn. 14:16), and the absence of His presence indicates a lost condition (Rom. 8:9)—there was that danger for the Old Testament believer. In the final analysis, then, the difference between the Holy Spirit's indwelling in the Old and New Testaments is one of degree. We must conclude, then, that regeneration and indwelling are distinct and not inseparable.

---

* This chapter was originally TOTT issue 43, February 2009.

I wonder, however, if the real problem here is that the doctrine of regeneration itself is not fully understood by many believers. (This complements our study in chapter 23, which deals with the result of salvation being a new creation.) Let us, therefore, first take a brief look at the doctrine of regeneration and then see how it applies to the Old Testament.

What Is Regeneration?

Like that wonderful word *charis* ("grace"), the Greek word behind "regeneration" (*paliggenesia*) is one of those ancient Greek words transformed by New Testament usage into something far deeper than it was before. It is a compound comprised of *palin*, "again," and *genesis*, "birth, origin." It, therefore, meant a restoration, return to former circumstances, or revivification. The Stoics believed that the earth would periodically perish through some conflagration, so they used this word to refer to "when the earth awakened in the blossoming of springtime from its winter sleep and revived from its winter death." Philo, the 1st-century Jewish philosopher, often used it to refer to the world emerging out of fire in a phoenix-like resurrection, a belief also held by the Stoics. Even of Noah and his family, Philo wrote, "They became leaders of a *paliggenesia* and chiefs of a second cycle."[2]

It's significant, then, that this word is used twice in the New Testament to refer to a *real* rebirth. It appears first in Matthew 19:28, where our Lord Himself says, "Verily I say unto you, That ye which have followed me, in the regeneration when the Son of man shall sit in the throne of his glory, ye also shall sit upon twelve thrones, judging the twelve tribes of Israel." The context, of course, is our Lord's teaching of future events, so He refers to the "regeneration," the "restoration," the "re-creation," of the world that will take place after His Second Coming. Many creationists and Bible teachers believe that this will be a restoration of the primeval perfections of the earth before the Genesis Flood. In stark contrast to pagan belief, this will be a true rebirth of the original world by the One True God who created it. As Acts 3:21 also declares, "Whom the heaven must receive until the times of restitution of all things, which God hath spoken by the mouth of all his holy prophets since the world began."

The other occurrence of *paliggenesia* is in Titus 3:5: "Not by works of righteousness which we have done, but according to his mercy he saved us, by the washing of regeneration, and renewing of the Holy Ghost." As God can restore a fallen world, He also restores those who were once spiritually *alive* and then *dead* in Adam (1 Cor. 15:22; Rom.5:17) to a *new life* in Christ (Rom. 6:4).

What, then, is regeneration? Theologian Emory Bancroft offers this excellent definition:

> Regeneration is the Holy Spirit's gracious sovereign, quickening act, in which the divine life and nature is imparted to the soul of man, causing a reversal of his attitude toward God and sin, the expression of which, in repentance and faith, is secured through the instrumentality of the Word of God.[3]

This doctrine has been variously described as: the new birth (Jn. 3:3–7; Jas. 1:18; 1 Pet. 1:23), a spiritual quickening or resurrection (Jn. 5:21, 25; Eph. 2:1, 10), the impartation of a new life (2 Pet. 1:4;), a spiritual translation (Col. 1:13), and a transformed life (2 Cor. 5:17).

Why Is Regeneration Necessary?

We would submit that this question is, in fact, the heart of the whole matter. At the root of today's misunderstanding of salvation in general, and the Doctrines of Grace in particular, is that we do not recognize man's spiritual state before God regenerates him. What is that state? He is **dead in trespasses and sins** (Eph. 2:1, emphasis added; cf. 5:14; Jn. 5:21; 2 Cor. 5:14; 1 Jn. 3:14).

The Greek for **dead** here is *nekros*, which literally speaks of a dead body, a corpse, as in James 2:26, "For as the body without the spirit is dead, so faith without works [as an evidence] is dead also." Before God regenerates a man, he is quite literally *a spiritual corpse*; his spirit is separated from God. Paul doesn't mean the man "looked dead" or was "in danger of death" or "standing on the precipice of death," or "looking death in the eye," but was really *dead*. As Scottish commentator John Eadie put it, it's a case of "death walking."[4]

So important is this truth that Eadie goes on to point out that **dead in trespasses and sins** implies three things:

First, it implies *previous life*, since to die one had to first be alive. When was man alive? In Adam, of course. But when Adam sinned, the entire race died spiritually. "For as in Adam all die, even so in Christ shall all be made alive" (1 Cor. 15:22). The distinction before and after Christ is clear and dramatic.

Second, it implies *insensibility*. Man is unaffected by anything spiritual. He feels nothing. He shrugs his shoulders at even the thought of the blessings of holiness or the threat of hell.

Third, and most significant of all, it implies *inability*. One of the basic controversies today about salvation is the biblical doctrine of man's inability. While controversy has raged for years about the doctrine of *election*, most people don't realize that the real issue is the doctrine of *depravity*, which is what makes election necessary. Most people simply do not (or will not) comprehend (or recognize) the depth of man's depravity. They simply don't take the words of Scripture literally. Some argue that man has a certain "spark of divinity," "glimmer of goodness," or "residual free will," which if properly motivated will produce salvation. But the Word of God is clear: man's will has been so affected by sin that he has lost all will or ability to any spiritual good. Why? *Because he is **dead**.* As Eadie again illustrates, "The corpse cannot raise himself from the tomb and come back to the scenes and society of the living world."

To illustrate, can a drowning man who has taken water into his lungs help himself? Can he sit up and say, "Oh, I'm not completely helpless. I have water in my lungs, but I'll be okay in a minute." Of course not. He is totally helpless, totally unable to give himself CPR. Likewise, the spiritually dead man can do nothing to resuscitate himself spiritually. He can do nothing righteous, nothing good, nothing to please God, and is in himself incapable of believing.

We can further illustrate by picturing a cadaver. Medical students can do anything to a cadaver that they want and that cadaver does not respond in any way. It is dead to any physical stimulus. Likewise, apart from Christ we were "spiritual cadavers." We could not respond to any spiritual stimulus. We were not "sick in a fever,"[5] "incapacitated," or even "hopelessly crippled" by sin. We were *dead*.

Commentator R. C. Sproul recounts an analogy that has been used many times to describe man's problem:

> Fallen man is so overcome by the power of sin, that he is like a person on his deathbed, who has no physical power left to save himself. If he is going to be healed he can't possibly do it through his own strength. The only way he can be made well would be if the physician gave him the medicine that is necessary to restore him. But the man is so desperately ill that he doesn't even have the power to reach out and take the medicine for himself. So the nurse approaches his bed, opens the bottle of medicine, pours it into a spoon, and then moves it over the dying man's lips. But he must, by his own power, his own will and his own initiative, open his mouth to receive the medicine.[6]

But if we take Scripture exactly how it reads, that analogy is false. A dead man isn't on his deathbed—he's already *dead*. He not only can't reach for the medicine, he can't even open his mouth to receive it if someone holds it to his lips. Taken to its final implication, in fact, that analogy says that the man must do something for himself to be saved. But that violates the whole concept of grace, which says that God alone has done it all. Does man believe? Yes, but as Ephesians 2:8–9 go on to declare, God even gives us the faith to believe (cf. Jn. 1:12; 6:65; Acts 18:27; Phil. 1:29; see our chapter 9), something we could never have done, or even been *inclined* to do, without His intervention. Why? Because we were **dead**, not just critically ill, not just gasping our last breath, not uttering that final death rattle, but **dead**.

Still another analogy, which I've heard at evangelistic crusades, goes like this: "Picture a drowning man. He's struggling to stay afloat. He's already gone down twice and is now going down for the third time, with only his desperately seeking hand still above the surface. His only hope is for someone to throw him a life preserver. That's what God does, but even if the preserver hits the man's hand, that's not enough. The man must close his hand around it and capture his salvation."

That's certainly dramatic and plays very well in the evangelist's emotional appeal, but it's obviously unbiblical. Is the lost person *drowning*? No! He's **dead**. He is as entombed at the bottom of the sea as are the over 1,100 men still entombed in the USS Arizona at the bottom of Pearl Harbor. His only hope is for God to reach down, pull his corpse to the surface, and breathe life into him, that is, *regenerate him.*

Pastor and commentator Ray Stedman quite graphically recounts how this truth was brought home to a friend of his. Stedman's friend was given an after-hours tour of a funeral home by a mortician friend, who took him into a room where several bodies were laid out on slabs. The mortician pulled back a sheet to reveal one of the bodies and said to his guest, "Tell him about Jesus." Needless to say, it was something the man never forgot, for that is exactly what the lost man is, dead and absolutely incapable of responding.[7]

Our Lord Himself cut to the heart of the matter when He declared, "No man can come to me, except the Father which hath sent me draw him: and I will raise him up at the last day" and "therefore . . . no man can come unto me, except it were given unto him of my Father" (Jn. 6:44, 65).

In sad contrast, popular teaching says that man is "free," that is, totally free in the sense that he can choose good from evil in the same way Adam was free to choose, but as noted earlier, "in Adam all die" (1 Cor. 15:22). The term "free will," in fact, has become, in the words of John Owen, an "idol."[8] This term is a symbol of man's arrogance in thinking that he can, in and of himself, choose God when Scripture and history prove that he always chooses sin and always runs from God.

It is fascinating, indeed, that the issue of "free will" was the crux of the whole Reformation debate, as seen in the story of Luther and Erasmus. Desiderius Erasmus (1466–1536) was a Dutch humanist and theologian. While ordained a priest in 1492, it seems that he never actively worked as a priest and, like Luther, criticized some of the Church's excesses. He and

Luther respected one another, but they had a fundamental disagreement over the human will. In 1524, Erasmus published his book *The Freedom of the Will*, which dealt with the issue of grace, but from a subtle, roundabout way. He chose to make the biggest issue of all the question of "free will," that is, how much impact sin had (or did *not* have) on man's will. He wrote, "By free choice in this place we mean a power of the human will by which a man can apply himself to the things which lead to eternal salvation, or turn away from them."[9] In other words, man has voluntary or free power in and of himself to choose the way which leads to salvation apart from God's grace (the same basic heresy Pelagius taught 1,000 years earlier). In Erasmus' mind, then, God and man work together to bring man's salvation.

Luther responded to Erasmus by publishing his most famous work, *The Bondage of the Will*, in 1525. Amazingly, while disagreeing with virtually everything Erasmus wrote, Luther actually commended Erasmus for recognizing the core issue separating Rome and the Bible believer. He wrote, in fact,

> that unlike all the rest, you alone have attacked the real thing, the essential issue. You have not wearied me with those extraneous issues about the Papacy, purgatory, indulgences and such like . . . you and you alone have seen the hinge upon which it all turns, and aimed for the vital spot. For that I heartily thank you.[10]

Erasmus was not so foolish as to defend any of the major points, for they are indefensible. Rather, he pointed out "the hinge upon which it all turns." The issue of "free will" to Luther was the crux of the whole thing. Is Christianity a religion of *pure* grace or *partial* grace, that is, either *all* of God or *partly* of God with man. Did God simply supply the grace and man in his own power supply the faith, or did God supply it all?

Is Regeneration in the Old Testament?

Again, I believe the above answers the whole matter of regeneration. While the above focuses on the New Testament development of this doctrine, we also find it in Old Testament thought.

This is true of many doctrines, in fact. Most New Testament doctrines have their basis in Old Testament theology. From sin, to salvation, to service, the New Testament is *enfolded* in the Old, while the Old is *unfolded* in the New. Or as Augustine put it, "The New is in the Old *contained*, the Old is in the New *explained*." While some theological truths (such as the Church) are foreign to the Old Testament, most New Testament subjects are rooted in the Old. These include such doctrines as: the nature of God, creation, man, morality, sin, redemption, worship, wisdom, truth, and many more. This also includes regeneration, at least in "seed form," if we may coin the term, which then comes to full bloom in the New Testament.

Therefore, has man's need changed form the Old Testament to the New? Is his spiritual state different in one over the other? Most importantly, is he regenerated in the New but left **dead** in the Old? While some teachers insist that Old Testament believers will be regenerated when they are resurrected and not before, this is foreign to Scripture. Some cite Daniel 12:2 as "proof," but it does not say that. It says, "Many of them that sleep in the dust of the earth shall awake, some to everlasting life, and some to shame and everlasting contempt." Clearly, this refers to resurrection not regeneration. While Old Testament believers will be resurrected to "everlasting life" (cf. Matt 19:29; Gal 6:8; etc.), unbelievers will be resurrected to "everlasting contempt."

This brings us to our second text, Isaiah 57:15. The word **revive** translates the Hebrew *chāyâ*, which appears about 270 times in the Old Testament and means to live, be alive, remain alive. The word is used often to indicate something going on in one who is already a believer.

In the Psalms, for example, especially 119, *chāyā* is often rendered "quicken" or "quickened" in the AV. In 119:25, David prays, "quicken thou me according to thy word." The idea here is reviving someone from sickness, discouragement, or despair, which only God can do. It will not come from self-determination, will power, psychological technique, or clever cliché. It will come only from God's Word working in our heart and mind. Further, as *chāyā* is used in several ways—to show that an object is safe (Num. 14:38), to indicate that something is reviving (Ezek. 37:5), and to demonstrate that something is flourishing (Ps. 22:26)—the Word of God, therefore, *brings* life, *sustains* life, and *is* our life.

Hebrew authorities point out, however, that *chāyā* is also used to mean "to cause to live." W. E. Vine writes of our text, "This word may also mean 'to bring to life or 'to cause to live.'"[11] Another classic lexicon also has "be restored to life."[12]

We also read twice in Ezekiel of God's promise to replace the "stony heart" with "a new heart" that is made "of flesh" (11:19–20; 36:25–26). Does that not sound like regeneration and transformation? Of Saul we also read that "the Spirit of the LORD" came upon him and "gave him another heart" (1 Sam. 10:6, 9).

While I unapologetically admit to being a "mild" dispensationalist (see chapter 29)—I recognize the obvious distinction between Israel and the Church and other equally obvious distinction—it is troubling to conclude that the Holy Spirit did not have to regenerate a spiritually dead creature in the Old Testament because of some supposed dispensational difference. If God did not regenerate hearts in the Old Testament, every Old Testament character is still dead. No, the doctrine of regeneration is not *fully developed* in the Old Testament, but it most certainly is *functionally declared.*

NOTES

[1] Millard Erickson, *Christian Theology*, 2nd Edition (Baker Books, 1983, 1998), p. 992.

[2] Richard Trench, *Synonyms of the New Testament* (Hendrickson Publishers, 2000 reprint), p. 75.

[3] Emory Bancroft, *Elemental Theology*, Third Edition (Zondervan, 1960), p. 196.

[4] John Eadie, *A Commentary on the Greek Text of the Epistle of Paul to the Ephesians* Wipf and Stock Publishers, 1998; reprint of 2nd Edition, 1861), pp. 120-121.

[5] Bishop Alford; cited in Eadie, p. 119.

[6] R. C. Sproul, *The Purpose of God: An Exposition of Ephesians* (Christian Focus Publications, 1994), p. 46.

[7] Ray Stedman, *Our Riches in Christ* (Discovery House Publishers, 1998.), p. 75.

[8] John Owen, *A Display of Arminianism* (Edmonton: Still Waters Revival Publishers, 1989 reprint), p. 12.

[9] E. Gordon Rupp, P. Watson, *Luther And Erasmus: Free Will And Salvation* (The Westminster Press, 1969), p. 47.

[10] Martin Luther, *The Bondage of the Will* (Grand Rapids: Fleming H. Revell, 1992), p. 319.

[11] *Vine's Complete Expository Dictionary of Old and New Testament Words* (electronic edition), "To Live" entry."

[12] *Brown, Driver, and Briggs Hebrew-English Lexicon* (electronic edition), entry for Strong's #2421.

The Bible is alive, it speaks to me; it has feet, it runs after me; it has hands, it lays hold of me.

Martin Luther
The Westminster Collection of Christian Quotations, p. 21

26

The Disagreement Between Paul and Barnabas[*]

Acts 15:36–41

And some days after Paul said unto Barnabas, Let us go again and visit our brethren in every city where we have preached the word of the Lord, and see how they do. And Barnabas determined to take with them John, whose surname was Mark. But Paul thought not good to take him with them, who departed from them from Pamphylia, and went not with them to the work. And the contention was so sharp between them, that they departed asunder one from the other: and so Barnabas took Mark, and sailed unto Cyprus; And Paul chose Silas, and departed, being recommended by the brethren unto the grace of God. And he went through Syria and Cilicia, confirming the churches.

This "tough text" is a somewhat troubling one for two reasons. First, it recounts an unfortunate disagreement between two men of God, and second, it is used by some teachers to criticize the Apostle Paul. What happened here? What brought about such a division? Is there a practical application in this? Let's examine this passage with a two-fold emphasis: the incident and its importance.

The Incident

The scene here is the beginning of Paul's second *church-planting* journey (which has always seemed to me to be a far better term than "missionary," which is somewhat ambiguous at best nowadays). While Barnabas wanted to include his cousin John Mark in the team (Col. 4:10), Paul did not. Why? The answer is back in Acts 13:13, which recounts, "Now when Paul and his company loosed from Paphos, they came to Perga in Pamphylia: and John departing from them returned to Jerusalem." While John Mark was a member of the team during the first journey, he left the team.

"Departing" translates the Greek *apochōreō*, from the root *chōreō*, "to depart," and the prefix *apo*, "from." This word occurs only two other times

---

[*] This chapter was originally TOTT issue 44, March 2009.

in the New Testament, the most graphic being when Jesus says that the day is coming when He will say to false professors, "I never knew you: depart from me, ye that work iniquity" (Matt. 7:23). The idea in this word, then, is total abandonment.

So why did John Mark abandon the team? Several reasons have been offered. One commentator summarizes:

> (1) Perhaps he was disillusioned with the change in leadership. After all, Barnabas, the original leader, was John Mark's cousin. (2) The new emphasis on Gentiles may have been too much of an adjustment for a Palestinian Jew like Mark. (3) Possibly he was afraid of the dangerous road over the Taurus Mountains to Antioch which Paul was determined to travel. (4) There is some evidence Paul became quite ill in Perga, possibly with malaria, as the city of Perga was subject to malarial infections. Furthermore, Paul preached to the people of Galatia "because of an illness" (Gal. 4:13). The missionary party may have gone inland to higher ground to avoid the ravages of malaria and Mark in discouragement over this may have returned home. (5) Some think Mark was homesick. His mother may have been a widow (Acts 12:12); perhaps Mark became lonesome for her and home.[1]

In the final analysis, however, we submit that the reason for John Mark's defection was (and is) irrelevant. He abandoned not only God's *work* but also God's *workers*. The word translated **departed** in verse 38 is not the same word used back in 13:13. The Greek here is the stronger *aphistēmi*, to withdraw, remove oneself, forsake, desert, retire, or cease from something. Of its sixteen other New Testament appearances, one of the most graphic is when Paul declares that in "the latter times some shall depart from the faith, giving heed to seducing spirits, and doctrines of devils" (1 Tim. 4:1). Paul later uses the same word to declare that believers are to "withdraw" themselves from all kinds of false teachers (6:5). There is no doubt, then, as to John's Mark's serious defection.

Paul, therefore, flatly refused to allow John Mark to return to the team. This offended Barnabas for the obvious reason that John Mark was his cousin. Can there be any doubt that this was the real issue as far as Barnabas was concerned? Was he looking at the situation objectively? Was he concerned for the ministry or simply his cousin's hurt feelings (or perhaps even wounded pride)?

We should also take careful note of the phrase **Barnabas determined to take with them John**, which in a sense is the key to the whole question. **Determined** is the Greek *bouleuō*, to resolve in council, to decree, take counsel, consult, determine, or deliberate with oneself or with one another in counsel. So, with whom did Barnabas take council? The answer lies in the fact that the verb is in the *aorist tense* and the *middle voice*. Please bear with me in this technical point because it is pivotal.

The aorist tense (which we have noted in previous studies) is used for simple, undefined action.[2] We can best understand the middle voice by contrasting it with active and passive voice. While the active pictures the subject of the verb doing the acting, and the passive pictures the subject being acted upon, the middle voice pictures *the subject acting in its own interest*, that is, it receives the benefit of the action. Putting it together, then, the "aorist middle represents non-continuous action by the subject as acting upon himself or concerning himself."[3]

To illustrate, the aorist middle is used in Ephesians 1:4—"According as [God the Father] hath chosen us in [Christ] before the foundation of the world"—declaring that God did the choosing independently in the past and did so *primarily* for His own interest, that is, "To the praise of the glory of his grace" (v. 6).

So, with whom did Barnabas take council? *Himself.* He **determined** the matter totally *in* himself and *for* himself. While the NIV, NASB, and ESV weakly render this "wanted," **determined** is better, as is "was determined" in the NKJV and "was minded" in the original ASV (1901). All three demonstrate Barnabas' self motivation. Jay Green's *Literal Translation* is also good with "purposed."[4]

Does this not graphically demonstrate that Barnabas was, to use a modern idiom, "way out of line"? He was acting in his own interest and for his own purpose. The language allows no other conclusion.

Some immediately argue that John Mark deserved a "second chance." Well, Paul didn't think so, and we need to be reminded that Paul was now in charge! He was the Apostle, and Barnabas should have submitted to that authority. Harry Ironside well explains Paul's view:

> Paul considered the work of the Lord so serious he could not think of linking up again with a man who had shown so little sense of the importance of service for the Lord. It was no picnic! It was severe testing, hard work, and service for the glory of God. Paul did not wish to take anyone who was not divinely guided nor ready to endure hardship.[5]

Sadly, **the contention was so sharp between them, that they departed asunder one from the other**. The word **contention** is the extremely strong Greek word *paroxusmos* (English *paroxysm*, a fit or outburst). The root *oxunō* means to sharpen, incite, or irritate, and the prefix *para* pictures movement toward a certain point. The idea then is to impel, incite, or rouse someone toward something. Used in a bad sense, *paroxusmos* speaks of sharp contention, or even an angry dispute (i.e., inciting to anger), as is evident here. Another instance of the word is in Acts 17:16, where Paul's "spirit was stirred [*paroxusmos*] in him, when he saw the city wholly given to idolatry." He was incensed to see how truly and totally pagan the city was. From this it would seem that Barnabas was just mad at Paul for his "unreasonableness," while Paul was incensed at the idea of taking along a man who had quit.

We would also submit that a factor that seems to be overlooked by many commentators is that the church at Antioch was the sending church. There is no indication whatsoever that there was a single voice of disagreement in the church regarding Paul's decision. Neither do we see a single repercussion from this incident in Paul's ministry. If this was really "sin" on Paul's part, should we not read of a hindrance to his ministry and his eventual repentance? Recall that Paul himself condemned the disunity of Euodias and Syntyche (Phil. 4:2), as well as other instances of disunity (e.g. 1 Cor. 3:1–7; etc.). But there is no condemnation from anyone anywhere in our text. Why? *We submit that it is because this is not really a matter of unity at all, rather a matter of spiritual qualification for ministry.* (We'll return to this point later in the chapter.)

It puzzles me that in their quest to reconcile this situation, some commentators make odd statements. One such anomaly is, "In God's providence, not one team of missionaries but two teams leave from Antioch," but the same writer goes on to negate such an idea with his very next comment: "Even if we know nothing about the result of the work performed by Barnabas and Mark, we still see God's marvelous care for the believers in Cyprus."[6] But wait! How can both be true? Is it probable that God would sovereignly decree a second great missionary team but never inspire the Scripture writer to report on the ministry of that team? Yes, the text says that Barnabas and John Mark went to **Cyprus**, but it says absolutely nothing about what was accomplished there, if anything. To say that "we still see God's marvelous care for the believers in Cyprus" is pure speculation; we know nothing of the sort. There is no record that they ever planted a church or even ministered effectively.

Further still, note that there is no direct evidence that Barnabas and John Mark actually continued in active ministry, at least for a time. Cyprus, in fact, was Barnabas' home (Acts 4:36), so is it not possible that the words **Barnabas took Mark, and sailed unto Cyprus** imply that they simply left the ministry for awhile, choosing to go home instead?

Even more significant, it is essential to note that at this point both John Mark and Barnabas vanish from the Acts narrative, their ministries never being mentioned again. We cannot help but be reminded of Demas (2 Tim. 4:10), who forsook the ministry and disappeared. Yes, John Mark appears again in 2 Timothy 4:11, where he and Luke are the only ones who are by Paul's side at the end, but this is an entirely different setting. It has nothing to do with preaching, planting churches, or any such ministry. He is mentioned twice more as Paul's co-worker (Col. 4:10; Phile. 24), but this says nothing of his ministry while apart from Paul.

Likewise, it seems Paul and Barnabas also later reconciled—Paul spoke of him in positive terms in 1 Corinthians 9:6—but once again, this is a different setting, with still no mention of ministry while divided from Paul.

In dramatic contrast to the ministry of Barnabas and John Mark (if there even was any), **Paul chose Silas, and departed, being recommended by the brethren unto the grace of God.** The word **recommended** renders the strong Greek word *paradidōmi*, which occurs some 120 times in the New Testament and is translated most often as "deliver" (or similar form), although at times as "give, gave, and betrayed." A study of this important word reveals much.

The root *didōmi* means "to give of one's own accord and with good will." The prefix *para* adds the idea of alongside or over to, providing the full meaning, "to deliver over to the power of someone." It was used in Classical Greek (before the New Testament) as a legal term for delivering a prisoner to the court. Likewise, the basic New Testament meaning is to deliver someone over to judgment and death. In Matthew 4:12, it's used of John the Baptist when he was "cast into prison" with the ultimate end of death.

With that in mind, it's noteworthy that most occurrences of *paradidōmi* refer to the Lord Jesus being delivered over for certain death. This was the whole reason He came to earth in His first advent. He did not come to live or even to "judge the world" (John 12:47); He came to die that sinners would be saved. We see this in every stage of His final days on earth: He was "betrayed" into the hands of men (Matt. 17:22), "betrayed" to the High Priest (20:18), "delivered" to the Gentiles (20:19), "delivered" to Pilate (27:2), "delivered" to the death sentence (Luke 24:20), and "betrayed" for crucifixion (Matt. 26:2).

It's also significant that *paradidōmi* is used of the Christian's response to what Christ did for them. Acts 15:25–26 describes Paul, Barnabas, and other "chosen men . . . that have hazarded [*paradidōmi*] their lives for the name of our Lord Jesus Christ." Can each of us say this of ourselves? Are we willing to "hand ourselves over" to whatever might come in the cause of Christ?

There is one other important meaning of *paradidōmi*. It's also used in the sense of "to hand down, pass on instruction from teacher to pupil"[7] This meaning is vivid in Jude 3, where Jude writes that every believer "should earnestly contend for the faith which was once delivered unto the saints." As "the faith" is the preaching and teaching of the apostles that was handed down and passed on, it is that *faith*, that body of truth which comprises historical, evangelical Christianity and is the faith we are to continue to hand down.

With that in mind, Luke used this strong word to demonstrate that the church **recommended**, that is, delivered up and handed over Paul and Silas for the ministry at hand. There is no word of rebuke towards them, only blessing. In contrast, no such word is used of Barnabas and John Mark because they had left the team and gone their own way.

I'm convinced that the weight of evidence overwhelmingly indicates that it was Barnabas and John Mark who were at fault in this incident, not Paul. Motivated out of sentimentality and misplaced family loyalty, Barnabas wanted to include a man in a difficult and demanding ministry who had once quit and thereby (at least temporarily) disqualified himself from ministry, and Paul would have none of it. That leads us to our second emphasis.

The Importance

Why is this incident important? We submit two reasons.

First, as mentioned above, the primary issue in this passage seems to be that of *spiritual qualification for ministry*. The common attitude of our day is that anyone can do anything he (or she) wants, regardless of God's calling, qualification, or examination, as noted in chapter 14, "Is There a So-Called 'Call' to Ministry?"

As noted in chapter 14, 1 Timothy 3:1 is pivotal: "If a man desire the office of a bishop, he desireth a good work." To summarize, "desire" is *oregō*, "to stretch one's self out in order to grasp something; to reach after or desire something."[8] It speaks of a deep longing, a complete disregard for all else. "Desireth," then, is *epithumeō*, "to long after, to have a passionate compulsion for something," in this context something "good." While *oregō* implies only the outward, *epithumeō* refers to the inward feeling of desire. Taken together, the two terms describe the man who pursues the ministry outwardly at all cost because of a driving compulsion inwardly.

John Mark, therefore, is a classic example of one who did not pursue the ministry in disregard of everything else. Something, whatever it was, turned him aside from the task at hand, thereby disqualifying him. While he returned later, and we rejoice in that, in this incident he was wrong and Paul was absolutely right in excluding him.

This incident further exposes another trend in our own day, namely, restoring men to the pastoral office no matter what the offense. To illustrate, commenting on the critical meaning and implications of a man being "blameless" (*anepilemptos* in 1 Tim. 3:2, "nothing which an adversary could seize upon to base a charge," and *anengklētos* in Titus 1:6, "not be called in," above reproach) one writer puts it far better than I could:

> One contemporary trend that is cause for great concern is the shocking moral sins pastors commit only to step back into ministry as soon as the publicity cools down. . . . The Bible clearly teaches that once a man fails in the area of sexual immorality, he is unqualified for pastoral ministry any longer. Certainly we want him restored to the Lord and to the fellowship, but biblical qualifications for one who preaches God's Word and is identified as pastor, overseer, or elder exclude him from that role in a church that is pleasing God. . . . This world overflows with sexual sin, and Paul directs the church to find as leaders men who have impeccable reputations . . . . This is the kind of man God is looking for to set up as the model in His church. . . . Sexual sin disqualifies any man from being a pastor. The Apostle Paul remained keenly aware of that fact, saying, "I buffet my body and make it my slave, lest possibly, after I have preached to others, I myself should be disqualified (1 Cor. 9:27, [NASB])." That is strong terminology. Paul maintained rigorous self-discipline to avoid being disqualified from pastoral ministry. He knew that any kind of sexual sin brings lifelong reproach.[9]

Of course, sexual sin was not the issue with John Mark, but the point here is *qualification*. Men do not just "jump in and out" of ministry as they feel like it. They cannot do whatever they want and remain in a place of leadership. The qualifications for leadership are high, irrevocable, and non-negotiable.

A corollary to this is the modern trend of "missionary trips," often involving a group of young people, an idea nowhere supported in Scripture. While sincere, such excursions are often little more than "school projects" at best, or vacations at worst, that demand very little in sacrifice and labor and certainly do not underscore the true hardships and *total dedication* of biblical ministry.

Second, we should also note the church's place in all this. Another modern trend is that people are either self-appointed to ministry or are appointed by any one of a thousand entities outside the local church (commonly called parachurch organizations). But it is beyond doubt that these practices are unsupported in Scripture. *The local church is to ordain and send out men for ministry*. In this incident, the church at Antioch blessed the ministry of Paul and Silas, but not that of Barnabas and John Mark.

So, as Paul (and by implication the church) recognized disqualified servants, we do well to recognize them today.

NOTES

[1] John F. Walvoord and Roy B. Zuck (ed.), *The Bible Knowledge Commentary* (Cook Communications Ministries), electronic edition.

[2] Only in the indicative mood does the aorist denote punctiliar action (action that happens at a specific point in time) in the past. With few exceptions, when the aorist is used in any other mood, it refers only to the reality of the action, not when it occurred.

[3] Spiros Zodhiates, *The Complete Word Study New Testament* (Chattanooga: AMG Publishers, 1991), p. 863.

[4] A note for the technical reader. While our discussion refers to the Textus Receptus' and Majority Text's *ebouleusato* (aorist tense), the Critical Text has *ebouletō*, which is the imperfect tense, indicating continuous action and Barnabas' persistence (e.g. Wuest's *Expanded Translation* renders: "Barnabas, after thinking the matter over, kept on insisting that they take along with them also John"). Both are middle voice, however, so the point is basically the same.

[5] Harry Ironside, *Lectures on the Book of Acts* (Loizeaux Brothers, 1943, 1977), p. 361.

[6] Simon J. Kistemaker, *Baker's New Testament Commentary: Acts* (Baker Books, 1990), p. 570.

[7] Colin Brown, *The New International Dictionary of New Testament Theology* (Zondervan, 1975), Vol. 3, pp. 772–773.

[8] Joseph Thayer, *Thayer's Greek-English Lexicon* (Hendrickson), p. 452.

[9] John MacArthur, *Rediscovering Pastoral Ministry* (W Publishing Group, 1995), pp. 89–91.

Ignorance of Scripture is ignorance of Christ.

Jerome
The Westminster Collection of Christian Quotations, p. 23

27

What Does Scripture Say About Women Teachers?[*]

1 Timothy 2:11–15

Let the woman learn in silence with all subjection. But I suffer not a woman to teach, nor to usurp authority over the man, but to be in silence. For Adam was first formed, then Eve. And Adam was not deceived, but the woman being deceived was in the transgression. Notwithstanding she shall be saved in childbearing, if they continue in faith and charity and holiness with sobriety.

Addressing the question raised by this "tough text" provided me a little insight into how a bomb squad technician must feel: "One wrong move and this thing will blow up in my face." To set the stage, therefore, I want to say right up front that the ministry of women is of incalculable value. To be honest, in fact, words truly fail to adequately express such worth.

First, and foremost, a woman is to be a "help-meet" to her husband (Gen. 2:18, 20), that is, "a fitting help," one who is tailor-made by God to meet every need of her husband and support and aid him in ministry. *Second*, a woman is to be a homemaker (1 Tim. 5:14; Titus 2:5), one who makes a warm nest for her family. *Third*, she is to teach her children and younger women how to serve the Lord (Titus 2:3–5). How can you put a price on all that? Such a woman's value is, indeed, "far above rubies" (Prov. 31:10; cf. 11–31). If I may interject, I have personally had the joy of being married to such a woman for 35 years, as of this very month.*

That is the role of women as set forth in the Word of God. Sadly, however, such incalculable worth is not good enough for modern thinking. Feminism has infiltrated the church, creating what can safely be dubbed "Christian Feminism," the attitude that women can do whatever they choose, they can "have it all," and other such humanistic nonsense.

Nowhere is this more evident, in fact, than in the area of preaching, teaching, and leading in the church. While we briefly mentioned this in chapter 16 ("What About the Deacon and Deaconess?"), there is today a need for further clarity. Never in Church History do we find as many

---

* This chapter was originally TOTT issue 45, April 2009.

women adopting these roles than today, in spite of the fact of how unmistakably clear it is in Scripture that they should not. This has arisen, of course, from the *Egalitarianism* that permeates our society, and which has infiltrated our churches, schools, and seminaries. This view, held not only by liberals but by several noted evangelicals,[1] maintains that men and women are equal in essence and function and no role distinctions can be made between them.

Adherents to this view often see Paul as either contradicting himself or at least being confused when he wrote to Timothy: **Let the woman learn in silence with all subjection. But I suffer not a woman to teach, nor to usurp authority over the man, but to be in silence.** Some hold that his attitudes were molded more from rabbinical teachers of his day than from Divine inspiration (a blatantly blasphemous idea to start with). Their "proof text" is Galatians 3:28, "There is neither Jew nor Greek, there is neither bond nor free, there is neither male nor female; for you are all one in Christ Jesus," which they say teaches that because we are all one in Christ, therefore most, if not all, order and authority structure in the church should be eliminated. Just reading the verse and its context, however, demonstrates that they have absolutely nothing to do with roles, rather *spiritual* position, possessions, and privileges.

Others try a more scholarly approach by saying that the word **authority** actually means "domination," so Paul was simply telling the women not to domineer, or run over the men in the church, not that they could not lead them at all. On this point, one modern commentator graphically demonstrates the modern trend of reinterpreting this passage:

> As is true in all of his letters, Paul is addressing specific people and specific situations. Rarely do we have access to the actual problems. But is it not safe to assume that some of these newly liberated women in Christ had become overly aggressive in the meetings of the congregation? . . . What the interpreter must decide, then, is the scope of application. Were these only local situations that needed the drastic remedy that Paul prescribed, or was Paul setting forth a universal rule to be applied in all churches, in all places? I prefer the former . . . . Paul is clearly referring to his personal practice. It seems to me that this practice is to be limited rather than universal in the church.[2]

While our desire is always to speak the Truth in love, such comments are truly appalling. The statement, "Rarely do we have access to the actual problems," is a subtle attack on biblical sufficiency, obviously implying that "since we don't have all the facts, we can't say for sure." Further, the words "it seems to me" are irrelevant. What matters is what the text says. Was Paul simply giving his opinion and dealing only with a local abuse?

Such ideas are preposterous, as his going back to the Old Testament precedent in verses 13–14 proves beyond doubt. In fact, Paul goes back to this precedent in the other major texts that deal with this issue (1 Cor. 11:7–9; 14:34). In all these Paul points out the authority structure that God created in the beginning.

We say again, like most of today's trends, *such reinterpretation is a wholly modern invention*. In contrast to the above, note another commentator's exposition, this one by the incomparable John Gill, who ministered in London 100 years before Spurgeon and who Spurgeon quoted often. Commenting on 1 Corinthians 11:5 (and also citing 14:34–35), he wrote: "Not that a woman was allowed to pray publicly in the congregation, and much less to preach or explain the word, for these things were not permitted them." On our text, Gill further comments:

> They may teach in private, in their own houses and families; they are to be teachers of good things, Titus. 2:3. . . . but then women are not to teach in the church. . . . one part of rule is to feed the church with knowledge and understanding; and for a woman to take upon her to do this, is to usurp an authority over the man: this therefore she ought not to do.[3]

Gill is not an isolated example. Unlike our day, when words can mean whatever each individual chooses them to mean, most expositors and theologians of yesterday knew Scripture and were not swayed by modern thought. We could cite one quotation after another. Commenting on 1 Corinthians 14:33–39, as well as our text, B. B. Warfield, wrote: "It would be impossible for the apostle to speak more directly or more emphatically than he has done here. He requires women to be silent at the church-meetings. . . . Neither the teaching nor the ruling function is permitted to woman."[4] Calvin adds that Paul "forbids them to speak in public, either for the purpose of teaching or of prophesying."[5] And the examples go on. If I may be so bold, is it that we are more *enlightened* today, or are we just *defiant*?

So, does **authority** actually mean "to domineer" as insisted today? Not precisely. While the Greek *authenteō* (English, "authority," etc.), which appears only here in the New Testament, includes the idea of domination, its primary meaning is more basic. As Greek scholar M. R. Vincent states, "The kindred noun *authentēs*, 'one who does a thing with his own hand,' [appears in Classical Greek] in Herodotus, Euripides, and Thucydides."[6] All this is derived from *autos* ("himself") and *entea* ("arms or armor"), indicating "a self-appointed killer with one's own hand, one acting by his own authority or power."[7] Further, Paul goes on to narrow the idea by saying a woman is not to **teach**, that is, not in the public assembly. The point could not be clearer.

The words **silence** and **silent** are also reinterpreted nowadays. The Greek in both instances (*hēsuchia*) unmistakably means "silence." Some argue that it can mean "a meek and quiet spirit," therefore, permitting women to preach or teach as long as they do it with the proper attitude. But not only is this reading something into the word that isn't there, if there were any doubt to the meaning, the word **subjection** would erase it. The Greek *hupotagē* literally means "to line up under" showing subordination and submission. As if that's not enough, God prefixes **subjection** with the words **with all**, emphasizing the *complete* subjection called for. In the context of all public meetings, women are to be silent and content in the role of the learner. If I may lovingly say, today's playing of word games and careless exegesis simply ignore the plain truth of Scripture.

Are we saying women are inferior? *Absolutely not!* That is precisely why Paul said, **Let the woman learn**. While it's obvious to us that women should be taught God's Word—they are spiritually equal in Christ and the commands of the New Testament are to all (1 Pet. 2:1–2)—it was not at all obvious to those who came from a Jewish background. First-century Judaism did not hold women in high esteem. While not barred from attending synagogue, neither were they encouraged to learn. In fact, most rabbis refused to teach women, and some likened it to throwing pearls to pigs. Nor was the status of women in both Greek and Roman society any better. They could not hold public office or even go into any public assembly.

What we see here, then, is the *exact opposite* of what Paul is accused of by our modern "liberated society." Far from being a "male chauvinist," what he said to Timothy, and by extension the Ephesian believers, was shockingly revolutionary. He didn't *suggest* that women be taught, rather *commanded* them to be taught. With that one statement, Paul did more for women than anyone else in his day or ours.

Now, while this was new to contemporary Jewish tradition, it wasn't new to men of God at all. The Old Testament clearly declared the spiritual equality of women to men. The Mosaic Law was given to all Israel, both men and women (Deut. 1:1). Both were to teach it to their children (Deut. 6:4–7; Prov. 6:20). Both were equally protected by the Law (Ex. 21:28–32). Both had inheritance rights (Num. 36:1–12). Both participated in the Jewish religious feasts (Ex. 12:3; Deut. 16:9–15). Both could take the Nazarite vow (Num. 6:2). And both were involved in spiritual service (Ex. 38:8; Neh. 7:67). We also see that God at times dealt directly with women (Gen. 3:13: 16:7–13; Judg. 13:3).

The same is true in the New Testament. Jesus revealed His messiahship first to a woman (Jn. 4:25–26). He also not only healed women

(Mk. 5:25–34; Lk. 13:11–13) but crossed the tradition of the rabbis by teaching women (Lk. 10:38–42). Women reciprocated this attitude by ministering to Jesus and His disciples (Lk. 8:2–3). The first person Jesus appeared to after His resurrection was a woman (Mk. 16:9; Jn. 20:11–18). Both women and men were involved in the prayer services of the early church (Acts 1:13–14). Peter reminds men that women are to be "[given] honor . . . as the weaker vessel and as being heirs together of the grace of life" (1 Pet. 3:7). The fruit of the Spirit (Gal. 5:22–23) is for both men and women. In short, all the promises, commands, and blessings of the New Testament apply equally to women and men.

The other side of this issue, however, is that *spiritual equality* does not cancel out *differing roles*. In the Old Testament, there were no "queens" in either Israel or Judah (Athaliah was a usurper; 2 Kings 11:1–16; 2 Chr. 22:10—23:15). Many people react to this by saying, "Oh, but Deborah served as a judge (Judg. 4:1—5:31) and proves that women can lead." Her case, however, was unique. Dr. Robert L. Saucy comments,

> There may be instances when the regular pattern of God's order may have to be set aside due to unusual circumstances. When, for example, the husband and father is absent, the woman of the house assumes the headship of the family. So it would appear, there may be unusual circumstances when male leadership is unavailable for one reason or another. At such times God may use women to accomplish his purposes even as he used Deborah.[8]

Indeed, all the men in Israel were paralyzed with fear at Jabin, the king of Canaan (4:2–3), so there was no one who would stand except one woman. She then encouraged Barak to pursue God's plan. It's significant, however, and often ignored, that Deborah declined to lead the military campaign against the Canaanites, deferring instead to a man, Barak.

Additionally, not a single woman ever served as a priest, was an Old Testament author, or had an ongoing proclamation or teaching ministry like that of Elijah, Elisha, or the other prophets. While it is true that Miriam (Ex. 15:20), Deborah (Judg. 4:4), Huldah (2 Kings 22:14), and Isaiah's wife (Isa. 8:3) are called "prophetesses," not one of them had a permanent calling to that office. *Even more significant, in not a single one of those instances is there even the slightest indication of this being done in a public setting.* Additionally, in fact, Isaiah's wife did not prophesy at all—she was called a prophetess only because she gave birth to a child whose name had prophetic meaning—and the other three prophesied only once each.

So while many today are desperate for any biblical justification they can conjure up to support women teachers, it is a futile exercise. One writer puts it well in his comment about Huldah:

Though Huldah was a prophetess, the solitary record of her prophesying involved some men going to her where they communed privately. . . . It is impossible to find public preaching here.[9]

Finally, Noadiah is the only other "prophetess" named, but she was a false prophetess (Neh. 6:14). So while there were instances when God spoke through women, it was rare and extremely limited. Not one had a permanent role of preaching or teaching and not one did it in public. Each served, as the Latin says, *exceptio probat regulum* (the exception establishes the rule[10]).

Undeterred, modern reinterpreters zealously turn to the New Testament to try to prop up their hopelessly sagging argument, but we find the same pattern there as we do in the Old. Totally ignored is the plain and simple fact that we find not a single woman pastor-teacher, evangelist, bishop, or elder (see chapter 15). Also like the Old Testament, no New Testament author was a woman, nor do we find a record of even one sermon or teaching by a woman.

Luke 2:36–38 is cited as evidence of women teachers because Anna was a prophetess who served in the Temple. But if one just reads the passage, he immediately sees that it clarifies that she "served God with fastings and prayers night and day." There is not the slightest intimation that she was involved in public teaching. In fact, as the 1st-century Jewish historian Josephus makes clear, on one side of Herod's Temple "there was a partition built for the women . . . as the proper place wherein they were to worship" and "when they went through their own gate could they go beyond their own wall."[11] Because of such separation from the men, public instruction was impossible.

Priscilla is also repeatedly appealed to as "proof" of women teachers because of her aid in the instruction of Apollos (Acts 18:26). But it should also be noted that Aquilla is mentioned first and was undoubtedly in charge, and the instruction was in private.

Appeal is also made to Acts 2:17–18 and 21:9, both of which say there were prophetess in the 1st-century church. But again, in neither case is either the occasion or the message included, so there is no justification in *assuming* that they taught during the public worship, much less that they had an ongoing preaching ministry. The book of Acts, in fact, nowhere records a woman teaching men in public. The same is true of Euodias and Syntyche. While they "laboured with [Paul] in the gospel" (Phil. 4:2–3), there is no indication that their aid was public preaching or teaching.

In addition to all that irrefutable evidence, *presbuteros* ("elder") is masculine. If women could be elders, the Bible would somewhere say so by using the Greek word *presbutera*, but we never find that term in the Bible as speaking of a female elder. While *presbuteras* does appear in 1 Timothy

5:2, it is used only to refer to older women not women elders.

Likewise, the requirements for leadership in 1 Timothy 3:1–7 speak specifically of "a man" desiring the office (v. 1) and the necessity of him being "the husband of one wife" (v. 2). With no sarcasm intended, I know of no way that a woman can be the husband of one wife.

To repeat a comment from chapter 16, in the meeting and ministry of the Church, a woman is neither to teach nor have a position of leadership. Men are to lead, and women are to follow. In short, women are to be *learners*, not *leaders*. Even Acts 6:1–6 clearly indicates that only men filled the office of deacon. (As demonstrated in chapter 16, "deaconess" is not a New Testament office.)

Does all this mean that women are inferior to men? As mentioned earlier, NO, NO, a thousand times NO. God simply commands differing roles as being in line with His design for the weaker vessel. The issue is not *superiority*, rather *authority*, which in turn results in *responsibility* and *accountability*. That is why God said through James, "Be not many [teachers], knowing that we shall receive the greater condemnation" (Jas. 3:1). Countless Christians today, both men and women, have no idea how foolish they are being to take on the responsibility of teaching, which they are not *called to*, *qualified for*, or *trained in*.

Alas, in spite of all the clear, indisputable evidence, the practice of women preaching, teaching, and leading has never been so rampant. From church worship, to "revivals," to seminars, to Bible colleges, and every other venue, this trend permeates today's church. With extremely rare exceptions, this practice has been virtually nonexistent in the Church until the 20th-century, and according to the clear teaching of the Word of God, it is wrong, regardless of the famous women who practice it and the popular teachers (both women and men) who defend it.

For the sake of unity, we will not list the many who are practicing this today, but sadly the list is a long one. If I may say from my burdened heart, it is a sad commentary on the Church today that a principle so crystal clear, an issue so beyond even the minutest dash of doubt, that it can still be readjusted, or even totally ignored, for the sole purpose of conforming to modern thought.

NOTES

[1] Examples: former professor at Moody Bible Institute, Stanley Gundry; Mennonite theologian Myron S. Augsburger; textual scholar F.F. Bruce; popular

speaker and writer Tony Campolo; commentators Gordon Fee, Walter Liefeld, and Lloyd J. Ogilvie; and noted pastor of Willow Creek Community Church, Bill Hybels.

[2] Lloyd J. Ogilvie, *The Preacher's Commentary* (Thomas Nelson, 1982-1992), electronic edition. The similar reading of personal opinion into the text appears in the *Life Application Study Bible* (Tyndale).

[3] *John Gill's Exposition of the Entire Bible* (electronic edition)

[4] B. B. Warfield, *Paul on Women Speaking in the Church* (http://www.apuritansmind.com/Pastoral/WarfieldBBWomenSpeaking.htm).

[5] *Commentaries* (1 Cor. 14:34).

[6] M. R. Vincent , *Vincent's Word Studies*, electronic edition.

[7] Spiros Zodhiates, *The Complete Word Study Dictionary* (AMG Publishers, 1993), electronic edition, #831.

[8] "The Negative Case Against the Ordination of Women," in Kenneth S. Kantzer and Stanley N. Gundry, eds., *Perspectives on Evangelical Theology* (Grand Rapids: Baker, 1979), p. 285.

[9] Wayne Jackson, "Woman's Role in the Church," *Christian Courier*, March 16, 2000 (http://www.christiancourier.com/articles/169-womans-role-in-the-church)

[10] The often used expression "the exception proves the rule" is imprecise, "leading the unwary to think that any self-respecting rules must have an exception. What is meant is that the existence of an exception to a rule provides an opportunity to test the validity of a rule: Finding an exception to a rule enables us to define the rule more precisely, confirming its applicability to those items truly covered by the rule" (Eugene Ehrlich, *Amo, Amas, Amat and More* [Harper and Row, Hudson Group, 1985], p. 121).

[11] *The Wars of the Jews*, Book 5, Chapter 5, Section 2.

Truth is the most orient pearl in Christ's crown. Let us contend for the truth, as one would a large sum of money, that it should not be wrested out of his hand.

Puritan Thomas Watson – *A Body of Divinity*, p. 208

28

Is There a "Carnal Christian"?[*]

1 Corinthians 3:1–4

And I, brethren, could not speak unto you as unto spiritual, but as unto carnal, even as unto babes in Christ. I have fed you with milk, and not with meat: for hitherto ye were not able to bear it, neither yet now are ye able. For ye are yet carnal: for whereas there is among you envying, and strife, and divisions, are ye not carnal, and walk as men? For while one saith, I am of Paul; and another, I am of Apollos; are ye not carnal?

To introduce this "tough text," is there anything wrong with the following scenario? A certain Christian fellow (we'll call him Rupert, since there aren't many of those around) shares this testimony of his salvation: "Well, I asked Jesus into my heart when I was young, but backslid and lived the sinful life of the carnal Christian for 20 years but then rededicated my life and now live for God."

Does such a testimony have the ring of a person who was truly converted, one who actually became a "new creature" (2 Cor. 5:17; see chapter 23)? Does Rupert sound like a guy who was truly born again at the young age he claims? Does the term "carnal Christian" refer to a person who "backslides" and then "rededicates" himself later on? Is this a pure theology of salvation and sanctification? We would submit that it is not. Sadly, however, Rupert's story has been told and retold many times.

Such teaching is, in fact, common in our day, and much of it is centered in the term "carnal Christian," a term which, as we'll see, is nowhere found in the New Testament. Yes, "carnal" is there and "Christian" is certainly there, but melding the two together to refer to a new "category" of Christian is an invention.

Worse, there are actually two problems with Rupert's statement before we even address the main issue of "carnal." One is the idea of "rededication." Where on earth did we get even this *idea*, much less the *term* itself? Neither the principle nor the term appears anywhere in the New Testament, yet "rededication" has become one of the most common expressions in Christianity. I have heard some people say that they have

---

[*] This chapter was originally TOTT issue 46, May 2009.

rededicated their life several times. In the final analysis, this term is not only misleading but ultimately meaningless.

The other troublesome term is "backslide," a term used exclusively in the Old Testament and one that is extremely interesting and enlightening.

Jeremiah 3:6—4:2 recounts Jeremiah's second message of his book (the first is in 2:1—3:5). He tells the story of two sisters, Israel (the Northern Kingdom) and Judah (the Southern Kingdom). Israel had committed spiritual adultery against God, that is, the worship of idols, specifically, the fertility cult of the ancient world. God waited for her to return, but she refused to do so, so He gave "her a bill of divorce" and sent her away (v. 8), a clear reference to the destruction of Israel and her Assyrian captivity in 722 BC. Despite the object lesson this provided Judah as she watched this scene, she did not learn from it, would not turn away from idolatry, becoming even worse than Israel, and was also taken into captivity, this time by the Babylonians beginning in 605 BC.

The word "backsliding[s]," which appears seven times (vv. 6, 8, 11, 12, 14, 22 [twice]), translates two separate Hebrew words. Most often used is *meshûbâ*. Coming from the root *shûb*, "to return or go back, bring back," the literal idea is "back-turning, backsliding," and so figuratively speaks of disloyalty, and faithlessness. Most of its twelve occurrences are here in Jeremiah, but its two appearances in Hosea are most significant, where the people were "bent to backsliding" (11:7); that is, *apostasy had become the way of life*, although it is still possible for them to be healed (14:4).

The other word for "backsliding" in Jeremiah is *shôbâb* (vv. 14, 22), which is again from the root *shûb*. In this form it is an adjective, appearing only one other place (Isa. 57:17, "forwardly"), to picture a continual unfaithfulness to God.

Now, while this passage is, of course, Jewish, it certainly provides a picture for the church to consider. Prior to the Protestant Reformation, for example, the Church had drifted far from God and His revelation in Scripture. It had become thoroughly pagan in worshipping idols, relics, and saints, and "salvation" was simply a matter of doing certain works (called "sacraments") to obtain God's grace. Disastrously, the church today is drifting back to those days, and desperately needs to return to the Truth.

That said, however, the picture ends there. Backsliding is a term used exclusively for the nation of Israel to indicate her apostasy. It is *not* used, and *should not* be used, for a New Testament Christian. It must not be construed to refer to a Christian who has "fallen away" (see chapter 19), one who needs to "rededicate" his life, or any such unbiblical concept.

This is further confirmed by the fact that the only place *meshûbâ* is used of an individual is an isolated appearance in Proverbs 1:32, where it is translated "turning away," indicating the destruction that comes to those who turn away from the Truth.

Sadly, then, in spite of the fact that this word appears not once in the New Testament, rather only a few times in the Old Testament in reference to Israel's apostasy, and one isolated instance of an individual, it is commonly used today in much the same way the term "carnal Christian" is used, as well as for one who needs to "rededicate" his life.

If we may interject here, it should deeply grieve all Christians, *especially* pastors, expositors, and all other leaders who desire to be discerning, that terms having no biblical foundation whatsoever continue to be added to our "Christian vocabulary." We could fill several pages just listing them. Words mean things, and our words must be exact. We need to take great care to not add to, subtract from, or simply misapply Scripture (cf. Rev. 22:18–19)?

That brings us to our tough text. As if this issue does not raise enough questions, the very first problem we encounter is actually with the Greek text itself. The *Textus Receptus*, as well as the more modern Majority Text, uses a single Greek word for **carnal** four times in these verses. The word is *sarkikos*, an adjective meaning "fleshly, pertaining to the flesh or body, having the nature of flesh, i.e. under the control of the animal appetites."

In stark contrast, based on only five so-called "older manuscripts" (instead of hundreds in the Majority), the Critical Text, on which is based almost all modern English translations, uses another adjective, *sarkinos*, instead of *sarkikos* for **carnal** in verse 1 (rendered "men of flesh" in NASB). So what's the difference? Generally, Greek words ending in *-inos* mean "consisting of," while words ending in *-ikos* mean "characterized by." That is, while *sarkinos* speaks of being *made* of flesh ("fleshy"), *sarkikos* speaks of something having the *nature* of flesh ("fleshly").

But how does all that help? Why would Paul make the point that they are *made* of flesh? Why change terms in the middle of his argument? In fact, the only occurrence of *sarkinos* in the *Textus Receptus* and Majority Text is in 2 Corinthians 3:3, where Paul declares that God not only wrote His law on "tables of stone" but also on "fleshly tables of the heart." To further confuse the issue, the NIV renders both *sarkinos* and *sarkikos* as "worldly," with which no lexicon agrees; "worldly" would demand the Greek *kosmikos* (e.g., "worldly lusts" in Titus 2:12).

Making already muddy water even thicker, the Critical Text uses neither of these words for **carnal** in verse 4. Instead, it has *anthropos*, a generic term for "man" which the NASB, for example, here renders "are you not mere men?"

In fact, a headache begins to develop when one reads expositors and exegetes who, because they defend this reading, go on for several paragraphs trying to sort it all out and then apply it.

While it is not our intention here to open up the whole textual/translation "can of worms" (and we know that some readers might disagree), we would humbly ask, Does not the Critical Text actually confuse more than clarify? Does it not make far more sense that Paul uses one word consistently to get across his point?[1]

We would also submit, as we'll see in a moment, the use of the adjective form *psuchikos* for the "natural" man in 2:14 and then *pneumatikos* in 2:15 further supports the use of *sarkikos* alone in our text. The repetition of the ending *-ikos* in all three terms seems to us to clearly indicate that *sarkinos* is out of place and incorrect.

So what *is* Paul's point? Let us now turn to an exposition of the passage. In a sense, the "chapter break" at 3:1 is unfortunate, for the thoughts here continue those of 2:14–16. As stated a moment ago, verse 14 speaks of the "natural man," which is *psuchikos anthropos*. The adjective *psuchikos* is derived from the noun *pseuchē*, meaning "soul, that immaterial part of man held in common with animals."[2] This is the sensual, unregenerate man. Because he is driven solely by his senses, he simply cannot in any way understand or accept the things of God. No one has put it better than the beloved Vance Havner:

> The wise Christian wastes no time trying to explain God's program to unregenerate men; it would be casting pearls before swine. He might as well try to describe a sunset to a blind man or discuss nuclear physics with a monument in the city park. The natural man cannot receive such things. One might as well try to catch sunbeams with a fishhook as to lay hold of God's revelation unassisted by the Holy Spirit. Unless one is born of the Spirit and taught by Him, all this is utterly foreign to him. Being a Ph.D. does not help, for in this realm it could mean "Phenomenal Dud!"[3]

In contrast, there is then the one who is "spiritual" in verse 15. The Greek adjective *pneumatikos* derives from *pneuma*, "breath or spirit," and therefore refers to that which pertains to or is dominated by the Holy Spirit. Here, in fact, is a person who can "judge" and "discern" truth from error, while the natural man cannot. Both "discerned" in verse 14 and "judged" in verse 15 translate the same Greek word, *anakrino*. From about 400 BC onwards, it expressed "the questioning process which leads to a judgment: to examine, cross-examine, interrogate, enquire, and investigate." Other concepts in the word are "scrutinize" and "sift."[4]

True spirituality, then, along with discernment and maturity (as noted in chapter 6, "Where Has Our Discernment Gone?"), mean that we examine everything, that we investigate, question, scrutinize, and sift through every aspect of what is being taught and practiced, not from the perspective of natural inclination, but by the domination of the Holy Spirit and God's Word. Most people are, just like the Corinthians, anything but *spiritual*; they are, in fact, the very opposite, looking at everything from a sensual perspective. The truly spiritual person does not accept everything that comes along; rather he or she first examines it biblically to see if it's right or wrong.

It is this backdrop that sets the stage for 3:1–4. It is here that Paul adds the third term, *sarkikos*, one who is fleshly, one who is *characterized* by fleshly behavior (again, not *sarkinos*, one who is *made* of flesh). The chief misunderstanding about **carnal** (*sarkikos*), then, is the false notion that it refers to a supposed separate category of Christian and can refer to any sin that indicates "carnality." Those ideas, however, are not in the text.

In his wonderful book, *Whatever Happened to the Gospel of Grace?* (a highly recommended read), James Montgomery Boice writes one of the best statements I have ever read on this issue:

> "Carnal" is not a biblical category for weak Christians. Where the term appears in Paul's writings, it means an unregenerate person, an unbeliever (see Rom. 8:5–11). Even in 1 Corinthians 3, where Christians are said to be acting in a "worldly" (carnal) way, the point is only that they are acting as if they were not Christians, which must not be. They need to stop that and begin to behave as what they really are.[5]

What makes Boice's statement doubly important is the modern trend he outlines *before* that statement. He mentions the Bible teachers who insist that repentance, commitment of life, obedience, and behavioral change are involved in salvation. "In fact," Boice writes, "one of the reasons this teaching eliminates obedience from the essence of saving faith is to include as Christians professing believers whose lives are filled with sin."[6] He goes on to quote one such a teacher who insists, "If only committed people are saved people, then where is there room for carnal Christians?"[7] How sad it is that much of today's church no longer knows what being a Christian means!

While such teaching was not widely popularized until the 20th-century, it is not without earlier precedent. Some 200 years before, Scottish nonconformist theologian Robert Sandeman (1718–1771) rejected the doctrine of imputed righteousness and taught that only the barest assent to the work of Christ was necessary for salvation, a view now known as Sandemanianism. Not surprisingly, like our own day, many churches sprang up, undoubtedly populated by many unbelievers.

Such teaching is a wholesale denial of the most basic truths of salvation, namely, a deliverance from sin that results in a change of life. As we have studied before in this publication, in fact, the Greek *pisteuō* ("faith") implicitly and indisputably carries the idea "to obey" (see chapter 23 again). How we need to review the statement of doctrine in Chapter 18, Section 1 of both the *Westminster Confession of Faith* (1646) and the *London Baptist Confession* (1689):

> Although hypocrites, and other unregenerate men, may vainly deceive themselves with false hopes and carnal presumptions: of being in the favor of God and estate of salvation; which hope of theirs shall perish: yet such as truly believe in the Lord Jesus, and love him in sincerity, endeavoring to walk in all good conscience before him, may in this life be certainly assured that they are in a state of grace, and may rejoice in the hope of the glory of God: which hope shall never make them ashamed.

So, as Boice observes, it is essential to recognize that "carnal" is actually used in Scripture to refer to an unregenerate person. The phrase "to be carnally minded is death" in Romans 8:6 clearly speaks of the lost person under God's wrath, while the words "to be spiritually minded is life and peace" refer to the true believer. Further, "the carnal mind is enmity against God: for it is not subject to the law of God, neither indeed can be" (v. 7).

We must conclude, therefore, that "carnal" is not a *category* of *Christian*, rather it is a *characteristic* of the *non*-Christian. It does not refer to a "new convert," "the backslidden Christian," or any other such category. It refers to a Christian who is acting like a non-Christian in some very specific ways and who needs to stop such behavior and who will, in fact, do so if a true believer.

That immediately brings us to the question: what kind of non-Christian behavior is characteristic of such carnality? Some teachers insist that it can be anything, but again, the text does not say that. The text clearly shows that carnality is not a *moral* problem. In other words, in this context the Corinthians were not guilty of habitual drunkenness, fornication, or other moral sin, things that unarguably demonstrate an unregenerate life. In fact, to say that the "carnal Christian" is one who can continue to live immorally like an unregenerate person is to violate the very thing that Paul also wrote to the same group of believers, namely, that a Christian is a "new creature" (2 Cor. 5:17; again, chapter 23).

If carnality is not a *moral* problem, then what is it? We would submit that it is rather a *maturity* problem, for Paul goes on to specify exactly what he means. He doesn't list *moral* issues rather *maturity* issues.

To illustrate, the third most wonderful day of my life (my conversion being the first and my marriage the second) was the birth of my son Paul. What utter joy it was to hear his first infant sounds and then the laughter that came to his mom and me when he mispronounced various words as he grew and began to talk. We even wrote down a list of them as a keepsake (although I would be in deep trouble if I shared any here). If he still made the same sounds and mispronounced the same words when he was 21, however, it would no longer be cute or humorous. It would, of course, be cause for great alarm. It would indicate arrested development, perhaps even mental deficiency.

That was the situation, in a spiritual way, among the Corinthian believers. Instead of acting like spiritual adults, they were acting like fleshly children. How? Through **envying . . . strife, and divisions**.

Envying is *zelos* (English "zeal" and "zealous") is derived from the verb *zeō*, "to be hot." It can be used positively (e.g., Rom. 10:2; Col. 4:13), but here it is clearly negative, meaning jealousy, envy and anger (Act 5:17, "indignation"; 13:45; Rom. 13:13; Gal. 5:20; Phil. 3:6; Heb. 10:27, "fiery indignation"; Jas. 3:14, 16).

Strife is *eris*, meaning strife, contention, and wrangling (Rom. 13:13; 1 Cor. 1:11; 2 Cor. 12:20, "debates"; Gal. 5:20, "variance"; 1 Tim. 6:4; Titus 3:9).

Finally, **divisions**, is *dichostasia*, which speaks of dissension and separation into factions (Rom. 16:17; Gal. 5:20, "seditions"), which Paul goes on to detail in verses 4–8.

All three of those words underscore the childish behavior every parent has observed. From fights over a toy, to sibling rivalry, to schoolyard jealousies, such is the behavior of those driven by fleshly impulse. Likewise, pettiness, partiality, and prejudice ruled in Corinth.

As if all this were not bad enough, they were also characterized by another sign of an infant, namely, choking on solid food. Unlike the spirituality, maturity, and discernment that characterize "he that is spiritual," one who can *feast* on **meat**, these childish, juvenile Christians could merely *feed* on **milk**. Instead of being able to chew and swallow the deeper things of Christian truth, they could only drink the simplest, most elementary doctrines of the faith.

So appropriate was this metaphor that Paul used it again in Hebrews 5:12–14 (see chapter 7 for a discussion of Pauline authorship of Hebrews). If there is one thing that is true of the church today, it is shallowness and even outright ignorance of much biblical truth. We need to examine our churches carefully to discern whether this is a temporary state of carnality or the permanent state of the natural man.

NOTES

[1] For the technical reader, what is described here is actually a prime example of the modern, rationalistic textual criticism that follows one of the seven arbitrary "rules" of choosing the "correct" reading of any given text. Starting with Johann A. Bengel (1687–1752) and continuing to our day, second only to the first "rule" that "the older reading is to be preferred," another chief rule is that "the more difficult reading is to be preferred." In other words, when there is a choice between a reading that is hard to understand and a reading that is easy to understand, the hard reading must be the genuine one because orthodox scribes always changed the hard readings to make them easy. Such an approach is not only totally arbitrary—and this can easily be proved historically—but it is also thoroughly rationalistic, discounts the sovereignty of God in preserving the text, and even accuses orthodox Christians of lying by deliberately corrupted their own New Testament text by making readings easier.

[2] Spiros Zodhiates, *The Complete Word Study Dictionary* (AMG Publishers, 1993), electronic edition, #5590.

[3] *Pepper and Salt* (reprinted by Baker Book House, 1983) , p. 27.

[4] Colin Brown, *The New International Dictionary of New Testament Theology* (Zondervan, 1971), Vol. 2, p. 362.

[5] James Montgomery Boice, *Whatever Happened to the Gospel of Grace?* (Crossway Books, 2001), p. 143.

[6] Ibid, p. 142.

[7] Ibid, quoting Charles Ryrie, *Balancing the Christian Life* (Moody Press, 1969), p. 170.

Bless God for the translation of the Scriptures. The Word is our sword; by being translated, the sword is drawn out of its scabbard.

Puritan William Gurnall
The Christian in Complete Armour, Vol. 2, p. 236

29

Distinctions, Divisions, and Christian Love*

Selected Texts

This chapter is a little different. While it certainly deals with a text (several actually), the "tough part" concerns the *application* of the text. The purpose is to share a deep burden that I have had for some time and hopefully encourage all of us to Christian love in a specific area.

Two Theological Perspectives

To lay the foundation, I would first share the barest essentials of the two main theological perspectives.

First, there is *Covenant Theology*, a system of biblical interpretation that develops the Bible's philosophy of history on the basis of two (or three) covenants. Most see two, the first of which is the "Covenant of Works," an agreement between God and Adam promising life for perfect obedience and death for disobedience. Adam sinned, however, and therefore mankind failed to meet the requirements of the Covenant of Works. This covenant covers the time from Genesis 1:27—3:6.

Because of man's failure, God instituted the "Covenant of Grace," an agreement between God and man in which God promises salvation through Jesus Christ for those who will receive Him by faith. This covenant covers the time from Genesis 3:7—Revelation 20:7, that is, through the rest of biblical history, Old and New Testaments. The other covenants of Scripture—Noahic, Abrahamic, Mosaic, Palestinian, Davidic, and New—are administered under the one overarching, all-encompassing Covenant of Grace.

Some covenant theologians see a third covenant prior to those two, the "Covenant of Redemption," which was made between God the Father and God the Son in eternity past in which the Son voluntarily agreed to die for the elect in exchange for His headship of the elect. This, then, became the basis for the Covenant of Grace.

Second, there is *Dispensational Theology*. Based upon the word "dispensation" (*oikonomia*: *oikos*, "house, dwelling place," and *nomos*, a

---

* This chapter was originally TOTT issue 47, June 2009. It is worth noting that this piece generated more reader response than any other we have published. It has been edited slightly here but only by adding two quotations by A. W. Pink.

law; 1 Cor. 9:17; Eph. 1:10; 3:2; Col. 1:25), the idea is "the law of a house." The word speaks of the oversight, management, or stewardship one has over the affairs of a household. Applied to Scripture, it simply means that as the owner of His "household-world" God is overseeing, managing, and administering everything according to His will and purpose and is doing so in various stages called "dispensations" (or "economies"). This view recognizes that there have been (and will be) seven specific ways in which God has (and will) deal with man. Each dispensation is marked in Scripture by a different way of dealing with classes or individuals in regard to man's responsibility and sin.

Further, there are four characteristics of a dispensation: 1) man's *condition*, that is, his state and standing at the beginning of that era; 2) man's *responsibility*, that is, the test God gives man for that age; 3) man's *disobedience*, his failure of the test that God gave; and 4) God's *judgment* on man for his disobedience to God's test. Each dispensation also has a *steward*, that is, the chief representative of that age, the one to whom the responsibility of carrying out the commands of the dispensation is given.

The Distinctions

With that basic background understood, these two systems—which, if we may honestly interject, were both developed and systemized by men and both have their problems—are often at great odds with each other. We mention this briefly because it is essential to the point of this chapter that we make later.

For example, in its practical outworking, Covenant Theology says there's only one people of God and no distinctions between them. Dispensationalism sees two distinct people, Israel and the Church, which are mentioned together in 1 Corinthians 10:32, along with a third group ("Gentiles"), which is comprised of the lost.

Another great divide involves the Church. Covenant Theology views the church (the Body of Christ) as existing in the Old Testament and consisting of all the redeemed from Adam on. Pentecost was not the *beginning* of the Church, rather the empowering of the New Testament *manifestation* of the church that has existed since Adam. Dispensationalism views the church as nonexistent in the Old Testament, beginning rather at Pentecost.

Still another gulf is formed by a difference in the purpose of history. A "philosophy of history" seeks to interpret and apply history in a meaningful way by: 1) recounting *what* and *why* something happened; 2) interpreting it according to a particular unifying principle that ties all events together; 3) demonstrating how this fulfills the ultimate purpose and goal of history. While the philosophy of history in Covenant Theology views the ultimate goal as the eternal state, Dispensationalism views the ultimate goal to be the earthly Millennial Kingdom, demonstrating the sovereignty of God over human history.

Also, while Covenant Theology views the unifying principle of history as the "Covenant of Grace" (or the Covenant of Redemption, as some covenanters prefer), that is, God's plan of salvation for men, Dispensationalism views the unifying principle of history as being God's glory, as His glory is exhibited in the differing ways that He manifests Himself in the various dispensations.

Another chasm, this one the size of the Grand Canyon, opens between the two views when it comes to prophecy. Covenant theologians are usually either "Amillennial" (believing the kingdom to be present and spiritual) or "Postmillennial" (believing the Kingdom is in the process of being established on earth with Christ's return being the climax). Dispensationalists believe that there will be a literal 1,000 year reign of Christ on the earth based upon the promise of David's perpetual throne.

For lack of a better term, there is also some tragic "in-fighting" between the two groups. For example, on the one hand Covenant theologians accuse the dispensationalist's emphasis on literalness as "wrongly dividing the people of God" (a play on words of 2 Tim. 2:15). On the other hand, dispensationalists make much of the fact that Covenant theologians spiritualize certain portions of Scripture, such as spiritualizing Old Testament circumcision into baptizing infants now, which immediately begs the question, "Why baptize baby girls?"

This leads us to the central purpose of this article.

The Division

In the above, I have not defended either view of theological thought. While back in chapter 25 I admitted to being a "mild" Dispensationalist—I do see a distinction between Israel and the church—I am not defending that here. In fact, I disagree with some of the more extreme strains of Dispensationalism. That, however, is not my purpose here. Rather my purpose is to challenge some of the unchristian statements that are leveled by advocates of one camp at their brothers in the other, *because we need to be reminded that we are brothers.*

As mentioned earlier, my burden started quite some time ago. While at a pastor's conference, where the preaching was good and the fellowship sweet, the latter was marred for me by a statement one Covenant brother made. Since the views on eschatology in that group are mixed, and because that subject is avoided as a result, he made what I viewed as an inappropriate comment. After sharing an anecdote about a particularly tough week he had had, he said, "I found myself rethinking the Rapture," which brought a round of laughter. Now, I most certainly do not wear my feelings on my shoulder, and I am the first to join in good-natured banter, but I did not view that as an appropriate venue.

Sadly, others nowadays are not as subtle (or friendly). There are those who laugh and scoff at dispensationalists and look on them condescendingly, considering them little more than unscholarly simpletons. I've read several jabs by one author whose sarcasm drips off the page in his monthly publication. I ultimately stopped my subscription to that otherwise wonderful periodical just because of such uncalled for remarks.

Still others are just downright mean spirited and unchristian. One writer—and for unity's sake, I will not document his statements with a footnote—calls Dispensationalism "a cult and not a branch of the Christian church" and calls dispensationalists "false teachers" and "heretics." Do such comments reflect Christian love? Frankly, I found those comments so discrediting that I had a hard time finishing the book.

I was also deeply distressed by a recent DVD release that was at one point titled, *The Late Great Planet Church: The Rise of Dispensationalism and the Decline of the Church.* While I admit that I am going by the title, description, and previews alone, I find those painful enough. The description calls Dispensationalism a "fraudulent system." Now, according to Webster, "fraud" and "fraudulent" speak of deliberate deceit, dishonesty, and trickery, so the accusation seems pretty clear. Added to that is the indictment that Dispensationalism is a "stumbling block to the Church and a distraction from the Great Commission." Are such accusations indicative of Christian love and a desire for unity with fellow believers?

The DVD description also, like every critic, mentions that Dispensationalism is of "relatively recent development." While that is true—Dispensationalism was not fully systemized until the early 19th-century—it is also a fact that Covenant Theology as a system is not much older. It is seldom mentioned in the writings of the Early Church Fathers, it does not appear at all in the writings of the Reformers (Luther, Calvin, Zwingli, and Melanchthon), and it was not actually systemized until the 16th-century.[1] It would seem, then, that this point hinges on one's definition of "recent."

The DVD's title is equally distressing in its accusation that Dispensationalism is part of the decline of the Church. I find such a charge shocking in light of the many movements today that truly *are* destroying the Church, such as: seeker-sensitivity, psychology, the Emerging Church, and many others.

I'm not implying that Dispensationalists are not guilty of attacks of their own. On the contrary, I have read such ridiculous statements that Covenant Theology is a "doctrinal, and therefore personal, menace" and that it is "a gospel of works." Some have also called it "heresy." One speaker I know of went so unimaginably far that he lumped Covenant theologians in with "agnostics, Mormons, and cults." My comments later about Christian love are, therefore, aimed at all of us.

At the heart of all this finger pointing, in my view, is the incredibly loose usage of the word "heresy." But what exactly is heresy and what teachings are dubbed with that label in Scripture? "Heresy" is actually transliterated right from the Greek *hairesis* and is an interesting word. In Classical Greek, it means "seizure, taking, acquisition, choice, desire for something, and purposeful decision." Later in Hellenistic Greek, it "denotes the teaching or the school of a particular philosopher with which a person identifies himself by his choice."[2] In the Septuagint, it speaks of choice, as it translates the Hebrew *nedābāh* in Leviticus 22:18 and 21 ("freewill offering").

The New Testament usage of *hairesis* follows that of Hellenism and the Septuagint. Heresy is a choice, a deliberate decision to "seize" upon a particular teaching that is not orthodox. Acts 5:17, for example, mentions "the sect [*hairesis*] of the Sadducees," a Jewish faction that denied the doctrine of resurrection. Acts 15:5 refers to another sect, the Judaizers, who taught salvation by works, such as adding circumcision as a requirement. That issue prompted the Jerusalem Council, as the following verses describe, which definitively stated the principle of salvation by grace alone through faith alone.

There has always been the plague of false teaching and teachers. That is why discernment is so crucial. The main thrust of Peter's second epistle is a warning against false teachers who will infiltrate the church. That is best summarized in 2:1: "There shall be false teachers among you, who privily shall bring in damnable heresies, even denying the Lord that bought them, and bring upon themselves swift destruction." We see here at least three principles.

First, false teaching is *deceitful*. "Privily" is *pareisagō*, to bring in by the side of, to bring something in by smuggling it. False teaching has to be "brought in the side door" lest someone see it for what it really is. *Second*, false teaching is *degrading*. False teachers deny the Lord and His work in one way or another and in so doing degrade and blaspheme Him. *Third*, false teaching is *destructive*. "Damnable" is *apōleia*, to destroy fully. False teaching not only destroys right doctrine and the lives of its *victims* but also the *propagators* ("swift destruction"). (Note also the other "works of the flesh" listed with "heresies" in Galatians 5:19–21 and the command Paul gives concerning heretics [*hairetikos*] in Titus 3:10.)

If we may now ask, In view of what we have just outlined, is it honest to call either Dispensationalism or Covenant Theology "heresy"? No one is denying the resurrection, the virgin birth, the Deity of Christ, inspiration, salvation by grace alone, or any one of another dozen or so cardinal doctrines of Christianity. To put it another way, I am ready at a moment's notice to "lock and load" when it comes to defending the Doctrines of Grace and passionately guarding the Five Solas of the Reformation as Christianity's very foundation, *but such things are not at issue here.*

If I may intereject, I was recently reminded of this statement by A. W. Pink:

> Will not the Lord yet say unto many an unfaithful occupant of the modern pulpit (and editors of religious magazines), "Ye have not spoken of me the thing that is right" (Job 42:7)? "You did not make known the high requirements of My holiness, nor teach My people those things which would most "adorn the doctrine" (Titus 2:10) they profess. You have been tithing mint and anise and cummin, but omitting "the weightier matters" (Matt. 23:23): concerned with politics, wrangling over forms of church government, speculating about prophecy, but failing to insist on practical godliness. No wonder the "churches"—Calvinistic, equally with others—are in such a low state of spirituality.[3]

Indeed, there are far greater priorities in the church today than "wrangling" over non-essentials. Let us be honest. The two theological systems outlined earlier are *not* cardinal doctrines of Christianity, regardless of how fervently we might defend one or the other. For example, while the Doctrines of Grace are most certainly cardinal doctrines, one's view of the Millennium is not. While one's view might put him in a different *denomination*, it doesn't place him into a different *faith* or *body*. We are all members of Christ's Body, and we need to start acting like it. After all, has your arm ever called your leg a heretic, or has your right big toe ever called your left little toe a cultist? This leads us to our final encouragement.

Christian Love

Please do not misunderstand my next three statements, because I do not wish to appear self-righteous or that I am the more spiritual thinker who is taking "the high ground." If I may say, however, while I do not agree with their position, I have never called an Amillennial or Postmillennial brother in Christ a heretic. Not once have I ever said of a brother who believes in infant baptism that he is a false teacher. And I have certainly never accused any Covenant theologian of propagating a cult that is not a branch of the Christian church.

If I may lovingly ask, Where is our brotherly love? Now, please understand, I'm not talking about today's syrupy sentimentality. I'm not implying we should all hold hands around the campfire and sway to the music of *Kumbaya* or *We Are the World*. What I *am* saying, however, is that our unkind words and snide remarks to, and about, one another need to stop.

To illustrate, it's often noted about many in the King James Only camp (and rightly so) that they say some pretty nasty things about anyone who even slightly disagrees with them. They label Christian brethren as heretics, liars, Roman Catholics, and a plethora of other epithets just because they don't agree with their view of the textual issue. But what is the difference in that behavior and what we have noted on the present issue? Is it appalling in them but justified for us?

In verse after verse, Scripture commands believers to love each other. Why? *Obviously because we need constant reminding.* As our Lord Himself declared in Matthew 22:35–40, second only to a love for God is a love for our fellow believers. In John 13:34–35, He adds that while love itself is not a new command, to love as sacrificially as Christ did is the new standard. He goes on to say that it is "by this shall all men know that ye are my disciples." Is it not a little odd to think that we love each other and can be a witness to the world while we are calling each other heretics? John Gill comments here:

> Love one another: as brethren in the same family, children of the same Father, and fellow disciples with each other; by keeping and agreeing together, praying one for another, bearing one another's burdens, forbearing and forgiving one another, admonishing each other, and building up one another in faith and holiness.

As one of my professors early in my training used to say, "We can agree to disagree agreeably." If we are sincerely burdened for what we think is a brother's error, what happened to "speaking the truth in love" to him and praying for him instead of maligning him in print?

So crucial, so fundamental is this principle, that our Lord declares again, "Greater love hath no man than this, that a man lay down his life for his friends" (Jn. 15:12–13, 17). Is that not a pretty tough order to carry out with brothers whom we are calling cultists?

Being profoundly impacted by Jesus' teaching, the Apostle John repeatedly emphasizes this in his first Epistle. In this crucial letter, John presents several tests for knowing whether we are truly saved and have "passed from death unto life" (3:14; 5:25). One, for example, is obedience: "we do know that we know him, if we keep his commandments" and "whoso keepeth his word, in him verily is the love of God perfected: hereby know we that we are in him" (2:3, 5). Well, in 2:8–10, we see another. A crucial test for whether or not we are true believers is whether we love other believers. As the always encouraging Lehman Strauss puts it: "Love for the brethren is an infallible test of one's salvation, a distinguishing mark of true conversion."

Now, we are judging no one here, but what is John saying? Is he saying that any hatred, despising, disgust, loathing, scorning, contempt, ridicule, mockery, or other such attitude for another Christian is simply wicked and ungodly and might even be coming from an unregenerate heart? It would certainly seem so. As Strauss adds, "So long as brotherly love is wanting, that is proof conclusive that the one with hatred in his heart 'abideth in death.'"

We will leave the reader to examine John's many other encouragements on this point: 3:10–11, 14–19, 23; 4:7–8, 20–21. As one reads each of those, it's hard to imagine being able to carry them out while writing scathing attacks on the character and teaching of sound, godly men. If we may add, who do we think is pleased by such name calling, Christ or Satan?

Although I know some readers will think this ridiculous, I would still lovingly ask, What if either the Covenanter or dispensationalist gets to Heaven and finds out he was wrong? Then again, what if *both* arrive and discover they were wrong? Again, let's be honest. To dogmatically declare that either system is 100 percent correct is ridiculous. If either is wrong in only a single tiny point, then it is not perfect and, therefore, does not deserve to be elevated to infallibility and absolute authority. This alone should end all condescending attitudes and unchristian comments.

I would close with an illustration and challenge. A Claymore antipersonnel mine is a lens-shaped block of C-4 explosive with 700 steel balls embedded in it. Embossed on the front surface of the mine are the words "Front Toward Enemy" to remind the soldier of the "business end" of the weapon. Dear brethren, we need a reminder as well, a reminder that our *real* enemies are secularism, humanism, pragmatism, relativism, mysticism, materialism, post-modernism, historical (higher) criticism, rationalistic textual (lower) criticism, and the list goes on. We need to start unifying against those enemies and, indeed, attack with all guns blazing and all our "Claymores" pointed in the right direction. Yes, we can certainly debate the issues and passionately defend our views, but the unloving attitudes and unchristian speech must cease. To quote Pink once again:

> There should be a happy medium between sectarian narrowness and the world's "broadmindedness," between deliberately compromising the Truth and turning away from some of the Lord's people because they differ from us on non-essentials. Shall I refuse to partake of a meal because some of the dishes are not cooked as I

like them? Then why decline fellowship with a brother in the Lord because he is unable to pronounce correctly my favourite shibboleth? It is not without reason that "Endeavouring to keep the unity of the Spirit in the bond of peace" is immediately preceded by "forbearing one another in love" (Eph. 4:2, 3).[4]

NOTES

[1] Significantly, renowned Covenant theologian Louis Berkhof admits, "In the Early Church Fathers the covenant idea is seldom found at all." In the system's defense, he adds, "Though the elements which it includes, namely the probationary command, the freedom of choice, and the possibility of sin and death, are all mentioned." But he then goes on to report that the system was not yet developed in the time of the Reformers and that Kasper Olevianus (1536-1587) "was the real founder of a well developed federal theology, in which the concept of the covenant became for the first time the constitutive and determinative principle of the entire system." (*Systematic Theology*; [Eerdmans, 1939, 1941], pp. 211-212.)

[2] Colin Brown, *The New International Dictionary of New Testament Theology* (Zondervan, 1971), Vol. 1, p. 533.

[3] A. W. Pink, *Studies in the Scriptures*, Vol. XXVI, March 1947, No. 3, p. 7. It is noteworthy that this quotation (and more we could include) has been totally removed from Moody Press' reprint of Pink's study, which they titled, *Gleanings from Paul: Studies in the Prayers of the Apostle* (1967, p. 237) and done so without informing the reader of the deletion.

[4] *Studies in the Scriptures*, Vol. XIV, March 1935, No. 3.

"Those who do "love the truth" (2 Thes. 2:10) are they in whom a divine work of grace has been wrought. They have something more than a clear, intellectual understanding of the Scripture: it is the food of their souls, the joy of their hearts (Jer. 15:16). They love the truth, and because they do so, they hate error and shun it as deadly poison. They are jealous for the glory of the Author of the Word, and will not sit under a minister whose teaching dishonors Him; they will not listen to preaching which exalts man into the place of supremacy, so that he is the decider of his own destiny."

A. W. Pink
Experimental Salvation

30

The Grace of Unity*

Ephesians 4:1–3

I therefore, the prisoner of the Lord, beseech you that ye walk worthy of the vocation wherewith ye are called, With all lowliness and meekness, with longsuffering, forbearing one another in love; Endeavouring to keep the unity of the Spirit in the bond of peace.

This chapter (and the next) addresses an ever-increasingly important issue in our day—*unity*. What *is* true unity, and *upon what* can it be based? Can there be unity between greatly diverse groups if we simply agree on some very general "common ground," or are there definitive, objective truths in Scripture that define the basis of unity?

The Epistle to the Ephesians is a life-long passion of mine. As I have shared in a full exposition of this letter—which I hope to publish before I "have shuffled off this mortal coil"—while Romans is the most thorough and comprehensive presentation of Gospel doctrine, Ephesians is the most basic, the most profound, and the most awe-inspiring. I am convinced (in my humble opinion) that it is the most basic and foundational New Testament book for the believer.

As is true of most of Paul's letters, the first half (1—3) deals mostly with *doctrine*, while the second (4—6) addresses mostly *duty*. Another way we can say this it that we first see our *riches* in Christ and then *responsibilities*; first comes our *wealth*, and then our *walk*. On the present issue, therefore, Paul first *states* the truth about unity in Christ in 1:22–23, 2:16, 21–22, and 3:6, and then *applies* that truth in 4:1–16 (for the sake of space, we will not quote the entire passage, but please open your Bible and follow along).

The key word in chapters 4—6 is **walk**, and we find it five times (4:1, 17; 5:2, 8, 15). The Greek in all five occurrences is *peripateō* (*peri*, "about" or "around," and *pateō*, "to walk"), and so literally means "to walk about, to walk around, to walk concerning." In Classical Greek, this word was used only in the literal sense and meant strolling and stopping, as someone would walk about in the market place. It was never used in a figurative sense as it is in the New Testament.[1] Used in such a figurative sense, it

---

* This chapter was originally TOTT issues 31 and 32, Feburary and March 2008.

speaks of "conduct of life," that is, "how we walk about," how we conduct ourselves as we walk through life. How, then, are we to conduct ourselves? Chapters 4—6 reveal seven ways in which we are to walk, each of which in-turn is based on related doctrine in chapters 1—3. We are to walk in: *unity* (4:1–16; cf. 1:22–23; 2:16, 21–22; 3:6); *purity* (4:17–32; cf. 1:4); *love* (5:1–7; cf. 3:17–19); *light* (5:8–14; cf. 1:18); *wisdom* (5:15–17; cf. 1:8, 17; 3:10); *submission* (5:18—6:9; cf. 3:8); *victory* (6:10–20; cf. 1:19–21).

It is extremely significant, therefore, that the very first practical reality in which Paul tells the Christian to walk is **unity**. This is not an accident. Paul, in fact, dealt with this first in another letter, his first letter to the Corinthians. With all the problems in that Church—and there were *many*—he dealt first, and at great length, with **unity** (1 Cor. 1:10—3:23). Why? Because without unity, there can be no growth, joy, or effective witness. So important is unity in the Body of Christ that our Lord prayed several times in His high priestly prayer (Jn. 17:11, 21–23) that His people "may be one." This was also the precedent set in the Early Church. All that they did—their worship, witness, and willingness to serve—was in **unity**. Please read Acts 2:47–48 and note that unity is again listed first ("continuing daily with one accord"). To understand this, we will examine two of four principles in 4:1–16: the *grace* of unity (vv. 1–3) and the *ground* of unity (vv. 4–6).[2]

In this chapter, we will first three principles concerning the *grace* of **unity**: its *meaning, motive,* and *maintenance.*

The Meaning of Unity

Perhaps never before in history have we heard as much about **unity** as we do today. But much of what we hear is not based upon a proper understanding of what *true* **unity** is. Let us, therefore, consider first what unity is *not* and then what it *is*.

What Unity is Not

First, unity is not "compromise," or another word that is prevalent today, "tolerance." Unity does not mean we throw out all doctrine so that everyone can "get along." This is perhaps the most common misconception of our day. It is argued, "Let's not have any distinctives or any doctrinal barriers that might divide us; let's just agree on love and unite on moral issues, such as fighting abortion and gay marriage."

Second, unity is not some common brotherhood or mutual camaraderie. Unity does not necessarily exist just because we are members of the same company, union, association, or even church denomination.

Third, unity is not uniformity. As Webster (11th Edition Collegiate) defines it, "uniformity" means "having always the same form, manner, or degree; not varying . . . of the same form with others . . . unvaried appearance of surface, pattern, or color." Unity does not exist just because everyone is a cookie cutter cutout who walks, talks, acts, thinks, and even dresses alike. Such uniformity is not biblical. As one can see in the *gifts* for unity in verses 7–11, this violates the context of the passage. God did not make us alike, and neither does He give us all the same spiritual gifts. God gives us *unity*, but He also gives us *diversity*. You can create uniformity from *pressure without*, but unity comes only from *power within*.

What Unity *Is*

The Greek for **unity** is *henotēs*, which basically means "unanimity and agreement." One Greek authority, however, provides a marvelous contrast between how the Greeks, the Septuagint (the Greek translation of the Old Testament), and the New Testament use this word:

> In Greek and Roman philosophy the unity of God and the world is demanded by educated *reason*. In the Old Testament [the Septuagint], the unity of God is a confession derived from *experience* of God's unique reality. The decisive advance in the New Testament, caused by God Himself, is the basing of the unity and uniqueness of God on *the unique revelation through and in the one man Jesus Christ*.[3]

To simplify, we base unity either on *reason, experience*, or *the person and work of Jesus Christ*. Most of today's so-called unity is based either on *experience* ("We've all experienced the same thing, so we're in this thing together") or *reason* ("To accomplish more, we'll get rid of our doctrinal differences"). While such platitudes sound noble, they are unscriptural and ultimately destructive. True, biblical unity is this: *the unanimous agreement concerning the unique revelation of God through Jesus Christ*. Unless we can agree on the person and work of Jesus Christ, there can be no unity. It's as simple as that.

As Paul told the Galatians, "As we said before, so say I now again, If any man preach any other gospel unto you than that ye have received, let him be accursed" (Gal. 1:9). The words "as we have said before" indicate that Paul had said this many times in his ministry. Doctrine, therefore, *must* be the ground of unity, as Paul makes clear here in verses 4–6.

Who, then, produces this unity? Certainly not man. This is not something we can produce like we would create "school spirit." Rather, as our text says, it is the Holy Spirit who *produces* this unity. What we are to do is *keep* the unity the Spirit has produced through Christ.

Notice the subtlety of the word **keep,** which translates the Greek *tēreō*, "to keep by guarding, to guard by exercising watchful care, to guard as with a fortress." The picture here is a fortress around which we post armed guards, set Claymore mines, erect concertina wire, and do all else that we can to guard this unity. But this is not enough for Paul, for he adds the word **endeavoring,** which is *spoudazō*, "to make haste, to be zealous or eager, to give diligence." It speaks of determined effort and exertion. It is, therefore, the responsibility of every believer to diligently, zealously, absorbingly guard the unity that Christ has provided. We do not *produce* unity because we *can't* produce it. When we try, we end up with a false unity. Rather we are to *guard* the unity that the Spirit produces in Christ. In essence, Paul is saying, "Don't muck it up. Don't try to make something you can't. Just guard what God has already done."

As commentator William Hendrickson observes, the unity in this passage "is not external and mechanical, but internal and organic. It is not superimposed, but, by virtue of the power of the indwelling Christ, proceeds from within the organism of the church. Those, therefore, who in ecumenical zeal are anxious to erase all denominational boundaries and to create a mammoth super-church can find no comfort here."[4]

A graphic example in recent history of such an attempt to *create* unity where there can *be* no unity was the "Evangelicals and Catholics Together: The Christian Mission in the Third Millennium" (ECT) document that was written by two evangelicals a few years ago and signed by several others. It was designed to bring together Roman Catholics and Evangelicals for the purpose of evangelism and a "betterment of life in America." While it clearly notes certain differences between Catholics and Protestants, it flatly denies the most important difference, namely, *what it means to be saved!* That fact immediately and fundamentally violates the true basis of unity we just examined. The ECT document also states that all Catholics and Evangelicals hold the same faith and are brothers and sisters in Christ, when in reality, *the two systems are exact opposites.* Roman Catholicism is based *solely* on a sacramental, works-oriented "salvation," not on God's grace alone, through faith alone, in Christ alone. All you have to do to prove this is ask anyone who was saved out of it. There can be no unity between these diametrically opposed systems.[5]

One of the authors of the ECT document compounds his error in a book he wrote on unity. In it he "expounds" on our text like no one before him (at least none I have ever read). He maintains that while doctrinal agreement is essential in the Local Church (what he calls "the church particular"), such agreement is not required in "the church universal." He further maintains that the reason it is essential at the local level is that without it the local church's ability to worship is destroyed. He concludes,

"The distinction is critical: uniformity within the church particular, but unity with diversity in the Body or church universal."[6]

Lest I be accused of promoting disunity, I'll say only one thing in love: that is appallingly unscriptural. The text simply does not say that, nor does the Bible *anywhere* differentiate between the local assembly and the universal body *in respect to doctrinal purity*. Scripture *repeatedly* speaks of right doctrine and discernment of error. Again, as Paul plainly states in Galatians 1:9, anyone who preaches another Gospel, and Roman Catholicism (like Mormonism, Jehovah's Witness, and others) *is* another Gospel, is cursed.

The author not only misuses the word "uniformity," but then makes an even more serious error by implying that "diversity" refers to "doctrinal differences," that we in the Universal Church can get along even in our diverse doctrinal positions. Such error is common when we fail to exposit the Scriptures, which this author fails to do. *The context of 4:1–16 clearly shows that "diversity" refers to spiritual gifts NOT doctrine.* Paul's point here is the same one he makes even more strongly in 1 Corinthians 12. Each one of us, having our own unique spiritual gifts, which have been imparted by the Holy Spirit, is as diverse in function and purpose as are an arm, a leg, and an eye on the body. But all those differences work together in harmony to edify the entire body.

Another even more appalling development is the more recent "A Common Word Between Us and You" document, which "identifies some core common ground between Christianity and Islam" and seeks unity between them. Unbelievably, this document has been endorsed by many noted "evangelicals," such as: Timothy George, Bill Hybels, Rick Warren, Rich Nathan, David Neff, and, not surprisingly, Robert Schuller. But we are compelled to ask here: *how can there be a "common word" between two groups with different Gods?*

So we say again, true biblical unity is this: *the unanimous agreement concerning the unique revelation of God through Jesus Christ.* Where that cannot be agreed upon, there can be no unity. Tragically, more and more evangelicals are abandoning this by redefining the Gospel and preaching Relativism, as seen in the ministries of those listed above, as well as the apostate "Emerging Church" movement and other false teaching.

Having emphasized that, let us not fail to recognize how truly sweet **unity** is when based upon the right doctrine concerning Christ. It is **unity** that transcends denominations. We can agree to disagree on *non-essentials*, but we can unify on the one *reality of Christ*.

There is no better illustration than in an incident recorded by Harry Ironside. Taken ill with typhoid during a series of meetings in Minneapolis, he was down for six weeks. After gaining enough strength to return home to California, friends helped him to the train and the conductor made up a special berth for him. As he lay in his berth the first morning out, he took out his Bible and began to read. As he read, a stout-looking German woman came walking by, noticed Ironside, and then stopped and asked, "Vat's dat? A Bible?" "Yes," Ironside replied. "Vell, you haf your morning vorship all by yourself?" she asked. "Vait, I go get my Bible and ve haf it together."

A little later a tall Norwegian gentleman came and stopped and said, "Reading ze Bible. Vell, I tank I get mine, too." After a few minutes, Ironside was amazed at how many had gathered. Every day a crowd gathered, one day totaling twenty-eight. The conductor walked through all the cars announcing, "The camp meeting is starting in car number so-in-so. Any wanting to take advantage are invited." They would sing, read, pray, and ask questions.

At the end of the trip in Sacramento, as people came to say goodbye, that dear German woman asked Ironside, "Vat denomination are you?" "Well," Ironside replied, "I belong to the same denomination that David did." "Vat vas dat?" she asked. "I didn't know David belonged to any." Ironside replied, "David said, 'I am a companion to all them that fear Thee and keep Thy precepts' [Ps. 119:63]." "Yah, yah," she said, "dat is a gute church to belong to."[7]

Ironside went on to write that no doubt there were many denominations represented in that group, but what mattered was that they were one in Christ. *Minor* points didn't matter; the *main* point did, *the unique revelation of God through Jesus Christ.* As we will go on to detail in the next chapter, Ephesians 4:4–6, in fact, lists doctrines that form the *ground* of unity.

The Motive for Unity

The motive for unity is two-fold in verse 1.

God Brought Unity Through Christ

The key here is the word **therefore**, and its importance cannot be overemphasized. It stands as a signpost to announce that there can be no separating *doctrine* from *duty*, that we simply cannot rightly *accomplish* the *duty* of chapters 4—6 until we *assimilate* the *doctrine* of chapters 1—3.

Space does not allow us to go into detail, but it is truly amazing how many times the word **therefore** appears in Scripture, and it is a worthwhile study in itself. Of its some 1,237 instances in our Authorized Version, about 356 are in the New Testament, and every one is significant. The **therefore** of Matthew 3:7–8, for example, demonstrates that true repentance results in fruit. The **therefore** of 28:18–20 shows that without

Christ's power the commission could have no success. And of special significance in our day are Paul's parting words to Timothy. In light of growing apostasy, what did Paul challenge Timothy to do? Did he challenge him to be an entertainer, or "appeal to seekers," or be "user-friendly" or "purpose-driven"? Hardly! He commanded, "I charge thee **therefore** before God . . . Preach the word . . . reprove, rebuke, exhort" (2 Tim. 4:1–2).

That great word, then, carries a three-fold significance in Scripture: *First*, it reminds us of the wholeness of scripture. It reminds us always to be looking at the context, as well as *analogia scripturae*, "the analogy of Scripture" (see the Appendix on "Principles of Biblical Interpretation"). *Second*, the word **therefore** is a word that indicates application. I am always struck here by Galatians 4:16, of which every Christian needs reminding. What is the application when we tell rebellious people the Truth? Bewildered, and perhaps even asking rhetorically, Paul writes, "Am I **therefore** become your enemy, because I tell you the truth?" *Third*, and most important of all, the word **therefore** shows not only *application* but also that *application is always a result of doctrine.*

That third application leads us to the importance of **therefore** in our present text. Since the passage deals with unity, the word **therefore** clearly and dramatically demonstrates that we cannot have unity without the doctrine of chapters 1—3. Martyn Lloyd-Jones rightly made this a major emphasis in his exposition of this passage:

> Whatever be the unity of which the Apostle speaks, it is a unity that results directly from all he has been saying in the first three chapters of the Epistle. You must not start in chapter 4 of the Epistle to the Ephesians. To do so is to violate the context and to ignore the word "Therefore." In other words, you cannot have Christian unity unless it is based upon the great doctrines outlined in chapters 1—3. "Therefore!" So if anyone comes to you and says, "It does not much matter what you believe; if we call ourselves Christians, or if we believe in God in any sense, come let us all work together," you should say in reply, "But, my dear sir, what about chapters 1 to 3 of the Epistle to the Ephesians? I know of no unity except that which is the outcome of, and the offspring of, all the great doctrines which the Apostle lays down in those chapters." Whatever this unity may be, we are compelled to say that it must be theological, it must be doctrinal, it must be based upon an understanding of the truth.[8]

Biblically, Lloyd-Jones was correct decades ago, and is still correct today. With few exceptions, people go right to Ephesians 4 when talking about unity without even acknowledging the doctrine that precedes it. The author we noted earlier is guilty of this; he builds his entire argument for unity upon his *opinion*, not on the *doctrine* outlined earlier in the Epistle. This doctrine appears in no less than three passages (please read 1:22–23; 2:16, 21–22; 3:6).

Both a *body* and a *building* must be unified, and all this has been accomplished by the true gospel of Christ. Most unity talk today is based upon one word—*love*. But the Bible says no such thing. Only when we acknowledge the finished work of Christ, that salvation is only in Him by grace through faith, can there be unity. As we will see in verse 5, there is only "one Lord" and "one faith."

As Lloyd-Jones also observes here, and I have verified this in my own reading, many commentators and expositors miss this point. While many mention the transition from doctrine to duty marked by the word **therefore**, it is tragic that most fail to drive home the principle that *doctrine matters when it comes to unity* and that the word **therefore** underscores this truth. It is essential that we recognize that if we do not base unity on the truths of chapters 1—3, we do *not* have and *cannot* have true unity. As noted earlier, true biblical unity is this: *the unanimous agreement concerning the unique revelation of God through Jesus Christ*, and it is this that Paul details in chapters 1—3. As we'll see later, Paul makes this even clearer in 4:4–6, where he gives us the *ground*, that is, the *basis*, for unity.

This leads to a second principle.

We Are Commanded to Keep this Unity

Once we recognize the true basis for our unity, we are then (and only then) commanded to "keep" (v. 3, *tereō*, "to guard as with a fortress") that unity. To show how imperative this is, Paul uses the word **beseech**. The Greek here is *parakaleō*, a compound word made up of *para*, "beside," and *kaleō*, "to call," yielding the picture "to call alongside." Originally, it spoke of summoning someone and at times "to summon to one's aid for help." Its main three meanings in the New Testament, however, are reflected in our Authorized Version by three translations: "beseech," that is, to plead with or implore (43 times), "comfort" (23 times), and "exhort" (21 times). In the present context, there is no doubt as to how Paul uses it; he implores and pleads with the Ephesians to certain behavior based upon the doctrine of chapters 1—3.

Specifically, Paul implores us to **walk worthy**. As noted earlier, **walk** is *peripateō*, "to walk about," and figuratively speaks of how we conduct ourselves as we walk through life. The Greek behind **worthy** is *axios*, which in Classical Greek carried the idea of balancing scales, of one side of the scale counter-balancing the other side.[9] We are **therefore** to **walk** in balance to something. And to what are we to walk in balance? What is the "counter-balance" on the scales? **The vocation wherewith [we] are called**. **Vocation** translates *klēsis*, "a call or invitation to a banquet." With only a few exceptions,[10] Paul uses this word and related words (such as the verb *kaleō* for the word **called** in our text) to refer to the Divine calling of the elect to salvation. So the full thrust of Paul's statement here is that we are to **walk** in balance to the salvation to which we've been **called**; in other words, we are to **walk** as believers ought to walk. *And the first way we are to walk is in unity.*

Just as a broken bone in the physical body brings pain and debilitation, it is a terrible thing to fracture the Body of Christ through disunity. Once the doctrinal truth of Christ is settled, there had better be unity, not warring factions (as in the Corinthian church), not individuals fighting for whatever reason (as the two women in Philippians 4:2–3), rather true unity.

It is also significant that Paul refers to himself for the second time as **the prisoner of the Lord**. Why a second mention of this (cf. 3:1)? It is a simple reminder that a worthy walk will be costly, but the blessings far outweigh the suffering. "For I reckon that the sufferings of this present time are not worthy to be compared with the glory which shall be revealed in us" (Rom. 8:18).

Oh, how important unity is! It is to be the *practical result* of a *doctrinal reality*. Let us do all we can to keep that unity. This leads us right to a third principle.

The Maintenance of Unity (vv.2–3a, c)

With all lowliness and meekness, with longsuffering, forbearing one another in love; Endeavouring to keep the unity of the Spirit in the bond of peace.

We cannot over-emphasize these two verses. The unity of Christians has been a perennial problem since the early days of Christianity. As early as Acts 6, in fact, unity was threatened. Additionally, in almost every one of Paul's Epistles there is something about unity. The most vivid picture is the analogy of the human body, which is not only mentioned here but elaborated in 1 Corinthians 12, where we see three principles: (1) there is one body but many members; (2) each member has a different function but still edifies the whole; (3) one member out of sorts effects the whole.

Tragically, there is little true unity in the Church, that is, the Body of Christ, today. There are preachers who break fellowship over minor points of doctrine and those who practice "secondary separation," which means they won't fellowship with one group because that group fellowships with another group. To illustrate tongue-in-cheek, I've seen this go even further to "thirdary" and "fourthdary" separation; one group won't fellowship with another group because they fellowship with another group that fellowships with another group that fellowships with another group. There is also disunity in many local churches, which is caused by petty squabbles over nothing, which in turn comes from spiritual immaturity. It is said that it was Spurgeon who first said this little jingle, and how true it is:

> To dwell above with saints we love,
> O that will be glory!
> But to dwell below with saints we know,
> Well, that's another story!

As we saw earlier, then, we are to "[endeavor] to keep the unity" (v. 3). It is the responsibility of every believer to diligently, zealously, absorbingly "guard as with a fortress" the unity that Christ has provided. But now the question arises: how can we maintain ("keep") the unity that God has produced in Christ? The answer lies in our text, where we see the "Fruit of the Spirit" of Galatians 5:22–23 in action. Let us first briefly examine that text and then see it applied here in Ephesians.

The "Fruit of the Spirit"

At the very core of the Christian life is the "Fruit of the Spirit," as Paul wrote to the Galatian believers:

> But the fruit of the Spirit is love, joy, peace, longsuffering, gentleness, goodness, faith, Meekness, temperance: against such there is no law (Gal. 5:22–23).

Here is the very essence of Christian living because it is the very essence of Christ's own character. In his classic reference Bible, C. I. Scofield writes:

> Christian character is not mere moral or legal correctness, but the possession and manifestation of the graces of vv. 22–23. Taken together they present a moral portrait of Christ, and may be understood as the apostle's explanation of 2:20, "Not I, but Christ," and as a definition of "fruit" in John 15:1–8. This character is possible because of the believer's vital union with Christ (John 15:5; 1 Cor 12:12–13), and is wholly the fruit of the Spirit. "Fruit" (singular), in contrast with "works" (plural, v. 19), suggests that the Christian's life in the Spirit is unified in purpose and direction in contrast with the life in the flesh, with its inner conflicts and frustrations.

Particularly important is that last statement, that "fruit" is singular to show the unified Christian life. These are not the *fruits* of the spirit, rather the *fruit* of the Spirit; they are a unified whole in the believer's life. The Galatian believers had been "bewitched" (3:1) by false teachers into believing that following the Mosaic Law was necessary for right living. But Paul makes it clear here that it is not the constraints of the Law that produce Christ-like character, neither our efforts that produce it, but the Holy Spirit working in us. Just as the "the works of the flesh" in 5:19–21 fall into three general areas (sex, religion, and human relationships), "the fruit of the spirit" also fall into three categories: personal, social, and philosophical.

First, "love," "joy," and "peace" are *personal*. By this we mean that they are the real basis of our growth in Christ and are the foundation of all the others. They come only by personal experience of Christ and are absolutely unique to Christianity. We must never forget this uniqueness. No other "religion" or faith can profess, much less manifest, these three. They form the very foundation of all that happens in the Christian life.

Second, "longsuffering," "gentleness," and "goodness" are *social*. They illustrate the command of our Lord, "Love thy neighbor as thyself." They describe how we should *appear to* and how we then *deal with* those around us.

Third, "faith," "meekness," and "temperance" are *philosophical*. These are given to demonstrate the basic contrast between the attitudes of God and the attitudes of the world. These three philosophical principles are the exact opposites of the world's philosophies.

The "Fruit of the Spirit" in Our Text

It is truly amazing that four of the nine "fruit of the spirit" appear in our text *and* that there is at least one from each category. The obvious reason for this is that *these are the characteristics that will maintain unity*.

First, from the *personal* category, we see **love** and **peace**. There can be no doubt why **love** is mentioned first. The first characteristic in Galatians 5:22 is **love** because from it all the others flow. As Paul declared just a few verses earlier, "For all the law is fulfilled in one word, even in this; Thou shalt love thy neighbour as thyself" (Gal. 5:14). We submit, therefore, that the underlying characteristic of unity is **love**. The Greek *agapē* refers to a sacrificial love, "a self-emptying self-sacrifice." God's love, then, could be defined as, "A self-emptying self-sacrifice in which God gave of Himself in the form of His only begotten Son who gave His life for us." Now we read that to maintain unity we are to have and practice the same kind of **love** toward other believers. Just think, how can there ever be disunity when we all have "a self-emptying self-sacrifice?" To put it in the reverse, when there is disunity, there is an obvious lack of "a self-emptying self-sacrifice." If there is some rumbling going on in the body, if there is some little fuss brewing, if a fight breaks out, it is because we are thinking of ourselves instead of someone else.

We might think that to speak of **love** would be enough, but Paul knew that it would not be enough because he understood human nature. So he adds that we are also to be **forbearing one another**. The Greek behind **forbearing** (*anechomai*) means "to hold one's self upright, to bear, to endure." This is the same word Paul uses in 2 Timothy 4:3 to describe people who will not "endure [put up with] sound doctrine" but will seek teachers who will tickle their ears. The idea here, then, is that sometimes we just put up with each other, that we bear with each other in misunderstandings, problems, and conflicts, that we **love** each other and sacrifice ourselves for others anyway. This does not mean we just put up with it but still boil within, rather we forbear in **love**. Without this kind of **love** and **forbearing**, unity will be destroyed and God's work right along with it.

Paul mentions another personal characteristic, **peace**. The Greek is *eirēnē*, "a state of tranquility; the opposite of rage and war." This word is related to the Hebrew word *shalom*, a common Hebrew greeting. This word, however, means not so much the opposite of war but of any disturbance in the tranquility of God's people. First, since we are in Christ, there is tranquility and harmony between God and man (Eph. 1:2), and second, since we are in Christ, there is tranquility and harmony between Jew and Gentile (2:14). We now see the third step in the progression: *there is, and must continue to be, tranquility between all believers because of Christ*. This is not just the opposite of war, not just the opposite of "going at one another," not just the opposite of suppressing our seething resentment of someone else, rather a tranquility, a freedom from any agitation or turmoil. We must allow the Holy Spirit to maintain this tranquility, because it is the **bond** that holds us together.

The word **bond** translates *syndesmos*. In Classical Greek, from the time of Homer onwards (8th–7th-century), the root *desmos* meant "chain."[11] In the New Testament, it meant "band, bond, ligament."[12] With the prefix *sun* ("with"), *syndesmos* means "that which binds together." In a negative sense, we see it in Acts 8:23, where someone is enslaved by a habit or attitude. Peter says of Simon the sorcerer, who was not a truly converted man, "I perceive that thou art in the gall of bitterness, and in the bond of iniquity." In Colossians 2:19, it refers to a tendon or ligament of the bones that holds the body together.

This, then, is the picture of true unity. It's not some superficial or sappy sentimentality, rather a **bond**, the very ligaments of the body, which hold us together. One commentator notes that the American Indians spoke of **peace** as a "chain of friendship."[13] That is, indeed, what the true Christian has with other Christians.

This challenges us that a lack of **peace** in the Body is sin, no matter what the reason. A vivid example of this appears in Philippians 4:2–3:

> I beseech Euodias, and beseech Syntyche, that they be of the same mind in the Lord. And I entreat thee also, true yokefellow, help those women which laboured with me in the gospel, with Clement also, and with other my fellowlabourers.

The only problem in the Philippian church was a single unnamed conflict between two women, but that one conflict threatened to do serious damage. Paul obviously doesn't tell us what the problem was because it didn't matter. Whether one woman's argument was right and the other wrong didn't matter either. Both were wrong because they were causing disunity in the body.

As Paul wrote the fractured Corinthians, "Now I beseech you, brethren, by the name of our Lord Jesus Christ, that ye all speak the same thing, and that there be no divisions among you; but that ye be perfectly joined together in the same mind and in the same judgment" (1 Cor. 1:10). When we are thinking more about what *we think* and what *we feel*, there will be division. As Paul writes later, we are being wise in the world, and that's foolishness (3:18–20). How many Christians there are who think they are wise in this age, that is, wise in contemporary human wisdom. But Paul says that they are just deceiving themselves. As a pastor, I am constantly troubled (and quite honestly terrified) about what disagreements and difference of *opinion* over paint color, carpet fiber, pew design, window trim, and other such ridiculous matters can do to church unity. Such things are merely personal taste and worldly wisdom and are foolishness to God. Such things can destroy unity in a heartbeat, so we must always be on guard.

Second, from the *social* category of the "fruit of the spirit," there is **longsuffering**. The Greek here is *makrothumia*, a compound word from *makro*, meaning "long," and *thumos*, meaning "temper." The idea, then, is simple; we are to be long-tempered in contrast to short-tempered, to suffer long instead of being hasty to anger and vengeance. This is one of the *social* characteristics of "the fruit of the spirit" because this is how we are to react to people and how we are to treat them. To maintain unity, we will set aside "self," set aside our own needs, and be willing to suffer last place instead of first place, even to look like we're wrong (in non-essential matters) if it will maintain unity. Again, we're not talking about doctrinal issues here—that is the point in the next passage (4:4–6). Rather we are speaking here of things that don't matter, the little things of personality and human interaction. What a marvelous testimony it is to be **longsuffering**, to have the ability to be long-tempered. "Love suffers long" (1 Cor. 13:4) and we must be "swift to hear, slow to speak, and slow to wrath" (James 1:19).

Chrysostom, that great 4th-century preacher, wonderfully defined this as the spirit that has the power to take revenge but does not do so. Commentator William Barclay offers a homey illustration. Have you ever seen a puppy and a large dog together? The puppy barks that high pitch puppy yap, pesters the big dog, and even nips him. But while the big dog could snap the puppy's neck with one bite and a shake, he just bears it with dignity. Perhaps you have even seen the big dog look up at you with an expression that says, "Look what I have to put up with." *That* is **longsuffering**, the attitude that bears attack, assault, affront, and abuse without bitterness or complaint.

When we are impatient with people and when we are short tempered, it is really because we are impatient with God. We are at that moment not trusting and not leaning upon Him to give us strength. A verse, which is not quoted enough and lived consistently by Christians, is Isaiah 40:31: "But they that wait upon the Lord shall renew their strength; they shall mount up with wings like eagles; they shall run and not be weary; and they shall walk and not faint." When we wait upon God and allow Him to rule in our lives, and let Him "right the wrongs" that people do to us, He renews our strength in three stages: 1) During the easy times we will soar like eagles. It's quite easy to live for the Lord when all goes well, but it is also during these times that we must lean upon Him lest we become puffed-up; 2) Then during the everyday difficulties of life we might not soar as eagles but we will still run and not grow tired if we are leaning on Him; 3) And then during the serious problems and tragedies we will still be able to walk along without collapsing if we are leaning on Christ.

Again, what a testimony it is to those around us when we can wait upon the Lord and manifest Him in our lives! This "social grace" comes only by allowing the Holy Spirit to produce it in us.

Third, from the *philosophical* category of the "fruit of the spirit," there is **meekness**. The common error is that **meekness** means "weakness," but that could not be further from the truth. The Greek is *prautēs* (or *praotēs*), which means gentleness and mildness. It has been truthfully stated many times that, "Meekness is not weakness, but strength under control." The Greek word was used, for example, of horses that were broken and trained and also of a strong but mild medicine, both of which have strength but is under control.

The ultimate example of **meekness** is the Lord Jesus in His humanity. As that well-known song proclaims:

He could have called ten thousand angels,

To destroy the world, and set Him free;
He could have called ten thousand angels,
    But he died alone for you and me.

Our Savior had the power of the universe at His command. Is that not strength? But still Scripture says He was meek. While our Lord will one day be vindicated and glorified, instead of being vindicated at that moment, He submitted to the greater need of redeeming the lost. Additionally, our Savior was strong physically. The liberals and the world would have us believe Jesus was weak and even effeminate, but could a weakling carry a timber weighing as much as 150–200 pounds? Jesus did! (see John 19:17). However, even with all that strength, Jesus was meek, for His strength was under control.

Again, meekness is strength and power under control. It is the opposite of self-interest, self-assertiveness, and self-direction. What is needed today are Christians who are meek and humble, Christians who know the power they have in Christ and the Holy Spirit, and Christians who are thereby controlled by Christ and His Spirit.

This word is inseparably coupled with another word—**lowliness**. The Greek here (*tapeinophrosunē*) pictures modesty, humility, and lowliness of mind, having a humble opinion of one's self, a deep sense of one's littleness. Think of that! Not a false humility, such as one that is spoken of often, rather a deep sense of how little we really are.

One of my favorite stories is the one told about a group of tourists who went in to see Beethoven's home in Germany. After the tour guide had showed them Beethoven's piano and had finished his lecture, he asked if any of them would like to come up and sit at the piano for a moment and play a chord or two. There was a sudden rush to the piano by all the people except a gray-haired gentleman with long, flowing hair. The guide finally asked him, "Wouldn't you like to sit down at the piano and play a few notes?" He answered, "No, I don't feel worthy." No one recognized him, but that man was Ignace Paderewski (1860–1941), Polish statesman, composer, and celebrated concert pianist. While he was the only person present who really was worthy to play Beethoven's piano, he did not think so.[14] *That* is **lowliness**. And if a concert pianist can think that he is lowly in the shadow of Beethoven, how little are we in the shadow of our Lord? Are our feelings, views, and opinions important enough to destroy unity?

The most fascinating aspect of the Greek word behind **lowliness** is that, as Greek scholar Richard Trench points out, "No Greek writer employed it before the Christian era, and apart from the influence of Christian writers, it is not used later."[15] The reason this was true was that to the Greek and Roman mind such an attitude was synonymous with weakness and cowardice. It was so abhorrent to their mind that they had no term to describe it. That philosophy still lives in today's pervasive "self-image" craze, and that is precisely why this is in the *philosophical* category of "the fruit of the Spirit." It is the very opposite of the world's basic philosophy of life—*the exaltation of self.* These words from Martyn Lloyd-Jones should challenge us:

> "Lowliness" is humility, and especially humility of mind. . . . It means modesty. It is the opposite of self-esteem, self-assertion, and pride. Humility is one of the chief of all the Christian virtues; it is the hallmark of the child of God. Humility means having a poor opinion of yourself, and of your powers and faculties. . . . It is the opposite of what is found in the so-called man of the world; it is the opposite of the worldly spirit which urges man to trust in himself, and to believe in himself. It is the opposite of all aggressiveness and self-advertisement and ambition and all the brazenness of life at the present time. There is nothing sadder about this present age than the appalling absence of humility; and when this same lack is found in the Church of God, it is the greatest tragedy of all.[16]

Lloyd-Jones said and wrote that in the middle of the 20th-century, and look where we are today, how "self" has been enthroned, just like the Greeks and Romans.

There is one other observation we should make. Notice Paul says **all lowliness and meekness**. The Greek behind **all** is *pas*. When used with an article, it conveys the idea of the sum total of something. Used *without* an article, however, as it is here, it means "each" or "every." Paul is saying, then, "every kind of lowliness and meekness possible, in each and every situation, we are to be as lowly and meek as possible." Someone has said that humility "is the first, second, and third essential of the Christian life."[17]

Humility truly is elusive, is it not? Why? Because if we focus on it too much, it can turn into the very opposite—*pride*. I once heard a preacher say from the pulpit, and I'm not making this up, "I have many shortcomings, but one virtue I know I have is humility." Sadly, he missed the whole point. *Humility is a virtue we seek but can never claim to have.* Probably the best we can ever say is, "God is still working on me."

Similarly, the story is told of a young man who fancied himself a preacher and who stood up at a pastor's conference and announced, "I am against education. I don't believe in education. I read no books except the Bible; I don't profess to know nothing about literature or anything of that kind; I am just an ignorant man. But the Lord has taken me up, and is using me, and I am not at all interested in schools, or colleges, or education. I am proud to be just what I am." An older preacher then arose and said, "Do I understand that our dear young brother is proud of his ignorance? If so, all I can say is that he has a great deal to be proud of."[18] To our shame, we have such men in pulpits today. But as someone has wisely said, "Knowledge is the discovery of ignorance," and it is only the humble mind that recognizes that truth.

In stark contrast, a story is also told about John Wesley. After the memorial service for George Whitefield, a staunch supporter of Whitefield approached Wesley, who had strongly disagreed with Whitefield's Calvinistic views, and asked him, "Mr. Wesley, do you think you will see Mr. Whitefield in heaven?" "No," Wesley answered quickly. "I was afraid you would say that," lamented the enquirer. But then Wesley added, "George Whitefield will be so near the throne of God, that men like me will never catch a glimpse of him."[19] Oh, that such humility would characterize us all!

There we have the *Grace* of Unity, its meaning, motive, and maintenance. Without **love, peace, [forbearance], longsuffering, meekness,** and **lowliness** we will not **keep the unity of the Spirit**, and that will have grave consequences. If our Lord could bring unity between God and man, between Jew and Gentile, and now between all believers, is it too much to ask that we do all we can to guard that unity?

NOTES

[1] Colin Brown, *The New International Dictionary of New Testament Theology* (Zondervan, 1975), Vol. III, p. 943.

[2] The other two are: the *gifts* for unity (7–11) and the *growth* of unity (12–16). This entire study, and the author's complete Ephesians exposition, are on our web site (www.TheScriptureAlone.com). It is our goal to publish this exposition in hardcopy.

[3] Brown, Vol. II, p. 722 (emphasis added).

[4] William Hendrickson, *New Testament Commentary: Exposition of Ephesians* (Baker Book House), p. 181–182.p. 181-182.

[5] Since this article first appeared in 2008, another such document, the *Manhattan Declaration*, has appeared (http://manhattandeclaration.org). Its "goal is to build a movement of Catholic, Evangelical, and Eastern Orthodox Christians . . . to advance the sanctity of life, rebuild and revitalize the marriage culture, and protect religious liberty." It looks good but is not based upon doctrinal soundness.

[6] Charles Colson, *The Body*, p. 105.

[7] Harry Ironside, *In The Heavenlies: Practical Expository Addresses on the Epistle to the Ephesians* (Loizeaux Brothers, 1977), pp. 173-175.

[8] Martyn Lloyd-Jones, *Christian Unity: An Exposition of Ephesians 4:1-16* (Baker Book House, 1982), p. 37.

[9] Brown, Vol. 3, p. 348.

[10] 1 Cor. 15:9, 10:27, and three quotations from the LXX: Rom. 9:7 (Gen 21:12), Rom. 9:25 (Hos. 2:23(25), Rom. 9:26 (Hos. 1:10). Brown, Vol. I, p. 275.

[11] Vol. 3, p. 591.

[12] Spiros Zodhiates, *The Complete Word Study Dictionary: New Testament* (AMG Publishers, 1992), p. 407.

[13] Albert Barnes, *Barnes Notes on the New Testament.*

[14] Adapted from J. Vernon McGee (*Thru the Bible*) and other sources.

[15] Richard Trench, *Synonyms of the New Testament* (Hendrickson, 2000) p. 163.

[16] Martyn Lloyd-Jones, *Christian Unity: An Exposition of Ephesians 4:1-16* (Baker Book House, 1982), p. 41. Note also the discussion of "self-esteem" in chapter 49, "What in the World is a Biblical Worldview?"

[17] Cited in William Hendrickson, *New Testament Commentary: Exposition of Ephesians.* (Baker Book House), p. 183.

[18] Cited in Harry Ironside, *In The Heavenlies: Practical Expository Addresses on the Epistle to the Ephesians* (Loizeaux Brothers, 1977), p. 169.

[19] Cited in Wayne Detzler, *New Testament Words in Today's Language* (Victor Book, 1986), p. 223.

I do verily believe that when God shall accomplish it (unity), it will be the effect of love, and not the cause of love. It will proceed from love, before it brings forth love.

Puritan John Owen
A Puritan Golden Treasury, p. 302

31

The Ground of Unity[*]

Ephesians 4:4–6

There is one body, and one Spirit, even as ye are called in one hope of your calling; One Lord, one faith, one baptism, One God and Father of all, who is above all, and through all, and in you all.

In our previous chapter, we began a look at the question of unity. With Christianity becoming more all-embracing every day, with the lines being increasingly blurred between what is "true" and what is "false," we must ask ourselves, "What is the true basis of unity and fellowship?" Having examined the *grace* of unity, we turn now to the *ground* of unity, which we find clearly presented in Ephesians 4:4–6.

The first observation we should make here is that this is perhaps the most important section of the second half of Ephesians. I say that because this section forms the very foundation of unity. What exactly unites us? Some today answer "love," others answer "our shared experience," and still others answer "a common goal." Many today, even professing evangelicals, insist, "Doctrine divides, love unites."

About 25 years ago, while preaching a week of meetings in a certain church, the pastor came to me with a burden about how his denomination was drifting towards Liberalism (which it has since fallen into). Asking me what he should do, I answered immediately, "Get out. You must separate yourself from those who deny the Truth." Appalled at that, he responded, "Oh, I could never do that. Our denomination views love and unity as supreme, so I could never pull out." But that is serious error. Love is never spoken of in Scripture as being superior to Truth. Not even I Corinthians 13, that great "Love Chapter," implies such an idea. Yes, it says that without "love" certain things, such as knowledge, faith, and giving are empty and meaningless, but neither does it say that love is meant to stand by itself or is meant to replace all those things.

We should ask a simple question: how can love unite people who deny Christ with those who embrace Him? As we saw in our previous chapter, how can there possibly be unity apart from *the unique revelation of God through Christ?* If we remove the very essence of Christianity, the very foundation of the faith, we have nothing. As we also noted, with few

---

[*] This chapter was originally TOTT issues 33–35, April–June 2008.

exceptions, people go right to Ephesians 4 when speaking of unity without considering the doctrine of chapters 1—3. Only when we understand the *doctrine* of unity there can we understand the *duty* of unity here. Let us say it clearly and with no ambiguity: *doctrine must be the ground for unity*. Of course, that principle is frowned upon in our day and is ironically considered "divisive," but there can be no other foundation.

To put it another way: *doctrine makes up the building blocks of unity, while love provides the energy to build*. One without the other is useless. If all we have is doctrine, the building materials will lie around and accomplish nothing. What good is Truth if you don't use it? What good is right theology if there is no energy? On the other hand, if all you have is love, you'll have everyone passionately running around looking for materials with which to build, but they will find nothing lasting. It is really here that most of Christianity is today. Everyone is looking for something around which to unify, but the last thing they consider is doctrine. We must, therefore, have both: *truth* and *love*. That is precisely why Paul says later in Ephesians, "Speaking the truth in love" (4:15). Truth is first; love is second. Again, we don't *build* unity, rather we *maintain* it. To maintain that "building," however, we must have the energy and use the right materials.

Once we accept the fact that doctrine is the ground for unity, a question immediately arises: *WHAT doctrine is the ground for unity?* This is vitally important. Some base their unity upon which translation of the Bible another uses, or where someone went to Bible College or Seminary, or what position another takes on a particular minor doctrine or practice, or what view someone takes of the Second Coming of Christ, and so on. But such divisions are not taught in Scripture.

What then *is* the basis? What doctrine *is* the ground of unity? What doctrine forms the foundation of our faith? The answer is in our text. *These verses list seven spiritual realities that unite all true believers.* Contained in these seven principles is the very essence of Christianity, that is, its foundational truths. If we could boil Christianity down to its bare elements, here they are. Our unity and fellowship must be based upon these. If someone accepts these, there can be unity, even when there is disagreement on minor points of doctrine or practice. But if one or more of these is rejected, there can be no unity and fellowship. Recall again our definition of unity: *the unanimous agreement concerning the unique revelation of God through and in Jesus Christ.* And these seven spiritual realities are *rooted in Christ and His Word.* Let's examine each of these, noting first its *meaning* and then its *application*.

One Body (v. 4a)

The Meaning

There can be no doubt that **one body** refers to the Universal Church, the Body of Christ, the Church as an *organism*, to which Paul has referred several times in this letter.

There are many other references to this in Scripture. In Matthew 16:18, Jesus said He would build His "Church" (singular), not "churches" (plural). While before his conversion Paul no doubt persecuted individual churches, he recounts in 1 Corinthians 15:9 how he persecuted "the church," that is, the entire Body of Christ. That is why the Lord Jesus asked, "Why persecutest thou Me?" (Acts 9:4), that is, My Body, all believers. Later in Ephesians 5:25, Paul also declares that Christ gave Himself for "the church," that is, the entire Body. That Body was formed on the Day of Pentecost and includes every true believer. He emphasized the same truth to the Romans: "For as we have many members in one body, and all members have not the same office: So we, being many, are one body in Christ, and every one members one of another" (Rom. 12:4–5).

So there is **one body**, not many. There is not one church that is for Jews, another for Gentiles, another for men, another for women, another for Caucasians, another for Negroes, and another for Asians. There is one, a single unified Body of Jesus Christ, of which all believers are part. As Paul states in 2:14–18, God has made us all one. Shame on us if we build back any walls that He has broken down.

What a joy it is to meet someone and find out they are a believer! A few years ago I had to fly back from vacation for an emergency in our local church. On the last leg of the trip, between Denver and Grand Junction, Colorado, I started talking with the man sitting next to me. As we chatted, it came out that he was a believer. What a marvelous time we had in the next few minutes! Regardless of race, denomination, or any other factor, to meet a true believer is a joy. There is an immediate connection, an instant fellowship that is incomprehensible to an unbeliever. Why? Because we both belong to the same body so our fellowship is instantaneous.

One word of caution is in order here. A common teaching in today's pragmatic atmosphere is that only the Universal Church is important. This emphasis tears down and de-emphasizes the Local Church, which is, in fact, actually more important in some ways. The Local Church is the Church as an *organization*. More precisely, it is the local assembly of believers, organized and functioning according to Scriptural guidelines, that carries out all outward ministry. The Local Church is God's instrument for working in the world today, and each is to carry out all ministry. That is why Paul founded local churches. As Warren Wiersbe aptly puts it:

The one body is the model for the many local bodies that God has established across the world. The fact that a person is a member of the one body does not excuse him from belonging to a local body, for it is there that he exercises his spiritual gifts and helps others to grow.[1]

That is precisely what the Local Church is for. It is for God's people to gather for worship, exercise their gifts, and equip them for service. As Paul makes clear later in 4:11–16, God has given certain men "for the perfecting of the saints, for the work of the ministry, for the edifying of the body of Christ," and this obviously takes place in the Local Church, as is also made plain in the book of Acts. Paul likewise wrote to Timothy, the pastor of a local church, "But if I tarry long, that thou mayest know how thou oughtest to behave thyself in the house of God, which is the church of the living God, the pillar and ground of the truth" (1 Tim. 2:15 with context). So, it is the Local Church (not parachurch organizations, as some insist) that is the training ground for ministry.

The Application

Simply stated, acceptance of the **one Body**, the Universal Church, is a basis of unity and fellowship. One example of those who don't accept this principle are certain denominations (or some groups who refuse to be even called a denomination) who maintain that their local assembly, along with other local assemblies who agree with them, are "The Church"; no one else is part of the Church, no matter what they believe. That is, of course, arrogance that is hard to fathom.

The most graphic example of false teaching concerning the Body of Christ is Roman Catholicism, which teaches that only it is "The True Church." If you are not Roman Catholic, you not a part of "The Church" and are, therefore, "accursed." But biblically, no earthly denomination or group can be called "The Church." Every true believer who is in *agreement concerning the unique revelation of God through and in Jesus Christ* is part of Christ's Body. Any other attitude destroys unity and any possibility of fellowship.

One Spirit (v. 4b)

The Meaning

One spirit can refer only to the Holy Spirit of God, the third member of the Trinity, who regenerates the sinner and then indwells, enlightens, equips, and empowers the believer. So vital is the Holy Spirit in living the Christian life that Paul mentions Him a dozen times in Ephesians.[2] While we could add several to the list, let's briefly note seven major ministries of the Holy Spirit to the Believer. What is the Holy Spirit doing in your life?

First, the Holy Spirit *regenerates* the sinner. As our Lord declared to Nicodemus, "Except a man be born again, he cannot see the kingdom of God . . . Except a man be born of water [physical birth] and of the Spirit [spiritual birth], he cannot enter into the kingdom of God" (Jn. 3:3–7). And as Paul reminded Titus, "Not by works of righteousness which we have done, but according to his mercy he saved us, by the washing of regeneration, and renewing of the Holy Ghost" (Titus 3:5). The new birth is the imparting of the Divine nature (2 Pet. 1:4), and it is the Holy Spirit who transmits that nature.

Second, the Holy Spirit gives the believer *assurance* of salvation. Romans 8:15 and 16 declare, "For as many as are led by the Spirit of God, they are the sons of God. . . . The Spirit itself beareth witness with our spirit, that we are the children of God." The Spirit gives the needed peace and rest that we are indeed in Christ and thereby a child of God. As stated in Ephesians 1:13, we have been "sealed with that holy Spirit of promise," which denotes absolute ownership and assurance. No other picture in Scripture gives a stronger affirmation of assurance than sealing of the Holy Spirit (see chapter 22 for an indepth study).

Third, the Holy Spirit *indwells* the believer. Regardless of how imperfect or immature we might be, 1 Corinthians 6:15–19 declares "that [our] bodies are the members of Christ" and "the temple of the Holy Ghost." Paul was writing to the most carnal bunch of Christians recorded in the New Testament, but they were still indwelt by the Holy Spirit. His presence within motivates us to holiness and purity and gives us a realization of His power in our lives. That leads to the next principle.

Fourth, the Holy Spirit *strengthens* the believer. As Ephesians 3:16 declares, "That he would grant you, according to the riches of his glory, to be strengthened with might by his Spirit in the inner man." Through the Holy Spirit, God gives us the power and ability to perform anything that He desires of us.

Fifth, the Holy Spirit *illumines and teaches* the believer. As Paul again wrote to the Corinthians, "Now we have received, not the spirit of the world, but the spirit which is of God; that we might know the things that are freely given to us of God . . . But the natural man receiveth not the things of the Spirit of God: for they are foolishness unto him: neither can he know them, because they are spiritually discerned" (1 Cor. 2:12, 14). Man's mind must first be illumined by the Holy Spirit before he can rightly understand the Word of God. As Jesus told His disciples:

> But the Comforter, which is the Holy Ghost, whom the Father will send in my name, he shall teach you all things, and bring all

things to your remembrance, whatsoever I have said unto you (Jn. 14:26).

> Howbeit when he, the Spirit of truth, is come, he will guide you into all truth: for he shall not speak of himself; but whatsoever he shall hear, that shall he speak: and he will show you things to come. He shall glorify me: for he shall receive of mine, and shall show it unto you (16:13–14).

There are no new revelations being given today, as an increasing number of people are claiming. The Holy Spirit illumines the believer concerning Christ, and brings to our remembrance what Christ has said and done. As we hear Truth preached and read it in Scripture, the Holy Spirit gives us understanding.

Sixth, the Holy Spirit *infills* the believer and empowers him for service. As Paul instructs in Ephesians 5:18: "Be not drunk with wine, wherein is excess; but be filled with the Spirit." The Greek behind "filled" is *pleroō,* which means "to influence fully, to control." The chief idea is that we are to be permeated by the Spirit, to be influenced by Him and nothing else, or, to put it simply, to be filled with the Spirit is to have our thoughts, desires, values, motives, goals, priorities, and all else set on spiritual things and spiritual growth. The purpose for this infilling is for an empowering for service, more specifically, an empowering to be a witness of Jesus Christ. As Acts 1:8 confirms the words of our Lord, "But ye shall receive power, after that the Holy Ghost is come upon you: and ye shall be witnesses unto me both in Jerusalem, and in all Judaea, and in Samaria, and unto the uttermost part of the earth."

Seventh, the Holy Spirit *produces the fruit of Christ-like character* in the believer. We read of the "fruit of the Spirit" in Galatians 5:22–23: "love, joy, peace, longsuffering, gentleness, goodness, faith, meekness, temperance." As noted in our last chapter, the Holy Spirit is producing the *fruit* of the Spirit, not *fruits.* Paul put it in the singular to demonstrate that these "Christ-like characteristics" are a unified whole in the believer's life, and only the Holy Spirit can produce them (it).

The Application

The pointed application of this spiritual reality is that this **one spirit** is the energy of unity and fellowship. In 38 years of ministry (as of 2012) I have seen some tragic examples of a lack of unity. I am convinced that the reason for this is a failure to allow the Spirit of God to rule. I am not questioning anyone's salvation, but I am doubting that we are allowing the Holy Spirit to work in us. If we divide over some silly thing, we have just denied the "unity of the Spirit" (Eph. 4:3) and have fractured the body of Christ (e.g., see chapter 29).

On the other hand, a rejection of this doctrine makes unity impossible. If one examines any cult or false religion, he finds the total absence of the idea of the personal indwelling and empowering presence of God through the Holy Spirit. Jehovah's Witness, for example, teaches that the Holy Spirit is not a part of the Godhead. Both the personality and Deity of the Holy Spirit (which is defined as "the invisible active force of Almighty God which moves His servants to do His will") are denied.[3] So as Romans 8:9 declares, "If any man have not the Spirit of Christ, he is none of his." A rejection of the **one spirit** of God who indwells every believer and who produces unity in the first place destroys any possibility of unity. Again, as we examined back in verse 3, "Endeavouring to keep the unity of the Spirit in the bond of peace." It is the Holy Spirit who produces unity. If we, therefore, do not possess the Holy Spirit, how can there be unity in the Body?

Tragically, there are Evangelicals today who advocate unity with political bodies as well as liberal denominations and even false religious groups for the sake of social ends. But this blatantly contradicts the doctrine of **one Spirit**. There can be no unity, and therefore no glory to God, when we join with those who do not possess the Holy Spirit of God.

One Hope (v. 4c)

The Meaning

The Greek behind **hope** here (*elpis*) does not picture uncertainty, such as a wish or want, as it does in English. Rather it speaks of *absolute assurance* and *rest* in that assurance. There is, therefore, **one hope**, one certainty to which the believer looks: *the return of Jesus Christ for His Church.* **Our calling** refers to our calling to salvation, and the final **hope**, the final *certainty*, of that salvation is the return of our Savior.

To apply this principle, there are, of course, differing views of the Second Coming of Christ: Amillennialism, Post-Millennialism, and Premillennialism. While there are very important differences between these views, they all do have one thing in common: *all of them hold that Jesus Christ WILL return.* That is what really matters most. Why? Because that is what Scripture says. As Revelation 19:11–16 records:

> And I saw heaven opened, and behold a white horse; and he that sat upon him was called Faithful and True, and in righteousness he doth judge and make war. His eyes were as a flame of fire, and on his head were many crowns; and he had a name written, that no man

knew, but he himself. And he was clothed with a vesture dipped in blood: and his name is called The Word of God. And the armies which were in heaven followed him upon white horses, clothed in fine linen, white and clean. And out of his mouth goeth a sharp sword, that with it he should smite the nations: and he shall rule them with a rod of iron: and he treadeth the winepress of the fierceness and wrath of Almighty God. And he hath on his vesture and on his thigh a name written, KING OF KINGS, AND LORD OF LORDS.

Then, in the last chapter of the Bible, we read twice our Lord's promise: "Behold, I come quickly" (Rev. 22:7, 12), and we then read it again intensified in verse 20, "Surely I come quickly."

That is our **one hope**, our certainty. As Paul wrote to the Colossians, "To whom God would make known what is the riches of the glory of this mystery among the Gentiles; which is Christ in you, the hope of glory" (Col. 1:27). Christ is, indeed, the only glory we should ever seek and the **one hope** to which we look.

The Application

In applying that truth we should see that unity exists with a proper view of Christ's return, that is, that He *will* return to the Earth as the Scripture says. Jehovah's Witness, for example, teaches that Christ returned *invisibly* in 1914 and set up His kingdom in Heaven, but that is in direct contradiction to Scripture. At Christ's ascension, two angels in the form of men announced, "Ye men of Galilee, why stand ye gazing up into heaven? this same Jesus, which is taken up from you into heaven, shall so come in like manner as ye have seen him go into heaven" (Acts 1:11). The Lord's coming, then, will be a *visible* one to *earth*, not an invisible one in heaven.

This brings up the question, "What about those who don't agree on their view of Christ's return? Can a Premillennialist, for example, possibly fellowship with an Amillennialist?" There is today much unnecessary division here. Some who believe one view would not even consider fellowshipping with someone who holds another. But can this possibly honor the Lord? Is that "[keeping] the unity of the Spirit in the bond of peace?" (v. 3). I, for example, am convinced that Premillenialism is correct. I believe without a shadow of a doubt that the reference in Revelation 20:4 and 6 to those who will "[live] and [reign] with Christ a thousand years" refers to a literal earthly Kingdom that will last 1,000 years. I am thoroughly persuaded that as every other number in Revelation is a literal number, so are the six instances of 1,000 in Revelation 20. At the same time, however, I can still fellowship with a brother in Christ who believes that the Kingdom is spiritual not literal. While I certainly think he is wrong and is missing an enormous blessing, what matters most is that we both know that our Lord is coming back to take us to glory.

One Lord (v. 5a)

The Meaning

Without question, this is the most pointed and the most important of all seven of these spiritual realities. It appears in the middle of Paul's list and does seem to be the very heart of our unity. There truly is only **one Lord**—*the Lord Jesus Christ who is Savior, Master, and God incarnate.*

How vividly this is demonstrated in Mark 12:28–34! A certain scribe came to Jesus and asked, "Which is the first commandment of all?" Jesus answered: "The first of all the commandments is, Hear, O Israel; The Lord our God is one Lord: And thou shalt love the Lord thy God with all thy heart, and with all thy soul, and with all thy mind, and with all thy strength: this is the first commandment. And the second is like, namely this, Thou shalt love thy neighbour as thyself. There is none other commandment greater than these."

The scribe responded with his own profound statement: "Well, Master, thou hast said the truth: for there is one God; and there is none other but he: And to love him with all the heart, and with all the understanding, and with all the soul, and with all the strength, and to love his neighbour as himself, is more than all whole burnt offerings and sacrifices."

Seeing the scribe's understanding, our Lord then said, "Thou art not far from the kingdom of God." While the man was not yet in the kingdom, he was close. Notice that he repeated everything Christ said *except* **one Lord**. He understood the importance of loving God; all that was left was to recognize Jesus Himself as **Lord** and believe and obey Him. As we'll see in our application later, it's amazing that the principle of lordship in salvation is a big issue. Here is a vivid example of its centrality.

After being arrested, Peter proclaimed to the Jewish rulers that the same Jesus that they had crucified was in reality the "corner stone" that they had rejected (as noted back in Eph. 2:20). He then declared, "Neither is there salvation in any other: for there is none other name under heaven given among men, whereby we must be saved" (Acts 4:1–12). The world says there are many lords, but God says there is only **one Lord**.

This serves to remind us of an often-overlooked truth, namely, that our salvation lies not in *our experience* but in *Christ's energy*. In other words, there's a tendency to judge someone's salvation because their experience was different than yours or mine. John Macneil, an early 20th-century Scottish preacher, wonderfully illustrated this in a sermon. He imagined a conversation between the two blind men our Lord healed: the one in John 9 and the other in Mark 8. As we recall, the one in John 9 was healed when Jesus took some clay, spat on it, placed it on the man's eyes, and then told him to go wash in the Pool of Siloam. In the case of the man in Mark 8, however, Jesus did none of this. Macneil imagined these two meeting one day and comparing their conversion experience. The man in John 9 asked the man in Mark 8, "What did you feel like when He put that mixture of clay and spittle on your eyes?" "Clay and spittle?" answered the man in Mark 8, "I don't know anything about clay and spittle." "What," said the man in John 9, "don't you remember how He spit on the ground and made the mixture and put it on your eyes? I am asking, What did you feel?" But the man in Mark 8 just answered, "There was nothing put on my eyes." The conversation continued until finally the man in John 9 said, "Look here, I do not believe you've been healed at all; you must still be blind. If He did not put the clay on your eyes, you are still blind." Macneil concluded, "In other words, two religious denominations came into being at once: the Mud-ites and the Anti-mudites."[4]

That is precisely what happens when we are looking at our own experiences instead of the **one Lord** who saved us. Some people had a dramatic conversion out of the depths of wickedness; others were saved when they were young and untouched by heinous sin. I've heard former gangsters and gang members give their testimony, almost to the point of glorifying sin, and thereby giving the impression that their conversion was "better" than someone else's. Others tend to think that being saved as a result of a particular preacher's ministry is in some way special.

But none of those things matter. It's interesting, in fact, that the Bible nowhere says that we have to cite that "moment in time" when we were saved. Of course, many people can do this, but that doesn't mean they have to. Neither is it required that we remember the name of the preacher we were listening to, or the verse he preached, or an illustration that he used. What matters is the **one Lord** who saved us.

The key to understanding this doctrinal reality is, of course, the term **one lord**. We dealt with the question of the Deity of Christ back in chapter 10 ("Is the Bible Unclear About the Deity of Christ?") so we will not repeat that material here. We would reemphasize, however, that the Deity of Christ is an absolute cardinal doctrine of Christianity, the central truth of the Gospel. Anyone who rejects that truth, in fact, is not a believer and cannot be saved, as our Lord Himself made clear: "I said therefore unto you, that ye shall die in your sins: for if ye believe not that I am he, ye shall die in your sins" (Jn. 8:24).

The Application

The application here is obvious: *unity can exist only with a proper view of Christ.* Christianity is Christ, so how we view Him is absolutely essential. As noted back in chapter 10, when used of Jesus in a confessional way, **Lord** clearly refers to His divinity. To argue that point is utter folly and blatant apostasy.

Countless cults and false religions, for example, deny the Deity of Christ. To the Jehovah's Witnesses, Jesus was not equal to Jehovah and was not God in human flesh but was rather a created being and was actually Michael the Archangel in his preexistent state, having a brother named Lucifer who rebelled against God.[5] Likewise, to the Mormon, Jesus—like all men, in fact—was a preexistent spirit who took his body at birth in this world; He is set apart from the rest of us only by the fact that He was "the Firstborn" of God's spirit-children.[6] Other cults, such as Christian Science, the Unity School of Christianity, The Way International, and others illustrate why they are all called "a cult," namely, because they deny the deity of Christ or in some way pervert that doctrine.

But all this is nothing new in Church History, rather simply a revival of the ancient heresy called Arianism. Arius, a 4th-century parish priest in Alexandria, taught that Jesus was not coequal with God and was, in fact, a created being.

A popular book called *The Da Vinci Code* by Dan Brown (Doubleday, 2003) is another graphic illustration. While seemingly just another thriller novel set in present-day, it has a hidden agenda that makes it far more. Starting with the murdered curator of a Paris museum, the hero and heroin of the story must decipher the clues left behind by the murdered man and thereby uncover an ancient and sinister plot. *And what is that ancient secret?* The supposed "true" story that Christianity has been trying to hide for 1,600 years, namely, that Jesus was just another man who actually ended up marrying Mary Magdalene.

Not only is that book Arianism and Gnosticism in a new wrapper, but it's also full of countless historical errors that reveal the author to be either incredibly ignorant or just a blatant liar. For example, referring to the Council of Nicea in 325, Brown claims that "until *that* moment in history, Jesus was viewed by His followers as a mortal prophet . . . a great and powerful man, but a man nonetheless." *But that simply is not so.* History proves beyond the slightest doubt that early Christians overwhelmingly worshipped Jesus Christ as their risen Savior and **Lord**. Before the appearance of complete doctrinal statements, early Christian leaders wrote summaries of doctrine called the "Rule" or "Canon" of Faith that stated this fact. The canon of well-known 2nd-century bishop Irenaeus, for example, was prompted by 1 Corinthians 8:6: "But to us there is but one God, the

Father, of whom are all things, and we in him; and one Lord Jesus Christ, by whom are all things, and we by him." There is no doubt whatsoever that those early Christians viewed our Lord as God.

This serves to illustrate a consistent practice of unbelievers, namely, *they must distort history to deny Truth.* Why? Because history, as the old expression goes, is "His Story." It is what God is doing in the world, what He is accomplishing. So to escape the plain truths of God's Word, men must revise the facts, reinterpret events, and rewrite the history books. Another example in our day is the rewriting of American history. To escape the fact of America being founded upon biblical and moral principles, revisionist historians totally ignore the godliness of many of our Founding Fathers.

The "lordship salvation" debate again comes into view here (see also chapter 23). There is something seriously wrong with a theology that teaches that there is a difference between "accepting Jesus" as *Savior* and then at some later day accepting Him as **Lord** when there is absolutely no such dichotomy or distinction in Scripture and is, in point of fact, *an invention of modern (not historical) Christianity.* It is clearly a denial of **one Lord** to say that all one must do is "believe in Jesus" to be saved. After all, "the devils also believe, and tremble" (Jas. 2:19). They believe in the facts concerning Christ, and that is exactly what many today view salvation to be, just some vague belief, where no repentance is necessary, no change of life is expected, and no responsibility is demanded. As mentioned earlier, Romans 10:9–10 makes it clear that salvation is based not only on the recognition of Christ as Savior but a confession of Him as **Lord**. How could it be plainer than this? "That if thou shalt confess with thy mouth the Lord Jesus, and shalt believe in thine heart that God hath raised him from the dead, thou shalt be saved. For with the heart man believeth unto righteousness; and with the mouth confession is made unto salvation."

What **one Lord**, and therefore so-called "Lordship Salvation" means, is that true salvation results in an *automatic change* in the person who believes. True "conversion" (Latin *convertere*, "to turn around, transform") fundamentally speaks of a "new lordship." No longer are *we* Lord, no longer is *Satan* Lord, but *Christ* is **Lord**. This is the very essence of salvation, as Paul wrote to the carnal Corinthians, "Therefore if any man be in Christ, he is a new creature: old things are passed away; behold, all things are become new" (2 Cor. 5:17).

So we say again, *unity can only exist with a proper view of Christ and His salvation.* Tolerating false doctrine and trying to create unity where none can possibly exist is an abomination. But when this principle is met, what sweet fellowship and unity it brings. As commentator Albert Barnes writes:

There is no better way of promoting unity among Christians than by reminding them that they have the same Saviour. And when jealousies and heart-burnings arise; or when they are disposed to contend about trifles; when they magnify unimportant matters until they are in danger of rending the church asunder, let them feel that they have one Lord and Saviour, and they will lay aside their contentions, and be one again. Let two men, who have never seen each other before, meet in a distant land, and feel that they have the same Redeemer, and their hearts will mingle into one. They are not aliens, but friends. A cord of sympathy is struck more tender than that which binds them to country or home; and though of different nations, complexions, or habits, they will feel that they are one. Why should contentions ever arise between those who have the same Redeemer?

Paul's point about **one Lord** leads right to another spiritual reality.

One Faith (v. 5b)

The Meaning

There has been some debate as to whether **one faith** refers to the *act of believing* or the doctrines that one believes, that is, *a system of Truth*. But as Paul notes several times in Ephesians (1:1–2, 15–17; 2:8), what matters most is the *object* of faith. Theologian and commentator Gordon Clark astutely makes this point when he writes:

> Many commentators understand *faith* as the subjective act of believing. But such acts are one only as they have the same object. Jews, Moslems, Hindus all believe; but they do not have the same faith. The faith here mentioned must be the doctrines believed. [French historian and agnostic Joseph] Renan believed that Jesus was just a moral teacher; [German philosopher and liberal theologian Albert] Schweitzer believed that Jesus was insane; [German existential theologian Rudolf] Bultman believed that we could not believe anything that Jesus is reported to have said or done. It is not the psychology of the act, but the doctrines believed that constitute the unity of the many Christians' many acts of believing.[7]

It seems obvious, then, that Paul is saying that *true unity is based upon common doctrine*, that is, the system of truth that we all have in common. Why introduce something totally *sub*jective into a list of *ob*jective truths? Paul's emphasis in this list is to present absolutes, not what we might feel, think, or even believe about it, but specific, unchanging realities. He wants to prove what is the basis for unity, so the last thing he would do is interject something subjective. Mark it down: *subjectivity never proves anything.* The evolutionist believes that the entire universe came from one Big Bang billions of years ago. Does that make it so? No, for it's not our belief that makes anything true. It's what God says that makes something true.

This is exactly the point Jude makes in his short but powerful letter, that believers "should earnestly contend for the faith which was once delivered unto the saints" (Jude 3). **One faith**, then, refers to "the body of revealed truth that constitutes Historical, Evangelical Christianity." This doesn't mean an entire system of theology on which we all can agree; that would be impossible. Rather it refers again to the unique revelation of God through Christ. Paul has, of course, dealt with this often here in Ephesians. Specifically, this body of truth is the very essence of the Gospel, *the redemption by blood and salvation by grace alone, through faith alone, in Christ alone.* This one faith is clearly stated in Romans 1:16–17: "For I am not ashamed of the gospel of Christ: for it is the power of God unto salvation to every one that believeth; to the Jew first, and also to the Greek. For therein is the righteousness of God revealed from faith to faith: as it is written, The just shall live by faith."

This was the **one faith** that was virtually lost for centuries and restored to prominence in the Protestant Reformation. This is the **one faith** for which John Huss and countless others died. This is the *sola fide* (faith alone) that Martin Luther stood for, against that dark, sinister power of Rome.

Also implicit in **one faith** is where this body of revealed Truth is located, namely, *the Scriptures.* In other words, it is obviously the completed Scriptures that contain the record of "the faith which was once delivered unto the saints." In fact, a basic acknowledgment of Scripture as the Word of God is automatic in salvation. Why? Because the person is saying, "I believe what the Bible says about sin, salvation, and the Savior." Here is an acknowledgment of Scripture being true in its revelation of Christ. As Paul also declared to Timothy, "The things that thou hast heard of me among many witnesses, the same commit thou to faithful men, who shall be able to teach others also" (2 Tim. 2:2). Those early Christians had a body of basic doctrine (the Apostles' doctrine; cf. Acts 2:42) that they believed and committed to others.

So important is right doctrine, that Paul spoke of those who "resist the truth: men of corrupt minds, reprobate concerning the faith" (2 Tim. 3:8) and instructed Titus to "rebuke [false teachers] sharply, that they may be sound in the faith" (Titus 1:13). We do not tolerate false doctrine or embrace false teachers. On the contrary, we rebuke them because they have violated "the faith." Among Paul's last words, in fact, was that confidence that, "I have fought a good fight, I have finished my course, I have kept the faith" (2 Tim. 4:7). Oh, that that would be our testimony as well!

The Application

The application here is two-fold.

First, unity can exist only with a proper view of salvation. The hallmark of all cults and false religions is works, that a person attains salvation either in whole or at least in part by his own efforts.

To the Jehovah's Witness, for example, as its founder Charles Russell wrote, "they must be recovered from blindness as well as from death, that they, each for himself, may have a full chance to prove, by obedience or disobedience, their worthiness of eternal life."[8] Likewise, according to Article 3 of the *Mormon Articles of Faith*, "All mankind may be saved, by obedience to the laws and ordinances of the Gospel." According to Herbert W. Armstrong, founder of the Worldwide Church of God, "Salvation, then is a process! But how the God of this world would blind your eyes to that!!! He tries to deceive you into thinking all there is to it is just 'accepting Christ' with 'no works'—and presto-change, you are pronounced 'saved.' But the Bible reveals that none is yet 'saved'"[9] And on it goes from religion to religion. Of course, the question arises, "But how many works are needed?" As Shakespeare put it, "Ay, there's the rub," that is, there's the big *obstacle* to their system, because they don't know how many works it takes![10]

Two world religions, however, stand out as leading more people into error than all others. One is Islam, which in our day is more in the spotlight than ever before and is enjoying unprecedented tolerance. But it, too, is just another religion of works. It is a legalistic system where a person must earn his salvation by holding to its five main doctrines, called the "Five Articles of Faith" (God, Angels, Scripture, Prophets, and Last Days), and especially following its "Five Pillars of Faith" (The Creed, Prayer, Almsgiving, Fasting, and the Pilgrimage to Mecca). This, of course, flatly denies Jesus' own words, "I am the way, the truth, and the life: no man cometh unto the Father, but by me" (Jn. 14:6). You might call your god "Allah" or anything else you wish, but the issue is the Lord Jesus Christ—one Lord and **one faith**. It's not your works, not what you might do, not how many "infidels" you might blow up, but in Jesus Christ alone.

But the most shocking tolerance of all among evangelicals is that of Roman Catholicism. *Many persist in ignoring that it, too, is just another works system.* As is made clear in its own *Baltimore Catechism*, Catholicism teaches "that among the chief means provided by Christ for our sanctification are the sacraments. They are outward signs instituted by Christ to give grace. . . . When the sign is applied to the one who receives the sacrament, it signifies inward grace and has the power of producing it in the soul."

Particularly troubling is Catholicism's teachings concerning Mary. She is considered to be the "Co-Redemptrix" with Christ, that is, she cooperates with Christ in the work of saving sinners. While the Vatican II council (1963–65) brought certain reforms, it changed nothing of Catholicism's underlying theology. In that council it was stated that Mary was "used by God not merely in a passive way, but as cooperating in the work of human salvation through faith and obedience. . . . She conceived, brought forth, and nourished Christ. She presented Him to the Father in the temple, and was united with Him in suffering as He died on the cross."[11] In other words, while the Church does not teach that Mary literally died for our sins, it does teach that by giving birth to Christ and nurturing Him through life, she indirectly contributed to the work of salvation.

Further still, Mary is also considered "Mediatrix," that is, she now dispenses God's grace and blessings to the spiritually needy. Again, Vatican II reaffirmed:

> This maternity of Mary in the order of grace began with the consent which she gave in faith at the Annunciation and which she sustained without wavering beneath the cross. This maternity will last without interruption until the eternal fulfillment of all the elect. For, taken up to heaven, she did not lay aside this saving role, but by her manifold acts of intercession continues to win for us gifts of eternal salvation.

> By her maternal charity, Mary cares for the brethren of her Son who still journey on earth surrounded by dangers and difficulties, until they are led to their happy fatherland. Therefore the Blessed Virgin is invoked by the Church under the titles of Advocate, Auxiliatrix, Adjutrix, and Mediatrix.[12]

How is it possible that any evangelical cannot recognize that that is an abominable perversion of the Gospel? It has nothing to do with the Gospel, for it is neither **one faith** nor "one Lord." It is "another gospel," as Paul said, which is actually not another gospel (good news) at all. He goes on to make it clear that any gospel other than what he delivered (salvation by grace alone, through faith alone, in Christ alone) is to be "accursed" (Gal. 1:6–9). Salvation is apart from any outward works that we can do (Eph. 2:8–9; Titus 3:5; etc.).

Second, because the Lord Jesus Christ is inseparably linked to His Word (Jn. 1:14), there is another application here that is equally obvious: *unity can exist only with a proper view of Scripture.* Another hallmark of cults is their rejection of the Scriptures as the sole, absolute, and sufficient authority. Mormonism, for example, says, "We believe the Bible to be the Word of God in so far as it is translated correctly."[13] But it also teaches that a correct translation is *impossible* because the Roman Catholic Church has subtracted from it. Orson Pratt, an early Mormon Church "apostle," wrote, "Who knows that even one verse of the Bible has escaped pollution, so as to convey the same sense now that it did in the original."[14] The real authority in Mormonism, therefore, resides in three "sacred books": *The Book of Mormon, Doctrine and Covenants*, and *The Pearl of Great Price*. Additionally, contemporary living prophets also contribute to authoritative pronouncements of the Mormon Church.

Likewise, while the founder of Christian Science, Mary Baker Eddy, claimed she got her teachings from the Bible, she also claimed in no uncertain terms that her revelations were higher than the Bible. Similarly, the writings of Ellen G. White are considered by Seventh Day Adventists to be inspired revelations. Some charismatics also claim to receive new revelations in visions and dreams. And again, while many today insist on unity between Protestantism and Roman Catholicism, that is patently impossible. While Catholicism does teach that the Bible is *inspired*, it denies that it is *sufficient*. That was, in fact, the very battleground of the Reformation. Added to the Bible are the teachings and traditions of the church. It is, in fact, quite open in this view. Its *Catechism of the Catholic Church* boldly states that the Church "does not derive her certainty about all revealed truths from the holy Scriptures alone. Both Scripture and tradition must be accepted and honored with equal sentiments of devotion and reverence." Further, added to that is the infallibility of the Pope when he makes "absolutely authoritative" pronouncements *ex cathedra* (from the chair).

Please mark this down: *the common thread through all false teaching is adherence to a second authority that supercedes the Bible when the Bible says something that men don't like.* Even evangelicals, though they say the Bible is their authority, actually replace Scripture with their own ideas and opinions. The modern "ministries" of Pragmatism, Relativism, seeker-sensitivity, user-friendliness, seeking the unchurched, and so on are man's philosophy not God's revelation. This issue is imbedded deep in my soul, because compromise of the Truth is commonplace, because what God says in Scripture is replaced by what men think based on their own experience.

The Bible in no uncertain terms speaks of itself being the sole and sufficient authority of God. A key verse here is 2 Peter 1:19: "We have also a more sure word of prophecy; whereunto ye do well that ye take heed, as unto a light that shineth in a dark place, until the day dawn, and the day star arise in your hearts." In verses 15–18 Peter writes about his witnessing Christ's transfiguration, but now he declares that there is something much surer than "personal experience." How important this is in light of how many people today speak of their "experience," that they saw Jesus at the foot of their bed, or they saw a statue of Mary weeping or Jesus bleeding. Peter declares here that he, too, had an experience but that it cannot compare with the "more sure word of prophecy," that is, *the written Word of God.* In essence Peter says, "Yes, my experience was exciting, but what makes it true is not that I saw it but that it coincides with the written Truth of God's Word."

The word "sure" is the Greek *bebaios*, which means "fit to tread on, having a firm foundation, durable, unshakeable, sure, reliable, and certain." Further, used in a legal sense, it meant "valid and legal." As one Greek authority writes, "Thus the hope and confidence of man is firmly secured as by an anchor, when the object of the trust is the Word of God, which He has legally confirmed with an oath (Heb. 6:16, 19)."[15] As another points out, this word "in the New Testament is not used of persons but objects (Heb. 6:19), that which does not fail or waver, immovable, and on which one may rely."[16] So, and please get this, *as long as we cling to the Word, we will be firm, unshakable, sure, and certain.* The reason for this "surer proof" is because the Word of God came by inspiration, as Peter goes on to write in verse 20–21: "Knowing this first, that no prophecy of the scripture is of any private interpretation. For the prophecy came not in old time by the will of man: but holy men of God spake as they were moved [literally, carried along] by the Holy Ghost."

So, the two-fold application of **one faith** is very clear: *unity can exist only with a proper view of salvation and Scripture.* The doctrine of salvation today has been reconsidered, redefined, and even rejected. Likewise, the Word of God has been mocked, maligned, and mutilated. But one of the very foundation stones of unity is that salvation is by grace alone, through faith alone, in Christ alone, apart from any merit or works and the acceptance of the Bible as the only inspired, infallible, authoritative, and sufficient revelation to man. Opinions will vary, experiences will change, methods will adjust, but *God's Word lasts forever.*

One Baptism (v. 5c)

The Meaning

Paul now says something quite fascinating—we have unity because of **one baptism.** As with "one faith," there has been debate as to what **one baptism** refers. Some commentators insist that it refers to water baptism because they view "one Spirit" back in verse 4 as implying Spirit baptism. As we saw, however, "one Spirit" goes much deeper. We must, therefore, lean toward Spirit baptism for three reasons.

First, consider the Greek behind **baptism** and the context. **One baptism** (*en baptisma*) is literally "one placing into." The verb *baptō* originally referred to dipping clothes into dye or drawing water, hence the idea of submerging, placing something into. So a placing into what? Water seems totally out of place because the context speaks of "one body" and "one spirit." Here is a single, definitive baptism that really does something, that accomplishes something. It isn't *symbolic*, as is water; it's *actual*. That is precisely the point, in fact, of 1 Corinthians 12:13: "For by one Spirit are we all baptized [placed, submerged] into one body, whether we be Jews or Gentiles, whether we be bond or free; and have been all made to drink into one Spirit." Greek born scholar Spiros Zodhiates writes this authoritative statement:

> The whole paragraph, Eph. 4:1–5, is indicative of Paul's desire that there should be unity of the Spirit in the body of Christ. No reference is made to water baptism at all. The verse says, "One Lord, one faith, one baptism." This baptism must be, therefore, the spiritual baptism, the baptism in the Spirit that was promised by John the Baptist that the One coming after him would accomplish (Matt. 3:11; Mark 1:8; Luke 3:16; John 1:33) and Jesus Christ Himself promised in Acts 1:5. This took place in Acts 2. . . . The purpose of this Spirit baptism is shown in 1 Cor. 12:13 as the incorporation of all believers into the body of Christ, the Church (Eph. 1:22, 23).[17]

It seems clear from the language and context that Spirit Baptism is Paul's emphasis. He is dealing with a single, definitive placing into, not something that has to do with our experience but with what God alone has accomplished.

One expositor argues for water baptism by writing that this view "is preferred because of the way Paul has spoken specifically of each member of the Trinity in succession. This is the Lord Jesus Christ's verse, as it were." We'll come back to this in a moment, but by this he means that since the Holy Spirit is in view in verse 4, the Son in verse 5, and the Father in verse 6, then it follows that one baptism speaks of water baptism because it is "the common New Testament means of a believer's publicly confessing Jesus as Savior and Lord." While that is true, it doesn't require water baptism here. Spirit Baptism fits just as well because it's what places us into Christ, thereby indicating that Christ is still in view in verse 5.

Second, the entire context (vv. 4–6) is supernatural. As Greek expositor Kenneth Wuest writes, why "[interpret] the Greek word as referring to the rite of water baptism when the entire context is supernatural?" In other words, everything here is divinely produced, not what we do, not some rite we observe, but the work of God alone. Why would Paul just throw in an earthly rite such as water baptism when that is not the point he is making in the passage? Further, if he's going to do that, why not also mention the Lord's Supper ("one communion," for example), since that is for the fellowship and oneness of God's people?

If we might also interject, while many Baptists take the view of water in this passage, John Bradbury, editor of the *Watchman Examiner*, the leading Baptist journal of the mid 20th-century, observed: ". . . in this passage, where ordinances are not before us but the truth concerning the organism called 'the body of Christ,' we have baptism mentioned on equal terms with 'hope,' 'Lord,' 'faith,' 'God.' This signifies that the baptism referred to is that of I Corinthians 12:13."[18] Indeed, water baptism is not a divine or supernatural act, but Spirit Baptism most certainly is.

We should also add that this verse has been used by countless false teachers through the centuries to teach baptismal regeneration. Such teaching reads Paul's statement this way: "One Lord, one faith in that Lord, and one regeneration into that Lord by way of, or through the instrumentality of, baptism." Roman Catholicism for example, teaches that baptism works *ex opere operato*, that is, it operates in and of itself, that it "infuses into the soul the new life of sanctifying grace."[19] While other groups don't go that far, they still believe that baptism is part of salvation. No, this **one baptism** is not something *outward* that *man* does; it is something *inward* that *God* does.

Third, water baptism could not possibly produce or maintain unity. Indeed, how could all believers possibly unify around water baptism? How many denominations disagree on the mode of baptism (immersion, sprinkling, pouring) and are anything but unified on the issue? Theologian Lewis Sperry Chafer addresses this very point in his classic *Systematic Theology*:

> It is easily discerned that the baptism of the Holy Spirit into one Body engenders the most vital and perfect union that could be formed among men; on the other hand, if the history of the Church on earth bears a testimony to the course of events at all, it is to the effect that ritual baptism has served more than any other one issue to shatter that manifestation of organic union which Christian fellowship is intended to exhibit.[20]

We must, therefore, view **one baptism** as referring to Spirit Baptism. Only the Holy Spirit can supernaturally place us into the Body of Christ and bring unity to that Body, as Paul has already stated back in verse 3 ("the unity of the Spirit"). Even though we might disagree on the mode of water baptism, we can all agree that we have been placed into Christ's Body and are, therefore, unified.

The Application

As with "one spirit," the application of **one baptism** is the right view of the nature and ministry of the Holy Spirit. The most serious departure from biblical teaching concerning the Holy Spirit is that Spirit Baptism, or as it is called by some, "the Baptism of the Holy Spirit," is a subsequent event in the Christian's life, which is then characterized by "speaking in tongues." This teaching results in a "spiritual elite," thereby not *unifying* God's people at all, rather actually *dividing* them into two classes: those who have "received the baptism" and those who have not.

I still recall riding next to a very sweet Christian gentleman on a plane trip from Denver to Indianapolis while I was still a Bible College student back in 1971. We got to talking and he finally asked me, "Have you been baptized by the Holy Spirit?" I answered, "Yes, sir, I have. I've been placed into the Body of Christ." "Oh, no," he replied, "there is more and I will pray that you will experience it soon." I've never forgotten that because it immediately put us into separate categories, one being on a higher level than the other. What is so tragic about this is that it is the exact opposite of what Paul is emphasizing, namely, *the unity of ALL believers equally in Christ.* Paul's intent is not to divide but to underscore unity. The cause of this error is a three-fold misreading of 1 Corinthians 12:13.

First, "baptized" is aorist tense in the Greek, which speaks of punctilliar action in the past and can literally be translated "were baptized." So when did it occur? On the Day of Pentecost. It was on that day that believers were placed into the Body of Christ. Each of us then takes part in the benefits of that day when we receive Christ as Savior and Lord. Neither here nor anywhere else in Scripture are we commanded to seek this baptism because it is something God has already done. *Nowhere does the Bible say,* "Seek the baptism of the Holy Spirit." Why? Because it has already been done by God alone.

Of course, it is argued that people spoke in "tongues" (Greek *glossa*) on that day and we should, therefore, do so today. But the so-called "ecstatic speech" that is taught today is another departure from language and history. (Note our indepth examination of this in chapter 4, "Temporary Spiritual Gifts.")

Second, another misreading of 1 Corinthians 12:13 simply misses the word "*all.*" Paul simply does not say that only a certain elite class of Christian receives the "Baptism of the Holy Spirit." We repeat: *the text does not say that.* It is, therefore, poor exegesis and bad theology to say or even imply that it does. Paul very clearly says that *all* Christians, even that incredibly carnal bunch in Corinth, whether Jew or Gentile, were placed into the Body of Christ and "have been all made to drink into one Spirit." *That is what the text says.* Again, Paul's whole point is oneness of *all* believers in Christ's Body, not two divided classes, one of which has "experienced" something the others have not.

Third, one other misreading of 1 Corinthians 12:13 overlooks a subtlety in the Greek. Regardless of what someone today might teach, the common phrase "baptism *of* the Holy Spirit" is actually not a correct translation of this verse (or any other verse in the New Testament for that matter). *It is a term without any biblical support whatsoever.* The words "by one Spirit" translate the Greek *en heni pneumati*. The word *en* is a common word that can be translated not only as "by," but also "with" and most commonly "in." *Young's Literal Translation* reads, "For also in one Spirit we all to one body were baptized." Similarly, Tyndale's 1534 New Testament reads, "For in one spirit are we all baptized to make one body."

We make this point for a very important reason. What did John the Baptist say of those he baptized? He declared, "I indeed baptize you with water unto repentance: but he that cometh after me . . . he shall baptize you with the Holy Ghost, and with fire" (Matt. 3:11). As the next verse makes clear, the baptism of "fire" speaks of the judgment of hell. So what John is saying is that every living person is in one way or the other baptized *by Christ*—believers are baptized with the Spirit into Christ's body, and unbelievers will be baptized with fire into judgment. The point, therefore, is that it's not that we are baptized **by** the Holy Spirit, but actually **by** Christ "with" or "in" the Holy Spirit. And it is this that places us into Christ's Body. Our Lord has done all the work through His Spirit.

How we should rejoice in this **one baptism**! It is this that truly makes us one in Christ. It is in this doctrine that we have unity.

One God (v. 6)

The Meaning

Here is the capstone of the passage. This is the culmination, the climax to which Paul has been building. He has built each of these spiritual realities, one on the other, until he now reaches the summit in **one God**. The entire Trinity is now in view:

- ❏ *One Spirit* (God the Holy Spirit, v. 4)
- ❏ *One Lord* (God the Son, v.5)
- ❏ *One God* (God the Father, v. 6)

We see this reemphasized in the present verse by three prepositions:

- ❏ **Above all** (God the Father)
- ❏ **Through all** (God the Son)

❑ **In you all** (God the Holy Spirit)

Those prepositions also *encapsulate the very nature of God*. Those glorious words **above all** speak of God's *omnipotence, omniscience, and sovereignty*. Please read the following verses here: Psalm 57:11; 96:4; 99:2; and Romans 11:34. Flowing from that are the words **through all**, which demonstrate His *providence*, as He sustains, guides, and controls all things "according to the good pleasure of his will" (Eph. 1:5). **In you all**, then, pictures God's *omnipresence*. Here please read David's exultation in Psalm 139:6–10.

There is a small textual issue here. While the Critical Text and, therefore, most modern translations omit **you**, the majority of manuscripts include it.[21] We submit that it should remain because it more clearly specifies those who are unified. As John Gill writes, this should be "understood, not of his being in his creatures, by his powerful presence, which is everywhere supporting them; but of the gracious union there is between him and his people, and of his gracious inhabitation in them by his Spirit." In other words, the point of the passage is unity of God's people and God in them creating that unity, not that He is in all His creation.

At any rate, expositor John Phillips expresses these prepositions beautifully when he writes that our Father is *absolute in His power*, *absorbed in His purpose*, and *abiding in His presence*.[22] And it is because of this unity of the Godhead that all believers have unity.

The emphasis in this verse, then, is **God** the **Father**. The word **all** further emphasizes this, as it is masculine in the Greek. Paul is, therefore, not writing about God being "all things" as the pantheist would suggest, but that He is all persons, all members of the Godhead. As we also see in 3:14–15, such a reference doesn't refer to the "Universal Fatherhood of God," for Christ is again in view in the context and any relationship with the Father depends upon the relationship with the Son.

So the point here in our text is a proper view of **God** *as the capstone of our doctrine*. Interestingly, Old Testament Jews saw five basic principles concerning God's Fatherhood: in terms of (1) His begetting, (2) His nearness to them, (3) His loving grace, (4) His guidance, and (5) their obedience to Him. Here is a true summary of the biblical doctrine of God. Any good theologian could write an entire work on the doctrine of God using those five views as an outline.

More importantly, Paul further emphasizes that there is only *one* **God**. We find this word combination seven times in Scripture. Besides here, for example, in Malachi 2:10–16, the prophet indicts the spiritual leaders of Israel as they lead the rest of the nation into intermarriage with foreign women and divorcing the wives of their youth. By speaking of God as "one father," he reminds them of that five-fold view mentioned earlier, especially of their requirement to obey Him.

As mentioned under "one Lord," Jesus' answer to the scribe who asked, "Which is the first commandment of all?" prompted the scribe to add later, "Master, thou hast said the truth: for there is one God; and there is none other but he." And it was that confession that demonstrated that the scribe was close to the kingdom (Mk. 12:28–34). While that kind of belief (mental assent) is not enough—as James writes, "Thou believest that there is one God; thou doest well: the devils also believe, and tremble" (Jas. 2:19)—the belief in **one God** is certainly the beginning.

Read also Romans 3:30, which declares there is, indeed, only **one God** who can justify men, that is, declare them righteous through the finished work of Jesus Christ. Also, countless cults and false religions ignore the truth that Paul wrote to the Corinthians (1 Cor. 8:6).

The Application

Once again, the application is obvious: *unity is possible only with a proper view of God.* The true God of the Bible is not the polytheistic god of Mormonism, the pantheistic god of Christian Science, the strict, harsh, emotionless god of Islam, or the god of any other cult or false religion. The true God of the Bible is a **father**, with all that that entails.

Another of the countless false views of God is the view of The Masonic Lodge, of which many Christians today need to be made aware. While most Masons adamantly deny that Masonry is a religion, its foremost authorities quite readily admit that it is precisely that. In his *Masonic Encyclopedia*, the leading authority of Masonry, Henry Wilson Coil, not only admits that Masonry is a religion according to the definition of religion given in *Funk and Wagnall's New Standard Dictionary* (1941), but goes on to say that it functions in the same way as does a church.[23] In his *Revised Encyclopedia of Freemasonry*, another authority, Albert Mackey, states, "Freemasonry may rightfully claim to be called a religious institution."[24]

Most Masons also deny that Masonry teaches a way of salvation, but again, its authorities say otherwise. Any manual that outlines the Ritual of the Blue Lodge, that is, the first three degrees of Masonry, clearly teaches a way of salvation. Malcolm C. Duncan's, for example, reads, "The All-Seeing Eye [God] . . . beholds the inmost recesses of the human heart, and will reward us according to our works."[25] And what is the coming reward? Concerning the wearing of the linen apron, or lambskin, Masonry teaches, "He who wears the lambskin as a badge of a Mason is thereby continually reminded of purity of life and conduct which is essentially necessary to his gaining admission into that celestial Lodge above, where the Supreme

Architect of the universe presides."[26] What is that if not a salvation by works just like any other religion?

So what does the Lodge teach about God? Is He the **one God** of the Bible? Far from it. The God of Masonry, "The Great Architect of the Universe," is very loosely defined. While Masonry insists that its members be monotheistic, each Mason can decide for himself whether he wants "a God like the ancient Hebrew Jahweh, a partisan tribal god, with whom they can talk and argue and from whom they can hide if necessary, or a boundless, eternal, universal, undenominational, and international Divine Spirit, so vastly removed from the speck called man, that He cannot be known, named, or approached."[27] Another authority, Carl H. Claudy, is even clearer: "[The Mason] may name Him [i.e., God] as he will, think of Him as he pleases; make Him impersonal law or personal and anthropomorphic; Freemasontry cares not. . . . God, Great Architect of the Universe, Grand Artificer, Grand Master of the Grand Lodge above, Jehovah, Allah, Buddha, Brahma, Vishnu, Shiva, or Great Geometer . . ."[28]

Such vagueness makes Masonry seem tolerant and open to all faiths. *But this is actually a very subtle deception.* In one of the later degrees (Royal Arch), the candidate is told that the *real* name of God is *Jahbulon*. This is a combination of Jehovah (*Jah*), the God of the Old Testament, Baal (*Bul* or Bel), the infamous Canaanite fertility god, and *On*, a probable reference to the Egyptian god Osirus, the brother and husband of Isis. The purpose of such a composite "God" is to show unity between all god-ideas, that all religions are essentially the same in their ideas of the divine. So, while claiming to tolerate all religions and views of God, Masonry in reality views its own idea as supreme.

But if we are to "speak the truth in love" (Eph. 4:15), we are compelled to say that to join the **one** true **God** of the Bible with pagan deities is beyond blasphemy, beyond sacrilege. Some of God's severest judgments were upon those who worshiped pagan deities. Please read Judges 2:13–14 and Jeremiah 32:29, 35–36. *God simply will not tolerate paganism*, especially when it is mixed in and blended with His name and worship.

In light of the other spiritual unities we've examined, Masonry also denies the very foundations of Christianity. In his 1879 book, *The Master's Carpet: Masonry and Baal-Worship Identical*, Edmond Ronayne, former Master of a Masonic Lodge in Chicago prior to his conversion to Christianity, writes (please read closely):

> Freemasonry "carefully excludes" the Lord Jesus Christ from the Lodge and chapter, repudiates his mediatorship, rejects his atonement, denies and disowns his gospel, frowns upon his religion and his church, ignores the Holy Spirit, and sets up for itself a

spiritual empire, a religious theocracy, at the head of which it places the G.A.O.T.U.—the God of Nature—and from which the only living and true God is *expelled by resolution . . .*" (emphasis added).[29]

The words "expelled by resolution" are especially significant. The true **one God** of the Bible doesn't fit into the concept of God taught in Freemasonry, so He must be done away with by official ruling. The book goes on to show that Masonry is the equivalent of the "Ancient Mysteries," that its ceremonies and symbols are identical in every detail with the initiatory rites that were practiced thousands of years ago in the worship of the pagan gods of Egypt, Babylon, and Canaan. It also reveals some shocking comparisons between Masonry and Roman Catholicism, demonstrating that both rest upon the same anti-Christian foundation.

Does there appear to be any doubt that Masonry is diametrically opposed to the **one God** of the Bible, not to mention "one faith" and "one Lord"? While various pastors, elders, Sunday School teachers, and other Christian leaders are Masons, should not all this challenge each of us to take a discerning look (cf. Eph. 4:14) and act accordingly? Is it possible to have unity with something so foreign, so opposed to the **one God** of Scripture?

Indeed, unity can come only from a right view of the **one God**. To illustrate, ponder for a moment a symphony orchestra. As the musicians are tuning up, they each are doing something different, and it sounds awful. But when they are done, the Conductor appears and leads them in a beautiful piece of music. Even though the instruments are tuned and the musicians could go ahead and play the music, the Conductor is still absolutely essential. Likewise, countless people today are playing their own tune, or as Henry David Thoreau put it, marching to their own drummer.[30] We so desperately need a Conductor, and we have Him in **one God**. He is **above all, through all, and in [us] all**.

Conclusion: Paul's Doctrinal Statement

To bring these seven unities together, *here we read the very essence of the Christian faith.* Down through the ages there have been creeds, doctrinal statements, statements of faith, catechisms, and other forms of stating doctrinal positions. But here we find a biblical statement of faith on which we base unity and fellowship. What is the doctrine to which we hold?

- ❑ *One Body* — Christ's Body, of which we are all members.
- ❑ *One Spirit* — the Holy Spirit who indwells, enlightens, equips, and empowers the believer.

- ❑ *One Hope* — the certainty of Christ's return to the Earth for His own.
- ❑ *One Lord* — the Lord Jesus Christ who is Savior, Master, and God incarnate.
- ❑ *One Faith* — salvation by grace alone, through faith alone, in Christ alone, apart from any merit or works, and the acceptance of the Bible as the only inspired, infallible, authoritative, and sufficient revelation to man.
- ❑ *One Baptism* — the Baptism of the Holy Spirit that places us into the Body of Christ.
- ❑ *One God* — the one and only True God who is the Father of all who receive the Son through the Spirit.

That is a truly biblical doctrinal statement, and it is the basis on which we can have true unity. Martyn Lloyd-Jones closes his exposition of this passage with these words:

> The end of all doctrine is to lead to the knowledge of God, and the worship of God; any knowledge we may have is useless if it does not bring us to that point. If your spirit is not humble, if you are not loving, if you are not concerned about this unity of God's people, you have nothing better than intellectual knowledge that is barren and may indeed be even of the Devil. Our Lord said, "If ye know these things, happy are ye if ye do them" (Jn. 13:17). Are you striving to realize that there is "one body, and one Spirit, even as ye are called in one hope of your calling; One Lord, one faith, one baptism, One God and Father of all, who is above all, and through all, and in you all?"[31]

Indeed, until Christianity today rids itself of artificiality and realizes that true unity can be based only upon doctrine, it will continue its downward spiral into Relativism and ultimately irrelevance.

NOTES

[1] Warren Wiersbe, *Be Rich: Ephesians.*

[2] 1:13; 2:18,22; 3:5,16; 4:3,4; 4:30; 5:9,18; 6:17,18.

[3] Jehovah's Witness publication, *Let God Be True*, p. 108.

[4] Cited in Martyn Lloyd-Jones, *Christian Unity*, pp. 87-88.

[5] Jehovah's Witness publication, *The Kingdom is at Hand*, p. 49.

[6] Mormon publication, *Doctrine and Covenants*, 93:21–23.

[7] Gordon Clark, *Ephesians*, p. 131.

[8] *Studies in the Scriptures*, Vol. 1, p. 158.

⁹ *Why Were You Born?*, p. 11.

¹⁰ *Hamlet*, III.1.73. "Rub" means "obstacle." It was a "technical term from the game of bowls, where a 'rub' is any obstruction that hinders or deflects the course of the bowl" (*Hamlet*, The New Folger Library Shakespeare (New York: Pocket Books, 1992), p. 126.

¹¹ Walter M. Abott, S.J., General Editor, *The Documents of Vatican II* (New York: Guild Press, 1966), pp. 88, 91.

¹² Ibid, p. 91.

¹³ *Articles of Faith of the Church of Jesus Christ of Latter Day Saints*, Article 8.

¹⁴ *Orson Pratt's Works*, 1891, p. 218.

¹⁵ Colin Brown, *New International Dictionary of New Testament Theology*, Vol. I, p. 658.

¹⁶ Sprios Zodhiates, *The Complete Word Study Dictionary: New Testament*, p. 331.

¹⁷ *The Complete Word Study Dictionary*, p. 314.

¹⁸ Cited in Lewis Sperry Chafer, *Systematic Theology*, Vol. VI, p. 148.

¹⁹ *Baltimore Catechism*.

²⁰ Chafer, Vol. VI, p. 147. Chafer also includes an excellent quotation of Merrill F. Unger from *Biblitheca Sacra* (CI, 244–247), which is too lengthy to include here (pp. 148-150).

²¹ The Majority Text reads *hēmin* (dative plural of *egō*), and the *Textus Receptus* (Traditional Text) reads *humin* (dative plural of *su*). In either case, the translation is "you" or perhaps "us."

²² John Phillips, *Exploring Ephesians*.

²³ *Coil's Masonic Encyclopedia* (New York: Macoy Publishing and Masonic Supply, 1961), p. 512. This work is recognized as the leading authority according to a poll taken of all 50 Grand Lodges in the US, as cited in John Ankerberg and John Weldon, *The Facts on the Masonic Lodge* (Eugene, OR: Harvest House Publishers, 1989), pp. 8–9.

²⁴ *Mackey's Revised Encyclopedia of Freemasonry*, Revised and Enlarged by Robert I. Clegg (Richmond, VA: Macoy Publishing and Masonic Supply, 1966), Vol. II, p. 847. This is considered the third leading authority of Masonry according to the poll cited above.

²⁵ Malcolm C. Duncan, *Masonic Ritual and Monitor* (New York: David Mckay Co., nd.), p. 129.

²⁶ Ibid, p. 50.

²⁷ *Coil's*, p. 516.

²⁸ Carl H. Claudy, *Introduction to Freemasonry*, 3 Volumes (Washington, DC: The Temple Publishers, 1984), Vol. II, p. 110.

²⁹ *The Master's Carpet; or Masonry and Baal Worship—Identical* (Chicago: Ezra Cook Company, 1879), p. 87. This work has also been reprinted.

³⁰ "If a man does not keep pace with his companions, perhaps it is because he hears a different drummer. Let him step to the music which he hears, however measured or far away" (from *Walden*).

³¹ *Christian Unity*, pp. 142–143.

Articles or rules for doctrine or practice in matters of religion to be imposed upon men, should be as few as may be; there is very greast danger in the unnecessary multiplying of them. This in all ages has caused division and exceeding disturbance in the churches of God.

Puritan Jermiah Burroughs
A Puritan Golden Treasury, p. 303

Unity without verity is no better than conspiracy.

Puritan John Trapp
A Puritan Golden Treasury, p. 304

32

Quietism or Pietism?[*]

Philippians 2:12–13

Wherefore, my beloved, as ye have always obeyed, not as in my presence only, but now much more in my absence, work out your own salvation with fear and trembling. For it is God which worketh in you both to will and to do of his good pleasure.

Have you ever noticed that we humans often tend to be creatures of extremes? One example of this in biblical matters is the doctrine of the Holy Spirit. Another example, of course, is the doctrine of election and its many related topics. One extreme is Arminianism (if not Semi-Pelagianism or even full-blown Pelagianism), which all see man's will as either unfallen, or at least not *totally* marred, by the fall and therefore able to cooperate with God in salvation. The other extreme is the equally unbiblical Hyper-Calvinism, which insists that the process is so much "of God" that Christians shouldn't even evangelize.

This chapter addresses still another example and the Scripture texts used to support each. The two extremes are *Quietism* and *Pietism*. The debate is actually an old one, dating back centuries. How exactly do we live the Christian life? Is it by God's power or our effort? Is it by *passive* trust *in* God or by *active* obedience *to* God? Or is it rather a combination of both? Let's first look at each of these and then try to find the balance in Scripture.

Quietism

The most famous axiom in Quietism, one that sums it up nicely, is, "Let go and let God." Another is, "I can't; God can." Also dubbed the "deeper life," or "higher life," movement, Quietism teaches that Christian living is simply a passive submission to God, who will live life totally for us. Popularized by the old Quakers, other advocates included the Keswicks and the extremely troubling Charles Finney. The most famous teacher of all was Quaker Hannah Whitall Smith, whose book, *The Christian's Secret of a Happy Life*, has become one of the main treatises on this teaching. In it she writes:

---

[*] This chapter was originally TOTT issue 48, July 2009.

To state it in brief, I would just say that man's part is to trust and God's part is to work. . . . Plainly the believer can do nothing but trust; while the Lord, in whom he trusts, actually does the work intrusted to Him. . . . We do not do anything, but He does it. . . . clay is put into the potter's hands, and then lies passive there, submitting itself to all the turnings and overturnings of the potter's hands upon it. There is really nothing else to be said about the clay's part. . . . What can be said about man's part in this great work but that he must continually surrender himself and continually trust? But when we come to God's side of the question, what is there that may not be said as to the manifold and wonderful ways in which He accomplishes the work intrusted to Him? It is here that the growing comes in. The lump of clay would never grow into a beautiful vessel if it stayed in the clay-pit for thousands of years. But once put into the hands of a skilful potter, and, under his fashioning, it grows rapidly into a vessel to his honor. And so the soul, abandoned to the working of the Heavenly Potter, is changed rapidly from glory to glory into the image of the Lord by His Spirit.[1]

Now, while God is indeed the Potter and we are the clay (Rom. 9:21)—although that image actually refers specifically to election, not sanctification—and while Galatians 2:20—another favorite verse of the quietist—declares "yet not I, but Christ liveth in me," Quietism takes it to the extreme. It maintains that the Christian is to put forth no effort whatsoever in holy living, that God does it all. For the quietist, in fact, it is futile and even unspiritual to fight against sin or discipline oneself to produce good works because it "gets in God's way."

As is true of Smith's book, a simple Internet "Google" search on "let go and let God" (with the quotation marks) exposes a serious deficiency of this teaching. A random reading of a few dozen of the 159,000 hits I received, for example, quickly demonstrated that such teaching is based mostly on anecdotes and feelings. One finds a lot of personal experience, poetry, and just downright mysticism, but Scripture exposition is virtually nonexistent, all classic examples of experience trumping Scripture.

The simple fact is that the Christian life is not *solely* about "letting go and letting God." It is not a life in which *only* God is working. Paul wrote, for example, "I press toward the mark for the prize of the high calling of God in Christ Jesus" (Phil. 3:14). Paul had not put himself in neutral and was not casually living the Christian life. Rather he was "pressing" toward the heavenly goal. While the Christian life is certainly a life a of *dependency*, it is not a life of *passivity*.

"Press" is *diōkō*, to chase, to pursue eagerly, to try to obtain. It's also in the present tense, showing continuous action. The Greeks used this word to speak of a hunter earnestly pursuing his prey, an attacker pursing the enemy, and an athlete endeavoring to reach the finish line. Using the same word, Paul also wrote that we are to "fight the good fight of faith" and "follow [*diōkō*] after righteousness, godliness, faith, love, patience, meekness" (1 Tim. 6:11–12). All this obviously indicates significant effort.

Even more graphically, in 1 Corinthians 9:24–27 Paul pictures the Christian life by comparing it with the Isthmian games, which were actually held in Corinth, so his readers immediately understood what he was saying. Contestants in the games had to prove rigorous training for ten months and spent the last month of training in Corinth itself, where they underwent supervised workouts in the gymnasium and athletic fields every day.

The Christian, therefore, is not a *spectator* at "the games," but rather a *participant.* He isn't to sit on the sidelines eating popcorn watching the Holy Spirit do all the work. The Christian life is a life of commitment, discipline, and struggle. We are in a no holds barred war. That is why Paul wrote that the Christian is to put on the spiritual armor of God to prepare for battle (Eph. 6:10–20; cf. 1 Tim. 6:12; 2 Tim. 4:7). No general fights the war by himself for his men; he leads and guides them as they fight. So, while Quietism flows from the purest of motives, it is not based upon sound biblical exposition and "comparing Scripture with Scripture."[2]

Pietism

Like the other side of a coin, Pietism could not be more opposite to Quietism. Pietism is a life of all out effort, giving 100 percent exertion during every waking moment. It is the life of self-discipline, strict obedience, study, and service. The key to the pietist is found in verses such as, "Let us cleanse ourselves from all filthiness of the flesh and spirit, perfecting holiness in the fear of God" (2 Cor. 7:1), and, "Even so faith, if it hath not works, is dead, being alone" (Jas. 2:17).

Reacting against the dead orthodoxy of many Protestant churches, Pietism arose in Germany late in the 17th-century. Credited as the "Father of Pietism," Philipp Jakob Spener (1635–1705) became convinced (and rightly so) of the need for moral and religious reform within German Lutheranism and so wrote *Pia Desideria* (*Pious Wishes*) in 1675. Various strains developed over the years in other countries, and the movement dramatically affected several groups, such as the Mennonites, as well as John Wesley and therefore Methodism and the Holiness Movement.

Like Quietism, Pietism has several praiseworthy aspects, but its inherent danger is the extreme that it usually goes to, namely, legalism. What frequently occurs is that certain practices are arbitrarily chosen as being unholy. Historically, for example, pietists dogmatically declared that card playing, the theater, "worldly" literature, certain kinds of dress, and other practices were unholy. Such teaching still exists today among some groups. The Amish took this so far, of course, that electricity, automobiles, and other modern conveniences and dress are "not plain" and therefore forbidden.

Now, we do not criticize the motives here. On the contrary. To be a Christian clearly implies and demands a changed life—each of us is a "new creature" (2 Cor. 5:17). But to create our own list of things that are either spiritual or unspiritual, when Scripture simply does not address those things, is a form of legalism. Sadly, byproducts of Pietism are self-righteousness, pride, inconsistency, and even hypocrisy. All this results because spiritual *living* is divorced from spiritual *power*, self-effort replaces Spirit control, and personal *preference* trumps divine *precept*.

Finding the Balance

Warren Wiersbe offers this practical illustration of these "competing" views:

> What quarterback would say to his team, "OK, men, just let go and let the coach do it all!" On the other hand, no quarterback would say, "Listen to me and forget what the coach says!" Both extremes are wrong.[3]

It is in our text, therefore, that we discover Paul's answer to this dilemma. At first reading, however, it doesn't look like a resolution to the problem at all. In fact, it strikes us as a staggering contradiction! Paul first commands that *we* are to work and then says that is *God* doing the work. First he's a pietist and then a quietist! How does that help the issue? That is precisely why these verses have often been a battleground.

Significantly, however, note that *Paul does not go on and try to rationally harmonize the two extremes.* Why? Because no one can. He simply states that both are true. Let's examine the wonderful paradox of this verse, which is, as Martyn Lloyd-Jones puts it, "one of the most perfect summaries of the Christian life to be found anywhere,"[4] and then see how they work together.

Recognizing Our Effort

Our effort in Christian living is stated in the words **work out your own salvation with fear and trembling**. As most commentators point out, the first thing to note here is that the verse does not say to work *for*

Truth on Tough Texts

salvation, but to work *out* salvation. Salvation does not come by works, rather works (obedience) are the evidence of salvation.

Work out translates a single Greek word, *katergazomai*, to work out, accomplish, or carry out a task until it is finished. Greek authority Kenneth Wuest well illustrates:

> We say, "The student worked out a problem in arithmetic." That is, he carried the problem to its ultimate conclusion. This is the way it is used here. The Philippians are exhorted to carry their salvation to its ultimate conclusion, namely, Christlikeness.[5]

Intensifying this basic idea is the fact that the verb is in the present tense, indicating continuous action, and the imperative mood, indicating a command. We could therefore expand the translation to read "continually keep on carrying out the task of completing your salvation until it's finished." Again, this is not working *for* but working *out* salvation. It is a command to diligent effort in obedient living that results from conversion and God's empowering as He works in us, which, as we will see in our next section, is the very point Paul goes on to add in verse 13.

Paul elsewhere repeatedly makes the point of our effort in Christian living. In addition to the verses cited earlier, he wrote to the Corinthians, "Let us cleanse ourselves from all filthiness of the flesh and spirit, perfecting holiness in the fear of God" (2 Cor. 7:1). He commanded the Ephesians to "walk worthy of the vocation wherewith ye are called" (Eph. 4:1) and goes on to list the attributes of such a calling (vv. 2–3). For the Colossians he even provided a list of negative traits to avoid and positive ones to cultivate as they labored (Col. 3:5–17).

What does Paul then mean when he adds that this labor is with **fear and trembling**? While the "let go and let God" mentality would have us sit back, kick off our shoes, and forget about our cares, Paul says something quite the contrary. Puritan Charles Bridges perfectly defines the "fear of the Lord" when he writes: "It is that affectionate reverence by which the child of God bends himself humbly and carefully to his Father's law. His wrath is so bitter, and His love so sweet; that hence springs an earnest desire to please Him, and—because of the danger of coming short from his own weakness and temptations—a holy watchfulness and *fear*, 'that he might not sin against Him.'"[6]

The phrase **fear and trembling** appears, for example, in Ephesians 6:5, describing how the slave (or employee) is to obey his master. This attitude is not cowering in fear, but rather a respect for another's position and authority. Deeper, however, is the thought of our fear of neglecting our responsibility and in so doing disobeying the Lord. In 1 Corinthians 2:3, Paul writes that he came to the Corinthians in **fear and trembling**. This was a fear of failing both the Corinthians and the Lord. Likewise, then, to **work out your own salvation with fear and trembling** means we labor with the attitude that we do not want to fail our Lord.

Realizing God's Empowering

So, does all the labor Paul speaks of flow from self-effort? Do we in our own strength and will power just grit our teeth and "keep on keepin' on"? No, for Paul goes on to add, **For it is God which worketh in you both to will and to do of his good pleasure.**

Worketh is the Greek, *energeō* (English "energy" and "energize") and means "to be at work, to effect something." It's extremely significant, as one Greek authority tells us, that the noun *energeia*, "energy, active power, operation") "in the [Septuagint] (as in the NT) is used almost exclusively for the work of divine or demonic powers."[7] In Ephesians 1:19, for example, it is God's power that is "working" (*energeia*) in us, while in 2:2, Satan is said to be working (*energeō*).

Another authority agrees, adding that this usage is predominant in the entire word group: "Only in Philippians 2:13 does the active *energein* [present active participle of *energeō*] refer to human activity,"[8] but we note that even then it's *still God* who is working. So why is it that we can work, why is it that we have the strength to labor and be victorious? Because God first is at work. Let us briefly note four principles.

First, the *Person* of the work again is God, not us. "The divine activity is literally an in-working (*ho energōn*)," writes pastor and commentator Robert Gromacki. "The literal translation of this participle is 'the one who enrgizes.' God's inner work deals with character, and man's outer work manifests his conduct."[9] *Second*, the *place* of the work is found in the words **in you**. God is at work in every aspect of our being. *Third*, the *purpose* of all this work is both to **will** and **do** what He purposes. Here is God's sovereignty in action. *Fourth*, the *point* of this work, the ultimate reason for it all, is God's **good pleasure**. As Paul declares in Ephesians 1, *everything*—election, predestination, redemption, sealing, and all else—is "to the praise of the glory of His grace."

Reconciling the Enigma

While these two truths might be viewed as *rationally contradictory*, they are *spiritually complementary*. As Kenneth Wuest well puts it: "In verse twelve, we have human responsibility, in verse thirteen, divine enablement, a perfect balance which must be kept if the Christian life is to be lived at its best. It is not a 'let go and let God' affair. It is a 'take hold with God' business."

To put it another way, this is not a *passive deference* rather a *positive dependence*. It is a mutual cooperation of Holy Spirit power enabling the Christian to labor victoriously. I am always blessed when I read Lehman Strauss. He offers an illustration here that wonderfully pictures how these two principles complement each other:

> When I visited the West Indies in 1956, I witnessed American aluminum manufactures removing millions of tons of bauxite from the hills of Jamaica. The rich ore was already there. God had worked it in by some catastrophic movement of nature or through some aging process. Man had only to operate and exploit in order to get the greatest worth out of that which already was his possession. As I watched I observed the process to be anything but simple and easy. It was a costly project. But be certain, the effort was sure to pay off in large dividends. Such, it seems to me, is the idea in the Holy Spirit's words, "work out your own salvation." It is my possession by gift of divine grace, but as Guy H. King has said: "I am to mine what is already mine," endeavoring to work out that precious nugget of humility.[10]

Neither is our text an isolated one. Paul wrote to the troubled Corinthian church: "But by the grace of God I am what I am: and his grace which was bestowed upon me was not in vain; but I laboured more abundantly than they all: yet not I, but the grace of God which was with me" (1 Cor. 15:10). He likewise wrote the Colossian believers: "Whereunto I also labour, striving according to his working, which worketh in me mightily" (Col. 1:29). Even in Galatians 2:20, he makes it clear that it is *both*, "I live . . . yet not I." In all these instances, believers are *striving* while God is *strengthening*.

In closing, Martyn Lloyd-Jones well sums up this issue when he writes:

> . . . desires for a fuller and better and more perfect Christian life are not self-generated or self-produced. When you have a desire to do something good, or a desire to pray, it is God who energizes it in your will, God working in us both to will and to do. He is the energy and power also in our breathing, in our ability to live this life. . . . The initiative is His from beginning to end. It is God who began [it], it is He who keeps it going, and it is He who is making it perfect.

And yet you and I are told to work it out, we are told to do something. Is this a contradiction? I suggest that it is not and we can put it like this. God carries on this work within us by placing these desires and powers in us. In other words, God is perfecting us, He is bringing His great purpose to pass in our Christian life, not by action upon us in a passive state or condition, but by controlling our will, our desires, our thoughts and aspiration, and everything. It is God who starts and He makes us do it. I do not say that God forces our will. Rather, God does something more gracious: He persuades our will, and gives us holy desires, so that we will those things, and our desire and ambition is to work it out because it is "God which worketh in us."[11]

Amen!

NOTES

[1] *The Christian's Secret of a Happy Life* (Revell, 1952), electronic edition, "Introduction" (italics in the original).

[2] This is the principle of *analogia scripturae*, "the analogy of Scripture," that is, comparing Scripture with Scripture. This is further explained by *Scripturam ex Scriptura explicandam esse* ("Scripture is to be explained by Scripture"), which is also related to *Analogia Fide* ("Analogy of Faith," i.e., Bible doctrine is to be interpreted in relation to the basic message of the Bible, which is the Gospel, the content of faith, or simply "The Faith" (cf. 1 Cor.2:13, 15:1-4).

[3] *Bible Exposition Commentary*, electronic edition, on Philippians 3:14.

[4] *The Life of Joy and Peace: An Exposition of Philippians* (Baker Books, 1999), p. 160.

[5] *Wuest's Word Studies*, electronic edition on Philippians 3:12–13.

[6] Charles Bridges, *Exposition of the Book of Proverbs* (Zondervan, 1959), pp. 3–4.

[7] Colin Brown, *The New International Dictionary of New Testament Theology* (Zondervan, 1975, 1986), Vol. 3, p. 1147.

[8] Gerhard Kittel (editor), *Theological Dictionary of the New Testament* (Eerdmans, 1964; reprinted 2006), Vol. II, p. 653.

[9] *Stand United in Joy: An Exposition of Philippians* (Kress Christian Publications, 2002), p. 106.

[10] *Devotional Studies in Philippians* (Loizeaux Brothers, 1959, 1970), p.121–122.

[11] *The Life of Joy and Peace*, pp. 169–170.

33

What Was Paul's Thorn in the Flesh?[*]

2 Corinthians 12:7

And lest I should be exalted above measure through the abundance of the revelations, there was given to me a thorn in the flesh, the messenger of Satan to buffet me, lest I should be exalted above measure.

So what exactly was Paul's thorn in the flesh? Many commentators and expositors have speculated about this, but is there any way of knowing? Let us examine this question by noting the interpretations, language, and purpose of our text.

The Interpretations of the Verse

Few verses of Scripture have generated as many interpretations as has this one. The speculation has, in fact, been enormous. Albert Barnes puts it well, "Every one who has become familiar with commentaries knows that almost every expositor has had his own opinion about this, and also that no one has been able to give any good reason for his own. Most of them have been fanciful; and many of them eminently ridiculous."[1]

He is correct. I read over twenty commentators and at least half that many opinions. The most popular has been some kind of eye trouble, brought on by his being blinded at his conversion, citing Galatians 6:11 as proof: "Ye see how large a letter I have written unto you with mine own hand." But there is quite clearly nothing in that verse that directly connects it with the apostle's thorn in the flesh; to connect them must be *assumed*, for it is not revealed. Additionally, the reason he wrote in large letters could have simply been for emphasis or dramatic effect. (See the last section of our "Reader Questions" chapter for a discussion of this statement.)

Other theories include: migraine headaches (which might or might not have been connected with eye trouble), malaria, epilepsy, gallstones, gout, rheumatism, an intestinal disorder, sexual temptation (the Roman Catholic view), or even a speech impediment. One old Scottish commentator said Paul's thorn in the flesh might have been his wife, a comment we will just leave alone, but one that is really no more speculative (or sillier) than any

---

* This chapter was originally TOTT issue 49, August 2009.

of the others. I heard one old preacher make it even simpler: "What was Paul's thorn in the flesh? Well, maybe Paul just had a thorn in his flesh."

Another popular view, as one expositor puts it, is that this was "a demonic messenger of Satan sent to torment him by using the deceivers to seduce the Corinthians into a rebellion against him." In other words, the language can simply be taken figuratively to refer to the false teachers that plagued the Corinthians and burdened Paul to such an extent that it became like a thorn. Such a view is an obvious stretching of the language. In my view, there is no warrant whatsoever to make the language figurative instead of taking it in its normal sense. That leads us right to our next point.

The Language of the Verse

If words mean anything, whatever this **thorn** was, it simply had to be something physical. This simply cannot be denied; the Greek permits no other possibility when taken in its normal sense. As the late Dr. David Cooper summed up the matter:

> When the plain sense of Scripture makes common sense, seek no other sense; therefore; take every word at its primary, ordinary, usual, literal meaning unless the facts of the immediate context, studied in the light of related passages and axiomatic and fundamental truths, indicated clearly otherwise.[2]

Again, there seems to us no justifiable reason to take the language here in a figurative manner, much less to virtually spiritualize it into something more.

We would submit, then, that the *first* word that proves this normal sense is the word **flesh**. The Greek here is *sarx*, which Paul used in three ways in his letters: 1) physical or that which pertains to the body (37 times; e.g., Eph. 5:29); 2) general term for humanity (25 times; e.g., Eph. 6:12); 3) inherent evil in the human nature (27 times; e.g., Eph. 2:3; often inaccurately called the "old nature," a term that never appears in Scripture; the accurate term is **flesh**, which Paul uses in this sense 11 times in Rom. 7 and 8).[3]

So, as **flesh** in our text obviously does not refer either to humanity in general or inherent evil in the human nature, it clearly refers to the physical body.[4] There was obviously something in Paul's physical body that ailed him with great severity.

The *second* word that indicates something physical is **thorn** itself. The term *hapax legomenon* refers to a word that occurs only once in either the written record of a language, the works of an author, or in a single text. Such words in Scripture are often very instructive, or at least significant.

Truth on Tough Texts

The Greek *skolops* (**thorn**) is such a word. Not only does it appear only once in the New Testament, but it's also not all that common even in Classical Greek (the Greek used prior to the Koine [common] Greek of NT times). As one Greek authority tells us:

> It means something pointed, and is probably connected with *skallo*, hack. Originally, it meant a pointed stake, used in defense (Homer, *The Odyssey*, 7, 45; *The Illiad*, 8, 343) or upon which the head of an enemy could be stuck (Homer, *The Illiad*, 18, 176). It was used in a similar sense to *stauros*, cross. But it is also found in the sense of a thorn or splinter in Aesop's *Fables* (279, 11), and in this sense well attested.[5]

Another Greek authority adds that *skolops* also referred to stakes used for the fortification of walls as well as ones used for impaling enemies in execution.[6]

What, then, is Paul expressing? It would certainly seem that he is saying that there is a severe physical issue plaguing him, something that causes him such savage pain that it is similar to a stake impaling him.

The *third* word that indicates something physical is **buffet**. The Greek here is *kolaphizō*. This word is one of several that are used to indicate literal physical violence, both in Classical and New Testament Greek. For example, *derō* (to beat, scourge, or flay; Lk. 22:63, "smote"), *phragelloō* (to whip or scourge, Matt. 27:26, "scourged"), and *mastigoō* (to whip or scourge, Jn. 19:1, "scourged") are all used of the Lord Jesus in His passion sufferings. *Kolaphizō* is likewise used of our Lord's suffering (note Matt. 26:67 again, "buffeted," as well as Mk. 14:65, "buffet"). It means to strike with the fist, beat, or cuff. It appears also in 1 Corinthians 4:11 and 1 Peter 2:20, both of which again indicate the physical sense of being "buffeted." It, therefore, seems clear once again that Paul is describing something physical in his life that keeps striking and beating him.

Physical infirmity seems all the more apparent in verses 9 and 10, where Paul uses the word *astheneia* three times ("weakness" and "infirmities"). This word means "to be sick or weak." It, along with the two related words *asthenēs* and *astheneō*, "are the most common expressions for illness and are used in the comprehensive sense of the whole man. However, it can also refer to a special form of bodily weakness or sickness. Figuratively, *astheneia* can mean general impotence [or] weakness (Rom. 8:26)."[7]

In addition to the internal evidence in our text, Galatians 4:13–14 adds some external evidence that Paul was plagued by something physical: "Ye know how through infirmity [*astheneia*] of the flesh [*sarx*] I preached the gospel unto you at the first. And my temptation which was in my flesh [*sarx*] ye despised not, nor rejected; but received me as an angel of God, even as Christ Jesus."

The Purpose of the Verse

What is most troubling concerning the various speculations about what this **thorn** specifically was is that such conjecture, at least in my view, misses the real point of the passage. Is the main point of this verse and its context to tell us what Paul's physical problem was? Obviously not, since there are so many opinions as to what it was.

We would submit, therefore, that after all such speculation is noted, the bottom line is that we do not know what the ailment was—the text simply does not say. *Period.* I am convinced that the reason for this is that it doesn't matter, and to speculate is missing the point.

What, then, *is* the point? The point is that whatever the affliction was, it was there to keep Paul humble. As the words **lest I should be exalted above measure through the abundance of the revelations** indicate, Paul had been given staggering **revelations**, and such truth could easily puff him up with pride. **Exalted above measure** is a single word in the Greek, *huperairō*, which means to lift above, elevate, exalt, be conceited, arrogant, or insolent. Its only other New Testament appearance is in 2 Thessalonians 2:4, where it is used of the anti-Christ, who will "[oppose] and [exalt] himself above all that is called God."

So, to keep him from being spiritually proud and self-confident, God gave Paul a physical affliction to keep him humble. Nothing, in fact, keeps us humble like a chronic, even debilitating, illness. Nothing reminds us that we are weak, frail, and human than does physical affliction. This would have been especially significant to the Corinthians. As in our own society, Corinthian society valued strength and success over weakness and failure. God loves to work through weakness because this puts his power on display. In his first letter to the Corinthians, Paul wrote that God "hath chosen the weak things of the world to confound the things which are mighty" (1 Cor. 1:27). And as Paul states later in our present passage, "when I am weak, then am I strong" (v. 10). In other words, "It is only when I am at my weakest that God's power makes me the strongest."

Another example of this truth that immediately comes to mind is Job. Satan directly afflicted Job, though God set limits for Satan, who could do only what God allowed him to do (see Job 1:12; 2:6). Likewise, as **Satan** afflicted Job, Satan's **messenger[s]** afflicted Paul and still afflict God's people. "In one sense, " writes William MacDonald, this is "an effort on Satan's part to hinder Paul in the work of the Lord. But God is greater than Satan, and He used the thorn to further the work of the Lord by keeping

Paul humble. Successful service for Christ depends on a weak servant. The weaker he is, the more the power of Christ accompanies his preaching."[8]

The point of this passage, and its application for us, should now be clear. No matter what affliction each of us has, it is there for our learning and humbling, and it is there so that God's grace for our endurance is magnified. In short, it is all for His glory and our good. As Paul wrote earlier in this letter, let us be reminded daily that "our light affliction, which is but for a moment, worketh for us a far more exceeding and eternal weight of glory" (2 Cor. 4:17). And as he also wrote the Romans, "For I reckon that the sufferings of this present time are not worthy to be compared with the glory which shall be revealed in us" (Rom. 8:18).

Soli Deo Gloria!

NOTES

[1] *Albert Barnes' Notes on the Bible*, electronic edition, comment on 2 Cor. 12:7.

[2] Cited in J. Vernon McGee's *Guidelines for the Understanding of the Scriptures* (Thru the Bible Books), p. 20.

[3] These totals do *not* include the five additional occurrences in the Epistle to the Hebrews, as some teachers dispute Pauline authorship (although this author does not; see chapter 7).

[4] J. Sidlow Baxter provides a very helpful chart of all these occurrences of **flesh**, divided into their three categories, in his wonderful book *A New Call to Holiness* (Zondervan, 1967, 1973), pp. 187–188.

[5] Colin Brown, *The New International Dictionary of New Testament Theology* (Zondervan, 1975, 1986), Vol. 1, p. 726.

[6] Gerhard Kittel (Ed.), *Theological Dictionary of New Testament* (Eerdmans, 1971, 2006), Vol. VII, p. 409.

[7] Spiros Zodhiates, *The Complete Word Study Dictionary* (AMG Publishers), electronic edition, word #769.

[8] *Believer's Bible Commentary* (Thomas Nelson Publishers), electronic edition.

34

What About Cremation?[*]

Selected Texts

What about cremation for a Christian? This is a question I have been asked many times throughout 38 years of ministry. Reasons for the question vary. Some ask for convenience sake, since it is obviously far easier to cremate than bury.

The chief reason, as one might assume, seems to be monetary. As TOTT reader TO in Texas recently wrote:

> I wanted to get your feedback on cremation as a choice for final interment. I find the open casket and burial in a high dollar casket a bit odd. When we lay down for our final rest, I have always felt as a saved Christian we have gone on to be with the Lord. All else seems to me to be for the benefit of the living.

We agree, and even empathize, here. While there are certainly Christian (or at least ethical) funeral directors who are not guilty of this, I have seen those who take advantage of bereaved people, selling them high dollar "packages" when there were several ways to lower the cost dramatically. So why not just go the cheap route of cremation? After all, we even have an urn for a memorial.

For those reasons and others, more and more people are opting for cremation. According to the Cremation Association of North America, for example, in 2005 there were 778,025 deaths in America, 30.88% of which were then cremated. Based on the current rate of increase, the CANC goes on to estimate that the percentage will grow to 38.15% in 2010. Another interesting statistic is the percentage of cremations in other countries: China (41%), New Zealand (58%), United Kingdom (70%), and Japan (97%).

We would submit, however, that the biblical evidence is overwhelming that cremation is not the best, that it is burial, in fact, that is the scriptural precedent.

The Biblical Precedent of Burial

The Hebrew *qāḇar*, which is also found in most of the other Semitic languages, appears about 130 times in the Old Testament, the vast majority

---

[*] This chapter was originally TOTT issue 50, September 2009.

of which are in the Pentateuch and historical books. It means to bury or entomb and in every instance except one (Jer. 22:19) refers to human burial.

This fact immediately and fundamentally underscores that burial was extremely important in Hebrew thinking. "A proper burial was a sign of special kindness and divine blessing," writes one authority.[1] Not to be properly buried, in fact, was considered great misfortune, calamity, and even judgment (1 Kings 13:22; 14:11; 2 Kings 9:37; Ps. 79:3; Jer. 7:33; 8:1; Ezek. 29:5; Rev. 11:9). In accordance with Genesis 3:19, burial was the accepted method of disposal of the dead. We repeatedly see God's people buried throughout Scripture, often in a family tomb, as with Sarah (Gen. 23:19), Abraham (25:9), Isaac, Rebekah, Leah (49:31), Jacob (50:13), and many others; the list, in fact, is long.[2]

The Pagan Practice of Cremation

There is no doubt whatsoever that cremation has always been practiced predominantly by pagans. The Greek Homeric heroes were burned, for example, cremation being introduced to them by the nomadic Achaeans and Dorians centuries before Christ.[3] First century Roman senator and historian Tacitus records that by the time of Christ cremation was almost universal among the Romans.[4]

Writing on this issue around the mid 20th-century, Scottish born missionary and pastor James W. Fraser recounts:

> I asked a missionary from India if the Christians of that land cremated their dead. With a look of surprise he said, "Positively not! Cremation is heathen. The Christians of India bury their dead, because burial is Christian."[5]

It's extremely significant that Tacitus also observed that in contrast to the Romans, it was a serious matter of piety with the Jews "to bury rather than to burn dead bodies."[6]

Cremation was, in fact, rare among the Hebrews: "According to the Mosaic law burning was reserved, either for the living who had been found guilty of unnatural sins (Lev. 21:9; [also 20:14; Gen. 38:24; 2 Kings 23:16, 20]), or for those who died under a curse, as in the case of Achan and his family."[7] It was also used to prevent disease epidemics in the case of mass death (Amos 6:10).

As a rule, then, burning was considered the ultimate desecration of the dead (1 Kings 13:2; 2 Kings 23:16, 20). Note that even though the bodies of Saul and his sons were burned, undoubtedly because the bodies were badly mutilated and/or decayed, the bones were still buried (1 Sam. 31:11–13), not crushed into powder as in modern cremation. While a question is sometimes raised over Asa, he was unquestionably buried but was then honored by "a very great burning," that is, a fire of incense and spices (2 Chron. 16:14). In contrast, Jehoram did not receive the honoring spice burning because of his shameful reign (21:19).

During my research of this question, I ran into one Christian leader who was asked, "My husband and I are considering cremation. Is cremation against the teaching of the Bible? Will those cremated also be resurrected?" In his nationally syndicated column, that very well known Christian leader answered this way:

> The aspect of cremation that worries some Christians is the thought of the total annihilation of the body. We need to get our thinking in a right perspective here. The body is annihilated just as completely in the grave as it is in cremation. The graves of our ancestors are no longer in existence, and soil in which they were buried has long since been removed elsewhere. We must therefore accept that what happens to the body or to the grave cannot be of any significance so far as the resurrection is concerned.
>
> Our resurrection is related to that of Christ's in 1 Corinthians 15, and we must realize that the resurrection of Jesus was quite different from that of say, Lazarus. Lazarus needed the body that had been buried, but when Jesus came forth from the tomb, his body was so changed that he could not be easily recognized.
>
> In that chapter, Paul states of the burial of our bodies: "thou sowest not that body that shall be" (v.37). The body that rises is not made of the same substances as the one that was buried, but is immortal and incorruptible.
>
> In 2 Corinthians 5, Paul makes the contrast between living in a tent, a temporary home that can be pulled down and put away, and living in a permanent home that will last forever. Our bodies are our temporary tents. Our resurrected bodies will be our permanent homes. They are similar in appearance but different in substance. Cremation is therefore no hindrance to the resurrection.[8]

The ignorance of Scripture and history in that answer is sad in light of it coming from a supposed great Christian leader. The resurrection is not the real issue here; it is the desecration of the body that is the issue, for the body is most certainly "significant." Even more tragic is the fact that many other Christians, including some Bible teachers of a more evangelical position than the above, are being deluded into believing that cremation is acceptable. This is due chiefly to the increase of pagan influence that has been going on in Christianity for centuries.

Perhaps most significant of all, it should also be noted that there is not a single instance of cremation in the New Testament, and that the body is always treated with respect, the burial of our Lord, of course, being the greatest example. A reading of 1 Corinthians 15:35–46 quickly demonstrates the obvious precedent of burial as well as the joyous event of future resurrection. Throughout Scripture, therefore, we see that it is *burial*, not *burning*, that honors the body. Let us be Christians, not pagans.

NOTES

[1] *Vine's Complete Expository Dictionary of Old and New Testament Words* (Thomas Nelsom, 1985 revision), p. 28 ("To Bury" entry).

[2] Just a few more include: Moses (Deut. 34:5–8), Gideon (Judg. 8:32), Samson (16:31), Samuel (1 Sam. 25:1), David (1 Kings 2:10–12; 1 Chron. 29:26–28), Solomon (1 Kings 11:41–43), and the long list goes on.

[3] See Will Durant, *The Story of Civilization II: The Life of Greece* (Simon and Schuster, 1939, 1966), p. 311 (cf. 37–38; 62–63).

[4] Tacitus (ca. 56 – ca. 117 AD), *Annals*, 16, 6.

[5] *Cremation—Is It Christian?* (Loizeaux Brothers). Reprinted by Sola Scriptura Ministries, 2001, p. 8.

[6] Tacitus, *The Histories*, Book V (ca. 110 AD).

[7] James Orr (General Editor), *International Standard Bible Encyclopedia* (electronic edition), "Burial" entry.

[8] Billy Graham, "My Answer," a nationally syndicated newspaper column.

A godly man holds no more than he will die for. The martyrs were so confirmed in the knowledge of the truth that they would seal it with their blood.

Thomas Watson, *The Godly Man's Picture*, p. 21

35

Teaching Faithful Men[*]

2 Timothy 2:2

And the things that thou hast heard of me among many witnesses, the same commit thou to faithful men, who shall be able to teach others also.

Romans 8:29–30 has often been called God's "Golden Chain of Salvation": "For whom he did foreknow, he also did predestinate to be conformed to the image of his Son, that he might be the firstborn among many brethren. Moreover whom he did predestinate, them he also called: and whom he called, them he also justified." That title is fitting because we see here five links that are absolutely unbreakable, five acts God alone has done in the past (since all the verbs are in the past tense) to provide and secure our salvation.

Well, there is another "chain" in Scripture, one that we could dub God's "Chain of Teaching." It is found here in 2 Timothy 2:2.

Responsibilities of the Pastor-Teacher

To introduce this key text concerning church ministry, let's very briefly note Acts 20:28–35. In a hurry to get to Jerusalem for Pentecost, Paul sends for the elders (pastors) of the church at Ephesus. In one of the most touching scenes in Scripture, we read the counsel and parting challenges Paul gives these dear men of God. He here lists six basic responsibilities of the pastor-teacher.

First, a pastor must guard his own life and ministry (v. 28). "Take heed" is *prosechō*, a nautical term meaning to holding a ship in a certain direction, sailing towards something. A pastor, therefore, is to hold to his course, pay attention to the "compass" so he doesn't drift from the right heading. He must at all times make sure he is right with God, live what he preaches, keep his life pure, and be disciplined in every area of his existence.

Second, he must "feed the church of God" (v. 28). This is without argument his number one responsibility. This man must be "apt to teach" (1 Tim. 3:2), that is, *skillful* in teaching and he must be committed to that

---

[*] This chapter was originally TOTT issue 51, October 2009.

single task. He is not an entertainer, psychologist, fund-raiser, or any other modern job description. His primary duty is to preach and teach the Word of God (2 Tim. 4:1–4).

Third, he is to "oversee," that is, lead the sheep (v. 28). "Overseers" is *episkopos*, which is rooted in Greek culture and referred to a superintendent or magistrate who was sent to an outlying city to organize and govern it. As a building superintendent doesn't own the building he manages, the pastor doesn't own the Church; he manages it, leads it, and governs it according to God's Word. Further, as a shepherd, he leads. He does not *drive* the sheep, as would a *dictator*, rather he *leads* the sheep as does a *shepherd*. As Peter declares, "Feed the flock of God which is among you, taking the oversight thereof" (1 Pet. 5:2).

Fourth, he is to protect the sheep (vv. 29–31). The pastor first protects the sheep from *danger from without* (v. 29), as he guards them against "grievous wolves" of false teaching and other risks. He also protects them from *disease from within* (v. 30), from those who would arise even within their midst "to draw away disciples after them."

Fifth, he is to study and pray (v. 32). "Commend" (*paratithēmi*) speaks of "a deposit, a trust." Preachers have been *entrusted* with the Word of God, *put in charge of* its use. What a responsibility this is and one we had better not take lightly! Most preaching today shows the shallow (or even non-existent) study of the preacher. So the number one *responsibility* of the pastor is to feed the sheep, but his number one *priority* must be his study time. A preacher who does not spend the majority of his "ministry time" in study will not be able to adequately feed his people. It gets harder every day to find men who are truly preaching the Word of God instead of philosophy, politics, and "warm-fuzzies." Many Bible colleges, seminaries, and pastor's conferences revolve around the latest marketing tools instead of the revealed Truth of God.

Sixth, he must be free of self-interest. Verses 33–35 end with a three-fold challenge: do not covet wealth, be satisfied with what God provides, and be generous in giving. A pastor must never be one who thinks of temporal gain and possessions. His motive and desire is to feed the sheep and see them grow and reproduce. There are, indeed, many false teachers today who instead of *feeding* the sheep are *fleecing* the sheep, who are "greedy of filthy lucre" (1 Tim. 3:3, 8), guilty of taking all they can get, and thereby ruining not only God's work but their own reputations.

God's "Chain of Teaching"

That brings us to our text, where Paul adds a seventh responsibility of the pastor-teacher, namely, *every pastor is to train other men of God*. Some commentators take this to refer simply to the pastor's duty to teach *all* Christians in his role as a shepherd. While he is certainly required to do that, the fact that this is a Pastoral Epistle suggests something more specific. This seems clear when we consider five "links" in this chain of teaching

First, there is the Lord Jesus Himself. While He is not mentioned in our text, He must be noted, for He is the one who personally taught the Apostle Paul. Not only did He reveal Himself to Paul on the road to Damascus (Acts 9:1–9), but Paul himself recounts something further in Galatians 1:16–19. Here he states that while in Nabataean Arabia—a region that stretched east from Damascus down to the Sinai peninsula—he "conferred not with flesh and blood," that is, any person—although he did see Jesus' brother James—nor did he go "up to Jerusalem to them which were apostles before [him]" to be taught by them.

Now, while this passage does not specifically state what occurred in Arabia, there is little doubt that it was here that Paul was prepared for ministry. In fact, the number "three" seems to reoccur repeatedly when it comes to training men for ministry. The disciples spent three years with the Lord, and Timothy was with Paul for three years during his second missionary journey (Acts 15:36; 18:22). Since Paul, therefore, was not taught by any of the other Apostles, just as none of them were taught by other men, there seems no doubt that Paul was taught for three years by the Lord Jesus Himself in Nabataean Arabia.

Second, Paul is the next link in God's chain of teaching. Having been taught by the Lord Jesus—again, just as the other Apostles had been—Paul became a trainer of men for ministry. Since the Lord Jesus was no longer on earth to carry out this crucial need, he appointed men to do so. And that is exactly what Paul did. Throughout his ministry, men accompanied him, aiding him and learning from him. These included: Barnabas (Acts 11:25–26); John Mark (12:25; 13:5, 13; 15:37; see chapter 26 for a study of "The Disagreement Between Paul and Barnabas" concerning John Mark in 15:36–41); Silas (15:36–41); and especially Timothy (16:1–3; etc.). Concerning Timothy, in fact, our text records that Paul specifically mentioned **the things that [Timothy had] heard** from him, that is, the things that Paul had taught him.

Heard is the Greek *akouō* and is the source of such English words as *acoustics* (the science of sound). It not only means to hear in general (e.g., Matt. 2:3), to hear with attention (e.g., Mark 4:3, "hearken"), and to understand (e.g., Mark 4:33), but also to *obey* (e.g. 1 Jn. 3:11). We can only imagine how many times Timothy heard Paul preach, how many times he heard Paul teach precept upon precept. We can only imagine the private times of teaching and counsel that these two men shared as they traveled hundreds of miles together. Paul taught, and Timothy listened and obeyed.

Third, Timothy is the next link in God's chain of teaching and brings us to the core of our text. Having taught Timothy, Paul now challenges him to teach others. The word **commit** is *paratithēmi*, a compound comprised of *para* (near or along side) and *tithēmi* (to place or deposit). The idea in this word, then, is to place something with someone for one's own sake, to commit it *to* them and entrust them *with* it. Such an act is a painstaking one. It requires diligent and disciplined teaching.

It's noteworthy that Paul does not *suggest* that Timothy teach other men but *commands* him to do so. The verb *paratithēmi* (**commit**) is here in the imperative mood, indicating a command. Just as the Lord Jesus left this earth and would no longer personally train His men, Paul also was close to departing this life and commanded Timothy to do what God had commanded him to do. This is not teaching some supposed "apostolic succession," as some foolishly teach, rather it demonstrates that each generation must teach the next.

Fourth, **faithful men** form the next link in God's chain of teaching. **Faithful** is *pistos*, which here refers not to the *act* of *believing* but to the *state* of being *trustworthy*. Paul used this word in reference to himself in his first letter to Timothy, where he wrote that "Jesus our Lord . . . enabled me" and "counted me faithful, putting me into the ministry" (1 Tim. 1:12). He wrote of the same quality to the Corinthians: "Moreover it is required in stewards, that a man be found faithful" (1 Cor. 4:2).

Proven faithfulness is, therefore, a crucial key in determining a man's qualification for ministry. As mentioned back in chapter 26, this is why John Mark disqualified himself when he abandoned Paul's team (Acts 15:36–41). This is also why the qualifications and requirements for leadership in the Church are extremely high, according to 1 Timothy 3:1–7 and Titus 1:6–8. God could not be clearer on this issue of qualified leadership. In spite of that, however, we see more and more people today leading who frankly should not be doing so. The common attitude is that anyone can lead, but this is worse than dangerous. Men must be *proven* before they can be *appointed*.

Fifth, the word **others** forms the "final" link in God's chain of teaching, although in reality there is no last link in this chain. It is designed to continue on—one link being added to the next and the next and the next—until our Lord returns. One more key word here, of course, is **teach**. This is the familiar New Testament word *didaskō*, which speaks of systematic teaching and appears (with other forms) no less than 26 times in the Pastoral Epistles.

Is there any doubt, then, what the preacher's job is? This is precisely why Paul mentions in 1 Timothy 3:2 that one of the required qualifications for the ministry is that a man is "apt to teach," as mentioned earlier. This is one word in the Greek (*didaktikos*) that means "*skilled* in teaching." As one expositor puts it: "Not merely *given to* teaching, but able and skilled in it. All *might teach* to whom the Spirit imparted the gift: but *skill* in teaching was the especial office of the minister on whom would fall the ordinary duty of instruction of believers and refutation of gainsayers."[1] Is it any wonder, then, that included in the pastor's teaching responsibility is the duty to teach and train other men for this very same ministry? This is, indeed, God's method of propagating the Church leadership offices. I appreciate expositor Jon Courson's comment here:

> In our educational system, there are few greater sins than that of plagiarism. "Be innovative, creative, and original," our teachers say—which is fine for schoolwork, but not for ministry. Because there is no such thing as plagiarism in ministry, Paul told Timothy to take the very things he had heard Paul teach and pass them on to others.[2]

In a day when innovation and creative thinking are the primary tools for church building, we need to be reminded of what Scripture says and proclaim that alone. I'm reminded often of what I heard Vance Havner say many years ago:

> We don't need to be in the novelty shop, as much as we need to be in the antique shop, where we find the old truths of God's Word. We don't need something new today half as much as we need something so old that it would be new if anybody tried it."[3]

A mantra of our day is, "We need something new, something culturally relevant, something that appeals to people's felt needs." No, what we need are men who will teach other men the historical doctrines of the church and biblical ministry. This leads us to further application of this principle.

Applying the Principle

I have been fascinated by this principle for several years. As I have meditated upon it, it has occurred to me that the "three year" pattern works out quite well in practical application. In modern terms, this translates to thirty-six months, which in-turn roughly equals a four-year degree program (assuming only nine months per year). This would seem, then, to be the absolute bare minimum for a man's training for ministry.

Sadly, this kind of thinking is becoming more "archaic" nowadays, as people of more modern thinking prevail. As mentioned earlier, more and more people (both men and women) are taking on leadership roles for themselves with no divine calling, training, or accountability to anyone (see chapter 14 for a study of the "Call to Ministry" and related issues). Also quite common is the two or three year "Bible Institute" that claims to prepare men (and again women) for leadership. Does this not seem woefully inadequate when we weigh it against the biblical precedents of narrow qualifications and intense training? After all, the "three years" spoken of in Scripture did not have either Christmas break or Spring break, not to mention three months off in the summer. For all practical purposes, those years were around the clock training, with the added daily pressures of persecution and threat of death.

If we might go one step further, while Bible colleges and seminaries certainly have their place, should they be the sole locations of such training? Let us remember, Paul was writing specifically to a *pastor*, not a seminary professor. He did, in fact, *command* that pastors train men for ministry. What, then, are we doing in our churches today to train men? Are we training them in any way before we ship them off to "school"? Do we provide an internship for them after they graduate to give them more practical experience? Or to be real "novel," how many churches could channel their resources into starting a Pastor's College, as did Charles Spurgeon? That would, in fact, be the ideal and most biblical approach to training men. What better method could there be other than training men *in* the church *for* the church? In the next chapter, we will build upon this very principle by offering a fascinating model from history.

NOTES

[1] Dean Alford in *Wuest's Word Studies* (Eerdmans), electronic edition, note on 1 Timothy 3:2.

[2] *Jon Courson's Application Commentary*, New Testament (Thomas Nelson, 2003), electronic edition, note on 2 Timothy 2:2.

[3] Interview with Vance Havner by Dennis Hester; October 1982.

36

A Model for Teaching Faithful Men[*]

2 Timothy 2:2

And the things that thou hast heard of me among many witnesses, the same commit thou to faithful men, who shall be able to teach others also.

In September of 2009, I had the opportunity to teach two courses at the Haiti Bible Institute.[1] That ministry prompted the article in our previous chapter, "Teaching Faithful Men," based upon 2 Timothy 2:2. In September of the following year, I was able to return to Haiti and teach again, which in part prompted this second article. The first ended with the thought that while Bible colleges and seminaries certainly have their place, they should not be the sole locations of such training, that churches should, indeed, be doing this as well. This second chapter goes a step further to submit how such a ministry, whether in the church or separate from it, should really operate in its philosophy of education and even curriculum.

To give credit where it is due, the other part of the impetus to this follow-up was Ian Murray's "Introduction" to Charles Spurgeon's classic book, *An All-Round Ministry*.[2] The vast majority of Christians today (and I fear many pastors) are totally unaware that from 1855 to 1891 Spurgeon (along with others who aided him) trained 845 men for the Gospel ministry in his Pastor's College, a ministry that was based firmly in the Local Church. Spurgeon was strong in his understanding of this principle, writing of our text:

> The Church at Antioch had its foreign mission; for it sent forth Paul and Barnabas on a missionary tour [Acts 13:3]. They had their Pastor's College; for Paul says to Timothy, "The things that thou hast heard of me among many witnesses, the same commit thou to faithful men, who shall be able to teach others also."[3]

So essential was the College that Spurgeon—who as the pastor was "also the president of the College"[4]—wrote that it had

> become the most important of all the Institutions connected with the Church at the Metropolitan Tabernacle. The place which it once held

---

* This chapter was originally TOTT issue 65, December 2010.

in the heart of the pastor alone, it now holds in the hearts of the elders and deacons with him. It is indeed a part of the whole Church.[5]

Many of the men trained at the College went out to plant new churches, or serve in existing ones, not only in England but throughout the world, *including America!*[6]

What especially caught my attention in Murray's Introduction, however, was that many people asked Spurgeon why he even started his College, since there were already several Nonconformist (Baptist being one) colleges in existence. He was even criticized for this. Many insisted that "the formation of a new college would excite jealousies and divisions in the denomination."[7]

Spurgeon's response was one we today should truly take to heart and use to analyze what we are doing (and *not* doing). In essence, Murray states, Spurgeon's response was that "there were no colleges which met the needs as he saw them." As Murray goes on to detail, Spurgeon differed in four essential respects. After reading that explanation and then doing further research, I would humbly offer the following using my own heading titles in place of Murray's and several additional quotations. Did Spurgeon leave behind a *biblical model* for us today? I hope these principles will stir Christian leaders to reevaluate what our education philosophy and teaching emphasis should be in training men for ministry.

Definite Calling

As noted back in chapter 14 ("Is There a So-Called 'Call' to Ministry?"), the popular notion is, "There's no such thing as God's 'inward call' to the ministry; that whole concept is nothing more than a person's subjective feeling. Anyone can be in the ministry simply if they choose to be." But as we then clearly demonstrated, both by biblical doctrine and precedent, God does, in fact, call men specifically and inwardly to ministry. Since Spurgeon's ministry is our focus here, we note again what he "hammered" into the minds of his students:

> In order to [be] a true call to the ministry there must be an irresistible, overwhelming craving and raging thirst for telling to others what God has done to our own souls. . . . "Do not enter the ministry *if you can help it*," was the deeply sage advice of a divine to one who sought his judgment. If any student in this room could be content to be a newspaper editor, or lawyer, or a grocer, or a farmer, or a doctor, or a senator, or a king, in the name of heaven and earth let him go his way; he is not the man in whom dwells the Spirit of God in its fulness, for a man so filled with God would utterly weary of any pursuit but that for which his inmost soul pants. . . .

> This desire should be one which *continues with us*, a passion which bears the test of trial, a longing from which it is quite impossible for us to escape, though we may have tried to do so; a desire, in fact, which grows more intense by the lapse of years, until it becomes a yearning, a pining, a famishing to proclaim the Word.[8]

While such teaching is shrugged off nowadays, it was at the very center of Spurgeon's thinking when it came not only to *training* men for ministry but even *admitting* them into the Pastor's College in the first place. This was, in fact, the first and foremost prerequisite:

> His call to the ministry is the first thing inquired into, and if it be not thought clear, the applicant is declined. Mistakes are doubtless made, for we are very fallible, but these do not arise from want of intense desire to help forward the chosen men, and to reject the incompetent and uncalled.[9]

Is this the first step schools use nowadays to admit men into their programs? Has any school in recent days actually declined a candidate admittance as did Spurgeon? He wrote more on this critical principle:

> It has often been a hard task for me to discourage a hopeful young brother who has applied for admission to the College. My heart has always leaned to the kindest side, but duty to the churches has compelled me to judge with severe discrimination. After hearing what the candidate has had to say, having read his testimonials and seen his replies to questions, when I have felt convinced that the Lord has not called him, I have been obliged to tell him so.[10]

> Certain of our charitable neighbors accuse us of having "a parson manufactory" here, but the charge is not true at all. We never tried to make a minister, and should fail if we did; we receive none into the College but those who profess to be ministers already. It would be nearer the truth if they called me a parson killer, for a goodly number of beginners have received their quietus from me; and I have the fullest ease of conscience in reflecting upon what I have so done.[11]

He goes on in the pages that follow the second quotation above to cite several examples of men who were turned down for admission for one reason or another. Such an idea would be appalling to most today. It would be counted as judgmental and even unloving. But Spurgeon was more concerned about his duty to Christ than he was popular opinion. Thus, we humbly submit, the *call* must be at the *core* of our theological schools.

Doctrinal Curriculum

While one will nowadays see courses offered in "Sunday School Administration," "How to Do a Puppet Ministry," and others, such was not the emphasis in the Pastor's College. Consider this course of study:

> The studies embrace the English language, Mathematics, Logic and Natural Philosophy, Intellectual and Moral Philosophy, Latin, Greek and Hebrew, Biblical Literature, Systematic Theology, which is always Calvinistic, and Homiletics. The studies on which special stress seem to be laid, are Mathematics, Logic, and Calvinistic Theology.[12]

That list does, indeed, form a core curriculum. It is a balanced blend of the elements of Classical education and strong Theology with the latter being the predominant emphasis, for we read again:

> Let theology, in a word, be the principal study of the professed teacher of theology, and all other sources of information and mental improvement as may become subservient to this, placed within their reach. . . . We have become daily more and more impressed with the conviction that theology should be the principal subject for instruction in a Theological College, and that a diversified course, of all other studies, prepares the young minister to enter upon his office in the full vigor of his mental powers, and with a capacity for continuing his research into all subjects that may at any time contribute to his own principal design.[13]

Tragically, we see today a continuing decline in a strong theological foundation in many schools (not to mention the biblical languages). In others where it does exist, it is sometimes tainted by popular thinking. In Spurgeon's day, Latitudinarianism was still a concern. Arising in the Church of England in the latter part of the 17th-century, the Latitudinarians were steeped in Plato, sympathetic with Arminians, felt that matters of doctrine were of little importance, emphasized "an intuitive consciousness of God," and fostered liberalism and a social gospel. Does not all that sound familiar? Spurgeon, therefore told his students:

> In the Pastors' College definite doctrines are held and taught. We hold by the doctrines of grace and the old orthodox faith, and have no sympathy with the countless theological novelties of the present day, which are novelties only in outward form: in substance they are repetitions of errors exploded long ago. Our standing in doctrinal matters is well known, and we make no profession of latitudinarian charity, yet we find no failure in the number of earnest

spirits who rally to our standard, believing that in truth alone can true freedom be found.[14]

Those are powerful words in light of the atmosphere and tolerance of our day. Also unlike our day, Spurgeon had no problem "naming names," that is, pointing out false teachers by name:

> We endeavor to teach the Scriptures, but, as everybody else claims to do the same, and we wish to be known and read of all men, we say distinctly that the theology of the Pastors' College is Puritanic. We know nothing of the new *ologies*; we stand by the old ways. The improvements brought forth by what is called "modern thought" we regard with suspicion, and believe them to be, at best, dilutions of the truth, and most of them old, rusted heresies, tinkered up again, and sent abroad with a new face put upon them, to repeat the mischief which they wrought in ages past. We are old-fashioned enough to prefer Manton to Maurice, Charnock to Robertson, and Owen to Voysey. both our experience and our reading of the Scriptures confirm us in the belief of the unfashionable doctrines of grace.[15]

In contrast to the great Puritans Thomas Manton, Steven Charnock, and John Owen, the church of Spurgeon's day was plagued with more popular voices. Anglican F. D. Maurice (1805–1872) was a "Christian Socialist." F. W. Robertson (1816–1853), while an evangelical, "great thinker, and a prompter of thought in other men," Spurgeon wrote, had to be "read with discretion" because his "doctrinal vagaries [were] well known."[16] Worse was Charles Voysey (1828–1912), who was condemned for heresy—such as denying the doctrine of eternal punishment—and went on to found the Theist Church of London.

Do we not, indeed, have our own versions of such men in today's church? And it was precisely because of the existence of such men that Spurgeon made the historic doctrines of the faith the core of the curriculum of his school. Is that what we are doing? Let us remember, as Spurgeon reminds us:

> Believing the grand doctrines of grace to be the natural accompaniments of the fundamental evangelical truth of redemption by the blood of Jesus, we hold and teach them, not only in our ministry to the masses, but in the more select instruction of the class room. . . . Our Lord has given us no permission to be liberal with what is none of ours. We are to give an account of every truth with which we are put in trust.[17]

Dogmatic Credo

The typical approach to teaching in our day addresses students using phrases such as: "What do you think this verse says?" Or, "Let's compare the various viewpoints and find common ground." Or, "Let's break up into groups and discuss the Scripture writer's intent and message and look for a consensus." Or, "Each of you must ultimately choose for yourself what this text means or is saying to you." While such disastrous drivel is the norm in our post-modern culture, this was the polar opposite of Spurgeon's teaching philosophy at the College:

> The College started with a definite doctrinal basis. I never affected to leave great questions as moot points to be discussed in the Hall, and believed or not believed, as might be the fashion of the hour. The creed of the College is well known, and we invite none to enter who do not accept it. The doctrines of grace, coupled with a firm belief in human responsibility, are held with intense conviction, and those who do not receive them would not find themselves at home within our walls. The Lord has sent us tutors who are lovers of sound doctrine, and zealous for the truth. No uncertain sound has been given forth at any time, and we would sooner close the house than have it so. Heresy in colleges means false doctrine throughout the churches: to defile the fountain is to pollute the streams. Hesitancy which might be tolerated in an ordinary minister would utterly disqualify a teacher of teachers. The experiment of Doddridge ought to satisfy all godly men, that colleges without dogmatic evangelical teaching are more likely to be seminaries of Socinianism than schools of the prophets. Old Puritanic theology has been heartily accepted by those received into our College, and on leaving it they have almost with one consent remained faithful to that which they have received. The men are before the public in every part of the country, and their testimony is well known.[18]

The "experiment" Spurgeon refers to is that of Nonconformist Philip Doddridge (1702–1751), who headed the famous Daventry Academy. While having many great qualities and authoring such classics as *The Rise and Progress of Religion in the Soul*, he had a fatal flaw in his teaching philosophy. Spurgeon explains:

> We remember the experiment of Daventry, under that eminently godly man, Dr. Doddridge, and we are not inclined to try the like under any circumstances. That worthy man did not dogmatize to the "dear young men" who came to his college, but adopted the plan of letting them hear the argument upon each side that they might select

for themselves. The result was as disastrous as if error had been taught, for nothing is worse than lukewarmness as to truth. Dissent became enervated with a fainthearted liberalism, and we had a generation of Socinians, under whom Nonconformity almost expired. Both General and Particular Baptists have had enough of this evil leaven, and we are not inclined to put it again into the people's bread.[19]

How serious is such a teaching method? It led to "a generation of Socinians." Socinianism was total apostasy; it rejected the pre-existence of Christ, the propitiatory view of atonement, and put a limitation on God's omniscience, all of which are still with us today. Worse, as we continue to entertain the same teaching philosophy, error is further propagated. We need the same authoritative teaching style that Spurgeon proved to be the only true method:

Calvinistic theology is dogmatically taught. We mean not dogmatic in the offensive sense of that term; but as the undoubted teaching of the Word of God. . . . The cross is the center of our system. "To this I hold, and by this I am upheld." is our motto. This is our stand-point from which we judge all things. We have no sympathy with any modern concealment or perversion of great gospel truths. We prefer the Puritan to modern divinity. From our inmost souls we loathe all mystic and rationalistic obstructions of the plain and full-orbed doctrines of grace, and foremost of all of justification by the righteousness of Christ and atonement by his blood.[20]

Dynamic Communication

The final way Spurgeon's College differed from the status quo was the priority of producing *preachers*:

It has appeared to us that the chief aim should be to train preachers and pastors rather than scholars and masters of arts. Let them be scholars if they can, but preachers first of all, and scholars only in order to become preachers.[21]

Most of the schools in Spurgeon's day, in fact, simply did not prepare men for preaching. They were plagued with "the curse of the idolatry of intellect" and were more concerned about "the fear of losing intellectual respectability"[22] than they were of falling short of biblical standards for building expositors. If I may be so bold, we have fallen into the same trap today with our obsession with so-called "accreditation" and other compromises with a humanistic world system. Many schools teach the same marketing, psychology, sociology, and other courses that secular schools teach so that we might all be "socially relevant." But that is not what God wants from the leaders He calls. He wants preachers of the Truth.

Let us not be swayed by the nay-sayers who insist, "Ah, such an approach can't work." There were such in Spurgeon's day. Perhaps Spurgeon himself had a doubt or two when he wrote during the fourteenth year of the College, "When it was commenced I had not even a remote idea of whereunto it would grow."[23]

Is it not high time that we step back and take a close look at *what* our schools are teaching and *why* they are teaching it? Is there a truly biblical model?

NOTES

[1] The Haiti Bible Institute was founded in 2009 by *On Target Ministries* (http://www.ontargetministry.org/), which is committed to the 2 Tim. 2:2 model by serving God through international education.

[2] Banner of Truth Trust, 1960, 1986. This work is a compilation of the 12 best of the 27 total addresses Spurgeon delivered at the Pastor's College annual Conference from 1865 to 1891.

[3] *The Sword and the Trowel* (electronic edition, Ages Software), Vol. 1, April 1865, 66.

[4] *The Sword and the Trowel*, Vol. 1, March 1886, 251.

[5] *The Sword and the Trowel*, Vol. 1, May 1865, 76.

[6] *The Sword and the Trowel*, Vol. 3, April 1873, 330.

[7] *The Sword and the Trowel*, Vol. 1, January 1866, 213.

[8] *Lectures To My Students* (Zondervan, 1974), 26–28.

[9] *The Sword and the Trowel*, Vol. 3, April 1873, 325.

[10] *Autobiography* (electronic ed., Ages Software), Vol. 3, Ch. 69, 114.

[11] *Lectures to My Students*, 35.

[12] *The Sword and the Trowel*, Vol. 2, July 1869, 317.

[13] *The Sword and the Trowel*, Vol. 1, March 1886, 248–49.

[14] *Lectures to My Students* (electronic ed., Ages Software), Vol. 1, 7–8.

[15] *Autobiography*, Vol. 2, Ch. 46, 163.

[16] *Lectures to My Students* (electronic ed.), Vol. 4, 318.

[17] *Lectures to My Students* (electronic ed.), Vol. 2, 6–7.

[18] *The Sword and the Trowel*, Vol. 6, May 1881, 423.

[19] *The Sword and the Trowel*, Vol. 5, May 1877, 96.

[20] *The Sword and the Trowel*, Vol. 1, March 1886, 249.

[21] *The Sword and the Trowel*, Vol. 3, April 1871, 317.

[22] Murray's "Introduction" to *An All-round Ministry*, xv.

[23] *The Sword and the Trowel*, Vol. 2, April 1870, 435.

Charles H. Spurgeon dared to say, "Many would unite church and stage, cards and prayer, dancing and sacraments. If we are powerless to stem this torrent, we can at least warn men of its existence and entreat them to stay out of it." A. J. Gordon dared to say, "The notion having grown up that we must entertain men in order to win them to Christ, every invention for world-pleasing which human ingenuity can devise has been brought forward till the churches have been turned into play-houses and there is hardly a carnal amusement that can be named from billiards to dancing which does not find a nesting place in Christian sanctuaries. Is it then Pharisaism or pessimism . . . to predict that at the present fearful rate of progress, the close of this [twentieth] century may see the Protestant church as completely assimilated to fourth-century paganism?" We smile at that today, but we are not overstocked with Spurgeons and Gordons.

Vance Havner
Pepper and Salt, p. 115

37

Forsaking the Assembly*

Hebrews 10:25

Not forsaking the assembling of ourselves together, as the manner of some is; but exhorting one another: and so much the more, as ye see the day approaching.

This "tough text" is one that has been close to my heart for most of my 38 years of ministry.* It has also been a cause of great burden—not the text itself, of course, but rather its implications and the lack of impact those implications seem to have on many believers and, sadly, even some pastors.

Dear Christian Friend, I would like to speak to you from two perspectives. First, I would speak from a *teacher's mind*, carefully examining the text exegetically and historically, for that must always come first. Second, however, I want to speak to you from a *pastor's heart*, sharing with you the profound implications of this principle both in the Christian's experience and the life of the church.

From a Teacher's Mind

While the recipients of Hebrews has been debated, there is no doubt that the audience was predominantly Jewish. The chief point of the letter—which reads more like a sermon than a letter—is the superiority of Christ (note the repetition of "better" throughout) over the levitical system. It is devoid of all things Gentile and is aimed solely at Jewish Christians to encourage them not to return to the old system, a system that has been rendered null and void because of the fulfillments of it in Christ.

Turning to our text, then, there was for some reason a tendency among these Jewish believers to neglect meeting together for worship. There have been several theories offered as to what this reason was. Perhaps they didn't think it was important, perhaps it was due to apostasy, or perhaps they simply had no interest in it.

One strong possibility was that they were dissatisfied with other church members. While the congregations were mostly Jewish, there would have been at least some Gentiles, since the "middle wall of partition" between them had been "broken down" by Christ (Eph. 2:14). The Jews

---

* This chapter was originally TOTT issue 53, December 2009.

had always been exclusive, however, and despised other nations. It's quite possible that, as Calvin puts it, "the Gentiles were a new and unwonted addition to the Church,"[1] causing many to forsake attendance altogether.

Another strong possibility—and we think it possible that more than one of these reasons existed—was they simply feared persecution. Persecution is referred to, in fact, further down in the passage (vv. 32–39; 12:4). It is reasonable to assume that this applied even to meetings in house churches, as the Romans, like all dictatorships, were suspicious of private meetings.

The challenge, therefore, given to these believers was not to **[forsake] the assembling of [them]selves together**. The language here is significant.

First, **assembling** is *episunagōgē*. The root *sunagōgē* (assembly or congregation), of course, was the name of the Jewish gathering, which is transliterated directly into the English *synagogue*. Many Bible students believe that it was during the Babylonian captivity that the system of synagogue worship was instituted due to the absence of the Temple.

Added to this root, then, is the preposition *epi*, which fundamentally differentiates this gathering from the strictly Jewish one. As Greek authority Spiros Zodhiates submits: "The preposition *epi*, "to," must refer to Christ Himself as the one to whom this assembly was attached. Thus it would have the meaning of not betraying one's attachment to Jesus Christ and other believers, not avoiding one's own personal responsibility as part of the body of Christ."[2]

That picture is all the more evident in the only other New Testament occurrence of *episunagōgē*: "Now we beseech you, brethren, by the coming of our Lord Jesus Christ, and by our *gathering together* unto him" (2 Thes. 2:1; emphasis added). This unique word, then, emphasizes that the Christian congregation is just that, a gathering of believers in Jesus Christ for the express purpose of worship, fellowship, and learning with Him at the center.

Second, is the word **forsaking**, *egkataleipō,*. While the root *leipō* means "to leave or forsake," *kataleipō* is stronger, as in "leave down, that is, leave behind or remaining." Adding the prefix *eg* (or *en*), "in, at, or by," further strengthens the word to its fullest: "to leave behind in any place or state . . . to leave in the lurch."[3]

That expression "to leave in the lurch" is itself an interesting one. It "alludes to a 16th-century French dice game, *lourche,* where to incur a 'lurch' meant to be far behind the other players. It later was used in cribbage and other games, as well as being used in its present figurative sense by about 1600," as in, "Jane was angry enough to quit without giving notice, leaving her boss in the lurch" (*The American Heritage® Dictionary of Idioms*).

The strength of *egkataleipō* is further seen in some of its other New Testament occurrences. Paul uses it to describe Demas, who had once been an active partner in ministry (Col. 4:14; Phile. 24) but had now "forsaken" Paul (2 Tim. 4:10). Six verses later Paul goes on to write that as he sat in prison in Rome, everyone had deserted him; all had indeed left him in the lurch. Stronger still, this is also the word Matthew used of our Lord when He cried from the cross, "My God, my God, why hast thou forsaken me?" (Matt. 27:46).

We should also note that the construction of this verb in out text is the present participle, which expresses continuous or repeated action. There was, therefore, a continuing habit of staying away from the gathering of the church, a consistent pattern of forsaking the church.

So what does it mean to forsake the assembling of ourselves together in the local church? It means to abandon those who remain in the congregation, to leave them in the lurch. In light of the reasons for leaving noted earlier, the reason is actually irrelevant. Because of that truth, one commentator pulls no punches with his very first comment on this verse:

> One of the first indications of a lack of love toward God and the neighbor is for a Christian to stay away from the worship services. He forsakes the communal obligations of attending these meetings and displays the symptoms of selfishness and self-centeredness.[4]

Those are strong words, indeed, but words that need to be heard in our day. They lead us, in fact, to our second emphasis.

From a Pastor's Heart

Dear Christian Friend, this issue is not a minor one. On the contrary, this is an extremely serious matter that every true pastor is burdened by. Commenting on our text, R. Kent Hughes shares his pastor's heart when he writes:

> People have a thousand reasons to stay away from church. This is not a new problem. The early Jewish church had had a fall-off in attendance due to persecution, ostracism, apostasy, and arrogance. Today persecution and ostracism may not be our experience, but people find many other reasons to absent themselves from worship, not the least of which is laziness. But de-churched Christians have always been an aberration, as Cyprian, Augustine, Luther, Calvin, and the various classic confessions repeatedly affirm.[5]

John Gill is equally candid: "This evil practice arises sometimes from a vain conceit of being in no need of ordinances, and from an over love of the world."[6] Commentator and professor E. Schuyler English also effectively "meddles" into the life of such Christians: "Point out a man or a woman who does not desire communion with other Christians, and you are pointing to one whose spiritual condition is low and whose testimony for Christ is weak indeed."[7]

Speaking from my own heart, in all my years of ministry, I have never quite gotten past this oddity. I simply don't understand it. I have seen countless things come before church, proving that such attendance is not only not the priority but is also flippantly considered as "no big deal." I've seen Christians abandon church for any number of reasons. I could make a list, but such a list would go on *ad infinitum, ad nauseam*. It would be far better if we each examine ourselves to see where our priority lies. One I just can't resist mentioning, however, is the lady I once heard say, "Oh, I can't be at church tonight because I'm getting my hair done."

If I may also say from my heart, I lovingly submit that there is something seriously wrong with the Christian whose priority is not faithful, consistent attendance in the local church. I know that might sound intolerant—or even that most terrible of words "legalistic"—but such nonchalance about unfaithfulness is a staggering contradiction. What can possibly be more important than our attendance in the local church, where we worship, fellowship, and receive the essential nourishment of God's Word?

I would, therefore, offer seven reasons for **not forsaking the assembling of ourselves together, as the manner of some is.**

To Obey Christ

This is first and actually should be enough. We have seen in our text that such attendance is not to be neglected. To neglect it, therefore, to abandon it and "leave it in the lurch," is simple disobedience. Attendance in the local church is repeatedly assumed (Acts 2:42; 20:7; 1 Cor. 5:4; 11:17, 18, 20; 14:23; 16:2). While there will certainly be times of illness, the yearly vacation, or the unforeseen emergency that keeps us away from church, these are the few exceptions that establish the consistent rule (Latin, *exceptio probat regulum* [8]).

To Praise and Worship Our God

While the common attitude in our day is that the local church is a place for entertainment and the meeting of our "felt needs," it is on the contrary, first and foremost, the place for corporate worship.

David's words in that well known verse lay an Old Testament foundation: "I will dwell in the house of the LORD for ever" (Ps. 23:6b). The Hebrew behind "dwell" (*yāšab*) primarily means to sit (Gen. 27:19;

Ex. 11:5; 2 Sam. 19:8; etc.). Several other meanings include "to inhabit, endure, or stay," but the most common is "to dwell" (e.g., Lam. 5:19, "remainest").

Significantly, the Septuagint renders *yāšab* here, and elsewhere, as the Greek *katoikeō*, "to inhabit a house." Elsewhere (e.g. Ps. 102:12), *yāšab* is translated *menō*, which denotes remaining in one place, keeping an agreement, and remaining valid, as in a law. The clear truth in all this, then, is permanence, continually dwelling in a place. Does not David, therefore, teach us about attendance in corporate worship? He speaks of spending the rest of his life worshipping God in the Tabernacle. Should that not encourage and challenge us? R. Kent Hughes again writes:

> We meet Christ in a special way in corporate worship. It is true
> that a person does not have to go to church to be a Christian. He does
> not have to go home to be married either. But in both cases if he
> does not, he will have a very poor relationship.

To Hear the Word of God

One of the most important reasons for our consistent attendance in the local church is that it is here we receive the teaching of the Word of God. The primary reason the office gifts were given (Eph. 4:11) was "for the perfecting of the saints, for the work of the ministry, for the edifying of the body of Christ" (v. 12).

"Perfecting" translates *katartismos*, which occurs only here in the New Testament. The root *artismos* comes from the related word *artios* (English *artist*) and means suitable, complete, capable, sound. With the intensifying prefix *kata*, "according to," the meaning of *katartismos* is very instructive: "to put in order, restore, furnish, prepare, equip." It was, therefore, the responsibility of the "apostle" and "prophet" in that day and is the responsibility of the "evangelist" and "pastor-teacher" today to put in order, restore, furnish, prepare, and equip the saints.

I am reminded often of a military illustration. As soldiers are trained as a combat unit at a specific training facility, Christians are likewise trained in a specific place. What would be the result if soldiers were as unfaithful to their training sessions as some Christians are to the church? What would that do to the quality of the unit in both combat readiness and morale? Likewise, we are in a war, and we are not only *required* to be in training, but we should also *want* such training because of the ferocity of the war.

To illustrate another way, what if we were as unfaithful to our daily job as we are to the local church? How long would we have that job?

Consider David again: "Behold, I have longed after thy precepts" (Ps. 119:40a). In stark contrast to the common dismissing of church today,

David's use of the words "longed after" are most instructive. The Hebrew *tā'ab* appears only twice in the Old Testament, both of which are right here in Psalm 119. David declares in verse 174, "I have longed for thy salvation, O LORD; and thy law is my delight." A derivative (*ta'abâ*) occurs once more back in verse 20: "My soul breaketh for the longing that it hath unto thy judgments at all times." This word speaks of an intense hunger, and David was broken hearted when deprived of God's Word. How many of us are broken hearted when we can't be under the preaching and teaching of the Word? Mark it down: the consistent Christian is one who has an insatiable appetite for God's Word.

To Edify Yourself

Another critical reason for faithful church attendance is that of your personal edification. Returning to Ephesians 4:11–12, our Lord gave the office gifts not only "for the perfecting of the saints, for the work of the ministry," but also "for the edifying of the body of Christ." The Greek *oikodomē*, along with its other forms, is a compound word comprised of *oikos*, "house or dwelling," and *dōma*, "to build." While the entire body of Christ, of course, is in view here, individuals comprise that body, so each is vital to the structure, which in-turn can obviously be applied to the local church. No single building material is isolated from the rest in building a literal house; none is meant to stand alone. Likewise, it is vital that every believer be present for God's use in building.

If I may change analogies, I read of a pastor who visited a man who wasn't attending church very faithfully. It was a cold, winter day, so they sat by a fire and warmed themselves as they talked. To this irregular attendee the pastor said, "My friend, I don't see you at church on the Lord's Day. You seem to come only when it's convenient, or only when you feel like you need to come. You miss so very often . . . I wish you'd come all the time." The man didn't seem to be getting the message, so the pastor said, "Let me show you something." He then took the tongs from beside the fireplace, pulled open the screen, and began to separate all the coals so that none of them were touching each other. In a matter of moments, the blazing coals had all died out. "My friend," he said, "that is what's happening in your life. As soon as you isolate yourself, the fire goes out." Likewise, the Christian will not survive alone out in this world.

Commentator Lloyd J. Ogilvie puts it still another way: "We Christians are like short-lived radioactive isotopes; we have a very short half-life. Get us away from the worship of God with other saints and our radioactivity dissipates quickly and we lose our effective radiance."[9]

To Encourage Your Pastor

I can tell you from personal experience, there are few things that discourage and grieve a pastor more than seeing Christians who are sporadic in their attendance. Scripture calls him a shepherd, and like a literal shepherd he wonders where in the world his sheep are when they are absent from the fold. He is concerned because those sheep need nourishment but have wandered from the rich pasture where the food is waiting. He is concerned because there are predators just waiting for such a moment to pick off a wandering sheep that is completely oblivious to the danger. The biblical pastor spends the majority of his time in the Word of God so he can feed those sheep. So when they don't care to show up to hear what God has laid on his heart, it grieves his spirit. If I may confess, more than once I have thought, "What's the point in going on?" but I then remember that God simply demands our *faithfulness* (1 Cor. 4:2) not our success or even our attendance numbers.

To Encourage Other Believers

Many people feel they can worship God by being out in nature or by viewing a church service on television. But what of other believers? What about the other Christian soldiers in our company? Just as literal soldiers depend upon one another, so do we. We encourage each other in spiritual combat. We love, encourage, and protect each other. Those who just shrug this off by not "showing up" discourage the others that do. Consider this often quoted statement by Martin Luther: "At home, in my own house, there is no warmth or vigor in me, but in the church when the multitude is gathered together a fire is kindled in my heart and it breaks its way through."

To Be a Testimony to Others

I again have grieved when I've seen Christians forsake their responsibility of church attendance in such a way that unbelievers see it. I have seen many other things take precedence even though unbelievers at those times knew that the Christians involved missed church to be there. What message does that send? How is this a testimony of our commitment and love for Christ? Is our faith and spiritual life important only when it is convenient and doesn't interfere with our schedule? Is our church life just a satellite that revolves around everything else, or does everything else revolve around it? What is really at the core of our "universe"?

Finally, our text goes on to declare: **exhorting one another: and so much the more, as ye see the day approaching.** Which day is approaching? The views vary: death, the last judgment, the destruction of Jerusalem, heightened persecution, or Christ's Second Coming. While I lean toward one of the latter two (perhaps even a combination of the two), in the final analysis does it really matter in practice? The point is that whichever event is in view, that event is **approaching**. This is the Greek *eggizō*, "to bring near, to be at hand." Today we might say, "It's just around the next corner." In light of that impending day, then, we should be **exhorting one another** (*parakaleō*), that is, comforting, beseeching, admonishing, and even imploring one another in this area of faithfulness to the assembly. As one commentator submits:

> To neglect Christian meetings is to give up the encouragement and help of other Christians. We gather together to share our faith and to strengthen one another in the Lord. As we get closer to the day when Christ will return, we will face many spiritual struggles, and even times of persecution. Anti-Christian forces will grow in strength. Difficulties should never be excuses for missing church services. Rather, as difficulties arise, we should make an even greater effort to be faithful in attendance. (*Life Application Study Bible*)

Dear Christian Friend, is there any doubt as to the critical importance of faithful attendance in the local church?

NOTES

1 *Commentaries*, note on Heb. 10:25.

2 Spiros Zodhiates, *The Complete Word Study Dictionary: New Testament* (AMG Publishers), p. 640 (entry 1997).

3 Zodhiates, p. 499 (entry 1459)

4 William Hendrickson and Simon Kistemaker, *Baker's New Testament Commentary* (Baker, 1984), electronic edition, comment on Heb. 10:25.

5 R. Kent Hughes, *Preaching the Word: Hebrews, Volume 2, An Anchor For The Soul* (Crossway Books, 1993), electronic edition.

6 John Gill, *Exposition of the Old and New Testaments*, electronic edition, comment on Heb. 10:25.

7 E. Schuyler English, *Studies in the Epistle to the Hebrews* (Findlay, OH: Dunham Publishing Company, 1955), p. 315.

8 The often used expression "the exception proves the rule" is imprecise, "leading the unwary to think that any self-respecting rules must have an exception. What is meant is that the existence of an exception to a rule provides an opportunity to test the validity of a rule: Finding an exception to a rule enables us to define the rule more precisely, confirming its applicability to those items truly covered by the rule" (Eugene Ehrlich, *Amo, Amas, Amat and More* [Harper and Row,

Hudson Group, 1985], p. 121).

[9] Lloyd J. Ogilvie (Ed.), *The Preacher's Commentary* (Thomas Nelson, 1982-1992), electronic edition, note on Heb. 10:25.

The world depends on promotion, prestige, and the influence of money and important people. The Church depends on prayer, the power of the Spirit, humility, sacrifice, and service. The Church that imitates the world may seem to succeed in time, but it will turn to ashes in eternity. The Church in the book of Acts had none of the "secrets of success" that seem so important today. They owned no property; they had no influence in government; they had no treasury . . . ; their leaders were ordinary men without special education in the accepted schools; they had no attendance contests; they brought in no celebrities; and yet they turned the world upside down.

Warren Wiersbe
We Wise, pp. 49–50

38

Is There an "Age" of Accountability?[*]

Selected Texts

A pastor friend recently dropped me an email asking my position on the "age of accountability." This term refers to the concept that those who die before reaching an age at which time they can understand sin and salvation are automatically saved by God's grace and mercy. As I shared with my friend, this question is, indeed, one of those that opens the proverbial "can of worms," but it is one that arises often and one of great importance.

A typical argument against this concept is: "The only ones under the blood of Christ are those whom God has chosen before the foundation of the world. (Eph. 1:4)." While that is most certainly true, applying that here is little more than a straw man argument. How do we know, for example, that the more than one million babies murdered in this country every year by abortion are not elect?

On the other hand, we should also point out that Scripture does not explicitly state such an age by number. In other words, Scripture nowhere says, for example, "Each person is responsible at the age of 12." It is interesting that the age of 12 or 13 (Jewish sources are not unanimous) was the age at which the Jews identified a child as being "an adult." The consensus of opinion is that at 13 a boy become *bar mitzvah* (a son of the Law), that is, he was now mature enough and responsible to keep God's Law. It is, in fact, in keeping with that tradition we find the Lord Jesus in the Temple at the age of 12 (Lk. 2:42). All males of a mature age were required to appear in the Temple three times a year.

All this, however, is just that—tradition. There is no Scripture that states a specific age that a child is now mature. While an argument can be made for "puberty" as being this age—as a child is now self aware and conscious of impulses, motives, drives, attitudes, and so forth, and probably capable of discerning sinfulness—Scripture does not say that. Besides, every child matures differently, so one child will be accountable earlier or later than another.

It is because of just such ambiguity that I personally do not like the term "*age* of accountability," simply because there is no explicit age. I would submit, however, that there *is* a "*point* of accountability" and that

---

[*] This chapter was originally TOTT issue 54, January 2010.

point is different for each child. I do believe there is biblical precedent for this principle for four reasons.

David and His Son

The classic illustration, of course, is David in 2 Samuel 12:13–23. This passage recounts the death of the son born from David's adultery with Bathsheba. In mental agony David pleaded with God to spare the child, but God's judgment was final. No one could console or comfort him. He couldn't eat, sleep, or even get up. The lessons in this are, of course, numerous.

Like turning on a light switch, however, David's response to the child's death changed from inconsolable despair to joyful expectation. He knew that while that child could not come to him, he would one day go to that child. In other words, David knew he was going to heaven and knew that his child was there as well.

What made David's reaction even more significant was how surprised his attendants were at it. Why? Because it was the custom in the East to mourn and not even leave the deceased for three or even four days (cf. Jn. 11:17), and relatives and friends would bring food and clothing. But David didn't act that way. There was an obvious assurance that "to be absent from the body [is] to be present with the Lord" (2 Cor. 5:8).

I have not read a single compelling reason to doubt this obvious, unambiguous meaning. In fact, one writer who disagrees with the position presented here is really puzzling when he says that verse 23 simply means "David will someday die as his child did. The child will not return to him but he will go to the child. He is united with the child in the fact of death, which all humans must face."[1]   But we must remember that David is rejoicing in all this. Why would he be rejoicing in future death if he wasn't assured of heaven? More puzzling is that while the same writer goes on to say of verse 23, "The child was saved and went to be with the Lord and David would someday follow him as he goes into the presence of Christ upon the moment of his physical death," he then denies that this passage is a precedent for all other children. But we must ask, "How did David know the child was saved?" We would submit that it was because the child was, in fact, "innocent"—a term we will detail later—and that other parents can have the same assurance.

The beloved Puritan Matthew Henry, therefore, well brings out the comfort of verse 23:

> Godly parents have great reason to hope concerning their children that die in infancy that it is well with their souls in the other world; for the promise is to us and to our seed, which shall be

performed to those that do not put a bar in their own door, as infants do not. *Favores sunt ampliandi— Favours received should produce the hope of more.* God calls those his children that are born unto him; and, if they be his, he will save them. This may comfort us when our children are removed from us by death, they are better provided for, both in work and wealth, than they could have been in this world. We shall be with them shortly, to part no more.

We would also submit that David's rejoicing came from his deep theological understanding of God's mercy and grace. It is insisted by some that no person (including an infant) can go to heaven without receiving the message of Christ in the Gospel. But does not David's reaction indicate that he understood God's character in showing mercy to an "innocent" child? Is it not probable that God does, indeed, look upon an "innocent" infant with a special mercy and grace?

An Understanding of Sin

"Where there is no law there is no transgression" (Rom. 4:15), and "sin is not imputed when there is no law" (5:13). Therefore, how can a small child, especially an infant, understand sin? And if they cannot understand sin, it is not imputed to them, and they are therefore innocent. This is what is meant by "the point of accountability." If one has not reached the point of understanding sin, he cannot be held accountable for it. Some might object, "Ignorance is no excuse," but we are not implying that it is. As we will see in a moment, there is a great difference between *ignorance* and *innocence*. This leads to a related principle.

Hearing by Faith

Paul clearly proclaims that a key truth of salvation is that "faith cometh by *hearing* and *hearing* by the word of God" (Rom. 10:17, emphasis added). *Hearing* is the noun form of the Greek verb *akouō*, from which we get such words as *acoustics* (the science of sound). It not only means to hear in general (e.g., Matt. 2:3), but also to hear with attention (e.g., Mark 4:3, "hearken"), understanding (e.g., Mark 4:33), and even obedience (Lk. 6:47; 8:21; 11:28; Jas 1:21–25). In the Septuagint, for example, *akouō* is used to translate the Hebrew *sāma*, as in Genesis 3:17, where God said Adam "hearkened unto the voice of thy wife" (cf. Isa. 6:9–10).

A graphic example of this word appears in the Parable of the Rich Man and Lazarus (Lk. 16:19–31); when the rich man asked Abraham to send Lazarus back from the dead to tell his five brothers about the torment of hell, Abraham answered, "They have Moses and the prophets; let them hear them" (v. 29). His point was piercing. As he goes on to explain, if they would not hear (obey) God's Law as revealed, they would not be convinced by someone who rose from the dead. That truth is proven every day as people reject the resurrected Lord Jesus.

We, therefore, submit that since an infant cannot hear in this capacity, faith cannot come. As we know, even faith is a gift of God (Eph. 2:8; cf. Jn. 6:65; Acts 18:27; Phil. 1:29; see our chapter 9), but a gift that cannot be received is a gift that cannot be used. This leads us to one final key word.

The Meaning of "Innocent"

A word that is often overlooked, and even more often misunderstood, is the word *innocent*, which we've mentioned already. For example, Jeremiah 19:4 refers to how Judah had been drawn into pagan worship, including the practice of child sacrifice, having "filled this place [Valley of Hinnom] with the blood of innocents." The word *innocents* translates *nāqiy*, which means blameless, innocent, guiltless, free, exempted, clean (of hands), and even carries a judicial connotation. It is often attached to *blood*, as in Proverbs 6:17, where one of the seven abominations God hates are "hands that shed innocent blood" (the Hebrew *dām* refers to literal blood, whether animal or human, and is synonymous with "life"; Gen. 9:4). This paints the picture of an innocent person, a life that is clean and free from guilt. *Nāqiy* is, in fact, also used several times of someone being taken to court and found not guilty. We would submit, then, that this is a strong indication that such children, while not *unfallen*, are indeed *innocent*, that is, not guilty.

This should make it clear that there is a difference between *ignorance* and *innocence*. Ignorance is a choice, innocence is not. Ignorance is a lack of desire to know, innocence is an incapacity to know. It's, therefore, not a child's ignorance that is the issue, but rather his innocence.

We would submit then that there are, indeed, more than valid reasons to rest in the thought that children who die before a point where they can hear and understand the Gospel are under God's special mercy and grace.

NOTES

[1] Ken Matto, Scion of Zion Internet Ministry, www.scionofzion.com/age.htm. Another writer agrees and adds a troubling bit of pagan myth for whatever reason: "Gilgamesh's mourning for his dead companion Enkidu includes the statement that he 'has now gone to the fate of mankind,' and the hero is reminded by Siduri in the same epic that 'when the gods created mankind, they ordained death for him'" (*The IVP Bible Background Commentary*).

39

The Old Paths[*]

Jeremiah 6:16

Thus saith the Lord, Stand ye in the ways, and see, and ask for the old paths, where is the good way, and walk therein, and ye shall find rest for your souls. But they said, We will not walk therein.

On occasion, we address a text that while not a "tough text" exegetically or interpretively, it is a hard, or at least a challenging, text to face. Jeremiah 6:16 is one of those, and is one that is desperately needed in our day. I once heard a comedian quip to his audience, "Have you noticed that everybody nowadays talks about 'new and improved'? I guess that means what we already have is old and lousy." As we'll see, that is, indeed, characteristic of today's church.

About 60 years after the great prophet Isaiah's death, God called another man to the terribly difficult task of proclaiming God's Word to his own perverted generation on the eve of their national disaster. It was 626 BC, and that man was 20-year-old Jeremiah. His name is a transliteration of the Hebrew *yirmeyāh* and seems to mean "Jah will rise." Jeremiah's contemporaries included: Ezekiel, who preached in Babylon; Daniel, who stayed faithful in Nebuchadnezzar's own palace; Habakkuk and Zephaniah, who aided Jeremiah in Jerusalem; Nahum, who predicted the fall of Nineveh; and Obadiah, who proclaimed the ruin of Edom. Bible teacher Irving Jensen well says of Jeremiah: "Amid all the bright stars of Old Testament history, there is not a name that shines brighter than that of Jeremiah."[1] I agree and return to Jeremiah often for encouragement in the responsibilities, rigors, and even rejections that come with biblical ministry and the proclamation of Truth.

God called Jeremiah to minister during the darkest days of Judah's history. Following in the footsteps of Israel (the Northern Kingdom), the spiritual condition of Judah (the Southern Kingdom) was horrific. There was flagrant idol worship (cf. chap. 2), including the sacrificing of children to the god Molech in the Valley of Hinnom just outside Jerusalem. King Ahaz had set up much of this in Isaiah's day. The godly Hezekiah had led in reforms and clean-up (Isa. 36:7), but his son Manasseh, the most wicked

---

[*] This chapter was originally TOTT issue 55, February 2010, and was based upon a sermon by the author.

king in Judah's history, continued to promote these practices into Jeremiah's time (Jer. 7:31; 19:5; 32:35). Many also worshiped the "queen of heaven" (7:18; 44:19), a title for Ishtar, the Babylonian goddess of love and fertility, whose worship involved abominable obscenities (44:17–19, 25). While King Josiah sincerely tried to bring reform, sin was too deeply imbedded in the people's hearts. As 3:10 recounts, "Judah hath not turned unto me with her whole heart, but feignedly, saith the LORD." He led the nation in a shallow *revival* but not in a heart-changing *repentance*. The idols were *removed*, the temple *repaired*, and the worship of Jehovah *restored*, but the people had not *repented*, had not turned to the Lord with their whole heart and soul. The same is true today of much so-called "revival," which often is emotionally driven and temporary at best. Another striking characteristic appears in 5:31: "The prophets prophesy falsely, and the priests bear rule by their means; and my people love to have it so." Like today, people loved what was preached even though it was not true! People simply do not want to hear the Truth (2 Tim. 4:1–4).

That brings us to our text. Its setting is Jeremiah's vivid description of Jerusalem's impending destruction at the hands of the Babylonians, which would, in fact, come in Jeremiah's own lifetime. He repeatedly warns that repentance is the only hope for escaping ruin.

The picture here is a traveler who is not sure of the way to his destination. He comes to an intersection of several paths but does not know which one he should take. He asks another traveler for directions, who points him in the right direction and tells him which path is the right one. There are two key words here.

First, there is the word **way** (or **ways**). This is the Hebrew *derek*, which in the literal sense speaks of a "road" or "trodden path." Metaphorically, then, it refers to a marked-out pattern of life, as in Proverbs 3:6: "In all thy [patterns of life] acknowledge him, and he shall direct thy paths." Deuteronomy 8:6 likewise commands, "Thou shalt keep the commandments of the LORD thy God, to walk in his [patterns of life], and to fear him." We find other verses that speak of either righteous, pleasant, or wise patterns of life (2 Sam. 22:22; Prov. 3:17; 6:6), but also patterns that are evil and dark (1 Kings 22:52; Prov. 2:13).

Second, there is the word **paths**. This is *natiyb*, which is similar to *derek* in meaning and at times modifies it, as it does here and in Proverbs 12:18: "In the way of righteousness is life; and in the *pathway* [combination of both words] thereof there is no death." An extremely significant verse is Psalms 119:35: "Make me to go in the *path* of thy commandments; for therein do I delight."

So Jeremiah was pleading with the people to follow **the old** trodden and true **paths**. The word **old** is *'ôlām*. While this word is used more than

300 times to indicate indefinite continuation into the distant future, there are at least 20 instances where it refers to the past. Joshua 24:2, for example, looks back to "the flood in old time," indicating previous generations. Here, then, it looks back even farther in the sense of generations, as it also does later in Jeremiah 18:15: "Because my people hath forgotten me, they have burned incense to vanity, and they have caused them to stumble in their ways [*derek*] from the ancient ['*ōlām*] paths, to walk in paths [*naṭiyḇ*], in a way not cast up."

Jeremiah also begged the people to follow **the good way**. The word **good** is *ṭôḇ*, which has a huge range of meanings: "good, pleasant, beneficial, precious, delightful, right, well-pleasing, fruitful, morally correct, proper, convenient." The Creation narrative of Genesis 1 best expresses all these aspects of meaning when God declares each facet of His handiwork to be **good**. Likewise, Jeremiah called the people to this kind of behavior.

What, then, are the **old paths**? It is obvious that the "new (or modern) paths" the people were taking were that of apostasy and idolatry. We would submit, therefore, that the **old paths**, both then and now, consist of two basic principles: *doctrine* and *duty*.

The Old Path of Doctrine

Today's popular "new paths" are clearly and proudly marked with what amounts to flashing neon road signs: entertainment, pragmatism, relativism, tolerance, user-friendliness, seeker-sensitivity, self-fulfillment, personal prosperity, motivational speeches, pop-music, social relevancy, and others. We want the "new and improved." Are you old enough to remember the some 7,000 wonderfully quaint Burma-Shave road signs that existed from 1925–1963? They were replaced by huge, unsightly billboards because people were now moving too fast to see the old signs. Likewise, the profound truths of Christianity are being replaced by the monstrosities we have just listed.

Henry David Thoreau wrote in his *Journal* on September 2, 1851: "The more we know about the ancients, the more we find that they were like the moderns."[2] Likewise, I have no doubt that today's "new paths" had their 626 BC equivalents when God called Jeremiah. The people in that day no more wanted doctrine and absolute Truth than do most people in our day, and so replaced it with things they thought were better. Worse, both then and now, is that leadership carries much of the blame. As 5:31 again indicates, and as has been observed often by many, responsibility, accountability, liability, and other characteristics lie squarely on the shoulders of leadership.

Is it not odd that some in the secular world seem to know more about true leadership than do so-called "Christian leaders"? We have many in church leadership today, for example, who proudly say they are "managers," but as writer and management consultant Peter Drucker (1909–2005) well puts it: "Management is doing things right; leadership is doing the right things." Where are the men of God who are driven by what is biblically right instead of what is popular? Similarly, Warren Bennis (1925–), organizational consultant, author, and widely regarded pioneer of the field of leadership studies, writes: "The manager accepts the status quo; the leader challenges it." Likewise, where are the men of God today who are challenging what is fashionable and proclaiming the Truth? I was also struck by this statement by noted Harvard professor and author Robert Coles (1929–):

> Abraham Lincoln did not go to Gettysburg having commissioned a poll to find out what would sell in Gettysburg. There were no people with percentages for him, cautioning him about this group or that group or what they found in exit polls a year earlier. When will we have the courage of Lincoln?

Indeed, where are the true leaders in today's church? Where are men who instead of taking polls and organizing focus groups to see what people want in a church, proclaim Truth no matter what the reaction of people might be? Arthur W. Pink (1886–1952) put it well when he wrote:

> It is *natural* that the preacher should wish to please his hearers, but it is *spiritual* for him to desire and aim at the approbation of God. Nor can any man serve two masters. As the apostle expressly declared, "For if I yet pleased men, I should not be the servant of Christ" (Gal. 1:10): solemn words are those! How they condemn them whose chief aim is to preach to crowded churches. Yet what grace it requires to swim against the tide of public opinion, and preach that which is unacceptable to the natural man.[3]

We would, therefore, submit that there is nothing as foolish and destructive as the de-emphasis, downplaying, and disregard of doctrine and theology. I must admit that words truly fail to adequately express this principle. Without doctrine, there is no direction, no compass, no foundation, no core. Everything is shallow, surface, superficial, and even spiritually suicidal.

Many years ago I heard Vance Havner make this statement, and I have never forgotten it: "Evangelism is to Christianity what veins are to our bodies. You can cut Christianity anywhere and it will bleed evangelism. Evangelism is vascular; it's our business." I agree with that totally, but I would like to build on the analogy: *Doctrine is to Christianity what bone marrow is to the physical body.* Bone marrow produces blood cells: *red* cells carry oxygen and have a lifetime of 120 days; *white* cells are part of the immune system and have a lifetime of a few days to years; and *platelets* are involved in blood coagulation and have a lifetime of about nine days. All that is what doctrine does. Some "cells" sustain and enrich our lives, others keep us healthy from things that would harm us, and still others heal us when we are injured. Further, as cells have limited life spans, the "marrow of doctrine" continues the work of replacing the exhausted cells with fresh ones. While some today insist that "doctrine is not practical," such an idea is ludicrous, as we will see in more detail.

Another statement, this one by Martyn Lloyd-Jones, is also one that often comes to mind: "The most foolish of all Christians are those who dislike and decry the importance of Theology and teaching. Does not that explain why they fail in practice?"[4] Why are many Christians weak and shallow? Why do many fall to any new trend that comes along? Why do many fail to discern false teaching? Why do many fail to be consistent, faithful, and obedient? Why do many succumb to temptation? Why do many collapse when someone challenges their faith? *Because they do not know doctrine.* Sadly, they are not being taught doctrine by their pastors; they are not being taught that God's Word *alone* is Truth. They are being taught that Truth is relative and can be found in many other places. *That* is why they fail, and that is why Christianity continues to degenerate. The more modern *trends* that arise, the more biblical *truths* that are sacrificed on the Altar of Change. As Charles Spurgeon so well said: "The Holy Ghost rides in the chariot of Scripture, and not in the wagon of modern thought."[5] Far too many Christian leaders today are sitting in wagons instead of standing in chariots.

Contrary to popular thinking, doctrine and teaching are repeatedly, over and over again, emphasized in Scripture. The word *doctrine*, in fact, appears 45 times in the New Testament, 11 of which are in reference to Jesus' own ministry. Regarding Jesus' Sermon on the Mount, we read: "And it came to pass, when Jesus had ended these sayings, the people were astonished at his doctrine, For he taught them as one having authority, and not as the scribes" (Matt. 7:28, 29). We also read in Mark 4:2: "He taught them many things by parables, and . . . doctrine." Parables, we should remember, were not for the shallow hearer. Matthew 13:10–17 makes it clear that parables were for Jesus' true followers. If I may be so bold, the Joel Osteen crowd, and other such groups, don't get them. Those with hardened hearts cannot understand deep truth. J. Wallace Hamilton wisely said, "Our modern age is a pushover for the shallow and the shortcut. We want to change everything except the human heart."[6]

What, then, was the emphasis at the birth of the Church? Acts 2:42 documents this for us: "And they continued stedfastly in the apostles' doctrine and fellowship, and in breaking of bread, and in prayers." Is it not interesting that there is nothing here about cultural relevance, "appealing to seekers," or addressing "felt needs"? There's not even a single word about music here (or anywhere else in Acts), while today this has become by far the main emphasis and prominent feature.

Coming to the Epistles, a key verse is 1 Timothy 4:13: "Till I come, give attendance to reading, to exhortation, to doctrine." "Give attendance" translates *prosechō*, which was a nautical term for holding a ship in a direction, to sail onward. The idea, then, was "to hold on one's course." And what course was Timothy to hold? Not entertainment or "felt needs," rather on the Word of God alone. Specifically, Timothy's course was to be set on three emphases.

First, *reading*. The definite article ("the") appears before "reading," indicating the specific practice of public reading. Because of the scarcity of manuscripts, the practice of reading and explaining Scripture in the synagogue (Acts 15:21 and Luke 4:16–19) was carried over into the church (Col. 4:16; 1 Thess. 5:27). First and foremost, then, it is the reading of God's Word that should fill our churches.

Second, Timothy's course was to be set on *exhortation*. The Greek (*paraklēsis*) refers to an admonition or encouragement for the purpose of strengthening and establishing the believer in the faith (see Rom. 15:4; Phil. 2:1; Heb. 12:5; 13:22). In short, *exhortation* is the *application* of the *exposition* of Scripture. Expository preaching has all but vanished today, but exposition—which by its very nature will be doctrinal—is what will challenge God's people to obey the Truth of God's Word and warn them of the consequences of not doing so.

Third, Timothy's course was to be set on *doctrine*. There's that word again. To the ancient Greeks, *didaskalia* meant imparting information and later the teaching of skills. Another Greek word translated *doctrine* is *didachē*. While its basic meaning is also "teaching," it places more stress upon what is taught than does *didaskalia*. A noted Greek authority says this about *didachē*:

> Paul's use of *didachē* in Romans and 1 Corinthians may be contrasted with the usage found in the Pastoral Epistles. In the former epistles the scope of the word is left undefined, whereas in the Pastorals (cf. 2 Tim 4:2; Titus 1:9) *didachē* has probably become a given body of doctrine which is to be inculcated as such.[7]

The vital meaning of *didachē*, then, is that it speaks of what is being taught, that is, *a body of doctrine*. A key verse here is 2 Timothy 4:2, where we find the crucial significance of *didachē*. Writing to pastor Timothy, Paul declared with no ambiguity, apology, or alternative: "Preach the word; be instant in season, out of season; reprove, rebuke, exhort with all longsuffering and doctrine." He goes on in verses 3 and 4 to give a reason for this, namely, that the time will come when people will not put up with this and will seek teachers (false ones) who will humor them and tickle their ears to entertain them. In spite of such attitudes, however, Paul commands Timothy to preach anyway, *to change absolutely nothing in his method*. The modern idea that methods must change with the times is a lie.

Writing to *another* pastor, Paul declared the exact same crucial responsibility of leadership: "Holding fast the faithful word as he hath been taught, that he may be able by sound doctrine both to exhort and to convince the gainsayers" (Titus 1:9). To further cement this concept, Paul added to Timothy: "Hold fast the form of sound words, which thou hast heard of me, in faith and love which is in Christ Jesus" (2 Tim. 1:13). "Form" is *hupotupōsin*, which refers to "a pattern, sketch, or outline." Paul impresses upon Timothy that there is a definite pattern or outline of doctrine that he taught his student. Why? So Timothy would be thoroughly grounded in the Word of God and thereby able to discern false teaching. Only doctrine does that.

What was Timothy to do with such doctrine? He was to teach other men so that they could in-turn teach others (2 Tim. 2:2). We also read in 1 Timothy 4:6: "If thou put the brethren in remembrance of these things [i.e., "the word of God and prayer" in verse 5], thou shalt be a good minister of Jesus Christ, nourished up in the words of faith and of good doctrine, whereunto thou hast attained." It is doctrine and prayer-soaked teaching that nourishes and builds up God's people and is the epitome of a "good minister."

Neither is all this confined to the New Testament. The Old Testament repeatedly emphasizes the critical nature of truth, doctrine, and teaching. A fascinating incident appears in Isaiah 28:9. The corrupt prophets and priests were disgusted by Isaiah and asked with contempt: "Whom shall he teach knowledge? and whom shall he make to understand doctrine? them that are weaned from the milk, and drawn from the breasts?" In other words, who are you to treat us like children with endless repetition of the same things? We can think for ourselves." They went on in verse 10 to mimic that great man of God as if he were speaking baby talk: "For precept must be upon precept, precept upon precept; line upon line, line upon line; here a little, and there a little." Likewise, many today say, "We are too sophisticated, too well-read, too well-informed for old, out of date doctrine. We are modern and relevant."

With all that in mind, and many more verses we could cite, it continues to amaze me that something as clear as this mandate to teach doctrine to God's people can be so easily ignored by much of the church's leadership today. *Popular thought* has replaced the *principles of Truth*.

This leads us to consider for a moment the true **old paths** of theology that have also all but vanished. Throughout the history of the Church, every time the historic Doctrines of Sovereign Grace have been challenged, those challenges have been humiliatingly defeated. Pelagianism, Semi-Pelagianism, Arminianism, and a whole horde of other heresies have repeatedly arisen in an attempt to destroy, or at the very least dilute, the true Gospel, and every time they have been exposed for what they are. And so it is again today, but sadly with unprecedented success. The historic doctrines of the Reformation, which themselves are woven into the very fabric of Scripture, are under violent attack, and the attackers are winning. It is sad, indeed, not to mention catastrophic, that Arminianism, Pragmatism, and Relativism rule most of today's church with an iron hand. Things that throughout church history were recognized as heresy are now the *status quo* of orthodoxy. Where are the men who will return to the **old paths**?

Having considered the old path of *doctrine*, this leads us to consider briefly the other side of that coin.

The Old Path of Duty

Again, a popular mantra nowadays is that doctrine is not practical. Such statements demonstrate either a total ignorance of Scripture at best or deliberate deception for ulterior motive at worst. Doctrine is most certainly practical. A case in point (or actually cases) is the consistent practice of Paul in his Epistles of first presenting *doctrine* and then *duty*. In Ephesians, for example, chapters 1—3 deal with *doctrine* (our *riches* in Christ), while chapters 4—6 apply that doctrine to *duty* (our *responsibilities* in Christ).

Of the many duties of the Christian, for example, the chief is godliness. Salvation is a transforming experience, and the result of true conversion is godly behavior. Paul made this clear in Ephesians 2:10: "For we are his workmanship, created in Christ Jesus unto good works, which God hath before ordained that we should walk in them," which he then enumerates in chapters 4—6. He also made this clear to the Corinthians: "Therefore if any man be in Christ, he is a new creature: old things are passed away; behold, all things are become new" (2 Cor. 5:17).

It is doctrine, therefore, that results in the production of godly behavior. Writing again to Timothy, Paul declared:

> If any man teach otherwise, and consent not to wholesome words, even the words of our Lord Jesus Christ, and to the doctrine

which is according to godliness; He is proud, knowing nothing, but doting about questions and strifes of words, whereof cometh envy, strife, railings, evil surmisings, Perverse disputings of men of corrupt minds, and destitute of the truth, supposing that gain is godliness: from such withdraw thyself. (1 Tim. 6:3–6)

The principle here could not be clearer: *There is a definite correlation between truth and godliness and error and ungodliness.* In other words, right doctrine will produce right conduct, while wrong doctrine will produce wrong conduct. *Period.* This truth is not only biblical, but also logical. Why? Because how can we *live* right and *do* right unless we *know* right? And knowledge *always* comes by doctrine. Truth cannot be *discovered*; it must be *revealed.*

Another duty of doctrine is obedience. The modern teachings of easy-believism, no lordship, no repentance, and others are simply additional heresies that have further contributed to the decline of the true Christian message. *Obedience is implicit in the Gospel.* Our Lord made the issue clear: "If ye love me, keep my commandments. . . . If a man love me, he will keep my words . . . He that loveth me not keepeth not my sayings" (John 14:15, 23, 24). The Apostle John picked up on this and wrote in his first Epistle:

> Hereby we do know that we know him, if we keep his commandments. He that saith, I know him, and keepeth not his commandments, is a liar, and the truth is not in him. But whoso keepeth his word, in him verily is the love of God perfected: hereby know we that we are in him. He that saith he abideth in him ought himself also so to walk, even as he walked. (1 John 2:3–6).

All this is *duty* that flows from *doctrine.* Is duty the *cause* of salvation? Of course not, for that would be works salvation. But duty (like works) is most certainly the *result* of salvation and evidence of it.

Another aspect of such obedience is that it continues in the believer's life as he or she is exposed to the Word of God. One might know the Bible from cover to cover, be able to recite every doctrine, plumb every prophecy, and quote entire passages, but if there is little or no obedience, knowledge means nothing. Knowledge without application is less than worthless—it's actually destructive. As Paul told the Corinthians, "knowledge puffeth up, but [love] edifieth" (1 Cor. 8:1). Facts simply make us arrogant. It's the application that makes us humble.

For example, when you *read,* "Lie not to one another, seeing that ye have put off the old man with his deeds" (Col. 3:9), then *obey* it by never saying anything with the intent to deceive, embellish, or mislead. When you *read,* "The words of a talebearer are as wounds, and they go down into the innermost parts of the belly" (Prov. 26:22), as well as, "The tongue can no man tame; it is an unruly evil, full of deadly poison" (Jas. 3:5), then *obey* it by never gossiping and being careful about every word you say. As Paul commands, "Let your speech be alway with grace seasoned with salt, that ye may know how ye ought to answer every man" (Col. 4:6). When you *read*, "Now I beseech you, brethren, by the name of our Lord Jesus Christ, that ye all speak the same thing, and that there be no divisions among you; but that ye be perfectly joined together in the same mind and in the same judgment" (1 Cor. 1:10), along with, "Endeavouring to keep the unity of the Spirit in the bond of peace" (Eph. 4:3), then *obey* it by striving never to be the cause of a disunity or disharmony among God's people. Reading a command of God without obeying it is *rebellion*, and if we disobey God's Word, *chastisement* will come in one form or another. And the more knowledge we have the more responsible we are for it and the more serious is the disobeying of it.

We could continue, but I think the challenge is clear. Are we going to walk the new paths of contemporary thought, which change daily and result in our wandering aimlessly through the wilderness? I fear we have not only left the **old paths**, but have reseeded them to erase that they ever existed. Or are we going to clear away the overgrowth and walk the **old paths** that lead straight and true to the destination of glory? Let us, indeed, walk the **old paths**, the paths that were trodden by such men as, to name only a few: Gresham Machen (1881–1937), Charles Spurgeon (1834–92), J. C. Ryle (1816–1900), Robert Dabney (1820–1898), Charles Hodge (1797–1878), John Dagg (1794–1884), Jonathan Edwards (1703–1758), George Whitefield (1714–1770), John Owen (1616–1683), John Gill (1697–1771), John Calvin (1509–64), John Knox (1505–72), Ulrich Zwingli (1484–1531), Martin Luther (1483–1546), John Huss (1369–1415), Augustine (354–430), Athanasius (293–373), the Apostles, and our Lord and Savior Jesus Christ Himself.

My dear Christian Friend, let us walk the **old paths** for the praise of God's glory and **rest for [our] souls**, not the new ones that lead to ruin. Let us never say, as did the Judeans, **We will not walk therein**.

NOTES

[1] *Jensen's Survey of the Old Testament* (Moody), p. 336.

[2] *The Writings of Henry David Thoreau* (Houghton Mifflin and Company, 1906), Vol. 8, p. 444.

[3] "Why Doctrinal Preaching Declines" in Ian H. Murray, *The Life of Arthur W. Pink* (Banner of Truth, 1981), pp. 217–18.

[4] *Life in the Spirit* (Baker), pp. 142–143.

---

[5] *Metropolitan Tabernacles Pulpit*, Vol. 37 (1891), p. 233 (on Eph. 6:17).

[6] *The Thunder of Bare Feet: Sermons on Christian Social Concerns* (Fleming H. Revell, 1964), p. 69.

[7] Colin Brown (Ed.), *The New International Dictionary of New Testament Theology* (Zondervan, 1975), vol. 3, p. 770.

It is all too plainly apparent men are willing to forego the old for the sake of the new. But commonly it is found in theology that that which is true is not new, and that which is new is not true.

Robert Shindler in Charles Spurgeon's
The Sword and the Trowel (1887)

40

"We Band of Brothers"*

1 John 4:20–21

If a man say, I love God, and hateth his brother, he is a liar: for he that loveth not his brother whom he hath seen, how can he love God whom he hath not seen? And this commandment have we from him, That he who loveth God love his brother also.

Among the many things I read on a daily basis, both joy and profit come from reading a little Shakespeare.[1] Among my favorites of his plays is *Henry V*. In one of the most dramatic scenes in the history of English literature, Henry is speaking to his troops before the Battle of Agincourt in France (1415). The heavily armed French knights were standing between the English troops and Calais, the port city that Henry's band needed to reach for their return to England. War weary and suffering from dysentery, morale was low as the dwindling band gazed upon the overwhelming, four-to-one, force of the French knights. Rising to the occasion, however, King Henry stood before his men and spoke words of encouragement that rallied them together and carried them to victory. While the incident was true, Henry's speech is fiction, but it still serves to underscore the critical nature of unity in a fighting force, whether in medieval or modern times. Dubbed the St. Crispen's Day Speech, the core of it reads:

> This story shall the good man teach his son;
> And Crispin Crispian shall ne'er go by,
> From this day to the ending of the world,
> But we in it shall be rememberèd;
> *We few, we happy few, we band of brothers*;
> For he to-day that sheds his blood with me
> Shall be my brother; be he ne'er so vile,
> This day shall gentle his condition:
> And gentlemen in England now a-bed
> Shall think themselves accursed they were not here,
> And hold their manhoods cheap whiles any speaks
> That fought with us upon Saint Crispin's day.[2]

---

* This chapter was originally TOTT issue 56, March 2010, and was based upon a sermon by the author.

Interestingly, there seems to be no doubt that Shakespeare was, in fact, the first to use the term *band of brothers* in classical literature. It has appeared several times since, such as in Friedrich Schiller's play *Wilhelm Tell* in 1803. We find it often during the American Civil War. Stephen Douglas used it during the great Lincoln-Douglas debates. Frederick Douglass also used it in reference to his days in slavery. It even became a line in the second most popular war song of the South, "The Bonnie Blue Flag": "We are a band of brothers, / And native to the soil, / Fighting for our liberty, / With treasure, blood, and toil." The line also appears in the song "Hail Columbia," which many have referred to as America's first national anthem: "Firm, united, let us be, / Rallying round our Liberty; / As a band of brothers joined, / Peace and safety we shall find." Finally, contemporary (though late) historian Stephen Ambrose titled one of his many books *Band of Brothers*, the true story of the 101st Airborne's Easy Company, which fought with distinction at Normandy, the Battle of the Bulge, and on to the end of the war.

The theme in all this, of course, is a martial philosophy, where unity and unit cohesion is absolutely critical for victory. This should strike us all profoundly because Christians are, indeed, in a war, and unity among this *band of brothers* (and obviously *sisters*) is crucial. One of the most serious and devastating things that can occur in a church body is a lack of love among believers for one another. Most of us have seen, to one extent or another, a lack of love among believers, and it is a heartbreaking thing to witness. I would, therefore, like to share my heart with you on this grave matter.

The story is told of an infant girl in a small Midwestern town who had been critically injured and was in desperate need of a blood transfusion, but no one could be found who had her rare blood type. Finally it was discovered that her 7-year-old brother had the same type of blood. The doctor took him into his office, held the youngster on his knee, and said, "Son, your sister is very, very sick. Unless we can help her, I'm afraid the angels are going to take her to heaven. Are you willing to give blood to your baby sister?" The young boy's face turned pale, and his eyes widened with fright and uncertainty. He appeared to be in great mental agony, but after a minute or so he half-whispered, "Yes, I will." The physician smiled reassuringly and said, "That's a fine, boy; I knew you would." The transfusion took place, but the 7-year-old, watching the tube carrying the life-giving fluid to his sister, seemed apprehensive. The doctor said, "Don't be nervous, son. It will all be over before long." At that moment big tears welled up in the little boy's eyes. "Will I die pretty soon?" he asked. It then became apparent that he thought he was giving up his own life to save his baby sister![3]

THAT is love, the New Testament *agapē* (self-emptying self-sacrifice) love, the putting of someone else ahead of ourselves.

As the Apostle John recorded the words of our Lord Himself, "Greater love hath no man than this, that a man lay down his life for his friends" (Jn. 15:13). What does that say to us today, who are so concerned about our feelings, preferences, and sensitivities that such a thought would never occur to us? True love, however, lays down its life for another. Picking up on that truth and building on it, John wrote much about love for fellow believers in his first Epistle. In fact, he repeatedly mentions that *brotherly love is a major test of true Christianity*. It's tremendously significant that the word "commandment" (singular) appears seven times in John's first letter and the word "commandments" (plural) appears another seven, *and that each and every instance of the singular refers to the commandment to "love one another"* (2:7–8; 3:23; 4:21). In other words, this singular commandment is crucial to the Christian faith. Our feelings are irrelevant. What matters is that we truly love one another. As we will see, in fact, if we do not love each other, we do *not* love God and should therefore not even call ourselves Christians.

To put it another way, while John's *Gospel* was written that men might *believe* on Christ and have life (Jn. 20:31), his first *Epistle* was written that men might *know* they have that life (1 Jn. 5:13). It is for that reason that John records many tests of true Christian life, *not the least of which is love for fellow believers*. Here is a major test of true Christianity. Let us meditate on two thoughts: the *necessity* and *expression* of brotherly love.

The Necessity of Brotherly Love

John expressed the need for love among the brethren earlier in the epistle:

> In this the children of God are manifest, and the children of the devil: whosoever doeth not righteousness is not of God, neither he that loveth not his brother (3:10).

> We know that we have passed from death unto life, because we love the brethren. He that loveth not his brother abideth in death (3:14).

I have witnessed some professing Christians who simply can't stand certain individuals, who can't get along and love them. I've seen church fights and splits, and no word better describes this than *SIN*. This is not a minor issue, as we just read, rather a major problem. It reveals a heart of unrighteousness and even spiritual death.

John reiterates this truth in our main text with even more thundering force. He makes it crystal clear: if you say you love the *Lord*, but don't love your *brother*, it is a glaring contradiction. J. C. Metcalfe once wrote in *The Overcomer*:

> There is much more that can be said about this link between the birth from above and the resultant entry into a completely new attitude, in which love is the predominant feature. The general life of the evangelical section of the church is a strange commentary on all this. The bitterness, strife, criticism, petty rivalry, and discourtesy which we so often meet raise the question as to the validity of our claims, and the value of those religious qualities and practices we consider to be so important. Do not Paul's pungent words in the first three verses of 1 Corinthians 13 need to be read again and again, and rigidly and honestly applied in our own lives? Experiences, gifts, soundness of knowledge, and ministry, faith, charity, and even supreme sacrifice are swept aside, and love is enthroned alone.[4]

Each of those listed practices are important, but without love none of them mean anything; they are vain, empty, and worthless. What practical effects this love has upon every relationship of the believer within the family of God! If we truly love *God* and keep His commandments, then we *will* love the *children* of God. That is an absolute. If we do not love other brothers, we do not love God, no matter how much we think or claim we do.

Paul's command to the Romans is equally unavoidable: "Wherefore receive ye one another, as Christ also received us to the glory of God" (Rom. 15:7). What a rebuke to, as Metcalfe just put it, our "bitterness, strife, criticism, petty rivalry, and discourtesy." How this exposes our excuses for mistreating our brethren in Christ, either in deed or in word! To claim a love for God and at the same time to reject, despise, mistreat, and criticize those who are brethren in the same family is a staggering contradiction. It shows a heart of selfishness, self-centeredness, and sin.

A striking illustration of the operation of love for the brethren appears in the experience of the early church at Jerusalem (Acts 11). In one Spirit the believers there had been baptized into one body. Subsequently, Simon Peter was sent by God to a Gentile household in Caesarea. Accompanying him were some believing Jews from Jerusalem, and they were astonished that the Gentiles had also received the Holy Spirit. The apostles and brethren that were in Judea had heard what happened in the household of one who was not a Jew. Peter was summoned to Jerusalem to explain why he had gone into the home of a "Gentile dog" (as Gentiles were dubbed). These Jewish Christians were filled with prejudice, *but that was inexcusable*, for they all, Jew *and* Gentile, had experienced the love of God in Christ. Peter concluded his report to them with these words, "Forasmuch, then, as God gave them the same gift as He did unto us, who believed on the Lord Jesus Christ, what was I, that I could withstand God?" (v. 17). The love of God in those Christians at Jerusalem then manifested itself in brotherly love for the new members of God's family who were Gentiles: "When they heard these things, they held their peace, and glorified God, saying, Then hath God also to the Gentiles granted repentance unto life" (v. 18).

What an indictment that is! If 1st-century Jews and Gentiles could lay aside their differences, and even centuries of hatred, and get along with each other, is it not reasonable that we today can set aside our feelings and petty differences and love each other?

Now, we can partially understand why those Jewish believers were at first unwilling to accept as brethren the Gentiles in Caesarea—after all, they were new to the group, from different backgrounds, practiced different customs, possessed different gifts, and so forth. *But their reluctance was still inexcusable.* For believers to refuse to accept in Christian love others who know the same Savior, who have been regenerated by the same Holy Spirit, and who are members of the same body, is to disobey the direct command of our Lord and causes us to question seriously their love for the Lord.

As John mentions earlier in the letter, "We love him, because he first loved us" (4:19). What else can we do? Romans 5:5 declares, "The love of God is shed abroad in our hearts by the Holy Spirit who is given unto us." We also read, "The love of Christ constraineth us" (2 Cor. 5:14). Therefore, love for fellow believers is the evidence of a true love for God. Remember, *we are all in the same family.* This love is to be active toward all who are of the household of faith. They may be agreeable or disagreeable, but that is not the issue. The reason for loving them is that they are born of God, saved by the same Savior, members of the same body. In the very next verse after our text (5:1), John adds, "Whosoever believeth that Jesus is the Christ is born of God: and every one that loveth him that begat loveth him also that is begotten of him." If we truly love our Lord, our "Elder Brother" (Rom. 8:29), we will also love every one of His "siblings." Part of the "divine nature" that Peter refers to (2 Pet. 1:4) is that of love, and this love fellowships not only with God but with all who know Him. "For this is the love of God," John writes in 5:3, "that we keep His commandments: and His commandments are not burdensome." Brotherly love must of necessity be a reality in the Christian's life. Anything less is incongruous, contradictory, and, as we'll see, destructive.

The Expression of Brotherly Love

It's one thing to *say*, "Okay, I love my brother in Christ," but quite another to *show* it. Consider the love that Thomas Steward's brother William had for him. Thomas injured one of his eyes with a knife. A specialist decided that it should be removed to save the other. When the operation was over and he recovered from the anesthesia, it was discovered that the surgeon had blundered by removing the *good* eye, so rendering the young man totally blind. Undaunted, Thomas pursued his studies in law at McGill University in Montreal. He was able to do this only by the aid of his brother William, who read to him and accompanied him through all the different phases of college life. The blind brother came out at the head of his class, while the other came second.

How many of us would be willing to do that for a fellow Christian? How many of us are even willing to do something far less dramatic for a fellow believer? In short, *how many of us are willing to be second?* Are we willing to set ourselves aside for another?

First John 3:17–18 provides a practical illustration of how to express our love for others:

> But whoso hath this world's good, and seeth his brother have need, and shutteth up his bowels of compassion from him, how dwelleth the love of God in him? My little children, let us not love in word, neither in tongue; but in deed and in truth.

In other words, "Okay, here is a Christian who sees a fellow believer who has a physical or spiritual need, but won't do a single thing to help him, won't pray for him, won't encourage him, nothing. Just how in the world, then, does God's love dwell in this Christian?" The answer is obvious—it doesn't. Words are cheap, as the adage goes, and to say we love each other is empty unless we show it in our actions. *If we do not love our brother and treat him as God has treated us (Rom. 15:7), we do not love the Lord.* There are plenty of needs around—needs of the body, of the mind, and of the soul—and we are to meet those as we are able.

John's point in our text is just such empty profession, professing that which actually is not true in one's life. **If a man say, I love God**—there's the *profession*—but **hateth his brother**—there's the *reality*—**he is a liar.** Strong words, indeed. John doesn't say the man is embellishing or just mistaken, rather knowingly lying. Our orthodoxy can be impeccable, our doctrine even precise—we've plumbed every prophecy, expounded every truth, exegeted every verse—but we can still hate our Lord because we hate one of His people. John continues, **for he that loveth not his brother whom he hath seen, how can he love God whom he hath not seen?** In other words, if you can't love the one in front of you, you can't love the

One above you. Finally John writes, **And this commandment have we from him, That he who loveth God love his brother also.** It's automatic.

It's interesting that at least six verses begin in a similar way, three using the phrase, "If we say" (1:6, 8, 10), and three opening with the words, "He that saith" (2:4, 6, 9). Love and hatred are incompatible; they are opposites. Again, to say we love God while we hate another believer is to speak a lie (2:9; 3:15). *There is no middle ground here.* As a "son of thunder" (Mk. 3:17), John was not a soft spoken milquetoast, rather he thundered out the truth that if we say we love God and really believe that we love Him, but at the same time hate another, we are deceived. If we say we love the Lord, and we know that we do not love Him, we are a hypocrite and a liar. Likewise, if we say we love God, but don't love other believers, that too is hypocrisy. Why? Because those believers are part of Christ. *To mistreat a child of God is to mistreat the Lord Himself.*

We should interject here that this is one practical reason for observing the Lord's Table every Lord's Day (see chapter 3). Our hearts should be right not only with God but with other believers before we come to that table (cf. Matt. 5:23–24 and 1 Cor. 11:27–29).

The beloved Bible teacher Lehman Strauss writes of his own struggle with our text:

> Some years back I found it difficult to understand the words, "He that loveth not his brother whom he hath seen, how can he love God whom he hath not seen?" It was easier for me to love God, because all I ever knew about Him was good. But I could see the flaws and faults and unattractiveness in some of my brethren, and I found it harder to love them. Then one day God made it clear to me, from this verse, that if I do not love my brother, whose failures and unattractiveness I see, it proves the love of God is not in me. Actually the verse assumes the two to be an impossibility.[5]

Could John have made the principle any clearer that the way you treat your brother is the test as to whether or not you really love the Lord? Anything less cannot be justified or defended. Neither can it be tolerated in a church and should be dealt with via church discipline, for it sows discord in the body (cf. Prov. 6:14, 19; Matt. 18:15–17; 1 Cor. 5:11, "railer"; Rom. 16:17–20).

Such behavior is nowhere exposed more dramatically than in our speech, which is why James takes such great pains in dealing with the tongue:

> If any man among you seem to be religious, and bridleth not his tongue, but deceiveth his own heart, this man's religion is vain. (1:26)

Even so the tongue is a little member, and boasteth great things. Behold, how great a matter a little fire kindleth! And the tongue is a fire, a world of iniquity: so is the tongue among our members, that it defileth the whole body, and setteth on fire the course of nature; and it is set on fire of hell. (3:5, 6)

But the tongue can no man tame; it is an unruly evil, full of deadly poison. (3:8)

How careful we must be in *what* we say and *how* we say it. One of the most tragic stories I have ever read was of the young sailor who called his parents after his release from the military. He said he was bringing his buddy home to stay with him. "You see, Mom," he said, "my friend is pretty badly broken up. He was severely wounded and has only one leg, one arm, and one eye." After a little reflection, the mother said grudgingly, "Of course, Son, I guess he can stay with us a *little while.* Her voice, however, carried the message that they would not like to be burdened very long with such a severely handicapped fellow. Two days later they received a telegram from the admiral's office, saying their son had plunged to his death from a hotel window. When his body arrived for burial, his parents saw that he had only one arm, one leg, and one eye! The memory of her last conversation with him lingered with that mother for the rest of her life. She often cried out, "Why didn't I speak more carefully, more lovingly? If only I could take back those thoughtless words 'he can stay with us a *little while.*' But it is too late now!"[6]

That woman's lack of love in her *heart* showed forth in her *voice.* And once she said it, the damage was irreparably done, just by the inflection of her voice. I have never forgotten one illustration of evil words I heard decades ago: Trying to take back something we said is like tearing open a feather pillow and then catching every feather before it hits the floor. We need to be reminded often that *we can say things that can never be fixed.*

As always, the beloved Harry Ironside forces us to meditate on God's Truth:

> The way you treat your brother is the test as to whether or not you really love the Lord. "And this commandment have we from Him, that he who loveth God love his brother also." If you do not keep His commandments, you are not walking in obedience to His Word. "A new commandment I give unto you, That ye love one another; as I have loved you, that ye also love one another" (John 13:34). We need to remember the word, "Let us not love in word, neither in tongue; but in deed and in truth" (1 John 3:18). Think of this the next time you feel provoked with somebody. Say to yourself, "How often I have grieved the Holy Spirit, but He loves me still.

How often I have provoked the Lord, but He loves me still. How often I have dishonored the Father, but He loves me still. Blessed God, by Thy Holy Spirit let that same divine all-conquering love be shed abroad in my heart, that I may never think of myself but of others for whom Christ has died, and be ready to let myself out in devoted, loving service for their blessing." This is Christianity in practice.[7]

My greatest passion in ministry is orthodoxy and right doctrine. I am driven by the absolute Truth of God's Word and desire accurate exegesis and correct Theology at all times. But as vital as that is, it is nothing without love for God's people; it is empty and meaningless. Regardless of how many hours I might pour over a verse or even a single word to make sure I get it right, it is a waste if I don't love the ones to whom I preach.

Oh, how often "self" raises its ugly head! We are more concerned with our feelings, our views, and our opinions, than that of others and ultimately the edification of the Body of Christ itself. In short, we are more concerned with *self* than the *Body* and totally unconcerned with how what we say or do might affect the Body. Without *unity*, the Body cannot function properly, and without *love* there can be no unity.

Mark it down: *Not loving a brother in Christ is a direct attack on the Body of Christ and therefore Christ Himself.* Would any of us look at our hand and say, "I just hate this hand?" Of course not, because it's part of the Body. Likewise, we must love every member of the Body of Christ.

"But does this really mean *everybody*?" we might ask. "Aren't some Christians less lovable than others?" If we may answer this way, name one single person on earth who is lovable, including you or me. Not one. "We love [God] because He first loved us" (1 Jn. 4:19), and we now love each other for the same reason. We love each other because He loves us all.

J. N. Darby offers a good illustration:

> We cannot love a person without taking an interest in his children. But suppose the case of a father having three sons; I love two of them, this does not testify that I love their father, for if I did, I should love the three sons.[8]

Try that if you dare! What would happen if you said to a father, "Well, I sure like those two boys of yours, but I just can't stand that girl." How well will that go over? But that is *exactly* what we do if we do not love all believers and treat them accordingly; we have attacked *one* member of the family and therefore the *whole* family.

Dear Christian Friend, we are, indeed, a *band of brothers* (and *sisters*). The question is: *Are we acting like it?* I'll close with this encouragement and challenge from Theodore Epp, to which I could add nothing:

The love that we have for God is measured by the love that we have for other people. *The closer we walk with God, the sweeter will be our love for others.* Here is a good test: Select someone who is seemingly unlovable. Ask yourself, How can I get along with that person? How can I show my love to him?

We may disagree with the person over issues or principles, but that need not affect our love for him or her. It is not necessary that we agree on all points with another person before we can love him. In fact, it is a greater expression of the life of Christ within us to show kindness and consideration to those with whom we disagree on certain things. This can indeed be a real test of our love for God. Our love for other people will prove how much we love the Savior. Seek to love the unlovable; this is the acid test of our love for God.[9]

NOTES

[1] See my review of the book *Shakespeare for Everyone to Enjoy*, by David R. Brown, on our website.

[2] *Henry V* (IV.3.58–69, emphasis added)

[3] Recounted in *Windows on the Word: Illustrations from Our Daily Bread* (Radio Bible Class, 1984), pp. 91-92.

[4] Cited in Paul R. Van Gorder, *In the Family: Studies in First John* (Radio Bible Class, 1978), pp. 140-41.

[5] *The Epistles of John* (Loizeaux Bothers, 1962, 1971), p. 122.

[6] *Windows on the Word*, p. 92.

[7] *The Epistles of John* and Jude (Loizeaux Bothers, 1931, 1958), p. 181-82.

[8] *The Collected Writings Of J. N. Darby*, Expository No. 7, Volume 28.

[9] *Tests of Faith: Studies in the Epistles of John* (Back to the Bible, 1957), p. 88.

41

What is the Unpardonable Sin?[*]

Matthew 12:31–32

Wherefore I say unto you, all manner of sin and blasphemy shall be forgiven unto men: but the blasphemy against the Holy Ghost shall not be forgiven unto men. And whosoever speaketh a word against the Son of man, it shall be forgiven him: but whosoever speaketh against the Holy Ghost, it shall not be forgiven him, neither in this world, neither in the world to come.

"Few passages of Scripture," writes one expositor, "have been more misinterpreted and misunderstood than these two verses." That is an understatement. This article, therefore, is my humble attempt to examine the text, consider some biblical examples of this sin, and finally exhort us all in the practical application.

Examination of the Text

First, we should get a handle on the meaning of **blasphemy**. This is a direct transliteration of the Greek noun that appears here, *blasphēmia*. In secular Greek it (and the verb form *blasphemeō*) refer not only to "abusive speech" but also to "the strongest form of personal mockery and calumniation." They're almost equal, in fact, to *loidoria*, railing in harsh, insolent, and abusive speech[1] (note "reviled" for *blasphemeō* in Matt. 27:39).

What is most significant about these words is that while our English word means speaking evil of *God*, the Greek means speaking evil of *anyone*. We find, in fact, no less than six usages in the New Testament for the objects of blasphemy: God (1 Tim. 1:13; 2 Thess. 2:4; Rev. 13:5–6); Christ (Matt. 27:39; Mk. 15:29; Lk. 23:39); Holy Spirit (our text; cf. Mk. 3:28–29); the Word of God (1 Tim. 6:1; and Titus 2:5); angels (1st-century Gnostics despised the idea of angels, and Jude 8 and 2 Peter 2:10–11 seem to refer to such teachers who "speak evil of dignities"); and even people (Paul was treated "slanderously," 1 Cor. 4:13, and "defamed," 10:30, "evil

---

spoken of"). So, regardless of the object, blasphemy is extremely serious sin.

Second, as our text indicates, while horrendously evil, all such **blasphemy** (except one) is forgivable. The text goes even further to say that not only **blasphemy** but also **all manner of sin** is forgivable. In this case, the Greek *pas* (**all manner**) means "all inclusively," which certainly includes a wide range of sin: lying, stealing, vulgarity, drunkenness, adultery, murder, even suicide (contrary to the teaching of Roman Catholicism), and the list goes on.

Third, what then is **blasphemy against the Holy Ghost**, the one sin that is not forgivable? One popular view is that this sin cannot even be committed today because, it is alleged, it could only be committed while Jesus was on the earth performing miracles in the Spirit's power and so only in this very limited context by the Pharisees. This seems odd, however. Why even mention this if it is the only time in history that it would ever be true? What's the point of bringing it up if it has no bearing on anyone else in the present or future?

We would also point out that Jesus' promise that He would send "another Comforter" (Jn. 14:6) should be considered. "Another" is not *heteros*, which means "another of a different kind" (Eng. *heterodox* and *heterosexual*), rather it is *allos*, "another of similar or identical nature." How thrilling! The Savior is saying in essence, "When I depart, I will send another in my place who is virtually identical to Me." No, He is not physically here doing miracles, but He is still here, still working mightily *for* us, *in* us, and *through* us. We would also add, since this incident is also recorded in Mark, it does not seem wise to insist that it's strictly Jewish, as some insist about the book of Matthew. We submit, therefore, that there is no good reason to relegate this incident to another age and thereby dismiss it as irrelevant today. In fact, as we will see, it has a very important significance in *every* age. Let us now note the *what* and the *why*.

What, then, is this sin? Jesus tells us that is it *the* **blasphemy against the Holy Ghost** (*tou pneumatos blasphēmia*). As always, the definite article is significant. It demonstrates here that a specific type of blasphemy is in view, namely, **against the Holy Ghost**, that is, attributing the great and mighty works of the Holy Spirit to Satan. We would submit further, as we'll see later, that this can still be done today.

The question now arises, however, *why* is this sin unpardonable? As is usually the case, if a *text* is not completely clear, the *context* is. As we look at the Pharisees (who we insist are representative of all men), we see not one hint of the acknowledgment of sin, which is an absolute prerequisite for forgiveness. In every case of forgiveness recorded in Scripture, such admission was present—for example, David (2 Sam. 12:13–23; Ps. 51); the woman in the city of Nain in Capernaum (Lk. 7:36–50); the prodigal son (Lk. 15:13, 21–24;); Peter (Matt. 26:74–75; Lk. 22:31–32; Jn. 18:15–18, 25–27; 21:15–17); and Saul of Tarsus (Acts 9:1; 22:4; 26:9–11; 1 Cor. 15:9; Eph. 3:8; Phil. 3:6). Not so the Pharisees. There was in them not only unbelief, but indifferent, intentional, and insolent unbelief. There was a coldness and callousness that with malice of forethought refused to acknowledge their sin, even to the point of ascribing to Satan the things of God that they had seen and clearly understood.

Paul actually provides us with an illustration in himself. As he wrote to Timothy:

> And I thank Christ Jesus our Lord, who hath enabled me, for that he counted me faithful, putting me into the ministry; Who was before a blasphemer [*blasphemos*], and a persecutor, and injurious: but I obtained mercy, because I did it ignorantly in unbelief. (1 Tim. 1:12–13)

Paul was actually a hairsbreadth from the unpardonable sin. He was indeed a blasphemer, but he did it all in *ignorant* unbelief, while the Pharisees in dramatic contrast did so in *knowing*, even *deliberate*, unbelief. In fact, just a few verses before our text we read: "And all the people were amazed, and said, Is not this the son of David?" (v. 23). Everyone who witnessed what Jesus did recognized that He did it in God's power and in fulfillment of Messianic prophecy. The only way one could reject Him was to do so willfully and deliberately and thereby ascribe what He did as *Satanic* power not *Spirit* power—and *that* was unforgivable.

There is one more aspect of this scene that makes the issue even clearer. A further reason that this sin is unpardonable is because it literally, and quite completely, *prevents* pardon and repentance. Despite irrefutable evidence, despite the clear proofs of what God is doing through the Spirit, they "call evil good, and good evil . . . put darkness for light, and light for darkness . . . [and] put bitter for sweet, and sweet for bitter!" (Isa. 5:20). As commentator William Hendrickson well says, "to be forgiven implies that the sinner be truly penitent. Among the Pharisees here described such genuine sorrow for sin is totally lacking." He goes on to add:

> For penitence they substitute hardening, for confession plotting. Thus, by means of their own criminal and completely inexcusable callousness, they are dooming themselves. Their sin is unpardonable because they are unwilling to tread the path that leads to pardon. For a thief, an adulterer, and a murderer there is hope. The message of the gospel may cause him to cry out, "O God be merciful to me, the sinner." But when a man has become hardened, so that he has made up his mind not to pay any attention to the promptings of the Spirit,

not even to listen to his pleading and warning voice, he has placed himself on the road that leads to perdition.[2]

This sin is not a *single* sin (such as murder), a *series* of sins (such as breaking all the 10 commandments), or even *succession* of a sin (persistence in a particular one). Rather this is a *state of mind* arrived at by the practiced refusal to acknowledge what God alone has accomplished through His Spirit.

Examples of this Trait

Based upon the consideration of our text, we would submit that there are vivid examples of this trait of deliberate, calculated, and impudent unbelief.

First, consider Pharaoh (Ex. 1—14). Here was a man who had been given evidence after evidence, proof stacked upon proof of what God was doing. Through a series of plagues upon the entire land of Egypt, God gave irrefutable proof that He was saying, "Let My people go," a phrase that appears nine times."[3] Could it have been clearer? A blind man could see it with a cane, as the expression goes. Yet, Pharaoh deliberately, defiantly, and determinately refused to relent.

In fact, no less than 14 times we read that Pharaoh's heart was "hardened" (or "harden").[4] In several of these instances, it was actually God doing the hardening. This is significant because it demonstrates God's response to man's impertinence. In effect, God's response is, "Very well, if you *wish* to be defiant, then you *shall* be defiant."

While some Bible students are troubled by the fact that God hardened Pharoah's heart, implying that God was "unfair" or "harsh," they overlook what God said to Moses before the incident even began. In 3:19 we read, "I am sure that the king of Egypt *will not* let you go, no, not by a mighty hand." As John Gill writes, "Mighty hand" refers to "the mighty power of God displayed once and again, even in nine plagues inflicted on [Pharaoh]."[5] Even with the evidence staring him in the face, Pharaoh would not relent, and *that* was unpardonable.

Second, does this not also help explain God's seemingly harsh judgment and destruction of the peoples of Canaan? Many Christians have wondered why God would command the children of Israel to annihilate whole cities of people, entire civilizations. The answer is quickly forthcoming when we read Joshua 2:9–11, where Rahab admits to the spies Joshua sent into Jericho:

> I know that the LORD hath given you the land, and that your terror is fallen upon us, and that all the inhabitants of the land faint because of you. For we have heard how the LORD dried up the

water of the Red sea for you, when ye came out of Egypt; and what
ye did unto the two kings of the Amorites, that were on the other side
Jordan, Sihon and Og, whom ye utterly destroyed. *And as soon as we
had heard these things, our hearts did melt,* neither did there remain
any more courage in any man, because of you: for the LORD your
God, he is God in heaven above, and in earth beneath (emphasis
added).

Word had spread quickly of what God had done for His people; the
Canaanites had heard it, considered it, and even feared it, but they still
rejected it. Case closed. As a result, they were beyond *pardon*, beyond
penitence, and beyond even *pleading*. This scene was repeated throughout
Canaan, as noted in 5:1. When people heard what God had done, their
hearts "melted." The Hebrew here (*māsas*) literally pictures melting wax
and so figuratively the dissolving of one's courage. People clearly heard but
did not heed.

Third, consider again the judgment of Judah. As we explored back in
chapter 39, Judah (the Southern Kingdom) was following the same road to
ruin as had Israel (the Northern Kingdom). This is, in fact, what makes
Judah stand out. While Israel, of course, had seen God's mighty acts and
willfully apostatized, Judah had the additional testimony of God's
judgment on Israel. As we recall, while under Josiah's reforms the idols
were *removed*, the temple *repaired*, and the worship of Jehovah *restored*,
the people had not *repented*, had not turned to the Lord with their whole
heart and soul. The only response to willful apostasy is judgment.

This is further substantiated by two other details. For one, God
instructed Jeremiah on three separate occasions *not* to pray for the people
(Jer. 7:16; 11:4; 14:11). What an a indictment! After all, God listened when
Moses interceded for sinful Israel (Ex. 32—33; Num. 14), and He had
allowed Abraham to pray even for the indescribably wicked city of Sodom
(Gen. 18:23–33). Yet, He forbid Jeremiah to plead for Judah.

One other detail appears in the words of Hosea. While he prophesied
to Israel, not Judah, the impact of his words are not lessened. In fact, they
show that even Israel had gone too far to repent. Since Ephraim was the
largest and strongest of the Northern Kingdom, it was used as a synonym
for all Israel, so Hosea's words tell the tale: "Ephraim is joined to idols: let
him alone" (Hosea 4:17). Indeed, if Israel wanted to live like a harlot, God
said in effect, "So be it. The warnings are over."

Fourth, King Herod the Tetrarch is a truly dramatic demonstration of
the unpardonable sin. Mark 6:20 says something very enlightening about
Herod:

Herod feared John, knowing that he was a just man and an holy, and observed him; and when he heard him, he did many things, and heard him gladly.

"Feared" is the Greek verb *phobeō*. It actually comes from a verb that does not even appear in the New Testament, *phobomai*, which literally means "to flee" and was used mostly by Homer. Later it refers to the physical emotion of fear, terror, and anxiety. It sometimes means respect, awe, and reverence, as in veneration of the gods. It is, of course, from this word group that we get the English *phobia*, an irrational fear of something. Why did Herod fear John the Baptist? Because he first *realized* who John represented and then *recognized* who empowered him.

But Herod had a problem, namely, his desire to marry Herodias, the wife of his brother Philip, unlawfully (Lev 18:16). So, Herod had to make a choice, and of course, he made the wrong one. It is Luke's account of this, however, that really paints the horrible picture:

> But Herod the tetrarch, being reproved by [John] for Herodias his brother Philip's wife, and for *all the evils* which Herod had done, *Added yet this above all*, that he shut up John in prison. (Lk. 3:19–20, emphasis added)

Later, of course, Herod went on to have John beheaded simply to please the offended Herodias (Mk. 6:27). Ignoring the evidence of who empowered John and disregarding what John said, Herod chose wrongly and willfully.

But that is not the end of Herod's story. Still racked by guilt, upon hearing of the spreading fame of Jesus, Herod cried in terror, "This is John the Baptist; he is risen from the dead; and therefore mighty works do show forth themselves in him" (Matt. 14:2). Still later, Herod even tried to kill Jesus (Lk. 13:31).

It is then that Herod's true unpardonable state is revealed when Jesus was brought before him. Luke 23:9 declares, "[Herod] questioned with [Jesus] in many words; but he answered him nothing." J. Sidlow Baxter masterfully concludes here:

> The voice of God which had been knowingly and systematically silenced in [Herod's] life *will not speak any more!* In his rage and frustration, Herod now has Jesus "set at naught" by his soldiers , and "mocked"; but Jesus remains mute. The voice of God speaks no more. The man who *would* not *shall* not . . . Such is the unpardonable sin, and such is the process leading to it.[6]

Fifth, Jesus' lament over Jerusalem. In a replay of history, Jerusalem is again in the depths of sin. As Jeremiah did in his day, it is our Lord Himself who weeps this time:

O Jerusalem, Jerusalem, thou that killest the prophets, and stonest them which are sent unto thee, how often would I have gathered thy children together, even as a hen gathereth her chickens under her wings, and *ye would not!* Behold, your house is left unto you desolate. (Matt. 23:37–38, emphasis added).

Like the belligerent Pharisees in our main text, the nation itself was too far gone to repent. While some would come to believe at the Day of Pentecost, and while Israel will be grafted back into the "olive tree," a symbol of privilege (Rom. 11), many in that generation (and in our own) are unpardonable.

Sixth and finally, no passages could be more graphic of this unpardonable state than those in Revelation. Note first 6:15–17:

The kings of the earth, and the great men, and the rich men, and the chief captains, and the mighty men, and every bondman, and every free man, hid themselves in the dens and in the rocks of the mountains; And said to the mountains and rocks, Fall on us, and hide us from the face of him that sitteth on the throne, and from the wrath of the Lamb: For the great day of his wrath is come; and who shall be able to stand?

While openly acknowledging that the disasters they have been experiencing have come from God, most people during the Tribulation will defiantly refuse to repent. We read again in □9:20–21:

□The rest of the men which were not killed by these plagues yet repented not of the works of their hands, that they should not worship devils, and idols of gold, and silver, and brass, and stone, and of wood: which neither can see, nor hear, nor walk: Neither repented they of their murders, nor of their sorceries, nor of their fornication, nor of their thefts. □

While by this time one-third of the earth's remaining population will have fallen to God's judgment, yet still, unimaginably, those that remain will not repent. In spite of years of indescribable suffering, tens of millions of deaths, coupled with the powerful preaching of the Gospel by the 144,000 Jewish evangelists (□7:1–8□), the two witnesses (□11:1–14□), an angel in the sky (□14:6–7□), and other believers (□Matt. 24:14□), there will have never been a time in history that men were as defiant as they will be then. Finally, we read yet again in 16:10–11:

And the fifth angel poured out his vial upon the seat of the beast; and his kingdom was full of darkness; and they gnawed their tongues for pain, And blasphemed the God of heaven because of their pains and their sores, and repented not of their deeds.

At this point, men's confirmed unbelief is total and complete. There comes a time when there is no more light, no more opportunity, and no more forgiveness.

Exhortation to Think

Some people have been troubled by the thought of whether they have committed the unpardonable sin. But to even ask that question is proof positive that they have not. The person guilty of this sin would never ask, for he is beyond such a notion.

That said, however, this sin can indeed be committed today and is, in fact, committed often. How many evolutionists, for example, are in this state? They witness the wonders of the world but in belligerent arrogance reject the obvious, even going so far as ascribing the works of "the Spirit of God [who] moved upon the face of the waters" to a "big bang." Such willful unbelief was demonstrated to me when I read one evolutionist who said, "I believe in evolution because the only other alternative is creation, and I refuse to believe that."

It seems clear in each case we've examined that the unpardonable sin begins with *rejection* in the mind, which morphs into *rebellion* in the emotions, which ultimately hardens into the *refusal* of the will. This should encourage us in our evangelism to alert people that "now is the accepted time; behold, now is the day of salvation" (2 Cor. 6:2)? We should strongly warn them that to *postpone* is to quite possibly be beyond *pardon*.

NOTES

[1] Gerhard Kittle (editor), *Theological Dictionary of the New Testament* (Grand Rapids: Eerdmans, 1964; reprinted 2006),, Vol. I, p. 621.

[2] William Hendriksen, *The Exposition of the Gospel According to Matthew* (Baker, 1973), p. 529.

[3] Exodus 5:1; 7:16; 8:1, 20, 21; 9:1, 13; 10:3, 4.

[4] Exodus 4:21; 7:13, 14, 22; 8:19; 9:7, 12, 35; 10:20, 27; 11:10; 14:4, 8, 17.

[5] *John Gill's Exposition of the Entire Bible* (electronic edition).

[6] J. Sidlow Baxter , *Studies in Problem Texts* (Zondervan, 1960, 1974), p. 127 (emphasis in the original).

42

What is the Sin Unto Death?*

1 John 5:16–17

**If any man see his brother sin a sin which is not unto death, he shall
ask, and he shall give him life for them that sin not unto death. There is
a sin unto death: I do not say that he shall pray for it. All
unrighteousness is sin: and there is a sin not unto death.**

Our text here is among a choice number that have generated much debate. It's right up there with Genesis 6:4, 1 Corinthians 13:10, 2 Corinthians 12:7, and others that we've addressed in this humble publication.

Since John makes this statement in such a matter-of-fact way—almost off-the-cuff, as it were, with no explanation—his readers obviously knew exactly what this sin was about, while we are left somewhat perplexed. But is there really that much of an enigma here? We would humbly submit that this statement is not that puzzling after all, that its meaning seems fairly obvious. We would, therefore, offer the following: the *promise*, the *problem*, the *precedents*, and the *prayer*.

The Promise

As with any text, we should not jump into this one without first looking before we leap. One of the most basic and critical principles of interpretation is the *context*.

First, the overall theme of John's First Epistle is stated, in fact, just three verses before our text: "These things have I written unto you that believe on the name of the Son of God; that ye may know that ye have eternal life, and that ye may believe on the name of the Son of God" (5:13). As noted in chapter 40 ("We Band of Brothers"), while John's *Gospel* was written that men might *believe* on Christ and have life (Jn. 20:31), his First *Epistle* was written that men might *know* they have that life. The Greek behind "know" is *eidō*, which means "to behold, look upon, contemplate, to see in order to know, to look at or into, examine,"[1] and therefore speaks "of absolute [knowledge], beyond the peradventure of a doubt knowledge, a positive knowledge."[2]

---

* This chapter was originally TOTT issue 59, June 2010.

First John is therefore about the Christian having assurance of his salvation based upon objective evidence in his life. While it addresses several themes, the overall theme can be expressed several ways, such as, "a recall to the fundamentals of the faith," "back to the basics of Christianity,"[3] "the evidences of faith," or perhaps best of all, "the tests of life."[4]

We see that overall theme in three major tests that reoccur many times throughout the letter, all of which flow from the words, "we know." First, is the test of *doctrine*, the test of orthodox belief in Jesus Christ as the Son of God (3:23; 5:5, 10, 13). Second, there is the test of *duty*, the test of obedience to God's Word and practical righteousness (1:5–6; 3:5, 9; 5:18). Third, there is the test of *devotion*, the test of whether we love other believers (2:9–11; 3:14; 4:7–8, 20–21). These are not arbitrary or unrelated. They are inseparably intertwined, for *faith, holiness,* and *love* are all works of the Holy Spirit. (3:24; 4:13). If even one of these is lacking, true salvation is not evident. So, as we will see, understanding this overall theme aids us in understanding our text.

Second, in addition to the overall theme is the immediate context around these verses, which is about having confidence in prayer. Verse 14 declares: "This is the confidence that we have in him, that, if we ask any thing according to his will, he heareth us." "Confidence" is *parrēsia*. In Classical Greek it was important in political situations, meaning "the right to say anything, an openness to truth, candor." Taken to extremes, it took on the negative sense of "insolence," being disrespectful. In each of its 31 New Testament occurrences (e.g., Acts 4:31), the basic idea is that the person has the right to speak and to speak it openly. The word is actually a compound, *pas* ("all") and *rēsis* ("the act of speaking"), so the most literal idea is "to tell all." In other words, we can come before our Father with total freedom of speech, pour out our hearts, and tell Him everything. What a blessed privilege! Verse 15 goes on to add, "And if we know that he hear us, whatsoever we ask, we know that we have the petitions that we desired of him."

While verses 14 and 15 speak of our overall *confidence* in prayer, verses 16 and 17 deal with *content*, specifically, intercessory prayer for other believers, as the word **brother** implicitly implies. It is argued by some that **brother** does not of necessity refer to a true believer, but as we will detail later, this fact is consistent throughout the letter. That leads us to our second emphasis.

The Problem

Based upon the promise of these verses, John makes an extraordinary statement, so much so, in fact, that it seems out of place, even a sudden change of subject. He makes what appears at first glance to be an exception to intercessory prayer. Is he actually saying that while we can pray for believers who are committing a sin that is **not unto death**, we should *not* pray for those who *are* committing **sin unto death**? Before answering that question, what *is* **sin unto death**? Let's examine the views.

First, some very sound Bible teachers equate this sin with the "unpardonable sin," which we examined in our previous chapter, viewing this as an act of extreme willful rebellion against God and His working by His Sprit. In our view, however, this does not seem to fit. However loosely one might define the term **brother**, which we will examine in a moment, we can't imagine John using it here in even the broadest sense of the term.

Second, others view this sin as a particularly heinous one, one that carried the death penalty. Since the Mosaic Law defined several sins as capital offenses (e.g., Lev. 20:1–27; Num. 18; cf. Rom. 1:32), it is argued, then it follows that such sins would still carry this ultimate penalty. It is further insisted that the Law differentiated between sins that were not deliberate and could be forgiven through sacrifice and those that were premeditated and could not. Such a view, however, not only smacks of the Roman Catholic teaching of "mortal" (which the RSV uses in our text) and "venial" sins, not to mention "the seven deadly sins," but also seriously blurs the distinctions between Old and New Testament economies. As John R. W. Stott puts it, "There is no New Testament warrant for such an arbitrary classification of sins, and certainly it would be an anachronism to apply it here."[5]

Third, still another view, a quite popular one, in fact, is that this sin refers to a Christian who apostatizes, that is, a former believer who repudiates Christ. Since Gnosticism[6] was growing at this time, which John addresses in this letter, some insist that John refers to such apostasy in our text. They further support this with passages such as Hebrews 6:4–6 (see chapter 19) and 10:26–27. The troubling aspect of such an idea, of course, is whether a true Christian can apostatize. A true Christian is a metamorphosis, a "new creature" (2 Cor. 5:17), a "[partaker] of the divine nature" (2 Pet. 1:4). The idea of such a one repudiating Christ is unthinkable and flies in the face of the doctrine of security. A variation, of course, is that these weren't believers *proper*, rather only believers *professed*, making it possible for them to ultimately reject Christ. But here again, this demands that we view the term **brother** in a way that simply does not match how John uses this term throughout the letter. Further, passages such as Hebrews 6:4–6 do not say anything about death. All three of these views, therefore, fall short of explaining John's meaning.

Fourth, this brings us to the view that, in our humble opinion, is the most natural sense of the language of the text. As Dr. David Cooper stated what many view as "The Golden Rule of Interpretation": "When the plain sense of Scripture makes common sense, seek no other sense; therefore; take every word at its primary, ordinary, usual, literal meaning unless the facts of the immediate context, studied in the light of related passages and axiomatic and fundamental truths, indicated clearly otherwise."[7]

In our view, therefore, this plain language indicates, as one commentator succinctly puts it: "Sometimes a Christian may sin so seriously that God judges that sin with swift physical death: 'a sin that leads to death.'"[8] We would humbly offer four reasons we accept this view.

1. The term **brother**. It is odd, indeed, that some expositors downplay the significance of this term here. The Greek, of course, is *adelphos*, a compound comprised of *delphus*, "a womb," and the prefix *a*. Not only is this prefix often used as the "alpha negative," which makes a word mean the exact opposite, it's also used in a "collative" manner, signifying unity. The picture in *adelphos*, then, is "one born from the same womb." Originally, it referred to a physical brother (or sister with the feminine *adelphē*). Later it came to refer to any near relative, such as a nephew or even a brother-in-law. Finally, there are several examples in the Septuagint where *adelphos* is used to refer even to fellow Israelites (e.g., Ex. 2:11; Lev. 19:17), showing a close relationship without any physical heritage. It's that very practice of using **brother** to refer to fellow Israelites that was carried over into the New Testament. The idea of fellow Christians being brothers, in fact, appears some 30 times in Acts and 130 times in Paul's Epistles, so this concept obviously carries great importance.

Likewise, the Apostle John uses *adelphos* 17 times in his First Epistle and three additional times in his Third Epistle.[9] Some insist here that John uses the term in a broad sense to refer to a "neighbor or nominal Christian, a church member who professes to be a 'brother.'"[10] But that simply is not supported by the data. With only a single exception, in fact, John clearly speaks of a believer. Only in 3:12 does he use it otherwise, in this case in reference to Cain and Abel as siblings.

It is argued that in verses such as 2:9—"He that saith he is in the light, and hateth his brother, is in darkness even until now"—**brother** might also include those who only *profess* to be a believer. But we humbly submit this is a misreading of the text! Note carefully who is actually being called **brother**. The term is clearly used to refer to *the one being hated*, not the one doing the hating; it is the latter whose salvation is in question, not the former. The same is true in verses 10, 11, and 3:15—**brother** refers to the genuine believer, not the one whose behavior makes it questionable. John's use of *adelphos* in his Third Epistle is also significant in demonstrating this consistency; all three uses dramatically indicate believers.

We, therefore, submit that the plain and consistent use of **brother** (*adelphos*) in Acts and the Epistles, including John's epistles, to refer to a true believer indicates that John does, in fact, have a Christian in mind here in 1 John 5:16. It simply cannot be demonstrated, in fact, that this term is ever used for an unbeliever in the spiritual sense.

2. The terms **death** and **life** seem to indicate the *physical*. It is argued that since **death** refers to spiritual death and **life** refers to spiritual life in 3:14, it therefore follows that they mean the same in 5:16. We submit, however, that does not follow of necessity. The verb tense of "we have passed (from death unto life)" in 3:14 is the *perfect*, a past action (or process) with results that continue. In other words, John says that we passed from death in the past and that state still continues (cf. Jn. 5:24). The verb tense of "he shall give (him life)" in 5:16, however, is the *future*, action that *will* take place. So, why would John say that spiritual life *shall* come when he said earlier that it already *has* come and continues? It seems possible instead that he is saying that for those who **sin *not* unto death** God **shall give** more physical life in contrast to those who commit **sin unto [physical] death**.

This explanation makes all the more sense in light of the phrase **unto death**. The preposition **unto** is the Greek *pros*, which in the construction here indicates the idea of "tending (or moving) toward death."[11] Only physical death makes sense. As we will see, a believer can commit sin that "moves him toward death."

3. The verb tense of **sin** (in the phrase **if any man see his brother sin**) indicates a continuing practice. This is the *present* tense, indicating continuing action in the present time. Coupled with this are the words **a sin**, which can actually read just **sin** because the article is not mandatory. In other words, the idea is not **a** particular **sin** that is in view, or an isolated act (which we all are guilty of), rather recurring sin, some sin, whatever it might be, that persists.

Now, this seems at first glance to contradict totally what John says previously. In 3:9, for example, the words "commit," "remaineth," and "(cannot) sin" are all in the present tense. Additionally, "cannot" is the negative particle *ou*, indicating complete and absolute negation. We could, therefore expand the verse to read: "Whosoever is born of God doth not [habitually] commit sin; for [God's] seed [continually] remaineth in him: and he [absolutely] cannot [habitually] sin, because he is born of God." So, if that is true, how can 5:16 say that a Christian can persist in sin?

It seems to us, however, that this is John's very point. He is saying in 5:16 that this sin is contradictory for a believer, that such a believer is in practice acting like an unbeliever in a particular sin, which cannot be allowed to continue. While a believer is *not* capable of the *perpetual condition* of sin—that is, a life that is permeated by sin—he *is* capable of the *practical circumstance* of sin, of allowing a particular sin to continue, allowing the flesh to win out over the Spirit (Rom. 7 and 8) in some particular action or attitude.

This also reminds us of the overall theme of this Epistle, as noted earlier: "the evidences of faith" or "the tests of life." The three tests of *doctrine* (orthodoxy), *duty* (obedience and practical righteousness), and *devotion* (brotherly love) are the rule by which we are measured. If any behavior begins consistently to contradict one of those, a believer is flirting with **sin unto death**. This idea should become clear as we examine a few examples in a moment.

4. Finally, the phrase **if any man see** indicates that this overt **sin** is quite probably effecting the entire body of believers. As 1 Corinthians 5:6–7 declares, and to which we will return later, "a little leaven leaveneth the whole lump" and must be purged. If a believer persists in some sinful attitude or action that has become obvious to others in the church, that sin must be removed, and God might indeed do so with physical death. That thought leads right to our third point.

The Precedents

The view we presented above is easy to accept—and indeed is hard to deny—when we recognize that there are many biblical illustrations of such sin and penalty.

First, without a doubt, Ananias and Sapphira are a graphic example of **sin unto death**. Their greed, hypocrisy, and lying were done in front of the whole church and God took their lives for it. They had publicly promised to give all the proceeds from their sale to the church but then publicly reneged. There is no indication whatsoever that they were unbelievers or just professing believers; Acts 4:32 implies that they were part of "the multitude of them that believed were of one heart and of one soul."

The question could arise, "But this situation seems to be one *act* of sin instead of a continuing practice as noted earlier." We submit, however, that just the opposite is true. It seems quite likely that this behavior was, in fact, not isolated at all, that their attitudes were known to Peter and others. A believer is capable of any sin under the right circumstances, which is all the more reason to guard against it. J. N. Darby makes a noteworthy comment here:

This does not seem to me to be some particular sin, but all sin which has such a character that, instead of awakening Christian charity, it awakens Christian indignation. . . . It was a lie, but a lie under such circumstances that it excited horror rather than compassion. We can easily understand this in other cases.[12]

Second, the incident of church discipline in 1 Corinthians 5 is another example. The scene there was a case of incest going on within the church, a truly disgusting and unthinkable situation. There is again no indication that this was an unbeliever or simply a professing believer. On the contrary, this was a believer who was put out of the church, "deliver[ed] . . . unto Satan for the destruction of the flesh, that the spirit may be saved in the day of the Lord Jesus" (v. 5). "Delivered" is *paradidōmi*, a compound of *didōmi*, to give of one's own accord and with good will, and *para*, alongside or over to, yielding the full meaning, "to deliver over to the power of someone." It was used in Classical Greek as a legal term for delivering a prisoner to the court. Likewise, the basic New Testament meaning is to deliver someone over to judgment and death. It's used in Matthew 4:12 of John the Baptist when he was "cast into prison" with the ultimate end of death. Thankfully, that man repented and was restored to fellowship about a year or year-and-a-half later (2 Cor. 2:5–8), but what would have happened if he had not? The language could not be clearer: this man was on his way to death. We don't know how that would have happened, but had he not repented, death "before his time" was assured. While difficult and heartbreaking, church discipline is absolutely mandatory for the purity of the Body of Christ.[13]

Third, we find another example of **sin unto death** within the troubled Corinthian church. Paul tells us that some believers were abusing the Lord's Table (1 Cor. 11:17–32) in both *action* and *attitude*. Overt action included drunken revelry, by partaking of it "unworthily" (*anaxios*). In Classical Greek, the root *axios* originally meant "tipping the scales, counterbalancing, of different weight," and finally came to mean "worthy." The negative (with the added *a*) form *anaxios*, then, means *un*worthy, not suitable. So in the present context, such unworthy, out-of-balance attitudes would include a plethora of things: indifference, unthinking ritualism, unconfessed sin, bitterness against another believer (cf. Matt. 5:23–24), or any other attitudes that undermine the whole purpose of this ordinance. Such abuse, therefore, had resulted in judgment through illness and even *death* ("sleep" was a common euphemism for death; cf. 1 Cor. 15:18; Matt. 27:52; Acts 7:60; 2 Pet. 3:4).

Fourth and finally, we find this sin rooted even in Old Testament history. Commentator Adam Clarke, for example, observes: "The disobedient prophet, 1 Kings 13:1–32, is . . . a case in point: many others occur in the history of the Church, and of every religious community."[14]

Others point out incidents such as Nadab and Abihu (Lev. 10), Korah (Num. 16:23–35), Achan (Josh. 7), and Joab (2 Sam. 3:22–39). Even David was well aware that he could have died for his sin (2 Sam. 12:13–14); on the other hand, perhaps worse was the fact that *others died* because of his sin.

So, we submit once again, the most natural sense of the language in our text, as well as Scriptural precedents, demonstrates that the **sin unto death** is the physical death of a believer for serious unrepentant sin.

The Prayer

Finally, what does John mean by **I do not say that he shall pray for** those overtaken by **sin unto death**? One expositor insightfully writes: "Why, then, doesn't John say that one should pray for them? The answer is because such prayer is useless. It is not that it is absolutely wrong to pray. While John clearly does not intend Christians to pray for the forgiveness of such people, he words himself carefully so as not to forbid it."[15]

The only question that remains, then, is: *How do we know?* It seems that the only answer is: *We don't.* We are not judges. Rather we pray for everyone, no matter what. We might see sin that concerns (or even) frightens us deeply, so we pray. Whether or not it does any good, we still intercede. When we pray according to God's will, He hears, and does according to His sovereignty, holiness, and justice.

Dear Christian Friend, this verse stands as a solemn, serious, and stern warning to every believer. God cannot allow sin to remain, so He will at times remove it for the purity of the Body. Let each of us, therefore, examine ourselves. A. T. Pierson encourages us:

> It has been my habit for years to spend the last half hour before I go to sleep in looking over the day, asking God to let me see where wood, hay, and stubble have found incorporation in my life building. I would ask him to judge me then and there, and to burn up the wood, hay, and stubble that nothing may stand but gold, silver, and precious stones. What a blessed thing for us to discern ourselves in daily judgment, deciding, with regard to God, to leave nothing for the last great trial that will not stand the fire.[16]

NOTES

[1] Spiros Zodhiates, *The Complete Word Study Dictionary: New Testament* AMG Publishers, 1992), entry #1492.

[2] Kenneth S. Wuest, *Wuest's Word Studies* (electronic edition), comment on 1 John

5:13.

[3] Both from *The MacArthur Study Bible.*

[4] Both of the following use *Tests of Life* as the title of their exposition: Robert Law (T. Clark, 1909; reprinted by Baker, 1968) and Theodore Epp in his short exposition (Back to the Bible, 1957).

[5] John R. W. Stott, *The Epistles of John: Tyndale New Testament Commentaries* (Eerdmans, 1964), p. 188.

[6] Influenced by Plato and others, Gnosticism was a dualistic philosophy, maintaining that while spirit was good, all matter was inherently evil. The result of such teaching was that while Christ was "some form of Deity," He could not have been truly human for such "matter" would have made Him evil. Coming to full bloom in the second century, it also boasted of a deeper, superior, mystical knowledge that was higher than Scripture and that only the properly initiated followers could acquire. Gnosticism is alive and well in our day, taking many forms in various cults and flavors of mysticism.

[7] David L. Cooper, *The World's Greatest Library: Graphically Illustrated* (Biblical Research Society, 1970), p. 11.

[8] John Walvoord and Roy Zuck, *The Bible Knowledge Commentary* (electronic edition), note on 1 John 5:16.

[9] 1 John 2:7; 9, 10, 11; 2:10, 11; 3:10, 12, 13, 14 (twice), 15, 16, 17; 4:20, 21; 5:16; 3 John 3, 5, 10.

[10] Stott, p. 190.

[11] While there are three "cases" (functions) for nouns in English, there are five in Greek. Two of those are the *nominative*, which indicates the subject of a sentence, and the *accusative*, which is used for a direct object, as is the word **death** in the phrase **sin unto death**. The rule is that when the preposition *pros* is used with the accusative (which it usually is), it marks the object toward or to which something moves or is directed.

[12] John Nelson Darby, *Synopsis of the Old and New Testaments*, note on 1 John 5:16.

[13] Look for a study on "Principles of Church Discipline" in a future issue of our monthly TOTT.

[14] *Adam Clarke's Commentary on the Bible*, note on 1 John 5:16.

[15] Walter Kaiser, Peter Davids, F. F. Bruce, and Manfred Brauch, *Hard Sayings of the Bible* (InterVarsity), "1 John 5:16-17. A Sin That Leads to Death?"

[16] Cited in *The Friend: A Religious and Literary Journal*, Volume LXXX, No. 35 (Printed by Wm. H. Pile's Sons, 1907), p. 278.

43

The Pestilence of Idolatry*

Selected Texts

At first it seems extremely odd to discuss a subject like idolatry in our modern society. After all, we are civilized, educated, sophisticated, cultured, and refined. We are surely far from the primitive, stone-age native who with painted face and drug induced frenzy dances around screaming and bowing down to a carved statue of his god. It might seem even odder still to talk about this with Christians. We "worship [God] in spirit and in truth" (Jn. 4:24) and would, therefore, of course, never worship some idol or false god.

This, however, begs the question, "Why, then, did Paul command a body of believers in a local church, **My dearly beloved, flee from idolatry** (1 Cor. 10:14)?" Why did the Apostle John do the same: **Little children, keep yourselves from idols** (1 Jn. 5:21)? Further, what is the deeper and more significant truth of the second commandment in the Moral Law: **Thou shalt not make unto thee any graven image** (Ex. 20:4)? Do not all those verses (and others) seem to indicate that idolatry isn't as far out a thought as we might think?

On Scriptural grounds, in fact, we would submit that idolatry is a far more prominent, pervasive, and persistent sin than we will ever allow ourselves to consider (unless the Holy Spirit is ruling our thinking). In his famous sermon, "Idolatry," the great 19th-century preacher J. C. Ryle declared:

> It is a pestilence that walks in the Church of Christ to a much greater extent than many suppose. It is an evil that, like the man of sin, "sits in the very temple of God" (2 Thes. 2:4). It is a sin that we all need to watch and pray against continually. It creeps into our religious worship insensibly and is upon us before we are aware.[1]

If we may build on the idea of "pestilence," idolatry can indeed be likened to a virus that we have contracted from someone else (in this case Adam), has an indefinite incubation period, can flair up at any time, ravage us, spread to others, and then go dormant for a time until the next flare-up.

---

* This chapter was originally TOTT issue 63, October 2010, and was based upon a sermon by the author.

Let us, therefore, consider four principles on this much ignored subject: the *meaning, motive,* and *manifestations* of idolatry, and then finally the *moratorium* on idolatry.

The Meaning of Idolatry

Our English word *idol* is derived from the Greek *eidōlon*. Homer used *eidōlon* for phantoms and apparitions. In later Classical Greek, it carried the other non-religious meanings of picture, copy, or "any unsubstantial form, an image reflected in a mirror or water, an image or idea in the mind."[2] In the Hebrew, there are no less than twelve words translated *idol*. One of the most significant is *pesel*, whose first appearance is in Exodus 20:4 and is translated **graven image**. It literally means "to hew or to cut in creating an idol." As we'll see, at the very foundation of God's Law was that man was not to make any image whatsoever to represent deity. Renowned Hebrew scholar Robert Girdlestone provides us with a pointed application that we will detail as we continue:

> Man is essentially an image-maker. . . . he seeks to make a visible representation even of God Himself, and gradually to transfer to the work of his own hands that reverence and dependence that properly belongs to the one living and true God. There is a strange fascination in exaggerated religious symbolism. It engrosses and excites the mind, but is by no means of a healthy character. It tends little by little to supplant the simplicity of spiritual worship, and to turn man into an idolater.[3]

What, then, is idolatry? The famous Noah Webster, who was a devout Christian, provides us with an interesting definition of idolatry in the 1828 edition of his *Dictionary of American English*, which is saturated with biblical definitions:

> 1. The worship of idols, images, or any thing made by hands, or which is not God. Idolatry is of two kinds; the worship of images, statues, pictures, etc. made by hands; and the worship of the heavenly bodies, the sun, moon and stars, or of demons, angels, men and animals. 2. Excessive attachment or veneration for any thing, or that which borders on adoration.

Idolatry, then, is: The worshiping of an object as *another* god, venerating an object as a representation of the *True* God, or adoring any object to the *level* of God. All this will become vividly clear as we continue.

The Motive of Idolatry

What is at the core of idolatry? What is its root cause and underlying motive? As noted earlier, it is essential to understand that man is an idolater by his very nature. Puritan Thomas Watson put it this way: "Our nature is prone to this sin as dry wood to take fire."[4] While we might not have a carved god on the mantle over our fireplace, we all love symbols, we love objects we can see and hold. Some Christians, for example, want to hold on to Old Testament symbols, celebrate feasts, hang "pictures of Jesus" on their walls, stick religious symbols on their car bumpers, and so forth. There seems to be a ribbon to wear for every cause nowadays, from AIDS awareness to anti-abortion. We love this kind of stuff because it "represents something."

Idolatry is a thread that is woven into the very fabric of human nature. History is inundated with examples that prove man's natural bent. Every single civilization has erected its gods: Assyrians, Babylonians, Syrians, Egyptians, Canaanites, Greeks, Persians, Romans, Celts, Vikings, Mayans, Aztecs, and the list goes on. But is idolatry only among pagan peoples? Indeed not. We repeatedly see God's people fall into the worship of Baal, Moloch, and Ashtaroth. Over and over again we see them worshipping idols among hilltop groves. As we'll see in more detail later, idolatry crept little-by-little into the church. None of this should surprise us. It is part of the fall. By nature we bring worship down to the level of the *senses* rather than the *spirit*. We want something we can see, touch, and feel. But Jesus Himself declared, as noted earlier, we are to be "true worshippers" who "worship the Father in spirit and in truth" (Jn. 4:23–24).

All this could not be more vividly demonstrated than it is in our third emphasis.

The Manifestations of Idolatry

How does idolatry demonstrate itself? What forms does it take? Overtly, of course, it does so in many ways. The idols of the civilizations mentioned above are all obvious examples. Also, while there have been many defenders of the statues and relics of Roman Catholicism, their use is a glaring and almost laughably indefensible example of idolatry. Relics include supposed pieces of the cross, bones of martyrs, pieces of the silver coins Judas took for betraying Christ, pieces of cloth woven by the Virgin Mary, and even vials of milk from her breasts. By visiting and venerating such relics, worshipers are promised less time in purgatory. There is also the veneration of statues of Mary and the saints by kissing them, bowing down to them, and burning candles and incense before them. Any defense of such paganism is pure folly and hardly worth refutation.

But what are the less obvious examples of idolatry? How does that inbred "virus" mutate, multiply, and manifest itself in our ordinary lives? The old Strict Baptist preacher J. C. Philpot discerningly preached in an 1855 sermon:

> There is an old Latin proverb, that "love and a cough are two things impossible to be concealed;" and thus, though an idol may be hidden in the heart as carefully as Laban's teraphim in the camel's saddle, or the ephod and molten image in the House of Micah (Judges 18:14), yet it will be discovered by the love shown to it, as surely as the suppressed cough of the consumptive patient cannot escape the ear of the physician.[5]

We submit, therefore, *an idol, can be anything that we love more than, or even as much as, God.* Every one of us must ask the question, "What do I love, and does it ever come before God?" The most common idols that come to mind, of course, are money, possessions, and success. For many people these are the sole drives in their lives and are the very gods they serve. But there are countless less obvious idols. Education can become an idol when it becomes the chief focus. Other people, such as family, can be an idol if they are given priority over God. A particular leader (whether Christian or non-Christian) can become an idol, if he is given position or authority equal to God. One of the most prevalent gods of our day is sports. This was graphically demonstrated after Super Bowl XLIV in Miami, when you could buy a 3-inch square of sod from the stadium that was freeze-dried, preserved, and encased in glass for $99.99, or "special moments" pieces where key plays occurred for $134.99. I recently spoke with a former salesmen who told me that if he didn't talk with clients about sports, there was no way he was going to make a sale. My own favorite sport is golf, which believe me could easily become an idol. Even children, grand-children, a friend, or a spouse can become an idol. How many possibilities are there? The list is endless because it includes anything that exists. We can make idols of our country, car, boat, home, job, leisure activity, furniture, clothing, books, yard, garden, pictures, art, collectibles, pets, or even a church ritual, church ordinance, church building, or particular Bible translation. And which idol is the greatest temptation of all? *Self,* when we (our feelings, views, opinions, etc.) become the chief focus.

Have you ever pondered, in fact—and I say this with all reverence—that even God Himself can be molded into an idol? How? When we fashion Him into an image of our own making. A common teaching today, for example, is that God is a Cosmic Genie who gives us whatever we want when we recite the Prayer of Jabez. Or He is One so loving that He will never judge sin. Or He is One who is always there to get us out of trouble even though we ignore Him the rest of the time. Or He is only a partially sovereign God, who must wait hat-in-hand for men to exercise their "free-will" instead of the God of sovereign grace.

This subject inevitably brings us to an issue that is usually overlooked, but even when mentioned is often defended, namely, the question of pictures of Jesus and other images. I know this is a sticky subject, but I am convinced of its importance and ask the reader to consider history and Scripture.

First, the history of the matter is most enlightening. Philip Schaff, among the most noted of all church historians, writes:

> The primitive church, says even a modern Roman Catholic historian, had no images of Christ, since most Christians at that time still adhered to the commandment of Moses (Ex. 20:4); the more, that regard as well to the Gentile Christians as to the Jewish forbade all use of images. To the latter the exhibition and veneration of images would, of course, be an abomination, and to the newly converted heathen it might be a temptation to relapse into idolatry. In addition, the church was obliged, for her own honor, to abstain from images, particularly from any representation of the Lord, lest she should be regarded by unbelievers as merely a new kind and special sort of heathenism and creature-worship. And further, the early Christians had in their idea of the bodily form of the Lord no temptation, not the slightest incentive, to make likenesses of Christ. The oppressed church conceived its Master only under the form of a servant, despised and uncomely, as Isaiah, 52:2–3 describes the Servant of the Lord.[6]

As several church historians consistently go on to observe, however, as more and more converted heathen came into the church, they brought their tendency toward images with them. One historian puts it this way: "The use of images and pictures in worship expanded rapidly as more and more untutored barbarians came into the church."[7] Another historian provides us with some crucial detail concerning the 4th-century:

> Pictures, especially those representing Bible scenes and ideas, like Daniel in the lions' den, or Christ under the image of the Good Shepherd, came into general use, and, to some extent, in the minds of the half-converted heathen, took the place of the artistic decorations of their abandoned temples. Churches built in memory of martyrs were often adorned with paintings portraying their sufferings. . . The evils to which this desire might lead, were pointed out by the more enlightened bishops, such as Eusebius of Caesarea. They especially resisted attempts to introduce representations of Christ, urging people rather to strive to be like him in their lives. But

towards the end of the fourth century, the use of images in the churches became general. People began to prostrate themselves before them, and many of the more ignorant to worship them.[8]

That historian's mention of the great exegete, polemicist, and historian Eusebius of Caesarea (c. 263–339) is extremely significant. He did indeed resist all this. In his classic work, *Ecclesiastical History*, he wrote about images in the church:

> Nor is it strange that those of the Gentiles who, of old, were benefited by our Saviour, should have done such things, since we have learned also that the likenesses of his apostles Paul and Peter, and of Christ himself, are preserved in paintings, the ancients being accustomed, as it is likely, according to a habit of the Gentiles, to pay this kind of honor indiscriminately to those regarded by them as deliverers.[9]

Commenting on that very citation, John Jewell, 16th-century English bishop of Salisbury, wrote:

> By these words of Eusebius it is plain that the use of images came not from Christ, or from the apostles . . . but from the superstitious custom of the heathens. Neither doth it appear that those images were set up in any church.[10]

Indeed, the whole idea of pictorially representing Jesus is based entirely upon the impulse of man, not the teaching of Scripture. Where in Scripture do we read even the minutest hint that we should paint a picture of Jesus?

We learn one other crucial fact from Eusebius. In a letter titled, *To Constantia Augusta*, he responded to Constantia, the sister of Constantine and wife of Licinius. She had written to Eusebius requesting him to send her a certain likeness of Christ of which she had heard. But Eusebius rebuked her in his response, and spoke strongly against the use of such representations, on the ground that it tends toward idolatry.[11]

But, as is often the case when men speak the Truth, the fallout from Eusebius' disapproval was severe. He fell into great disrepute in the later image-worshiping Church. His writing against such practices was cited years later during the Iconoclastic Controversy at the second Council of Nicæa (787). Incredulously, in fact, even his orthodoxy was fiercely attacked by the defenders of image-worship, who dominated the council, and won the day.[12]

Eusebius wasn't totally alone, however. The great apologist Jerome (c. 347–420) agreed. Commenting on Jeremiah 10:4, he expressly stated that "the errors of images hath come in and passed to the Christians from the

Gentiles, by an heathenish use and custom."[13] Jerome also translated a document written by the church father Epiphanius, 4th-century bishop of Salamis in Cyprus. In that document Epiphanius tells how in a church at Anablatha he tore up a curtain bearing an image and replaced it with a plain curtain, declaring that images in churches is "contrary to the Christian religion." He rejected not only carved, graven, and molten images, but also painted images, out of Christ's church. [14]

Despite those who stood against this practice, it got worse. About the middle of the 5th-century, representations of Christ Himself appeared, which many people shockingly claimed to be accurate portraits of the original. Recognition of images of Christ, especially of the Madonna and Child, even became a test of orthodoxy. In the 6th-century, according to the testimony of Gregory of Tours, pictures of Christ were hung not only in churches but in almost every private house.[15]

The issue finally came to a head in the 8th and 9th-centuries in what was dubbed the Iconoclastic Controversy, which shook the entire Byzantine Empire. Emperor Leo III triggered the dispute with an open condemnation of icons in 726, but that was soon reversed by the Council of Nicea in 787. Opposition continued, but the matter was for all practical purposes settled at a council in Constantinople in 843, where icon veneration was formally restored for good. This issue was, in fact, a major contributor to the division between the Western and Eastern Church.

It seemed that only something truly earth shattering could ever address such practices, and that was exactly what the Reformation did. John Calvin is one focal point. Citing the incident of Epiphanius mentioned above, he writes, "It was [Epiphanius] who termed it a dreadful abomination to see an image either of Christ or of some saint painted in the churches of Christians."[16] Calvin goes on to quote the decision of the Council of Elvira (Illiberitanum) in Spain (ca. 305): "There ought not to be images in a church, that what is worshiped and adored should not be depicted on the walls."[17] So critical was this to Calvin (and other reformers), that he wrote an entire work on this issue, his famous *Treatise on Relics*.

Now, we are well aware that the typical argument in defense of pictures and other images goes something like this, "We have a picture of Jesus but we don't worship it. Such things are okay if they do not become an object of worship." That very argument, however, has been made throughout church history. One historian puts it this way, "The defenders of this practice said that they were merely showing their reverence for the precious symbols of an absent Lord and his saints."[18] This was certainly the motive in the 5th-century, when Pontius Paulinus, Bishop of Nola (Italy), had the walls of the temple painted with Old Testament stories for the purpose of teaching the people and exhorting them to turn from their vice.

But the sad reality was that little-by-little idolatry was the result, as the pictures themselves began to be revered.

We also read of the excuses that Augustine heard from people of his own day (late 4th and early 5th-centuries). Many insisted that "they were not worshiping that visible object but a presence that dwelt there invisibly." Others, who claimed a "purer religion," stated that "they were worshiping neither the likeness nor the spirit; but that through the physical image they gazed upon the sign of the thing that they ought to worship." In other words, they were "not content with spiritual understanding," rather they "thought that through the images a surer and closer understanding would be impressed upon them."[19] Many today use the same flawed reasoning.

It should be clear to any spiritually minded believer that the temptation to idolatry is simply too great with regard to any kind of image. In the end, an image will invoke some type of veneration, however subtle, small, or sincere it might be. An illustration I have used many times has proven itself accurate. If we had a Rembrandt painting and a picture of Jesus hanging side by side, would we esteem or respect the picture of Jesus more highly, even in the minutest degree? If so, that is the veneration of an image. Likewise, during the Christmas season, manger scenes and numerous other images are erected as items of special spiritual significance, and that is no less than idolatry.

J. C. Ryle weighed in on this issue, and we do well to listen. Emphasizing again our natural bent to idolatry, he writes:

> There is a natural proneness and tendency in us all to give God a sensual, carnal worship, and not that which is commanded in His Word. We are ever ready, by reason of our sloth and unbelief, to devise visible helps and stepping stones in our approaches to Him, and ultimately to give these inventions of our own the honor due to Him.

Second, with the aforementioned history in mind, this brings us to the basis for the thinking of those who have stood against such practices, namely, *Scriptural command*. All of them took Exodus 20:4, in its plain meaning: **Thou shalt not make unto thee any graven image, or any likeness of any thing that is in heaven above, or that is in the earth beneath, or that is in the water under the earth.** Some Bible teachers insist that this commandment merely forbids art or other images of *false* gods, but that is patently false. The context makes it clear. The First Commandment commands us to worship God alone: "Thou shalt have no other gods before me" (Ex. 20:3). The Second Commandment tells us to do so not by our own devices but only by His self-disclosure. Verse 5 goes on to detail how pagans make images of heavenly and earthly objects to represent their gods, but this must *never* be so of the True God.

This clear meaning of the text has been consistently held by faithful theologians, expositors, and commentators. Calvin, for example, wrote:

> By these words he restrains our waywardness from trying to represent him by any visible image, and briefly enumerates all those forms by which superstition long ago began to turn his truth into falsehood. . . . We believe it wrong that God should be represented by a visible appearance, because he himself has forbidden it [Exodus 20:4] and it cannot be done without some defacing of his glory.[20]

Puritan Thomas Watson agreed: "To set up an image to represent God, is debasing Him. . . . What greater disparagement to the infinite God than to represent Him by that which is finite?"[21] Also citing this commandment, the great theologian Charles Hodge concurred: "Idolatry consists not only in the worship of false gods, but in the worship of the true God by images."[22] R. W. Dale, the famous 19th-century English Congregationalist preacher and theologian, likewise wrote:

> The second Commandment condemns a very different sin from that which is condemned in the first. The first condemns the worshipping of false gods; the second condemns the making of any image or symbol even of the true God.[23]

That great expositor G. Campbell Morgan similarly wrote: "The first forbids us to have any other gods . . . The second . . . forbids the creation of anything which is supposed to be a representation of Him, to assist man in worship." Morgan then goes on to add a critical point:

> Man declares that he must have something to help him in his worship of God. Devout souls . . . avow that they do not worship the image, but the God behind it . . . *Yet this is exactly what is forbidden in this commandment.* . . . that they should not be used as representations to help in worship. "God is a Spirit, and they that worship Him must worship in spirit and in truth." The *material* cannot help the *spiritual.*[24]

Is not the golden calf a vivid example of this very fact? The thought of renouncing or replacing God never entered the people's minds as they prodded Aaron into making the golden calf. On the contrary, "Here are your gods," they announced, "who brought you up out of Egypt." And the festival in honor of the calf was kept as a "feast to the LORD" (Ex. 32:4–5). When Jeroboam set up the calves of gold in Dan and Bethel, it never occurred to him to tell the ten tribes to cast off their allegiance to God. Rather, he simply said, "It is too much for you to go up to Jerusalem: behold thy gods, O Israel, which brought thee up out of the land of Egypt" (1 Kings 12:28).

In both instances, the idol was *not* set up as a *another* God, rather it was erected as being a *helper* in His worship and even a *springboard* to His service. But none of that made this terrible sin any less horrific. It is an inescapable fact that no image whatsoever should be made as a replica, representation, or reminder of God. We say again, the temptation is simply too great. biblically and historically, the use of images always degenerates. Nothing *material* must be allowed to be lifted to the level of *spiritual*. Once again, "True worshippers . . . worship the Father in spirit and in truth: for the Father seeketh such to worship him" (John 4:23; v. 24).[25]

The Moratorium on Idolatry

While we have already noted Scriptures that command and warn against idolatry, I pray this final thought will bring it home to our minds with particular force. There must, indeed, be a moratorium, a cessation, a halt, an end to idolatry in the hearts of God's people. While it is a result of the fall, idolatry can be reversed by God's power. If we do not purge it, however, there will be judgment. God's severest judgments of His people throughout history, in fact, were because of this sin.

We close, therefore, by considering once again 1 John 5:21: **Little children, keep yourselves from idols.** While the precise date John wrote this epistle is unknown, there is strong evidence that it was late in the 1st-century. Since we do know that John's later years were spent in Ephesus, and because church tradition consistently maintains that John spent those years in extensive writing, the date had to be 85–95. The whole tone of the Epistle supports this view, as John's use of the term **little children** (nine times) strongly indicates that he was much older than his readers.

That being the case, this last verse of the Epistle was among the last words of Scripture that were written. While Revelation was last, of course, its theme is vastly different. John's Epistle, however, contains the final words of personal counsel and pointed command from the last of the Apostles, the words of an aged saint to his spiritual **little children**. So what did he tell them in his final words? **Keep yourselves from idols. Keep** translates *phulassō*, "to keep watch, to guard," and was used of the garrison of a city guarding it against outside attack. It is also in the aorist imperative, marking a crisis point at which time obedience to a command must begin at that very moment. Idolatry stops here and now!

The eloquent William Alexander, 19th-century preacher and poet, wrote, "Two things especially hated by John were lying and idolatry." Alexander then refers to John's appeal in this final verse as "an eloquent shudder."[26] I cannot think of a better way to end this chapter (as I did the sermon on which it is based) than that. Let us pray that any thought of idolatry will, indeed, give us an eloquent shudder.

NOTES

[1] J. C. Ryle, *Knots Untied*, reprinted by Charles Nolan Publishers (now in public domain).

[2] Colin Brown (Ed.), *The New International Dictionary of New Testament Theology* (Zondervan, 1975), Vol. 2, p. 284.

[3] *Girdlestone's Synonyms of the Old Testament*, Third Edition (Baker Book House, 1983 reprint), p. 328.

[4] Thomas Watson, *The Ten Commandments* (Banner of Truth Trust, 1965; originally published 1692), p. 62.

[5] J. C. Philpot, "The History of an Idol, its Rise, Reign, and Progress." The Latin is, *amor tussisque non celantur*, literally, "love and a cough cannot be concealed."

[6] Philip Schaff, *History of the Christian Church* (electronic edition), Vol. 3, Chapter 8, §100.

[7] Earle Cairns, *Christianity Thorough the Centuries* (Zondervan, 1964, 1966), p. 175.

[8] George Park Fisher, *History of the Christian Church* (New York: Charles Scribner's Sons, 1887, 1915), p. 117.

[9] *Eusebius Pamphilius: Church History, Life of Constantine, Oration in Praise of Constantine* [Philip Schaff, Editor, 1819-1893 and Rev. Arthur Cushman McGiffert, Translator], Book VII, Chapter XVIII, para. 4.

[10] *The Works of John Jewel* (Cambridge University Press, 1847), Vol. 2, p. 652.

[11] Prolegomena, §2. Catalogue of his Works, VIII. Epistles.

[12] From footnote in the above citation from Eusebius' *Church History*.

[13] *Hieron. in Jerem* 10:3–5; Opp. IV, 911.

[14] *Letters 51:9, Corpus Scriptorum Ecclesiasticorum Latinorum* (CSEL 54. 411; tr. *A Select Library of the Nicene and Post-Nicene Fathers*, second series, 6. 89).

[15] Schaff, Vol. 3, Chapter 8, §110.

[16] *Institutes of the Christian Religion*, ed. by John McNeill, tr. by Ford Lewis Battles (Westminster Press, 1960), Vol. 1, p. 20 (PA.4).

[17] Ibid, footnote 21 cites C. J Hefele,, ed. and H Leclercq, *Histoire des conciles d'apres les documents originaux* (1. 240; Mansi 2. 264).

[18] Fisher, p. 117.

[19] Calvin, *Institutes*, Vol. 1, p. 110 (I.11.9). Calvin here cites Augustine, *Psalms*, Psalm 113:2:4–6 and 115.

[20] Calvin, *Institutes*, Vol. 1, p. 100 (I.11.1).

[21] Watson, pp. 59–60.

[22] *Systematic Theology* (Eerdmans, reprint 1989), Vol 1, p. 149.

[23] R. W. Dale, *The Ten Commandments*, Fourth Edition (Hodder and Stoughton, 1884), p. 39.

[24] G. Campbell Morgan, *The Ten Commandments* (The Bible Institute Colportage Association of Chicago, 1901), pp. 25–27 (emphasis added).

---

²⁵ We also call the reader's attention to J. I. Packer's wonderful discussion of this in *Knowing God* (InterVarsity), pp. 43–51. E.g., "Images dishonor God, for they obscure His glory" and they "mislead us, for they convey false ideas about God."

²⁶ William Alexander, *Primary Convictions* (James R. Osgood, McIlvaine & Co, 1893), p. 213–214.

Too many ministers are toying with the deadly cobra of "another gospel," in the form of "modern thought."

Charles Spurgeon
The Sword and the Trowel (1887)

44

The King and Mephibosheth:
A New Testament Portrait*

2 Samuel 9

There are many great Bible stories we all know and love. There are wonderful stories of triumph, such as: Creation; God's providing the ram in place of Isaac; Joseph and Potiphar's wife; the Exodus from Egypt; David and Goliath; Daniel in the lion's den; and many more. There are also sad stories of tragedy: man's fall in the Garden; Cain and Abel; Sodom and Gomorrah; Samson and Delilah; David and Bathsheba; and others. Such is the great value of the Old Testament, where we read stories that are "for [ex]amples . . . written for our admonition" (1 Cor. 10:11).

We all have our favorite Bible story, but mine is one that is not as well known, one that is rather obscure, in fact. It is recorded in 2 Samuel 9. Please pause and read that passage.

In my humble opinion, there is no Old Testament story of greater beauty than this one. I've preached this several times over the years in several churches, refining it a little each time, and did so again recently (you can listen to this message online[1]). This is, in fact, my favorite message I have ever preached in over 38 years of ministry (as of 2012). While an *Old* Testament *tale*, we find here absolutely amazing illustrations of many *New* Testament *truths*. This story paints a graphic picture of salvation and service, of how God deals with man and how man should respond. King David is representative of God in His place and power, and Mephibosheth is a vivid portrait of man in his helplessness. Here is a story of mercy, grace, and love that illustrates what God has done for man through Jesus Christ. Let us make twelve observations.

Mephibosheth Was Crippled by a Fall

Back in 4:4, we read: "And Jonathan, Saul's son, had a son that was lame of his feet. He was five years old when the tidings came of Saul and Jonathan out of Jezreel, and his nurse took him up, and fled: and it came to pass, as she made haste to flee, that he fell, and became lame. And his name

---

* This chapter was originally TOTT issue 68, March 2011, and was based upon a sermon by the author.

was Mephibosheth." The news that came from Jezreel, of course, was that David's dear friend Jonathan had been killed in battle and Saul had taken his own life to prevent being captured by the Philistines. Out of fear that the Philistines might destroy the rest of Saul's family, especially an heir to the throne, the little boy's panicked nurse dropped him and either broke a bone that didn't heal properly or caused some other debilitating injury.

The first feature we note in our story, therefore, is that *Mephibosheth was crippled by a fall.* That, too, is what happened to all humanity—it was crippled by Adam's fall. Because of that fall, man is lame and totally helpless; he is sinful and will forever fall short of what God demands. As Romans 3:10 declares, "There is none righteous, no, not one." Verse 23 goes on to add, "All have sinned, and come short of the glory of God." Paul goes on to conclude in 5:12, "Wherefore, as by one man sin entered into the world, and death by sin; and so death passed upon all men, for that all have sinned."

What is worse, just as Mephibosheth could do nothing in himself, man was left with his own paralyzing inability. Romans 1:21 sums up this state: "When they [fallen men] knew God, they glorified him not as God, neither were thankful; but became vain in their imaginations, and their foolish heart was darkened." "Vain" is *mataioō* from the noun *mataios*, "devoid of force, truth, success, result; speaks of that which is futile, without result or success." This word refers to the unsuccessful attempt to do or be anything. How did Solomon put it? "Vanity of vanities, all is vanity" (or "Futility of futilities, all is futile," Ecc. 1:2). So, the plight of the human race is that in refusing to glorify or thank God, it became futile (unsuccessful) in all its thoughts and reasoning.

All this is further intensified by where Mephibosheth lived. **Lodebar** literally means "pastureless," which, as William MacDonald puts it, pictures "an unconverted soul living in a barren land."[2]

So, just as David intervened on Mephibosheth's behalf, God must do the same. Why? Because we "were [spiritually] dead in trespasses and sins" and unable to help ourselves, as Paul makes clear in Ephesians 2:1–4. That leads us to our second observation.

King David Desired to Show Kindness

Verse 1 again declares, **Is there yet any that is left of the house of Saul, that I may shew him kindness.** The word **kindness** is the key word of the whole story. The Hebrew word here is *chesed*, which is "one of the most important [words] in the vocabulary of Old Testament theology and ethics,"[3] appearing some 240 times. It speaks of kindness, loving-kindness, mercy, goodness, faithfulness, loyal love, and acts of kindness.

It was likewise God's desire to show kindness to man. If there is a single word, in fact, that could summarize God's dealing with His men, it would be the word *mercy*. One example, and by far the most notable appearance of *chesed*, is in Psalm 136, where the psalmist declares twenty-six times of God, "His mercy endureth for ever." This psalm is a study in worship, with God's mercy at the forefront, displaying what wondrous works He has done. Mercy is at the *foundation* of His character (vv. 1–3), the *function* of His creative work (vv. 4–9), the *fountain* from which all His blessings flow to His people (vv. 10–25), and the *force* behind His Rulership in heaven (v. 26).

The whole point of mercy, therefore, is to relieve the affliction that man suffers (just as David relieved Mephibosheth) because he cannot relieve it himself. Mercy is always to the helpless, to the crippled, to the dead, in fact. This again leads to another observation.

Mephibosheth Did Not Earn David's Kindness

This fact is also clearly indicated in verse 1 and implied in the whole passage. Nowhere do we read that Mephibosheth did anything to earn the king's kindness. He had nothing to do with any of it. After all, what could he possibly offer the king? He was a helpless cripple. Likewise, while every religion of the world claims that salvation comes by works that we do for God, that is not what we see in God's revelation. "Surely I can do enough that God will have mercy on me," it is claimed. "Surely I can do enough good works to merit salvation." No, man cannot earn salvation; he is dead, worthless, and totally at the mercy of God.

Paul made this clear in Titus 3:5, "Not by works of righteousness which we have done, but according to his mercy he saved us, by the washing of regeneration, and renewing of the Holy Ghost." Even more direct was Isaiah when he graphically pictured the sinfulness of man and what his good works amount to: "But we are all as an unclean thing, and all our righteousnesses are as filthy rags; and we all do fade as a leaf; and our iniquities, like the wind, have taken us away" (Isa. 64:6). The Hebrew behind "filthy rags" literally refers to "a menstrual cloth" (Lev. 15:33; 20:18). Think of it! All of man's good deeds and good intentions are as useless and offensive to God as a menstrual cloth is to us. Isaiah adds that all we might do will simply wither like a leaf and blow away.

No truth is clearer in Scripture, in fact, than that salvation is apart from any merit or works of men, that works cannot save. Writing again to the Romans, Paul declared that if salvation is "by grace, then is it no more of works: otherwise grace is no more grace. But if it be of works, then is it no more grace: otherwise work is no more work" (Rom. 11:6). To the Ephesians he made it clear that "by grace are ye saved through faith; and that not of yourselves: it is the gift of God: Not of works, lest any man should boast" (Eph. 2:8, 9). Verse after verse declares this truth (Job 9:20; Rom. 3:20, 28; 4:5; 9:11, 16, 30; Gal. 2:16; 3:16–21).

David's Kindness was for Jonathan's Sake

Recall a moment the closeness of David and Jonathan. First Samuel 18:1 tells us that their souls were "knit with" each other. Here was one of the closest friendships in human history. So, the kindness David wanted to show was for the sake of Jonathan and was to be toward *Jonathan's offspring*. Now for the parallel: Oh, how God loved Adam, and how God loves Adam's offspring, that is, *us*! But even more than that, as Jonathan typifies the first Adam, he also typifies the second Adam (Christ), for "as in Adam all die, even so in Christ shall all be made alive" (1 Cor. 15:22). How often we think that God showed us grace primarily for *our* sake, when actually He showed grace toward us primarily for *Christ's* sake, because of the love He has for His dear Son, the Creator.

Why did kindness come to Mephibosheth? No, it wasn't his works, it wasn't what he could do for the king. It was because of who he was related to. The same is true for us. It is only because of our relationship to Jesus Christ that God bestows mercy and grace.

The King Summoned Mephibosheth

Verse 5 tells us that **king David sent, and fetched** Mephibosheth. We often hear it said of certain people that they are "seeking God." Many church ministries, in fact, have been specifically tailored to appeal to what are called "seekers." But such so-called seekers are seeking a wide range of things, such as: philosophy, debate, religion, morality, political correctness, religious toleration, or just plain entertainment. Such people are not seeking truth at all, for when they are confronted with Christ, who *is* "the way, the truth, and the life," they reject Him.

Romans 3:11–18, in fact, categorically declares that man in no way seeks God, does nothing to please God, and actually runs away from God. Adam is a proof of that. Knowing he had sinned against God, he and Eve "hid themselves from the presence of the LORD God amongst the trees of the garden" (Gen. 3:8). Jonah, even as a prophet, tried to hide from God. Jesus sought each of His disciples; they did not seek Him. In the Last Days, men will try to hide themselves from God's judgment (Rev. 6:15–17). And it is because of man's natural tendency to run from God, that Jesus had "to come to seek and to save that which was lost" (Lk. 19:10).

We can also add that if any one appears to be truly seeking God, it is only because God, through His sovereign grace, is drawing him. As our

Lord Himself declared in John 6:44: "No man can come to me, except the Father which hath sent me draw him." Such an effectual call is absolutely necessary simply because man's depravity makes him run from God.

The King Sent Messengers to Fetch Mephibosheth

Verse 5 also tells us that David used others to actually go get Mephibosheth. Could David have done this personally? Certainly. But he chose to use others to carry out the task.

The application could not be clearer. There is no better picture of evangelism in the Old Testament than this. God could certainly save anyone without using what we might call "a middle man," but He has chosen to use us as His messengers. He has declared all believers, in fact, to be His witnesses, as we read in Acts 1:8: "ye shall receive power, after that the Holy Ghost is come upon you: and ye shall be witnesses unto me both in Jerusalem, and in all Judaea, and in Samaria, and unto the uttermost part of the earth."

"Witnesses" is the Greek *martus* (English *martyr*), which was a legal term, just like today. The witness gives solemn testimony to that which he knows and offers evidence. The Christian, therefore, is one who testifies of Christ and gives evidence through his or her life. So, it's not just that we witness for Christ with our *lips*, but rather what we also do through our *life*. It's not so much that the local church evangelizes through "programs of evangelism" or "evangelistic campaigns," but rather individual believers are the outreach.

Mephibosheth Reverenced the King

Verse 6 tells us that **when Mephibosheth . . . was come unto David, he fell on his face, and did reverence.** The word **reverence** is the Hebrew (*shāchāh*) that is commonly used for worship, but its primary meaning is simply "to bow down." This is important because Mephibosheth was undoubtedly bowing not out of worship but simply out of **fear**. In that day, being summoned before the king was not a good thing, especially in this case. Mephibosheth was a member of a deposed royal family who could claim throne rights, and it was common practice to destroy the household of one's predecessor. That is why David says in verse 7 **fear not**. This further underscores David's mercy and grace.

It is such **fear**, in fact, that must be the starting place for man. "The fear of the LORD," Solomon wrote, "is the beginning of knowledge" (Prov. 1:7) and "the beginning of wisdom" (9:10). In other words, *true knowledge begins with a fear of God*. If we are to know anything, we must begin with the presupposition of God. How, for example, can an intelligent person believe (and then brag about believing it) that the universe sprang from nothing and then evolved? How can truly brilliant people say something so absurd and irrational? Simple: because they do not start with God. Without Him, we can know nothing. Such knowledge begins with the fear of God.

It is then, and *only* then, that we can truly worship. It is a sad fact that "worship," as carried on in many churches today, is based almost exclusively on man-centered methods and on the feelings of the worshipper. Just as Mephibosheth undoubtedly was thinking only of all the king had done for him and not himself, so should our worship be. This leads to another observation.

Mephibosheth Responded as a Servant

Verse 6 tells us something else about Mephibosheth's response; he answered David with the words, **Behold thy servant!** I am blessed by that statement every time I read this passage. Let us get the picture. Handicapped people of that day were often carried by some kind of litter. Unlike such folks today who, because of modern technology, can live very productive lives, such was not the case in ancient times. Begging or some very simple trade was all they could possibly imagine.

To further underscore his worthlessness, he asks in verse 8, **What is thy servant, that thou shouldest look upon such a dead dog as I am?** The words **dead dog** reflect the attitude of the day that such were useless, contemptible. Dogs were nothing but scavengers and merited no kindness. But still Mephibosheth says, **Behold thy servant!** What could he possibly do for the king of Israel or for the furtherance of the Kingdom? Well, if nothing else, he was and still is today a challenge to others to be servants of the King of Kings. He is still proclaiming that we as crippled individuals can be useful to the King. While we can not help ourselves, when we give ourselves to the King, He will find a way to use us.

Today we tend to think only certain people can serve to the fullest, only those with great talent and natural abilities. But what we need are more Mephibosheths who realize their worthlessness (and even contemptibleness) until the King comes along to use them for His purpose.

Mephibosheth Received Riches

In verses 7 and 9 we read David's promise, **I will surely shew thee kindness for Jonathan thy father's sake, and will restore thee all the land of Saul thy father; and thou shalt eat bread at my table continually. . . . Then the king called to Ziba, Saul's servant, and said unto him, I have given unto thy master's son all that pertained to Saul and to all his house.** Mephibosheth didn't have to go back to his old home, his old world. He was now in a new world with a new inheritance. The same is true of each of us, who now "know what is the hope of his calling, and what the riches of the glory of his inheritance in the saints" (Eph. 1:18) and "the exceeding riches of his grace in his kindness toward us through Christ Jesus" (2:7). Oh, what we have in Christ! Salvation, sanctification, eternal life, spiritual gifts, a heavenly home, and more. We also, like Mephibosheth, have daily provision, knowing that "God shall supply all [our] need according to his riches in glory by Christ Jesus" (Phil. 4:19).

Mephibosheth Had Absolute Security

Again verse 7 declares, that from that day forward, with no interruption or possibility of loss, Mephibosheth would **eat** at David's **table continually**. Here is one of my favorite parts of the story. After supper, David did not say, "Well, Mephibosheth, it's been a nice evening, and I'll have you back sometime, but it's time for you go now." Indeed not. He said, in effect, "You are here to stay," and words like that from the king were absolute security.

I still recall preaching an early version of this message on Mephibosheth many years ago in a church that did not believe in the security of the believer and was promptly asked to leave and not finish the rest of the scheduled services. There are few things sadder than rejecting the security of the believer because it demonstrates a total ignorance of grace. The same unmerited favor that saves us is the same unearned kindness that keeps us. God doesn't say to his adopted sons and daughters, "Drop over once in awhile for a meal," rather He says, "You will now eat at my table forever." And it is that very thought that leads us to another observation.

Mephibosheth Became One of the King's Sons

Verse 11 is the true capstone of the whole story: **Then said Ziba unto the king, According to all that my lord the king hath commanded his servant, so shall thy servant do. As for Mephibosheth, said the king, he shall eat at my table, as one of the king's sons.** Here is a subtle but crucial point. Mephibosheth was not David's son before this incident. *He became a son only when King David declared it so because of Jonathon's sake.*

We hear countless people today say, "Oh, all people are God's children, all fellow members of the family of God." But that is a lie that Satan is thrilled with. John 1:12 makes it explicitly clear, "As many as received him [Christ], to them gave he power [i.e., the right or privilege] to become the sons of God." The Apostle echoed that truth in Galatians 3:26: "For ye are all the children of God by faith in Christ Jesus."

This is, in fact, the foundation of the biblical doctrine of adoption. We who were once "of [our] father the devil" (Jn. 8:44), have now been "predestinated . . . unto the adoption of children by Jesus Christ to himself, according to the good pleasure of his will" (Eph. 1:5). Indeed, through Christ we are forever King's sons, which again demonstrates our security. That leads to one other observation.

Mephibosheth's Crippled Condition Was Hidden

Verse 13 provides us with a beautiful parting shot before our story "fades to black": **So Mephibosheth dwelt in Jerusalem: for he did eat continually at the king's table; and was lame on both his feet.** Once again, there is no better way to grasp this principle that to get a mental picture of the scene. In the earliest Old Testament times, a **table** was no more than an animal hide or rug spread on a floor or even the ground. Royalty, on the other hand, often used a low table, around which were stools or low chairs. In the latter case, then, when we imagine Mephibosheth seated at the king's **table**, we can easily picture that his crippled condition was hidden. Besides, as everyone ate and communed together, no one cared anyway. So, as long as Mephibosheth was at the king's table, his crippled condition was hidden.

When this thought occurred to me years ago, its application struck me profoundly. As long as the Christian is seated at God's table feeding on His Word, no one will know our crippled state. While we are certainly lame in ourselves and will fall on our face if we try to leave the table, God's Word will hide our condition. We must **eat continually at the king's table**. This is why I "nag" about the importance of church attendance, because it is critical that God's people are constantly being fed the Word.

Well, we have come to the end of our story. C. I. Scofield sums it up this way: "Here is a striking picture of salvation by grace. Grace [gives] kindness to a helpless one (vv. 1–3; Eph. 2:1, 4–7) . . . gives a place of privilege to its recipient (v. 11; Eph. 1:3–6) . . . and sustains and keeps him (v. 13; John 10:28–29)."[4]

Let us each ask ourselves, "Now that I know this story, am I familiar with it by experience? Do I know God's grace for salvation? In my helpless state, am I depending upon God's mercy and grace alone? Am I committed to His service even though I have nothing to offer? Am I seated at His table and feasting on His Word?"

In a day of almost cultish emphasis on self-esteem and an arrogantly, even narcissistically, high view of man, this story should humble us. Let us not consider ourselves as a King David, but rather as a Mephibosheth.

NOTES

1 www.thescripturealone.com/MP3_New.htm

2 *Believer's Bible Commentary.*

3 *Vine's Expository Dictionary* ("Loving-kindness" entry)

4 *Scofield Reference Bible.*

Our Christian faith does not hang upon air but is firmly grounded in divine revelation. God reveals Himself in the universe which He has created, in human history, especially the history of the Christian Church, and in the preaching of the Gospel. But above all God reveals Himself in the pages of the Holy Scriptures. For without the Scriptures these other modes of divine revelation would avail us little. As John Calvin observed, the Scriptures are the spiritual eyeglasses which enable our sin-blinded minds to see aright the revelation which God makes of Himself in nature. Also the Scriptures are the key which unlocks the mysteries of history and reveals to us God's plan. And finally, the Scriptures are that pure well of divine truth to which the preachers of the Gospel must continually repair and fill their silver pitchers. The Scriptures, therefore, are the foundation of faith. In them, alone God's revelation of Himself is found unobscured by human error. They are the Word of God, which liveth and abideth forever (1 Peter 1:23).

Edward F. Hills
Believing Bible Study, 2nd Edition, pp. 3–4
[Calvin reference: *Institutes*, I.6.1]

45

The "Only Begotten" Son[*]

John 3:16

For God so loved the world, that he gave his only begotten Son, that whosoever believeth in him should not perish, but have everlasting life.

One reader of our publication sent along a question concerning the modern rendering of John 3:16. While the KJV (as well as the NKJV, NASB, and YLT), reads "only begotten Son," the NIV (as well as the NCV and MSG) reads "one and only Son." Other translations (ESV, NRSV, NLT, CEV, and GWT) simply read "only." While I provided an answer then, I later felt compelled to go a little deeper. My reason was simply because this issue is actually more important than we realize. There is, in fact, something at stake here, namely, *doctrine*.

As I always do before approaching anything having to do with the issues of textual criticism or Bible translations, I want to make it clear up front that I know some TOTT readers embrace the Critical Text and the modern translations based on it, so I do not wish to offend or inflame. While there are godly men on both sides of the issue, I do defend the historic (and what I believe is the providentially preserved) text of the New Testament (i.e., Traditional or Ecclesiastical Text) instead of the modern Critical Text.

With that said, the issue at hand has nothing to do with the underlying text, but rather accuracy in translation and, most importantly, the teaching of Scripture that results from a particular rendering. In other words, saying Christ is the "only begotten" Son of God is *vastly* different than saying He is the "only" or "one and only" Son of God. I hope we can all agree in that. Words mean things and these words are most certainly very different.

Since our initial examination of this, I have come across some additional resources that discuss it. For one thing, when this change appeared in the Revised Standard version of 1952, it actually caused quite a stir. Why? Simply because this was a blatant departure from a reading that had stood for centuries. Even the original Revised Version of 1881, as well as its American counterpart, the American Standard Version of 1901 (both of which were based, of course, on the Critical Text of Westcott and Hort)

---

[*] This chapter was originally TOTT issue 70, May 2011.

retained "only begotten." Along comes the RSV, however, and *poof* "begotten" vanishes.

I for one simply do not understand why so many evangelicals just shrug this off as apparently irrelevant. At the time of its publication, and for several years after, the RSV was notorious for being the most liberal translation to date. One of its greatest errors, for example was rendering the Hebrew *'almāh* in Isaiah 7:14 as "young girl" instead of the correct "virgin" (an error still retained in the NRSV but fixed in the ESV). But now, lo and behold, we have several translations that retain the same reading. This is not surprising for either the NRSV or ESV because they are both based on the RSV (the increasingly popular ESV, in fact, is 91% the same). But why doesn't this bother NIV users, who insist that this is a great Bible? Something is seriously amiss here.

Interestingly, this rendering was not totally novel with the RSV. Several lesser known translators had offered it before.[1] Because of the endorsement of the RSV by the National Council of Churches, however (which also owns the NRSV and the ESV), not to mention a huge marketing campaign at its launch, the now missing "only begotten" was noticed by many.

Also interesting (and revealing) was the reaction of some of the RSV committee members when they were criticized for this change. One, Frederick C. Grant, was down right indignant. In an article in *The Bible Translator* in 1966, he wrote:

> . . . perhaps the great truth expressed in the Gospel of St. John is better expressed, and better safeguarded, *in modern English*, by the perfectly correct, entirely accurate, and theologically far more adequate expression 'only son', than the cumbersome, antiquated (antiquated in 1611) translation 'only begotten son.' One needs only to study it a little and the Greek behind it, and to become a little more familiar with the new version as a whole, to realize its superiority over the older rendering.[2]

Well, setting aside his mildly condescending attitude, I did just what Grant challenged. I studied it. What I found is that this reading is far from "correct," "accurate," and "theologically adequate." It is, in fact, error textually, doctrinally, and historically.

"Only Begotten" in the Language and Theology

In addition to the great truths in this verse concerning God's *love* (*agapē*) for His own and the eternal life that comes by *faith* (*pisteuō*) in Christ, it is also distinctive because the Apostle John is the only Scripture writer who uses the term *monogenēs* to describe the relationship of Jesus to the Father. *Monogenēs* is a compound, comprised of *monos* (English *monograph*), "only, alone, without others," and *genos* (English *gene*), "offspring, stock." The idea then is "only offspring," "only physical stock," or, as one commentator puts it, "only born-one."[3] In ancient Greek, this word was used to refer to a unique being.

This makes it very clear that something is unique here, but saying that Christ is the "only son" or "one and only son" is not unique. Why? Because, as we will see, He is neither one of those. There are other sons, so we must say something that actually sets Him apart from those, and that is what "only begotten" ("one physically born one") does.

To go a little deeper first, however, the massive 10-volume *Theological Dictionary of the New Testament*, edited by Gerhard Kittel, has been recognized as a chief authority for many years. Within its four large pages on *monogenēs*, we read the following:

> The *mono-* does not denote the source but the nature of derivation. Hence, *monogenēs* means "of sole descent," i.e., without brothers or sisters. This give us the sense of only begotten. . . . It is found only in later [New Testament] writings. It means "only-begotten." . . . [It] occurs in John 1:14, 18; 3:16, 18; 1 John 4:9. What is meant is plainest in John 3:16 and 1 John 4:9. . . . It is only as the only-begotten Son of God that Jesus can mediate life and salvation from perdition. . . . In John [it] denotes the origin of Jesus. He is *monogenēs* as the only-begotten.[4]

There is undoubtedly no specific connection, but it is at least interesting that this dictionary was published only a year after Grant's article appeared (1967). While Grant calls this reading "cumbersome [and] antiquated," this dictionary has no problem using it a dozen times.

As for his comment that "only begotten" was even "antiquated in 1611," he is actually correct but for the wrong reason. The same is true, for example, of the "thees" and "thous" that are so maligned nowadays and replaced with modern pronouns. Most people mistakenly say, "That's the way they talked then, but we don't talk like that anymore." But that shows the misinformation that is propagated nowadays. The fact of the matter is that they did *not* talk like that. These pronouns were purposely used because they alone could accurately convey the singular and plural indicated in the Greek and Hebrew; only they can differentiate between single and plural in second person pronouns.[5] William Tyndale knew all this almost 100 years before and *deliberately* revived words that had already passed from common use for the sole purpose of accuracy. The KJV translators likewise understood this and left them untouched, as the

KJV is 90% Tyndale's work. I often have to just smile and walk away when I hear someone say, "Oh, the KJV is not accurate," because the fact is that because of the "antiquated" pronouns, it is fundamentally more accurate than modern translations in over 19,000 instances.[6]

Added to that, if the Apostle John had really wanted to indicate "only son" or "one and only son," why didn't he actually say that and erase all question? For the former he could have used *monos huios* and for the latter he could have written *heis kai monos huios*. No, he uses a term that underscores physical birth, something that is indeed unique.

It is here that Grant launches into a long peroration of how often *monogenēs* is used in classic Greek writings, as well as in Scripture, to indicate "only son," not "only begotten son." As Bible scholar Jacob van Bruggen well says, however, while it is true that *monogenēs* can refer to an only child, *it does so only when this fact is actually true*.[7] In Luke 7:12, for example, the widow's son at Nain is said to be "the only son of his mother." In 8:42 we also read that Jairus "had one only daughter," and in 9:38, the father of the demon possessed boy says "he is mine only child." But again, in each case that was the real state of things.

Based on that, Grant confidently concludes, "Jesus is the *only* son of the Father" (emphasis Grant's). But, is that, in fact, true? Is it true that God only has one Son or "one and only Son"? Of course not. If modern translations read "only unique son" we could agree, because that is clearly what *monogenēs* implies, but "only" or "one and only" is simply not so. If it were, then Paul was wrong when he wrote that Christ is "the firstborn among many brethren" (Rom. 8:29). Who are those brethren? We are! As 2 Corinthians 6:18 and other verses make crystal clear, all believers are "sons and daughters." Christ is the only Son of God by *natural* means ("one physically born one"), the only one actually *begotten* (born into the world) as a son of God, while we are children by *adoption*. Jesus, however, is, as one translator renders it, "His Son, the uniquely begotten one,"[8] or another, "His Son—the only begotten."[9]

John makes this same point earlier in his Gospel when he writes that Christ is "the only begotten of the Father, full of grace and truth" (1:14) and is "the only begotten Son, which is in the bosom of the Father" (v. 18). He writes again in his first epistle "that God sent his only begotten Son into the world, that we might live through him" (4:9).

While Grant and modern translations get these wrong too, "only begotten" is the only rendering that makes sense and matches Scripture elsewhere. This term "only begotten," in fact, is a wonderful summary of Psalm 2:7: "Thou art my Son; this day have I begotten thee," a glorious reference to coming Messiah, which in-turn is quoted and applied to Christ in Acts 13:33 and Hebrews 1:5 and 5:5.

So, this issue is not one of just vocabulary or grammar; it also has to do with underlying biblical truth. Neither of the two can ever be forced to stand alone. If that is not enough, however, there is something else to consider.

"Only Begotten" in History

While it is certainly true that "only begotten" is, as Grant insists, the "older rendering" (like that is automatically bad), what seems to be missed is that it's also the *historic* rendering. Why was it that latter 20th-century Christianity consistently ran as fast as it could away from historic doctrine, historic texts, and virtually all other things historic? And it is still running.

While many today insist this is "no big deal," history very pointedly rebukes such a lack of wisdom. The framers of both the original *Nicene Creed* of 325 and the later 381 version recognized this fact. That creed is the most widely used brief statement of the Christian Faith, and both versions declare Christ to be the "only begotten" Son of God.

It seems that even Jerome understood the importance of this doctrine. While his 4th-century Latin Vulgate has its problems, he correctly chose to use the Latin *unigenitus*, "only begotten."

Another important historical document was *The Definition of Chalcedon* in 451. While the *Nicene* established the eternal, pre-existent Godhead of Christ, the *Chalcedon* came as a response to certain heretical views concerning His nature. In addition to declaring His virgin birth, sinless nature, and co-equality with the Father, it also declared that His "nature being preserved, and concurring in one Person and one Subsistence, not parted or divided into two persons, but one and the same Son, and only begotten, God the Word, the Lord Jesus Christ."

This was also recognized by the great theological minds that penned *The Heidelberg Catechism* (1576). In answer to Question 33—"Why is Christ called the only begotten Son of God, since we are also the children of God?"—it states: "Because Christ alone is the eternal and natural Son of God; but we are children adopted of God, by grace, for his sake," adding Scripture proofs for both sentences.

The Canons of Dort (1619) likewise used this term. Speaking of Christ's death, it declares: "This death is of such great value and worth for the reason that the person who suffered it is—as was necessary to be our Savior—not only a true and perfectly holy man, but also the only begotten Son of God, of the same eternal and infinite essence with the Father and the Holy Spirit" (Third Point of Doctrine, Article 4).

Of enormous significance are the two greatest statements of faith of all: *The Westminster Confession of Faith* (1646), and *The London Baptist Confession* (1689). In both we read:

It pleased God, in his eternal purpose, to choose and ordain the Lord Jesus, his only-begotten Son, to be the Mediator between God and men, the prophet, priest, and king; the head and Savior of the Church, the heir or all things, and judge of the world; unto whom he did, from all eternity, give a people to be his seed, and to be by him in time redeemed, called, justified, sanctified, and glorified. (8.1).

This demands a question: Why is it that the ancient church, as well as the church of the Middle Ages, could recognize the unique sonship of Christ but we today cannot? It continues to puzzle me that so many evangelicals support the NIV. Here is one of the most graphic examples why they should not. It goes completely contrary to historic statements of faith on the present subject. We would lovingly submit that it makes no sense for evangelicals who are truly historic to support the NIV.

For those who still have doubts, I would strongly recommend Robert Martin's *Accuracy of Translation*.[10] This is a book of tremendous significance. Martin is *not* a "King James Only" advocate, and the book is published by the rock solid Banner of Truth Trust, a publisher that has consistently offered books that champion the historic positions of the faith. His point is to explain the principles lying behind contemporary translations and carefully analyze the NIV. While I don't agree with his Appendix C, and while his book is not quite equal to Jacob van Bruggen's *The Future of the Bible* (noted earlier), it is the best analysis available today from a mainstream publisher.

Conclusion

There is no ambiguity here. Grant is defending the indefensible. He is wrong, plain and simple, and so are modern translations. They are wrong textually, doctrinally, and historically. Let's be honest. The fact that Jesus was "the only begotten" is basic doctrine, baby's milk, Theology 101. If a Bible translation can't get this right, what else is in danger? We need to humble ourselves and admit that several modern translations are retaining a reading that is clearly not "correct," "accurate," or "theologically far more adequate"—plain and simple.

NOTES

[1]   Examples: Ferrar Fenton's *Holy Bible in Modern English* (1853); R. F. Weymouth's *The New Testament in Modern Speech* (1902); James Moffatt's *The*

448 *Truth on Tough Texts*

New Testament: a New Translation (1922); William G. Ballantine's *The Riverside New Testament* (1923); Edgar J. Goodspeed's *The New Testament: an American Translation* (1923); Helen Barrett Montgomery's *Montgomery New Testament* (1924); Charles B. Williams' *The New Testament in the Language of the People* (1936); and J. B. Phillips' *New Testament in Modern English* (1958).

2   Frederick C. Grant, "'Only-Begotten'—A Footnote to the R.S.V.," *The Bible Translator* 17 (1966), pp. 11–14. Quotation from p. 14 (emphasis in the original). Grant was Edwin Robinson Professor of Biblical Theology at Union Theological Seminary, New York, and President of Seabury-Western Theological Seminary, Evanstaon, IL.

This article was first brought to my attention by Jacob van Bruggen, *The Future of the Bible* (Institute for Biblical Textual Studies, 2003 reprint of the 1978 original), pp. 134–135. I was then able to locate it online (http://www.ubs-translations.org/tbt/1966/01/TBT196601.html?seq=13) and there thoroughly investigate it. van Bruggen is professor Emeritus of New Testament exegesis at the Reformed Theological College in Kampen, The Netherlands. While difficult to find, the book is available from the Institute For Biblical Textual Studies; 5151 52nd Street; Grand Rapids, Michigan; 49512; 616-942-8498; email@kjv-ibts.org.

3   John F. Walvoord and Roy B. Zuck, *The Bible Knowledge Commentary* (Wheaton: Scripture Press Publications, Inc., 1983, 1985).

4   Gerhard Kittel (editor), *Theological Dictionary of the New Testament* (Eerdmans, 1964; reprinted 2006), Vol. IV, p. 738–741.

5   For example, John 3:7 reads, "Marvel not that I said unto *thee, Ye* must be born again" (emphasis added), while new translations replace both "thee" and "ye" with "you." But "you" does not indicate whether the second person pronoun is singular or plural. In contrast, "ye" is plural and "thee" is singular. In fact, this is 100% consistent throughout the KJV. Every pronoun that begins with "y" (ye, you, and your) is plural, and every pronoun that begins with "t" is singular (thou, thee, thy, and thine).

Another example of the importance of this is how the KJV uses "you" and "thee" *in the same verse* no less than 382 times. Just one of these is Romans 1:11, where Paul writes: "For I long to see *you*, that I may impart unto *you* some spiritual gift, to the end *ye* may be established" (emphasis added). In other words, "I long to see *all of you as a group*, that I may impart unto *all of you* some spiritual gift, to the end that *each one of you individually* may be established."

6   Using *QuickVerse* 4.0, the data for the appearance of the second person pronouns is as follows: "thee" (3,827 times); "thy" (4,604 times); "thyself" (214 times); "thou" (5,474 times); "thine" (937 times); and "ye" (3,983 times); total 19,039.

To say that these pronouns are not significant is simply foolish. Just a few other examples, picked at random, one from each NT book (except 2 and 3 John), are: Matt. 5:11; Mk. 16:7; Lk. 6:31; Jn. 16:12; Acts 3:22; Rom. 12:1; 1 Cor. 1:10; 2 Cor. 2:4; Gal. 1:6; Eph 4:11; Phil. 1:27; Col. 1:9; 1 Thes. 2:2; 2 Thes. 3:4; Heb. 5:12; Jas. 2:16; 1 Pet. 5:10; 2 Pet. 1:12; 1 Jn. 2:1; Jude 1:3; Rev.

2:10. Every instance plainly shows the difference between the singular and plural and provides better understanding of the verse.

[7] van Bruggen, *op cit.*

[8] *Wuest's Expanded Translation* (Grand Rapids: Eerdmans Publishing Company, 1961).

[9] *Young's Literal Translation* (1862, 1898).

[10] Martin is Pastor of Emmanuel Baptist Church (Seattle, WA) and the author of *A Guide to the Puritans*, also published by Banner of Truth.

To account for such an amazing book with its continuity of development on natural means would demand a greater miracle than inspiration itself.

Louis Sperry Chafer, *Major Bible Themes*, p. 13

46

GOD Was Manifest in the Flesh[*]

1 Timothy 3:16

And without controversy great is the mystery of godliness: God was manifest in the flesh, justified in the Spirit, seen of angels, preached unto the Gentiles, believed on in the world, received up into glory.

Have you ever stopped to think that there are over 750,000 words in the Bible? Since there are that many, can a single one make much difference or really matter all that much? Can it effect doctrine one way or another?

It would seem that each word is, indeed, important. Since our Lord said that His "words shall not pass away" (Matt. 24:35), even to the extent that not one jot (the smallest letter of the Hebrew alphabet, *yod,* ˈ) or tittle (a small line or projection on a Hebrew letter) would "pass from the law, till all be fulfilled" (5:18), it would seem that each word is significant and important.

Well, there is a word in our text that has been a major point of question since the days modern textual criticism began. In fact, it's believed to be the only text that has been examined with a microscope in an attempt to verify what the letters are.

The issue is basically this: There is no clearer statement in the New Testament of the deity of Jesus Christ than 1 Timothy 3:16—**And without controversy great is the mystery of godliness: God was manifest in the flesh, justified in the Spirit, seen of angels, preached unto the Gentiles, believed on in the world, received up into glory**—but the Word **God** does not appear in modern translations, being replaced with either "He" or "who."

Once again, we broach an issue in which there is disagreement, but we would submit that this text is especially critical in the debate and should be considered with the greatest of care. Some TOTT readers embrace the Critical Text and the modern translations based on it, so I do not wish to offend or inflame. While there are godly men on both sides of the issue, I do defend the historic (and what I believe is the providentially preserved) text of the New Testament (i.e., Traditional or Ecclesiastical Text) instead

---

[*] This chapter was originally TOTT issue 71, June 2011.

of the modern Critical Text. (Neither am I of the radical "King James Only" camp.)

There is, however, a twist on this particular text. As we will see, the evidence, both internal and external, is absolutely overwhelming that **God** is the correct reading in this verse. The twist comes in with one of today's most quoted defenders of modern textual criticism. Being careful to speak the Truth in love, we would quote and then graciously comment on a statement he makes in his very popular book about "King James Onlyism":

> There is much to be said in defense of the King James rendering of 1 Timothy 3:16 as "God was manifest in the flesh." In fact, I prefer this reading, and feel that it has more than sufficient support from the Greek manuscripts. I can agree with the majority of the comments made on the topic long ago by Dean Burgon.[1]

Dean John Burgon was a contemporary of Westcott and Hort, the original developers of the Critical Text, on which was then based the English Revised Version (1881), American Standard Version (1901), and most translations since. Burgon, however, an unimpeachable scholar of enormous qualifications, but who was (and still is) virtually ignored, wrote against this revolution in textual studies. Of several works, his 300-page book, *The Last Twelve Verses of Mark*, for example, proved beyond even the tiniest tinge of doubt that those verses are authentic, despite the marginal notes to the contrary in modern translations.

So, what makes the above statement so surprising (and, if I may be so blunt, inconsistent) is that Burgon uses the same arguments in defense of dozens of other verses that he uses for 1 Timothy 3:16, but the above author apparently ignores this. If I may submit, one cannot "have his cake and eat it too," nor can he mix oil and water.

The Textual Evidence and Theology of "God"

Let us first look at the textual evidence concerning the correct reading in this verse and also demonstrate that it does matter theologically which one we choose. We will try to present this as simply as possible.

The Problem

The problem is basically this. Like English, Greek has upper and lower case letters. From about the 3rd- to the 9th-centuries, manuscripts were written entirely in capital letters, called "uncials"—such large, block letters were used for public notices because they were easy to see—while "minuscules" (or "cursive," small letters) were used from the 9th-century onward.

Now, because copying uncial manuscripts was such a laborious task, a common practice was to abbreviate the name of **God** using only the first and last letter and a line above them to indicate such a contraction. Therefore:

Θεὸς (*theos*) is ΘΕΟΣ (uncial) and abbreviated $\overline{ΘΣ}$

The other half of the problem, then, is the relative pronoun "who." This is the Greek ὃς (*hos*). The little apostrophe makes a big difference, adding the aspirate "h." This was not written in the uncial form, however, and so would just be ΟΣ. Note, therefore, that the little line inside the letter and the line above the two letters was the only way to differentiate **God** from "who." This is made even worse in some manuscripts that read "which," the Greek ὃ (*ho*).

In an uncial manuscript, therefore, which has no spaces or punctuation, here's how just part of the verse reads in both versions:

ΜΥΣΤΕΡΙΟΝΟΣΕΦΑΝΕΡΩΘΗΕΝΣΑΡΚΙ
mystery,   who was manifested   in the flesh

ΜΥΣΤΕΡΙΟΝΟ̅Σ̅ΕΦΑΝΕΡΩΘΗΕΝΣΑΡΚΙ
mystery,   God   was manifested   in the flesh

Based upon this, it borders on the ludicrous to say, as many do, "It doesn't really make any difference." Are we really to believe that weakening the name **God** to a relative pronoun is irrelevant? To soften this result, some modern translations actually create a new reading, "He" (NIV, ESV), which is clearly wrong—"who" does not mean "He." Others, such as the NASB, reads, "He who," since *hos* is masculine. Either one, however, seems an obvious admission that "who" is not sufficient, so we must therefore "help" the reading. There is no way to avoid the harsh reality that Jesus Christ as **God** in the flesh is no longer clear because we have removed the word that makes it so.

At this point it is often insisted that "the *obvious* antecedent of who is, of course, Jesus Christ." But just how is this obvious? How are we supposed to know that? The last time His name appears in the preceding text is up in verse 13, but this is an entirely different context than verse 16. One of today's greatest expositors is honest enough to admit that "no antecedent for *hos* is given" but then adds that the verse "can only be describing Jesus Christ." But again, how do we know that? The plain truth of the matter is that this is deplorable grammar, something we should not accept as coming from the Apostle Paul.

In fact, this is such bad grammar that the result is the *masculine* pronoun "who" follows the *neuter* noun "mystery." This simply "cannot be," as Burgon writes: "Such an expression is abhorrent alike to Grammar and to Logic; it is intolerable in Greek as in English."[2]

The Evidence

As one reads various commentators in studying this verse, he encounters such statements as "the word 'God' is not in most manuscripts."[3] While we again strive for love and unity, we are compelled to say that such a statement is extremely shocking and makes one wonder why a commentator would say it because it simply is not so and is easily proven such. While others are not that inaccurate, they still err by saying, "*Some* manuscripts read **God**."[4]

On the contrary, the clear, demonstrable fact is that *most* manuscripts read **God**. What is the evidence? The primary debated manuscript is that of Alexandrinus, an important 5th-century uncial that resides in the British Museum and includes almost all the New Testament.[5] Many critics assert that it reads ΟΣ ("who") and that a later, passionately orthodox, scribe added the needed marks to make it read **God**.

That idea has been a popular one for over a century, that is, orthodox scribes actually altered the ancient text to make it read more strongly orthodox. In plain English, we are being told that godly men, men who were handling the sacred text of God, deliberately lied by making the text "read better." One of the chief modern proponents of this is the self-proclaimed agnostic scholar Bart Ehrman. While professing to have been a born again believer in his youth, it was during his graduate studies—under Bruce Metzger at the then and now liberal Princeton Seminary—that he turned away from orthodoxy because of what he viewed as the problems of evil and suffering and the Bible's own contradictions. His books are nothing short of blatant, in your face apostasy (which is why I do not withhold his name as I have done with others in this article). His latest book, for example—*Forged: Writing in the Name of God: Why the Bible's Authors Are Not Who We Think They Are*, released in March 2011—"reveals which New Testament books were outright forgeries" and demonstrates "how widely forgery was practiced by early Christian writers."

In an earlier work, one wholly dedicated to the above theory, Ehrman writes concerning our present text:

> We cannot overlook what the reading [*theos*] provides for the orthodox scholar—a clear affirmation of the doctrine that God became incarnate in the person of Jesus Christ. . . .The change must

have been made fairly early, at least during the third century, given its widespread attestation from the fourth century on. It can therefore best be explained as [a] . . . corruption that stresses the deity of Christ."[6]

Think of it! Here is an agnostic who dubs the strongest statement of the deity of Christ in all Scripture as being a *corruption*. How can any evangelical say that theology is not at issue in textual criticism? It continues to baffle me why true evangelicals today continue to defend a textual theory that utilizes this and many other such God dishonoring conjectures that are obviously agenda-driven. They originated in ungodly minds bent on not only the diluting of God's Word but also even slandering the character of his servants whom God has used to preserve it through the ages. It is sad, indeed, that while not actually quoting Ehrman, many evangelicals have still bought into this and other fantasies.

Let us just stop and think: Are we to believe that early godly scribes—who apparently weren't really godly at all if they deliberately altered the sacred text—were so successful that no one ever noticed? Are we to believe that such error was duplicated hundreds of times without anyone ever discerning such horrific error and deception?

The evidence for the true reading of Alexandrinus, in fact, along with the weight of other manuscripts, exposes the critic's fiction. Several outstanding scholars of the last 300 years examined this manuscript. As Burgon notes, "A man need only hold up the leaf to the light on a very brilliant day—as [Samuel] Tregelles, [Frederick] Scrivener, and many besides (including [myself]) have done"[7] to see that the marks were authentic. Scrivener, in fact, a brilliant, impeccable scholar, wrote in 1894:

> I have examined [Alexandrinus] at least twenty times within as many years, and . . . seeing (as every one must see for himself) with my own eyes, I have always felt convinced with . . . earlier collators that Codice A reads [*theos*].[8]

(If I may interject, the entire textual issue is one that I wish every Christian leader would objectively examine with his "own eyes.")

Burgon goes on to note several other scholars who attested to **God** as the correct reading. Patrick Young (1584–1652), a Scottish scholar, royal librarian to King James VI and I and King Charles I, as well as *the original collator* of Alexandrinus and had it in his possession for over 20 years, stated that **God** was the original reading. This is important, Burgon notes, since overuse and handling over 150 years ultimately resulted in the fading of the marks, but the marks were there nonetheless. Among others, Burgon also notes Bishop John Pearson (1612–1686), an English theologian and scholar who stated, "We find not *hos in any copy*" (emphasis in the original). Burgon also mentions J. Berriman,

> (who delivered a course of Lectures on the true reading of 1 Tim. 3:16, in 1737–8) [and] attests emphatically that he had seen it also. "If therefore" (he adds) "at any time hereafter the old line should become altogether undiscoverable, there will never be just cause to doubt but that the genuine, and original reading of the manuscript was **God**."[9]

That evidence, and much more we could report, demonstrates that, as Burgon's successor Edward Miller puts it, "There can be no real doubt, therefore, that [Alexandrinus] did witness for *Theos*."[10]

But Alexandrinus is far from the only evidence. In fact, Burgon discusses two other disputed uncials and then lists nearly 300 minuscules (cursives) as well as 36 lectionaries[11] that give undisputed support to **God** in this verse.

In stark contrast, *only six* manuscripts in all read *hos*, not one of which is a cursive, and only three lectionaries. So why is this reading retained? Because of the popular (though illogical) myth that "the oldest manuscripts are the best" (see the importance of the Greek Church Fathers in this regard below.)

The History of "God"

Not only are the manuscripts on the side of *Theos* in this verse, but Church History is as well. Of special note are the Greek Church Fathers. As Miller notes: "The overwhelming testimony of Fathers to manuscripts in their use, reaching back further than any existing manuscripts, adds a very powerful witness."[12] In other words, these men reach back to the days before any of the manuscripts that exist today were copied, so their testimony carries great weight. Besides other factors, this one does much to negate the "older is better" mantra. In this case, while *hos* is attested to "*not for certain by a single Greek Father*,"[13] some 20 Greek fathers confirm *Theos*.

Ignatius of Antioch (ca. 35–107), for example, who was a student of the Apostle John, made three clear allusions to this verse: "God Himself being manifested in human form"; "There is one Physician who is possessed both of flesh and spirit; both made and not made; God existing in flesh"; "There is one God, who has manifested Himself by Jesus Christ His Son, who is His eternal Word, not proceeding forth from silence."[14] Space does not permit further quotations, but other Fathers include: Dionysius of Alexandria (died 264), Barnabas (late 1st-century), Hipplytus (220);

Gregory of Nazianzus (329–390); John Chrysostom (344–407); Gregory of Nyssa (335–394); etc.

We must agree with Burgon in his response to Bishop Ellicott, who passionately opposed *Theos* in this verse: "How you can witness a gathering host of ancient Fathers illustrious as these, without misgiving, passes my comprehension."[15]

I once read the following from a very popular writer/scholar/commentator in his book on textual criticism: "I cannot think of a single great theological writer who has given his energies to defend a high view of Scripture and who has adopted the [*Textus Receptus*], since the discovery of the [older manuscripts]."[16] That puzzles (and shocks) me every time I read it because a man of his learning and stature should be familiar with Robert L. Dabney. Dabney was an outstanding theologian; his *Systematic Theology* (1871) is a classic. A. A. Hodge (son of Charles Hodge), in fact, wrote of him, "The best teacher of Theology in the United States if not the world." Well, in Volume 1 of his three volume work *Discussions: Evangelical and Theological*, Dabney clearly defended the TR against the then new Critical Text Theory. For example, after outlining the basic "few old manuscripts" *vs.* "the many recent manuscripts" debate, Dabney wrote: "Now, shall these few, which are claimed to be old, discredit the many more recent? We reply, No."[17] (Note chapter 51 for more on Dabney.)

On the present text, therefore, this "single great theological writer" states without apology that "the *theos* is changed to *hos*, thus suppressing the name of God in the text." He goes on:

> This is but an expedient, unwarranted by [the reviser's] own preferred text, to cover from the readers' eyes the insuperable internal evidence against reading the relative *os* instead of *Theos*; that for the relative there is no antecedent in the passage. So they intrude an antecedent! Yet this does not give them, still, a tenable sense; for Christ is never called by Paul the mystery, or blessed secret, of godliness. It is the doctrine about Christ which he always so calls. Nor are the defenders of this innovation even candid in their statement as to the testimony of the manuscripts, when they say, no old uncial has *Theos*. The Alexandrian indisputably has it. . . . the *prima facie* [at first view or appearance, or on first examination] evidence of the Alexandrian manuscript is for *Theos*.[18]

Additionally, the aforementioned writer has surely heard of Charles Hodge. In his monumental *Systematic Theology* (1871–73), he likewise defended the TR: "The internal evidence, so far as the perspicuity of the passage and the analogy of Scripture are concerned, are decidedly in favour of the common text."[19]

Neither can we ignore earlier comments, such as one from the great 17th-century theologian Francis Turretin: "[Paul] does not say simply that the divinity in the abstract, but 'God' (*Theon*) in the concrete, was manifested (to wit, the person of the *Logos* was manifested because incarnation is not of the divine nature absolutely, but of a person)."[20] Likewise, in his wonderful work, *Manual of Theology* (1857), the great theologian John Dagg quotes the verse, "God was manifest in the flesh,"[21] as did the equally illustrious John Gill (1839) before him,[22] and Puritan Thomas Watson long before both (1692).[23] And even before them, Calvin wrote in his *Commentaries*: "All the Greek copies undoubtedly agree in this rendering, 'God manifested in the flesh.'. . . I have no hesitation in following the reading which has been adopted in the Greek copies."

Do we not see a pattern in such men? They did not permit their heads to be turned by the "new scholarship," but rather stayed with biblical and historical truth.

Conclusion

Please ponder this: Does it not give us pause when we open the Jehovah's Witness "Bible" (*New World Translation*) and read, "He was made manifest in the flesh," just as in our modern translations? Is this not the same "Bible" that mutilates John 1:1? Do we really think there is no agenda here? This underscores that "He" could refer to anyone from Adam to Moses to John the Baptist. *Only the word* **God** *tells us exactly who is meant.*

This verse has often been called the *crux criticorum*, Latin for "the cross for critics, a riddle or puzzle for the critics." But may we ask (and pity my simplicity if you wish), does God give us word puzzles that we must solve? Does He lay out the crossword grid and then give us clues to figure out how all the words will match vertically and horizontally? Does He pose riddles for us to unravel in our rationalism? I for one simply cannot accept such an idea.

Whether *hos* is a deliberate perversion of the text by Arians or Gnostics, as some argue, or simply an unintentional error by a copyist, it really doesn't matter. Either way it cannot be tolerated. It is wrong textually, theologically, and historically.

NOTES

[1] James White, *The King James Only Controversy* (Bethany House Publishers, 1995), 207.

[2] *The Revision Revised* (Conservative Classics, reprint of 1883 edition), 426.

[3] E.g., Lloyd J. Ogilvie (editor), *The Preacher's Commentary* (electronic edition).

[4] E.g., Gordon Clark, *The Pastoral Epistles* (Trinity Foundation, 1983), 65 (emphasis added).

[5] Only Matthew 1:1—25:6; John 6:50—8:52; and 2 Corinthians 4:13—12:6 are missing.

[6] *The Orthodox Corruption of Scripture* (Oxford, 1993), 78.

[7] Burgon, 431.

[8] *A Plain Introduction to the Criticism of the New Testament* (London: George Bell & Sons, 1892), Vol. II, 392.

[9] Burgon, 433.

[10] *A Guide to the Textual Criticism of the New Testament* (London: George Bell and Sons, 1886), 136.

[11] "Lection" comes from a root word in Latin that means "to read." One way to describe Lectionaries is "church service books," copies of portions of Scripture that were read in the churches.

[12] Miller, 137.

[13] Burgon, 496 (emphasis his).

[14] *The Ante-Nicene Fathers*, Vol. 1: The Epistle of Ignatius to the Ephesians (Ages Software), chap. 19, 115; chap. 7, 103; chap. 8, 125.

[15] Burgon, 457. Note his discussion of the Fathers, 455–476.

[16] D.A. Carson, *The King James Version Debate: A Plea for Realism* (Baker Book House, 1979), 71.

[17] *Discussions: Evangelical And Theological* (Carlisle, PA: Banner of Truth Trust, 1969, first published in 1891), Vol. 1, p. 365.

[18] *Ibid*, 393–94.

[19] *Systematic Theology* (Eerdmans, 1989), Vol. 1, 518.

[20] *Institutes of Elenctic Theology* (P&R, 1994), Vol. 2, 315.

[21] *Manual of Theology* (Gano Books, 1990 reprint), 183.

[22] *Body of Divinity* (Baptist Standard Bearer reprint, 1995), 165.

[23] *Body of Divinity* (Banner of Truth reprint, 1992), 110, 163, 192.

We hold that neither man nor angel is any wise to add or detract any thing, to change or to alter any thing from that which the Lord hath set down in His Word.

Puritan John Penry
A Puritan Golden Treasury, p. 33

47

Fasting: Ritual or Relationship?[*]

Mark 2:19–22

And Jesus said unto them, Can the children of the bridechamber fast, while the bridegroom is with them? as long as they have the bridegroom with them, they cannot fast. But the days will come, when the bridegroom shall be taken away from them, and then shall they fast in those days. No man also seweth a piece of new cloth on an old garment: else the new piece that filled it up taketh away from the old, and the rent is made worse. And no man putteth new wine into old bottles: else the new wine doth burst the bottles, and the wine is spilled, and the bottles will be marred: but new wine must be put into new bottles.

Fasting has become a very popular trend in recent years. In the secular world, for example, there is the book, *Juice Fasting and Detoxification: Use the Healing Power of Fresh Juice to Feel Young and Look Great.* Other books include, among many: *Fasting: The Super Diet*; *Fasting As a Way of Life*; and of course, *Fasting Made Easy* (surprisingly, there isn't *Fasting for Dummies*, but there is *The Complete Idiot's Guide to Fasting*.)

While such things might have some benefit, they have nothing to do with Scripture or spiritual reality. A fundamental principle, in fact, is that Scripture never, not once, speaks of fasting for physical reasons. Some argue that Isaiah 58:8 speaks of physical benefit because it uses the word "health." The Hebrew word (*'ărûkâh*) and context, however, clearly indicate that this is used in a metaphorical sense and pictures spiritual restoration from past sin.

Far more serious is what we read in Christian books nowadays. One popular one, for example, published in 2009, insists, "Those who seek God through fasting can expect tremendous rewards both for their personal lives and the church. They will see breakthroughs in many areas, such as healing, finances, bondages broken, and children set free." As evidence, of course, the author provides us with the usual plethora of "stories of those who have reaped miraculous rewards from this simple act of faith." You can also

---

[*] This chapter was originally TOTT issue 72, July/August 2011.

keep a record of your fasts using the companion *Fasting Journal* (sold separately, of course).

Another author claims that there is "hidden power in prayer and fasting, which holds keys that will unlock the resident power of the Holy Spirit within you! Through this book you will receive an impartation from a man who has lived these truths and has seen the power of God released for total victory against impossible odds, resulting in revival and literal resurrection." Others maintain that one must fast so he can "hear from God" and "experience crucifixion moments."

Such unbiblical teaching immediately reminds me of the *Prayer of Jabez* fad of a few years back. These, and many other such trends, dramatically demonstrate the mysticism that permeates Christianity today.

While not as far out as the above, even one of today's leading, highly respected evangelical leaders insists in his book on the subject that fasting for the right reasons will bring us immeasurable gifts from our Father. Still another solid evangelical and university professor writes in his book that fasting can have such results as: solve a problem, break negative emotional habits, meet the need of others, and protect from demonic attacks.

Again, these are very troubling trends, for they do not reflect biblical precedent, rather they smack of eastern mysticism. Mystics, in fact, have always been passionately committed to fasting as a major contributor to higher levels of consciousness and new revelation.

So, what does Scripture tell us about fasting? Where does it fit into practical Christian living? Let us examine four emphases.

Fasting in the Old Testament

The most critical fact to note in the Old Testament concerning fasting is that one, and only one, fast was suggested, namely the one on Yom Kippur, the Day of Atonement (Lev. 16:29–34; 23:26–32). The phrase "afflict your souls" translates the Hebrew *'ānâ*, "to be afflicted, to be oppressed, to be humbled" and commonly included the idea of refraining from food. What is most significant here is that fasting was inseparably linked to the people's deep mourning for sin and spiritual anxiety, which indicates the essence of what fasting is about.

As time passed, however, fasting increased almost exponentially. Many such fasts were inarguably sincere—such as Moses on the mount (Exod. 34:28; Deut. 9:9), David weeping over his child (2 Sam. 12:16–23), and Daniel's reflecting on Judah's captivity (Dan. 9:3; 10:2–3)—and flowed from the basic attitude of mourning for sin and spiritual anxiety noted above.

On the other hand, it is also common knowledge that great distress often results in a person simply losing his appetite (although some still immediately jump to the conclusion that the person is "deliberately fasting for spiritual result"). Hannah, for example, was greatly distressed on account of her childlessness and therefore "wept, and did not eat" (1 Sam. 1:7). This was certainly true in David's case of mourning mentioned above, as it was when the valiant men of Israel buried and mourned over the bones of Saul and his sons (1 Sam. 31:13; 2 Sam. 1:12).

It's also significant that anger can produce the same result, as when Jonathan was angry with his father and wouldn't eat because of his mistreatment of David (1 Sam. 20:34), and when Ahab sulked and "would eat no bread" because Naboth refused to part with his estate (1 Kings 21:4). Likewise, it is difficult to tell in such passages as Ezra 10:6 and Esther 4:3 whether fasting carries a religious sense or is simply a natural expression of sorrow.

A key to all this presents itself in the fact, as Eugene Merrill writes, that

> by the ninth century B.C. fasting had become institutionalized or formalized to the extent that days or other periods of fasting were called as occasions for public worship. The usual way of describing such convocation is "to call for" or "proclaim" a fast. . . . Jehosphat . . . called for such an assembly in order to implore God's intercession on Judah's behalf (2 Chron. 30:3).[1]

There are, in fact, many examples of a king proclaiming a fast, as Jehoiakim did in Judah (Jer. 36:9). Such "extraordinary fasts," writes Merrill F. Unger, "were appointed by the theocratic authorities on occasions of great national calamity in order that the people might humble themselves before the Lord on account of their sins, thus averting His wrath and getting Him to look upon them again with favor (Judg. 20:26; 1 Sam. 7:6; 2 Chron. 20:3; Joel 1:14; Joel 2:12; Jer. 36:9; Ezra 8:21; Neh. 1:4)."[2]

It should be emphasized again, however, that none of these, and other examples we could list (e.g., Esther 9:31–32), were commanded or mandated by God. The danger, in fact, is that such fasting could become nothing more than outward ritual, and even hypocrisy, because the inner man did not reflect true spiritual worship. This is exactly what we see in Isaiah 58:3–6, where the prophet levels a scathing rebuke of the people because they were only going through the motions. They were more *concerned* by a *ritual* than they were a *reality*, more *consumed* by an *object* than they were *obedience*, more *captivated* by an outward *act* than they were an inward *attitude*.

As Jeremiah 14:12 also records (about 100 years after Isaiah), because of the people's rebellion, God declared, "When they fast, I will not hear their cry; and when they offer burnt offering and an oblation, I will not accept them: but I will consume them by the sword, and by the famine, and by the pestilence." Writing about another century later, Zechariah asked the priests: "When ye fasted and mourned in the fifth and seventh month, even those seventy years, did ye at all fast unto me, even to [the LORD]?" (Zech. 7:5). Both their *fasting* and their *feasting* (v. 6) were for themselves, not for God.

This sets the stage for our next observation.

Fasting in the New Testament

In the 400 years between Malachi and the events in the Gospels, the situation only grew worse. By the time the Lord Jesus stepped onto the scene, anyone who was truly serious about his religion, especially a Pharisee, was required to keep two fast-days every week, Monday and Thursday, as proudly proclaimed by the boasting Pharisee in Luke 18:12. As commentator Adam Clark adds, "The Pharisees had many superstitious fasts. They fasted in order to have lucky dreams, to obtain the interpretation of a dream, or to avert the evil import of a dream. They also fasted often in order to obtain the things they wished for." (Sounds pretty familiar to our own day, does it not?) For the most part, however, fasting had become no more than routine ritual that reflected no true piety, but instead was simply "a pious achievement"[3] of the observer.

This is vividly illustrated in Matthew 6:16–18. The Pharisees wanted everyone to know they were fasting so people would know they were spiritual. To that end they would put on a "sad countenance" (*skuthrōpos*; grim, gloomy face) and "disfigured their faces" (probably by putting ashes on their heads). Our Lord categorically condemned such false piety, calling such men "hypocrites." In fact, our Lord's strongest condemnation was reserved for "hypocrites" (Matt. 23). The English transliterates the Greek *hupokritēs* (*hupo*, "under," denoting secrecy, and *krinō*, "to judge"). The hypocrite is a pretender, one who professes to be something he is not. In Classical Greek, it originally meant to explain or interpret something but later came to be used in the theatre—the *hupokritēs* was "the 'answerer' who appeared on stage and turned the self-contained speeches of the chorus into dialogue form, or the 'interpreter' who explained the situation to the audience."[4]

Interestingly, however, the Classical meanings of *hupokritēs* never appear in the New Testament; it's the figurative idea that we find every time. The hypocrite is one who "plays the part," who says the right words, who convincingly acts the role, but who is not what he claims to be. Our Lord used it, for example, in Matthew 15:7–9 (a quotation of Isa. 29:13): "Ye hypocrites, well did Esaias prophesy of you, saying, This people draweth nigh unto me with their mouth, and honoureth me with their lips;

but their heart is far from me. But in vain they do worship me, teaching for doctrines the commandments of men."[5]

That serves as a sobering warning for us today. Some Christians want others to know they are fasting and work it into the conversation somehow. But whatever spiritual value there might be in it is negated because of such pride and hypocrisy. As we will see, the practice of fasting that still remains is to be a very personal and private thing.

That brings us to our main text. As one authority submits, here is an "entirely new view to the question of fasting." He continues:

> The irruption of the Kingdom of God, the presence of the Messiah, the good news of salvation not dependant on good works—all this means joy which is something excluded by fasting in the Jewish sense. . . . Such fasting is a thing of the past, belonging to a by-gone era. . . . The answer to the question . . . is linked to the parables of [Mk. 2:21–22]. We must take this as an indication that fasting has been superseded by Jesus. In fact, there is no evidence from the 1st-century that Christians voluntarily imposed fasting on themselves. The epistles of the NT make no reference to it [except 1 Cor. 7:5, 2 Cor. 5:5 and 11:27, which we will address later], and even in those passages which concentrate on the ascetic tendencies of some (Rom. 14 and Col. 2), fasting remains unmentioned.[6]

I am convinced that this is the key to understanding this whole issue. The context concerns the disciples of John the Baptist (possibly a former Essene), who according to Jewish tradition practiced twice-weekly ritual fasting. They noticed, however, that Jesus' disciples did not do this and asked why. Our Lord's response was dazzling. He likened Himself to a bridegroom; as long as He was with them, it made absolutely no sense to fast. A wedding feast usually lasted seven days and was a time of rejoicing, not mourning. While the time would come when He would be **taken away** (even "violently removed," *apairō*) and mourning would be appropriate, this was not the time.

To make His point—and here, indeed, is the crux—He adds two illustrations in verses 21–22 of mixing the **old** with the **new**. Patching a garment with **new**, unshrunk **cloth** will result in the patch shrinking and tearing the **garment** when it's washed. Likewise, putting **new wine** into **old** wineskins will result in the weak wineskins bursting during fermentation. "The life and liberty of the Gospel," writes William MacDonald, "ruins the wineskins of ritualism."[7] Such, then, is the result of mixing Judaism with Christianity. As A. C. Gaebelein well says:

> A Judaistic Christianity which, with a profession of Grace and the Gospel, attempts to keep the law and fosters legal righteousness

is a greater abomination in the eyes of God than professing Israel in the past worshipping idols.[8]

We would submit, therefore, that all this underscores the difference between *ritual* and *relationship*. By the time of Christ, any semblance of personal relationship with God had vanished from Judaism; it was little more than empty ritual. (That is still true today, as I witnessed repeatedly in my recent trip to Israel.) Our Lord, however, was speaking of personal relationship, that He was present with His people, so why would fasting be necessary? As all else in the old Mosaic System is passed, so is ritual fasting.

Now, before we say, "Well, but He's gone now, so fasting is appropriate," let us just stop and think a moment. Is He really gone? Yes, he told the disciples that He would be **taken away**, but let us remember He rose again. Equally significant, He told them that when He departed, He would come again (Jn. 14:18), but in the meantime He would "give [them] another Comforter, that he may abide with [them] for ever" (14:16), adding, in fact, that this was actually profitable for them (16:7). The Greek behind "another" is all important. It is not *heteros*, "another of a different kind" (English "heterodox" and "heterosexual"), rather it is *allos*, "another of similar or identical nature." How thrilling! The Savior is saying in essence, "When I depart, I will send another in My place who is virtually identical to Me."

Yes, physically our Lord is gone and will return. But this in no way diminishes the reality of His personal indwelling presence through the Holy Spirit right now and forever. *That* is a relationship that should replace any trace of ritual. Why would we mourn when He is still here and closer to us than ever in history?

Fasting in Church History

An examination of the practice of fasting in Church History further underscores this difference between ritual and relationship. As noted earlier, there is no evidence from the 1st-century that Christians voluntarily imposed fasting on themselves. This dramatically changed in the 2nd-century, however, when the Jewish ritual tradition of Monday and Thursday took hold in Christianity, although the days chosen were, as Philip Schaff notes, "Wednesday and especially Friday, as days of half-fasting or abstinence from flesh, in commemoration of the passion and crucifixion of Jesus." Also arising at this time was "the custom of Quadragesimal fasts before Easter," that is, the 40-day fast of Lent. Such fasts were rigidly practiced especially by the heretical Montantists. In addition to these, in fact, they observed special *Xerophagiae* ("dry eating") fasts (a "dry" diet excludes meat, dairy products, fish, alcohol, and foods cooked in oil).[9]

The Montanists are especially noteworthy. Founded by Montanus in the early 2nd-century, he claimed that he and his two prophetesses (Prisca and Maximilla) "spoke in a state of ecstasy [i.e., so-called tongues], as though their personalities were suspended while the Paraclete spoke in them. [He] was convinced that he and his prophetesses were the God-given instruments of revelation." So authoritative was he that to him any "opposition to the new prophecy was blasphemy against the Holy Spirit," and he even "claimed the right to push Christ and the apostolic message into the background. . . . Christ was no longer central. In the name of the Spirit, Montanus denied that God's decisive and normative revelation had occurred in Christ."[10] We see the same attitudes in some groups today, with their "revelations" often coming "through prayer and fasting."

It's also noteworthy that the early Church Father Clement of Alexandria (c.150–c.215) was opposed to such "over-valuation of fasting" and quoted "the word of Paul" against it: "The kingdom of God is not meat and drink, therefore neither abstinence from wine and flesh, but righteousness and peace and joy in the Holy Spirit [Rom. 14:17]."[11]

Such overemphasis continued virtually unabated nonetheless. As the years unfolded, "Wednesday and Friday continued to be observed in many countries as days commemorative of the passion of Christ (*dies stationum* [guard or watch days]), with half-fasting."[12] "By the sixth century," writes Merrill Unger, "fasting was made obligatory by the Second Council of Orleans (A.D. 541), which decreed that anyone neglecting to observe the stated time of abstinence should be treated as an offender. In the eighth century it was regarded as praiseworthy, and failure to observe subjected the offender to excommunication. In the Roman Catholic and Greek churches fasting remains obligatory, whereas in most Protestant churches it is merely recommended."[13]

What should be glaringly obvious in all that, and more history we could recount, is that there is not a trace of biblical authority in any of it. It is all opinion, tradition, and even superstition, with obvious overtones of paganism. To repeat an earlier statement, it is an "over-valuation of fasting," an over-emphasis that started very early and has continued to this very day. It totally ignores the change of emphasis that came in the New Testament and clings to *ritual* instead of a *relationship*.

So, where does all that place the believer today?

Fasting Today

While we will come back to instances of fasting in the book of Acts in a moment, we should first strongly emphasize that there are only three occurrences of the Greek *nesteia* (fasting) in all the New Testament *Epistles*. Two (2 Cor. 5:5 and 11:27) are included in lists of Paul's trials and tribulations, obviously referring simply to a lack of food.

The only remaining instance appears in 1 Corinthians 7:5 in the context of marriage. With overtones of paganism again, some believers in Corinth were practicing celibacy but with only one partner consenting, tempting the other one to adultery. Paul's counsel, therefore, was that one partner should not deprive the other. The only exception is that, if both agree to a specific time frame, they could abstain for the purpose of concentrated "fasting and prayer" on the part of either one or both.

This clears up the matter wonderfully. There will be times when we are so engaged in the Word and prayer that food is not only unimportant but even distracting. Since the whole matter is also between husband and wife (who are one), no one else knows anything about it, so there is no pretentious display.

So, *should* a Christian fast today? No, not in the manner prescribed in the Old Testament, for we have a relationship with the living Savior who abides in us through His Spirit. But *will* a Christian fast at times? Yes, whether it might be either losing one's appetite out of distress, or simply a lack of interest in food because of concentrated spiritual activity. Both the instances of fasting in Acts, in fact, fit the latter idea (13:2–3; 14:23). Contrary to popular mystic teaching, it is neither mandated nor commanded. Neither does it promise any special spiritual effect—there will be no "hearing from God" or "unlocking the resident power of the Spirit." It is an extremely personal reality between the believer and his Lord.

NOTES

[1] Walter A. Elwell (ed.), *Baker Theological Dictionary of the Bible* (Baker Books, 1996), 246.

[2] *New Unger's Bible Dictionary* (electronic edition), entry on "FAST, FASTING."

[3] Colin Brown (ed), *The New International Dictionary of New Testament Theology* (Zondervan, 1975, 1986), Vol. 1, 612.

[4] *Ibid*, Vol. 2, 468.

[5] Word study taken from the author's book, *A Word for the Day* (AMG Publishers, 2006), 343.

[6] Brown, Vol. 1, 612–13.

[7] *Believer's Bible Commentary* (Thomas Nelson, electronic edition).

[8] A. C. Gaebelein, *The Gospel of Matthew* (Loizeaux, 1910), 193.

[9] Philip Schaff, *History of the Christian Church* (electronic edition), Vol. II, Chapter VIII, § 101.

[10] Bruce L. Shelly, *Church History in Plain Language*, 3rd Edition (Thomas

Nelson, 2008), 65.

[11] Noted in Schaff, *op. cit.*

[12] Schaff, Vol. III, Chapter VII, § 75.

[13] Unger, *op. cit.*

I will give you this as a most certain observation, that there never was anything of false doctrine brought into the church, or anything of false worship imposed upon the church, but either it was by neglecting the Scripture, or by introducing something above the Scripture.

Puritan John Collins
A Puritan Golden Treasurey, p. 33

48

The Most Terrifying Words in the Bible[*]

Matthew 7:21–23

Not every one that saith unto me, Lord, Lord, shall enter into the kingdom of heaven; but he that doeth the will of my Father which is in heaven. Many will say to me in that day, Lord, Lord, have we not prophesied in thy name? and in thy name have cast out devils? and in thy name done many wonderful works? And then will I profess unto them, I never knew you: depart from me, ye that work iniquity.

If I may, I would like to encourage you with something that has been on my heart for a *long* time. I think of these verses often and each time I shudder and examine my own heart. I would begin with the old adage, "It's one thing to be a *professor* of Christ, but it's quite another to be a *possessor* of Christ." There has probably never been a preacher of the true Gospel in the history of the church who has not at some point said those words, or words to that effect.

In recent years, however, that truism has been relegated to an older, more unenlightened era and is considered narrow and judgmental. What matters in the minds of many in the church today, in fact, is simply what a person *does* profess, regardless of how nebulous it is. For example, if someone says, "Oh, I asked Jesus into my heart at Vacation Bible School when I was eight," or, "I went forward at a Billy Graham Crusade and made a decision for Christ," or, "I raised my hand at a revival meeting," or any one of a plethora of other clichés, such a profession is considered to be "good enough." After all, it's insisted, no one has the right to doubt someone else's salvation.

Taken to its final end, however, such an idea implies that a profession such as the following would qualify one as being a Christian: "Hence today I believe that I am acting in accordance with the will of the Almighty Creator: *by defending myself against the Jew, I am fighting for the work of the Lord.*" Who said that? Adolph Hitler![1] Or consider this even clearer profession by Hitler, who was raised Roman Catholic: "My feelings as a Christian points me to my Lord and Savior as a fighter. It points me to the

---

[*] This chapter was originally TOTT issue 73, September/October 2011, and was based upon a sermon by the author..

man who once in loneliness, surrounded only by a few followers, recognized these Jews for what they were and summoned men to fight against them and who, God's truth! was greatest not as a sufferer but as a fighter."[2] Take note of "Christian, "Lord", Savior," and even "God's truth."

Consider also porn king Larry Flynt. After being "born-again," reportedly from the witness of former president Jimmy Carter's sister, Ruth Carter Stapleton, Flynt continued to publish the worst filth that industry has to offer.

Now, would any evangelical today actually view Hitler as a true Christian? Would any discerning believer accept Flynt's "profession" as genuine? We certainly hope not. Why? Obviously because their lifestyle does not demonstrate the life transforming reality of Christ. On the other hand, many view other people with similar "testimonies" as being believers, so why not "a devil incarnate" or a smut peddler? Writing in the early 1940s, Arthur W. Pink addresses our own times with this comment on our text in his *Exposition on the Sermon on the Mount*:

> If it be true that Matthew 5–7 is more hated by our moderns than any other portion of God's Word, it is equally true that none is more urgently needed by them. Never were there so many millions of nominal Christians on earth as there are today, and never was there such a small percentage of real ones. Not since before the days of Luther and Calvin, when the great Reformation effected such a grand change for the better, has Christendom been so crowded with those who have "a form of godliness" but who are strangers to its transforming power. We seriously doubt whether there has ever been a time in the history of this Christian era when there were such multitudes of deceived souls within the churches, who verily believe that all is well with their souls when in fact the wrath of God abideth on them. And we know of no single thing better calculated to undeceive them than a full and faithful exposition of these closing verses of our Lord's Sermon on the Mount.

While we addressed the issue of so-called "Lordship Salvation" back in chapter 23, here in our text we encounter an especially significant group of those who profess Christ. This group, in fact, is on a whole new level of "profession." No text of Scripture is clearer than this one in demonstrating the truth that calling oneself a Christian doesn't make it so. Our Lord is very specific here of who *is* and who is *not* a true believer.

The Truth of the Text

In the introduction to his exposition of this passage, Martyn Lloyd-Jones wrote: "These, surely, are in many ways the most solemn and solemnizing words ever spoken in this world."[3] In my own preaching I have often read these verses from my pulpit and then added: "Here are, I am convinced, the most terrifying words in the Bible." I can think of nothing more frightening than to be so deceived and deluded as to think I am a Christian only to one day discover that I am not. How horrifying is the thought that I could preach, pray, and perform ministry only to have it revealed in the end that it was all a sham.

The setting of our text, of course, is our Lord's Sermon on the Mount, which underscores the gravity of the passage. These are not the words of a man but of God Himself. The immediate context (vv. 15–20) is about false teachers, who while looking and acting like sheep are actually wolves whose sole purpose is to devour the sheep (cf. 1 Pet. 5:8). The only way to discern them, our Lord adds, is to examine their fruit, as we would any individual (Jn. 15:1–17; cf. Prov. 12:12; Matt. 13:23; Rom. 7:4; etc.).

It is profoundly significant that our Lord has already finished the major teaching of His sermon but then ends with an explicit warning about false teachers. In a day when false teachers are everywhere while tolerance and open-mindedness of them is at an all-time high, this warning has never been more critical. All the Apostles recognized our Lord's emphasis of this (cf. Matt. 24:5, 11, 24) and repeatedly warned of it in Acts and their own epistles.[4] This was no less true in the Old Testament, as God's true prophets warned of Satan's false ones.[5]

Through four emphases, then, our Lord delineates those who *profess* but to do not *possess*.

Their Profession

First, we note this is a *purist* profession; it's orthodox, in fact. The word **Lord** is *kurios*, and understanding it here is critical. It appears in the Septuagint over 9,000 times, some 6,156 of which translate the Hebrew *YHWH* (Yahweh, Jehovah), thus reemphasizing the meaning of divinity. It appears then in the New Testament 717 times, the majority of which occur in Luke's gospel and Acts (210) and Paul's epistles (275). The reason for this, of course, was that they both wrote for readers who were dominated by Greek culture and language and who, therefore, understood the deep significance of this word in implying deity.

So, while **Lord** is sometimes used as simply a title of honor, such as Rabbi, Teacher, Master (Matt. 10:24; cf. Luke 16:3), or even a husband (1 Pet. 3:6), *when used of Jesus in a confessional way, it without question refers to His divinity*. The confession *Kurios Iēsous* (Lord Jesus) is rooted in the pre-Pauline Greek Christian community and is probably the oldest of all Christian creeds.

Early Christians unarguably recognized Jesus as God, as Paul wrote to the Philippians: "And that every tongue should confess that Jesus Christ is Lord, to the glory of God the Father" (2:11). Even more significant, when Thomas saw the risen Jesus, he called Him, "My Lord and my God" (John 20:28). Even salvation is based on a confession of Jesus as **Lord** as Divine Authority (Rom. 10:9–10).

It is, therefore, extremely significant that some people actually call Jesus **Lord** but are still unbelievers. While the profession of a Jehovah's Witness, Mormon, or other cult, for example, is easy to dismiss because they reject the deity of Christ and are therefore lost (cf. Jn. 8:24), others appear quite orthodox but are still unconverted. In other words, a person can be totally correct in his theology, have all his doctrine systematically outlined and memorized, and still be lost. Contrary to popular heresy, salvation is not just knowing and assenting to a few facts about Jesus.

Second, this is a *passionate* profession. The repetition of the term **Lord** (**Lord, Lord**) demonstrates enthusiasm, fervor, zeal, and perhaps even some level of "commitment." Oh, yes, such professors are earnest and sincere, but still they are not genuine. Yes, there are many who want to talk about Jesus, wave their hands in a worship service, and practice other outward displays of zeal, but still there is something missing.

Third, this is a *public* profession. Such people are not shy about their "faith." They let it be known where they go to church and what they do for God. But as we'll see, something is still amiss. This leads to a second observation.

Their Proclamation

While the Greek *propheteuō* (**prophesied**) can refer to proclaiming truth already revealed (implied in Acts 13:1), it also refers to speaking *immediately* of the Holy Spirit, that is, speaking under the direct inspiration of the Holy Spirit. Ponder a moment: How many teachers on radio and television nowadays claim new revelation? How many "testimonies" do we hear that claim, "God spoke to me last night and told me to share it with you." Is this not terrifying?

Our **Lord** warns us, however, that although such people do all this even **in [His] name**, they are false. Never in history, in fact, have more people claimed new revelation than in our own day, much of which flows from the mysticism that continues to grow in prominence. Later in Matthew our Lord declares that "many false prophets shall rise, and shall deceive many" (24:11), and such is indeed the case.

On the other hand, do such teachers have to be claiming new revelation to be considered false? Certainly not. Some simply deny historic doctrine and preach prosperity, pragmatism, purpose, or any one of a plethora of other deceptions. Oh, yes, they give Jesus lip-service, but there has been no life-transformation, no obedience to the Truth.

Their Performance

Oh, how impressive their performance is! Our Lord declares, in fact, that such people have even performed **wonderful works**, such as **[casting] out devils** and other "miracles." **Wonderful works** translates a single Greek word, *dunamis* (English "dynamic"), which speaks not just of power but here miraculous power. While some charlatans today fake their "miracles," it is quite possible that some are real. But since Christ is here condemning such people, it is obvious that their power is not coming from God. That leaves only one alternative: some such people are empowered by Satan.

The most graphic biblical example of this reality is Pharaoh's magicians in Exodus 7—9. When Moses and Aaron came before Pharaoh, Aaron "cast down his rod before Pharaoh . . . and it became a serpent" (7:10). Pharaoh's magicians (Jannes and Jambres according to 2 Tim. 3:8) appeared to duplicate this (v. 11), but it was, at the very least, a trick. Egyptian magicians had long ago mastered the art of inflicting a temporary paralysis on a cobra, making him appear stiff like a rod. The word "enchantments," in fact, comes from the Hebrew *lahaṭ*, meaning "to flame or to set on fire." Magicians often use fire for dramatic effect, so their feat was nothing more than, as the expression goes, "just smoke and mirrors."

As the miracles increased in complexity, however, it appears the magicians had some outside help. The word "enchantments" in 7:22, 8:7, and 18 is a different Hebrew word, *lāṭ*, a noun meaning secrecy, enchantment, mystery, or privacy and there conveys the idea of secret or magical arts known only to a select group. Scripture declares several times that Satan empowers men to perform "lying wonders" (2 Thes. 2:9–10; Matt. 24:24; Rev. 13:11–15).

Bringing this back to our text, commentator William MacDonald puts the matter well:

> From these verses we learn that not all miracles are of divine origin and that not all miracle workers are divinely accredited. A miracle simply means that a supernatural power is at work. That power may be divine or satanic. Satan may empower his workers to cast out demons *temporarily*, in order to create the illusion that the miracle is divine. He is not dividing his kingdom against itself in such a case, but is plotting an even worse invasion of demons in the future.[6]

While the performance of false teachers is often *dazzling*, such ones are *deadly* because they are not true believers.

Their Problem

William Hendriksen eloquently states the problem of these professors of Christ:

> The reason why the men described here in Matt. 7:22 are condemned is not that their preaching had been wrong and/or their miracles spurious but that they had not practiced what they preached![7]

How practical! This principle, in fact, is at the very core of the entire debate of Lordship that sadly continues to rage today. To say that we can believe in Christ but have absolutely no intention of following Him, obeying Him, or surrendering to Him is totally incongruous to the Gospel and is heresy. Our **Lord** clearly identifies who **shall enter into the kingdom**, namely, those who **[do] the will of my Father which is in heaven.** Frankly, why is there controversy? How much clearer could Jesus be? People can talk about Him, sing songs in a worship service, lead the worship team, preach sermons, teach a Sunday School class, do mission work, write books, and do all sorts of Christian service, but none of that is proof of conversion. Our Lord could not be clearer: If they do not do the **will** of God, as is revealed only in His Word, they are not true believers. While that is not a popular view, it is what Scripture everywhere declares. As noted in our discussion of this issue in chapter 23, there is absolutely no doubt whatsoever that biblical faith (*pistos*) implies obedience. To argue this is foolish. "I will put my spirit within you," God declared through the prophet, "and cause you to walk in my statutes, and ye shall keep my judgments, and do them" (Ezek. 36:27). Writing before this modern trend got its strangle hold on Christianity, Martyn-Lloyd-Jones observed:

> The difference between faith and intellectual assent is that intellectual assent simply says, "Lord, Lord," but does not do His will. In other words, though I may say "Lord, Lord" to the Lord Jesus Christ, there is no meaning in it unless I regard Him as my Lord, and willingly become His bondslave. . . . True faith always shows itself in the life; it shows itself in the person in general, and it also shows itself in what he does. . . . Faith shows itself in the whole personality.[8]

Further, to underscore that such professors are not true believers, our Lord says **then [i.e., at the final judgment] will I profess unto them, I never knew you: depart from me, ye that work iniquity.** The word **knew** is *ginoskō*, which means "to know by experience" and is practically synonymous with love and intimacy. Joseph, for example, "did not know" Mary before Jesus was born, that is, they had not yet been physically intimate (Matt. 1:25).

It's extremely significant that Peter uses *ginoskō* with the prefix *pro* in 1 Peter 1:1–2 to speak of God's election being according to "foreknowledge." Again, it is an absolute fact of the language that this does *not* mean just "precognition," that God simply elected those He knew would believe the Gospel. This is beyond all doubt when we read another verse in this chapter, one often either overlooked or ignored: "[Christ] verily was foreordained [*proginoskō*] before the foundation of the world, but was manifest in these last times for you" (v. 20). Obviously this doesn't mean that God simply foresaw that Christ would be manifested. Rather, He was, as we are, foreordained and foreknown by an intimate relationship before the foundation of the world. In other words, foreknowledge is not to *foresee* but to *"fore-love."* This is exactly what we see when we read what God said to Jeremiah: "Before I formed thee in the belly I *knew* thee; and before thou camest forth out of the womb I sanctified thee, and I *ordained* thee a prophet unto the nations" (Jer. 1:5, emphasis added). What a thought that is! Christ knew us in the elective and saving sense before we even existed.

With that in mind, our **Lord**, therefore, uses *ginoskō* to say that He never knew these false professors intimately as their Savior and Lord. He never knew them in eternity past in the elective sense. They were never believers.

If any doubt remains as to the character of such false professors, our Lord adds that at the final judgment He will also say, **Depart from me, ye that work iniquity. Work** is *ergazomai*, to labor, and **iniquity** is *anomia*, literally without law, that is, the violation of law. Further, the verb tense (present participle) indicates continuous, habitual practice. Everything these professors have done, therefore, is totally worthless because they have habitually violated God's revelation. We see many people today doing a lot of things, but how much of it plumbs with God's revelation?

All this is, in fact, the point of the parable of the two house builders our **Lord** goes on to offer in verses 24–27. The wise man "built his house upon a rock," while the "foolish man . . . built his house upon the sand." Now, to what exactly does "rock" refer? While our first impulse is to answer that this refers to Christ—after all, He is called "that spiritual Rock" in 1 Corinthians 10:4—we would submit that this is not precise. Since He refers in verse 21 to doing God's **will** (which is revealed in His Word), and then refers to hearing and doing His "sayings" (*logos*) in verses 24 and 26, it is clear that the foundation on which we must build is more specifically

God's Word. "Hear, then, the imperial claim of Christ," writes G. Campbell Morgan. "He says: Take these sayings of Mine and build on them; and no storm can destroy your building."[9]

This works out when we consider the two builders. On the outside, both buildings look fine, so it takes close examination of the foundation to see the problem. The foolish builder is impatient and doesn't want to be bothered with reading a building manual or consulting blueprints. He even arrogantly thinks he knows more than those who have come before him. He builds on the shifting sands of his own opinion. The wise builder, however, "reads the rules"; he obeys the sound principles of construction that have been proven repeatedly to be true. So, "The foundation in this parable," writes Warren Wiersbe, "is obedience to God's Word—obedience that is an evidence of true faith (James 2:14ff)."[10] It is tragic, indeed: while many people today appear to be believers, they are not. How terrifying!

The Pointedness of the Principles

We would close with two principles that flow from the truth of this text.

The Risk of Self-delusion

The greatest delusion on our little blue planet is how many people believe they are Christians but are not, simply because they give absolutely no evidence of it by their obedience to the Word of God. Is there any doubt why James wrote, "Be ye doers of the word, and not hearers only, deceiving your own selves" (Jas. 1:22)? How many people today are fatally deceived?

Consider this: According to *The World Almanac and Book of Facts*, there are about two billion "Christians" in the world. This number includes the categories: Roman Catholic, Protestant, Orthodox, Anglican, and Independent. Now then, is there *evidence* that out of the over 6.8 billion people in the world over one-third are *true* Christians? Or, is there evidence that out of some 300 million Americans, 100 million of them love God, are committed to Him, and do His will? Bringing it closer to home, do you consider one-third of those at your workplace to be Christians? One-third of your neighborhood? One-third of our government? One-third of our schools, colleges, and universities?

There's obviously no evidence for any of that. On the contrary, as our Lord says earlier in this passage (v. 14), few go through the narrow gate that leads to life. They might look, sound, and act like sheep (v. 15), but they are not. To make this even more practical (and blunt), expositor John MacArthur courageously writes:

When a couple lives together without being married, when a person practices homosexuality, is deceptive and dishonest in business, is hateful and vengeful, or habitually practices any sin without remorse or repentance, such persons cannot be Christian—no matter what sort of experience they claim to have had or what sort of testimony they now make. God's Word is explicit [in] 1 Cor. 6:9–10 [and] Eph. 5:5–6. In each of those extremely somber warnings Paul pleads with his readers not to be deceived.[11]

Indeed, self-delusion is a terrifying reality. Countless people today consider themselves heaven bound Christians simply because they go to church, prayed a prayer, walked an aisle, "asked Jesus into their heart," gave on offering, "spoke in tongues," or even read their Bible, but their lives are utterly devoid of obedience of the Truth. An unknown penman long ago wrote:

> You call me Master, and obey me not; You call me Light, and see me not; You call me the Way, and walk me not; You call me the Life, and live me not; You call me Wise, and follow me not; You call me Fair, and love me not; You call me Rich, and ask me not; You call me Eternal and seek me not. *If I condemn thee, blame me not!*

Countless people fail to remember the simplest principle of all: "Be not deceived; God is not mocked: for whatsoever a man soweth, that shall he also reap" (Gal. 6:7).

The Requirement of Self-examination

Is it not odd that many evangelists, pastors, and "crusade workers," routinely tell people, "Oh, you should never doubt your salvation," when Scripture says the exact opposite? Yes, it says we can have assurance (1 Jn. 5:20), but never does it say not to question. As Peter pleads in 2 Peter 1:10, "Make your calling and election sure." And how do we do that? By comparing ourselves to the list of seven qualities in verses 1–9 to see if they exist in us. Likewise, both John in his first epistle and James in his epistle go to great lengths to present tests of genuine Christian faith.

The Apostle Paul was no less direct when he wrote to the carnal Corinthians: "Examine yourselves, whether ye be in the faith; prove your own selves" (2 Cor. 13:5). "Examine' is *peirazō*, "to make trial of, to test. It was used in Classical Greek to refer to a medical test, which would prove either health or disease. "Prove," then, is *dokimazō*, which means "test, pronounce good, establish by trial." A related word, *dokimos*, was originally used as a technical term for coins that were genuine. This principle was nothing new, appearing throughout Scripture (e.g. Job 13:23; Ps. 17:3; 26:2; 139:23–24; Lam. 3:40; Hag. 1:5, 7; 1 Cor. 11:28, 31; etc.). "Examine, examine, examine," is what Scripture declares.

Whether a preacher, a parson, or a pew-sitter, let us each closely examine our lives. Who are truly Christian believers? Those who do the will of God.

NOTES

[1] *Mein Kamph* (Houghton Mifflin Company Boston, 1927; 1971 renewed), 65 (emphasis in the original).

[2] From a speech in the Bürgerbräukeller in Munich in April 1922. Reported by Richard Steigmann-Gall, *The Holy Reich: Nazi Conceptions of Christianity, 1919-1945* (Cambridge University Press, 2003), 37.

[3] Martyn Lloyd-Jones, *Studies in the Sermon on the Mount* (Eerdmans, combined volume, 1971, 1982), Vol. 2, 261.

[4] E.g., Acts 20:28–31; 2 Cor. 11:3, 13–14; Eph. 4:14; Phil. 3:2; Col. 2:8; 1 Tim. 1:8–20; 6:20-21; 2 Pet. 2:1–2; 1 John 4:1; Jude 4; etc.

[5] E.g., Deut. 13:1–5; Jer. 23:16, 21–22, 25–32; 27:14–16; 29:8–9; etc.

[6] *Believer's Bible Commentary* (Thomas Nelson), electronic edition.

[7] *Baker's New Testament Commentary: Matthew* (Baker Academic, 1973), electronic edition.

[8] Lloyd-Jones, Vol. 2, 309–10.

[9] *Studies in the Four Gospels*, 4 volumes in 1 (Scripture Truth Book Company, previously by Fleming H. Revell, 1927, 1929), Vol. 1, 80.

[10] *Bible Exposition Commentary* (David C. Cook, 2007), electronic edition.

[11] John MacArthur, *The MacArthur New Testament Commentary: Matthew* (Moody Bible Institute, 1985), electronic edition.

49

What in the World is a Biblical Worldview?[*]

Psalm 119:11

Thy word have I hid in mine heart, that I might not sin against thee.

There has been in recent years much discussion of what has been dubbed a "Biblical Worldview," or, "Christian Worldview." While much of that discussion is good, some of it is lacking not only in *clarity* (that is, what such a worldview actually *is*), but more importantly, in my view, in *application* (that is, what such a worldview demands in *practice*). This subject has been bothering me for quite some time, for while I have heard several Christians say they have a Biblical Worldview, their practice actually speaks much louder of something quite different. I would, therefore, like to offer a few thoughts that I hope you will prayerfully consider.

What Is a Worldview?

The word *worldview* actually comes directly from a German word that was coined in the mid 19th-century, *weltanschauung* (pronounced ˈvelt-ˌän-ˌshaủ-ən), which can be literally rendered "look onto the world." Webster defines this as "a comprehensive conception or apprehension of the world especially from a specific standpoint." James W. Sire, author and former editor for InterVarsity Press, offers a more detailed definition:

> A commitment, a fundamental orientation of the heart, that can be expressed as a story or in a set of presuppositions (assumptions which may be true, partially true, or entirely false) which we hold (consciously or subconsciously, consistently or inconsistently) about the basic construction of reality, and that provides the foundation on which we live and move and have our being.[1]

Michael J. Vlach, Associate Professor of Theology at the Master's Seminary, offers this simpler alternative: "A worldview is any philosophy, ideology, religion, or movement that provides an all-encompassing approach to understanding reality."[2] Based upon all that, we would humbly offer the following:

---

[*] This chapter was originally TOTT issue 74, November/December 2011.

A worldview *is the perspective from which a person, with all his presuppositions, attitudes, and beliefs, perceives and approaches, either consciously or subconsciously, the world, life, and everything in them.*

With that in mind, it is easy to see that every single person, whether he knows it or not, has a worldview. Every person *perceives* the world and everything in it and therefore *approaches* it in a way that satisfies him. Francis Schaeffer wrote much about the decline of Western thought and culture. Addressing our present subject, he noted:

People have presuppositions, and they will live more consistently on the basis of these presuppositions than even they themselves may realize. By *presuppositions* we mean the basic way an individual looks at life, his basic world view, the grid through which he sees the world. Presuppositions rest upon that which a person considers to be the truth of what exists. People's presuppositions lay a grid for all they bring forth into the external world. Their presuppositions also provide the basis for their values and therefore the basis for their decisions.[3]

While many people will add their own unique twist, there are several basic worldviews to choose from. For example, if you approach everything in life from the perspective of acquiring money and possessions, your worldview is Materialism. If you approach everything from a desire for pleasure, your worldview is Hedonism. If you approach everything from an exclusively intellectual perspective, appealing to reason as the only source of knowledge or justification, your worldview is Rationalism. If you approach everything from the perspective that nothing is absolute, that all value and "truth" depends upon each person's perception, your worldview is Relativism. And the list goes on.

The key principle to understand in all this, then, is that your worldview will automatically apply itself to what you think and do. "Keep thy heart with all diligence," Solomon declares, "for out of it are the issues of life" (Prov. 4:23).

What is a *Biblical* Worldview?

With the forgoing as our foundation, and after several months grappling with all this, we would offer the following definition of a biblical worldview:

A Biblical Worldview, created by the regeneration of the Holy Spirit and the justifying work of Christ, views, understands, and approaches everything in life through the lens of Scripture, that

Scripture alone defines *reality,* delineates *truth, and* dictates *our attitudes and actions.*

Now, does this mean that every issue and question has a "proof text." Well, yes and no. *Yes* because everything *is* addressed in Scripture, whether in specific word or general principle. *No,* however, because a biblical worldview, we submit, goes deeper than that. It considers the full revelation of Scripture, understanding what all of it says on a given issue, both in philosophy and practice. This will become clearer in our third point below.

While one might think that every born again Christian would automatically have such a view, nothing could be further from the real state of affairs. In a 2003 survey conducted by the Barna Group, it was discovered that only 9% of born again Christians have such a perspective on life. Shocking? Yes. Surprising? Not at all. Why? The reason is obvious. The church has become so immersed in the world, through a plethora of worldviews, that it has become tainted and infected. One cannot live in a hog barn 24 hours a day, for example, and not become contaminated, unless he wears plenty of protective gear. Likewise, unless Christians "put on [and never take off, as the Greek verb tense indicates] the whole armour of God," they will not "stand against" (*stēnai pros,* hold one's ground) Satan and his systems (Eph. 6:11).

The sad fact is that the vast majority of the church, as this survey inarguably confirms, does not *think biblically.* A case in point is the following statement by one of today's leading "Christian leaders": "The ground we have in common with unbelievers is not the Bible, but our common needs, hurts, and interests as human beings. *You cannot start with a text.*"[4] Is that a biblical worldview? Of course not. It's obviously a secular humanistic view. What is even more appalling is how many evangelicals have followed this man and his secular thinking and then built churches based on, at the very least, a mild form of humanism.

We, therefore, want to start with a text, Psalm 119:11: **Thy word have I hid in mine heart, that I might not sin against thee.** The Hebrew word translated **hid** (*tsāphan*) means to hide, to keep secret. It's used of concealing something, often of great value, as that precious picture of when the baby Moses was hidden (Ex. 2:2–3) and when Rahab hid the spies (Josh. 2:4). Used figuratively, it speaks of "laying up in the heart, putting back that which we value." The Word of God is, indeed, priceless, the most valuable thing we can own.

If we could pick one verse that is representative of all 176 verses in this Psalm, this is probably it. It strikes us as the essence of the psalmist's point. In the many months of my study and preaching of this psalm, this verse seemed to be the key to the whole matter. To hide the Word of God in our hearts is to be totally *captive in* it, *committed to* it, and *controlled by* it.

Further, to hide God's Word in the **heart** is to recognize that it alone is sufficient to fill that **heart** with all that is needed for living.

Heart (*lēb*) has a wide range of meanings. While it refers to the physical organ, it much more often refers to one's inner self and nature, including the intellect, emotions, and will, that is, the human personality. So where do we hide God's Word? *In our whole personality!* The Word of God must govern our entire being. We find this very picture, for example, in Genesis 6:5, where "GOD [YHWH, *yahweh*] saw that the wickedness of man was great in the earth, and that every imagination of the thoughts of his heart was only evil continually." Everything about man in that day was evil; not a single thought, emotion, or choice was righteous.

Spurgeon well said of the Psalmist: "He did not *wear* a text on his heart as a *charm*, but he *hid* it in his heart as a *rule*."[5] While many today wear a cross around their neck, some kind of religious symbol on a charm bracelet, a bumper sticker on their car that says, "I love Jesus," or other outward symbolism, the psalmist says he **hid** God's **word** in his **heart**, that is, his whole self. *Symbolism* is one thing; *substance* is quite another.

What, then, is the end of all this? Simply that it is such an immersion in God's Word that keeps us from **sin**. We would submit, therefore, that this verse encapsulates a biblical worldview. If God's Word is at the core of our entire being, it is going to dictate everything that pertains to life and then protect us from any other worldview. We will *think* biblically (the intellect), *react* biblically (the emotions), and we will *choose* biblically (the will).

With the footing and foundation laid, we are now prepared for the structure.

What Is the Application of a Biblical Worldview?

The Principle

In researching this article, I came across another in which the writer well says that the Christian worldview hangs on four strategic events. First, the *Creation* addresses how we got here; a perfect eternal God created all things. Second, the *Fall* explains what went wrong; sin, evil, suffering, and death entered by a single act of disobedience to God. Third, the *Incarnation* explains the solution; God's Son in the flesh, Jesus Christ, paid for sin. Fourth, *Restoration* tells us where history is headed, namely, a New Heaven and New Earth in which righteousness dwells.

What that article seemed to me to lack, however, was another "strategic event," *Transformation*, that is, the transformation of life that occurs in a person who receives Christ as Savior and Lord. While some argue that this is covered by Incarnation, that is clearly not true for certain evangelicals who argue against Lordship in salvation, who maintain that no repentance is required and no obedience implied when someone "asks Jesus into their heart."

We would submit, therefore, such transformation not only *means* something but also *demands* something. As noted in chapter 23, 2 Corinthians 5:17 declares that "if any man be in Christ, he is a new creature: old things are passed away; behold, all things are become new." "New" here is *kainos*, which refers to something new in *quality* (not *time*, as *neos* means). It, therefore, pictures a creature that has never existed before, a creature with a new character ("the divine nature," 2 Pet. 1:4). When Christ comes into a life, that life changes. To talk about a "conversion" (Latin *convertere*, "to turn around, transform") that doesn't change anything is ludicrous, to say the least. There is no such thing as spiritual *life* without spiritual *living*. "New" means *new*, not "improved, renovated, or enhanced old."

So, to have a true *biblical* worldview means that because we are regenerated and are new creatures with a divine nature, we think, feel, act, react, and live differently than those who live by any other worldview. This does not mean thinking biblically about just "*spiritual* things" (a great misnomer about this issue), but about *all* things.

The Application

The survey mentioned earlier makes this point to a certain degree. It points out that those who have a biblical worldview (the mere 9% of born again Christians remember) live a life that is much different from those who do not. For example, they are much less likely to engage in non-marital sex, use profanity, gamble, view pornography, get drunk, approve of homosexuality, or condone abortion.

But while all those are certainly well and good, are they really *proofs* of a biblical worldview? I know many non-Christians who are just as opposed to those things as Christians are. In fact, most of those things are opposed by Muslims—do they have a biblical worldview? It can be easily demonstrated further from history that many non-Christian cultures have been opposed to many of those things simply because such behavior has a negative effect on society.

I am, therefore, convinced that there is something much more important that we are missing here. Yes, the above things are obviously biblical mandates, but they do not prove that one has a biblical worldview. That is why we said earlier that such matters are not just about "proof texts," but rather the underlying philosophy of the totality of Scripture. In other words, we examine not only *precepts* and *precedents*, but also underlying general *principles*.

In all the research I did for this article, there was oddly very little practical application offered. To illustrate, what benefit would there have been if after men discovered the physical phenomenon of "lift" it had not then been applied in the real world in making airplanes fly? I would, therefore, dare to offer a couple of examples of how this *theory* of a biblical worldview can be put into *practice*. The world, with its multiple worldviews, has so seriously infected our thinking that we no longer think, react, and choose biblically. I know this might "rattle a few cages," but I also believe that such a reaction will prove the point all the more. If we really think, react, and choose biblically, if we really view the world through the lens of Scripture, we will recognize each issue for what it is.

With that in mind, there is a whole gamut of things we could examine, but here are just two that will illustrate how we should put this principle into practice.

First, modern psychology immediately comes to mind. Now, we are not referring here to true *biblical* counseling, which relies on Scripture *alone* for diagnosis and remedy. Rather we are talking about the man-centered, humanistic philosophy that underlies modern thought. There are few things in today's world, in fact, that are as openly anti-God and anti-Scripture as this, but still Christianity has bought into it. Oh, many have tried to sanitize and Christianize it by sprinkling it with Bible verses, but that does not change its underlying philosophy. There is no better illustration than one of the core emphases of modern psychology, namely, the centrality of "self-esteem," a philosophy diametrically opposed to Scripture (Mk. 8:34; Rom. 1:25; 12:3; Phil. 2:3; 2 Tim. 3:1–2; Jas. 4:6; etc.).

In an eye-opening article that appeared in several newspapers, including conservative weekly *The Washington Times*, well-known *secular* psychologist, parenting expert, and syndicated columnist John Rosemond reveals the facts about "self-esteem." He first describes how this approach was hatched back in the 1960s, "that high self-esteem is a good thing and parents should do all in their power to make sure their children acquire it." It didn't matter, he goes on to say, that there was "absolutely no empirical evidence . . . to support this claim," but that it "sounded good" and "was easy to market."

Rosemond then goes on to show that the real evidence is now in. "People with high self-regard, the evidence says, possess low regard for others . . . seek to manipulate others . . . [and] tend to antisocial behavior. People incarcerated in maximum security prisons have very high self-regard, for example." He then convincingly submits, "Self-esteem doesn't pass the common-sense test either. Would you rather be employed by, work alongside, be close friends with or be married to a person with high self-esteem or a person who is humble and modest? See what I mean?" [6]

The underlying philosophy of Scripture, however, is not *self*-esteem, but *Christ*-esteem. When the church as a whole swallowed the self-esteem bait hook, line, and sinker—along with all the accompanying trappings of psychology—it jettisoned a biblical worldview. How did Jesus or Paul minister effectively without such modern thinking? On the contrary, they used Scripture alone. Any compromise with modern psychology immediately and fundamentally denies the sufficiency of Scripture. The two are oil and water. Psychology, like philosophy, has no answers, only more questions. God alone has the answers. Biblical Counseling—which is one of the responsibilities of a pastor as he shepherds the flock—is essential, but when we mix it with humanistic thought, we have abandoned a biblical worldview.

Second, as alluded to earlier, most of today's church ministry is clearly not based upon a biblical worldview. It is, in fact, based upon several other worldviews, depending upon which false teacher you listen to.

Today's prosperity teachers are a prime example. They tell us that if we give to God (which means, of course, sending your money to the teacher himself), God will return our "investment" and make us rich. Such teaching is built upon a materialistic worldview.

Another example is the "seeker-sensitive" movement, which appeals to people's "felt needs." A "felt need" is simply anything a person *perceives* as a need, regardless of what the *real* need is, which is always Truth. "Seekers" are also referred to as the "unchurched" and are appealed to through entertainment and other fleshly methods. While it might seem a little harsh to say so, it is an inescapable conclusion that this reflects a hedonistic worldview.

Another graphic example is that of the Emergent Church movement, which rejects all certainty. It dismisses the possibility of a sure and settled knowledge of Truth. In fact, to say that we can know anything for sure is actually arrogant to Emergent leaders, who are obviously deeply committed to a relativistic worldview.

So, as is unambiguously clear, not one of those things, or others we could list, is committed solely and exclusively to Scripture. Their proponents do not think, react, and choose biblically, and it is this that is at the root of the problems in the church today.

A Final Encouragement

There are certainly many other things we could examine, and we could even do so by lengthening this chapter considerably. It's probably better, however, to just leave the matter here and allow each of us to examine other things on our own. The first essential, as we've seen, must be to recognize that all such issues go far beyond just "proof texts," that such things are not just "up for grabs" and open to each person's opinion or preference. To have a biblical worldview means that the whole of Scripture—its precepts, precedents, and principles—weighs in on every subject.

As I mentioned at the beginning of this chapter, this subject has been bothering me for quite awhile, for I fear that instead of a *biblical worldview*, many have a *worldly biblical view*; that is, instead of approaching everything in life through the lens of Scripture, they approach Scripture through the lens of the world. Or to say it another way, instead of Scripture molding their thinking toward the world, they force Scripture to conform to the image of the world. We all will be guilty of this at some time or another, so it calls for vigilance and courage.

Let us each, therefore, ask ourselves a few probing questions: Is my claim of a biblical worldview a *reality* or just *rhetoric*? Do I really have a biblical worldview, or have I combined it with elements of one or more other views? Do I have instead a "worldly biblical" view? Have I truly **hid** God's **Word** in my entire being for the purpose of shielding me from any of the world's views and the consequences of those views? Are the first words that form in my mind when any attitude, action, issue, subject, question, or problem (in short, *anything*) arises, "What saith the Scripture?" (Rom. 4:3; Gal. 4:30).[7] As Schaeffer challenges us:

> As Christians we are not only to know the right world view, the world view that tells us the truth of what is, but consciously to act upon that worldview so as to influence society in all its parts and facets across the whole spectrum of life.[8]

Postscript

During the preparation of this book, I encountered an insightful statement by preacher Phillips Brooks (1835–1893), who while not an expositor was still a powerful proclaimer of the Truth. It struck me so profoundly that I wanted to add it here:

> The Bible is like a telescope. If a man looks through his telescope he sees worlds beyond; but if he looks at his telescope, he does not see anything but that. The Bible is a thing to be looked through to see that which is beyond; but most people only look at it and so they see only the dead letter.[9]

I too fear that many today just look *at* their Bible instead of look *through* it, many who consider it merely as a collection of *letters* instead of a single *lens* through which they view everything in the universe. And so it is that until our attitude changes toward the Word of God, much of the Church today will continue its flirtatious affair with a plethora of worldviews.

NOTES

[1] James W. Sire, *The Universe Next Door: A Basic World View Catalog* (InterVarsity), 15–16.

[2] http://www.theologicalstudies.org/christian_worldvidew.html

[3] Francis Schaeffer, *How Should We Then Live?* (Fleming H. Revell, 1976), 19 (emphasis in the original).

[4] Rick Warren, *The Purpose Driven Church*, 295 (emphasis added).

[5] *The Treasury of David* (Ps. 119:11, emphasis added)).

[6] http://www.washingtontimes.com/news/2009/apr/12/rosemond-high-self-esteem-for-kids-a-sham/

[7] Other related chapters: 1 ("The Sufficiency of Scripture") and 6 ("Where Has Our Discernment Gone?").

[8] Schaeffer, 256.

[9] *The Westminster Collection of Christian Quotations* (Westminster John Knox, 2001), 23.

The Word shows us what is truth and what is error. It is the field in which the pearl of price is hidden. How we should dig for this pearl! A godly man's heart is the library to hold the Word of God; it dwells richly in him (Col. 3:16)

Thomas Watson
A Godly Man's Picture, p. 61

50

The Lord's Supper: Memorial or More?[*]

1 Corinthians 11:23–26

For I have received of the Lord that which also I delivered unto you, That the Lord Jesus the same night in which he was betrayed took bread: And when he had given thanks, he brake it, and said, Take, eat: this is my body, which is broken for you: this do in remembrance of me. After the same manner also he took the cup, when he had supped, saying, This cup is the new testament in my blood: this do ye, as oft as ye drink it, in remembrance of me. For as often as ye eat this bread, and drink this cup, ye do shew the Lord's death till he come.

Way back in the second issue of TOTT we examined the question, "How Often Should the Lord's Supper Be Observed?" (see chapter 3). While this study is not really a follow-up, it does address another aspect of this critical activity of the church.

Our main text is part of the Apostle Paul's discussion of the Lord's Supper in 1 Corinthians 11:17–34. After rebuking the Corinthians for their abuses of this supper, he assures them in verse 23a that the Lord Jesus Himself had revealed to him what had occurred on the night this observance was instituted. He then recounts:

> That the Lord Jesus the same night in which he was betrayed took bread: And when he had given thanks, he brake it, and said, Take, eat: this is my body, which is broken for you: this do in remembrance of me. After the same manner also he took the cup, when he had supped, saying, This cup is the new testament in my blood: this do ye, as oft as ye drink it, in remembrance of me (23b–25).

Theologian J. Oliver Buswell makes an interesting statement that well introduces our discussion:

> Although the Lord's Supper has been more of a question of controversy in church history than baptism has ever been, yet in the latter part of the twentieth century, the Lord's Supper is not a matter of controversy among evangelical Bible-believing, Christian

---

[*] This chapter was originally TOTT issue 75, January/February 2012.

denominations. The break with Rome is now so wide, so far as true evangelicals are concerned, that the Roman Catholic doctrine of the mass is really nothing but a subject for study in church history.[1]

While that is certainly true in the context of the Roman Catholic mass, there actually is a small amount of controversy among evangelicals on at least one aspect of the Lord's Supper, namely: What precisely is its significance? Is it memorial only, or is there something more in it?

Sacrament or Ordinance?

I am convinced that how we view the significance of Lord's Supper is at least partly related to how we refer to it. Words mean things, and in themselves they carry implications. While this section is a little technical, I ask your patience because it forms a very necessary foundation to the more devotional thoughts that follow.

The term "sacrament" transliterates the Latin *sacramentum*, the root of which is *sacrare*, to dedicate, consecrate, render sacred or solemn. With the suffix *-mentum*, "the act or process of," the full idea is an act of taking an oath of dedication or consecration. Historically, in the age of the Roman Empire, it was used in the context of taking the oath of fidelity the Roman soldier swore to the Emperor.

While this word appears valid, perhaps even appropriate, the fact of what it ultimately became simply cannot be ignored or minimized. In Roman Catholicism, *sacrament* came to refer to an act that infuses or produces grace. As one of the most authoritative works of Catholicism, *Fundamentals of Catholic Dogma* by Ludwig Ott, states:

> Scholastic Theology coined the formula: *Sacramenta operantur ex opere operato*, that is, the Sacraments operate by the power of the completed sacramental rite. The Council of Trent sanctioned this expression which was vigorously combated by the Reformers. . . . All Catholic theologians teach that the Sacraments are not merely conditions or occasions of communication of grace, but true causes (*causae instrumentales*) of grace . . . The Council of Trent declared against the Reformers, who, following the precedent of Wycliffe, denied the sacramental character. . . . As there are various Sacraments having various signs, and as the differences in the sacramental signs also point to a difference in the effecting of grace, it must be assumed that each individual Sacrament, corresponding to its special purpose, conveys a special or specific sacramental grace.[2]

Now, it is certainly true that while Reformed thinkers also use the word *sacrament*, they use it quite differently. Augustus Strong well states:

An ordinance is a symbolic rite which sets forth the central truths of the Christian faith, and which is of universal and perpetual obligation. Baptism and the Lord's Supper are rites, which have become ordinances by the specific command of Christ and by their inner relation to the essential truths of his kingdom. No ordinance is a sacrament in the Romanist sense of conferring grace but, as the *sacramentum* was the oath taken by the Roman soldier to obey his commander even unto death, so Baptism and the Lord's Supper are sacraments, in the sense of vows of allegiance to Christ our Master.[3]

That said, however, we submit that there is still a weakness in using the term *sacrament*. Note Strong's use of the word *ordinance*, a term that many prefer over *sacrament* for several reasons. One is simply because of the Roman Catholic overtones in the former and how easily the correct use of it can be obscured.

Another reason is that *ordinance* is, in our view, more accurate. It simply means, in fact, an authoritative rule or law; a decree or command (from the Latin *ordināre*, to set in order). This reflects the fact that our Lord Himself instituted both ordinances of the Church—Baptism and the Lord's Supper. Henry Thiessen well says: "We may define an ordinance as an outward rite instituted by Christ to be administered in the church as a visible sign of the saving truth of the Christian faith."[4]

One other reason we prefer this term is because it is actually a biblical one. The word appears in the very context we are discussing. In 1 Corinthians 11:2 Paul writes to that troubled church, "I praise you, brethren, that ye remember me in all things, and keep the ordinances, as I delivered them to you."[5] The Greek is *paradosis*, which is derived from *paradidōmi*, which in this sense means "to deliver in teaching." The idea then in *paradosis* is "a tradition, doctrine, or injunction delivered or communicated from one to another, whether divine or human."[6] Oh, the danger of *human* tradition! We must take great care that we do not "transgress the commandment of God by [our] tradition" (Matt. 15:3). Let us never violate God's Word by any tradition we embrace. We must test each carefully.

In stark contrast, however, are the traditions (doctrines, ordinances) of God's truth. In 2 Thessalonians 2:15, for example, we read: "Therefore, brethren, stand fast, and hold the traditions which ye have been taught, whether by word, or our epistle." Likewise, here in our text, as John Gill submits, "ordinances" refers to "baptism and the Lord's Supper, which [Paul] received from Christ, and delivered unto them (see 1 Cor. 11:23)."[7]

So, while solid, godly men of the past (and present) used the term *sacrament*, we would lovingly submit that *ordinance* is obviously the better term. As Thiessen submits, it "avoid[s] the mysticism and sacramentalism characterized by the term sacrament."[8]

Memorial or More?

Inseparably linked, then, to the term used for the Lord's Supper is the significance this act carries. There are four views concerning this significance.

The Roman Catholic View

Only a brief statement is needed here. The Roman Catholic view of the Lord's Supper is *transubstantiation* ("a change of substance"). The Council of Trent declared against the Reformers in 1562: "In the sacrament of the most holy Eucharist are contained truly, really, and substantially, the body and blood together with the soul and divinity of our Lord Jesus Christ" and "in the mass a true and proper sacrifice is . . . offered to God."[9]

That, of course, as any true evangelical immediately discerns, is apostasy, paganism, and blasphemy of the grossest sort. It is a blatant departure from Hebrews 9:25, 28; 10:10, 12, and 15, which declare Jesus Christ alone was the once-for-all sacrifice that ushered Him "into the holy place," where He "obtained eternal redemption for us." It is hard to imagine any teaching that is more repulsive than one that claims a priest actually calls Christ down from heaven to sacrifice Him again, who "crucify to themselves the Son of God afresh, and put him to an open shame" (6:6). Additionally, would God actually sanction the drinking of blood, a revolting act he forbade in Genesis 9:3–5?

The Lutheran View

As is commonly known, Luther's view of the Lord's Supper was *consubstantiation*, although he actually never used that term. He did use an analogy, however, that reflects that concept, namely, the picture of an iron bar being heated in a fire: "The two substances of fire and iron are so mingled in the heated iron that every part is both iron and fire. Why could not much rather Christ's body be thus contained in every part of the substance of the bread?"[10] In other words, "the metal was directly affected because it was immersed within the fire and heated; likewise, the elements of the Lord's Supper are in some sense affected by an engulfing presence of Christ."[11]

So, while Christ is not *personally* present in the elements, He is *permeationally* present—while He is not there in *substance*, He is there in *spirit*. This view is obviously troubling, however, because it reads a mystical idea into the observance that is simply not there, being implied neither by the Lord Jesus nor the Apostle Paul. There can be little doubt that as much as we commend Luther for some enormous contributions, it seems clear that he was still a little tainted by Rome when it came to the Lord's Supper.

The Reformed View

In a reference to an illustration by Calvin, Millard Erickson well summarizes the Reformed view: "Using the sun as an illustration, Calvin asserted that Christ is present influentially. The sun remains in the heavens, yet its warmth and light are present on earth. So the radiance of the Spirit conveys to us the communion of Christ's flesh and blood."[12] In other words, Calvin neither viewed Christ as present *personally* (Rome) nor *permeationally* (Luther), rather *persuasively.* Partaking of the bread and wine, then, nourishes believers and brings them into closer communion with Christ. In a sense, as Thiessen notes, "His presence in the Supper is similar to His presence in the Word."[13]

A key idea in the Reformed view (which in practice seems to go a little further than Calvin did) is that the Lord's Supper is "a means of grace." Wayne Grudem well defines this term for us: "The means of grace are any activities within the fellowship of the church that God uses to give more grace to Christians."[14] Perhaps no Reformed writer better articulates this position than does Charles Hodge: "[This term] is intended to indicate those institutions which God has ordained to be the ordinary channel of grace, *i.e.*, of the supernatural influences of the Holy Spirit . . . [namely] the word, sacraments, and prayer."[15] He goes on to specify the significance of the Lord's Supper itself:

> As the Word when attended by the demonstration of the Spirit, becomes the wisdom and power of God unto salvation; so does the sacrament of the Lord's Supper, when thus attended, become a real means of grace, not only signifying and sealing, but really conveying to the believing recipient, Christ and all the benefits of redemption.

Hodge goes on to bring together several concepts: communion in 1 Corinthians 10:16, Jesus' words in John 6:53 concerning the supper, Christ living in the believer (Gal. 2:20), and believers being members of one body (1 Cor. 12:13). "In being thus united to Christ as their common head," he concludes, "believers become one body, in a mystical sense."[16]

While all this paints a beautiful picture—and our highest respect goes to Hodge and others—such an emphasis on mysticism is a little disquieting. Again, as with Luther, the simple fact is that such teaching is reading something into the text that is not explicitly stated. For example, while some refer to the Lord's Supper (as well as Baptism for that matter) as some kind of "seal," it is *never* called that in Scripture; the Holy Spirit is a seal (Eph. 1:11; 3:30), not the ordinances.[17]

The question that inevitably arises here is, "What exactly does our Lord mean when He talks about eating His body and drinking His blood?" Well, obviously, it's not literal, as maintained by Rome. Neither, we believe, does it mean that there is some mystical connection. Rather it is clearly symbolic language. In the same way He referred to Himself as the "bread of life" (Jn. 6:35), "the door" of the sheepfold (10:7–9), and "the vine" (15:1, 5), He speaks here of being represented by the elements.

This brings us to the fourth and final view.

The Zwinglian (Memorial) View

As A. A. Hodge (son of Charles) recounts, the great Swiss reformer Huldrych Zwingli (1484–1531) "held that the bread and wine are simply memorials of the Body of Christ absent in heaven." It is also significant that, as Hodge goes on to add, Zwingli's "view at first prevailed among the Reformed churches and was embodied" in several confessions of faith between 1530 and 1536.[18]

To set the tone for this view, we note a wise comment from Millard Erickson:

> We need to be particularly careful to avoid the negativism which has sometimes characterized this view that the Lord's Supper is essentially a memorial. Out of a zeal to avoid the conception that Jesus is present in some sort of magical way, some have gone to such extremes as to give the impression that the one place where Jesus most assuredly is not to be found is in the Lord's Supper.[19]

Yes, we can overreact to a concept and thereby swing too far the other way. As we will see, however, a *memorial* actually implies far more than what many realize—it's more than *just* a memorial. We would, therefore, offer a six-fold significance of the Lord's Supper,[20] all of which, we submit, emerge solely from the biblical text.

First—and out of which flow the others—the Lord's Supper is primarily a *perpetual memorial* of Christ on the cross. There are, in fact, three strong evidences of the strictly memorial nature of the Lord's Supper.

1. The Greek for **remembrance** is *anamnēsis*, which (along with several others in this large word group, e.g., *mnemoneuō*) refers not only to the mental capability to recall something, but also "to be mindful" of it and "take [it] into account." Other concepts include: remind oneself, consider, ponder, and reflect.[21]

The same is true of the Hebrew *zākar*, which not only means to remember but also "to think of or pay attention to." The fact that it appears so often (about 238 times, 57 of which in the Psalms) demonstrates that *remembrance in ancient Israel was a major part of proper worship* (e.g., Psa. 22:27; 45:17; 63:5–6; 77:11, 13; etc.).

So, when our Lord said, "Do this in remembrance of Me," He was saying infinitely more than what my wife means when she says to me, "Remember to get milk while you're running your errands." The Lord's Supper is a time of deep spiritual worship, a time to be reminded (and be mindful) of the cross, to take into account what our Lord suffered, to ponder the spiritual riches He provides, and to reflect on our responsibilities.

2. The backdrop of the instituting of the Lord's Supper was immediately after the Passover Supper. Luke 22:20 declares that the Lord Jesus "took the cup after supper," for that was the current occasion (v. 15). The Passover, of course, looked back to God's delivering Israel from bondage in Egypt, calling them to **remembrance** of that key event. In fact, a form of the Hebrew *zākar*, which we noted earlier, is the word used in Exodus 12:14 for the word "memorial" that marked this feast. Likewise, the Septuagint renders *zākar* using a Greek word from the group mentioned earlier (*mnemosunon*).

What better backdrop, then, could there have been to our Lord's "new call" to **remembrance**? Further, we would ask, if we are truly practicing **remembrance** at this level, is some mystical idea even necessary or can it really add anything more?

3. We would also briefly submit that this is a memorial because no outward act we perform imparts or confers grace. As we contribute nothing to salvation, we contribute nothing to the furtherance of "a means of grace."

Second, the Lord's Supper is the *promise* of the New Covenant now fulfilled. As our Lord declared, **This cup is the new testament in my blood.** This refers to the covenant (**testament** is *diathēkē*) that God promised to the nation of Israel in Jeremiah 31:31–34 ("covenant" is *beriyt*), the terms of which are then expounded in Hebrews 8:10–12 (*diathēkē* again). The blood of Christ ratified that covenant, which is now in force but tragically rejected by Israel.

Third, the Lord's Supper is a *proclamation* of Christ's death and resurrection. It is through this that we **show** [*kataggéllō*, declare plainly, openly, aloud] **the Lord's death till he come.**

Fourth, the Lord's Supper is a *prophecy* of Christ's return. The words **till he come** introduce an amazing feature of the Lord's Supper—and this was also true again of the Passover Feast—that it not only looks *backward* but also *forward*. The early 2nd-century church document *The Didache*

(Teaching of the Twelve Apostles), written by an unknown author, contains teachings on church order. While it wasn't recognized as part of the canon of Scripture, it was very highly regarded in the early church (and still should be). Chapter 10 records that after taking "Communion" (note our sixth point) the people gave thanks in prayer, almost half of which looked to the future:

> Remember, Lord, Thy Church, to deliver it from all evil and to make it perfect in Thy love, and gather it from the four winds, sanctified for Thy kingdom which Thou have prepared for it; for Thine is the power and the glory for ever. Let grace come, and let this world pass away. Hosanna to the God (Son) of David! If any one is holy, let him come; if any one is not so, let him repent. Maranatha [Our Lord, come!]. Amen.

The true Christian believer desires to be with His Lord, and the supper He instituted declares that with a passion.

Fifth, the Lord's Supper is **a *point* of confession of sin**. Verses 28–29 declare that one must **examine** himself (*dokimazō*, "test, pronounce good, establish by trial") before partaking of this supper. Why? Because this a place of worship, and there is no room here for sin. In the context of the fleshly and divisive Corinthians, there is no place for such actions and attitudes at this table. This leads to and is inseparable with a final significance.

Sixth, the Lord's Supper is a *period* of fellowship for the church. In his previous reminder concerning the Lord's Supper, Paul writes in 10:16 about the "cup of blessing" and "the bread which we break" being for "the communion of the body of Christ." "Communion" is *koinōnia*, which speaks of a partnership, close union, and brotherly bond and is perhaps the best term to use for the Lord's Supper. Kenneth Wuest well expresses the meaning: "joint participation in a common interest or activity."[22] Oh, the wondrous time of fellowship this ordinance was designed by our Lord to be! Together we commune, we commemorate, and we comfort. It reminds us, too, that we *are* a body, which while having many members all labor together in unity and love for each other. It's significant, indeed, that it was at the institution of this ordinance that Jesus washed the disciples' feet (Jn. 13:14–15). While not commanded or adopted as a church ordinance, it graphically illustrates the service each body member should render to the others.

Conclusion

In his wonderful book on this subject, that great Puritan Matthew Henry writes:

Remember him! Is there any danger of our forgetting him? . . . Ought we not to remember, and can we ever forget such a friend as Christ is—a friend that is our near and dear relation? . . . A friend in covenant with us? . . . A friend that has so wonderfully signalized his friendship? . . . A friend, who, though he be absent from us, is negotiating our affairs, and is really absent for us? . . . A friend, who, though he be now absent, will be absent but a while?[23]

Yes, the Lord's Supper is a *memorial*, but it's certainly not *just* a memorial.

NOTES

[1] *A Systematic Theology of the Christian Religion* (Singapore: Christian Life Publishers PTE LTD, 1994; originally published by Zondervan, 1962), 267–68.

[2] Ludwig Ott, *Fundamentals of Catholic Dogma* (Tan Books and Publishers, 1955, 1960, 1974), 329–330, 332–333.

[3] A. H. Strong, *Systematic Theology* (Judson Press, 1907, 1993), 930.

[4] Henry Thiessen, *Lectures in Systematic Theology*, Revised Edition (Eerdmans, 1949, 1994), 323.

[5] Other translations read "traditions" (NASB, ESV) or "teachings" (NIV, which is imprecise).

[6] Spiros Zodhiates, *The Complete Word Study Dictionary* (AMG Publishing, 1992), entry #3862.

[7] *John Gill's Exposition of the Entire Bible*, comment on 1 Cor. 11:2. Note also Albert Barnes, as well as Jamieson, Fausset, and Brown (*A Commentary on the Old and New Testaments*).

[8] Thiessen, *op. cit.*

[9] Session 13, Canon 1 (see also Canons 2 and 5); session 22, canon 1.

[10] *The Babylonian Captivity of the Church* in *The Works of Martin Luther*, Vol. 2 (Ages Software), 136.

[11] Paul Watson, *A Study of What Takes Place During the Lord's Supper* (unpublished paper, Calvary Bible College), 4. My thanks to Mr. Watson, whose research for a college theology paper contributed to my own.

[12] Millard Erickson, *Christian Theology*, 2nd Edition (Baker, 1983, 1998), 1127. (See Calvin, *Institutes* (IV.17.12.)

[13] Thiessen, 329.

[14] Wayne Grudem, *Systematic Theology* (Zondervan, 1994), 950.

[15] *Systematic Theology*, Vol. 3 (Eerdmans, reprint 1989), 466.

[16] *Ibid*, 622.

[17] John Gill well comments: "The seals of God's will or testament are not the ordinances; circumcision was no seal of the covenant of grace; it was a seal to Abraham, and to him only, that he should be the father of believing Gentiles; and that the same righteousness of faith should come upon them, which came upon

him, when in uncircumcision: nor is baptism, which is falsely said to come in the room of it, and much less is it a seal of the covenant; nor the ordinance of the Lord's Supper; for though the blood of Christ, one of the symbols in it, is yet not that itself: but the seals are the Holy Spirit of God, and the blood of Christ" (*A Body of Doctrinal and Practical Divinity* [The Baptist Standard Bearer, 1995 reprint of 1839 edition], 242).

[18] *Outlines of Theology* (Banner of Truth, 1879, 1991 reprint), 640.

[19] Erickson, 1130.

[20] Partially adapted from five points by Thiessen (327–28) plus one additional.

[21] Colin Brown, *New International Dictionary of New Testament* (Zondervan, 1967, 1986), Vol. 3, 230.

[22] Kenneth Wuest, *Word Studies in the Greek New Testament* (electronic edition by Logos Library Systems), comment on Philippians 2:1.

[23] *The Communicant's Companion* (SGCB, 1843; reprint 2005), 43–44.

Chrysostom compares the scripture to a garden; every line in it is a fragrant flower, which we should wear, not in our bosom, but our heart. Delight in the word causeth profit: and we must not only love the comforts of the word, but the reproofs. Myrrh is bitter to the palate, but good for the stomach.

Thomas Watson
How We May Read the Scriptures with Most Spiritual Profit,
Direction 12

51

1 John 5:7–8:
Beyond a Reasonable Doubt?*

F ew texts of scripture have spurred as much controversy as has 1 John 5:7–8. A portion of these verses has been dubbed the "Johannine Comma" (Latin *comma Johanneum*, "the phrase of John"). Here is how the verses read in the King James Version, with the bold words indicating the Comma:

> 7 For there are three that bear record **in heaven, the Father, the Word, and the Holy Ghost: and these three are one.**
>
> 8 **And there are three that bear witness in earth**, the Spirit, and the water, and the blood: and these three agree in one.

The issue, as many Christians are aware, is whether those words actually belong to the sacred text or should rather be rejected due to the lack of evidence of genuineness.

I want to approach this subject, however, from a little different direction than it is usually broached. To do so, I would first like to quote the following from a distinguished law professor at Rutgers University who explains "the prosecutor's burden of proving guilt *beyond a reasonable doubt*":

> The defendant never has the burden of proving his innocence. The burden is entirely on the prosecutor, and if the prosecutor fails to carry that burden, an acquittal is required. The defense attorney may choose as a matter of trial strategy to convince the jury that the defendant is innocent, but it is equally appropriate simply to cast doubt on the prosecutor's story so that the burden is not met.
>
> Reasonable doubt is a much higher standard than the burden of proof elsewhere in the law. . . . Reasonable doubt is a doubt about guilt that remains after the jury has weighed all of the evidence and seriously considered the matter.[1]

---

* This chapter was originally TOTT issue 52, November 2009. The original article was shorter than desired because of space limitation. The present version, therefore, is slightly expanded.

In other words, the standard of proof does not require that the prosecutor establish absolute certainty by eliminating all doubt, but it *does* require that the evidence be so conclusive that all *reasonable* doubts are removed from the mind of the ordinary person.

So what's the point? Simply this: I want to approach this issue from the perspective of *beyond a reasonable doubt.* The "prosecutor" (modern textual critic) insists that the "defendant" (our text) is "guilty," if you will, of being false and not belonging here. One argument, in fact, is that there was deliberate tampering by zealous copyists who forged manuscript evidence.

My purpose, therefore, is not to prove that the Johannine Comma is authentic (or that the accused copyists were innocent), because as the "defense attorney" I don't have to do that. Rather, my purpose is to allow the critics to present their evidence and just see if they meet their burden of proof. Let us see whether they do indeed prove their case *beyond a reasonable doubt* or if it is at least *possible* that the Comma is genuine. As the great theologian Robert L. Dabney put it in 1891: "All the critics vote against it. But let us see whether the case is as clear as they would have it."[2]

Before continuing, I want to interject that my purpose is not to turn this into a polemic for "King James Onlyism," for *that is **not** my position on the textual issue* (see chapter 8, "What's *Really* at Stake in the Textual Issue?"). While I do defend the historic (and what I believe is the providentially preserved) text of the New Testament (i.e., Traditional or Ecclesiastical Text) instead of the modern Critical Text, that is not my purpose here. Nor is my purpose to attack said critics, for that is neither constructive nor Christian. I know that some TOTT readers embrace the Critical Text and the modern translations based on it, so I do not wish to offend or inflame. My only purpose is to examine this issue from what I hope is a fresh perspective.

If I may also interject, while some in the "Kings James Only" camp stoop to unfortunate name calling, some critics react by lumping everyone who defends the Comma into that camp. But there have been several very solid and brilliant men through the ages who have defended the Comma, such as: John Calvin, Francis Turretin, Matthew Henry, John Gill, Robert L. Dabney, Edward F. Hills, and others. To shrug off men such as those as being unscholarly, or even fanatical simpletons, is not wise.

Let us now allow the prosecution to charge the defendant and present its evidence.

Charge #1: Lack of Greek Manuscript Evidence

By far, this is the most relied upon proof that the Comma does not belong here. One modern critic seriously blunders by writing that the

Comma "disappear[s] from the Greek manuscript tradition without leaving a single trace,"[3] but that is simply not so. Most critics agree that out of all the Greek manuscripts that contain 1 John, one (but only one) does contain the Comma: Miniscule 61, a 15th or 16th-century Italian copy named Codex Montfortii (Britannicus by Erasmus), which now resides at Trinity College, Dublin. One is left puzzled by the above dogmatic assertion.

We submit, however, that there is a problem of consistency in that argument, which plants at least the seed of reasonable doubt. While in this instance the critics insist that only one manuscript supports this reading, they accept other readings based on minority evidence. For example, in 1 John 1:7, the Traditional Text reading *Iesou Christou* ("Jesus Christ") appears in 477 manuscripts, but the critics prefer the Critical Text reading *Iesou* ("Jesus") even though it appears in only 27 manuscripts. Also, while 491 manuscripts support *panta* ("all things") in 1 John 2:20, the critics prefer *pantes* ("all") even though its support is only 12 manuscripts. Again, much ado is made about nothing when it comes to the words "in Ephesus" (Eph 1:1). While the critics cast doubt that these words are genuine, relying on only six manuscripts, thousands of others support this reading. And these are only three of hundreds of illustrations. It seems the prosecutor wants to have the best of both worlds.

We should also point out here the reason for this obvious partiality toward the minority. It is usually due to the critic's number one criteria for a "correct reading," namely, that it is supported by the so-called "older manuscripts." It is consistently *assumed* (repeat *assumed*) that the older are closer to the original. But does that hold up in court? Is a jury actually going to believe the testimony of only a few over the testimony of a thousand?

To illustrate very simply, ponder the following scenario: Assume 100 people witness an accident and write down what they saw. The reports of 98 of the witnesses are very much the same. The other two, however, differ greatly with the 98, and even with each other at times, even though they wrote their statements a month before the other 98. Now, let's be honest: which story are we going to believe?

The prosecution goes one step further by even challenging Miniscule 61. This brings us to Erasmus. The Comma did not, in fact, appear in the first two editions of his Greek text (1516 and 1519) because he could not find a Greek manuscript that contained it (only Latin),[4] but did appear in his third edition (1522). Now, it is here that the following story has been popularized. We cite Bruce Metzger's own rendition of this story (written in 1968) because of his prominence in modern textual criticism:

> In an unguarded moment Erasmus promised that he would insert the Comma Johanneum, as it is called, in future editions if a single

Greek manuscript could be found that contained the passage. At length such a copy was found—or was made to order. As it now appears, the Greek manuscript had probably been written in Oxford about 1520 by a Franciscan friar named Froy (or Roy), who took the disputed words from the Latin Vulgate. Erasmus stood by his promise and inserted the passage in his third edition (1522), but he indicates in a lengthy footnote his suspicions that the manuscript had been prepared expressly in order to confute him.[5]

Based much on Metzger's scholarship, this story has been retold countless times for decades, so we now call to the stand a rebuttal witness: Henk J. de Jonge of Leiden University (who is *not* a *Textus Recpetus* advocate). In 1980 he published his paper *Erasmus and the Comma Johanneum*. As an expert on Erasmus, de Jonge went through every word Erasmus wrote and found not a trace of this story. As an example, he cites a work by T.H. Horne in 1818 that contained the first mention of the story, but Horne himself cited no documentation for the story.

There is, in fact, not a shred of proof that this incident ever happened. In my own research, I have found not a single person who retells this story who then cites a source. While apologist James White does cite Professor Erika Rummel as a source, all she does is cite de Jonge and then still inexplicably maintain that Erasmus did issue the challenge.[6] Most significantly, however, in light of de Jonge's work, Metzger himself finally admitted in the 3rd Edition of his classic, *The Text of the New Testament*, that this story "needs to be corrected."[7] I ask the jury, does not all this cast some reasonable doubt?

Further, if we may add, as for the theory that Miniscule 61 was a deliberate forgery to deceive Erasmus, any defense attorney worth his salt would rise and say, "Objection, Your Honor! Speculative." By law, the judge would have to respond, "Objection sustained." He might even add, "The jury will disregard the prosecutor's remarks because there is no proof of his allegation." As Dabney submits, "The recent [1891] critics are not so infallible as they pretend to be,"[8] and we would submit that neither are the ones of today.

We can also call O. T. Dobbin (1807–1890) to the stand. He was, in fact, the last collator of this manuscript and was convinced that it was not written "by any one 'bold' critic" as has been averred, nor by any unprincipled forger."[9] Perhaps even more significantly, as Roland Bainton maintained, Erasmus defended the verse in his fourth edition (1527). Bainton writes: "His own defense was that the verse was in the Vulgate and must therefore have been lost in the Greek text used by Jerome."[10]

While Miniscule 61 is regarded as the only possibly credible Greek manuscript that contains the Comma, the fact is that there are a few others.

There is, for example, Minuscules 110 (Codex Ravianus), a 16th-century manuscript. It is widely held that Ravianus was "obviously a forgery" and is therefore rejected by critical scholars. Again, however, the defense can justifiably object—this is speculation. If we may also add, in view of the fact that Ravianus contains the entire New Testament, does it not seem odd that a forger would put this much time and effort into such a task?

It must also be noted that three other manuscripts contain the Comma: 629 (Codex Ottobonianus, 14–15th-centuries), 918 (16th-century), and 2318 (18th-century). The prosecutor shrugs off all these by saying that none are dated before the 14th-century, but this once again flows from the *presupposition and assumption* that older is always better and younger is irrelevant. We also note that the Comma is found in the margins of Minuscules 88 (Codex Regis, 11th-century with margins added in the 16th), 221 (10th-century with margins added in the 15th–16th), 429 (14th-century with margins added in the 16th), and 636 (16th). There are also some variant readings in lectionaries (ancient church service books). All this evidence, however, is also discounted with improvable (and objectionable) allegations such as tampering and forgery.

While the Greek evidence is admittedly weak, giving the prosecution some weight, the Latin evidence makes up for that. As John Gill wrote in the 18th-century, "it is certain [that the Comma] is to be seen in many Latin manuscripts of an early date, and stands in the Vulgate Latin edition of the London Polyglot Bible."[11] We'll continue our look at the Latin evidence in Charge #2.

We again ask, has the prosecution proven it's case beyond a reasonable doubt?

Charge #2: Not Found in Greek Writers or Ancient Versions

Similar to Charge #1, this one points out the fact that the Comma is not quoted by a single Greek writer, who would surely have done so in the face of the Arianism of the day. Arius, a 4th-century parish priest in Alexandria, taught that Jesus was not coequal with God and was, in fact, a created being. If genuine, it is argued, the Comma would have been the perfect weapon against Arius.

There is again, however, room for reasonable doubt because it most certainly is cited by Latin writers. As John Gill documents, it is "cited by many of them" such as "Fulgentius [of Ruspe, North Africa] in the beginning of the 6th-century, against the Arians, without any scruple or hesitation." Edward Freer Hills (1912–81), who not only graduated from

Yale and Westminster Seminary but also earned a PhD in textual criticism from Harvard Divinity School, well sums up the data for us:

> Evidence for the early existence of the Johannine comma is found in the Latin versions and in the writings of the Latin Church Fathers. For example, it seems to have been quoted at Carthage by Cyprian (c. 250) . . .

> The first undisputed citations . . . occur in the writing of two 4th-century Spanish bishops, Priscillian, who in 385 was beheaded by the Emperor Maximus on the charge of sorcery and heresy, and Idacius Clarus, Priscillian's principal adversary and accuser. In the 5th-century the *Johannine comma* was quoted by several orthodox African writers to defend the doctrine of the Trinity against the gainsaying of the Vandals, who ruled North Africa from 489 to 534 and were fanatically attached to the Arian heresy. And about the same time it was cited by Cassiodorus (480–570), in Italy. The *comma is* also found in *r*, an Old Latin manuscript of the 5th or 6th century, and in the *Speculum*, a treatise which contains an Old Latin text. It was not included in Jerome's original edition of the Latin Vulgate, but around the year 800 it was taken into the text of the Vulgate from the Old Latin manuscripts. It was found in the great mass of the later Vulgate manuscripts and in the Clementine edition of the Vulgate.[12]

At this point, the question arises, How did this verse drop out of the Greek text but preserved in the Latin? Critical scholars answer this by theorizing that it was merely a Trinitarian interpretation of verse 8. In other words, as Hills explains, they assume that the "spirit" (signifying the Father), the "blood" (signifying the Son), and the "water" (signifying the Spirit) in verse 8 simply created the interpretation of verse 7, which was inserted by Latin writers. Besides the obvious problem that this is simply a theory, there is another difficulty. If this was simply an interpretation, why use "Word" instead of "Son?" Nowhere else in Scripture do we find the Trinitarian formula "Father, *Word*, and Holy Spirit." Critics explain this by saying the interpreter was copying John's style by using "Word," but this assumes blatant deceit, which would undermine the interpreter's purpose. Additionally, it seems unlikely that such an interpreter would abandon the accepted formula "Father, *Son*, and Holy Spirit."[13]

Charge #3: Probably an Interpolation

Here is a particularly serious charge. It is alleged that the only reason that the Comma appears is that a scribe deliberately inserted it to strengthen the teaching of the Trinity. A less accusatory contention is that one scribe made a comment in the margin and then a later scribe assumed it belonged in the text. All such accounts have one thing in common, however, namely, words such as "must have occurred" or "probably happened." The defense once again is justified in his objection on the grounds of speculation.

Is there not, in fact, something amiss when one resorts to such tactics as accusing pious scribes of emendation, questioning their very integrity, and in effect calling them liars, or at the very least accusing them of incompetence? We call Matthew Henry to the stand:

> It was far more easy for a transcriber, by turning away his eye, or by the obscurity of the copy, it being obliterated or defaced on the top or bottom of a page, or worn away in such materials as the ancients had to write upon, to lose and omit the passage, than for an interpolator to devise and insert it. He must be very bold and impudent who could hope to escape detection and shame; and profane too, who durst venture to make an addition to a supposed sacred book.[14]

John Calvin also testifies on this text's behalf:

> Some omit the whole of this verse. Jerome thinks it happened through malice rather than error, and that only among the Latins. But, since even the Greek MSS do not agree, I hardly dare assert anything. But because the passage reads better with the clause added and as I see that it is found in the best and most approved copies, I also readily embrace it.[15]

Instead of being *added*, in fact, it is much more likely that the Comma was *deleted*. While critics surmise that it was a Latin interpreter's addition, in view of history it's much more likely that either an early scribe accidentally left it out or that heretics deliberately deleted it, the latter of which seems most likely. As Jerome, Turretin, John Wesley, and others have suggested, it's quite possible that Origen or Arius, both of whom rejected the doctrine of the Trinity, or even one of their followers in the 3rd or 4th centuries surgically removed the problem text. John Wesley, for example, testifies:

> That we can easily account for its being, after that time, wanting in many copies, when we remember that Constantine's successor was a zealous Arian, who used every means to promote his bad cause, to spread Arianism throughout the empire; in particular the erasing this text out of as many copies as fell into his hands. And he so far prevailed, that the age in which he lived is commonly styled, Seculum Arianum, — "the Arian age."[16]

Hills, however, maintains that the deletion could have occurred even earlier. Before Arianism raised its ugly head, there was a heresy called Sabellianism in the 2nd and 3rd centuries. Named after Sebellius, this heresy taught that the Father, Son, and Holy Spirit were identical. While the words "these three are one" would seem to Sabellians to teach their view, verse 7 would confuse the issue. The struggle against Sabellianism was the most severe in the Greek-speaking East, so it is reasonable to deduce that the verse was widely rejected and deleted as copies were made.[17]

The highly respected theologian Robert L. Dabney—who was a contemporary of Westcott and Hort, the progenitors of much of this controversy—also comes to the defense:

> The Sabellian and Arian controversies raged in the third and fourth. Is there no coincidence here? . . . The curious coincidence, we repeat, that only one vital doctrine should be touched in any of its supposed testimonies, by all the myriads of variations, almost irresistibly impels the mind to the conclusion, that not the chance errors of transcribers, but some deliberate hand, has been at work in these instances. And when we remember the date of the great Trinitarian contest, and compare it with the supposed date of these exemplars of the sacred test, the ground of suspicion becomes violent.[18]

It should be noted again that Dabney carries much weight. He "was the most conspicuous figure and the leading theological guide of the Southern Presbyterian Church," B. B. Warfield wrote, "the most prolific theological writer that the church has yet produced, and for a period of over forty years, one of the most distinguished and probably the most impressive teacher of its candidates for the ministry."[19] As noted back in chapter 46, it seems he is conveniently ignored on these issues.

If we may once again ask, has the prosecution proven its case beyond a reasonable doubt?

Charge #4: Destroys the Passage's Continuity

The final charge, that the inclusion of the Comma destroys the continuity of John's thought, is particularly odd. It is insisted, as commentator Albert Barnes puts is, that he "is speaking of certain things which bear 'witness' to the fact that Jesus is the Messiah, certain things which were well known to those to whom he was writing [Spirit, water, and blood]," so "how does it . . . strengthen the force of this to say that in heaven there are 'three that bear witness'—three not before referred to, and having no connection with the matter?"[20] This is odd thinking because it calls into question the possible thinking process of an inspired author.

The same commentator further insists that the "language is not such as John would use," adding that John does use "the term 'Logos,' or 'Word' (Jn. 1:1, [etc.], but it is never in this form, 'The Father, and the Word.'" That, of course, as the jury immediately discerns, proves nothing. Just because John doesn't use this term anywhere else as he does here does not negate this usage. Interestingly, while Barnes was certainly not a liberal, the same kind of argumentation is, in fact, used by liberal scholarship to "prove" that Paul did not pen Ephesians. One such argument insists that Paul was not the author since almost 100 words and phrases appear in Ephesians that are not found in any other of his letters.[21] We submit, then, that ignoring the obvious significance of John's characteristic use of "Word" (*Logos*) is self-defeating.

The defense must now caution the jury before continuing. We must present some technical evidence for a moment to demonstrate further reasonable doubt. Critics consistently gloss over a grammatical fact concerning this text and dismiss it as irrelevant, despite several noted scholars who point it out.[22]

To put it simply, words in Greek have gender. For example, "man" is the masculine *anthrōpos*, so if we wanted to modify it with "good," the modifier must also be masculine, *agathos*. Likewise, to modify the feminine form *genē* would require the feminine *agathe*. Turning to our text, then, here is how it lays out according to gender:

> For there are three (masculine) that bear record **in heaven, the Father** (masculine)**, the Word** (masculine)**, and the Holy Ghost** (neuter)**: and these three** (masculine) **are one. And there are three** (masculine) **that bear witness in earth**, the Spirit (neuter), and the water (neuter), and the blood (neuter): and these three (neuter) agree in one.

In verse 6, therefore, "water" (*hudōr*), "blood" (*haima*), and "spirit" (*pneuma*) are all neuter in gender. Likewise the participle "bear witness" is neuter (*oi marturoun*), as it should be. If we immediately jump to verse 8, however, the same three words are treated as if they were masculine because the same basic participle, "that bear witness," is now in the masculine (*oi marturountes*). That is poor grammar, or as Dabney bluntly puts it, "an insuperable and very bald grammatical difficulty."[23] This also results in the masculine "three" modifying three neuters. Something appears to be missing. The problem is easily solved, however, when we include verse 7, where we find two masculine nouns, **Father** (*patēr*) and **Word** (*logos*), and one neuter, **Holy Ghost** (*pneuma*). Because of the influence of these masculine nouns in verse 7, it is quite proper to treat the usually neuter nouns in verse 8 as masculine using the masculine participle (*oi marturountes*).

It is also interesting to note Gregory of Nazianzus (330–390), a great orator of the Greek Church whom even Jerome enjoyed listening to. While he didn't necessarily confirm the authenticity of this verse, he did mention the flawed grammar that results if it is removed. Referring to John, he writes:

> . . . (he has not been consistent) in the way he has happened upon his terms; for after using Three in the masculine gender he adds three words which are neuter, contrary to the definitions and laws which you and your grammarians have laid down. For what is the difference between putting a masculine Three first, and then adding One and One and One in the neuter, or after a masculine One and One and One to use the Three not in the masculine but in the neuter, which you yourselves disclaim in the case of deity.[24]

If we may submit, there is no adequate rebuttal that the prosecution can bring here, and we are once again left with reasonable doubt. In fact, and in stark contrast, it's extremely significant that some of the leading critical scholars, such as Metzger, Vincent, Alford, Vine, Wuest, Bruce, and Plummer, never mention this problem when dealing with this passage. We are left wondering why. There is a common expression that every good litigator knows: "Don't ask a question unless you know the answer." Perhaps that is why these scholars remain silent.

The Defense's Closing Argument

Ladies and gentlemen of the jury, this controversy really boils down to one question: Why *is* there a controversy? This is the clearest statement of the Trinity in Scripture, so why challenge it in the first place? Dabney again speaks the blunt truth, that the Apostle John tells his readers

> the purpose of his writing was to warn them against seducers (ii. 26), whose heresy, long predicted, was now developed, and was characterized by a denial of the proper sonship (ii. 26) and incarnation (iv. 2) of Jesus Christ. Now we know that these heretics were Ebionites, and chiefly Cerinthians and Nicolaitanes. Irenseus, Epiphanius, and other fathers, tell us that they all vitiated the doctrine of the Trinity. . . . It can scarcely be doubted that these are the errors against which John is here fortifying the faith of his "children." . . . If we let the seventh verse stand, then the whole passage is framed, with apostolic wisdom, to exclude at once both

heresies [and] . . . declaring the unity of the Father, Word, and Spirit, and with the strictest accuracy.[25]

While the defenders of the Comma are the ones often accused of making this a "big deal," it is on the contrary the critic who has made it such and for no good reason. Incalculable time has been wasted on this question when there is absolutely no constructive reason to do so. If we may presume upon Shakespeare a moment, "The [critic] doth protest too much, methinks."[26] Is there some deeper reason for such loathing of these words? Is there an agenda?

"Why would God allow this text to be lost to antiquity?" the persecutor insists. "If He has supposedly providentially preserved the biblical text, why would He permit these words to be so ambiguous in the textual record?" If I may be so simple-minded and naïve for a moment, could it just *possibly* be to see if we will truly trust His providence—as puzzling as that might appear to our human thinking—instead of resorting to rationalism and sewing the seed of doubt in the sacred text to no good end? I submit that retaining 1 John 5:7 is perhaps the best example of accepting the "logic of faith." Critics rely on rationalism, while what we should be relying on is God's sovereign, providential preservation of His Word. (See the "The Contribution of Edward F. Hills" section of chapter 8 for more on the "logic of faith.")

The great theologian Francis Turretin pointedly wrote in the 17th-century that "some formerly called it into question, and heretics now do." Can we say the same today for those who attack this verse? Turretin adds, "To no purpose do the adversaries . . . endeavor to weaken confidence in this passage."[27] Indeed, there is no spiritual purpose for what the critics do here, and their actions certainly do not edify the Church.

Finally, it is noteworthy in the extreme that 1 John 5:7–8 stood unchallenged in the English Bible for a full 500 years. It was in the first English Bible by John Wycliffe in 1380, in Tyndale's New Testament of 1525, the Coverdale Bible of 1535, the Matthew's Bible of 1537, the Taverner Bible of 1539, the Great Bible of 1539, the Geneva New Testament of 1557, the Bishop's Bible of 1568, and the Authorized Version of 1611. These verses did not disappear from a standard English Bible until the English Revised Version of 1881 omitted it. This begs the question, Were the countless translators, theologians, and preachers who have accepted the Trinitarian statement in 1 John 5:7–8 of these English Bibles through the centuries really so ignorant and naïve? Or is it that today's critics are just so arrogant that they feel compelled to delete it?

No, we cannot prove beyond doubt that the Comma is authentic, but as noted at the beginning of this trial, we don't have to do that. It is the prosecutor, the textual critic, who has made this allegation, and the burden of proof has been upon him. We submit, therefore, that he has not met that burden and has, indeed, left a reasonable doubt.

The defense rests.

NOTES

[1] Jay M. Feinman, *Law 101: Everything You Need to Know About the American Legal System* (Oxford University Press, 2000), pp. 325–6.

[2] Robert L. Dabney, "The Doctrinal Various Readings of the New Testament Greek" in *Discussions: Evangelical and Theological*, Vol. 1 (Banner of Truth, 1891, reprint 1982), p. 377.

[3] James White, *The King James Only Controversy* (Bethany House), 62.

[4] An oddity here is that while Erasmus refused to include the Comma based solely on Latin authority, he did that very thing with the disputed words of Acts 9:5 ("it is hard for thee to kick against the pricks") and 6 ("And he trembling and astonished said, Lord, what wilt thou have me to do? And the Lord said unto him").

[5] *The Text of the New Testament* (Oxford, 1968), p 101.

[6] Henk J. de Jonge, *Erasmus and the Comma Johanneum* (an extract from *Ephemerides Theologicae Lovanienses*, 1980, t. 56, fasc. 4, pp. 381-389). This extract is posted on our website: www.thescripturealone.com. James White, 61, 85(n29). Erika Rummel, *Erasmus' Annotations on the New Testament* (University of Toronto, 1986), p. 133.

[7] *The Text of the New Testament*, 3rd Edition (Oxford, 1992), p. 291.

[8] Dabney, p. 377.

[9] O. T. Dobbin, *The Codex Montfortianus: A Collation of This Celebrated MS . . .* (London: Samuel Bagster, 1854).

[10] Roland Bainton, *Erasmus of Christendom* (New York: Charles Scribener's & Son, 1969), p. 137.

[11] *John Gill's Exposition of the Entire Bible*, electronic edition, 1 Jn.5:7.

[12] *The King James Version Defended* (Christian Research Press, 1956, 1984), p. 210. (Hills copiously documents these statements, but for space sake we have not included his notes.)

[13] Hills, pp. 210-11.

[14] This is actually John Reynolds, one of those who finished Henry's commentary (completed through Acts) upon his death in 1714.

[15] *Calvin's New Testament Commentaries, St. John, Part II*, p. 303

[16] *The Complete Works of John Wesley*, Vol. 6, p. 228

[17] Hills, pp. 212-13.

[18] Robert L. Dabney, *Discussions: Evangelical and Theological*, Vol. 1, pp. 375.

[19] Quoted on the rear jacket of Dabney's *Systematic Theology* (Banner of Truth Trust).

[20] *Albert Barnes' Notes on the Bible*, electronic edition, 1 Jn.5:7.

[21] Andrew Lincoln, *Word Biblical Commentary: Ephesians* (Word Publishing,

---

1990).

[22] E.g., Dabney (p. 378), Hills (p. 211–212), Henry, etc.

[23] Dabney, *Discussions*, 378.

[24] *Theological Orientations, Fifth Orientation: The Holy Sprit.*

[25] Dabney, *Discussions*, 379–80

[26] *Hamlet* (New Folger Library, 1992), Act 3, scene 2, line 254.

[27] Francis Turretin, *Institutes of Elenctic Theology* (P & R Publishing, 1997), Vol. 1, pp. 115, 268.

As the title set over the head of Christ crucified, was the same in Hebrew, Greek, and Latin, so are the Scriptures the same, whether in the original, or other language into which they are faithfully translated. Yet, as the waters are most pure, and sweet in the fountain, so are all writings, Divine and human, in their original tongues; it being impossible, but some either change, or defect, or redundancy will be found in the translation, either by default of the translator, or of the tongue, into which it is made.

Puritan John Robinson
The Works of John Robinson, Vol. 1, p. 47

52

Reader Questions

This final chapter compiles several articles from the monthly publication that were dedicated to questions from readers on various "tough texts" of Scripture. Such questions did not demand a full article to answer, so we simply devoted various issues of TOTT to such correspondence.

What does "Baptized for the Dead" Mean?

Question: What is the "baptism for the dead" referred to in 1 Corinthians 15:29? I know that Mormons teach that baptism is a saving ordinance; because many have died before baptism, those now living must be baptized for them if they are going to be saved. *I know this is wrong.* Please expound on this passage. I have read the context and cannot see where/how it fits. (CW)

Answer: Here is probably the most controversial verse in the entire Bible: **Else what shall they do which are baptized for the dead, if the dead rise not at all? why are they then baptized for the dead?** It has bothered many a Bible reader. There have actually been upwards of 200 explanations of its meaning, many heretical, but others legitimate possibilities. Here are just a few.

As you pointed out, it simply *cannot* refer to "proxy baptism." Paul would have immediately condemned such a practice. If baptism cannot save a *living* person, it certainly cannot save a *dead* one. Long before Joseph Smith came up with this idea, it was adopted by ancient Gnostic apostates such as Marcion, and it is just as apostate today as it was then.

There is also evidence of such vicarious "baptism" among ancient pagans. Because of the presence of so much error in the Corinthian church, some of which came from pagans, some interpreters think that it's possible that some in that church had adopted this error, since Paul uses the term **they**, not "we."

One of the plausible interpretations is that the term "the dead" refers to the Lord Jesus in His death, the plural being used for the singular, meaning "the dead one."

Another is that the word "baptized" simply refers to the idea of washing, cleansing, purifying (Matt. 8:4; Heb. 9:10), and so pictures the dead being carefully washed and purified when buried, with the hope of the resurrection, and, as it were, preparatory of that.

Because one of the meanings of the Greek word behind **for** (*huper*) is "because of," others think Paul is simply saying that people were being saved (baptism being the sign) because of the exemplary lives and witness of faithful believers who had died.

Still another view is that this might mean that a Christian friend was baptized for symbolic effect on behalf of a new convert who had died before being able to be baptized (perhaps by martyrdom or perhaps on his or her deathbed).

One other view says that this phrase means "baptized to take the place of those who have died." In other words, if there is no resurrection, why bother to witness and win others to Christ? Why reach sinners who are then baptized and take the place of those who have died? If the Christian life is only a "dead-end street," get off it.

Well, we could go on, but the view that I lean toward (which is similar to the one immediately above) is well stated by William MacDonald in his wonderful single-volume, *The Believer's Bible Commentary*, and held by others:

> The interpretation which seems to suit the context best is this: At the time Paul wrote, there was fierce persecution against those who took a public stand for Christ. This persecution was especially vicious at the time of their baptism. It often happened that those who publicly proclaimed their faith in Christ in the waters of baptism were martyred shortly thereafter. But did this stop others from being saved and from taking their place in baptism? Not at all. It seemed as though there were always new replacements coming along to fill up the ranks of those who had been martyred. As they stepped into the waters of baptism, in a very real sense **they** were being **baptized for**, or *in the place of* (Greek *huper*) the dead. Hence **the dead** here refers to those who died as a result of their bold witness for Christ. Now the apostle's argument here is that it would be foolish to be thus baptized to fill up the ranks of those who had died if there is no such thing as resurrection from the dead. It would be like sending replacement troops to fill up the ranks of an army that is fighting a lost cause. It would be like fighting on in a hopeless situation. **If the dead do not rise at all, why then are they baptized for the dead?**[1]

What does "Born of Water and of the Spirit" Mean?

Question: What does being born of the *water* and the Spirit mean in John 3:3–6? (BH)

Answer: Several "interpretations" have been offered: (1) it refers to baptism as a requirement for salvation. This, however, would contradict many other New Testament passages that speak of grace alone (e.g., Eph. 2:8–9); (2) it stands for the act of repentance that John the Baptist's baptism signified; (3) it refers to natural birth (specifically, the fluid released when the amniotic sac breaks prior to labor); thus it means "unless one is born the first time by water and the second time by the Spirit"; (4) it means the Word of God, as in John 15:3; (5) it is a synonym for the Holy Spirit and may be translated, "by water, even the Spirit."

I tend toward the simplicity of #3 simply because the context, verse 4, *specifically* refers to physical birth. Further, it cannot possibly refer to baptism because not only is baptism not required for salvation, but also because baptism had not yet been given or commanded when Jesus spoke these words. In short, I believe our Lord is simply saying, "Physical birth is not enough; one must be born again spiritually to enter the kingdom of heaven." In fact, that very contrast between "flesh" and "spirit" is then made in verse 6! In my view, any other interpretation violates the context and is looking for some deeper meaning that simply is not in the text.

On Which Day of the Week Did Jesus Die?

Question: Based on Matthew 12:40, where Jesus says He would be **three days and three nights in the heart of the earth**, on what day of the week did He die? I have been reading some who object to the idea of a Friday crucifixion. (DP)

Answer: This verse has caused many over the years to wonder. Some teachers, in fact, make a *huge* issue of it, going so far as to make it alone pivotal concerning the day of Jesus' death. Actually, the issue is not at all serious because of Jewish history and time rendering. To get the whole picture, we will note two things.

First, the Old Testament contains two kinds of prophecy regarding Christ. One is the "verbally predictive," in which specific and sometimes detailed predictions are given. Such prophecies include those that the Christ would be born of a virgin (Isa. 7:14), that He would be a descendant of David who would rule the entire earth with justice and righteousness (Jer. 23:5), and that He would be born in Bethlehem (Mic. 5:2).

The second type of messianic prophecy is "typical," in which an Old Testament person or event foreshadowed the person or work of Christ. We can be certain of typical predictions only if they are specifically identified as such in the New Testament. Here Jesus Himself tells us that Jonah's spending **three days and three nights in the whale's belly**; before he was vomited up on the shore typified the burial of **the Son of Man**, for **three days and three nights in the heart of the earth** before His resurrection. It was a predictive prophecy in picture rather than in specific word. Just as Jonah was buried in the depths of the sea, Jesus was buried in the depths of the earth; and just as Jonah came out of the great fish after three days, Jesus came out of the grave after three days.

Jesus obviously believed in the full literalness of the biblical account of Jonah. If Jonah had not been literally swallowed and miraculously protected while submerged for **three days and three nights in the whale's belly**, that event could not have typified Jesus' literal burial and resurrection. In light of Jonah's hardhearted stubbornness, it is not difficult to believe that he would lie about his experience; but it is difficult indeed to believe that Jesus would join Jonah in such duplicity or be mistaken about the historicity of the story. In declaring Jonah's experience to be a type of His own burial and resurrection, Jesus also verified the authenticity of Jonah's account of himself.

Second, the matter of **three days and three nights** is often used either to prove Jesus was mistaken about the time He would actually spend in the tomb or that He could not have been crucified on Friday afternoon and raised early on Sunday, the first day of the week. But such elaborate schemes are silly and pointless. Just as in modern usage, the phrase "day and night" can mean not only a full 24-hour day but also any representative part of a day. For example, let us say that my family and I went to a neighboring town on Monday. We went in the morning and came home after dark, *but this was not a 24-hour period*. In the same way, Jesus' use of **three days and three nights** does not have to be interpreted as 72 hours, three full 24-hour days; in fact, *it should not be interpreted that way*. Why? Because *it is an absolute fact* that the Jewish Talmud (commentaries on the Law) held that "any part of a day is as the whole." *Jesus was simply using a common, well-understood generalization.*

A similar expression in Luke 13:32–33 is another example, in fact. As Jesus weeps over Jerusalem, we read, "The same day there came certain of the Pharisees, saying unto him, Get thee out, and depart hence: for Herod will kill thee. And he said unto them, Go ye, and tell that fox, Behold, I cast out devils, and I do cures **to day and to morrow, and the third day** I shall be perfected. Nevertheless I must walk to day, and to morrow, and the day following: for it cannot be that a prophet perish out of Jerusalem." This expression signified only that Christ was on His own divine timetable; it was not meant to lay out a literal three-day schedule. Again, *expressions like this were common in Semitic usage*, and were rarely employed in a literal sense to specify precise intervals of time.

At any rate, I hope that clears up the matter for you. I mean no offence, but some Bible teachers make mountains out of molehills. There are issues that are *far more* crucial in our day than one such as this that is so simply answered by understanding biblical history. In fact, *much* false interpretation in our day comes from such ignorance. History is one of the most important principles of biblical interpretation.

Are There "Guardian Angels"?

Question: I ran across a verse in the Bible during a group Bible study; I should have written it down, but didn't. It talked about angels watching over us. I asked if all people are protected by the angels or just the elect. No one knew the answer to this question. One person suggested everyone but then they said "everyone who is saved has stories from early-on knowing of God" but she wasn't sure that question could be answered. (JP)

Answer: [2] The term angel is obviously a transliteration of the Greek *angelos*. As far back as Homer, it simply refers to "a messenger," but the role of such a messenger was sacred, and he was supposedly under the special protection of the gods.[3]

While such pagan concepts have no basis in Scripture, neither do some of the misconceptions that arose in Judaism. Many Jews, for example, believed that angels form a council that God consults before doing anything. Many also believed that various angels control the stars, seas, rain, snow, and other such things. Still others believed that "recording angels" write down everything people say and that every nation and child has a "guardian angel."

The latter idea is still popular in our day, no doubt as a result not only of Jewish tradition, but also from the writings of Thomas Aquinas, who was notorious for mixing human philosophy (especially Aristotle) with Christian thought. In his view, before birth each person is protected by the mother's guardian angel and then has his or her own assigned at birth.[4]

Scripture, however, nowhere says such things. What it *does* say, we find in Hebrews 1:14, for example: "Are they not all ministering spirits, sent forth to minister for them who shall be heirs of salvation?" We also read in Matthew 18:10: "Take heed that ye despise not one of these little ones; for I say unto you, That in heaven their angels do always behold the face of my Father which is in heaven." What we see here is that angels serve believers collectively (as the pronoun "their" is collective). The picture is that they are always looking at the face of God so as to hear His command to help believers.

Henry Morris well sums up: "They accomplish their ministry on behalf of the heirs of salvation in various ways, including: instruction (Acts 10:3–6), deliverance (Psalm 34:7; 91:11), comfort (Matthew 1:20; Luke 22:43) and, finally, reception at death (Luke 16:22). They were created to be ministering spirits, continually sent forth to minister (that is, serve) those who shall be heirs of salvation."[5]

What is the Meaning Of Mathew 7:6?

Question: I thank you greatly for your response to my last question on three days and three nights [see "On Which Day of the Week Did Jesus Die?" above]. My question this time is on Matthew 7:6. I have read this verse many times and am in question about it. I know this is a book written with Jewish readers in mind, but I am confused as to what they would have understood. It almost seems to me to be out of place. (DP)

Answer: I am very thankful for this question. It addresses a verse that is much needed in our day: **Give not that which is holy unto the dogs, neither cast ye your pearls before swine, lest they trample them under their feet, and turn again and rend you.**

This verse is not at all "out of place." On the contrary, it comes on the heels of a crucial passage on "judgment" and "discernment." As mentioned back in chapter 6 ("Where Has Our Discernment Gone?"), many today read verse 1—"Judge not, that ye be not judged"—and then immediately cry, "See there, Jesus says we are not supposed to be critical of anyone; we should not criticize what they believe or say." That, of course, is always the cry of tolerance: "Just leave me alone; don't judge what I say; don't ask any questions; just let things be."

But that is clearly not what Jesus is saying when you take the time to read the context, verses 2–5. He says, in effect, we are not to judge and discern *hypocritically* or judge someone's *motives and attitudes*, which have nothing to do with what someone *teaches*. They might have the purest motive and sweetest attitude, but that is never the issue; *the issue is what they teach*. Each of us is tempted to hold others to a higher standard than we hold ourselves, which is hypocrisy, so we must first make sure of our own life, make sure our standard is consistent, and *then* discern actions. In fact, that is exactly what Jesus says: "First, get the *log* out of your own eye and *then* you can remove the *splinter* that's in your brother's eye." Our Lord did not say, "Leave the splinter where it is." He said, "Deal with the error in your life first and then address the error in your brother."

Now we come to verse 6, which clearly shows once again that Jesus did not forbid every kind of judgment (or discernment). He instructs His disciples here that when they discern certain people to be either **dogs** or **swine**, they should not cast before them things that are holy (**pearls**). In that day, dogs were not the sweet, lovable pets we have in our homes today, rather most of them were wild, savage scavengers. Pigs also were wild, vicious scavengers and were the quintessential picture of filth and uncleanness. Jesus' Jewish listeners (and readers), then, would have immediately understood His meaning. As unthinkable as it would be to cast anything of value to such animals—for they would just **trample** them into the filth—it is equally unimaginable that we would continue to share the

Gospel or other holy truths with people who do nothing but mock, malign, and molest such spiritual riches. People do enough of this without our giving them more opportunity and even an open forum.

This was, in fact, precisely the reason our Lord began to speak in parables. Read Matthew 13:10–15, 34, noting that Jesus deliberately chose to hide certain truths from unbelievers, thus fulfilling the prophecy of Isaiah 6:9–10.

There will, therefore, be times when you will witness to someone who reacts with abject scorn, from whom we should turn away and "shake off the dust of [our] feet" (Matt. 10:5–15). In his wonderful single-volume commentary, *The Believer's Bible Commentary*, William MacDonald writes:

> When we meet vicious people who treat divine truths with utter contempt and respond to our preaching of the claims of Christ with abuse and violence, we are not obligated to continue to share the gospel with them. To press the matter only brings increased condemnation to the offenders. Needless to say, it requires spiritual perception to discern these people. Perhaps that is why the next verses take up the subject of prayer, by which we can ask for wisdom.[6]

If I may, I would dare apply this principle to an increasingly common practice today that is really quite appalling. More and more we see evangelicals (some calling themselves "Christian Apologists") holding discussions and debates with atheists, evolutionists, Muslims, and every other apostate and enemy of Christ under the sun. While we most certainly do *not* doubt the pure motives and evangelistic zeal of such "apologists," what else can we call this except "casting pearls before swine"? While Paul could have stood toe-to-toe with the Greek philosophers in Corinth and debated them right out of the forum, that is *not* what he did; rather he simply preached the Gospel (1 Cor. 2:1–5). It is not our well-argued points or our refutation of the other person's position that wins anyone to Christ, rather God's power that does the work. It is "the gospel of Christ" *itself* that is "the power of God unto salvation" (Rom. 1:16).

What does Proverbs 8:22–31 Mean?

Question: Proverbs 8:22–31 has frustrated me so much, and no one has been able to give me a direct answer. What does this mean? Is this talking about Christ, and if so, does this means He was a created being? I believe in the always existent Triune Godhead. (WL)

Answer: Well, I will certainly try to give you a "direct answer," and I do pray it will help alleviate your frustration.

While this passage has been interpreted as representing a picture of Christ, there is really no justification for doing so. The context is about the eternal character of *wisdom*, and there is no merit to the idea that it is Messianic. Yes, Christ is the Word (Jn. 1:1, 14), He is the revelation of God's wisdom (1 Cor. 1:24), and He possesses all wisdom and knowledge (Col. 2:3), but this passage is not prophetic.

One glaring reason that it is not a reference to Christ is that we are forced to conclude that He was **brought forth**, that is, created. Such an idea, of course is apostasy, for He "was in the beginning with God. All things were made by him; and without him was not any thing made that was made. In him was life; and the life was the light of men" (Jn. 1:2–4). Another reason is if Christ is "wisdom" here, to be consistent every other reference to wisdom in Proverbs would also have to refer to Him, an odd idea to say the least.

The view that this is a reference to Christ is actually not at all new. The Targum—oral Aramaic paraphrases (not translations) of the Old Testament made from the 2nd-century to about the 7th-century AD—makes this wisdom a living entity by translating the passage: "God created me in the beginning of his creatures." As Commentator Adam Clarke observes, "This is as absurd and heretical as some modern glosses on the same passage." This is also how the Septuagint—the Greek translation of the Old Testament—handles the passage, which is what Arius—a 4th Century parish priest in Alexandria—used to teach his apostate doctrine that Jesus was not coequal with God but was a created being. Arianism has been taught in numerous forms ever since, one of the most recent variations being the 2003 book, *The Da Vinci Code* by Dan Brown.

What we see here, then, is wisdom as a personification of God's own attribute of wisdom. "The passage shows," writes Charles Ryrie, "that wisdom is older than creation and is fundamental to it (v. 23), that it assisted in creation as a master workman (v. 30), and that it rejoiced in creation (vv. 30–31)."[7] This leads to a related question.

What Does Colossians 1:15 Mean?

Question: I need some clarification on Colossians 1:15. What does it mean in this context to be the firstborn of all creation? (WL)

Answer: At first glance, this verse is, indeed, troublesome: **[Christ] is the image of the invisible God, the firstborn of every creature**. Is this saying that Christ was a created being? If so, then God also gave Christ the power of creation, as verse 16 goes on to say: "by him were all things created." Such an idea, of course, is fraught with problems. This would also mean that verses that ascribe worship to Christ (Jn. 13:13; Heb. 1:6; 1 Cor.

1:2; etc.) are false and teach an apostate idea, for only God can receive worship (Matt. 4:10; etc.), not something that God created.

So what about that word **firstborn**? This word is used in three distinct ways in Scripture. In the *literal* sense, it speaks of physical birth, as when Mary "brought forth her firstborn son" (Lk. 2:7). In the *figurative* sense, it is used to refer to a distinctive place that something has, as when God called Israel His "son, even my firstborn" (Ex. 4:22). Finally, it is also used to denote *superior or supremacy*, as when God said He would make David His "firstborn, higher than the kings of the earth" (Ps. 89:27).

It is, therefore, in that last sense that Paul asserts that Christ, as the eternal Son, holds the position of supremacy in relation to all creation. He was *before* all things (v. 17), He *created* all things (v. 16), and He *sustains* all things (v. 17).

Should We Pray to Jesus?

Question: How would you respond (or *would* you respond) to those who address prayers to Jesus instead of God the Father when praying aloud? (BM)

Answer: In case other readers need clarification, the biblical method for prayer is: pray *to* the Father *through* the Son *in* the power of the Holy Spirit.

First, Scripture is clear that we are to pray *to* the Father; He is the *Object*. This is the guideline in "The Model Prayer" (Matt. 6:9–13). After saying, "After this manner [or, "in this way"] therefore pray ye," the first principle Jesus states is: "Father, which art in heaven. Hallowed be Thy name." This is foundational.

Second, Jesus then is the *Mediator*. We could not pray in the way we do if it were not for Him. It is by His merits and through His work that we can even approach the Father. John 14:13 declares: "And whatever ye shall ask in my Name, that will I do, that the Father may be glorified in the Son." We read again in 16:23–24: "Verily, verily, I say unto you, Whatsoever ye shall ask the Father in my name, he will give it you. Hitherto have ye asked nothing in my name: ask, and ye shall receive, that your joy may be full."

The Beloved J. Vernon McGee insightfully observes, "Someone may ask whether we can't pray to Jesus. I think you can if you wish to, but why do you rob yourself of an intercessor? Jesus is up there at God's right hand for you, praying for you. That is the reason that we should pray to the Father in the name of Jesus.[8]

Third, The Holy Spirit then is the *Interpreter*. Romans 8:26–27 explains: "Likewise the Spirit also helpeth our infirmities: for we know not what we should pray for as we ought: but the Spirit itself maketh intercession for us with groanings which cannot be uttered [or, "dismayed sighs that cannot be expressed in words"]. And he that searcheth the hearts knoweth what is the mind of the Spirit, because he maketh intercession for the saints according to the will of God." It is the Holy Spirit who gives us the power to pray. He takes our prayers to the Father; He interprets them because we do not know all there is to know about prayer. How could we possibly approach God without the Holy Spirit to interpret?

If we may add briefly, Paul writes elsewhere, "Praying always with all prayer and supplication in the Spirit" (Eph. 6:18). Without question, praying "in the Spirit" is the master key to an effective prayer life. It means we are yielded to the Spirit's wishes, not our own (cf. 1 Jn. 5:14). As R. C. Sproul writes, we are to pray "not in a perfunctory manner, not by reciting our favorite syllable or empty repetitions, but praying from the depths of our souls. To pray in concert with the Holy Spirit means that the communication is earnest in its origin and its passion."[9]

Now, with all that in mind, it is always awkward (and can be offensive) to "criticize" how someone prays, even when we are trying to help. Prayer is a *very* personal activity, so telling someone they're "doing it wrong" can make for hard feelings to say the least. I certainly would not mention it right after someone prays or anytime soon thereafter. One way to approach it would be to do so indirectly during a discussion of Scripture. For example, you could bring up the subject of prayer, talk about its wonderful privileges and blessings, and then at some point insert the correct model without even mentioning what you heard the person say. Another approach would be to give, or at least recommend, a good book on prayer that deals with this subject.

What are the Origins of "Pope"?

Question: What are the origins and meaning of "Pope." (BM)

Answer: The word "pope" itself is from the Latin *pāpa*, which in-turn is from the Greek *pappas*, "father." It refers, of course, to the leader of the Roman Catholic "church." While the Pope is referred to as "Holy Father," the Lord Jesus expressly forbade His disciples from calling any man "father" in the spiritual sense: "Call no man your father upon the earth: for one is your Father, which is in heaven" (Matt. 23:9).

The entire shaky foundation for this title is based upon only two texts of Scripture, according the *Catholic Encyclopedia*. The first is Matthew 16:16–19. For 1500 years Rome has taught, "Here then Christ teaches plainly that in the future the Church will be the society of those who acknowledge Him, and that this Church will be built on Peter." It goes on to say, "The word for Peter and for rock in the original Aramaic is one and the same; this renders it evident that the various attempts to explain the term 'rock' as having reference not to Peter himself but to something else are misinterpretations." [10]

This teaching, however, is not faithful to the Greek text. The words behind "Peter" and "rock" in the Greek are most certainly *not* the same. In Classical Greek, *petra* ("rock") refers to a large rock, such as a boulder, cliff, bedrock, or even a mountain chain. It (with *petros*, "Peter," a smaller stone that a man can throw) is, of course, where we get English words such as *petrify* (turning organic matter into rock) and *petroleum* (oil that comes from the earth or even from rock, as in the case of oil shale). It also carries the figurative meaning, as Homer used it in his *Odyssey*, of firmness and immovability of character. Aeschylus and Euripides also used it to denote hardheartedness.

Using a play on words, then, our Lord is plainly saying that He will build His church, *not* on Peter (*Petros*, a throwable stone), as Catholicism teaches, but on Himself, who is the large rock, the bedrock, the foundation stone, the "cornerstone," (Eph. 2:20; 1 Pet. 2:4–8; cf. 1 Cor. 3:11). Jesus then adds that it is because of that foundation that nothing will ever "prevail against" (*katischuō*, "overcome, overpower, vanquish") *His* church, not "Peter's church."

The other text on which the "Papacy" (the name for the Pope's office) is built is John 21:15–17, and this teaching is even more absurd than that on the Matthew passage. It insists that the Greek *poimainō*, "feed" in verse 16, which also means "rule," fulfills the promise Jesus made to Peter in the Matthew passage. Such a conclusion is transparent conjecture, concocted to prop up a feeble theory. There is not a single word in this passage that states, or even implies, Peter's supremacy, rather that he, like all other pastors, will teach and lead God's people (cf. Acts. 20:28; Eph. 4:11–12; etc.).

As mentioned earlier, Rome's teaching has existed for 1500 years. So what about before that time? A fact Rome tries to downplay is that the Papacy did not even exist until 590, when Gregory I (590–604) was the first bishop to be appointed "supreme bishop." In order then to defend the idea of "apostolic succession"—the tracing of the Papacy back to Peter—Rome went back through history picking certain bishops and dubbing them as links in the chain back to the supposed "first pope." That list, which has been revised several times and is currently at 63 bishops,[11] is questionable at best. A quick glance at the first ten, for example, confirms that very little is known about them, and several of those that follow are not even clearly defined figures of history.

To say, therefore, that the Roman Catholic papacy can be traced back through history to Peter is one of the most patently ridiculous, blatantly dishonest, and appallingly unscholarly statements to be made in the history of the world. Does that surprise us? Not in the least. Roman Catholicism is the most evil perversion of Christianity Satan could devise. It is pagan, wicked, and deceptive. It is a works-oriented system that perverts the work of Christ in many blasphemous ways (the Papacy being one) and was the reason the Protestant Reformation was necessary. How sad it is that many "evangelicals" today are trying to undo it.[12]

Do Matthew 5:32 and 19:9 Refer to the Betrothal Period?

Question: "In Matthew 5:32 and 19:9, what does the 'exception clause' refer to? Is this sort of like our engagement period?" (FG)

Answer: When I first received this question, I thought, "Oh, boy! If I answer this one, I'll sure put my head in the noose." This is one of those truly volatile texts that get some folks really upset. So, I will try to answer this question only to the extent of the question. I know some will disagree, but we can agree to disagree agreeably.

What the reader refers to is the *Betrothal Period View* of divorce, which maintains that a man could divorce his "wife" only if he found that she had committed sexual sin during the engagement period, not after the actual marriage. While this view has been around a long time, I am convinced that it is simply grammatically and historically unprovable at best and indefensible at worst for at least three reasons.

First, the Greek for "fornication" in Matthew 5:32 and 19:9 is *porneia.* In later Rabbinical language, which carried over into the New Testament, it came to be used for *any* sexual relations outside of marriage, including: premarital sex, extramarital sex, homosexuality, lesbianism, sodomy, pedophilia, incest, and bestiality. As Greek authorities agree, it simply cannot be narrowed to indicate *premarital* relations exclusively in *any* context. One says, for example, "In both [Mat. 5:32 and 19:9] *porneia* refers to extra-marital intercourse on the part of the wife, which in practice is adultery."[13] Native Greek scholar Spiros Zodhiates concurs: "Noun from *porneuō,* to commit fornication or any sexual sin. Fornication, lewdness, or any sexual sin. . . . Any sexual sin; coupled with *moicheía,* adultery (Mk. 7:21). . . . Specifically of adultery (Matt. 5:32; 19:9); of incest (1 Cor. 5:1)."[14]

Second, the *Talmud* (the ancient Rabbinical commentaries on the Law) without a shadow of a doubt, speaks of divorce *both* after *engagement* and after *marriage.* A reading of *The Tractate Gittin* 18a and 18b,[15] as well as other parts of *Gittin*[16]—which is concerned largely with questions of legal procedure and terminology—erases any ambiguity. It simply does not allow a case to be made historically for the exception being only during betrothal. This leads to one other point.

Third, there seems no doubt whatsoever that our Lord and the Pharisees were discussing marriage (Matt. 5:32, 19:9), *not* betrothal. In fact, the passages they were discussing were Deuteronomy 24 and Genesis 2, which *clearly* refer to people who are married, *not* betrothed. The text simply does not limit it as the Betrothal View insists. This view is simply not historical.

For the sake of the diversity that exists on the other issues concerning divorce, we will not go any further. My concern here is that whatever one's view(s) concerning divorce are, the so-called Betrothal View simply cannot be defended. It is a noble, well-meaning position, but it does not (and cannot) hold up in the end (IMHO). If I may be so bold, I have yet to read a defense of this view that can cite a respectable number of exegetes and other scholars that hold it simply because the grammar and history do not support it. While a little direct (which is his style), I think Jay Adams puts it well:

> The engagement theory has no support in the Scriptures and, indeed, the usage of the entire Bible annihilates it. The popularity of teachers who may espouse the theory is no basis for its acceptance.[17]

What Does "Private Interpretation" Mean?

Question: "Second Peter 1:20 says that 'no prophecy of the scripture is of any private interpretation.' What does 'private interpretation' mean? Don't Roman Catholics teach that this means that the laity cannot interpret Scripture?" (NT)

Answer: You are correct. Both the Council of Trent (Session IV; April 8, 1546) and Vatican I (Session III; April 24, 1870) stated that the interpretation of Scripture contrary to the Church or the unanimous agreement of the Fathers was explicitly forbidden. Trent, for example, stated that no person "shall dare to interpret the said Sacred Scripture contrary to that sense which is held by holy mother Church, whose duty it is to judge regarding the true sense and interpretation of holy Scriptures."

So what does this term mean? It's actually not hard in light of the language and context. "Private" is *idios*, which means "pertaining to oneself or one's own." It appears 114 times in such verses as John 10:3 ("own"), 1 Corinthians 3:8, and 1 Peter 3:1.

Likewise, how many people there are today who sit in private and alter God's Word to suit *their own* purposes! How many there are who sit in private and twist the Word of God to fit their lifestyle and justify their actions and attitudes!

"Interpretation," then, is *epilusis* (found only here in the New Testament). One Greek authority is weak here: "'A loosening, unloosing', *metaphorically* 'interpretation.'" Much stronger is Spiros Zodhiates: "*Epilusis*; genitive *epiluseos*, feminine noun from *epiluō*, to solve. Exposition, interpretation. In 2 Pet. 1:20, 21, it indicates that no prophecy comes from any private source, referring to the exposition of the will and purposes of God by the prophets themselves."[18] Another adds, "*Epiluō, epilusis*. Literally meaning 'to release,' *epiluō* means 'to resolve' (an issue) in Acts 19:39 and 'to explain' in Mk. 4:34. *Epilusis* means 'exposition' or 'interpretation' in 2 Pet. 1:20."[19]

So, "interpretation" is not a *metaphorical* meaning, but rather, it is *the* meaning. The emphasis here is that the prophets themselves did not *originate* ("unloose") the Scriptures or even *interpret* the words God gave them to write. In other words, the central point is not *interpretation*, but rather *origination*.

This point is vitally important in light of a common expression we often hear when it comes to the Bible. We've all heard people say after we quote the Bible, "Well, that's just your interpretation of the Bible; everybody has their own interpretation." It also applies to Roman Catholicism, which has become its own exclusive "private interpreter."

If we may add, an essential principle of biblical interpretation is *allowing Scripture to interpret itself.* This principle is called *analogia scripturae*, "the analogy of Scripture," that is, comparing Scripture with Scripture. The way to "interpret" the Bible is to take it as it reads. What matters is not how men *interpret* God's words, but what God's words plainly *say*.

What is "Effectual, Fervent" Prayer?

Question: "I've heard some preachers say that if we just pray fervently enough for something, we'll get it. They use James 5:16 as proof. Do you have any comment on this? Thanks." (BT)

Answer: This verse has, indeed, caused some questions among Christians. It declares, "The effectual fervent prayer of a righteous man availeth much." This has been variously translated as: "Very strong is a working supplication of a righteous man" (Young's Literal); "The prayer of a righteous man is powerful and effective" (NIV); and, "The effective prayer of a righteous man can accomplish much" (NASB).

None of those, however, adequately reflects the central truth. Many people take this verse to mean, "If I pray fervently and intensely, if I just pray hard enough, long enough, and often enough for a particular thing, it will happen." I do not wish to offend, but such an idea flies in the face of the principle that prayer involves conforming our will to God's will (1 Jn. 5:14).

The expression "effectual fervent" is actually only one word in the Greek, *energeō*, from which is derived English words such as *energy* and *energize*, and means "to be at work, to effect something." It is extremely significant, as one Greek authority tells us, that the noun *energeia*, "energy, active power, operation" in the [Septuagint] (as in the NT) is used almost exclusively for the work of divine or demonic powers."[20] In Ephesians 1:19, for example, it is God's power that is "working" (*energeia*) in us, while in 2:2, Satan is said to be working (*energeō*).

Another authority agrees, adding that this usage is predominant in the *entire word group*: "Only in Philippians 2:13 does the active *energein* [present active participle of *energeō*] refer to human activity,"[21] but notice that even then it is *still God* Who is working "in you both to will and to do of his good pleasure."

You might also want to read the following verses, noting in each that *energeō* refers to God's energy: 1 Corinthians 12:6, 11 ("worketh"); Galatians 2:8 ("effectually"); 3:5 ("worketh"); Ephesians 1:11, 20 ("wrought"); 3:20; Colossians 1:29; 1 Thessalonians 2:13 ("effectually").

When we also note that the word *availeth* is *ischuō*, "strength and ability," it's then easy to see exactly what James is saying. He's not telling us that we accomplish much by our own energy in prayer, but rather that *our prayers are strong because they are energized by God*. We could translate this verse, "The God-energized prayer of a righteous man is strong."

That is a wonderful encouragement for us to pray in the energy of God and with a view to accomplishing His will.

What Does "Image and Likeness" of God Mean?

Question: "Genesis 1:26 says, 'God said, Let us make man in our image, after our likeness.' What does that mean? What is the difference between *image* and *likeness*? (WD)

Answer: That's a good question, indeed. We'll get to the difference in a moment. First, we need to examine the words. "Image" is the Hebrew *ṣelem*. It refers essentially to a representation of something. Most of its eighteen appearances refer to a literal statue that represents a god—that is, an idol (Exod. 20:4; 2 Kings 11:18). But it's also used in the more metaphorical sense of something having the essential nature of what it represents, as when Adam "begat a son in his own likeness, after his image; and called his name Seth" (Gen. 5:3).

It is that latter sense that we find in the very first occurrence of *ṣelem* here in Gen. 1:26 (cf. 5:3). It is also here that *ṣelem* is coupled with our second word, "likeness," the Hebrew *demût*. Appearing about 25 times, this word refers to something being the same pattern, shape, or form of something else (e.g., 2 Kings 16:10, "fashion"; 2 Chron. 4:3, "similitude"; Ezek. 1:10).

Now, it has been debated whether these two words are synonymous or clearly distinct. Some early church fathers, for example, thought that while *image* pictured the physical aspect of likeness to God, *likeness* pictured the ethical.[22] It is generally accepted, however, that the words are synonymous, being used elsewhere interchangeably (*ṣelem* alone is used in Gen. 1:27, while *demût* is used alone in 5:1), and are therefore used together for the sake of emphasis.

So what does it mean that man is made in God's essential nature, pattern, and form? For one thing, it is certainly unique from the animals. In the face of the evolutionist, humanist, and other such ilk of pseudo-truth, Bible teacher and commentator John Phillips wonderfully writes, "God does not begin with man's body and relate man to the beasts. He begins with man's moral and spiritual nature, and relates man to God. Indeed, reference to the creation of man's body is relegated to a footnote at the end of the creation story (2:7)."[23]

We might also add that our being created in God's image is the reason why murder is such a heinous crime. Since we are made in His image, murdering an innocent person is an attack upon God. So terrible is this that God instituted capital punishment (Gen. 9:6; cf. Matt. 26:52; Rom. 13:4; Rev. 13:10).

So, think of it! Man was originally created in the moral and spiritual pattern of God. Man's entire personality—intellect, emotion, and will—was a reflection of the divine essence of the Creator. Yes, the entrance of sin seriously marred that image, but Jesus Christ restored it. No, we are not "gods" as some teach, but we are in *God's image*.

Soli Deo gloria!

Is the Sonship of Jesus Eternal?

Question: "I've heard a lot about whether Jesus was only considered the Son of God when He came to the earth and that He was not the Son before that. Any input you would offer would be appreciated." (TN)

Answer: This question always brings to mind Hebrews 1:3: "Who being the brightness of [the Father's] glory, and the express image of his person." We'll get to your question, but please bear with me for a moment.

"Brightness" is *apaugasma* (found only here in the NT), which comes from the verb *augazō* ("illuminate or shine"). We find *augazō*, for example, in 2 Corinthians 4:4: "In whom the god of this world hath blinded the minds of them which believe not, lest the light of the glorious gospel of Christ, who is the image of God, should shine [*augazō*] unto them."

With the addition of the prefix *apo*, "from," *apaugasma* therefore pictures radiant splendor emitted from a luminous body. Here is a wonderful allusion to nature. As John Gill comments: "The allusion is to the sun, and its beam or ray: so some render it 'the ray of his glory'; and may lead us to observe, that the Father and the Son are of the same nature, as the sun and its ray; and that the one is not before the other, and yet distinct from each other, and cannot be divided or separated one from another."[24]

Think of it! The Lord Jesus Christ is the very radiant splendor of God the Father's glory. While *personally distinct* from the Father, the Son is still *essentially one* with the Father, as our Lord Himself states in John 10:30 ("I and my Father are one"). What a paradox!

Now to your question. Since the Son is the radiant splendor of the Father, and since the light is eternal (John 1:1–4), we have a clear demonstration that the Son is also eternal. This forever discounts anyone who rejects the *deity* of Christ or doubts the *eternal Sonship* of Christ. While there has been debate on the latter among Bible teachers, we must insist that His Sonship is from all eternity (John 8:58; 17:5, 24; Col. 1:17; Rev. 22:13).

This is further underscored in our text by the word *being*. The Greek is *hōn*, which is the masculine present participle of *eimi*, "to be." "This means," as Greek authority Spiros Zodhiates tells us, "that there has never been a time when Jesus Christ has not been the [radiant splendor] of the Father," which not only includes eternity past, but also "even in His incarnation when He purged our sins."[25]

Oh, Dear Christian Friend, may you meditate today on God's radiance and set your mind on his glory!

What is the difference Between "Kingdom of Heaven" and "Kingdom of God"?

Question: "What is the difference between the Kingdom of Heaven and the Kingdom of God?" (MH)

Answer: Various Bible teachers have made a huge issue of this by insisting they are distinct. I am convinced, however, that there is no difference in these terms. Here's why.

During the Intertestament Period—the 400 years between the events of the Old Testament and the New—the Jewish people developed a superstitious fear of using God's name. Because they believed it was too holy, they didn't use the covenant name of God (Yahweh or Jehovah, indicated by the word LORD (note the small capital letters) in most English Bibles. As a result, they substituted other words for the name of God, and "heaven" became a common substitute. By New Testament times, in fact, that practice was so ingrained that the Jewish people instantly understood any reference to the kingdom of *heaven* as a reference to the kingdom of *God.*

Again, while some Bible teachers insist these two terms speak of two different things, they simply do not. Matthew is the *only* writer who uses Kingdom of Heaven" (32 times) because his audience was Jewish and would have been offended by the term *God.* While I do believe in certain distinctions in Scripture, I am convinced that this one has been needlessly manufactured. Scripture simply does not say they are different.

Parallel accounts in the other Gospels prove this beyond any doubt. Matthew 4:17, for example, recounts that Jesus preached, "Repent: for the kingdom of *heaven* [*ouranos*] is at hand," while Mark's account (1:15) of the same scene states that Jesus preached, "The kingdom of *God* [*theos*] is at hand: repent ye, and believe the gospel." If these terms refer to two totally different things, then the inescapable conclusion is that either Matthew or Mark misspoke. Likewise, in the Beatitudes, Matthew records Jesus saying: "Blessed are the poor in spirit: for theirs is the kingdom of *heaven* [*ouranos*]" (5:3), while Luke's account reads, "Blessed be ye poor: for yours is the kingdom of *God* [*theos*]" (6:20). If I may be so blunt, arguing over these terms is just silly and even counterproductive.

So, to what do these refer? Both refer to the sphere of God's dominion over His people. While presently that is God's rule over the hearts of believers (Luke 17:21), it will be fully realized in the literal, earthly millennial kingdom (Rev. 20:4–6).

Is it Important to Know the Moment of Salvation?

Question: "If a Christian doesn't remember the exact time in their life when they were saved, is that bad? Is that detrimental to their testimony? And if one does not remember, should they 'renew their vows'?" (AC)

Answer: That is a touchy question and one that many Christians have had. The camp of Christianity in which I grew up staunchly insists that a person must know the "precise moment in time when he or she asked Jesus into their heart." In over 38 years of ministry, however, I have met people who simply do not remember that "moment in time" but their lives are no less a clear testimony of the reality of Christ.

I think a fair illustration can be found in marriage. Is there an exact moment when a couple is "married"? Is it at the point in the ceremony when they exchange vows? Most of us would say, "Nope, not yet." Some argue, "It's when the pastor says, 'I now pronounce you husband and wife.'" Legally, however, that's not true either, since the marriage license hasn't been signed and witnessed. The true romantic says, "Ah, it's the kiss that seals the deal." Others view the wedding night consummation as the moment when they become "one flesh." But in the final analysis, none of that is the real issue because marriage is far more than just "a moment in time."

Similarly, the issue of salvation is infinitely more than just "a moment in time." Whether one remembers the microsecond when they received Christ is far less important than if their life now demonstrates that Christ *is* their Savior and Lord. Tragically, I have met many people who profess Christ and trace it back to the day they "walked the aisle" or "asked Jesus into their heart," but whose lives are little different now than before they supposedly "accepted Christ." That is why 1 John, James, and 2 Peter 1:3–10 are so critical. They methodically demonstrate the transformed behavior that exists in the true believer. To illustrate further, none of us remembers the moment of our physical birth, so how do we know that we are alive? Well, obviously because we demonstrate the evidences of life: walking, talking, breathing, and so forth. The same is true of spiritually life. We might not know that exact moment it began, but we sure give evidences of it now.

As for the idea of "renewing our vows," such a concept, along with others, such as "rededicating my life to Christ," are not biblical. Such ideas have no biblical precedent, rather were invented by well-meaning folks who simply misunderstand salvation and Christian living.

Part of this issue stems from one's assurance of salvation. This is why, in fact, God commands us to "examine [ourselves], whether [we] be in the faith" (2 Cor. 14:5) and to "give diligence to make [our] calling and election sure" (2 Pet. 1:10). Assurance of salvation is not a feeling; it's not because we did something. Rather, assurance of salvation comes by objective proof of living a Christ-like life. We know we are Christians not because we remember that "crisis moment," but because we have the objective proof of obedience to our Sovereign Lord. It's not the *moment* of salvation that is important, rather it's the *manifestation* of salvation that is crucial.

What is Authentic Christianity?

Question: I was speaking to someone recently who brought up the idea that there is *an authentic Christianity*. Can you tell me what you think it is? In other words, what do the people in authentic Christianity believe? Thanks. (JB)

Answer: I have yet to find a better summary of authentic Christianity than what we find in the the the five "solas" (Latin "alone") of the Reformation. Putting them together: "It is *Scripture* alone that declares that salvation comes by *grace* alone, through *faith* alone, in *Christ* alone, by which *God* alone is glorified."[26]

I believe that well summarizes True, biblical Christianity itself, and differentiates it from every other religion, cult, philosophy, or faith. We should note that it is also this that is (and has been) attacked more violently than any other faith in human history, for Truth is seldom embraced, and only then by the sovereign will of God.

What does "Spirits in Prison" and "Baptism" Mean in 1 Peter 3:19–22?

Question: What does 1 Peter 3:19–22 mean? I have read this several times and just don't understand it. (CH)

Answer: This is, indeed one of the most debated passages in Scripture. There are actually two "tough texts" in this passage.

First, there is the identity of **the spirits in prison** to whom Christ **went and preached.** The verb behind **preached** is *kērussō*, which referred to the imperial herald. In the ancient world, heralds would come to town as representatives of the rulers to make public announcements or precede generals and kings in the processions celebrating military triumphs, announcing victories won in battle.

To whom, however, did Christ make proclamation? That is the debate. Some believe Peter here referred to the descent of Christ's Spirit into *hades* between His death and resurrection to offer people who lived before the Flood a second chance for salvation. However, this interpretation is no less than heresy. After death there is eternal judgment, and there is no longer any hope of salvation.

Others also insist this passage refers to Christ's descent into *hades* after His crucifixion but only to proclaim His victory to the imprisoned fallen angels, but as John Gill says of this, it is "absurd, vain, and needless." This very popular notion is based upon the idea that these were the fallen angels of Genesis 6 who supposedly had sexual relations with women, which in-turn produced a race of giants. As we detailed in chapter

5, however, the fallen angel theory is based exclusively in pagan myth, not biblical precedent.

Both of those views are also bothersome, in fact, because they flirt with the teaching of Roman Catholicism on this passage. This is a text used to prop up the heresy of *limbus patrum*, that is, "limbo of fathers." As detailed in chapter 17, the literal idea of *limbus* is "fringe or border," and the basic idea in the word "limbo" is "a state or place of confinement." So the teaching in the term *limbus patrum*, which was chosen in the Middle Ages, refers to a place on the border of Hell that, as the *Catholic Encyclopedia* puts it, the place where "the just who had lived under the Old Dispensation, and who, either at death or after a course of purgatorial discipline, had attained the perfect holiness required for entrance into glory, were obliged to await the coming of the Incarnate Son of God and the full accomplishment of His visible earthly mission. Meanwhile they were 'in prison'" awaiting "the higher bliss to which they looked forward."[27] But Scripture simply nowhere teaches that Christ, after His resurrection and prior to His ascension, descended into hell. Such an idea is appalling. It continues to grieve me how often modern teachers and expositors allow themselves to be influenced by pagan ideas and Roman Catholic tradition.

Still others think the phrase **to the spirits** should be understood of Christ's going to preach, through His apostles, to the Gentiles, as in Ephesians 2:17. But one problem here is that living men are not called "spirits" in Scripture. Another is that it seems very odd that Peter, while speaking of the apostles, would then suddenly, as though forgetting himself, refer back to the time of Noah.

Therefore, in view of the context, this simply refers to the preincarnate Christ's preaching through Noah to those who, because they rejected that message, are now (in Peter's day) **spirits in prison**. John Gill again well puts it, "The plain and easy sense of the words is, that Christ, by his Spirit . . . went in the ministry of Noah, the preacher of righteousness, and preached both by words and deeds, by the personal ministry of Noah." Albert Barnes also well illustrates using the 17th-century minister of New Haven Colony, John Davenport. He writes: "Thus it would be proper to say that . . . Davenport came from England to preach to the dead men around us." That is, indeed, "the plain and easy sense of the words," not the fanciful ideas that seem popular to modern thought. Puritan Matthew Henry is equally good, emphasizing, in fact, the false teaching of Catholicism:

> **He went and preached**, by his Spirit striving with them, and inspiring and enabling Enoch and Noah to plead with them, and **preach righteousness to them**, as 2 Pet. 2:5. . . . The hearers . . . were dead and disembodied when the apostle speaks of them, therefore he properly calls them spirits now **in prison**; not that they

were *in prison when Christ preached to them,* as the vulgar Latin translation and the popish expositors pretend.

Some expositors object to such a view because they insist that if Peter meant to imply preaching the Gospel he would have used *euangelizō* (to announce good news, to evangelize). By using *kērussō*, they insist, Peter is saying that Christ was heralding something else. But such an idea is not quite accurate. Paul used *kērussō*, in fact, in 1 Corinthians 1:23 when he wrote, "We preach Christ crucified, unto the Jews a stumblingblock, and unto the Greeks foolishness" It's hard to fathom how one is not heralding the Gospel when he is preaching Christ crucified. *Kērussō* is also used to refer to preaching the word of faith (Rom. 10:8), preaching the resurrection (1 Cor. 15:12), and even preaching the Gospel (Gal. 2:2; Col. 1:23; 1 Thess. 2:9). Romans 10:14 is also significant: "How then shall they call on him in whom they have not believed? and how shall they believe in him of whom they have not heard? and how shall they hear without a preacher?" What exactly is the preacher heralding here if not the Gospel?

So, if we may say once more, "the plain and easy sense of the words" is best. This is consistently the view of older expositors, in contrast to modern opinion. Happily, some today do agree with this view, such as *The Bible Knowledge Commentary*: "The Spirit of Christ preached through Noah to the ungodly humans who, at the time of Peter's writing, were 'spirits in prison' awaiting final judgment." In fact, it goes on to add that this matches the theme of the letter:

> This interpretation seems to fit the general theme of this section (1 Peter 3:13–22)—keeping a good conscience in unjust persecution. Noah is presented as an example of one who committed himself to a course of action for the sake of a clear conscience before God, though it meant enduring harsh ridicule. Noah did not fear men but obeyed God and proclaimed His message.

Second, there is also debate over the idea that **baptism doth also now save us**. The setting is that Peter saw here an analogy not only of the proclamation of Truth, as we discussed earlier, but also the triumphant salvation provided through Christ. He, therefore, writes, **eight souls were saved by water**. The word **by** translates the Greek preposition *dia*, which in the present construction speaks of "intermediate agency," that is, it was by the intermediate working of the water in lifting up the ark that brought the eight survivors safely through the flood.

Now, the advocate of baptismal regeneration pounces here and says, "Aha! See there? It was water that saved them and it is water that saves us now, since Peter goes on to say, **The like figure whereunto even baptism doth also now save us**.

But hold on a minute. It is just such hasty "interpretation" that produces apostasy. If we may interject, in fact, baptismal regeneration was one of the earliest heresies to enter the church. Tertullian (c.160–c.220) was one of the earliest church fathers to teach it, and Roman Catholicism has always held it. Incredulously, even some *Protestant* churches teach this, which is especially contradictory because it is one of the doctrines they should be *protesting*! Zacchaeus (Luke 19:9), the thief on the cross (Luke 23:42–43), new believers at Pentecost (Acts 2:41), Paul (9:17–18), and Cornelius (10:47) were all declared saved *before* baptism. Salvation is by grace *alone*. Any other "gospel" is *not* the Gospel (Gal. 1:6–9).

The phrase **like figure**, therefore, is *antitupon*, from which is derived the theological term "antitype." Literally, *tupos*, "type," means "to strike with repeated strokes." From that came the idea of an image, impression, or mark created by such repeated strokes. Figuratively, then "a type is a model of some reality which was yet to appear, a prototype of that which was yet to be developed and evolved" (Spiros Zodhiates).[28] Specifically, certain Old Testament persons and events anticipate Christ or specific New Testament teachings. Joseph, for example, was a type, a model, of Christ as the rejected kinsman who becomes their Savior (Gen. 37:1–50:26; Acts 7:9–14). An antitype, therefore (*anti* meaning against or instead of), corresponds to, resembles, or is similar to a type. So, is Peter saying that just as water saved Noah it now saves us? No he is not. He's saying that all this is a *resemblance*, not that it is identical.

What, then, is the resemblance? How does it correspond? The key, of course, is the word **baptism**. While some insist this is water and therefore part of salvation, it can't possibly refer to that since Peter himself repudiates such an idea with his very next statement: **not the putting away of the filth of the flesh** (body). More basic than that is the misunderstanding many have over the word *baptizō* (**baptism**). While many read that word and immediately assume it implies water, that simply is not the case. The word simply means "immerse; place into." The verb *baptō* originally referred to dipping clothes into dye or drawing water by placing the container into the water.

First Corinthians 12:13, for example, declares, "By one Spirit are we all baptized into one body, whether we be Jews or Gentiles, whether we be bond or free; and have been all made to drink into one Spirit." This has nothing to do with water, rather the placing of every true believer *into* the Body of Christ. The same is true of the "one baptism" of Ephesians 5:5, where Paul is dealing with a single, definitive placing into, not something that has to do with our experience but with what God has accomplished (see the "One Baptism" section in chapter 31, "The Ground of Unity" for a detailed exposition of this text).

Peter's meaning, therefore, seems clear. He uses **baptism** in a figurative sense. As Noah and his companions were immersed in water, we are immersed in **the resurrection of Jesus Christ**, as Peter goes on to specify. It is *that* immersion that is our salvation, not one in water.

Why is the Word "Murders" Absent in Galatians 5:21?

Question: I have a question as to why the New King James Version includes a notation about the word "murders" in Galatians 5:21, saying "murders" is left out of NU. I found that NU refers to the prominent modern Critical Text of the Greek New Testament. I noticed the word "murders" is also left out of other versions of the Bible in this verse. Thanks for your insight. (CH)

Answer: This is one of those questions that opens the proverbial can of worms, for it brings up the controversial issue of textual criticism and Bible translations. As we have noted several times, while there are godly men on both sides of the issue, I do defend the historic (and what I believe is the providentially preserved) text of the New Testament (i.e., Traditional or Ecclesiastical Text) instead of the modern Critical Text. I know some TOTT readers embrace the Critical Text and the modern translations based on it, so I do not wish to offend or inflame.

That said, virtually every modern translation (NIV, NASB, ESV, etc.) is, indeed, based upon the Critical Text, which does not contain certain words, phrases, and sometimes entire verses and even whole passages that *do* appear in the Traditional (or Ecclesiastical) Text. (We also discussed the reasons for this in chapter 8.)

Now, as for the New King James Version, it *is* based on the Traditional Text (also called the *Textus Receptus*, Received Text), which itself is based upon a textual tradition that is represented by thousands of manuscripts, in contrast to the Critical Text that is, in point of fact, based upon a very few so-called "older manuscripts." The reason for the marginal notes in the NKJV, however, is that the editors chose to include data from the Critical Text, thereby telling the reader that certain words, phrases, verses, and passages that are in the English translation they are reading do not actually appear "in the best Greek manuscripts." (The acronym "NU" refers to the 27th edition of the Nestle-Aland Greek New Testament [N] and the United Bible Society's 4th edition [U]).

So what is the practical result? Well, perhaps there are two possibilities. As the last paragraph in the NKJV's Preface states, "The textual notes reflect the scholarship of the past 150 years and will assist the reader to observe the variations between the different manuscript traditions of the New Testament." On the other hand, could such a mixture actually betray both sides of the controversy? I guess it depends upon your perspective.

Is there a Contradiction Between 2 Kings 24:8 and 2 Chronicles 36:9?

Question: The Bible appears to contradict itself in the case of Jehoiachin. Second Kings 24:8 states that he was **eighteen** years old when he began to reign while 2 Chronicles 36:9 says he was **eight** years old. How can this be reconciled? (BD)

Answer: **Eight** is *shemōneh.* **Eighteen** is *shemōneh āśār,* the latter being used in combination with other numerals from eleven to nineteen. Most commentators chalk this "contradiction" up to "scribal error." That bothers me, however, because it's two separate words and would be a huge error on the part of a copyist. It's one thing to copy one or two letters incorrectly, but to insert an entire word and thereby drastically alter the meaning seems a pretty big stretch. Textually, in fact, the majority of Hebrew manuscripts actually read **eight** in 2 Chronicles 36:9. It's also odd that such commentators shrug off the clear implication that such a "contradiction" damages the doctrine of inspiration.

A couple of explanations have been offered, the most likely being that it was at eight years of age that his father designated him as the next king, but he did not assume that role until he was eighteen. A variation offered in a note in the Geneva Bible of the Reformation was that "he began his reign at eight years old, and reigned ten years when his father was alive, and after his father's death, which was in his 18th year, he reigned alone three months and ten days." Another variation is that "at the age of eight his father took him into partnership in the government. He began to reign alone at eighteen" (Jamieson, Fausset, and Brown). In any case, is this not better than casting doubt upon the text, which seems to be an ever popular practice?

Who is the the Persian Queen in Nehemiah's Day?

Question: In its lessons on the book of Nehemiah, our home school curriculum refers to the Persian queen in Nehemiah as probably being Esther. This didn't seem right to me. Would you have any insight here? (HH)

Answer: This question arises because of Nehemiah 2:6: "And the king said unto me [Nehemiah], (the queen also sitting by him,) For how long shall thy journey be? and when wilt thou return? So it pleased the king to send me; and I set him a time." There are some who believe that the queen mentioned here was Esther, but that just doesn't fit, as you indicate. She was the queen of the previous king, Xerxes (Ahasuerus; ca. 486–464 BC). It is now 446 BC and Artaxerxes (Longimanus, Esther's step-son) is on the throne. What seems likely, therefore, is that Esther (who might actually have still been alive) influenced her step-son, and his queen, to show some favor to the Jews. Extra biblical historical sources, in fact, tell us that this queen's name was Damaspia.

What is the Significance of the "Folded Napkin" in Jesus' Tomb

Question: I recently received an e-mail forward containing the following explanation for the "folded napkin" in Jesus' tomb:

> The Gospel of John (20:7) tells us that the napkin, which was placed over the face of Jesus, was not just thrown aside like the grave clothes. The Bible takes an entire verse to tell us that the napkin was neatly folded, and was placed at the head of that stony coffin. Early Sunday morning, while it was still dark, Mary Magdalene came to the tomb and found that the stone had been rolled away from the entrance. She ran and found Simon Peter and the other disciple, the one whom Jesus loved. She said, "They have taken the Lord's body out of the tomb, and I don't know where they have put him!" Peter and the other disciple ran to the tomb to see. The other disciple outran Peter and got there first. He stopped and looked in and saw the linen cloth lying there, but he didn't go in. Then Simon Peter arrived and went inside. He also noticed the linen wrappings lying there, while the cloth that had covered Jesus' head was folded up and lying to the side.

> Is it really significant? In order to understand the significance of the folded napkin, you need to understand a little bit about Hebrew tradition of that day. The folded napkin had to do with the Master and Servant, and every Jewish boy knew this tradition. When the servant set the dinner table for the master, he made sure that it was exactly the way the master wanted it. The table was furnished perfectly, and then the servant would wait, just out of sight, until the master had finished eating, and the servant would not dare touch that table, until the master was finished. Now if the master were done eating, he would rise from the table, wipe his fingers, his mouth, and clean his beard, and would wad up that napkin and toss it onto the table. The servant would then know to clear the table. For in those days, the wadded napkin meant, "I'm finished." But if the master got

up from the table, and folded his napkin, and laid it beside his plate, the servant would not dare touch the table, because the folded napkin meant, "I'm coming back."

Do you have any sources to verify or deny this? (JB)

Answer: I included all the above to provide a vivid example of what is so typical of the misinformation on the Internet and another proof of how critical discernment is in our day (see chapter 6). It is sad, indeed, that several online sermons include a yarn that is found *only* on the Internet, not in historical record. This tale, in fact, if I may be so blunt, is patently ridiculous. Commentator William Hendrickson puts it perfectly when he calls such things "exegetical (?) embellishments" (the question mark indicating that this is not true exegesis at all). The first such embellishment, in fact, is in the third line. Neither our text nor Luke 24:12 say the grave cloths were "just thrown aside." Most notable, however, is the word "napkin," which is the Greek *sudarion*, a handkerchief or sweat band or cloth, *not* a dinner napkin; such an idea comes from a western application of an Elizabethan English term and immediately proves this story to be fiction, pretty good fiction we admit, but fiction nonetheless.

A study of historical sources, in fact, reveals not a shred of evidence for a supposed Jewish custom of "the folded napkin." Further, I could not find a single orthodox Jewish authority who has ever even heard of such a custom. How odd that "every Jewish boy knew this tradition" but one can't find one today who does. The only places it can be found are on the Internet and seems to have first popped up in 2007.

The simple explanation of the text, which virtually all commentators agree, is that this little detail demonstrates that the Lord's departure was orderly and unhurried. The words **wrapped together** translate the Greek *entulissō*, a verb meaning "to roll up in, wrap in, to fold or wrap together." The clothes were, therefore, carefully rolled up or folded. If someone had stolen the body, which God knew would be the Jewish leaders' preposterous explanation for the missing body, the cloth would not have been so carefully handled. As expositor Bengel Johann notes, "Doubtless the two attendant angels (Jn. 20:12) did this service for the Rising One, the one disposing of the linen clothes, the other of the napkin." These facts, Hedrickson goes on to add, "are wonderful enough without exegetical embellishments."

A bonus benefit of this historical fact is that it also totally discredits the modern myth (if not deliberate hoax) of the so-called "Shroud of Turin." Have you seen the pictures? They show the imprint of the crucified victim from head to toe in a single piece of cloth. But that is impossible; there was a separate piece of cloth around the head. "The Shroud" is just one more of thousands of instances of fallen man's predilection for "sacred relics" (see chapter 43, "The Pestilence of Idolatry").

What does "Sent the Hornet" Mean?

Question: What does it mean that God "sent the hornet" before Israel (Josh. 24:12)? (WD)

Answer: This description, which also appears in Exodus 23:28 and Deuteronomy 7:20, is a striking picture of God Himself fighting to help Israel (Deut. 23:3, 5, 10, 18). Using some overwhelming force, He caused the enemy to flee. The **hornet** has been interpreted several ways: (1) literal hornets, (2) a symbol of Pharaoh, (3) a sense of panic or despair caused by God, (4) some kind of plague, such as leprosy, or (5) an angel of the Lord (cf. Ex. 23:27, 28; Deut. 7:20). Whichever it was, the point is that God did it. The two kings are probably Adoni-Zedek (Josh. 10:1) and Jabin (11:1), who led the southern and northern coalitions.

That said, I see no reason not to take this to refer to literal hornets. Classic Commentator Adam Clark writes of Exodus 23:28:

> The hornet, in natural history, belongs to the species crabro, of the genus vespa or wasp; it is a most voracious insect, and is exceedingly strong for its size, which is generally an inch in length, though I have seen some an inch and a half long, and so strong that, having caught one in a small pair of forceps, it repeatedly escaped by using violent contortions, so that at last I was obliged to abandon all hopes of securing it alive...How distressing and destructive a multitude of these might be, any person may conjecture; even the bees of one hive would be sufficient to sting a thousand men to madness, but how much worse must wasps and hornets be! No armor, no weapons, could avail against these. A few thousands of them would be quite sufficient to throw the best disciplined army into confusion and rout. [Here in] Josh. 24:12, we find that two kings of the Amorites were actually driven out of the land by these hornets, so that the Israelites were not obliged to use either sword or bow in the conquest.

The always historically thorough John Gill also offers some compelling data:

> [It is not] any strange or unheard of thing for people to be drove out of their countries by small animals, as mice, flies, bees, &c. and particularly Aelianus relates, that the Phaselites were drove out of their country by wasps: and it has shown that those people were of a Phoenician original, and inhabited the mountains of Solymi; and that

this happened to them about the times of Joshua, and so may probably be the very Canaanites here mentioned.

While the Bible does, of course, use figurative language, it always makes it clear that the language *is* figurative, either in the immediate context or larger context of Scripture. When there is ambiguity, therefore, the wisest course is to take the language literally and historically. There is already enough allegory, spiritualizing, and mysticism in the church today. Literal (or plain) interpretation is the only consistent and wise method.

What About Church Associations?

Question: What [does] the Bible say regarding churches "associating" with one another, as I've [recently] returned to the land of [a particular evangelical denomination] (along with others, various smaller "associations" within the state convention, within a larger convention, etc.)? As a tandem to that thought, [what about] the issue of churches of various beliefs associating with each other through a "ministerial alliance" type of thing? (MB)

Answer: Addressing the second question first, I have never been a part of a Ministerial Association simply because of who I would be associating with. Such associations include men (and women nowadays) from liberal denominations, some of who aren't even believers, as well as even apostates and cult members. While I certainly do not wish to offend, it is simply impossible to "fellowship" with people who are not true Christians. What are we going to talk about? Social reform? The community calendar? The weather? *By definition*, such groups are built upon the foundation of setting all doctrine aside for the sake of "unity." Several years ago our local newspaper gave free space to *all* the churches in town in which the ministers would rotate in writing a weekly column. After writing a couple, however, I was compelled to withdraw because of the content of most of the others. I did not want God's Truth to be lumped in with everyone else's "opinion."

Second, as for "churches 'associating' with one another," I taught on this at great length in an exposition of Ephesians 4:1–16, where we see: the *grace* of unity (1–2), the *ground* of unity (4–6), the *gifts* for unity (7–11), and the *growth* of unity (12–16). (Note chapters 30 and 31 for the first two; the complete exposition is on our website.)

As noted in chapter 31, cerses 4–6, therefore, list the foundational doctrines of "The Faith," the seven spiritual realities that unite all true Believers. Contained in those seven principles is the very essence of Christianity, its basic truths. Our unity and fellowship must be based on those. If someone accepts them, there can be unity, even when there is disagreement on minor points of doctrine or practice. But if one or more of those is rejected, there can be no unity and fellowship. Biblical unity can be defined as: *the unanimous agreement concerning the unique revelation of God through and in Jesus Christ.* And those seven spiritual realities are rooted in Christ and His Word.

As for "denominations" themselves, while they are tragically a necessity to mark distinctions between the many groups that exist and to keep doctrine pure, they have their own set of problems. Perhaps that's a subject for a future article.

What Does Paul's Words "How Large a Letter" Mean?

Question: I've read several views on the meaning of Galatians 6:11: **Ye see how large a letter I have written unto you with mine own hand.** Which view do you take? (WD)

Answer: Good question. This is a tough one. Let's examine the three major views, followed by my own humbly contribution.

First, the most common view is that Paul's secretary wrote most of the letter but Paul finished it, as was a common practice. He had to use "large letters," however, because of his poor eye sight. Many have conjectured that the physical infirmity that Paul mentions in 2 Corinthians 12:7, his "thorn in the flesh," was eye disease. But I simply cannot accept this view for two reasons. For one, it *is* conjecture (see chapter 33). For another, and most important, this whole idea doesn't fit the context. In the preceding verses (vv. 9–10) Paul admonishes Christians to do good, and in the following verses (vv. 12–15) he again warns them about the Judaizers. This doesn't seem like an appropriate place for him to draw attention to himself by mentioning his own physical affliction.

Second, a much more likely possibility is that the words **large letters** refer to capital letters, called "uncials." Such large, block letters were used for public notices because they were easy to see (see also chapter 46). "Minuscules" (or "cursive," small letters), however, were far more attractive and economical—since writing materials were expensive—so a professional scribe usually used these instead of uncials. So, to emphasize *content* over *form*, it is possible that Paul wrote the entire letter with his **own hand** using uncials for emphasis. In contrast to the Judaizers, who were more concerned about outward appearances—making "a fair showing in the flesh" (v. 12)—Paul's use of the unattractive uncials would have served to show his deeper inward motives.

This view, in fact, fits the context. If it is correct, Paul was saying in effect, "What I have to say is so important and urgent that I want you to have this letter in your hands as soon as possible, with as bold of lettering as possible. I am not like the Judaizers, who have tried to impress you with scholarship, rhetoric, or empty flattery. This letter, therefore, was not written to please the eye, rather to draw attention to the urgency of the Truth."

The *third* possibility, if we accept the translation as here in the AV—**how large a letter** (not "letters," although the Greek allows either rendering)—the verse simply refers to the length of the letter. This was the view of the highly respected John Gill. In other words, because of his love and concern, Paul writes a rather lengthy letter. His desire is to deliver them from error and set forth the correct doctrine. This, too, fits the context.

Whichever of these views is correct (I lean toward the second), the importance of the verse lies in the words **with my own hand**. For one thing, they show the importance and gravity of the letter. For another, they indicate that Paul normally dictated his letters to a secretary (amanuensis) who did the actual writing. To prove the genuineness of the letter, however, Paul customarily added his own salutation in his own handwriting (see 1 Cor. 16:21; Col. 4:18; 2 Thess. 3:17). Forged documents were common in the early years of the church and such forgers would use the names of the Apostles to gain credibility. Paul cautioned Thessalonian believers, in fact, about that very practice: "be not soon shaken in mind, or be troubled, neither by spirit, nor by word, nor by letter as from us, as that the day of Christ is at hand" (2 Thess. 2:2). So, since it is likely that the Judaizers deceitfully claimed to speak for the Jerusalem apostles (Acts 15:1–5), they would have had no scruples in claiming to speak for Paul if that would serve their purpose. Paul, therefore, not only wanted the Galatians to understand clearly *what* he was writing but also to recognize that *he* was, in fact, the one writing it.

Further, after studying the Greek behind this, I am convinced that Paul did, indeed, write the entire letter. The Greek verb behind **I have written** is *egrapha*, which is the aorist active indicative of *graphō* and refers to the past tense, that is, something *already* written, not to something *yet* to be written. In other words, Paul refers here to the letter as a whole, not some small portion he is preparing to add. Paul desperately wanted to get this letter to the Galatians, but perhaps there was no amanuensis available to meet the pressing need. It seems more likely, however, that he wrote it with his **own hand** simply because of the sternness of what he was going to write.

NOTES

[1] William MacDonald, *Believer's Bible Commentary* (Thomas Nelson Publishers, 1995), p. 1807.

[2] This answer taken from the author's book, *A Word for the Day: Key Words from*

the New Testament (AMG Publishers)].

[3] Gerhard Kittel, *Theological Dictionary of the New Testament* (Eerdmans, 1964), Vol. I, p. 74.

[4] *Summa Theologica*, Part 1, question 113.

[5] *Defender's Study Bible* (Heb. 1:14).

[6] William MacDonald, *Believer's Bible Commentary* (Thomas Nelson Publishers, 1995), p.1228.

[7] *Ryrie Study Bible.*

[8] J. Vernon McGee, *Thru The Bible* (comment on Jn. 16:23–24).

[9] R. C. Sproul, *The Purpose of God: An Exposition of Ephesians* (Christian Focus Publications, 1994), p. 153.

[10] *Catholic Encyclopedia.* You can read the entire article at: http://www.newadvent.org/cathen/12260a.htm.

[11] Ibid, http://www.newadvent.org/cathen/12272b.htm.

[12] The reader might want to listen to *The Five Solas of the Reformation* series on our website, available there in MP3 media. A book is planned based upon this series and other TOTT issues not included in the present compliation.

[13] Gerhard Kittle (editor), *Theological Dictionary of the New Testament* (Grand Rapids: Eerdmans, 1964; reprinted 2006), Vol. VI, pp. 592.

[14] Spiros Zodhiatus, *The Complete Word Study Dictionary: New Testament* (AMG Publishers, 1992), #4202.

[15] http://www.come-and-hear.com/gittin/gittin_18.html

[16] http://www.come-and-hear.com/gittin/index.html

[17] Jay Adams, *Marriage, Divorce, And Remarriage* (Baker Book House, 1980), p. 56.

[18] Spiros Zodhiates, *The Complete Word Study Dictionary: New Testament* (AMG Publishers, 1992), p. 630.

[19] "Little Kittle," p. 544.

[20] Colin Brown, *The New International Dictionary of New Testament Theology* (1975, 1986), Vol. 3, p. 1147.

[21] Kittle, Vol. II, p. 653.

[22] A good summary appears in the *International Standard Bible Encyclopedia* (electronic edition; "Image" entry), which is too lengthy to include here.

[23] *Exploring Genesis: An Expository Commentary* (Kregel Academic, 2001), p. 45.

[24] John Gill, *The New John Gill's Exposition of the Entire Bible*, comment on Hebrews 1:3.

[25] Zodhiates, #541.

[26] We deal with these "Five Solas" in more depth in TOTT Issues 60 and 61, although they are condensed from the original lectures. A book is planned on this subject that will also include a few TOTT articles that are not in the present compilation.

[27] "Limbo" in *Catholic Encyclopedia* (http://www.newadvent.org/cathen), Classic 1914 Edition

[28] Spiros Zodhiates, *The Complete Word Study Dictionary: New Testament* (AMG Publishers, entry #5179.

We should set the Word of God always before us like a rule, and believe nothing but that which it teacheth, love nothing but that which it prescribeth, hate nothing but that which it forbideth, do nothing but that which it commandeth, and then we try all things by the Word.

Puritan Henry Smith
A Puritan Golden Treasury, p.36

Conclusion

As I sat and pondered how to conclude this collection, I came across these words by Thomas Watson, one of the dearest (and easiest to read) of the old Puritans:

> The Book of God has no errata in it; it is a beam of the Sun of Righteousness, a crystal stream flowing from the fountain of life. All laws and edicts of men have had their corruptions, but the Word of God has not the least tincture, it is of meridian splendour. Psalm 119:140, "Thy word is very pure," like wine that comes from the grape, which is not mixed nor adulterated. It is so pure that it purifies everything else. (*A Body of Divinity* [Banner of Truth Trust, 1992 reprint], 27–28).

It was that first sentence—"The Book of God has no errata in it."—that caught my eye, because unlike Scripture the present book does have errata in it. Only the most arrogant man would think that he is always right, that his conclusions are armored and impervious to the shells of refutation. (To help minimize such errata, as I have encouraged other writers, it's probably wise not to publish before your fortieth birthday and at least twentieth year of ministry.)

But as I made clear in the Introduction, agreement on all points was never the purpose of either the original monthly articles or this compilation. Rather the goal always was, still is, and ever shall be to drive us to the Book. Watson goes on to write:

> This blessed Book will fill your head with knowledge, and your heart with grace. God wrote the two tables with his own fingers; and if he took pains to write, well may we take pains to read. Apollos was mighty in the Scriptures. Acts 18:24. The Word is our *Magna Charta* for Heaven; shall we be ignorant of our charter? Col 3:16. "0 Let the word of God dwell in you richly." The memory must be a tablebook where the Word is written. (34)

We live in a day of serious biblical ignorance. What's ironic, however, is how many Christians are unaware of their ignorance and actually think they know a great deal of the Bible, when in reality they are simply driven by their own cultured opinions, or worse their mystic feelings. Scripture is hardly the sufficient authority in much of the Church today. The humble scribblings in this book, therefore, have been offered to remind us of Absolute Truth and the only place we will ever find it.

Finally, as my name sake goes on to add:

Though we should not be of contentious spirits, yet we ought to contend for the Word of God. This jewel is too precious to be parted with. Prov 4:13. "Keep her, for she is thy life." The Scripture is beset with enemies; heretics fight against it, we must therefore "contend for the faith once delivered to the saints." Jude 3. The Scripture is our book of evidences for heaven; shall we part with our evidences? The saints of old were both advocates and martyrs for truth; they would hold fast Scripture, though it were with the loss of their lives. (37)

Does that describe us? Is the Word of God everything to us? Do we stand courageously for its promises, principles, precepts, and precedents, and then even willing to die in its protection?

Well, my Dear Christian Friend, thank you for reading. It is an honor and priviledge to write for those who wish to read. I pray that God will use these studies in at least a small way to enlighten you, encourage you, and equip you.

Soli Deo Gloria.

The Author
April 2012

News may come that Truth is sick, but never that it is dead.

Puritan William Gurnall
A Puritan Golden Treasury, p. 299

Appendix

Principles of Biblical Interpretation[*]

2 Timothy 2:15

Study to shew thyself approved unto God, a workman that needeth not to be ashamed, rightly dividing the word of truth.

Much has been said and written about interpreting the Bible. We have all heard more than one person say, "Oh, that's just your interpretation of the Bible," or "The Bible can be interpreted in different ways." Naturally, such statements are made by the skeptic and the infidel so that he can ignore the Scriptures.

If I may humbly submit, however, that is not only true of lost people, for professed Christians are also guilty of the same tendency. We sometimes "reevaluate" or "reinterpret" those parts of Scripture that we don't want to face. We sometimes justify our actions and attitudes with such statements as: "Well, that passage of Scripture was written in a different time and place; things are different now," or, "That is in the Old Testament, which *never* applies to the New Testament believer."

A vital key to understanding biblical *authority* is understanding biblical *interpretation.* How are we to interpret Scripture? The story has often been told of the man who wanted to be guided by Scripture, so he closed his eyes, opened his Bible, and pointed to a verse, which read, "And he [Judas] cast down the pieces of silver in the temple, and departed, and went and hanged himself" (Matt. 27:5). He thought he should try again, so repeating the process he came upon Luke 10:37, "Go and do thou likewise."

Obviously, that is a ridiculous story, but in some ways it is characteristic of exactly how some people interpret Scripture. They rip verses from their context, ignore to whom the words were written, ignore the historical setting of the verse or passage, ignore the words and grammar used in the verse, and in general *violate every rule of interpreting literature.*

Please note those last six words. As I present some principles of biblical interpretation here, some people might accuse me of simply creating principles that fit my viewpoint, but that is not the case. In fact, in the final analysis, interpreting Scripture is little different than interpreting

---

[*] This chapter was originally a two-part study that appeared in TOTT issues 26 and 27, September and October 2007.

any literature. Now please do not misunderstand me; I am *not* equating the Bible with all other literature. "God forbid!" The Bible is inspired, infallible, and authoritative literature, but it is still literature and is to be interpreted by certain rules that are universal to literature.

While the Word of God is deep, it is not complex. It says what it means and means what it says. God is not the One who has muddied the waters of His Word, rather it is man who has done so—he has complicated the Scriptures so much that it is no longer clear, no longer means what the words *seem* to say.

Again, Scripture cannot rule in our lives if we do not know what it says. Therefore, in a moment we will examine twelve principles for proper biblical interpretation. Before doing so, however, there is one general truth concerning biblical interpretation on which the other principles are built: *Scripture interprets Itself.* As *The Westminster Confession of Faith* (1646) puts it (and the *London Baptist Confession of 1689* is virtually identical):

> The infallible rule of interpretation of scripture is the scripture itself: and therefore, when there is a question about the true and full sense of any scripture [which is not manifold, but one], it must be searched and known by other places that speak more clearly (Acts 15:15, 16; John 5:46; see 2 Pet. 1:20, 21).

While the aforementioned statement, "Oh, that's just your interpretation of the Bible," is often true of some interpreters, proper biblical interpretation simply allows the Bible to interpret Itself. In other words, we simply allow the Word of God to tell us what it means. *There is nothing mystical or magical about interpreting the Bible. If we just get out of the way, it will make itself clear.*

Let us turn now to twelve basic principles of biblical interpretation. (See chapter 18, "What About the Head Covering?" for a representative example of using these principles to develop the biblical teaching on a specific subject.)

The Reverence Principle

Of all the principles of biblical interpretation, none today is violated more than this one. No longer is the Bible revered. It has been diluted, added to, subtracted from, treated flippantly, and generally considered by many as irrelevant. Often it is not consulted at all, but when it is, it is usually just added to the list of opinions collected from other sources.

This is true not only of Liberalism, but is true of Evangelicalism and Fundamentalism as well. Liberals attack the Bible by denying its truth. Other groups undermine the authority of Scripture by claiming new revelation through visions and other experiential means. We submit, however, that evangelicals and fundamentalists often undermine the Word of God as well. One way is in their failure to exposit the Word. Many preachers, while saying they believe in biblical authority, nonetheless stand in their pulpits every Sunday and fail to boldly and authoritatively expound on the Truth of the Scripture in depth and then apply it to people's lives.

Another way the holiness and seriousness of God's Word is undermined is by what I call "biblical humor." By this I mean making a joke at the expense of the Bible. Why is it that we teach our children not to make a joke at someone else's expense, but then turn around and do this with God's holy Word?

This practice is common today in cartoons. I was appalled, for example, at the cartoon of two doctors talking about a man they had just put in cryogenic freeze. The caption read, "In his will he said he wanted to be frozen until someone can see if his name's in the Book of Life; if it's not, leave him frozen." How can any Christian think something that blasphemous is funny?"

And what does this say about the "Christian comedians" that characterize "preaching" today? The argument that says, "Well, if you keep people laughing, you can get your point across" is worldly nonsense. *Truly spiritual people will desire spiritual Truth.* I certainly don't mind the occasional humorous comment or illustration, and use them on occasion myself, but "stand up comedy" has no place anywhere near the pulpit. We are dealing with holy, sacred things, and we had better treat them as such. That is God's demand. So-called "Christian comedy" is one of the most serious errors of our day and is a scourge that should be excised. The pulpit is a place of *solemnity*, not *slapstick*. The man who God esteems is "him that is poor and of a contrite spirit, and trembleth at my word" (Isa. 66:2). How many men in pulpits today tremble at the Word of God and teach their people to do the same?

So, first and foremost, we must approach the Bible with reverence and the utmost respect. Note the psalmist's declarations (for the sake of space, we mention only the references): Ps. 138:2; 119:72, 127, 161. Note also Job's conviction in Job 23:12.

How can we treat something that is this holy and highly esteemed flippantly?

The Diligence Principle

The second principle of biblical interpretation is found in our text, 2 Timothy 2:15. This pivotal verse reveals four things concerning proper biblical interpretation.

The Method of Proper Biblical Interpretation

Study is the Greek *spoudazō*, which speaks of being diligent or eager. Some think that a newer translation of the Bible that says "Be diligent" (NASB) or "Do your best" (a terrible translation in the NIV) is better here. One popular commentary says, "'Study,' (KJV) is obviously too narrow a term, usually referring today to the studying of books."[1] On the contrary, the beauty of the Old English here actually says more. After all, in his unabridged dictionary, Webster says that study, to be diligent, and to be eager are all "akin," and then defines study as, "A state of absorbed contemplation." Now, in all honesty, isn't that better?

Indeed, our attitude and approach to the interpretation of Scripture must be one of "absorbed contemplation." How much slip-shod, shallow, and sentimental biblical interpretation there is today! Many think they can just sit down, read a few verses, make a quick "application," and then hurry on to their next activity. Many preachers do likewise in their sermon preparation, spending an hour or two in the Word and coming away with a shallow, topical "sermonette for Christianettes" consisting of three points and a poem. Many Bible colleges are the guiltiest because that is the approach they teach.

Another deadly danger to honest interpretation is the common practice of approaching the Scriptures with preconceived ideas. In other words, there is always the danger of formulating an idea, opinion, or position and then going to the Bible to defend it. The story is often told of the preacher who said, "I've got a really good sermon in mind; all I need is a Scripture verse to go with it." That might be humorous, but it is more common than you think. It is also common among folks who have been taught a certain position all their lives and refuse to consider any other teaching. If we may say it as frankly as possible: get out of the way and allow God to speak. Lay aside whatever *you think*, and then go to the Scripture to find what *God says*.

Our text goes on to say that the pastor (and by application, every Christian) is a **workman**, one who labors over the Word of God, one who works at his study and interpretation. The words **to show thyself approved unto God** reemphasize this fact by showing that the workman is totally dedicated to God and God's Word. This is first and foremost the responsibility of the pastor, since this Epistle is written to a pastor, who is called by vocation to do this and has the time to devote to this. By application, however, all Christians can (and should) study the Word under the guidance of their pastor.

The Goal of Proper Biblical Interpretation

Often we incorrectly think that the reason and goal for studying the Scriptures is knowledge. While it is true that we want knowledge ("Truth"), our chief goal should be to "*rightly divide* the Word of Truth." The Greek word used here for **rightly dividing** (*orthotomeō*) is actually comprised of two words, *orthos*, meaning "straight" (as an orthodontist straightens teeth), and *temnō*, which means "to cut or divide." The word was used in ancient times for cutting a straight furrow, something that a farmer is always concerned about as he plows. Similarly, a carpenter is concerned about making a straight cut on a board, and a seamstress is concerned about sewing a straight seam.

This, then, is the goal of the interpreter of Scripture, to cut it straight, to rightly divide it so that it is clearly understood and plainly applied. Our goal is spiritual, not intellectual. How, then, do we accomplish this? Again, it takes work, hours of laborious study. We will not properly interpret if we grab a verse here and a principle there. We must labor to rightly divide. That is our goal.

The Difficulty of Proper Biblical Interpretation

This rightly dividing will inevitably and unavoidably cause problems from time to time. In other words, we will at times run into either textual or practical problems. Tragically, what often happens nowadays is that when problems occur, they are simply ignored. A commentator, for example, might simply skip over a textual problem. Or a pastor might just avoid dealing with an issue so as not to upset anyone.

This practice, however, is not only dishonest, but it also violates the clear admonition of Paul to the Ephesian elders, "For I have not shunned to declare unto you *all* the counsel of God" (Acts 20:27). He goes on to say that the shepherd is to "oversee" (v. 28), "feed," and "warn" (v. 31) the sheep, all of which might "step on toes" once in awhile.

Diligent study, therefore, demands that we deal with problems. For example, some Bible students have problems with the verse that instructs older women to teach the younger women to be "keepers at home" (Titus 2:4–5). Does that mean a woman can never go out of the house? Or what does Paul mean when he speaks of being "baptized for the dead" (1 Cor. 15:29)? Or what does the Bible mean when it says that "God repented?" (Gen. 6:6 and Jon. 3:10).

Using the proper principles of biblical interpretation will reveal the solution to these problems and all others, but only if we are committed to diligence.

The Result of Proper Biblical Interpretation

Finally, Paul assures his pupil of the result of this kind of diligence. What will be the result of diligent study? *We will never be ashamed* (**needeth not to be ashamed**). This assurance is really twofold. First, our diligent study of the Word of God is a testimony to others that we are not ashamed of it, that we are not ashamed to stand on Its authority. Second, since we *are* diligent laborers in the Word, we won't be **ashamed** when our Lord inspects our works.

The Plain Principle

There have been Bible interpreters through the ages who interpret the Bible with an allegorical approach. This type of approach doesn't take the words of Scripture as they are, rather it looks for some deeper "spiritual" meaning. This approach is often used by those who want to escape some theological or practical difficulty or by those who want to teach some far out religious view. One of the most notorious of this type of interpreter was the 3rd-century scholar Origen. His allegorical approach to Scripture and "spiritualizing" of it is well-known, going so far as to turn the entire Law and the Gospels into an allegory; in his own words, in fact, he said, "The Scriptures are of little use to those who understand them as they are written."

But does this approach make any sense? Do we take this approach with other types of literature? Do we just automatically assume a book or magazine article is allegorical? On the contrary, if a piece of literature is supposed to be allegorical, does it not plainly tell you so as you begin to read it? Likewise, as we'll see, *the Bible is to be taken in its plain meaning unless it makes it clear that it is to be taken otherwise.*

The chief danger of the allegorical approach is obvious. Using this approach, Scripture no longer means what it says, and therefore, for all practical purposes, is no longer authoritative. Interpretation of Scripture now depends upon the mind of the interpreter, not God.

In contrast to allegorical interpretation, there is what is commonly called "literal interpretation." In regard to this term, however, Charles Ryrie makes a very important distinction: "Since the word "literal" has connotations which are either misunderstood or subjectively understood, labels like "plain" or "normal" serve more acceptably. "Literal" is assumed to preclude figures of speech, etc. (which is not the case)."[2] To interpret plainly is to explain the original sense of the speaker or writer according to normal, customary, and proper usage of words and language.

There is actually more allegorical interpretation among evangelicals than one might think. One of the chief areas in which we find this is in the interpretation of prophecy. One example is how some fancifully interpret Revelation 9, where we find the description of the plague of locusts that sting like scorpions, which will inflict mankind during the Tribulation Period. One commentator writes about his Vietnam veteran friend who thought this has to be describing Cobra attack helicopters and that the torment of the sting will be nerve gas sprayed from the aircraft's tail. The commentator admits that this might be "conjecture" but that it does "fit the composite description."[3]

Another commentator writes that these locusts might be of the insect or animal variety, but that they could also be men with jet packs strapped to their backs, who emit a chemical substance from a canister that inflicts a painful sting.[4]

Still another commentator says that the old opinion of this being B-29 bombers that sting from their tail (because of the tail guns) is "fanciful," but then turns right around and says they are "spirit-beings who probably will not be seen by men, but whose effects will be strongly felt." He continues by saying that "they are not to be taken literally, nor symbolically, but spiritually."[5]

May we ask these men, what's wrong with the plain interpretation that this plague will be a literal plague of locusts that sting like scorpions? Why ignore Revelation 9:5 that plainly says the plague will last five months, *which is the natural life-span of locusts*? Compare these fanciful interpretations with that of rock solid expositors, such as William Newell, who not only brings out what we've noted here, but who also has this to say about other "interpretations":

> Now no one who believes the Bible has any trouble believing the record of that last plague. Nor has any one any *right* to have any difficulty about the terrible locust plague of Revelation 9. It is because of *the fog of unbelief*, and *the super-fog of "historical interpretation,"* that this passage has been considered "hard to understand." If we do not *believe* that God means what He so plainly and explicitly says in Revelation 9, let us *say* we do not believe it, and be honest. But let us not dare to bring in vain imaginations and call them interpretations of Scripture.[6]

All this is a vivid illustration of allegorizing and spiritualizing Scripture. This kind of biblical interpretation is dangerous because it allows every person to think of something different. Was this God's intention? Certainly not! It matters not what we *think* Scripture means, rather what it really *does* mean according to the plain language of Scripture.

Spiritualizing Scripture is also a common practice among preachers. I recently read about the pastor who preached on Jericho. He told how God gave the Israelites the city, how they marched around the city seven times, and how the walls fell down. His "application" of this truth was that if a young man believed God had given him a girl, he could claim her, march around her seven times, and the walls of her heart would fall down! Believe it or not, that couple (and other couples) got married on that basis, but as you might expect, marital problems came soon after.[7] Other preachers are "hyper-typers," teaching such things as each pillar of the temple having a deeper spiritual or symbolic meaning.

Another result of non-literal interpretation is the total rejection of a literal 1,000-year reign of Christ on the earth, that is, Premillenialism. With a wave of an allegorical hand, Postmillennialists and Amillennialists dismiss countless Old Testament prophecies that speak of a *literal* Kingdom. Inexplicably, while they take *non*-prophetic subjects literally—the virgin birth, the cross, the resurrection, salvation, etc.—they view the millennium as non-literal. Such an arbitrary departure makes no sense whatsoever, especially when they teach that *other* prophecies—Christ's *first* coming, His *Second* Coming, the Great White Throne judgment, and the new heavens and the new earth—*are* literal.

Does this mean that the Bible never speaks figuratively? Of course not. *But when Scripture is used figuratively, it makes it plain that it is doing so.* When Paul writes about putting on the "armor of God" (Eph. 6:10–20), for example, he makes it clear that this is figurative, illustrative language. Certainly, the Word of God is not a literal sword, but it is our only offensive weapon (as was the soldier's sword), and it is used in much the same way. Hebrews 4:12 gives us the same analogy, saying the Word of God is sharper than a two-edged sword, cutting through pretense, and discerning not only our thoughts but even our very intentions.

The late Dr. David Cooper summed up the matter very well when he said: "When the plain sense of Scripture makes common sense, seek no other sense; therefore; take every word at its primary, ordinary, usual, literal meaning unless the facts of the immediate context, studied in the light of related passages and axiomatic and fundamental truths, indicated clearly otherwise."[8]

Again, the main reason many shy away from a plain interpretation of the Bible is to escape what it demands. Taking the Bible plainly is, indeed, demanding. The Word of God has something to say about every aspect of human life; it leaves nothing to chance and never leaves us to "decide for ourselves."

The Grammatical Principle

Just as grammar and word usage is vital to understanding any literature or spoken word, it is likewise indispensable in interpreting Scripture. I once heard a well-known speaker and author speak on Jude 3. He read the verse

(" . . . earnestly contend for the faith") and then proceeded to speak about *subjective* faith, that is, our personal faith. While much of what he said was true, this verse has nothing whatsoever to do with subjective faith or the *action* of faith. Because of the definite article, the words "the faith" refer to *the body of revealed Truth that makes up historical, evangelical Christianity.* This meaning is further emphasized by the words "once delivered," which refer to the preaching and teaching of the Apostles as the historical basis of our faith. In fact, "deliver" (*paradidomi*) means "to hand down, pass on instruction from teacher to pupil"[9] (see 1 Cor. 11:2, 23; 15:3).

Countless errors have resulted from improper grammatical interpretation. The modern Charismatic Movement builds much of its foundation on a glaring grammatical error. It teaches that the "baptism of the Holy Spirit" is something we must seek now. But 1 Corinthians 12:13 *plainly* says that *all Christians* (even the appallingly carnal Corinthians) have been baptized (*past tense*) into the Body of Christ, that is, placed into His body. The grammar is absolutely inarguable.

Speaking of "baptism," the entire doctrine of baptism has been perverted due to improper grammatical interpretation. The Greek *baptizō* means "to dip, immerse, or plunge" and was used to describe the dying of clothes.[10] The whole point of baptism is being placed into something to show *identification.* Baptism pictures our being placed into Christ and our identification with His death, burial, and resurrection (Rom. 6:3–6). Other modes of baptism (sprinkling and pouring) are wrong because they do not properly picture this identification, this *placing into.* After all, how many of us would dye a piece of clothing by sprinkling or pouring the dye on it?

It is also extremely significant that there is absolutely no doubt whatsoever, and non-immersionists admit, that immersion alone was the universal practice of the Apostolic church, a fact John Calvin points out in his *Institutes.*[11] In a footnote, Calvin even admits that deviation from immersion is seen in the *Didache* (*Teaching of the Twelve*), a 2nd-century apocryphal book. It says that if running water was not available, "Pour water on the head three times." That is clearly unscriptural and serves as an excellent example of how men add to the Word of God by saying, "Well, this a special circumstance, so we can add this practice to meet the need of the moment." What men need to do is *obey* the Word of God, not *add* to it.

One of the most beautiful illustrations of this grammatical principle appears in Nehemiah 8:7–8, where we are told that Ezra and the Levites read from the Law, "gave the sense, and caused the people to understand." After the Babylonian captivity, Hebrew had been largely replaced by Aramaic as the spoken language of God's people. So when the Law was read in Hebrew, few understood it; it had to be explained in their own language. How this is needed today! Preachers need to know the language and must be able to exposit the deep truth of the Word.

Several years ago I was preaching this principle in a church, strongly emphasizing the need for pastors to know something about the biblical languages. Without having any knowledge of the pastor of that church, I made it clear that a pastor does not have to be a Greek scholar, but that he at least needs to know how to use the Greek tools that are readily available today and how to present the Word with grammatical accuracy. The pastor was offended by this and later said to me, "If you're right, I'm not even qualified to be in the ministry." It is sad, indeed, that he is not the only one of whom that is true; there are many men in pulpits today who simply do not adequately study the Scriptures and, therefore, disqualify themselves from the very office they occupy.

The Historical Principle

Another vital principle in proper biblical interpretation is the understanding of social customs, historical names and events, political climate and rulers, and even geographical references.

One example of the historical principle appears in Revelation 2:17 (for the sake of space, we will mention only Scripture references as we continue). In our Lord's letter to the church at Pergamum, a church that was tolerant of the world, He appeals to anyone who will listen and promises them two blessings if they will obey. First, He says He will give them "hidden manna." This is fairly easy to understand. As Israel was nourished with "physical food" in the wilderness, Christ is our "spiritual food," as He is spoken of as the "Bread of Heaven" and the "Bread of Life" (see Jn. 6:30–35).

The second blessing the Lord promises here, however, is impossible for us to understand without the historical principle of interpretation. What is this "white stone?" John's readers knew that a prisoner in court was either given a white stone (acquittal) or a black stone (conviction). They also knew that a white stone was often used as an invitation to a feast; the stone often had the recipient's name on it. Both meanings beautifully apply to the Christian believer. We have been acquitted from sin's guilt by justification through Christ, and we now have a "personal invitation" to the Marriage Feast of the Lamb (see Rev. 19:7–9).

Coming back to the armor of God (Eph. 6:10–20) mentioned earlier, we find another example of historical interpretation. Paul speaks there of having our "loins girded about with truth," but, again, we can't possibly understand this without knowing the historical background. The most important article of clothing in Paul's day was the tunic, a knee-length, kimono-like garment worn next to the skin. Holes were cut for the head and arms in a square piece of cloth and the garment was then worn loosely over the body. Poorer people wore only this in warm weather, while wealthier people wore this by itself only in private, never appearing in public without an outer garment (a coat or cloak).

For a soldier, however, wearing a loose tunic was dangerous, so the tunic was cinched up and tucked into the girdle, which held the tunic close to the body. The girdle was a broad leather belt, usually about six inches in width, and was the foundational piece of the soldier's armor; other pieces of armor were kept in place because they were attached to the girdle.

Knowing this historical meaning yields the powerful spiritual application of the "spiritual girdle of truth" we must all wear. Truth is absolutely foundational. Without the *objective* truth of the Word of God *and* the *subjective* truth of our personal honesty and integrity, there can be nothing else of value.

Peter uses this same expression in 1 Peter 1:13, where he says, "Gird up the loins of your mind," that is, discipline your mind, pull your thoughts together, prepare for battle.

Even a seemingly insignificant act can be filled with meaning when we know the historical background. John 18:1, for example, tells us that on His way to the Garden of Gethsemane, Jesus crossed over the Brook Kidron. This seems insignificant until you know that at that time of the year (Passover), the Brook Kidron was filled with blood because the blood from thousands of lambs drained out of the back of the Temple right into it. How significant this must have been for our Lord as He was reminded that He was the Lamb of God!

Consider also the historical significance of the term "body of this death" (Rom. 7:24), which Paul uses to graphically describe man's sin and his struggle with the flesh. A fascinating story is told of the ancient people near Tarsus, the city where Paul was born. Convicted murders were sentenced to an unimaginable execution. The corpse of the murdered person was tightly lashed to the murderer and remained there until the murderer himself died. In a few days, of course, the decay of the corpse would infect and kill the murderer. It is quite possible that Paul had this story in mind when he used this term.

History, then, is a vital principle of interpretation. No study of Scripture is complete (or honest) without the historical context.

The Contextual Principle

Probably the most violated principle of biblical interpretation is the ripping of verses from their context. Just as we can take any writer's words out of their context and, therefore, make him say the exact opposite of what he is actually saying, we can take a verse out of its context and quite literally prove anything we want to prove. In this way, countless "interpreters" have done tremendous violence to God's Word.

The Contextual Principle involves examining the *words* that surround the word in question, the *verses* that surround the verse, and the *basic theme of the book* where the verse appears.

One example of the importance of the context appears in 1 Corinthians 2:9. Taken out of its context, this verse indicates that the promise is to be fulfilled in the future, when, in fact, the context, verse 10, clearly shows that it is to be fulfilled *now*.

First Corinthians 9:27, where Paul writes about not becoming a castaway, has been used by some to "prove" that believers can lose their salvation, but the context clearly talks about rewards for Christian service, not salvation.

Even more dramatic is what the modern Charismatic movement does to 1 Corinthians. Portions of chapters 12–14 are used to prove Charismatic doctrine, while the context, when viewed as a whole, clearly demonstrates the temporary nature of the gifts listed in chapter 12. But even more shocking is what I heard a Charismatic say some years ago. During an excited radio broadcast, a Charismatic was *praising* the Corinthian believers and finally even said, "Oh, how I wish our churches today were like the one in Corinth!" I couldn't help but think that many churches *are* like the one in Corinth, but that is not something to be desired. *The occasion of the entire letter is rebuke.* The Corinthians had perverted virtually every aspect of Christianity.

Many preachers are guilty of taking verses out of context. A pastor friend of mine, a dedicated and careful student of the Word, was talking one day to another pastor in the area. As they chatted about ministry and preaching, the other pastor said, "I don't ever want to preach when you are in the congregation because I take a lot of verses out of context." How can a man deliberately do such a thing?

I don't know who to credit for this thought, but it has been well said that, "A text without a context is pretext."

The Comparison Principle

No Scripture verse stands by itself. Indeed, comparing Scripture with Scripture is absolutely essential to arriving at the proper interpretation of a given text. This principle is what is called *analogia scripturae*, "the analogy of Scripture," that is, comparing Scripture with Scripture.[12] In other words, we allow the Scripture to interpret Itself. The old adage, "Well, that's just your interpretation," is a smoke screen to hide from the truth of what the text says. Our motto must be, *What does the text say?*—not, "What do you think it says?" Or "How does it make you feel?"—rather, *what does it say?* If we ignore this principle, we are headed for disaster.

In my early days in Bible College (some 40 years ago), for example, I was required to read a book on prayer. Even in those early days of being a know-nothing neophyte, the book grieved me because the author's basic premise is that prayer is primarily "asking and receiving." What a narrow view of prayer! A worse problem with the book, however, is the author's contention that we never have to pray according to the will of God, that we can simply ask God for anything and He will give it to us. The author is quick to quote such verses as Matthew 21:22, which is, indeed, a blessed verse that promises power for overcoming obstacles to those who have faith, as the context (vv. 18–21) clearly indicates. But this verse must not be taken apart from 1 John 5:14–15, which speaks of praying "according to [God's] will." Prayer is *never* divorced from God's sovereign will. Prayer is not us getting our way done in heaven, rather God getting His way done on earth. *Our will must always come into conformity with His will.*

The great theologian Charles Hodge comments on this principle and provides another example:

> God cannot teach in one place anything which is inconsistent with what He teaches in another. Hence Scripture must explain Scripture. If a passage admits of different interpretations, that only can be the true one which agrees with what the Bible teaches elsewhere on the same subject. If the Scriptures teach that the Son is the same in substance and equal in power and glory with the Father, then when the Son says, "The Father is greater than I" [Jn 14:28], the superiority must be understood in a manner consistent with this equality. It must refer either to subordination as to the mode of subsistence and operation, or it must be official. A king's son may say, "My father is greater than I," although personally his father's equal. This rule of interpretation is sometimes called the analogy of Scripture. . .[13]

Again, many today, no matter what the issue, are fond of saying, "Well, that's just your interpretation." On the contrary, as the Reformers and the Puritans were fond of saying, "Scripture interprets Scripture."[14]

Another aspect of this principle is that any conclusion we come to in our study must not contradict the Scripture elsewhere. A very typical example of this today is Bible teaching that contradicts the nature of God, as when Bible teachers emphasize God's love as His motivating attribute. Upon this premise, then, they proclaim everything from "easy believism" salvation to unity at any price. As a result of today's ignoring of God's sovereignty, holiness, justice, and other attributes, we have a plague of false Bible teaching.

The next principle follows this one.

The Outline Principle

Coupled with the previous principle, this one looks for the organization and structure of the text, as well as the principles that the text presents. In other words, what is the logical flow of the text? What are the points or principles the author is trying to convey?

This process is often easy. For example, Galatians 5:22–23 lists nine "Christian Graces," that is, an outline of the believer's godly behavior. Each one of these principles, then, can be traced through the Scripture and reinforced using the Comparison Principle. The Comparison Principle and the Outline Principle then become the foundation for the Application Principle, which we will examine last.

Other texts will not be as obvious but will fall into place as you read and study them. Second Timothy 3:16–17, for example, provides a good example. As I studied the text, it became apparent that these two verses, and their context, give us three foundational truths about the Word of God: 1) The *Recording* of God's Word (v 16a), which is by Inspiration, and which we could then trace throughout Scripture; 2) the *Result* of God's Word (vv. 16b–17), which in turn involves four principles that form the foundation for our application; and 3) the *Reason* for God's Word (3:1–7; 4:1–4), which, as the surrounding context indicates, is so we have a record of absolute truth in contrast to that which is false.

Again, by using these two principles, we allow the Scripture to interpret Itself.

The Progressive Principle

Another principle we must not ignore when interpreting the Bible is that God's revelation is progressive; that is, God reveals His truth in steps, "a little at a time," if you will. Undoubtedly, one reason for this is that man could not possibly absorb all God has to say if He revealed it all at once. Can we imagine, for example, Adam's reaction if God had revealed to him His entire plan for the ages?

Such progressive revelation appears repeatedly in Scripture. Matthew 10:5–7, for example, records Jesus' sending forth the twelve to "the lost sheep of the house of Israel" but not to the Samaritans or the Gentiles, but He then commands all believers to go to "all nations" in Matthew 28:18–20. Another example appears in Genesis 17:10, where God institutes circumcision of every male child as a sign of the Abrahamic covenant, while Paul says in Galatians 5:2 that circumcision profits nothing. Likewise, God instituted the Sabbath as the day of worship in Exodus 20:8, but then replaced it with something better, "the first day of the week" (Acts 20:7), the day our Lord rose from the grave.

The Illumination Principle

As we study the Word of God, we must ever remember that what we are doing is not some intellectual exercise. Our ultimate purpose is not intellectual but spiritual. Therefore, no matter how much we study the Word, no matter what tools we use, no matter how many principles we employ, nothing can substitute for the illumination of the Holy Spirit. A key text hre is John 14:26: "But the Comforter, which is the Holy Ghost, whom the Father will send in my name, he shall teach you all things, and bring all things to your remembrance, whatsoever I have said unto you."

Head knowledge, *by itself*, is of little or no value. A person might have a string of degrees, but without the Comforter's *application* it will all be empty. Just like a baby's rattle, which is cute but means very little, knowledge in itself is empty. Now, knowledge is good and very important, but the greatest seminary is at Jesus' feet, the greatest textbook is the Scriptures, the greatest Tutor is the Holy Spirit, and the only tuition we must pay is the surrendering of ourselves to the authority of God's Word.

The point here is that it is the Holy Spirit who teaches us. We should key in on the word "He" in our text. Ponder a moment: in the technical sense, no man really "teaches." As a pastor I can only *present* the Truth of God's Word to God's people. It is then the Holy Spirit who does the teaching, as declared in John 16:13–14 and 1 John 2:27. Those verses have been used (and abused) to teach that Christians don't need a pastor or regular attendance to a local church, that they can just read their Bibles and get all they need. But that contradicts Ephesians 4:11–12, where God tells us that God gave certain men "for the perfecting of the saints for the work of the ministry." God calls certain men to be pastors so they can devote their time to study. Few Christians, because of vocation, can spend large amounts of time in study, but that is what God calls pastors to do. God's people, then, by being faithful in their attendance to the local church, benefit by the hours of study the pastor invests in preparation. We can put the contrast this way: the Christian should *desire* preaching and teaching but must *depend* upon the Holy Spirit.

Paul also emphasizes this Illumination Principle in 1 Corinthians 2:12 and 14. Spiritual study is the only avenue to spiritual truth. We must approach the Scriptures *reverently* and *prayerfully*. Indeed, the only way we will put ourselves under total biblical *authority* is to first put ourselves under total Holy Spirit *dependence*. At best, study apart from the Holy Spirit is *arrogance*, and at worst, it is *apostasy*.

The Paradox Principle

The dictionary definition of "paradox" is, "A seemingly contradictory statement that might nonetheless be true: [e.g.] the paradox that standing is more tiring than walking."[15] "Paradox" actually comes from the Latin word *paradoxum*, which in-turn comes from the Greek *paradoxos*. The root *doxa* means "opinion, expectation, or glory," and the prefix *para* means "beyond." In Greek, then, a paradox was something that was beyond expectation, something that surpassed all the opinions and anticipations of men.

This word does appear in the New Testament, but only once. Note the "strange things" (*paradoxa*) in Luke 5:28. The scene was the healing of the paralytic. When Jesus healed him and he got up and walked, the people were amazed and said that they had seen something that was beyond expectation, something that surpassed all the opinions and anticipations of men.

Applying this to biblical interpretation, there will be times when we will encounter things that are simply beyond our expectations, our opinions, and our anticipations. To put it simply, there will be things that we simply cannot comprehend, just as those spectators could not comprehend Jesus' miracle. As Deuteronomy 29:29 puts it, "The secret things belong unto the LORD our God."

For example, was Jesus God or man? Yes. He was both one hundred percent God from before the beginning (Jn. 1:1, etc.), and He was one hundred percent man in His incarnation (Jn. 1:14, etc.). Can we comprehend this seeming contradiction? No, but we believe it anyway.

Another question: Did God author the Bible or did men author the Bible? Yes. "Holy men of God spake [using their own words, style, and personality] as they were moved by the Holy Spirit [who controlled the entire process]" (2 Pet. 1:20–21). Can we comprehend this seeming contradiction? No, but we believe it anyway.

Still another question: Do I live my Christian life or does Christ live my Christian life? Yes. Paul states both principles in Galatians 2:20. While Paul said in one place that *he* constantly struggled to discipline his body to keep it in submission (1 Cor. 9:27), he says in another that "we are *His* workmanship, created in Christ Jesus unto good works, which *God hath before ordained* that we should walk in them" (Eph. 2:10). Which is true? Both. Can we comprehend this seeming contradiction? Can we possibly comprehend that someone else lives in us and through us? No, but we believe it and rejoice in it anyway. (Also, see the exposition of Phil. 2:12–13 chapter 32.)

Another question that constantly arises is: Is God sovereign, or is man responsible to choose? Yes. The Word of God clearly declares the absolute sovereignty of God in salvation. Ephesians 1:4–5 declares that "[God] hath chosen us in [Christ] before the foundation of the world" and that He "predestinated us unto the adoption of children by Jesus Christ to himself, according to the good pleasure of his will."

We can briefly state the matter this way: *God's sovereignty never tramples over man's "free choice," but neither is God's sovereignty ever at the mercy of man's will.* Because God knows (and therefore decrees) every choice a man might make, He anticipates everything so His will is still accomplished. Did you get it? No matter what man does, God's plans and purposes are *never* thwarted. Why? *Because He is God!* As A. A. Hodge so ably put it:

> We have the fact distinctly revealed that God has decreed the free acts of men, and yet that the actors were none the less responsible, and consequently none the less free in their acts.[16]

Acts 4:27–28 also illustrates this. Does this passage say that God decreed the suffering and death of our Savior at the hands of these wicked men? Indeed, it does. But does it say that these men were coerced or even forced to do what they did? No. While God knew and decreed the actions of Herod and Pilate, they still did them of their own accord. We can sum it up this way: Man is free to *choose*, but God is sovereign in *control*.

Commenting on John 19:31–37, where it speaks of the Roman soldiers fulfilling Old Testament prophecy concerning the death of Christ, Charles Spurgeon said:

> Shall we never be able to drive into men's minds the truth that predestination and free agency are both facts? Men sin as freely as birds fly in the air, and they are altogether responsible for their sin; and yet everything is ordained and foreseen by God. The fore-ordination of God in no degree interferes with the responsibility of man. I have often been asked by persons to reconcile the two truths. My only reply is, They need no reconciliation, for they never fall out. Why should I try to reconcile two friends? Prove to me that the two truths do not agree. In that request I have set you a task as difficult as that which you propose to me. These two facts are parallel lines; I cannot make them unite, but you cannot make them cross each other. . . I believe, but I cannot explain. I fall before the majesty of revelation and adore the infinite Lord.[17]

There is a humble man. There is a man who knows his place and realizes the greatness of the almighty, infinite God.

To adapt Spurgeon's idea of "parallel lines," perhaps we can think of our understanding of this depth as standing between a set of railroad tracts and looking toward the horizon. Where we are standing, they are separate, but only in eternity do they converge.

The trouble with much biblical interpretation and teaching today is an unwillingness to accept the paradoxes of Scripture. In our arrogance, we just have to "make sense of it all." But let us ask the same question as does the Apostle Paul in Romans 11:33–36:

> O the depth of the riches both of the wisdom and knowledge of God! how unsearchable are his judgments, and his ways past finding out! For who hath known the mind of the Lord? or who hath been his counsellor? Or who hath first given to him, and it shall be recompensed unto him again? For of him, and through him, and to him, are all things: to whom be glory for ever. Amen.

The Practical Principle

Finally, and because of all we have seen, we must interpret the Word of God practically. By this I do not mean that we sit back and say, "What is the Bible saying to me?" No, this is the trap of Liberalism and today's Post-modernism. Nor do we mean that we just read a verse and make a quick application. Rather, we sit back and say, "In light of my diligent study of what the Bible *says*, what is it now *demanding* of me?" Further, once we go through the interpretation process, the application reveals itself. We don't have to *look* for the application (or make one up, which is quite popular nowadays), for *it becomes self-evident.*

As mentioned earlier, as we study the Scriptures we must ever remember that our ultimate goal is not intellectual but spiritual. To put it another way, our goal is not primarily to *know* something, but to *do* something. As James declares, "To him that *knoweth* to do good, and *doeth* it not, to him it is sin" (Jas. 4:17). And as Paul told Timothy, "These things command and teach" (1 Tim. 4:11). Bible knowledge is not conceptual or theoretical; rather it is concrete and practical.

Second Timothy 3:16–17 declares that the Word of God is profitable for doctrine, reproof, correction, instruction in righteousness, and equipping for service. Many don't think the Bible is practical. On the contrary, how much more practical could it be? When properly interpreted, it provides us with the answer to every question, every need, every issue, and every problem.

NOTES

[1] Frank E. Gaebelein (General Editor), *The Expositor's Bible Commentary*, Vol. 11 (Grand Rapids: Zondervan Publishing House, 1978), p. 402.

[2] *Basic Theology*, p. 111.

[3] Hal Lindsay, *There's a New World Coming* (Santa Ana: Vision House Publishers, 1973), pp. 138-139.

[4] Salem Kirban and Gary Cohen, *Revelation Visualized* (Chicago: Moody Press, p. 201.

[5] Tim F. LaHaye, *Revelation: Illustrated and Made Plain* (Grand Rapids: Zondervan Publishing House, 1974), p. 185.

[6] William Newell, *The Book of the Revelation* (Chicago: Moody Press, 1935), p. 129-131.

[7] Cited in John *MacArthur's Charismatic Chaos*, p. 90.

[8] Cited in J. Vernon McGee's *Guidelines for the Understanding of the Scriptures* (Pasadena: Thru the Bible Books), p. 20.

[9] Colin Brown (Editor), *The New International Dictionary of New Testament Theology* (Zondervan), Vol. 3, pp. 772-773.

[10] Kittel, *Theological Dictionary of the New Testament.*

[11] Calvin, *Institutes*, Book IV, Chapter XV, Section 19 (abbreviated, IV.15.19).

[12] This is further explained by the principle: *Scripturam ex Scriptura explicandam esse* ("Scripture is to be explained by Scripture"). This principle is related to another: *Analogia Fide* ("Analogy of Faith," i.e., Bible doctrine is to be interpreted in relation to the basic message of the Bible, which is the Gospel, the content of faith, or simply "The Faith" (cf. 1 Cor.2:13, 15:1-4).

[13] Charles Hodge, *Systematic Theology*, Vol. I, p. 187.

[14] One of the most helpful books for Bible study is *The Treasury of Scripture Knowledge*, which contains over 500,000 Scripture references and parallel passages. In his Introduction, R. A. Torrey alludes to the Comparison Principle: "There is no other commentary on the Bible so helpful as the Bible Itself. There is not a difficult passage in the Bible that is not explained and made clear by other passages of the Bible, and [The Treasury of Scripture Knowledge] is marvelously useful in bringing to light those other parts of the Bible that throw light upon the portion that is being studied. But not only does the book illuminate dark places, it also emphasizes the truth by bringing in a multitude of witnesses."

[15] *The American Heritage Dictionary.*

[16] A. A Hodge, *Outlines of Theology* (Carlisle, PA: Banner of Truth Trust, 1991 Reprint), p.210.

[17] *Metropolitan Tabernacle Pulpit*, Vol. 33, p. 198-199.

The motions of the Spirit are always consonant with the Word. The Word is the chariot in which the Spirit of God rides; whichever way the tide of the Word runs, that way the wind of the Spirit blows.

Puritan Thomas Watson
The Godly Man's Picture, p. 68

Subject Index

Person Index

Scripture Index

Genesis
1 385
1:1 119, 217
1:26 525
1:27–28 191
1:27—3:6 282
2 522
2:7 525
2:18, 20 266
3:6 75
3:8 436
3:13 269
3:16 191
3:17 381
3:19 352
5:3 525
6 529
6:3, 5 51
6:4 47–64
6:5 54, 481
6:6 549
6:8, 9 55
6:22 17
9:3–5 490
9:4 382
9:6 525
15:6 13
16:7–13 269
17:10 559
18:23–33 408
21:10, 12 13
23:19 352
25:9 352
27:19 374
32:1, 3 137
38:24 352
49:31 352
50:13 352

Exodus
1—14 407
2:2–3 480

2:11 415
3:19 407
3:14 121
4:22 518
7:10–11, 22 472
8:7 472
11:5 374
12:3 269
12:21 160
15:20 270
16:23–29 242
16:29 243
18:20–21 160
19:7 160
20:2 243, 245
20:3 429
20:4 421, 524
20:5 429
20:8 559
20:8–11 242
20:10 243
20:11 428–29
21:24 244
21:28–32 269
23:27, 28 537
26:34 188
32—33 408
32:4–5 430
34:28 460
35:3 243
38:8 269

Leviticus
10 418
15:33 435
16:8–10 24
16:29–34 460
18:16 409
19:17 415
20:1–27 414
20:14 352
20:18 435
21:9 352

22:18, 21 286
23:26–32 460

Numbers
6:2 269
11:16, 17 160
13:33 51
14 408
15:32–36 243
16:23–35 418
18 414
20:14 137
36:1–12 269

Deuteronomy
1:1 269
1:13–17 160
6:4–7 269
7:20 537
9:9 460
13:1–5 477 (n4)
16:9–15 269
23:3, 5, 10, 18 537
24 522
27:1 160
29:29 560
31:9–13 18
31:9 160
34:5–8 354 (n2)

Joshua
2:4 480
2:9–11 407
5:1 408
7 419
8:35 21
10:1 537
11:1 537
24:2 385
24:12 537

Foreign Words Index

Hebrew (H), Greek (G), and Latin (L)

A

a- (G), 200, 415, 418
adelphē (G), 415
adelphos (G), 415–16
adunatos (G), 200
agapē (G), 301, 396
agathe (G), 505
agathos (G), 505
ah-ayrh (H), 33
aichmalōsian (G), 182
aichmalōtos (G), 182
aichmalōteuō (G), 182
aiōn (G), 199
akatakaluptos (G), 188
akouō (G), 357, 381
allos (G), 405, 464
anamnēsis (G), 493
'ānâ (H), 460
anakrinō (G), 79, 277
analogia fide (L), 345
    (n2), 563 (n12)
analogia scriptuea (L),
    42, 297, 345 (n2),
    523, 557
anengklētos (G), 264
anechomai (G), 302
anepilemptos (G), 264
angeloi (G), 136–37
anomia (G), 474
anthropos (G), 205,
    276, 505
anti (G), 188, 192, 532
antitupon (G), 532
apairō (G), 463
apaugasma (G), 526
aphistēmi (G), 259

apo (G), 210, 259, 526
apochōreō (G), 259
apōleia (G), 286
apologia (G), 210, 217
archē (G), 56, 60
autos (G), 148, 268
arrabōn (G), 230
'ărûkâh (H), 459
āśār (H), 534
astheneō (G), 348
asthenēs (G), 348
artios (G), 374
artismos (G), 374
augazō (G), 526
authenteō (G), 268
authentēs (G), 268
anaxios (G), 418
axios (G), 299, 418

B

bar mitzvah (H), 379
baptizō (G), 41, 225,
    532, 553
baptō (G), 327, 532
bebaios (G), 326
ben (H), 48
ben elohim (H), 48
beriyt (H), 493
blasphemeō (G), 404
blasphēmia (G), 404
bouleuō (G), 260

C

causae instrumentales
    (L), 488
cernere (L), 65
chara (G), 77

charis (G), 251
chāyâ (H), 256
chesed (G), 434–35
chōreō (G), 259
comma Johanneum (L),
    497–509
convertere (L), 235, 320
crux criticorum (L), 457

D

dām (H), 382
delphus (G), 415
derek (H), 384, 385
derō (G), 348
descensus ad inferos (L),
    182
demût (H), 525
desmos (G), 302
dia (G), 531
diakoneō (G), 172–73,
    175
diakonia (G), 172–73,
    175
diakonos (G), 172–73,
    177
diakrinō (G), 78
dichostasia (G), 280
didachē (G), 388–89
didaskalia (G), 388
didaskalias (G), 67
didaskalos (G), 153, 157,
    164, 358
didōmi (G), 262, 418
diatheke (G), 493
dikē (G), 145
diōkō (G), 340
diokonissa (G), 176
dis (L), 65

About the Author

D r. J. D. "Doc" Watson (ThD, DRE) entered the ministry in 1974, serving in several capacities including 29 years in the pastorate, 26 of which at Grace Bible Church in Meeker, Colorado. He also speaks at a few Bible Conferences and other venues.

In addition to his other published books, he continues to write and edit the monthly publication *Truth on Tough Texts*, on which the present book is based. His driving passion is the exposition of the Word of God as the sole and sufficient authority in all matters. This is demonstrated in no better way than in his 3-1/2 year (500,000 word) exposition of the Epistle to the Ephesians, which he hopes to publish in the future.

Dr. Watson also serves on the board of On Target Ministry (www.ontargetministry.org), which is committed to international education, based upon the 2 Timothy 2:2 model. He has had the opportunity to serve overseas in this capacity, including teaching at the Haiti Bible Institute, which was founded by OTM. He likewise serves on the board of the Institute for Biblical Textual Studies, which is committed to defending the Traditional Text of the New Testament.

Dr. Watson has also contributed articles to other publications, including a weekly column in his local newspaper based upon his pulpit ministry. He also maintains the blog, *Expositing Ephesians: The Christian's Wealth and Walk* (http://expositingephesians.blogspot.com).

The other three loves of his life are his wife, Debbie (since 1974), his son, Paul (since 1988), and golf (since 1968 and, thankfully, in that order). Contact him at: 970-618-8375 or docwatson3228@gmail.com. Website: www.TheScriptureAlone.com.

Also by the Author

A Word for the Day: Key Words from the
New Testament

A Hebrew Word for the Day: Key Words from the
Old Testament

Both from AMG Publishers
www.AMGPublishers.com

A Final Thought

Unless I am convinced by Scripture and plain reason—I do not accept the authority of popes and councils, for they have contradicted each other—my conscience is captive to the Word of God. I cannot and I will not recant anything, for to go against conscience is neither right nor safe. Here I stand; I cannot do otherwise. God help me. Amen.

Martin Luther before the Diet of Worms, April 18, 1521
(as report by Roland Bainton in *Here I Stand*, p. 144)

Made in the USA
Charleston, SC
27 April 2012